An A-to-Z Guide to
Biblical Prophecy
and the
End Times

An A-to-Z Guide to
Biblical Prophecy
and the
End Times

J. DANIEL HAYS • J. SCOTT DUVALL • C. MARVIN PATE

Previously published as *Dictionary of Biblical Prophecy and End Times*

ZONDERVAN®

ZONDERVAN.com/
AUTHORTRACKER
follow your favorite authors

We want to hear from you. Please send your comments about this book to us in care of zreview@zondervan.com. Thank you.

ZONDERVAN

An A-to-Z Guide to Biblical Prophecy and the End Times
Formerly titled *Dictionary of Biblical Prophecy and End Times*
Copyright © 2007 by J. Daniel Hays, J. Scott Duvall, and C. Marvin Pate

Requests for information should be addressed to:

Zondervan, *Grand Rapids, Michigan 49530*

This edition: ISBN 978-0-310-49600-7 (softcover)

The Library of Congress has cataloged the original edition as follows:

Hays, J. Daniel.
    Dictionary of biblical prophecy and end times / J. Daniel Hays, J. Scott Duvall,
and C. Marvin Pate.
        p. cm.
    Includes bibliographical references and index.
    ISBN 978-0-310-25663-2
    1. Bible — Prophecies — Dictionaries. I. Duvall, J. Scott. II. Pate, C. Marvin, 1952- III. Title.
BS647.3.H39 2007
220.1'503 — dc22   2007000461

Cover design: Ron Huizinga
Cover photography: (clockwise) iStock Photo / Nikada; Andy Dean; Amanda Rohde; Oleg Babich
Interior design: Mark Sheeres

Printed in the United States of America

12 13 14 15 16 17 18 19 /DCI/ 23 22 21 20 19 18 17 16 15 14 13 12 11 10 9 8 7 6 5 4 3 2

CONTENTS

PREFACE

Biblical prophecy is a relevant and important topic for the church today. Not only does biblical prophecy provide hope for the future and strength for today, but its broad-sweeping themes help us to understand the entire Bible. Indeed, prophecy ties the Bible together from Genesis to Revelation.

Unfortunately, the study of this topic is often surrounded by controversy and argument. Evangelicals and other Bible-believing Christians, who agree on many crucial aspects of theology, frequently find themselves disagreeing over the interpretation of biblical texts that deal with prophecy. Adding to the problem is the fact that some writers on this subject express their views with absolute certainty—they are convinced that their interpretation is without error and that those who disagree are simply wrong. All too often, writers and teachers on this subject abandon the virtue of academic humility and show little concern about the possible validity of the biblical arguments raised against their view or arguments in favor of a countering viewpoint.

This book was conceived with the purpose of helping laypeople in the church study and understand biblical prophecy. The three authors of *An A-to-Z Guide to Biblical Prophecy and the End Times* have no theological agenda to push or prophetic viewpoint to champion, other than a strong commitment to the Scriptures and a passion to interpret the biblical texts in accordance with the intention of the biblical writers. In fact, the three of us (J. Daniel Hays, J. Scott Duvall, and C. Marvin Pate) are not in complete agreement ourselves regarding the end times. Yet what unites us is a common commitment to sound, scholarly study of the Scriptures and a respect for differing evangelical viewpoints that nonetheless have substantial scriptural evidence. We are not only coauthors but also colleagues and friends, working together in harmony to try to strengthen the church through writing, teaching, and pastoring.

An A-to-Z Guide to Biblical Prophecy and the End Times is designed primarily for laypeople in the church. However, its goal is to move beyond the oversimplified and self-convinced viewpoints and discussions of some of the popular writers on this subject to provide nuanced, but understandable explanations and discussions based on the top evangelical scholarship available today. In addition, the goal for this book is to provide a solid explanation for and defense of all serious views on prophecy held by evangelicals, along with an appropriate critique pointing out each view's weaknesses as well.

Following the tradition of most modern English Bible translations, when referring to the Old Testament Hebrew covenant name of God (Yahweh), the English term LORD (in caps) is used. Occasionally Yahweh is used, usually with a brief explanation of the term.

We wish to thank Ouachita Baptist University students Garrett Ham and Eric Michalls, who contributed to this book through proofreading and checking the many biblical citations.

J. DANIEL HAYS

J. SCOTT DUVALL

C. MARVIN PATE

Abomination of Desolation

The "abomination of desolation," "abomination that causes desolation," or "desolating sacrifice" is a phrase that refers to the desecration of the Jerusalem Temple (see TEMPLE). The description occurs or is alluded to in the following texts: Daniel 8:11; 9:27; 11:31; 12:11; Matthew 24:15; Mark 13:14; Luke 21:20; and 2 Thessalonians 2:4, as well as in the noncanonical (apocryphal) book 1 Maccabees 1:54–64. These passages seem to attest to two or three stages of fulfillment of the prophecy.

(1) Daniel 8:11; 9:27; 11:31; 12:11; and 1 Maccabees 1:54–64 clearly speak of the actions of the Syrian ruler Antiochus IV (Epiphanes) against the Jerusalem Temple in 167 B.C., who decreed that Temple sacrifices and offerings should cease (see ANTIOCHUS EPIPHANES). To add insult to injury, he profaned the Most Holy Place by placing in it a statue to Zeus (the chief Greek god) and then sacrificing a pig to Zeus on the altar (described in Dan. 9:27 as the winged or horned altar). This terrible action is referred to as the abomination of desolation (lit., "and upon the wings of abominations shall come one who makes desolate"). Daniel 9:27, however, promises that the desolater (Antiochus) will be defeated, an event that occurred in 164 B.C. when Judas Maccabeus led the Jewish revolt that expelled Antiochus from Jerusalem. Judas then rededicated the Temple to God in December 164 B.C., celebrated today as Hanukkah (cf. 1 Macc. 4:36–61).

(2) Daniel's prophecy apparently was not completely fulfilled with Antiochus, for Luke 21:20 labels the Roman assault on Jerusalem in

A.D. 70 as the "desolation." In fact, the Roman destruction of the Holy City and its Temple was an intensification of the reality of the Old Testament prediction.

(3) Some interpreters extend the application of the prophecy of the abomination of desolation into the distant future. These scholars contend that the ultimate fulfillment of Daniel's prediction will occur in connection with the end-time Temple to be built by Israel, which the Antichrist will desecrate (see ANTICHRIST; ISRAEL, MODERN STATE OF). This viewpoint appeals to Matthew 24:15; Mark 13:14; and 2 Thessalonians 2:4 in support of its perspective (cf. Rev. 11).

But those who identify only two stages of fulfillment for Daniel's prophecy understand Matthew 24:15 and Mark 13:14 to pertain not to a future end-time Temple, but to the fall of Jerusalem in A.D. 70, as Luke 21:20 does. Furthermore, they see in 2 Thessalonians 2:4 an allusion to Emperor Caligula's (Gaius) failed plan to place a statue of himself in the Jerusalem Temple in A.D. 40, which, because of that ruler's assassination, did not occur (see CALIGULA; DANIEL, BOOK OF; TEMPLE).

Abrahamic Covenant

The Abrahamic Covenant, also called "The Promise to Abraham," plays a central role in biblical prophecy, providing one of the main prophetic themes that connect the Old Testament to the New. This covenant is presented in three central passages: Genesis 12:1–7; 15:1–20; and 17:1–8.

In Genesis 12:1–7 God promises to bless Abraham (the word "bless" occurs five times in 12:2–3). As part of this blessing, God promises to make Abraham into a great nation and to make his name great (12:2). He also promises to "bless those that bless you, and whoever curses you I will curse" (12:3). God also stresses that Abraham will be a blessing (12:2); indeed, in Abraham "all peoples on earth will be blessed" (12:3). God restates this aspect of the promise in 18:18, declaring that all *nations* will be blessed in Abraham. Finally, God promises to give the land of Canaan to Abraham's descendants (12:1, 7).

In Genesis 15:1–20 God formalizes his promise to Abraham into a "covenant." In the ancient Near Eastern world, a covenant was a legal agreement between two parties. There were numerous ceremonies that could be used to ratify or solemnize the covenant. One of the most serious ceremonies involved cutting an animal in half and then separating the two halves on the ground. The two parties then walked together between the two halves, apparently implying a vow of sorts, as if the participants were each saying, "May this happen to me if I break this covenant." In Genesis 15 God tells Abraham to bring five animals and to cut each of them in half. However, unlike in normal human covenant ceremonies, in this one God passes through the cut animals *by himself,* implying that he is instituting a one-sided or unilateral covenant that binds only one party—himself.

In Genesis 15 God also promises Abraham that his descendants will be as numerous as the stars (15:5). God then predicts four hundred years of bondage for Abraham's descendants, followed by their return and possession of the land of Canaan. Additionally, imbedded within this covenant dialogue and ceremony is the important statement in 15:6, "Abram believed the LORD, and he credited it to him as righteousness."

God appears to the aging Abraham again in Genesis 17 and promises to "confirm/establish" this covenant. God then repeats several aspects of the Abrahamic Covenant, expanding on the promise. He repeats the promise of numerous descendants, but expands on this by saying that Abraham will be the "father of many nations" (17:4–6) and that Sarah, his wife, will be "the mother of nations" (17:16). In addition, a "royal" aspect of the promise is added, for God promises that kings will come from Abraham and Sarah (17:6, 16). Once again God promises the land of Canaan to Abraham (17:8) and states that this covenant is to be an "everlasting covenant" (17:7). God then states that circumcision will be the sign of the covenant between himself and Abraham (17:9–14). Several of the promises that comprise the Abrahamic Covenant are also restated later in Genesis, both to Isaac (26:3–5) and to Jacob (28:13–15).

A Unilateral Covenant

In contrast to the later Mosaic Covenant, the Abrahamic Covenant appears to be a unilateral covenant to which God bound himself by his promise. Various scholars refer to it as a "one-sided" covenant, an "unconditional" covenant, a "divine commitment" covenant, or a "covenant of grace." God appears to have pledged himself to fulfilling this covenant without placing conditional stipulations on Abraham and his descendants. This is in strong contrast to the Mosaic Covenant as presented in the book of Deuteronomy. Indeed, in Deuteronomy 28 God clearly presents strict stipulations of keeping the law that were required in order to receive the blessings of that covenant. So the Mosaic Covenant was a "two-sided" or "bilateral" agreement; indeed, it was a covenant of law (although certainly God's grace can be seen in this covenant as well).

The Abrahamic Covenant was quite different. The unilateral aspect of that covenant is stressed by the fact that God passes through the halves of the animals by himself in Genesis 15. The one-sided binding or "grace" aspect of this covenant is illustrated in the story at the beginning, immediately after the promise to Abraham in 12:1–7. In 12:8–20 Abraham leaves the Promised Land (apparently in disobedience), goes to Egypt, and lies to Pharaoh about his wife, Sarah. God, however, in keeping with his unilateral promise, rescues Abraham and blesses him anyway (12:20; 13:2).

As with grace in the New Testament, even though the Abrahamic Covenant was a one-sided or unilateral covenant, God still calls on Abraham and his descendants to walk in obedience. In Genesis 12 God tells Abraham to go to the Promised Land, and in Genesis 17 God commands Abraham to circumcise the males in his family. But this obedience appears to be in response to the covenant, not as a means to covenant blessing. As the Old Testament story unfolds, it reveals that disobedience by Israel can delay the Abrahamic Covenant blessings or hinder the blessings from coming to a particular generation, but not stop the eventual fulfillment of the covenant. Thus, when the people of Israel disobediently refuse to enter the Promised Land (Num. 14), God sends that generation into the desert to die, but then he brings the next generation into the Promised Land in order to fulfill the Abrahamic Covenant.

The Abrahamic Covenant in the Old Testament

The prophetic promises of the Abrahamic Covenant are critical to the rest of the Old Testament story. In fact, it is the fulfillment of this covenant that drives that story along.

Genesis begins with the wonderful creation of God (Gen. 1–2), but is followed immediately by repeated human sin and disobedience (chs. 3–11). Adam and Eve ate of the forbidden fruit, Cain killed Abel, sin spread and brought the flood, and then people rebelled against God at the tower of Babel. The Abrahamic Covenant (ch. 12) is God's response to the universal sin of chapters 3–11. Although a hint of salvation can perhaps be seen prophetically in Genesis 3:15 (see SEED OF THE WOMAN), it is in the Abrahamic Covenant that the story of redemption really begins to unfold.

The book of Genesis ends with the patriarchal family residing in Egypt. As Exodus opens, the Abrahamic Covenant is clearly driving the story. The descendants of Abraham have indeed multiplied as God promised, and they find themselves in Egyptian bondage, as God predicted. Yet when Pharaoh defies God and tries to stop the Abrahamic Covenant fulfillment of proliferation by killing the babies of God's people, he finds himself on the punishment end of God's promise to Abraham, "I will bless those who bless you, and whoever curses you I will curse" (Gen. 12:3). Indeed, in response to Pharaoh, God sends ten plagues on Egypt (Ex. 7–11), completely destroying that country.

Numerous other critical connections between the Exodus story and the Abrahamic Covenant exist. When Pharaoh oppresses the Israelites, they cry out to God. Exodus 2:24–25 reads, "God heard their groaning and *he remembered his covenant with Abraham, with Isaac and with Jacob.* So God looked on the Israelites and was concerned about them" (italics added). In the next passage God responds to remembering the covenant by raising up Moses to deliver the Israelites from Egypt. It is important to recognize that the Exodus event (delivering Israel from the oppression of the Egyptians) is perhaps the central picture or paradigm of salvation in the Old Testament. It is likewise crucial to see that this great deliverance by God is tied integrally into the fulfillment of the Abrahamic Covenant. God had promised Abraham that his descendants would be a great nation, that they would possess the land of Canaan, and that they would be blessed. The story from Exodus to Joshua traces the fulfillment of that promise.

Because the Abrahamic Covenant was a unilateral covenant or a covenant of grace, it plays a critical role in Israel's relationship to God, especially when the people are disobedient. For example, in Exodus 32, the people build and worship a golden calf while Moses is receiving the Ten Commandments. God's anger burns against the people and he tells Moses he intends to destroy them (Ex. 32:10). Moses, however, argues with God, using the Abrahamic Covenant as a basis for asking for grace: "Remember your servants Abraham, Isaac and Israel, to whom you swore by your own self: 'I will make your descendants as numerous as the stars in the sky and I will give your descendants all this land I promised them, and it will be their inheritance forever" (32:13). God's response? "Then the LORD relented and did not bring on his people the disaster he had threatened" (32:14).

Likewise, as the Old Testament story continues to unfold, Israel receives the Promised Land and is offered tremendous blessings, but the people disobey and turn away to idols. The Mosaic Covenant promises punishment for such sin. However, throughout the story, God appears to be longsuffering and patient with them, apparently because of his promise to Abraham. In the book of 2 Kings, for example, as the nation hurtles downward in sin and apostasy, the text reminds the reader of the reason for God's forbearance: "But the LORD was gracious to them and had compassion and showed concern for them *because of his covenant with Abraham, Isaac and Jacob*. To this day he has been unwilling to destroy them or banish them from his presence" (2 Kings 13:23, italics added).

Eventually, however, the sin and apostasy of Israel lead to judgment, in keeping with the Mosaic Covenant. The prophets preach this continually, calling on the people to repent and to obey the Mosaic Covenant (especially the book of Deuteronomy). Yet the prophets realize that the people will not repent. Thus they proclaim that judgment is inevitable, as the Mosaic Covenant and God's justice demand. However, the prophets also proclaim that although judgment is coming (based on the Mosaic Covenant), after the judgment will come a glorious restoration and time of blessing, based on the Abrahamic Covenant and the Davidic Covenant (see DAVIDIC COVENANT), the one-sided covenants of grace.

The prophetic promise of the coming Messiah is tied to these two covenants. Likewise, as prophets such as Isaiah proclaim that the Gentiles will be included in this future time of deliverance, they are prophesying the actual fulfillment of Genesis 12:3: "All peoples on earth will be blessed through you."

The Abrahamic Covenant and the New Testament

The Abrahamic Covenant is one of the central themes that ties the Old and New Testaments together. The New Testament usage of the Abrahamic Covenant reflects a broad, but consistent, theological and prophetic understanding of God's ancient covenant with Abraham. The Abrahamic Covenant is not cited merely as an illustration of faith, but as a central, prophetic foundation on which much of New Testament doctrine relating to Christ and his salvation for us is built.

The prophets in the Old Testament proclaimed that the Messiah would come in fulfillment of the Abrahamic and Davidic Covenants. Moving from the prophets to the New Testament, one observes that the New Testament immediately alludes back to these two covenants, introducing Jesus Christ in Matthew 1:1 as "the son of David, the son of Abraham."

The coming of Jesus is likewise connected to the Abrahamic Covenant twice in Luke 1. In Luke 1:54–55, Mary proclaims, "He has helped his servant Israel, remembering to be merciful to Abraham and his descendants forever, even as he said to our fathers." Then Zechariah, the father of John the Baptist, states clearly that the coming of the Messiah is in fulfillment of the Abrahamic Covenant:

Praise be to the Lord, the God of Israel,
　because he has come and has redeemed his people.
He has raised up a horn of salvation for us
　in the house of his servant David
(as he said through his holy prophets of long ago),
salvation from our enemies
　and from the hand of all who hate us—
to show mercy to our fathers
　and to remember his holy covenant,
　　the oath he swore to our father Abraham. (1:68–73)

Abraham and the Abrahamic Covenant play central roles not only in the Gospels, but also in Paul's letters. Paul generally uses the term *promise* when referring to the Abrahamic Covenant; indeed, for Paul this term is practically a synonym for the Abrahamic Covenant. Thus Paul frequently alludes to the promises God gave to Abraham (Rom. 4:9–11; 15:8; Gal. 3–4), and these promises combine with Abraham's faith to provide a critical foundation for Paul's understanding of the gospel and the inclusion of the Gentiles.

In Galatians Paul declares: "Understand, then, that those who believe are children of Abraham. The Scripture foresaw that God would justify the Gentiles by faith, and announced the gospel in advance to Abraham: 'All nations will be blessed through you.' So those who have faith are blessed along with Abraham, the man of faith" (Gal. 3:7–9). Paul also argues that when the Abrahamic Covenant makes promises regarding the "descendants" of Abraham, this refers to those who believe in Christ, both Jew and Gentile: "If you belong to Christ, then you are Abraham's seed, and heirs according to the promise" (Gal. 3:29) (see SEED OF ABRAHAM).

The Abrahamic Covenant, therefore, plays a critical foundational and prophetic role in the story of salvation. The promises that God made to Abraham serve as prophetic guidelines that drive the story along the path of salvation history throughout the Old Testament and into the New, leading directly to the climactic fulfillment in Jesus Christ.

Advent

"Advent" means "coming" or "arrival." For Christians, "Advent" is often used to refer to that part of the church calendar encompassing the four Sundays prior to Christmas, in celebration of Christ's "coming" to earth. The term *First Advent* is used in a broader theological sense, referring to the coming of Jesus Christ to earth to provide salvation through his birth, life, death, resurrection, and ascension. Likewise, the term *Second Advent* references the return of Jesus in glory at the end times (see SECOND ADVENT).

There are numerous Old Testament prophecies that pointed to and predicted Christ's First Advent. Many of these are identified in the New Testament as fulfilled prophecies about Christ. These prophecies can be grouped into nine general categories:

1. *Christ's birth.* Several aspects relating to Christ's birth were foretold in the Old Testament. The Old Testament prophesied that Christ would be a descendant of David (cf. Ps. 110:1 with Matt. 22:43–44; Mark 12:36; Luke 20:42–43), but also of divine origin (cf. Ps. 40:6–8 with Heb. 10:5–9; Ps. 2:7 with Acts 13:33 and Heb. 1:5; 5:5; Isa. 7:14 with Matt. 1:21–23). Micah foretold the place of birth, Bethlehem (cf. Mic. 5:2 with Matt. 2:6; John 7:42). Several Old Testament prophets alluded to the opposition that the Messiah would face at birth, seen in the attempt by Herod to kill all the babies in Bethlehem (cf. Hos. 11:1 with Matt. 2:15; Jer. 31:15 with Matt. 2:16–18).

2. *Christ's forerunner.* The Old Testament prophesied that the Messiah would be preceded by a forerunner, fulfilled by John the Baptist (cf. Isa. 40:3–5 with Matt. 3:3; Mark 1:3; Luke 3:4–6; John 1:23; Mal. 3:1 with Mark 1:2; Luke 7:27; Mal. 4:5–6 with Matt. 11:14; 17:12; Mark 9:12–13; Luke 1:17) (see JOHN THE BAPTIST).

3. *Christ's ministry.* Various aspects of Christ's ministry were foretold in the Old Testament. The Messiah was to be a prophet (cf. Deut. 18:15–16, 19 with Acts 3:22–23; 7:37; Ps. 69:9 with John 2:17; see also Matt. 21:12–16; Mark 11:15–17; Luke 19:45–47), beginning with his ministry in Galilee (cf. Isa. 9:1–2 with Matt. 4:15–16). Likewise he was identified as the Suffering Servant of the Lord (cf. Isa. 53:4 with Matt. 8:17; Isa. 61:1–2 with Luke 4:18–21; Isa. 53:12 with Luke 22:37; Isa. 53:3ff. with Mark 9:12; Luke 18:32; 24:24–25, 46) (see SERVANT SONGS). The Old Testament also pointed to Jesus' eternal priesthood (cf. Ps. 110:4 with Heb. 5:6; 7:17, 21). Numerous texts prophesied that the Messiah would be a king (cf. Zech. 9:9 with Matt. 21:5; John 12:14–15) (see KING, MESSIANIC).

4. *Christ's opposition by the Jews.* The Old Testament indicated that the Messiah would be opposed and oppressed by his own people (cf. Isa. 6:9–10 with Matt. 13:14–15; Mark 4:12; Luke 8:10; Isa. 53:1; 6:9–10 with John 12:37–41; Ps. 118:22–23 with Matt. 21:42; Mark 12:10–11; Luke 20:17; Acts 4:11; 1 Peter 2:7–18).

5. *Christ's betrayal by Judas.* Two Old Testament texts described the betrayal of the Messiah by a close friend (cf. Ps. 41:9 with John 13:18;

17:12; Zech. 11:12–13 with Matt. 27: 9–10; see also Ps. 109:8; 69:25 and Acts 1:20).

6. *Christ's arrest and abandonment.* The Old Testament prophets declared that the Messiah would be arrested and then abandoned by his friends and supporters (cf. Zech. 13:7 with Matt. 26:30–31; Mark 14:27).

7. *Christ's death.* The violent death of the Messiah is mentioned in several places in the Old Testament (cf. Ps. 22:18 with John 19:24; Ps. 22:15 with John 19:28; Ex. 12:46; Num. 9:12; Ps. 34:20 with John 19:36; Zech. 12:10 with John 19:32; Isa. 53:7–9 with Luke 18:32; Acts 8:32–35; 1 Cor. 15:3; Deut. 21:23 with Gal. 3:13).

8. *Christ's resurrection.* The New Testament also identifies several Old Testament texts as pointing to the resurrection of the Messiah (cf. Ps. 16:8–11 with Acts 2:25–28; 2 Sam. 7:12–13 with Luke 18:33; 24:46; Hos. 6:2 with John 2:19–22; 1 Cor. 15:4).

9. *Christ's ascension.* The Old Testament predicted not only the suffering of Christ, but also his glorification, seen in his ascension to sit at the right hand of God (cf. Ps. 110:1 with Acts 2:34–35; Ps. 2:7 with Acts 13:33–35; Ps. 68:18 with Eph. 4:8).

Thus the New Testament points out numerous Old Testament prophecies fulfilled by Christ at his First Advent. (For a discussion regarding prophecies in both the New Testament and the Old Testament about Jesus' return to earth, see SECOND COMING.)

Agabus

Agabus is one of the prophets from Jerusalem who came to Antioch and prophesied that there would be a severe famine over the entire Roman world (Acts 11:27–30). This happened during the reign of Emperor Claudius (A.D. 41–54). Later this same prophet went from Jerusalem to Caesarea and acted out his prophecy that Paul would be bound in chains if he proceeded with his plan to go to the Holy City (21:10–11), which indeed came true (21:27–36).

Ahijah the Shilonite

Ahijah lives and prophesies during the tumultuous times of the final days of Solomon, the civil war that ensued after Solomon's death, and the early days of the split kingdoms of Israel and Judah. He is from the city of Shiloh, the site where the Tabernacle resided during the days of Samuel. Ahijah is a true prophet and plays a significant role during these troubled times.

In 1 Kings 11:1–13, Solomon, the son of David, turns away from God and leads the nation into idol worship. As punishment, God declares that he will take away the northern ten tribes from Solomon's descendants and will create a new nation (the northern kingdom, Israel) out of these ten tribes. Yet for the sake of David, God promises to leave the house of David (and Solomon) one tribe in the south (Judah). Ahijah the prophet delivers this message to Jeroboam (11:26–39). Ahijah also tells Jeroboam that God has chosen him to be king over this new kingdom. If Jeroboam remains faithful to God, Ahijah prophesies, following the pattern of David and not the idolatrous pattern of Solomon, he will be blessed and his dynasty will be established.

However, although God does bring Jeroboam to power, Jeroboam turns away from God and becomes an evil, disobedient king (1 Kings 13:33–34; 14:9). When Jeroboam's son becomes ill, Jeroboam sends his wife in disguise to Ahijah to find out what will happen to the boy. Ahijah sees through the disguise and prophesies severe judgment on Jeroboam and his entire household, including the death of the sick son, thus declaring an end to Jeroboam's dynasty — an ironic reversal to what would have happened if Jeroboam had been obedient. This action of the prophet Ahijah (declaring the death of the king's son) stands in strong contrast to the event in 17:7–24, where the prophet Elijah raises the son of a widow from the dead. Thus, the disobedient king's son dies, while the faithful widow's son is raised from the dead. Faithful prophets are involved in each event.

Alexander the Great

Alexander, born in 356 B.C., was the son of Philip, king of Macedon. The amazing, swift conquests of Alexander are alluded to in Daniel. Daniel 8:5–8 (cf. 2:40–43; 7:19–24) portrays Alexander the Great as the "goat" from the west (Greece) with a notable horn between his eyes that defeats the ram (the Medo-Persian army). This prophecy is fulfilled when Alexander leads the Greek armies across the Hellespont into Asia Minor in 334 B.C. and defeats the Persian forces at the river Granicus. Alexander again meets and quickly defeats the Persians at Issus ("without touching the ground"; Dan. 8:5).

Alexander then turns south, moving down the Syrian coast and conquering Egypt without difficulty. He then moves east again, defeating Darius the Persian for the last time, east of the Tigris River. Babylon, Susa, and Persepolis (the last two were capitals of Persia) all fell to the young warrior king. Alexander marches his armies as far eastward as the

Hydaspes River in India and wins a decisive battle there. But because his armies refuse to go any further, Alexander is forced to return to Persepolis and then to Babylon. There he dies in 323 B.C. at the age of thirty-three.

Alexander's chief contribution to posterity is Hellenization — the merging of Greek culture with the customs of the peoples he conquered (*Hellas* is the Greek word for Greece). Thus *koine* (common) Greek becomes a universal trade language from 330 B.C. to ca. A.D. 300, and the language of the Septuagint (the earliest translation of the Old Testament), the New Testament, and some of the early church fathers' writings. After Alexander's sudden death, his empire is divided among his four generals: Cassander (Greece), Lysimachus (Asia), Seleucus (Babylonia and Syria), and Ptolemy (Egypt), probably reflecting the prophecy of Daniel 8:8–22.

Allegory

An allegory is a story in which the details correspond to a deeper level of meaning than the literal sense. Duvall and Hays elaborate, "An allegory is a story that uses an extensive amount of symbolism ... that is, most or many of the details in the story represent something or carry some specific nuance of meaning." As those authors point out, John Bunyan's *Pilgrim Progress* is a well-known Christian book devoted to allegory. Thus, to understand allegory, one must read it figuratively and not as history.[1] Some classic examples of allegory in the Bible include Isaiah 5:1–7 (Israel is the vineyard of God) and John 15:1–8 (the vine and the branches). See also Galatians 4:21–27. Thus, allegory has its rightful place in Scripture.

However, allegory can be used in inappropriate ways, especially in regard to biblical prophecy. Sometimes narrative material in Scripture can be interpreted incorrectly in an allegorical manner instead of a more literal historical manner, as the material was probably intended to be understood. This method has its origin in Alexandria, Egypt, a Christian center of scholarship led by Clement of Alexandria in A.D. 190 and then by Origen in A.D. 202. The Alexandrian school was influenced by Platonic philosophy and understood the task of biblical interpretation as seeking the allegorical or symbolic meaning of the Bible, which lay behind the literal sense.

While the motivation of this school of thought was laudable (it sought to show that the Old Testament is filled with messianic predictions fulfilled in Jesus Christ), its methodology (reading the New Testament back into the Old Testament without the latter having a say in its own right) was incorrect. Regrettably, such an interpretation paved the way for later theologians to see Christ everywhere in the Old Testament, without regard for the authorial intent of the inspired author.

For example, the Tabernacle as described in Exodus has been the breeding ground of fanciful allegorical readings. Thus the tent pegs of the holy tent are thought to anticipate the cross of Christ. (Never mind the fact that the tent pegs were *not* wood, but bronze, the latter of which is supposedly symbolic of our salvation in Christ that does not decay!) And the pins were buried in the ground but emerged from the ground when the Tabernacle moved, thus bespeaking the death and resurrection of Christ! And on and on the messianic interpretation of the Tabernacle goes. Now there is certainly a connection between the Tabernacle and Christ (see the book of Hebrews), but it is the general point that Christ is the superior replacement to the ancient holy tent, not the far-fetched details often teased from the Exodus narrative regarding the tabernacle.

Thus, it is important to recognize that the interpreter today is not free to use allegorical methods to interpret Scripture whenever the interpreter feels as if it might be appropriate. It is critically important to first identify whether a passage was intended by the biblical author to be allegorical in nature. While, as noted above, allegories do occur in Scripture, they are rare, and today's interpreters should exert extreme caution before using this method to interpret most biblical texts.

Alpha and Omega

The introduction to the book of Revelation culminates in a vivid declaration of who God is: " 'I am the Alpha and the Omega,' says the Lord God, 'who is, and who was, and who is to come, the Almighty' " (Rev. 1:8). This is one of two occasions in Revelation where God himself clearly speaks (see also 21:6). Both instances echo Isaiah, where God uses similar language to communicate that he is not only the Creator, but also the sovereign Lord of history who will bring all things to fulfillment (see Isa. 41:4; 44:6; 48:12).

In the Greek alphabet, the first letter is alpha (α) and the last letter is omega (ω). This designation for God or Christ occurs in Revelation 1:8; 21:6; 22:13. In all three occurrences the "alpha" is spelled out ($\H{\alpha}\lambda\phi\alpha$) while the omega is written as a single letter ($\mathring{\omega}$). Perhaps this explains why many ancient inscriptions capitalize the alpha ("A") to capture the word alpha, while they use the letter "ω" that is used in the text rather than the capital omega ("Ω").

On the use of letters as descriptions of God, Craig Keener points out that "some Jewish writers used the first and last letters of the Hebrew alphabet (Aleph and Tav) to make the same point."[2] Bauckham contends that John emphasizes the phrase "the Alpha and the Omega" (listed first in 1:8) as a connection to the divine name:

> The biblical name of God YHWH was sometimes vocalized Yāhôh and so transliterated into Greek (which has no consonant "h") as IAΩ (Iota, Alpha, Omega). In the context of Jewish theological speculation about the divine name, the occurrence of the first and last letters of the Greek alphabet in this Greek form of the name could have suggested that the name itself contains the implications that God is the first and the last.[3]

In Revelation, the "Alpha and Omega" (and similar designations) are used for both God and Christ:

God—"I am the Alpha and the Omega" (1:8)
Christ—"I am the First and the Last" (1:17)
Christ—"the First and the Last" (2:8)
God—"I am the Alpha and the Omega, the Beginning and the End" (21:6)
Christ—"I am the Alpha and the Omega, the First and the Last, the Beginning and the End" (22:13)

This interchange asserts not only the deity of Christ and his oneness with the Father, but also the Triune God's complete control of history. He is both the origin and goal of history—quite literally, the first and last word. Also, if one considers Revelation 2:8 to be a continuation of 1:17, then these phrases are used a total of seven times in Revelation as yet another way of emphasizing the completeness of God's sovereign control. In 21:6–7 the phrase is used of God in the context of finalizing salvation: "It is done. I am the Alpha and the Omega, the Beginning and the End. To him who is thirsty I will give to drink without cost from the spring of the water of life. He who overcomes will inherit all this, and I will be his God and he will be my son." In 22:12–13 the phrase is used of Christ in the context of his return and judgment: "Behold, I am coming soon! My reward is with me, and I will give to everyone according to what he has done. I am the Alpha and the Omega, the First and the Last, the Beginning and the End." God the Father accomplishes salvation through the Son, a "salvation *through* judgment."[4]

The prophetic meaning of the title for the early church was to reinforce their faith in God as sovereign over their personal circumstances.

He is Lord of creation and Lord of the new creation. He is victorious over every contender, and no rival power can keep him from accomplishing his purpose and plan. Knowing that God is in control of history encourages Christians who are being threatened by worldly powers. While economic, religious, and military powers such as Rome may seem invincible from a human perspective, they are in reality under the ultimate control of the Triune God, who holds all of time and eternity in his hands.

Already – Not Yet

The *already – not yet* concept is closely tied to Jesus' teachings about the kingdom of God and to New Testament eschatology in general. The kingdom of God is the rule or reign of God. When Jesus began to minister publicly, his main message was, "The kingdom of God is near. Repent and believe the good news!" (Mark 1:15; cf. also Matt. 4:17, 23; Luke 4:42 – 44). Jesus healed the sick, cast out demons, fed the hungry, and forgave sinners — all signs that the kingdom had arrived. In Jesus, the kingdom of God became a present reality (Matt. 11:11 – 12; 12:28; 18:1 – 5; Luke 17:20 – 21). The "age to come" had already begun.

The disciples were operating from a typical Jewish understanding of eschatology (doctrine of the last things). They believed that when Messiah arrived, the new age of God's complete rule would begin. As a result, Jesus' disciples expected him to establish the kingdom fully and totally during their lifetime. When he was crucified, not only did they suffer emotionally because of the death of their friend and leader, but their entire understanding of God's plan encountered a crisis. If Jesus was Messiah, the one to bring about the messianic kingdom, why was he crucified? Was all hope lost for God's kingdom of peace, righteousness, and blessing to arrive? After Jesus' resurrection and ascension and the coming of the Spirit at Pentecost, however, the disciples began to understand God's greater plan (see the chart on next page).

At Jesus' first coming, the kingdom of God broke into this world. A world filled with sin, rebellion, Satan, darkness, and evil was invaded by Jesus the King and his messianic kingdom of peace, righteousness, life, and God. At conversion, believers begin to experience eternal life (lit., "age-to-come" life). The apostle Paul speaks of being "rescued ... from the dominion of darkness and brought ... into the kingdom of the Son" (Col. 1:13). Believers are new people living in an old world. God has started his kingdom project, but he has not completely finished it. The kingdom of God has *already* arrived, but it has *not yet* come in all

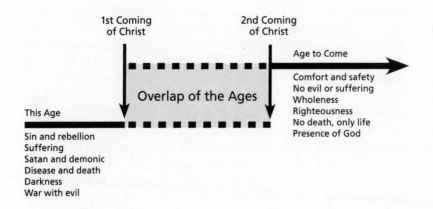

its fullness. The grand project has been launched, but it has not been finished.

Yet the kingdom of God also has a future dimension (Matt. 6:10; 25:34; 26:29; Luke 19:11–27). Believers are living in enemy-occupied territory between God's initial invasion (Jesus' first coming) and his total defeat of evil (Jesus' second coming). Believers live in the overlap between this age and the age to come. This situation explains many elements of the present Christian experience:

- Believers experience God's forgiveness, but they still sin and will never be perfect in this life.
- Believers have victory over death, but will one day die physically.
- Believers still get sick, and not all Christians experience healing.
- Believers live in the Spirit, but Satan will continue to attack and may do damage.
- God lives within believers, but they do not yet live in God's complete presence.

Because of the *already – not yet* reality of the kingdom of God, those who belong to Christ will experience victories as well as struggles until Jesus returns. (See also ESCHATOLOGY; KINGDOM OF GOD; SECOND COMING.)

Amos, Book of

Amos was a farmer/shepherd from the southern kingdom Judah who was led by God to prophesy briefly against the northern kingdom Israel. Amos prophesied during the reign of Jeroboam II (786–746 B.C.), a time when Israel was experiencing economic prosperity.

For most of the book, Amos proclaims how Israel has broken the Mosaic Covenant (primarily Deuteronomy). He accuses the king and the people of idolatry, social injustice (especially in association with affluent living), and hypocritical worship. Amos also describes the terrible consequential judgment that is coming. Amos is quite colorful, but brutally harsh and scathing in his criticism of Israel.

Amos barely touches on the theme of future restoration, and his brief glimpse of hope does not come until the final chapter (Amos 9). However, earlier in the book, as he describes judgment and destruction, he does allude to the survival of a remnant (3:12; 7:1–6; 9:8), even though his description of the remnant is rather grim: "As a shepherd saves from the lion's mouth only two leg bones or a piece of an ear, so will the Israelites be saved" (3:12) (see REMNANT).

In the last five verses of this book (Amos 9:11–15) the prophet Amos finally mentions future hope and restoration. God declares in 9:11 that he will restore "David's fallen tent," an allusion to fulfilling the promises of the Davidic Covenant (see DAVIDIC COVENANT). God then promises a time when Israel will be restored back in the Promised Land, a time characterized by agricultural blessings (9:13–15). (For an overview of the differing views on the restoration of Israel, see RESTORATION OF ISRAEL.)

Amillennialism

This view on the millennium is the notion that there will be no earthly reign of Christ after his coming ("a" means "no"). The "thousand years" mentioned in Revelation 20 symbolize the heavenly reign of Christ with Christians who have already died and gone to be with Christ. The return of Christ at the end of the age will be immediately followed by a general resurrection, the last judgment, and the eternal state. Amillennialists contend that these primary end-time events will occur in rapid succession, ruling out an earthly millennial kingdom. They look to the following passages to support this claim: John 5:28–29; Romans 8:17–23; 1 Corinthians 15:20–26; 2 Thessalonians 1:5–10; and 2 Peter 3:3–14, which they view as clear sections of Scripture to use for interpreting the less clear, more difficult portions of the Bible, such as Revelation 20:1–6.

Amillennialists take the Bible seriously, but not usually as literally as do certain types of premillennialists. For example, they conclude that the promises granted to Israel will find ultimate fulfillment in the church and that all Old Testament prophecies either have all been fulfilled in Christ and the church or will be fulfilled in the eternal state. Amillennialism acknowledges the symbolic power of prophetic literature and interprets it accordingly. As a result, the "last days" are defined as the time between the first coming and the second coming of Christ. Rather than supplying a strict chronological map of future events, Revelation describes these last days of tribulation through repeated visions. Consequently, the order in which these visions appear in Revelation is not necessarily the order of their fulfillment.

In terms of Revelation 20:1–10, amillennialists draw several conclusions:[5]

1. The visions of 20:1–3 and 20:7–10 go together to represent the situation on earth, while 20:4–6 provides a vision of the situation in heaven. All three visions refer to the same time period.
2. The number "one thousand" indicates a complete period of time when God's will is accomplished. It may also highlight the glory of reigning with Christ in heaven when compared to the brief period of tribulation experienced on earth.
3. The "binding of Satan" mentioned in 20:2 is a restatement of the clear record of Satan's binding presented in Revelation 12. In fact, the New Testament emphasizes two climactic phases of Christ's victory over Satan—the cross and his second coming (e.g., John 12:31; Col. 2:15; Heb. 2:14–15; 1 John 3:8). Revelation 20 provides a symbolic restatement of these two victories.
4. The "battle" mentioned in 20:8 is the same battle mentioned in 16:14 and 19:19. This last record of the same battle specifies what happens to Satan as a result of his defeat.
5. Revelation 20:4–6 offers a glimpse of the saints reigning with Christ in heaven (e.g., the reference to "thrones" and "souls" locate the scene in heaven). This reign occurs after these saints have died and as they are waiting for Christ's return, their resurrection, and the eternal state.
6. Believers experience one death (physical death) and two resurrections. The first resurrection occurs when a believer dies and is brought into God's presence (though some amillennialists view the first resurrection as what happens when a person receives new life in Jesus' name). The second resurrection is a bodily resurrection and occurs at Christ's return to prepare believers for the eternal state (1 Cor. 15:35–57).

Augustine is credited with developing amillennialism in a systematic way, although the close identification of amillennialism and postmillennialism in the early years explains why both groups claim him as an early proponent. Amillennialism has been the favored position of many Catholics, Anglicans, Lutherans, and Reformed groups, as well as many Baptists. In the twentieth century with the decline of postmillennialism, many shifted to amillennialism rather than make the major jump to premillennialism.

Amillennialism features a number of strengths. Compared to the other positions, amillennialism focuses on the central truths of biblical eschatology such as the return of Christ and avoids getting bogged down in overly complex details. This simplicity is appealing to many. Amillennialism takes seriously the nature of biblical literature and attempts to interpret according to the rules of each literary genre. In addition, amillennialists do serious exegesis on a wide variety of relevant biblical passages, attempting to use the clear passages to make sense of the more obscure passages. In contrast to postmillennialism, this view adopts a realistic view of the difficulty of living in the last days.

The primary weakness of amillennialism lies in its exegesis of Revelation 20:1–10, especially its understanding of the two resurrections. Verses 4–6 reads as follows:

> I saw thrones on which were seated those who had been given authority to judge. And I saw the souls of those who had been beheaded because of their testimony for Jesus and because of the word of God. They had not worshiped the beast or his image and had not received his mark on their foreheads or their hands. They came to life and reigned with Christ a thousand years. (The rest of the dead did not come to life until the thousand years were ended.) This is the first resurrection. Blessed and holy are those who have part in the first resurrection. The second death has no power over them, but they will be priests of God and of Christ and will reign with him for a thousand years.

Amillennialists have interpreted "come to life" in Revelation 20:4 either as new spiritual life given at conversion or as a heavenly reigning with Christ after death. In other words, the first resurrection is a spiritual resurrection of sorts. But they take the next reference to resurrection in 20:5 (the "rest of the dead did not come to life until the thousand years were ended") as a physical resurrection. Premillennialists in particular have noted the inconsistency of interpreting the same verb within the same immediate context in two completely different ways—the one as spiritual resurrection and the other as physical resurrection.

In addition, the phrase "the rest of the dead" in 20:5 indicates an entirely different group of people from the group referenced in 20:4. Since these interpretive inconsistencies occur in the central passage related to the millennium, the amillennial interpretation has been called into question by some. (See also DISPENSATIONALISM, CLASSIC; DISPENSATIONALISM, PROGRESSIVE; MILLENNIAL KINGDOM; POSTMILLENNIALISM; PREMILLENNIALISM, HISTORIC.)

Ancient of Days

The Ancient of Days personage occurs in two key biblical prophetic passages: Daniel 7:9 and Revelation 1:14–16. The first text, all agree, describes the LORD seated on the heavenly throne (see THRONE). The white clothing symbolizes God's righteousness. The hairlike wool implies his antiquity, and the fiery throne depicts his awesome power. A second figure, described in Daniel 7:13–14, is that of the heavenly Son of Man (see SON OF MAN), who receives the kingdom of God from the Ancient of Days (see KINGDOM OF GOD). Two prominent understandings of the Son of Man are that he either personifies the struggles and triumph of God's ancient people Israel, or he foreshadows the coming messianic deliverer.

The religious background of the two Daniel personages could be that of Canaanite religion. Like the Ancient of Days in Daniel 7, the head of the Canaanite pantheon of deities was El, the aged god who was addressed by the title "father of years." Moreover, the Canaanite myth depicts El's son, Baal, as riding on the clouds in his ascent to heaven, recently victorious over Yamm, the god of the chaotic sea. This is reminiscent of 7:13–14 (cf. vv. 1–8). If that is indeed the background of the Ancient of Days, then Daniel's portrait of the LORD nevertheless exalts him above any supposed Canaanite rival deity, as it does also the heavenly Son of Man.

The second relevant prophetic passage dealing with the Ancient of Days is Revelation 1:14–16. Exiled by Roman authorities on Patmos because of his faith in Jesus, John receives a vision from God. In that vision, he sees a heavenly person in whom is combined the features of the heavenly Son of Man and the Ancient of Days. Similar imagery characterizing the latter figure (white hair, fiery presence) is now applied to Jesus, the heavenly Son of Man. Clearly John here asserts that Jesus, the heavenly Son of Man, is none other that the Ancient of Days. That is to say, Jesus is God.

Angels

Angels, or messengers, in the Bible perform four general services: they worship God and his Son (Rev. 5:11–14), they minister to the righteous (Ps. 34:7; 91:11; Matt. 18:10–11; Heb. 1:14), they deliver messages from God (see, e.g., Matt. 1:20–23; 2:13; Luke 1:11-17, 26–38; 2:8–14), and they oppose evil human beings and fallen angels.

The relationship between angels and biblical prophecy unfolds in two categories: righteous angels and fallen angels or demons. A righteous angel who appears numerous times in the Old Testament is called the "angel of the LORD" (Gen. 16:7; 19:1, 21; 22:11; 31:11, 13; Ex. 3:2, 4; Judg. 2:1–5; 6:11–12, 14; 13:3, 6, 8–11, 13, 15–17, 20–23; Zech. 3:1–6; 12:8). Some scholars maintain this personage was a preincarnate manifestation of Christ, implying that many of these texts serve as indirect prophecies of the Messiah to come. That interpretation, however, is contested, for the angel of the Lord may simply be God's personal messenger who represented him and bore God's credentials.

Another righteous angel is Michael. He appears in Daniel 10:13–14, 21; 12:1, and is clearly connected to biblical prophecy (see MICHAEL). Those passages envision Michael as defending Israel during the future great tribulation, a time when Jews in mass will embrace God and his Messiah (see GREAT TRIBULATION). According to many interpreters, Revelation 12:7–9 is a further depiction of Daniel's prophecy. Michael and the angels of heaven will cast out Satan and his angelic followers to earth. Although the serpent will persecute Jews during the messianic woes, or the great tribulation, his fall from heaven is the beginning of the end of his evil reign.

Another key passage mentioning Michael is Jude 9, which refers to Michael's confrontation with the devil over the body of Moses, a noncanonical episode. The point made by Jude is that even Michael the archangel did not dare rebuke Satan, but rather deferred to God that task. In contrast, the false teachers of the end times will claim for themselves spiritual authority beyond their domain (Jude 10).

Yet another key angel in the Bible is Gabriel. He reveals the end times regarding Israel to Daniel (Dan. 8:16–26; 9:20–27) and announces the births of John the Baptist (Luke 1:11–20) and of Jesus (1:26–38).

Finally, a number of New Testament texts associate righteous angels with events that will attend the second coming of Christ (see SECOND COMING): sealing and protecting the people of God in the great tribulation (Rev. 7; 14); executing the judgments of God on the wicked during that same time period (Rev. 8–11; 15–18), including Satan (Rev. 20:1–3, 7–10); and accompanying Christ at his return (Matt. 24:30–31; Mark 13:26–27; 2 Thess. 1:7; Rev. 1:7).

The other major connection between angels and biblical prophecy is that of demons or fallen angels, who are led by Satan. Two key parallel texts dealing with fallen angels are Jude 6 and 2 Peter 2:4, where we read that certain angels did not remain in their divinely assigned positions. Consequently, they were consigned to hell (*tartaros*), the term used by Greeks to refer to the place where wicked spirits were sent to be punished.

Two views compete in their interpretations of Jude 6 and 2 Peter 2:4. (1) Some believe these angels' sin is described in Genesis 6:2, where the sons of God are said to have intermarried with the daughters of men (i.e., angels married human women). The offspring of those marriages are thought to have been giants, the Nephilim of Genesis 6. This is why God judged the earth by the flood. The Jewish noncanonical book *1 Enoch* certainly interprets Genesis 6 that way.

(2) But because many assume that angels, who are spirits, cannot have sexual relations with human women, they consider the sin referred to in Jude 6 and 2 Peter 2:4 as having occurred before the fall of Adam and Eve. These supernatural beings became fallen angels and are probably the demons and evil spirits referred to in the New Testament. They are confined in hell, awaiting the judgment of the second coming of Christ. Why some evil angels are imprisoned now and others not yet, allowing them to serve Satan as demons, is not explained in the Bible. It may be that the demons currently in *tartaros* are those who will be unleashed on the earth during the great tribulation (see Rev. 9). That prophetic chapter describes hideous, locust-like creatures as being let out of the Abyss (hell) for the purpose of inflicting torment on the followers of the Antichrist. Interestingly enough, that scene witnesses righteous angels calling the fallen angels into action, the implication being that the latter are subject to the former.

The leader of the fallen angels is known in Scripture by various names: the serpent (Gen. 3:1; Rev. 12:9; 20:2), Satan (Job 1:6; Zech. 3:2; Matt. 12:26; etc.), the devil (Matt. 4:1, 5, 8, 11; etc.), the god of this age (2 Cor. 4:4), and Lucifer (Isa. 14:12, Latin Vulgate). Some interpreters think Satan's fall from the ranks of righteous angels occurred at the time of the Garden of Eden (cf. Gen. 3 with Isa. 14:12–15; Ezek. 28:1–19). But these last two passages more likely allude to the falls of ancient Babylon (see BABYLON) and Tyre, respectively. If that is true, then Satan's fall is a matter of fact by the time we read Genesis 3.

Several key end-time activities characterize what Satan did as described in the New Testament. (1) He opposed the first coming of Christ and the dawning of the kingdom of God by tempting Jesus to avoid the cross (Matt. 4:1–11; Luke 4:1–13; cf. Mark 8:31–33). (2) That failing, Satan and his demons attacked Christ head-on through the evil intentions of Judas and the Jewish leadership (John 13:27–30; 1 Cor. 2:8). (3) Satan continues to oppress the church in the time before the second coming of Christ (Rev. 12:13–17; 13:1–18). (4) Yet, Christ on earth defeated Satan through the power and holiness of the kingdom of God (Luke 10:18–20; Col. 2:15). The exorcisms and healings he and his followers did were a sign of that. Whether or not Revelation 20:1–3, 7–10 refers to the defeat of Satan at the first coming of Christ is debated. Those who disagree with that perspective relegate the fulfillment of Revelation 20 to a future millennium, inaugurated at the return of Christ (see MILLENNIUM).

Anna

Anna (Luke 2:36–37) was an elderly, widowed prophetess who, at the time of Jesus' birth, lived at the Jerusalem Temple, fasting and praying. The emphasis of Luke's description of Anna is on her piety and on her reliability as one who could recognize the Messiah. In addition, her constant fasting and praying may not have been merely ritual, but rather were probably a sign of mourning, an acknowledgment that the spiritual situation in Israel and in the Temple at that time was deplorable. Along with Simeon (Luke 2:25–35) she represents those pious Jews who were faithfully looking for the coming Messiah.

Seeing Jesus in the Temple, Anna recognizes him immediately as the Messiah. She then gives praise to God for him and speaks of him to all of the others who, like her, were "looking forward to the redemption of Jerusalem" (Luke 2:38). As the story unfolds, the religious establishment associated with the Temple in Jerusalem rejects Christ and ultimately has him crucified. Anna, however, represents the true remnant, those connected with the true prophetic tradition of the Old Testament who were looking expectantly for the Messiah (see REMNANT).

Self-centered and self-seeking people like the scribes and Pharisees did not acknowledge the Messiah, reacting to Jesus with hostility rather than faith. People like Anna, by contrast, recognized him readily and proclaimed him as Messiah to all who were really looking for the Coming One.

Antichrist

Surprisingly, the term *antichrist* (Gk. *antichristos*) is only used four times in the Bible (1 John 2:18, 22: 4:3; 2 John 7). John warns his "dear children" that it is already the last hour and that just as they "have heard that the antichrist is coming, even now many antichrists have come" (1 John 2:18). The spirit of Antichrist, John says, is "already in the world" (1 John 4:3). He defines the Antichrist as a man who "denies the Father and the Son" (1 John 2:22), as "every spirit that does not acknowledge Jesus" (1 John 4:3), and as a "deceiver" who "does not acknowledge Jesus Christ as coming in the flesh" (2 John 7). John seems to rely on the false prophet theme common in the Old Testament when describing the antichrist(s).

Although the specific term is only mentioned a few times in Scripture, the concept of antichrist-type figures surfaces elsewhere in the New Testament. Jesus mentions "false Christs and false prophets" who will "perform signs and miracles to deceive the elect—if that were possible" (Mark 13:22). This description closely parallels the "beast from the earth" mentioned in the last half of Revelation 13 (this beast is often referred to as "the False Prophet"). Paul speaks of a "man of lawlessness" who will "oppose and will exalt himself over everything that is called God or is worshiped, so that he sets himself up in God's Temple, proclaiming himself to be God" (2 Thess. 2:3–4). In Revelation 13, John describes the most famous antichrist figure of all—the "beast from the sea." Before examining the beast of Revelation more fully, it will be helpful to know a bit about what led to the development of the image.

There could not be "Antichrist" before there was a Christ, that is, before Jesus came to be recognized as Messiah (see MESSIAH). As a result, the early Christians were responsible for officially developing the teaching about the Antichrist. They did, however, draw on and modify common Jewish traditions. Throughout the Old Testament, the false prophet tradition (e.g., Deut. 13, 18; Jer. 23; Ezek. 12–14) describes religious individuals from within the community who attempt to deceive God's people. Also, there was a common belief in an oppressive ruler from outside the community who would persecute the righteous (e.g., Dan. 8, 11). By the late first century when Revelation was written, people would have been familiar with a host of pagan rulers who had exalted themselves as gods (Babylon in Isa. 14; Pharaoh in Ezek. 29; Antiochus IV Epiphanes perhaps in Dan. 11; Roman emperors such as Caligula, Nero, and Domitian). The evil-ruler tradition and the false-prophet tradition seem to converge in Revelation 13 as the beast from the sea (the Antichrist) and the beast from the earth (the false prophet).

Most scholars agree that the original beast described in Revelation 13 was the Roman emperor (either Nero or Domitian), who demanded to be worshiped as God. Supported by a second beast, the cult of Caesar worship enforced by priests throughout the empire, the imperial system demanded that Christians choose between two opposing confessions— Caesar is Lord or Jesus is Lord—and those who chose the latter faced persecution, even death.

More specifically, Revelation indicates that the "beast from the sea" is empowered by Satan (Rev. 13:1–2, 4), masquerades as Christ (13:1, 3, 12, 14), accepts worship as a god (13:4, 8), wields extensive power (13:4, 7), blasphemes and slanders God (13:1, 5–6), and ruthlessly persecutes the saints (13:7). The "beast from the earth" (emperor cult) is also empowered by Satan (13:11, 14), promotes the worship of the first beast (13:12, 14–15), performs signs and wonders designed to deceive (13:13–15), and causes those who refused to worship the first beast to be put to death physically (13:15) or economically (13:16–17). Together with the dragon or Satan, these three are often identified as the unholy or satanic trinity.

Whereas John wrote to warn Christians at that time about the dangers of the Roman emperor and the imperial cult that opposed Christ and persecuted Christians, the images of the Antichrist and the false prophet remain an ongoing threat to God's people. As John argues in his letters, there will always be antichrists who continue in the wicked tradition of the originals. There will always be systems and institutions controlled by Satan, personified in individuals, and promoted with religious fervor that set themselves against Christ and persecute those who follow him. There continues the expectation of a future, final embodiment of the Antichrist who, empowered by Satan, will deceive humanity, blaspheme God, contend for the worship that only Christ deserves, and persecute believers who persevere in their allegiance to Christ alone. In spite of a final effort to take God's place and conquer his people, Christ will return to destroy the Antichrist and the false prophet in the lake of fire (Rev. 17:8; 19:19–21). (See ARMAGEDDON; BEASTS OF REVELATION; NERO; NERO REDIVIVUS; SIX HUNDRED SIXTY-SIX.)

Antiochus Epiphanes

Antiochus IV Epiphanes (175–164 B.C.) was the younger son of Antiochus III, ruler of the Seleucid empire. The name Epiphanes means "manifest," implying "manifest as a god." After his father was assassinated and his older brother taken as hostage by Rome, Antiochus IV assumed the throne over Syria. His veritably insane behavior and his tyrannical demeanor earned him the nickname "Epimanes" ("utterly mad").

Antiochus's ambition was to use the common culture of the Greeks (Hellenism) to unite the diverse Seleucid empire. He especially set his sights on Egypt and, along the way, Israel. Antiochus accepted the bribe of Jason, leader of the pro-Greek faction in Jerusalem, naming him high priest in place of the rightful priest, Onias III. In return, Jason agreed to hellenize Jerusalem by turning it into a Greek polis (city) and exposing the city to Syrian religion. According to the noncanonical Jewish history of 2 Maccabees 4:7–22, this stage of development occurred from 174 B.C. to 171 B.C.

After a series of events that culminated in the attempt of Menelaus (who supplanted Jason as high priest) to stage a coup against Antiochus's government in Israel, the Seleucid ruler retaliated against Jerusalem (169 B.C.), butchering its inhabitants and looting the Temple (see 2 Macc. 5:11–23; Josephus, *Antiquities* 12.5.3/246–47). Two years later, after being repelled from Egypt by the Romans, Antiochus unleashed his fury on Jerusalem. His soldiers attacked the city on the Sabbath, killing much of the male population and enslaving the remaining women and children (1 Macc. 1:29–36; 2 Macc. 5:24–26).

Then followed the prohibition of all Jewish rites, along with the rededication of the Jewish Temple to the Greek god Zeus. Anyone caught reading the Torah, observing the Sabbath and dietary laws, or circumcising their male babies was killed (1 Macc. 1:54–64; Josephus, *Antiquities* 12.5.4–5/248–64). In December 167 B.C., the first pagan sacrifice was offered on the altar in the Most Holy Place in the Jerusalem Temple (1 Macc. 1:54).

Antiochus at first met with pockets of resistance from faithful Jews, who opposed the ruler's orders and were therefore martyred (2 Macc. 6:10–7:42). But with a man named Mattathias and his five sons, open defiance against Antiochus's policies ensued. Mattathias, a priest in the town of Modein, refused to sacrifice to heathen gods and killed the Syrian representative. This incident sparked a Jewish rebellion led by his family (the Maccabees), culminating in his son Judah's defeat of Antiochus's forces in December 164 B.C. At that time Judas reconsecrated the Temple to Yahweh, the God of Israel, and Israel resumed the observance of the Jewish law (1 Macc. 4:52–59). Later that year, Antiochus, who had unsuccessfully tried to invade Persia, died of illness (1 Macc. 6:1–17; Josephus, *Antiquities* 12.9–1/354–59; 2 Macc. 1:13–17; 9:1–29).

Antiochus Epiphanes IV intersects with biblical prophecy in Daniel 8:11; 9:27; 11:31; 12:11. Those passages highlight the Seleucid ruler's attempt to hellenize the Jews, culminating in "the abomination of desolation." As such, many interpreters see in Antiochus's profaning of the Jerusalem Temple a foreshadowing of the coming of the Antichrist's desolation of a future, rebuilt Jewish Temple (see ABOMINATION OF DESOLATION; DANIEL, BOOK OF; ANTICHRIST)

Apocalypse

The term *apocalypse* comes from the Greek word *apokalypsis*, meaning "revelation" or "unveiling." An apocalypse is a work that features a heavenly figure (usually God or an angel) using apocalyptic language to reveal a "secret" message, often having an eschatological focus (e.g., relating to heaven or the kingdom of God or the end of the world). The book of Revelation is described as "the revelation [*apokalypsis*] of Jesus Christ" (Rev. 1:1), meaning either that the book reveals something about Jesus or that Jesus reveals something about God's plan in the book (or perhaps both). In either case, a message is being revealed or disclosed. Many interpreters refer to Revelation as "the Apocalypse" (see APOCALYPTIC LITERATURE; REVELATION, BOOK OF).

Apocalypse of Baruch

Not to be confused with the biblical Baruch who served as Jeremiah's scribe or with the apocryphal book of Baruch (ca. 150 B.C. and pseudonymously attributed to Jeremiah's scribe), the *Apocalypse of Baruch*, or *2 Baruch*, is a first century A.D., noncanonical Jewish book. It was written in the aftermath of the fall of Jerusalem in A.D. 70, though it purports to originate soon after the Babylonian destruction of the holy city in 587/586 B.C.

The core issue in *2 Baruch* is not theodicy (i.e., why did God permit Zion [see ZION] to fall?) but rather promise/fulfillment (i.e., when will God fulfill his promise to restore Jerusalem, see *2 Bar.* 1:4–5; 5:3?). The author attempts to show all Jews that, in the meantime, their only hope is God and his law: "We have nothing now apart from the Mighty One and his Law" (85:3).

Obviously, then, the Mosaic Law is of paramount importance in *Apocalypse of Baruch*. Two matters in it regarding the Torah can be highlighted here. (1) The law is viewed as God's gift explicitly to Israel, not to the nations in general (*2 Bar.* 32:1; 44:3, 7; 46:4–5; 77:3; 15–16). Only in 82:6 are the heathen said to have known the law, but they still transgressed it (cf. perhaps 15:5, though the reference here to "man" most likely refers to the Jew). (2) The law is ethical-eschatological in nature. Faithfulness to the law in this evil age ensures for the obedient the glory of the age to come (51:7–10; cf. 31:5–32:7; 44:3–15; 46:5–6; 77:5–7, 13–15).

Key to interpreting *2 Baruch* is the story of Israel (sin–exile––restoration), which governs the seven units of the book. From the author's perspective, because Israel sinned against God's law, divine judgment and exile came upon the nation in the form of Roman occupation. But the hope of restoration is also an ever-present theme in *2 Baruch*.

The overarching message of this first-century Jewish work is that the curses (see CURSE) of the covenant rest on Israel in this present age because of her sin, but in the age to come, God's blessing will once again reside on her, because she returned to the law and to the Lord. This apocalypse is important background for New Testament prophecy in general because of its apocalyptic orientation and in particular because of its description of the new Jerusalem.

Apocalyptic Literature

The term *apocalyptic* describes a genre or type of literature popular between the Old and New Testaments. Most scholars believe that apocalyptic literature grew out of Hebrew prophecy and actually represents an intensified form of prophecy written during a time of crisis. In apocalyptic there is a divine revelation through a heavenly intermediary to some well-known figure, in which God promises to intervene in human history to overthrow evil and establish his kingdom. In an apocalypse God's message is confirmed by the otherworldly way it is communicated; the readers experience the visions of the messenger, and they are challenged to change the way they think and behave based on that experience. In other words, desperate circumstances call for the desperately shocking genre of apocalyptic.

In the Old Testament, apocalyptic is often associated with the books of Daniel and Zechariah as well as select passages in other prophets (e.g., Isa. 24–27; 56–66; Ezek. 38–39). Several Jewish apocalypses became popular during the intertestamental period (e.g., *1 and 2 Enoch*, *Jubilees*, *2 and 3 Baruch*, *4 Ezra*, and the *Apocalypse of Abraham*). The apocalyptic literary style continues through the New Testament period. In addition to Revelation, such material appears in Jesus' Olivet discourse (Matt. 24–25; Mark 13) (see OLIVET DISCOURSE).

Apocalyptic literature contains fantastic visions and bizarre characters. In Revelation, for example, we read of four living creatures covered with eyes and wings, a red dragon with seven heads and ten horns, locusts with human faces and tails that sting like scorpions, and so on. Brent Sandy offers a list of what readers might encounter in Old Testament apocalyptic:[6]

- jaw-dropping scenes of animals, rivers, mountains, and stars that jump off the page with movie-like special effects (Dan. 8:2–14; Zech. 6:1–7)
- natural catastrophes producing cosmic chaos throughout the universe, ushering in the dreadful day of judgment (Isa. 24:18–20; Ezek. 38:19–22)
- pernicious and disruptive evil contributing to constant crises and producing a seemingly hopeless pessimism with the course of current events (Isa. 57:3–13; Dan. 7:19–25)
- an underlying determinism resting in the unquestioned conviction that somehow God maintains sovereign control (Isa. 25:1; 26:1–4)
- ecstatic expectation that God will intervene and suppress all evil forces working against his predetermined plan (Zech. 14:3–9; Mal. 3:1–5)
- visions of celestial scenes and beings with an otherworldly perspective (Dan. 10:4–19; Zech. 3:1–10)
- heavenly interpreters explaining the scenes in language that may be figurative (Ezek. 40:3–4; Dan. 8:15–17)
- a dualistic perspective that categorizes things into contrasting elements such as good and evil, this age and the age to come (Dan. 12:2)
- God's promise to act in the last days to restore his people and establish a new and glorious world order (Isa. 27:12–13; Zech. 8:1–8).

Certain themes are common to apocalyptic literature.

1. Apocalyptic assumes a situation of growing hopelessness. Hostile powers are becoming more powerful as the situation for God's people deteriorates. While the wicked appear to prosper, the righteous suffer.
2. No matter how bleak the outlook, God is sovereign and his heavenly reign will one day descend to earth in all its fullness. The Lord can be trusted.
3. Apocalyptic literature uses visions to bring perspective. Visions transport readers to another world in order to give them heavenly perspective. This renewed perspective allows them to endure.

4. Evil is no match for God. One day God will intervene to punish the wicked and destroy evil. No evil power will be able to withstand his coming judgment.

5. As the world system tempts believers to compromise, they are called to holy and blameless living.

6. God's people are called to persevere. Since God will win in the end, believers need enduring devotion to the true God. God alone is worthy of worship.

7. God will restore creation and will live forever with his people in a perfect community.

To expand on the above list, note Sandy's twelve themes of New Testament apocalyptic literature:[7]

Twelve Themes of New Testament Apocalyptic	
Striking presentation of the transcendent Lord	Horrors experienced by the animal world
Unprecedented turmoil in the world	Preservation of God's elect (the remnant)
The end of history as near	Coming of a new society for the righteous
God's terrifying judgment of evil	Rewards for the righteous
Horrors in the heavens	Satanic forces to attack God's people
Horrors on earth	Backlash of evil experienced by saints

Apocalyptic presupposes a crisis of faith among the believing audience. If God is truly in control, why are evil powers allowed to oppress his people and disrupt his plan? Readers are given a dramatic reminder that God is indeed sovereign and that nothing can frustrate his plan to defeat evil, vindicate his people, and establish his eternal kingdom.

For example, Revelation uses vivid images to create a symbolic world for the readers to inhabit. When they enter this symbolic world, their whole way of thinking is transformed so that their "normal" perspective on the world is changed. They are able to see things from a heavenly perspective because they have been changed by the visions of Revelation. As they are transported to the final future, they can see the present from the perspective of God's ultimate victory over his enemies. In this way Revelation provides Christians with a set of "prophetic counter-images" to purge their imagination of the pagan view of the world and replace it with a mind-set of what things will be like after God's ultimate restoration.[8] Richard Bauckham illustrates using Revelation 17:

> For example, in chapter 17 John's readers share his vision of a woman. At first glance, she might seem to be the goddess Roma, in all her glory, a stunning personification of the civilization of Rome, as she was worshipped in many a temple in the cities of Asia. But as John sees her, she is a Roman prostitute, a seductive whore and a scheming witch, and her wealth and splendor represent the profits of her disreputable trade. For good measure there are biblical overtones of the harlot queen Jezebel to reinforce the impression. In this way, John's readers are able to perceive something of Rome's true character—her moral corruption behind the enticing propagandist illusions of Rome which they constantly encountered in their cities.[9]

When Christians who are facing hostile circumstances hear again and again the message of Revelation, they are reminded that "what they believe is not strange and odd, but truly normal from God's perspective."[10]

By using images in this way, Revelation answers the larger question, "Who is Lord?" During times of oppression and persecution, the righteous suffer and the wicked seem to prosper. This begs the question, "Is God is still on his throne?" Revelation says that in spite of how things appear, Jesus is Lord and he is coming soon to restore his creation and establish his eternal kingdom. Satan, sin, and death will not have the final word. The main message of Revelation is that "God wins!" Those who are being pressured by the wicked have their hearts and minds immersed in hope and their eyes opened to see God's future. Those who are selling their souls to the pagan powers are shown God's future in order to shock them into repentance.

While the abundant use of visual images makes apocalyptic effective, those same images can puzzle and frustrate interpreters. Often readers encounter strange and bizarre picture language that they see nowhere else in Scripture. Even if the images are familiar, they are often combined in apocalyptic literature in ways that make them extraordinary. For example, we know about women and we know about the sun, but we don't know much about a woman clothed with the sun (Rev. 12:1). Revelation regularly combines images in unusual ways to accomplish its purpose. How should interpreters approach apocalyptic literature?

The following interpretive principles from Duvall and Hays provide guidance for interpreting apocalyptic literature such as Daniel, Ezekiel, Zechariah, and Revelation.[11]

1. Approach apocalyptic with humility since it is not easy literature to interpret and interpreters must sometimes live with uncertainty about the details of a passage.
2. Try to discover the message to the original readers. Apocalyptic was familiar to the ancient listener, particularly those experiencing a crisis of suffering. Rather than moving immediately to contemporary application, readers today should familiarize themselves with the mind-set of apocalyptic and seek to discover how the first audience would have understood the message.
3. Resist the temptation to discover in apocalyptic a strict chronological map of future events. Apocalyptic doesn't always move in a neat linear fashion. For example, there is considerable debate in Revelation about the relationship between the trumpet, seal, and bowl judgments. Rather than searching for a precise map of future events, interpreters are better off focusing on the main message in each vision.
4. Take apocalyptic seriously, but don't always take it literally. Expect this type of literature to use picture language to describe literal events. Techniques such as metaphor, hyperbole, irony, numerical patterns, and exaggeration are used to portray heavenly realities vividly. To say that the image of a woman sitting on seven hills is figurative (Rev. 17:9) is not to deny its historical reality, but simply to acknowledge that picture language is being used to describe Rome, the city built on seven hills.
5. When the author himself directly identifies an image, contemporary readers should take notice. For example, in Revelation 1:17 the Son of Man is Christ, in 1:20 the golden lampstands are the churches, in 5:5–6 the Lion is the Lamb, in 12:9 the dragon is Satan, and in 21:9–10 the heavenly Jerusalem is the wife of the Lamb or the church.
6. Readers should pay close attention to the historical-cultural context when attempting to discover what the images and symbols refer to. When interpreting New Testament apocalyptic material, readers should also look to the Old Testament for help. For instance, Revelation contains more echoes and allusions to the Old Testament than any other New Testament book.
7. Perhaps most important, focus on the main idea of each episode and don't press all the details. Since the first audience would have

listened to the book being read aloud, apocalyptic literature was designed to make an emotional impression on listeners. With most literary genres in the Bible, the interpreter begins with details and builds toward an understanding of the whole. In apocalyptic, however, readers should start with the big picture or main idea and work toward a grasp of the details. The concern over details should never take the focus off the main point of each section or vision.

When read using these and other appropriate guidelines, apocalyptic literature has a unique ability to touch the imagination and deepen the faith of contemporary Christians, especially those suffering for their faith. (See APOCALYPSE; REVELATION, BOOK OF.)

Apocrypha/Pseudepigrapha

The Apocrypha (the "mysterious writings") consists of fifteen additional books found in the Catholic Bible but not in the Protestant Bible: 1 and 2 Esdras, Tobit, Judith, Additions to Esther, Wisdom of Solomon, Sirach, Baruch, Epistle of Jeremiah, Prayer of Azariah and the Song of the Three Young Men, Susanna, Bel and the Dragon (the last three-mentioned pieces are supplements to Daniel), Prayer of Manasseh, and 1 and 2 Maccabees. Some other traditions accept Psalm 151 and 3 and 4 Maccabees.

Catholics defend the canonicity of the Apocrypha by three key rationales. (1) The New Testament draws on the Apocrypha (cf., e.g., Rom. 1:20–29 with Wisd. Sol. 1:20–29; Rom. 2:1–11 with Wisd. Sol. 15:1; 2 Cor. 5:1 with Wisd. Sol. 9:15; Matt. 11:28–30 with Sir. 6:18–31; James 1:9 with Sir. 5:11; Heb. 11:35 with 2 Macc. 7:20–23). This gives the impression that New Testament authors alluding to the Apocrypha believe it to be inspired. (2) The Septuagint (the Greek translation of the Hebrew Scriptures, ca. 250 B.C.) may have included the Apocrypha, judging from the oldest copies of the Septuagint (ca. fourth century A.D.). (3) Church fathers such as Origen (third century A.D.) and Augustine (fifth century A.D.) apparently believed the Apocrypha to be inspired.

Protestants, however, disagree. (1) In answer to the first point, just because a New Testament author alludes to the Apocrypha does not mean it was considered inspired. Note how Paul quotes pagan philosophers (Aratus in Acts 17:28; Menander in 1 Cor. 15:34; Epimenides in Titus 1:12–13), but no one seriously thinks he attributed canonicity to those writers. (2) Whether or not the Apocrypha was in the original Septuagint (and that is debatable since there are no copies of the original), those books certainly were never included in the Hebrew Bible. Not even

Philo (ca. 40 B.C.), who lived in Alexandria, the home of the Septuagint, believed the Apocrypha to be sacred Scripture. (3) While key church fathers accepted the Apocrypha as inspired because their Bible was the Septuagint, many did not—most notably Jerome, the author of the Latin translation, the Vulgate (fifth century A.D.).

But if it turns out that the Apocrypha is rightly excluded from Protestant Bibles, why bother to study the material? Several reasons quickly come to mind. (1) Textually, the Apocrypha, as it is reflected in the Septuagint, provides a valuable witness for reconstructing the original Hebrew Old Testament. (2) Hermeneutically, the Apocrypha marks an important transition between the Old and New Testaments: for the former, culmination of central convictions; for the latter, indispensable background. (3) Ethnically, Christians have an obligation to understand the Jewish community from which Christianity sprang. The Apocrypha helps do that, providing a vibrant witness to Israel's struggle to forge her faith between 400 B.C. and A.D. 100. In short, even though the Apocrypha does not have canonical status, Protestants neglect the Apocrypha to the detriment of their own understanding of the Bible.

The Pseudepigrapha (false writings), a related term to the Apocrypha, is comprised of approximately fifty Jewish intertestamental pieces (e.g., *1, 2, 3, Enoch, Jubilees, Psalms of Solomon, 2 Baruch, Testaments of the Twelve Patriarchs, Letter of Aristeas*) and is usually classified as either Palestinian (written in Aramaic in Israel) or Alexandrian (written in Greek in Alexandria, Egypt, and beyond). While no religious tradition views these works as canonical, the same three reasons for studying the Apocrypha pertain to the Pseudepigrapha (it should be noted that in form and content the Pseudepigrapha differs little from the Apocrypha). Probably some of the noncanonical works in the Dead Sea Scrolls (a collection of over 850 manuscripts dating from about 150 B.C.) should also be classified in this category. If so, then the Pseudepigrapha includes hundreds of works.

Ark of the Covenant

The Ark of the Covenant is also called the "ark of the LORD," "ark of God," "ark of the testimony," or "ark of the covenant of the LORD." The ark was a rectangular-shaped box (approx. 4 feet by 2½ feet by 2½ feet), covered with gold inside and out. It held the Ten Commandments, a pot of manna from the wilderness wandering, and Aaron's rod (Heb. 9:4). On top of it was the "mercy seat" (NIV "atonement cover"), a gold cover with gold cherubim on either side (see CHERUBIM). The ark was the focal point for the very presence of God. It was kept in the Most Holy Place, first in the Tabernacle and then in the Temple.

The prophet Jeremiah prophesies that in the coming days there will no longer be an Ark of the Covenant, and, furthermore, no one will miss it (Jer. 3:16). In addition, Jeremiah proclaims, after the original ark is gone, a new one will not be built. Later in Jeremiah's life the Babylonians destroy Jerusalem and the Temple, and the ark disappears from history. Most scholars suspect that the Babylonians probably melted it down and carried the gold away, although rumors and speculations about the fate of the ark have circulated for centuries.

A questionable Jewish tradition states that Jeremiah took the ark and hid it under the Temple Mount (or elsewhere) prior to the Babylonian capture of Jerusalem. Most scholars maintain that this is unlikely.

The Ethiopian Orthodox Church claims to have the original Ark of the Covenant at a church in the ancient city of Aksum. According to Ethiopian folk legend, the Queen of Sheba, an Ethiopian queen, had a child by King Solomon. This child, Menilek, returned to Jerusalem to visit his father, and then stole the ark and brought it to Ethiopia, where it remains today, although the Ethiopian Orthodox Church keeps it secluded and will not let anyone see it. Menilek went on to found the ruling dynasty of the Aksumite kingdom.

The problem with this legend is that Menilek and the Aksumite kingdom do not appear in history until about one thousand years *after* Solomon. So it is unlikely that Solomon was Menilek's father. However, the Ethiopians do apparently have *something* that is very old and quite special related to the ark in that church in Aksum. Furthermore, the Ark of the Covenant plays an important role in the festivals of the Ethiopian Orthodox Church, and has played this role for hundreds of years. How did such a custom get started?

One plausible explanation is that the Ethiopians have a very, very old copy of the original ark. Around 590 B.C. the Egyptians hired Jewish mercenaries to defend a fort on the island of Elephantine on the Nile River. These mercenaries built a Jewish community on this island in Upper Egypt. After two hundred years they disappeared from history. It is possible that these Jewish mercenary/settlers built a model of the Temple on Elephantine and likewise constructed a model of the ark as well. At some point perhaps they migrated east to Ethiopia and settled there, bringing the ark model with them. This may explain how the Jewish Ark of the Covenant came to play such an important role in Ethiopian religious life. If this is the case, then the Ethiopians have a very old (and significant) religious box in Aksum, but not the original Ark of the Covenant. It is most probable that the real ark was destroyed by the Babylonians. At any rate the ark disappeared, just as Jeremiah predicted.

The point of Jeremiah's prophecy, however, is that in the future, during the time of the New Covenant, the presence of God will not be limited to one small location, such as the Ark of the Covenant. Jeremiah's prophecy is fulfilled, not only by the disappearance of the ark around 587/586 B.C., but by the fact that in the New Testament era, God's presence indwells each believer. The people of God today do not miss the ark because they have direct access to God through Christ, and God's presence dwells directly within them through the Holy Spirit.

Armageddon

The only place "Armageddon" is mentioned in the Bible is Revelation 16:16: "Then they gathered the kings together to the place that in Hebrew is called Armageddon." This reference occurs in the context of the seven bowl judgments (16:1–21). As the sixth angel pours out his bowl, demonic spirits deceive the "kings of the whole world" and "gather them for the battle on the great day of God Almighty" (16:14). The outcome of this battle is reported in 17:14; 19:11–21; 20:7–10 as the forces of evil are totally annihilated by God Almighty and the Lamb. The gathering of the wicked for destruction was a common Old Testament theme (Joel 3:11–16; Zeph. 3:8; Zech. 12:3–4; 14:2–5). The battle reported in Revelation 16 is said to be fought at a place called "Armageddon."

The word "Armageddon" in Hebrew is *har-měgiddôn*, meaning "the mount of Megiddo." The city of Megiddo was strategically located in northern Palestine on a plain in the Valley of Jezreel or Esdraelon. Although Megiddo was not a "mountain," it was the site of many significant battles in Israel's history (e.g., Judg. 5:19; 2 Kings 23:29; 2 Chron. 35:22; Zech. 12:11). Often these battles featured righteous Israel being attacked by unrighteous nations. Greg Beale summarizes the battle background of Megiddo:

> John's reference to this place name [Megiddo] may ring with the following typological and prophetic associations: the defeat of kings who oppress God's people (Judg. 5:19–21), the destruction of false prophets (1 Kings 18:40), the death of misled kings, which led to mourning (2 Kings 23:29; 2 Chron. 35:20–25), and the expectation, in direct connection with the one "whom they have pierced," of a future destruction of "all the nations that come against Jerusalem" and mourning by all Israel's tribes (Zech. 12:9–12).[12]

Revelation 16:16 may also draw on the Gog–Magog tradition of the end-time defeat of enemy nations on "the mountains of Israel" (Ezek. 38–39). Regardless of the questions that remain about the specific background of the "mount of Megiddo," this much can be known for certain: Megiddo was connected to warfare.

How should Armageddon be interpreted? Some see real armies gathered at the exact geographical location in northern Palestine for a future battle. Satan will deceptively gather the military powers of the world in the Holy Land to combat the armies of heaven. The battle will rage for some time, ending in the defeat of the forces of evil at the return of Christ.

Other interpreters see Armageddon as a symbol of the final conflict between the forces of evil and the forces of God that occurs throughout the earth. As a result, "Armageddon" does not refer to a specific geographical location (as with other place names, such as "Babylon" or "Euphrates"), but to the whole world as a battlefield.

Regardless of whether Revelation 16:16 is interpreted literally or figuratively, the passage clearly describes a real, final battle in which Christ is victorious simply by his appearance. Revelation 19 describes the opposing armies and the battle in greater detail:

The rider on the white horse and the armies of heaven (Rev. 19:11–16):

I saw heaven standing open and there before me was a white horse, whose rider is called Faithful and True. With justice he judges and makes war. His eyes are like blazing fire, and on his head are many crowns. He has a name written on him that no one knows but he himself. He is dressed in a robe dipped in blood, and his name is the Word of God. The armies of heaven were following him, riding on white horses and dressed in fine linen, white and clean. Out of his mouth comes a sharp sword with which to strike down the nations. "He will rule them with an iron scepter." He treads the winepress of the fury of the wrath of God Almighty. On his robe and on his thigh he has this name written:

KING OF KINGS AND LORD OF LORDS.

The beast and his armies (Rev. 19:19):

Then I saw the beast and the kings of the earth and their armies gathered together to make war against the rider on the horse and his army.

The actual battle (Rev. 19:20–21):

But the beast was captured, and with him the false prophet who had performed the miraculous signs on his behalf. With these signs he had deluded those who had received the mark of the beast and worshiped his image. The two of them were thrown alive into the fiery lake of burning sulfur. The rest of them were killed with the sword that came out of the mouth of the rider on the horse, and all the birds gorged themselves on their flesh.

What is often lost in debates about Revelation 16:16 is what Jesus says to his followers in 16:15: "Behold, I come like a thief! Blessed is he who stays awake and keeps his clothes with him, so that he may not go naked and be shamefully exposed" (cf. 3:4–5, 17–18). Verse 15 is like a parenthesis between verses 14 and 16, thus providing the central spiritual message for the readers. In light of the approaching final battle, Christians should remain faithful without compromise because Jesus will return suddenly and unexpectedly. (See GOG AND MAGOG; SECOND COMING OF CHRIST.)

Astronomical Signs

The terms *prodigy* (Lat., *prodigium*) and *portent* (Lat., *portentum*) are words in ancient Roman religion for extraordinary occurrences in the natural realm, especially astronomy, understood to be an omen of coming divine judgment. Various phenomena often comprised such prodigies that occurred in Greco-Roman literature. These include: eclipses of the sun and moon, the raining of blood and stone, unusual hail, lightning, thunderclaps in a clear sky, comets, meteors, earthquakes, the behavior of birds, the sight and sounds of armies in the sky, the sound of clashing arms and horses, and the sweating, weeping, or moving of statues. The Roman historian Tacitus provides a summary of the role of prodigies in the period following A.D. 69 in his *History* 1.3.3:

> Besides the manifold misfortunes that befell mankind, there were prodigies in the sky and on the earth, warnings given by thunderbolts, and prophecies of the future, joyful and gloomy, uncertain and clear. For never was it more fully proved by awful disasters of the Roman people or by indubitable signs that the gods care not for our safety, but for our punishment.

In the Old Testament, similar prodigies or images regarding nature often accompanied end-time forecasts. Thus Joel 2:28–32 predicts that the sun will be darkened and the moon will turn to blood in the last days. Similar images are described in ancient noncanonical Jewish literature.

Relating to the New Testament era, the Jewish historian Josephus reported that a number of similar astronomical signs occurred in ancient Palestine, believed by many of that day to signal the divine destruction of

Jerusalem by the Romans in A.D. 70. These signs included: a comet that lasted a year, a light that shone around the Temple altar at midnight, a cow intended for sacrifice that gave birth to a lamb, an appearance of chariots and armed soldiers in the sky, and a voice that said, "We are departing from here" (*Jewish Wars* 6.289–300). The New Testament itself uses similar language as that used to refer to prodigies in the Greco-Roman world, as well as images from the Old Testament. David E. Aune lists the prodigies occurring in Revelation:

> The plagues of Revelation are restricted to certain categories of phenomena: (1) heavenly phenomena: (a) thunder and lightning (8:5; 16:18), (b) hail and fire mixed with blood (8:7), (c) comets falling to the earth (6:13; 8:8, 10), (d) darkening of the sun, moon, and stars (6:12–13; 8:12), (e) the moon turning to blood (6:12), and (f) gigantic hailstones (16:20); (2) terrestrial phenomena: (a) earthquakes (8:5; 16:18), (b) the sea turning to blood (8:9; 16:3), (d) rivers and springs turn to blood (16:4), (e) famines (6:6, 8), and (d) wild animals attacking people (6:8).[13]

These, no doubt, are what the Synoptic Gospels envision will characterize the return of Christ (Matt. 24:26–31; Mark 13:24–27; Luke 21:25–28). It should be noted that the biblical catalogues of prodigies, while forecasting divine judgment on the enemies of God, also portray the positive changes in the heavens and the earth (i.e., the new creation) that will result from the Parousia (the second coming of Christ).

Atbash

An atbash is a simple cryptogram or "code" based on the letters in the alphabet in which the first letter of the alphabet is used to replace the last letter and the second letter replaces the second from last letter, etc. In English, for example, this would involve substituting "a" for "z," "b" for "y," "c" for "x," and so forth. Likewise "z" would be substituted for "a," etc.

Two clear biblical examples of atbash are in Jeremiah 25:26 and 51:41. In 25:15–29 Jeremiah proclaims that various nations will drink the cup of God's wrath. In 25:26 the prophet finishes his summary of those nations who are included in this wrath by stating: "and all the kings of the north, near and far, one after the other—all the kingdoms on the face of the earth. And after all of them, the king of Sheshach will drink it too." The term *Sheshach* is an atbash. "Sh" is the second from the last letter in the Hebrew alphabet, and it represents "b," the second letter in the alphabet. "Ch" is the eleventh letter in the Hebrew alphabet and represents "l," the eleventh letter from the end. So the three Hebrew letters "sh, sh, ch" yield the Hebrew letters b, b, l," or Babylon.

In the previous verse, Jeremiah 25:25, the "king of Zimri" is mentioned. There is no known ancient city or country with the name Zimri. Some scholars have suggested that Zimri is an atbash for Elam. Others disagree, noting that Zimri is simply a derogatory term, a summary insult to the kings mentioned in 25:21–24.

The same word "Sheshach" also appears in Jeremiah 51:41, where the text itself clearly identifies it as synonymous with Babylon.

Atoning Tribulation

"Atoning tribulation" was a label coined in the early twentieth century by Albert Schweitzer, an important New Testament scholar of the late nineteenth and early twentieth centuries. Schweitzer's greatest contribution to New Testament studies was his demonstration that the theology of Jesus and the early church should be rooted in Jewish apocalypticism, a term that refers to the concept that "the age to come has broken into this age" (see APOCALYPTIC LITERATURE).

Schweitzer makes an important contribution to the study of the great tribulation. He explores the question, "Will Christians undergo the messianic woes?" To answer this, he delineates three stages of development of this subject in the New Testament. (1) There is the foundational stage of Jesus' self-understanding concerning his own suffering. Schweitzer argues that at this level, Jesus' concept of suffering changes from his earlier belief that he, along with his disciples, must endure the premessianic tribulation to the later belief that his death will be offered as atonement for the elect, and that they will consequently be exempted from the messianic woes.

(2) At the second level early Christianity, unaware of the later change in Jesus' thinking, latched onto the former notion that it, like Jesus, must experience the premessianic tribulation before the Parousia. Such suffering on the part of believers is connected to, and continues, their Lord's passion, the endurance of which ensures their future glory.

(3) With the third stage, Schweitzer connects the great tribulation with Paul's understanding of suffering with Christ—suffering is dying with Christ because of the believer's mystical union with him. This theory involves a number of components: (a) Paul commonly characterizes suffering as dying with Christ. (b) This is so because the suffering that believers experience is actually the death of Christ manifested in their

afflictions, resulting from their mystical union with him. (c) This last element is necessitated because Paul realizes, like early Christianity, that Christ had *already* endured the premessianic tribulation and thereby brought it to its climax:

> The concept of the fellowship of suffering with Christ did not, there-fore, as is often assumed, originate with Paul; it follows immediately from the concept of the pre-Messianic Tribulation. Paul shares it with Jesus and with primitive Christianity but, in accordance with his mys-tical doctrine, must necessarily intensify it into that of the dying with Christ. After the death and resurrection of Jesus there cannot, according to this view, be any further pre-Messianic Tribulation; for the Messianic time is already present. The only course open is to treat suffering as a dying with Christ.[14]

The upshot of this hypothesis is that, in actuality, two basic view-points are presented in the New Testament with regard to the question of whether or not the church will endure the great tribulation: according to Jesus and Paul, no; but according to the rest of the New Testament, yes. The phrase "atoning tribulation" refers to the first viewpoint. That is, Jesus' death on the cross was both eschatological (see ESCHATOLOGY) and atoning in nature—he endured the messianic woes on the cross in the place of the disciples (and, by implication, the church). Paul continued that tradition; believers are exempt from the great tribulation because they have died and have been raised with Christ. According to Schweitzer, this insight was lost to the rest of the New Testament authors.

Recent New Testament scholarship has called this view into question. The tension that Schweitzer sees in the New Testament is readily resolved by understanding the "already–not yet" viewpoint of the New Testament regarding the kingdom and the end times.[15] (See ALREADY–NOT YET.)

B

Babylon/Babylonians

Babylon was the capital city of Babylonia, a kingdom in the famous ancient region of the world called *Mesopotamia*. Mesopotamia means "between the rivers," and the term applies roughly to the territory between the Tigris and Euphrates Rivers, an area encompassed by the modern country of Iraq.

History of Babylon

Mesopotamia, the large region that spawned Babylonia, is one of the richest areas of ancient history and culture. In fact, many scholars refer to this region as the "cradle of civilization," for it was here that some of the world's earliest civilizations arose. As early as 3000 B.C., in the southernmost region of Mesopotamia, near where the Tigris and Euphrates Rivers flow into the Persian Gulf, the Sumerian civilization flourished. The Sumerians developed writing, and they used it extensively for recording government activities and even mundane business transactions. Many of the clay tablets they used for writing have been well preserved, and during the last hundred years archaeologists have recovered more than a quarter million clay tablets inscribed in the Sumerian language.

Besides writing and government documentation, many other developments critical to the rise of civilization are attributed to the Sumerians: the city-state, the accumulation of capital, the wheel, the potter's wheel, monumental architecture, the number system based on the number sixty (we still use this for time as well as for geometry, i.e. sixty minutes in an hour, 360 degrees in a circle, etc.), schools, and the cylinder seal.

By 2350 B.C., however, the region of Sumer had been conquered by Sargon, who had established one of the first Mesopotamian empires. With his capital at Akkad, Sargon established Akkadian as the main language of Mesopotamia, a feature that remained for many centuries. During Sargon's reign the city of Babylon first appears in nonbiblical literary documents, but it did not play an important role in his empire; it was a minor provincial city during this time.

Soon after Sargon came to power, Amorites (lit., "those from the west") began migrating into southern Mesopotamia and growing in power. They adopted the Akkadian language and the old Sumerian-related culture of the region. By 2000 B.C. they were well entrenched in the region, and under their influence the city of Babylon developed into one of the most powerful and important cities in the region. Thus, the next four hundred years are generally referred to as the "Old Babylonian Empire." The most famous king of this era is undoubtedly Hammurabi (many current scholars now refer to him as Hammurapi). The spectacular rise to power of Babylon during this time was due to Hammurabi's extensive diplomatic and military skill. Although the life of the empire he created was brief, his name for this region endured. For more than a thousand years, the entire southern region of Mesopotamia was known as Babylonia.

Not long after Hammurabi's death, the fortunes of Babylonia began to decline. For the next several hundred years an ongoing power struggle ensued in Mesopotamia. Numerous nations and migrating groups contested over the rich region. One of the strongest powers to emerge was Assyria, which lay to the north of Babylonia, toward the upstream end of the Tigris-Euphrates region. By 800 B.C. the Assyrians dominated the entire area, and during the next few generations they extended their control over Syria, Palestine, (including the biblical nations of Israel and Judah), and down into Egypt. The Assyrians play a major role in the Bible, appearing frequently in 2 Kings and in Isaiah.

However, Assyrian power began to wane and Babylonian power in the southern area of Mesopotamia began to rise again. By this time a fairly large migration of Arameans into Babylonia had taken place, and the region now spoke Aramaic as the main language. This was not the biblical country of Aram, which lay to the west in what is now Syria. But the language was the same, and this similarity can be confusing at times. The Chaldeans and the descendants of these migrating Arameans merged together to become what is known as Neo-Babylonia (see CHALDEA/CHALDEANS). This new Babylonia with its revitalized capital of Babylon continued to grow in power until it eventually defeated the Assyrians and their Egyptian allies in 612 B.C., establishing an empire that controlled much of the ancient Near East.

Although this empire lasted less than one hundred years (it fell to the Persians in 539 B.C.), Babylon during this time was powerful and spectacular. The Babylonians controlled much of the Middle East, including Mesopotamia, Syria, and Palestine. The most famous Babylonian king of this era was Nebuchadnezzar, the king who besieged Jerusalem and destroyed it completely in 587/586 B.C. He appears in the Bible numerous times, especially in 2 Kings, Jeremiah, and Daniel. He was responsible for taking the surviving Jews into exile in Babylonia.

Babylon in Biblical Prophecy

Without doubt the city of Babylon, the country of Babylonia, and the Babylonian people play a huge role in the Bible. In fact, the terms Babylon, Babylonian, Chaldea, and Chaldean appear over three hundred times in the Bible. The vast majority of these usages occur in the Old Testament, and the bulk of the references occur in 2 Kings, Isaiah, and Jeremiah, although there are references scattered throughout, including Genesis, as discussed below.

The Tower of Babel. Genesis 2:14 names two of the rivers flowing out of the Garden of Eden as the Tigris and Euphrates. However, this text is complicated by the mention of two other rivers, the Pishon and the Gihon, whose location is uncertain. Likewise, Genesis 10:10 states that Babylon was one of the first centers of the kingdom of the mighty warrior Nimrod, but the puzzling nature of Nimrod and the difficulties encountered in interpreting Genesis 10 make it difficult to state much about this reference with certainty.

The third and most famous incident in Genesis regarding Babylon is the story about the tower of Babel (Gen. 11:1–9):

> They said to each other, "Come, let's make bricks and bake them thoroughly." They used brick instead of stone and tar for mortar. Then they said, "Come let us build ourselves a city, with a tower that reaches to the heavens, so that we may make a name for ourselves and not be scattered over the face of the whole earth." (11:3–4)

The reader hears echoes of Genesis 9:1–7 in this passage, for in that text God commanded Noah and his family to *scatter* over the earth and replenish its population. So the builders of the Tower of Babel were doing the opposite of the divine injunction.

The Tower of Babel was located in "a plain of Shinar" (Gen. 10:10; 11:2; 14:1), the broad, alluvial plain of the Tigris and Euphrates Rivers south of modern Baghdad. Most likely, the Tower of Babel was a ziggurat (an elevated temple tower), where worshipers climbed the ramps of stairs to offer sacrifices to their gods. At the top of the ziggurat was a temple shrine, know as the "gateway to the gods." It was there that humans and their deities supposedly met. In the language of Mesopotamia, Babel (as well as Babylon) meant "gateway to the gods" or "gate of the gods."

In Hebrew, however, the word *babel* means "to confuse." Genesis 11:9 thus contains a parody, or wordplay, on the name of Babel. It does not really refer to the "gate of the gods" as the Mesopotamians intended, but rather alludes to the confusion and scattering that God brought against them. Thus, rather than reach to the heavens, the tower was abandoned in its construction because God turned the language of the builders into *babel* ("confusion").

Thus from early in Scripture, the connotations of Babel/Babylon are negative ones. Indeed, later in Israel's history, the city of Babylon will once again carry negative connotations, a symbol of human arrogance and rebellion against God.

The Babylonian destruction of Jerusalem. When God delivered the children of Israel from Egypt during the time of Moses, he made a covenant with them and led them to the Promised Land. In Deuteronomy, God spelled out the terms by which the Israelites could live in the land and be blessed by God. They were commanded to be faithful to God alone and to worship him alone. If they failed in this commitment, Deuteronomy warned (see esp. Deut. 28), God would punish them with foreign invasions (among other things), and ultimately they would be evicted from the Promised Land.

Unfortunately, by and large, the Israelites ignored God's warning, and as time goes by they turn to worshiping other gods. The northern ten tribes break off and form the country of Israel, while the southern tribes of Judah and Benjamin form the country of Judah. The northern tribes fall immediately into apostasy, worshiping golden calves. But even Judah eventually follows suit, worshiping the pagan gods of the Canaanites and their other neighbors. Old Testament prophets such as Isaiah, Jeremiah, and Micah preach against this serious backsliding of God's people into apostasy. The prophets call the people to repent. But they also warn of imminent judgment if they do not repent.

The prophets first warn the northern kingdom of Israel, but Israel ignores them. Thus, as the prophets predicted, the Assyrians invade and destroy the northern kingdom Israel (722 B.C.). They carry off most of the people and scatter them throughout the Middle East.

The prophets then preach to the southern kingdom of Judah, warning them of serious consequences if they continue to ignore God and worship other deities. Failure to repent, the prophets warn, will result in an invasion and in terrible destruction by the Babylonians. The prophet Jeremiah is at the center of this message, for he lives through the terrible times of spiritual decline, and he actually witnesses the horrendous Babylonian invasion. Jeremiah thus refers to the Babylonians 198 times. In chapters 20 to 39, Jeremiah warns the people of Jerusalem that God will raise up the Babylonians to judge them.

When the Babylonians finally arrive and the city comes under siege, Jeremiah urges the people of Jerusalem to surrender and thus save themselves; otherwise they will be destroyed. They cannot overcome the ones whom God has raised up to judge them. He preaches in vain, however, because the people ignore him, and thus Jeremiah 39 and 52 describe the actual fall of Jerusalem to Nebuchadnezzar and his Babylonian army and the resulting devastation (cf. the same grim story in 2 Kings 24–25). In 587/586 B.C. Nebuchadnezzar and his army completely destroy Jerusalem, burning the city and its Temple to the ground. They then carry off most of the population into exile in Babylonia.

This terrible event remains etched into the minds of the Old Testament writers, and Babylon becomes the literary symbol and epitome of Israel's enemies. In the Old Testament no other foe created such havoc and destruction on Jerusalem as the Babylonians did.

The Old Testament prophecies against Babylon. Accordingly, the Old Testament prophets not only preached judgment on Israel and Judah because of their apostasy, they also prophesied judgment on the surrounding pagan nations that had exploited Israel and Judah or had directly attacked them. Jeremiah, for example, prophesied against Egypt (Jer. 46:1–28), Philistia (47:1–7), Moab (48:1–47), Ammon (49:1–6), Edom (49:7–22), Damascus (49:23–27), the Arab cities of Kedar and Hazor (49:28–33), Elam (49:34–39), and especially Babylon (chs. 50–51).

As a result of the devastation of Jerusalem and because Babylon set herself against God, the LORD speaks through Jeremiah to announce judgment on Babylon:

> Announce and proclaim among the nations,
>   lift up a banner and proclaim it;
> keep nothing back, but say,
> "Babylon will be captured...

Her images will be put to shame
  and her idols filled with terror."
A nation from the north will attack her
  and lay waste her land.
No one will live in it;
  both man and animals will flee away. (Jer. 50:2–3)
Take up your positions around Babylon,
  all you who draw the bow.
Shoot at her! Spare no arrows,
  for she has sinned against the LORD. (50:14)
So desert creatures and hyenas will live there,
  and there the owl will dwell.
It will never again be inhabited
  or lived in from generation to generation. (50:39)

Isaiah also proclaims a scathing indictment on Babylon and announces a coming judgment on the Babylonians. He devotes a considerable amount of his book to this theme, and the Babylonian judgment fills most of chapters 13, 14, 21, and 47. For example, in Isaiah 13:19–20 the prophet declares:

Babylon, the jewel of kingdoms,
  the glory of the Babylonians pride,
will be overthrown by God
  like Sodom and Gomorrah.
She will never be inhabited
  or lived in through all generations.
No Arab will pitch his tent there,
  no shepherd will rest his flocks there.

The fall and destruction of Babylon. What happened to Babylon? When Jeremiah proclaimed the coming judgment on Babylon, the city was perhaps the most spectacular and powerful city in the world. Yet when German archaeologists began excavations of Babylon in 1899, the entire site was desolate and unoccupied. What is the history of the city between the time of Jeremiah and the era of modern archaeology? Here is a brief overview of its history.

(1) Nabonidus, the king who followed Nebuchadnezzar, tried to move the Babylonians away from the worship of their main god, Marduk, which alienated him from much of the population. Nabonidus even moved away to Arabia for ten years, leaving his son Belshazzar in charge. When Cyrus the Persian began to threaten Babylon, Nabonidus returned to Babylon, but it was too late. One of the most powerful Babylonian princes, Ugbaru, defected to the Persians, allowing Cyrus to defeat the Babylonians (539

B.C.) and take control of Babylon without any substantial resistance. The inhabitants of Babylon greeted Cyrus more as a liberator than as a conqueror. This was the beginning of the end for Babylon.

(2) Later, Babylon revolted against the Persians, but Xerxes recaptured the city for Persia in 482 B.C., sacking it, demolishing its fortifications, burning the great temple of Marduk, and carrying away the statue of Marduk as a spoil of war. Yet Herodotus (450 B.C.), the Greek historian, records that Babylon still was not completely destroyed.

(3) When Alexander the Great and his Greek army defeated the Persians in 331 B.C., the young king treated Babylon with kindness and was therefore warmly welcomed by its remaining citizens. However, in 324 B.C. Alexander's dear friend Hephaestian died, and the young king had a funeral pyre arranged in his honor in Babylon. Part of the city wall east of the royal palace was demolished to provide rubble for the platform.

(4) After Alexander's premature death in 323 B.C., one of his four generals, Seleucus, seized Babylon (312 B.C.). A fragmentary Babylonian chronicle records that at that time there was "weeping and mourning in the land" and "plundering of the city and the countryside." Seleucus' successor, Antiochus I (281–261 B.C.), issued two decrees that eventually sealed the fate of Babylon. He decided to build a new capital (Seleucia-on-the-Tigris) ninety kilometers to the north of Babylon. Then he moved the civilian population of Babylon to the new capital. These decrees, along with the physical damage Babylon had suffered earlier when the Seleucids first conquered southern Mesopotamia, ensured the increasing desolation and isolation of the once-great capital. Except for a brief period of renewal under Antiochus IV (173 B.C.), Babylon for all practical purposes ceased to exist.

(5) By the time of the Parthian takeover of Mesopotamia, Mithradates II (122 B.C.) apparently found Babylon in desolate ruin. In A.D. 116, the Roman emperor Trajan wintered in Babylon, finding nothing except ruins. Babylon's desolation, like Nineveh before it, by now was proverbial. A second century A.D. piece written by Lucian said that Nineveh vanished without a trace, and that soon men will search in vain for Babylon. Thus, in fulfillment of biblical prophecy, the city of Babylon went from being the most important and most spectacular city in the world to being a desolate, insignificant pile of rubble.

Will the literal city of Babylon rise again in the end times? Several contemporary writers argue that since Babylon was not destroyed explicitly and literally, exactly as prophesied by Old Testament prophets like Jeremiah and Isaiah, then it must necessarily be resurrected, restored to world prominence, and then destroyed again exactly and literally as predicted.

The issue revolves around how one interprets the poetic and figurative language of the Old Testament prophets (see FIGURES OF SPEECH; POETRY). Further complicating the issue is how one interprets the term "Babylon" in Revelation 17–18. There is much disagreement over this issue.

In these two fascinating chapters, John portrays the nemesis of God's kingdom as a harlot dressed in scarlet and riding on a beast. She is covered with blasphemous names and rules over the kings of the earth in opposition to God. Those who argue for the resurrection of a literal city of Babylon identify the harlot in Revelation 17–18 with the literal city of Babylon. They offer three reasons. (1) The city that the harlot represents is called "Babylon" (Rev. 17:1–5). (2) Babylon is said to sit "on many waters" (17:1), which recalls the moat that surrounded the ancient city. In addition, the Euphrates River flowed through the middle of the ancient city, and the encompassing region was crisscrossed with canals and irrigation ditches. (3) The case for a literal reading of Babylon is strengthened by an actual reference to the Euphrates River (cf. Rev. 16:12 with 17:1). Since ancient Babylon lay on the banks of the Euphrates, this reference is taken as clear connection to Babylon.

Nevertheless, many scholars maintain that the harlot of Revelation 17–18 symbolizes ancient Rome rather than modern Babylon. They offer several reasons for this view. (1) They note that Revelation is filled with symbolic, figurative language (see REVELATION, BOOK OF). If the term *Babylon* is used symbolically, they argue, it probably refers to the first-century city of Rome rather than to a resurrected modern-day city of Babylon. Indeed, there are numerous connections in Revelation 17–18 with the ancient city of Rome. Note how 17:9 portrays the great harlot and the beast as seated on "seven hills." The ancient city of Rome was comprised of seven hills; indeed it was famous for these hills. There is no known association of Babylon with seven hills.

(2) Another argument cited for identifying the harlot and beast of Revelation 17–18 as ancient Rome can be observed from a coin minted in A.D. 71 in Asia Minor, known as the *Dea Roma* coin (see DEA ROMA COIN). This coin depicts Roma, a pagan goddess of Rome, as sitting on seven hills. This image of a woman sitting on seven hills was an obvious way of representing Rome in the symbolic art of the day. John's readers would certainly have understood it that way.

(3) A third argument cited in favor of understanding the use of Babylon as a "code" for Rome is drawn from Peter's usage of the term. Peter uses "Babylon" to refer to Rome at the end of his first letter. He writes, "She who is in Babylon, chosen together with you, sends you her greet-

ings, and so does my son Mark" (1 Peter 5:13). Neither Peter nor Mark is ever associated with the literal city of Babylon. However, the Scriptures do describe Peter's ministry as moving northward from Palestine and then westward in the direction of Rome. Early Christian writings place both Peter and Mark in Rome at the end of Peter's ministry. The near consensus of New Testament scholarship is that Peter's use of "she" refers to the church and that his use of Babylon is a coded or symbolic reference to Rome.

Balaamites

On three occasions the New Testament refers to those who follow the way of Balaam: 2 Peter 2:15; Jude 11; Revelation 2:14. Peter provides a detailed description of false teachers who plague the church of Jesus Christ. These immoral and arrogant men "have left the straight way and wandered off to follow the way of Balaam son of Beor, who loved the wages of wickedness" (2 Peter 2:15). Jude compares the false teachers to three famous Old Testament sinners: "Woe to them! They have taken the way of Cain; they have rushed for profit into Balaam's error; they have been destroyed in Korah's rebellion" (Jude 11). In the message to the church at Pergamum in Revelation 2, Jesus rebukes the congregation for having "people there who hold to the teaching of Balaam, who taught Balak to entice the Israelites to sin by eating food sacrificed to idols and by committing sexual immorality" (Rev. 2:14).

In every instance, the example of Balaam is used to characterize the false teachers as those whose rebellion against God promoted idolatry and sexual immorality. Most interpreters think the Balaam group, the Nicolaitans (Rev. 2:6, 15), and the followers of Jezebel (2:20) are closely related, if not identical.

Numbers 22–25 tells the story of Balaam, the pagan prophet hired by Balak, the king of Moab, to curse Israel. Although God prevented Balaam from cursing Israel, Balaam influenced some Moabite women to entice Israelite men to commit sexual immorality and participate in pagan worship. The character of Balaam became associated in Jewish tradition with false teachers who encouraged compromise with the surrounding pagan culture. Just as Balaam had misled Israel into sexual and spiritual fornication, so the false teachers at Pergamum were encouraging Christians to participate in pagan worship feasts, where they faced enormous pressure to compromise their faith through idolatry and immorality. (See JEZEBEL; NICOLAITANS; PERGAMUM.)

Balfour Declaration

The Balfour Declaration was a British government policy document, written in 1917 by the British Foreign Minister Lord Balfour, that played a critical role in the Zionist movement of the early twentieth century (see ZIONISM). In this document the British government viewed with favor the establishment of a national home for the Jewish people in Palestine and promised to work toward that end. However, the document also stated that "nothing shall be done which may prejudice the civil and religious rights of existing non-Jewish communities in Palestine."[16] This document provided momentum for the establishment of a modern Jewish state in Palestine, while politically dodging the issue of how that state might impact the existing non-Jewish residents; this helped create the violent situation that exists in Israel/Palestine/West Bank today.

Balm of Gilead

Gilead is the mountainous region east of the Sea of Galilee, in the modern country of Jordan. It was famous for a medicinal ointment, or balm, most likely derived from a local plant. In Genesis 37:25 a caravan from Gilead is said to be carrying balm, spices, and myrrh on their way to Egypt. Jeremiah uses the expression "balm of Gilead" in Jeremiah 8:22: "Is there no balm in Gilead? Is there no physician there? Why then is there no healing for the wound of my people?" This prophet frequently compares the sinful situation of the people of Judah to a serious sickness or wound. Thus, "balm of Gilead" is a figure of speech to underscore that the sin (sickness) of the people is so pervasive that no balm or physician can heal them (see HEALING).

Beasts of Revelation

Revelation speaks of two beasts: the "beast ... out of the sea" (Rev. 13:1) and the "beast ... out of the earth" (13:11); both are apocalyptic symbols of antichristian forces empowered by Satan. The first beast is commonly referred to as the "Antichrist" (although Revelation never uses that term); the second is the "false prophet." The chart on the next three pages summarizes the origin, alliances, characteristics, and destiny of both beasts, as well as their relationships with the unrighteous and the righteous.

Beast from the Sea	Beast from the Earth
Origin	
11:7—comes up from the abyss	
13:1—comes out of sea	13:11—comes out of the earth
Alliances	
13:2, 4—derives power, throne, authority from the dragon	13:12—exercises all authority of first beast
16:13–14—allied with dragon, false prophet, and kings of the earth	16:13–14—allied with dragon, first beast, and kings of the earth
17:3, 7—ridden by the great prostitute	
Characteristics	
13:1; 17:3, 7—has ten horns with ten crowns and seven heads, each with a blasphemous name	13:11—has two horns like a lamb, but speaks like a dragon
13:2—resembles a leopard, with feet like a bear and a mouth like a lion	
13:3—one of its heads has a fatal wound that is healed	
13:18—number of the beast is man's number = 666	17:3—scarlet beast
17:3—scarlet beast	
17:8, 11—beast "once was, now is not, and will come"	
17:9–10—seven heads of the beast are seven hills and also seven kings—five have fallen, one is, and other is yet to come	
17:11—the beast is an eighth king who belongs to the seven	
17:12—the ten horns are ten kings who will give their power and authority to the beast	

Beast from the Sea	Beast from the Earth
Relation to the unrighteous	
13:3—whole world is astonished and follows beast	13:13–14—through great and miraculous signs (e.g., fire from heaven) performed on behalf of the first beast, he deceives the inhabitants of the earth
13:4—people worship the beast	13:14–15—orders inhabitants of the earth to set up an image in honor of the first beast who was wounded by sword and yet lived. He is given power to give breath to the image so that it can speak
13:7—given authority over every tribe, people, language, and nation	13:16—forces everyone (great/small, rich/poor, free/slave) to receive mark of first beast on right hand or forehead
13:8—worshiped by all inhabitants of the earth—all whose names have not been written in Lamb's book of life	13:12—makes earth and its inhabitants worship the first beast
17:8—the beast will astonish the inhabitants of the earth whose names have not been written in the book of life	
17:16–17—will take the power and authority of the ten kings to fight against the prostitute	
17:16—The beast and the ten horns (ten kings) will hate the prostitute and destroy her	
	19:20—performs miraculous signs on behalf of the first beast and deceives those who have received the mark of the beast and worship his image

Beast from the Sea	Beast from the Earth
Relation to the righteous	
11:7—attacks, overpowers, and kills two witnesses	
13:5—exercises authority for 42 months	
13:5–6—utters proud and blasphemous words, blasphemes God, God's name, God's dwelling place, and those who live in heaven	13:15—causes all who refused to worship the image of the first beast to be killed
13:7—wages war against saints and conquers them	13:17—no one can buy or sell except those who have the mark of the beast (name of beast or number of his name)
17:12–13—will take the power and authority of the ten kings to war against the Lamb	
19:19—gathers with the kings of the earth to battle the Lamb	
Destiny	
16:10—fifth bowl judgment poured out on beast's throne and his kingdom plunged into darkness	
17:8, 11—doomed to destruction	
17:14—Lamb will overcome beast and ten kings	
19:20; 20:10—The Lamb captures the beast and throws him alive into the fiery lake of burning sulfur, where he is tormented night and day forever and ever	19:20; 20:10—The Lamb captures the false prophet and throws him alive into the fiery lake of burning sulfur, where he is tormented night and day forever and ever

Some scholars think John may be drawing on an ancient Jewish tradition that God made two beasts on the fifth day of creation—the sea creature Leviathan and the land creature Behemoth (see Job 40–41; also the noncanonical books *1 Enoch* 60:7–10; *4 Ezra* 6:49–52; *2 Bar.* 29:3–5). Both beasts came to be associated with evil. But although this tradition may lie in background of Revelation 13, the Old Testament book of Daniel appears to be in the foreground. Whereas Daniel 7 describes four beasts arising from the sea to persecute God's people (with the fourth beast traditionally understood as Rome), Revelation 13 pictures one beast who is a composite of the different beasts (13:2). John also uses the vivid image of a beast to describe the final oppression of God's people at the end of history. Richard Bauckham notes a number of parallels between Revelation 13 and Daniel 7:[17]

Revelation	Daniel
13:1	7:2–3, 7
13:2	7:3–6
13:4	7:6, 12
13:5a	7:8, 25
13:5b	7:25 (cf. 12:7, 11–12)
13:6	7:25 (cf. 8:10–11; 11:36)
13:7a	7:21
13:7b	cf. 7:14

The first beast has "ten horns" and "seven heads," showing his close connection to the dragon, who also has ten horns and seven heads (Rev. 12:3; 13:1). The ten horns are ten kings (17:12), who will give their allegiance to the beast in waging war against the Lamb (Dan. 7:7, 20, 24). While the ten kings could represent ten client kingdoms of Rome, ultimately they symbolize the complete number of nations on earth who follow the beast and dragon. The seven heads are the "seven hills" (Rev. 17:9), a clear reference to Rome as the city built on seven hills. One of the seven heads has a fatal wound that is healed, perhaps referring to the *Nero redivivus* legend (13:3) (see NERO REDIVIVUS). Also, the wounded head clearly portrays the beast as a parody or counterfeit of the Lamb, who was crucified and resurrected.

The seven heads are also "seven kings" of which "five have fallen, one is, the other has not yet come" (Rev. 17:10). Also the beast is said to be "an eighth king," who is "of the seven" (17:11). Most interpreters have identified the seven kings as a series of Roman emperors or as a symbol of the complete period of Roman domination. Some interpreters have identified the seven kings as seven kingdoms or nations who have opposed Israel. The beast could refer to one of the emperors (e.g., Domitian) or to an end-time Antichrist figure, foreshadowed by Nero or Domitian (see DOMITIAN; NERO).

The second beast (the one from the earth) is also called the "false prophet" (Rev. 16:13; 19:20; 20:10; cf. Dan. 8:3). This beast "had two horns like a lamb, but he spoke like a dragon" (Rev. 13:11), showing that although he appears innocent and harmless, his message is deceptive and deadly (see Matt. 7:15; 24:11, 24; Mark 13:22; 1 John 4:1). Many scholars relate the second beast to the cult of Roman emperor worship and its priesthood, which was entrenched throughout the Roman empire when John wrote Revelation. While not discounting this historical association, many also see the second beast as representing false religion in general, whose purpose is to convince human beings to worship the Antichrist through deceptive teaching and miracles. If the dragon, the beast, and the false prophet comprise the satanic trinity, the false prophet serves as the demonic counterpart to the Holy Spirit.

Whomever or whatever the beasts symbolize, their authority and purposes remain clear. Both beasts derive their authority from Satan himself (Rev. 13:1–2, 4; 16:13–14). The first beast craves power and worship. He amazes the whole world (13:3; 17:8) so that people respond with worshipful devotion (13:4, 8). He develops alliances with earthly kings and empires in pursuit of his goal of achieving worldwide power (13:7; 17:3, 7, 16–17). The second beast is bent on using miraculous signs to deceive the world (13:13–14; 19:20). He erects an image in honor of the first beast and empowers the image to speak (13:14–15). He enforces devotion to the first beast by means of an identifying mark (13:16).

Because the first beast blasphemes God and all that belongs to God (Rev. 13:5–6), he violently opposes the Lamb (Jesus) and his followers. The beast uses the power and authority of the ten kings to battle the Lamb (17:12–13; 19:19). Unsurprisingly, he wages war against the saints and even conquers them (13:7). This beast also attacks, overpowers, and kills the two witnesses, an image that many take to represent the witnessing church (11:7) (see TWO WITNESSES). The second beast punishes those who refuse to follow the first beast with economic ruin (13:17) or death (13:15).

In Revelation the saints "overcome" the powers of evil by accepting martyrdom and by relying on God to judge evil, avenge their suffering, and give them eternal life (Rev. 2:10–11; 12:11; 14:12–13; 15:2). The beast's victory over the two witnesses is temporary, since the witnesses stay faithful unto death and God raises them from the dead (11:11–12). After describing the first beast in Revelation 13, John adds this warning (13:9–10):

He who has an ear, let him hear.

> If anyone is to go into captivity,
>   into captivity he will go.
> If anyone is to be killed with the sword,
>   with the sword he will be killed.

This calls for patient endurance and faithfulness on the part of the saints.

This paraphrase joining Jeremiah 15:2 and 43:11 (cf. Ezek. 14:12–23) affirms that the faithful remnant of God's people should be willing to suffer. Interestingly, both Old Testament prophets mention wild beasts (see WILD BEASTS). After warning anyone who worships the beast or his image and receives the mark to expect to incur the tormenting wrath of God (Rev. 14:9–11), John adds the following admonition encouraging believers to persevere (14:12–13):

This calls for patient endurance on the part of the saints who obey God's commandments and remain faithful to Jesus.
    Then I heard a voice from heaven say, "Write: Blessed are the dead who die in the Lord from now on."
    "Yes," says the Spirit, "they will rest from their labor, for their deeds will follow them."

Believers overcome through their willingness to stay loyal even unto death (Rev. 12:11). Although the beast may conquer them physically and appear to conquer them for good, they are actually conquering the beast. In the end God raises believers from the dead, and they enjoy life rather than the wrath reserved for those who oppose God. This paradoxical path to victory follows the way of the Lamb, who conquered through sacrifice (15:2–3; 20:4).

Revelation leaves no doubt about the ultimate destiny of the two beasts. While they temporarily overcome believers, they are overcome by the Lamb's sacrifice and believers' faithful perseverance, and one day the beasts will be overcome by the warrior Lamb (Rev. 17:8, 11, 14). At the return of Christ "the beast was captured, and with him the false prophet" (19:20). Both will be "thrown alive into the fiery lake of burning sulfur" (19:20; 20:10), where "they will be tormented day and night for ever and ever" (20:10). (See ANTICHRIST; FALSE PROPHET; IMPERIAL CULT; SEA; REVELATION, BOOK OF.)

Belshazzar

Belshazzar is featured in Daniel 5, where the story of the Babylonian king's fall from power is recorded. Two issues emerge pertinent to that chapter: the historicity of Belshazzar and the biblical prophecy concerning him. Although the Bible matter-of-factly portrays as historical the narrative of Belshazzar's ruin, liberally inclined theologians have doubted the accuracy of Daniel 5 here, primarily because Babylonian king lists do not mention Belshazzar. Furthermore, there seemed to be no evidence that Belshazzar was the son of Nebuchadnezzar, as 5:2, 18 suggest (see NEBUCHADNEZZAR). Rather, Nabonidus was the son of Nebuchadnezzar.

These two objections to the reliability of Daniel 5, however, have been answered. The discovery of the Nabonidus Cylinder in 1929 by R. P. Dougherty answers the first concern. That document refers to one Belsharusur (Belshazzar), who is called the son of Nabonidus. The Babylonian record relates that Belshazzar was co-ruler with Nabonidus, who was absent from Babylon for several years while residing in Tema in Arabia. Such a discovery also explains how Belshazzar could be called the son of Nebuchadnezzar, for "son" in the ancient Near East could be applied to the son, grandson, and other relatives. Thus Nebuchadnezzar's grandson, Belshazzar, is rightly called his "son."

Daniel 5:24–28 prophesies that Belshazzar will lose his kingdom to the Medes and Persians. Although Daniel does not tell the reader how that will happen, three ancient writings do: the Nabonidus Cylinder (sixth century B.C.), the Cyrus Cylinder (sixth century B.C.), and the comments of the Greek historian Herodotus (fifth century B.C.). These combined testimonies relate that Cyrus (see CYRUS), the ruler of the Persians and the Medes, intercepted Nabonidus's forces on their way from Tema to Babylon, defeating them and leaving Babylon essentially undefended. Cyrus then diverted the Euphrates River, which flowed through Babylon, so that his troops could march into the city on the riverbed. The Babylonian capital fell to Cyrus on October 11 or 12, 539 B.C., therefore fulfilling Daniel's prophecy (cf. Isa. 13:17–22; 21:1–10; Jer. 51:33–58).

Beth Togarmah

Beth Togarmah is a name occurring in the Table of Nations (Gen. 10:3; 1 Chron. 1:6), along with Ashkenaz and Riphath as the sons of Gomer and grandsons of Japheth. In Ezekiel 38:6 (cf. 27:14), Beth Togarmah is a nation north of Israel that trades in horses and mules. Beyond that identification, interpreters debate the significance of this group of people in history. Some believe that Beth Togarmah will combine with Gog and Magog to invade Israel in the end times; others do not attach eschatological meaning to Ezekiel 38:1–6 (see GOG AND MAGOG).

Bible Codes

In 1997 Simon and Schuster published a startling book by reporter Michael Drosnin entitled *The Bible Code*. In this book Drosnin claimed there was a special letter sequence code hidden in the Hebrew text of the Old Testament that could now be unlocked with the use of computers. Furthermore, he argued that this code contained predictions of dozens of significant modern people and events, including President Clinton, Watergate, the 1929 stock market crash, the Apollo moon landings, Adolph Hitler, Thomas Edison, the Wright brothers, the assassination of Israeli Prime Minister Yitzhak Rabin, and numerous others. Drosnin's book became an immediate bestseller.

However, biblical Hebrew scholars reflecting a wide range of theological positions, along with numerous mathematicians, studied Drosnin's *Bible Code* and concluded that his arguments were not valid and that there was no special letter sequencing code in the Hebrew Bible. Perhaps the most thorough and most devastating critique of this theory is Randall Ingermanson's 1999 book, *Who Wrote the Bible Code? A Physicist Probes the Current Controversy*.

In spite of this scholarly consensus, Drosnin soon followed up on his first book with a sequel, *Bible Code II: The Countdown*, and the idea of a Bible Code continues to flourish in some quarters of the popular imagination. Indeed, numerous books on this subject have appeared and continue to be popular. Likewise, several websites on this topic have appeared. What exactly is the "code," and what should Christians make of it? Does it contain hidden prophecies? And how does the "code" work?

Equidistant Letter Sequencing (ELS)

Equidistant Letter Sequencing (ELS) is the system propagated by Drosnin in The Bible Code. First, the entire Hebrew Bible (or occasionally just the

Pentateuch, depending on the researcher) is loaded into a computer. All spaces between the words are ignored, and the computer thus generates a long continuous stream of consecutive letters. The operators tell the computer to look for words or patterns of words by selecting equidistant letters. First the computer looks at every other letter. Then it looks at every third letter, every fourth letter, every fifth letter, and so forth, until it is looking at letters spaced thousands of letters apart. The computer then looks at the sequences that it has produced and tries to find matches with the words the operators are searching for.

For a small, simple example of how ELS works, consider a short biblical passage. Numbers 4:3 reads: "Count all the men from thirty to fifty years of age who come to serve in the work in the tent of meeting." Now suppose that a "researcher" wants to employ ELS and find out if this text (in English) says anything in code about *cats*. The first step is to remove all of the spaces between the words, thus yielding:

Countallthemenfromthirtytofiftyyearsofagewhocometoservein-theworkinthetentofmeeting

Next the researcher (or computer) will look at every other letter, then every third letter, fourth letter, and so on, until they find *cat*. Lo and behold, in Numbers 4:3 one does find *cat*, encoded with a 32-letter spacing! Starting with the *c* in *count*, skip over 32 letters and arrive at *a* in *years*, followed by a 32-letter skip to *t* in *the*. The results are shown below in bold:

CountallthemenfromthirtytofiftyyeArsofagewhocometoservein-theworkinThetentofmeeting

This is *ELS* or *equidistant letter sequencing*. Each letter is separated by the exact same number of letters (in this case 32). Of course three-letter words are easy to find. This one could be found without a computer in about 10 minutes. Longer words are more difficult to find, but if one searches a large enough text with the aid of a computer, even large words can be discovered fairly easily.

In one of Drosnin's famous examples, the computer was told to search for the Israeli Prime Minister Yitzhak Rabin.[18] This is a twelve-letter sequence, not an easy one to find. Fortunately computers can handle such challenges. Indeed, the computer did find a sequence containing the name Yitzhak Rabin. The first letter in his name occurs in Deuteronomy 2:33. The computer then skips 4722 letters to find the next letter in his name in 4:42, followed by another skip of 4722 to 7:20, and so forth, skipping 4722 letters each time until reaching the last letter in 24:16.

However, it is not the mere occurrence of the encoded name that convinces the ELS code proponents. It is the presence of other additional connecting or predicting aspects in the near vicinity of the texts that are intercepted by the letters of the name. Thus in Drosnin's example, the second letter of Yitzhak Rabin's name shows up in Deuteronomy 4:42. This verse, Drosnin points out dramatically, contains the phrase "the assassin will assassinate" and thus predicted the assassination of the Israeli prime minister thousands of years before it happened. Impressed? (Note: Drosnin has translated 4:41–42 rather poorly. The NIV text reads, "Then Moses set aside three cities east of the Jordan, to which anyone who had killed a person could flee if he had unintentionally killed his neighbor without malice aforethought." The text deals with cities of refuge for those who kill someone unintentionally; it has nothing to do with assassination.)

So how should one assess Drosnin's *Bible Code*? Drosnin's equidistant letter sequence (ELS) theory smacks of the current cultural infatuation with computers and technology and the postmodern desire for mysticism. The consensus view of respected biblical scholarship is that there is nothing other than coincidence behind Drosnin's (and others) secret messages that they find hidden in the Bible with ELS. The scholarly rebuttals to the *Bible Code* have been devastating and have provided strong evidence that there is nothing mystical, prophetic, or divine about the ELS Bible Code.

Analysis of ELS

The arguments leveled against the ELS Bible Code fall into two basic categories—one relating to probability and the other relating to textual variations.

Probability. The most important argument of Drosnin (and others) is that the patterns they have found are incredibly beyond normal probability and are therefore divine in nature. They cite incredible odds against names and connections appearing in the text with equidistant spacing merely by chance. This is the critical defense for the Bible Code.

However, this argument has been pretty well shattered by those who have critiqued the code. Large texts with several hundred thousand letters present *billions* of ELS options. One scholar, for example, points out that, assuming equal letter distribution, the chance of randomly selecting a six-letter word (with a twenty-two letter alphabet, as Hebrew has) is 1 in 110,000,000. This seems incredible, and the ELS proponents cite these fantastic odds as the certification of their method. However, as this scholar notes, the Pentateuch by itself contains over 300,000 letters. Based on ELS methodology, names can be read forward or backward and the skip sequence can range from 2 to around 30,000. Under these criteria the 300,000-letter Pentateuch yields 18 *billion* six-letter combinations.

Thus using an ELS computer search, any random six-letter name or other letter combination will show up in the Pentateuch around 160 times (18 billion divided by 110,000,000).[19] With 160 options it should not be hard to find one that intersects a verse that can be loosely connected to the name, especially if the imagination is used (or poor translation techniques, as Drosnin is prone to do).

Underscoring this reality has been the results of ELS searches run on nonbiblical literature. Any literary work of significant length will yield hundreds of modern names with hundreds of different associations in adjacent phrases. One research team, for example, loaded the English text of *Moby Dick* into their computer and ran ELS searches through this classic work to look for "predictions" about assassinations of other twentieth-century leaders. They found numerous names with significant connections to the topic of death in the nearby texts. For example, the name Samoza (president of Nicaragua, assassinated in 1956) showed up intersecting near the words "he was shot," "dies," and "gun."[20] This example is similar to Drosnin's Yitzhak Rabin example. Unless we view *Moby Dick* as divinely inspired, this evidence demolishes the argument behind the Bible Code.

Textual variations. Another flaw in the ELS approach is that its proponents seem completely unaware of variations in the Hebrew text of the Old Testament. The Bible was transmitted for many years through handwritten manuscripts. Because of the mammoth size of the Old Testament and the difficulties involved in hand copying, there are no two hand-written ancient Hebrew manuscripts that are exactly alike — that is, identical down to the very letter.

For one thing, spelling was not standardized during the production and during the early transmission of the Old Testament. Numerous words had two different spelling options, and the ancient manuscripts varied frequently in their spelling. Indeed, after the return of the Jews following the Babylonian captivity, the scribes not only changed the letter style from the old angular Hebrew in which it was written to the newer square Aramaic letters (as used in Hebrew Bibles today), but they also frequently inserted consonantal vowels, additional letters inserted into the spelling of words in order to help with reading and pronunciation. So the specific letter length of the Hebrew Old Testament was never uniform or fixed.

This is a critical problem for a method that searches for names with letters spaced apart by thousands of letters. Remember that Drosnin's example of Yitzhak Rabin has a letter spacing of 4772 letters for each letter. It extends through twenty-two chapters of Deuteronomy. If one letter is missing or if one extra letter is added, the system collapses. Drosnin used an edition of the Hebrew Bible called the Second Rabbinic Bible. This edition of the Hebrew Bible was the standard (but not universal) printed Hebrew text from the sixteenth century until the early twentieth century. The Second Rabbinic Bible was based on earlier printed Hebrew Bibles and on late medieval manuscripts. None of the earlier printed editions are exactly the same in letter length as the Second Rabbinic Bible.

Likewise, hand-written manuscripts that predate the Second Rabbinic Bible by hundreds of years, such as the Leningrad Codex (the oldest complete hand-written Hebrew Bible), differ in numerous ways — ways that are minor or insignificant in regard to meaning but major and critical in regard to counting letter spacing. Likewise, most twentieth-century editions of the Hebrew Bible are based on older manuscripts like the Leningrad Codex. So contemporary editions of the Hebrew Bible differ from the Second Rabbinic Bible in the number of letters that appear. We do not know of *any* Christian scholar today who uses the Second Rabbinic Bible as a Hebrew text.

For example, the modern edition referred to as *Biblia Hebraica*, which was also available to Drosnin in electronic form, differs from the Second Rabbinic Bible by forty-one letters in Deuteronomy alone! Thus Drosnin's Yitzhak Rabin "prediction" does not appear in any modern Hebrew Bible editions, nor does it appear in any of the ancient handwritten manuscripts. In each edition of the Hebrew Bible and in each ancient manuscript, the computer will find a completely different set of encoded names and "predictions." Thus to argue for the validity of one particular set of supposedly encoded names from one specific edition of the Hebrew Bible seems arbitrary. Drosnin reveals a total ignorance of the current textual situation of the Hebrew Bible when he writes, "Every Hebrew Bible that now exists is the same, letter for letter."[21] His statement is simply not true.[22] (See ATBASH; GEMATRIA.)

Book of Consolation

Jeremiah 30–33 is often called "The Book of Consolation." In contrast to chapters 1–29, which focus primarily on the covenant violation by Judah and the resulting imminent judgment, chapters 30–33 deal with future hope and restoration, "consoling" the people Jeremiah has been preaching judgment to. In this respect Jeremiah 30–33 is similar to Isaiah 40–66 (see ISAIAH, BOOK OF).

One feature of the Book of Consolation is that the prophet Jeremiah takes many of the judgment images or symbols used in chapters 1–29 and reverses the symbol or image to one of restoration and hope. For example, throughout Jeremiah 1–29 the prophet declares that Judah's wound (symbolic of her sin and rebellion) is too serious and cannot be healed. In Jeremiah 30–33 God declares healing and health for his people (see HEALING). Likewise, in Jeremiah 1–29 the prophet proclaims the end to weddings, joy, and singing, while in Jeremiah 30–33 he describes the new coming time of restoration as one characterized by weddings, joy, and singing. Tearing down is replaced by building up, scattering is replaced by regathering, uprooting is replaced by planting, and Israel as a harlot is replaced by Israel the virgin bride.

Central to the Book of Consolation is the New Covenant in Jeremiah 31:31–34, where Jeremiah prophesies a "new covenant" that will be written on people's hearts rather than on stone, and that will be characterized by forgiveness. Jesus Christ inaugurates the New Covenant of Jeremiah and becomes the fulfillment and climax of that covenant. (See NEW COVENANT; JEREMIAH, BOOK OF.)

Book of Life

In Revelation the "book of life" refers to a divine record of all true believers —those who will live eternally with God in the new heaven and new earth (see Rev. 3:5; 13:8; 17:8; 20:12, 15; 21:27; cf. Luke 10:20; Phil. 4:3; Heb. 12:23). The Christian understanding of the phrase as a roster of the righteous is rooted in Old Testament passages such as Exodus 32:32–33; Psalm 69:28; 87:6; Malachi 3:16; and especially Daniel 7:10; 12:1 where the context is one of final judgment.

David Aune notes three types of books mentioned in the Old Testament and early noncanonical Jewish and Christian literature: (1) the *Book of Life*, which records the names of the righteous, (2) the *Book of Deeds*, which keeps track of all the good or bad deeds a person has performed, and (3) the *Book of Destiny*, which records the history of the world and/or the destinies of people before birth.[23] There is no clear allusion to the *Book of Destiny* in the New Testament, but the other two categories of books certainly appear (see a clear example of both types in Rev. 20:12). For the purposes of judgment, then, God keeps track of a person's deeds (the "books") and keeps a register of those whose citizenship is in heaven (the "book of life").

The Christians of Asia Minor were also familiar with citizenship registers. The city of Sardis even housed the royal archives. There are references (especially in Athens) where names of citizens were erased from the city register just before they were executed for a crime. When the citizenship was forfeited, the name was blotted from the register. This is probably the background for Revelation 3:5, where Jesus promises the faithful believers in Sardis that he will never blot out their names from his heavenly register (see SARDIS).

In fact, throughout the New Testament and especially in Revelation, the "book of life" carries significance as a book of salvation or redemption. Jesus promises the faithful believers at Sardis not only that he will never blot their names out of the book of life, but also that he will acknowledge them before his Father and the angels (Rev. 3:5). Having one's name in the book of life is synonymous with being acknowledged by Christ before the Father on the last day (cf. Matt. 10:32–33; Luke 12:8–9).

By way of contrast, the "inhabitants of the earth" (an expression for unbelievers in Revelation) are described as those "whose names have not been written in the book of life belonging to the Lamb" (Rev. 13:8; 17:8). Here the worship of the beast stands in contrast to belonging to and following the Lamb. At the final judgment, the dead are "judged according to what they had done as recorded in the books" (20:12), and anyone whose name is not found in the book of life is thrown into the lake of fire (20:12, 15). Inclusion in the book of life stands opposite eternal punishment.

Finally, when depicting the heavenly city, John says that "nothing impure will ever enter it, nor will anyone who does what is shameful or deceitful, but only those whose names are written in the Lamb's book of life" (Rev. 21:27). Again, the distinction is between entering the heavenly city and being denied entrance. More than a book of deeds, the book of life is a book of destiny. (See GREAT WHITE THRONE JUDGMENT; JUDGMENT; JUDGMENT SEAT OF CHRIST; LAST JUDGMENT.)

Book of the Twelve

An ancient Jewish scribal practice placed all twelve Minor Prophets (Hosea, Joel, Amos, Obadiah, Jonah, Micah, Nahum, Habakkuk, Zephaniah, Haggai, Zechariah, and Malachi) on one scroll. This scroll was known as "the Book of the Twelve." Thus, these twelve books were preserved, transmitted, referenced, and received into the canon as one book.

The Hebrew Bible has three main divisions: the Law, the Prophets, and the Writings. The Prophets are broken down into two main divisions: the Former Prophets (Joshua, Judges, 1–2 Samuel, 1–2 Kings) and the Latter

Prophets. The Latter Prophets are comprised of Isaiah, Jeremiah, Ezekiel, and "the Twelve" (see MINOR PROPHETS).

Bowl Judgments

The three sets of judgments that occur in the central section of the book of Revelation include the seven seals (Rev. 6:1–17; 8:1), the seven trumpets (8:6–9:21; 11:15–19), and the seven bowls (16:1–21). The bowls, like the trumpets, draw from the plagues of Exodus to depict the pouring out of God's wrath on unbelievers. Unlike both the seals and trumpets, the bowl judgments contain no interlude between the sixth and seventh elements.

The seals and trumpets are also partial judgments, affecting one-fourth and one-third of the earth respectively, whereas the bowl judgments are universal. These are the final judgments of God's wrath. The bowls do contain three added features: (1) an exchange of praise for God's justice (Rev. 16:5–7), (2) the evil trinity gathering the nations for war (16:13–14), and (3) a warning from Jesus that he will return unexpectedly (16:15).

The first four bowl judgments are poured out on the earth, but the results are experienced by people who have the "mark of the beast and worshiped his image" (Rev. 16:2). The first bowl of "ugly and painful sores" parallels the sixth Egyptian plague of boils (Ex. 9:9–11). The second and third bowls, reminiscent of the first Egyptian plague, are poured out on the sea and bodies of fresh water, turning them into blood and resulting in death (Rev. 16:3–4). The fourth bowl is poured out on the sun, not to darken it as in the previous series, but to intensify its heat so that it scorches people (16:8–9). Between the third and fourth bowls there appears an exchange of praise between the angel in charge of the waters and the altar (16:5–7):

> Then I heard the angel in charge of the waters say:
>
> "You are just in these judgments,
>> you who are and who were, the Holy One,
>> because you have so judged;
>> for they have shed the blood of your saints and prophets,
>>> and you have given them blood to drink as they deserve."
>
> And I heard the altar respond:
>
> "Yes, Lord God Almighty,
>> true and just are your judgments."

The purpose of this praise song is to affirm the justice of God in judging evildoers and vindicating his people. The martyrs' cry for vengeance in Revelation 6:10 is now being answered, resulting in praise to God (cf. 15:2–4; cf. Deut. 32:4; Ps. 7:11; 9:4, 8; 19:9). As the wicked have spilled the blood of his people, so God has given them "blood to drink as they deserve." The Lord God Almighty, the Holy One who is and was, is worthy to be praised, for his judgments are perfectly true and just.

At the end of the first four bowl judgments, unbelievers "curse the name of God" and "refuse to repent and glorify him" (Rev. 16:9). Instead of responding to God's character of truth and justice by turning to him for mercy, the rebellious harden their hearts even further and continue their blasphemies (13:6; 16:9, 11, 21; cf. 2:22; 9:20–21).

The fifth bowl is poured out directly on the throne of the beast, causing darkness to cover his entire kingdom (Rev. 16:10–11). The Antichrist's throne is mentioned only here in Revelation, and this passage refers to his temporary dominion or authority. As a possible background, the "throne of Satan" in Pergamum (2:13) connects the worship of pagan gods with the emperor cult (see PERGAMUM). Building on the ninth Egyptian plague, the beast's kingdom was "plunged into darkness" so that people cursed the God of heaven (the location of the eternal throne). They respond to their suffering by moving farther away from God rather than returning to him in repentance.

When the sixth bowl is poured out, the great river Euphrates dries up to prepare the way for "the kings from the East" (Rev. 16:12) (see EUPHRATES RIVER). Some view these kings as specific oriental rulers who will invade Palestine from the east, while others take the expression to represent pagan political powers allied with the beast for the purpose of attacking God's people. The most likely background is either the war of Gog and Magog against the people of God (Ezek. 38–39) or a revived Nero returning as the leader of a Parthian army to retake Rome and continue his persecution of Christians (see GOG AND MAGOG; NERO REDIVIVUS).

At this point the dragon, the beast, and the false prophet (the evil trinity) speak forth demonic spirits. The unclean or evil spirits resemble frogs and recall the second Egyptian plague (Ex. 8:1–15). That they are spoken forth by the satanic trinity and perform miraculous signs probably refers to the deeply deceptive nature of their rhetoric (cf. Rev. 13:3, 12–14). Their mission is to gather the kings of the whole world at a place called "Armageddon" (16:16) for the "battle on the great day of God Almighty" (16:14). This so-called "battle" is described in greater detail in 19:11–21, where Christ conquers evil simply by appearing. The "battle of Armageddon" refers to the final defeat of the forces of evil by God Almighty (see ARMAGEDDON).

The third unusual feature of the bowl judgments appears at this point. John records Jesus himself warning his followers to stay awake and alert because his coming will be unexpected, like a thief in the night (cf. Matt. 24:43; Luke 12:39; 1 Thess. 5:2, 4; 2 Peter 3:10; Rev. 3:3). The one who stays awake and is clothed will be blessed (third of seven beatitudes) rather than shamefully exposed (cf. Rev. 3:4–5, 17–18). This "parenthesis" of 16:15 provides the central spiritual message for John's readers—in light of the approaching battle, believers should remain faithful without compromise.

The seventh bowl judgment brings history to a close. The voice from the Temple and throne proclaims, "It is done"—that is, it is over, it is finished (cf. Rev. 10:7; 21:6; also John 19:30). The storm-earthquake of previous series (Rev. 8:3–5; 11:19) appears again here in much greater detail. God divides and conquers the "great city" or Babylon the Great (the symbolic center of rebellious humanity and satanic oppression of God's people) by making her drink "the cup filled with the wine of the fury of his wrath" (16:19) (see BABYLON/BABYLONIANS). The disappearance of earthly elements is mentioned again in 20:11 at the Great White Throne Judgment of God.

The huge hailstones that follow recall the seventh Egyptian plague (Ex. 9:13–35) and vividly portray God's awful wrath (cf. Ezek. 38:19–22). Once again, unbelievers curse (or blaspheme) God because of the plague of hail (Rev. 16:21). God's decisive judgment of evil described in the seventh bowl is developed more fully in Revelation 17–19. (See LAST JUDGMENT; SEAL JUDGMENTS; TRUMPET JUDGMENTS; WRATH OF GOD.)

Branch

In several prophetic texts the image of a branch is used to describe the coming Messiah (Isa. 11:1; Jer. 23:5; 33:15; Zech. 3:8; 6:12; perhaps Isa. 4:2). Frequently the branch imagery is connected to the fact that the new messianic King will be from the lineage of David (Isa. 11:1; Jer. 23:5; 33:15). The imagery suggests a tree or a stump from which a new branch emerges, something that is both connected, yet different and unique. The imagery suggests not only connection to the tree (i.e., lineage of David) but also fruitfulness (Isa. 4:2; 11:1). Likewise, in several texts, the righteousness and justice of the branch is stressed. In Zechariah 6:12 the Branch is identified as the one who will build the Temple.

Branches, Ingrafted

In Romans 11:17–24 Paul uses the grafting of an olive tree as a metaphor to illustrate the inclusion of Gentile Christians in the people of God (see PEOPLE OF GOD). The normal process of ancient grafting was to remove a shoot from an olive tree that bore good fruit, though it did not grow vigorously, and to insert it onto a wild olive stock, whose fruit was poor but did grow vigorously. This results in a tree with vigorous growth that bears good olives. Paul, however, reverses the process by referring to grafting a wild olive branch onto the stock of a good olive tree and later even grafting back some of the good olive branches that have been cut out. Paul, however, knows he is describing the exception to the rule (see 11:24, where he calls such a procedure "contrary to nature").

The theological message from Paul's illustration is to be found in the symbols he uses. The olive tree represents Israel (Jer. 11:16; Hos. 14:6), the Old Testament people of God. They are the "natural branches" that have been broken off because of their rejection of Jesus as the Messiah. The Gentile Christians are the wild branches that have been grafted into the tree of the people of God. But Paul says that this should not result in Gentile pride and arrogance, because Christian Gentiles are only part of God's people. Should they at some time in the future embrace unbelief, they too will be broken off from the tree. Thus, the spiritual message of Romans 11:17–24 is that of a warning to Gentile Christians not to become complacent in their faith.

The eschatological perspective governing this passage is that the present salvation of Gentiles, who are currently grafted into the tree of God's people by faith in Christ, is the divine method of stirring up jealousy in Israel for its Messiah (cf. 11:17–24 with 11:11–16). According to 11:25–27, that day awaits Jews in the future at the Parousia (the second coming of Christ).

Bride of the Lamb

The "bride of the Lamb" refers to the community belonging to the Lamb, Jesus, who is the divine bridegroom. The background for this image of the church lies in God's relationship with his people in the Old Testament. Several prophets speak of Israel as betrothed to God or as his wife (Isa. 49:18; 54:5–6; 62:5; Jer. 2:2; Ezek. 16:15–63; Hos. 2:14–23). While she should have responded to God's steadfast love with loyalty and faithfulness, Israel's disobedience is often compared to the prostitution of an adulterous wife (Jer. 3:20; Ezek. 16:15–63; Hos. 2:1–13; 4:12, 15). Yet God remains the faithful husband, and these same prophets hold out hope for a time when he will restore his bride under his New Covenant (e.g., Isa. 62:1–5; Ezek. 16:60–63). The passage from Hosea 2:16–20 summarizes God's new-covenant promise to purify his bride:

"In that day," declares the LORD,
  "you will call me 'my husband';
  you will no longer call me 'my master.'
I will remove the names of the Baals from her lips;
  no longer will their names be invoked.
In that day I will make a covenant for them
  with the beasts of the field and the birds of the air
  and the creatures that move along the ground.
Bow and sword and battle
  I will abolish from the land,
  so that all may lie down in safety.
I will betroth you to me forever;
  I will betroth you in righteousness and justice,
  in love and compassion.
I will betroth you in faithfulness,
  and you will acknowledge the LORD.

The New Testament details the fulfillment of this New Covenant promise. The bride image is expanded and enriched as Jesus is now clearly identified as the bridegroom (Matt. 9:14–17; John 3:22–30; 14:1–4) and the New Covenant community as the "bride of Christ" (2 Cor. 11:2; Eph. 5:25–27, 31). The imagery reaches a climax in Revelation with its dramatic picture of God's love relationship with his people and his desire to live with them in intimate fellowship (Rev. 19:7; 21:2, 9; 22:17).

Following typical Jewish wedding customs, when the day arrives the bride makes herself ready by bathing and adorning herself with special clothes. Revelation 19:7–8 reflects this custom:

Let us rejoice and be glad
  and give him glory!
For the wedding of the Lamb has come,
  and his bride has made herself ready.
Fine linen, bright and clean,
  was given to her to wear.
(Fine linen stands for the righteous acts of the saints.)

The verb "make ready" or "prepare" is used seven times in Revelation (8:6; 9:7, 15; 12:6; 16:12; 19:7; 21:2) to indicate a necessary part of God's plan that will not be hindered. In contrast to the "fine linen" of the pros-titute (18:12, 16), the bride adorns herself in clean and bright linen, repre-senting the "righteous acts of the saints" (cf. 19:8, 14; Isa. 49:18; 52:1–10; 61:10). Theologically, membership in the bridal community received by grace through faith needs to be authenticated by righteous behavior as part of the preparation process. The church is repeatedly warned at the end of these bride passages in Revelation to reject the world system and follow Christ no matter what the cost (e.g., Rev. 21:7–8, 27). To love the world is to commit spiritual adultery against the Lamb, the divine bridegroom.

As the bride image unfolds in Revelation, John describes seeing the "Holy City, the new Jerusalem, coming down out of heaven from God, prepared as a bride beautifully dressed for her husband" (Rev. 21:2). Just as John is carried away in the Spirit to view the great prostitute in the desert in 17: 1–3, now he is transported by the Spirit to a great and high mountain for a glimpse of the "bride, the wife of the Lamb ... coming down out of heaven from God" (21:9–10).

Above all, the language of the bride and bridegroom communicates deeply about God's perfect love for his people. Although human marital love can only reflect dimly the perfect love of God, a healthy husband-wife relationship includes a touch of the relational joy, intimacy, and ful-fillment that God's people long for and will only experience fully in the presence of Jesus, the bridegroom. No wonder Revelation ends with the bride's longing for the bridegroom to arrive so that the marriage proper may begin: "The Spirit and the bride say, 'Come!' " (Rev. 22:17). (See BRIDEGROOM; HARLOT; MARRIAGE SUPPER OF THE LAMB.)

Bridegroom

Against the Old Testament background of God as the husband of Israel, Jesus identifies himself as the "bridegroom." Early in his ministry, John the Baptist clarifies his role as the "best man" and points to Jesus as the bridegroom:

> "You yourselves can testify that I said, 'I am not the Christ but am sent ahead of him.' The bride belongs to the bridegroom. The friend who attends the bridegroom waits and listens for him, and is full of joy when he hears the bridegroom's voice. That joy is mine, and it is now complete. He must become greater; I must become less." (John 3:28–30)

Later, when John's disciples ask Jesus why his disciples do not fast, he answers using the image of the bridegroom, "How can the guests of the bridegroom mourn while he is with them? The time will come when the bridegroom will be taken from them; then they will fast" (Matt. 9:15). In the Olivet Discourse of Matthew 24–25, Jesus uses the parable of the ten virgins to illustrate the need for people to be ready for the coming of the Son of Man, even though the coming is delayed. In this story Jesus portrays himself as the bridegroom who will come for his bride and escort her to the wedding banquet (25:1–13). Many also see the bridegroom image as the background to Jesus' comforting words in John 14:1–3: "I am going there to prepare a place for you ... I will come back and take you to be with me."

The word "bridegroom" is used only once in Revelation (18:23), where it occurs in the ordinary sense of a human bridegroom. But the more-developed image of the "bride" at the end of the book assumes Jesus as the bridegroom. The "husband" of the bride (21:2) is God himself (21:3–7). The bride is the "wife of the Lamb" (21:9). When the Spirit and the bride say, "Come!" (22:17), Jesus is the one who answers, "Yes, I am coming soon" (22:20; cf. 22:7, 12).

For Christians suffering abuse and persecution under tyrannical rule, the image of Jesus as the bridegroom and husband conveys deep emotional assurance and comfort. The bridegroom is providing a new-creation home that is beautiful, peaceful, and safe; a magnificent wedding feast with joyous celebration; endless nourishment from the river of life and tree of life; and an intimate, sacred experience of the personal presence of God himself. (See BRIDE OF THE LAMB.)

Caesar

See EMPERORS.

Caligula

Gaius Caligula (A.D. 37–41) was Rome's fourth emperor, preceded by Julius Caesar (48–44 B.C.), Augustus (31 B.C.–A.D. 14), and Tiberius (A.D. 14–37). Gaius was the son of Tiberius's nephew Germanicus, a popular commander-in-chief of the Roman army of the Rhine. As a little boy, Gaius lived at his father's headquarters on the Rhine and was dressed in diminutive military uniforms, boots and all. Hence the soldiers nicknamed him Caligula ("Little Boots").

Gaius's reign was marked by conflict with the Jews. His distaste for Jewish customs sparked an anti-Jewish riot in Alexandria, Egypt, in A.D. 38. Consequently, a Jewish embassy led by Philo, a leading Jewish philosopher of Alexandria, appeared before Gaius to make their case, but to no avail. Matters only grew worse for the Jews. In A.D. 40 Jews in Jamnia (Israel) tore down an altar erected to Gaius. The emperor retaliated by commanding that a statue of himself be set up in the Temple of Jerusalem. This, of course, would be disastrous, reminding Jews of the abomination of desolation perpetrated on the Jerusalem Temple by Antiochus Epiphanes in 167 B.C. (see ANTIOCHUS EPIPHANES). Before Gaius's order was executed, however, members of the Praetorian Guard (the elite Roman soldiers of the emperor) assassinated him in A.D. 41. War with the Jews was thereby delayed.

Some interpreters believe certain prophetic passages in the New Testament regard Caligula as the Antichrist (see ANTICHRIST). Thus they maintain that Mark 13:14–19 (cf. Matt. 24:15; Luke 21:20), in its prophecy of the tribulation that was to come on Jerusalem, especially the abomination of desolation (v. 14), alludes to Caligula's attempt to set up his statue in the Jewish Temple (see ABOMINATION OF DESOLATION). Moreover, 2 Thessalonians 2:4 is thought to predict the same event: "He will oppose and will exalt himself over everything that is called God or is worshiped, so he sets himself up in God's Temple, proclaiming to be God." Other interpreters, however, see these passages as being fulfilled in the distant future, with the arrival of the Antichrist at that time.

Callousness of Israel

The title of this article is based on the Greek word *pōrōsis*, a medical term for the hardened swelling of a bone after it had been broken, resulting in a callus that is dull and insensitive.[24] This word and its related verb occur in three places in Paul's writings: Romans 11:7, 25; and 2 Corinthians 3:14.

Romans 11:7 labels ancient unbelieving Jews as "calloused" toward God. In doing so, Paul enlists Isaiah 6:10: "God gave them a spirit of stupor, eyes so that they could not see and ears so that they could not hear to this very day." The context of Paul's argument is that non-Christian Jews in his day were repeating the sin of their ancestors by refusing to believe that Jesus was the Messiah and by refusing to accept that the way of righteousness was by faith instead of by the works of the law. Similar to this passage, in 2 Corinthians 3:14 Paul declares that non-Christian Jews in his day are callous of heart and spiritually blind not to see that the New Covenant of faith righteousness has dawned in Jesus the true Messiah.

Romans 11:25 resumes the same theme, but in an end-time setting. The key verses are 25–27:

> I do not want you to be ignorant of this mystery, brothers, so that you may not be conceited: Israel has experienced a hardening in part until the full number of the Gentiles has come in. And so all Israel will be saved, as it is written:
>
> "The deliverer will come from Zion;
>   he will turn godlessness away from Jacob.
> And this is my covenant with them
>   when I take away their sins."

Three key phrases in these verses call for comment. (1) "Israel has experienced a hardening [*pōrōsis*] in part" (Rom. 11:25a). In light of 11:1–10, Paul no doubt here refers to the fact that while some Jews have received Jesus as Messiah (including Paul himself), many (perhaps most) have not. The apostle reserves the verb related to *pōrōsis* (i.e., *pōroō*) for the Jews in their persistent unbelief in Romans 11:7 and 2 Corinthians 3:14. In one passage (Eph. 4:18), Paul uses *pōrōsis* of the Gentiles.

(2) Paul states that Israel's spiritual hardness will continue until "the full number of Gentiles has come in" (Rom. 11:25b; cf. Luke 21:24). Most likely this phrase means that Gentiles will come to faith in Christ until they reach the appointed number intended by God. This will happen during the extended period of disbelief on the part of Israel.

(3) The phrase "and so all Israel will be saved" is difficult to interpret with certainty. Scholars have debated this text, with three core problems at the heart of the discussion. (a) What does "Israel" mean? If it means *spiritual* Israel, then the referent would include Gentiles as well as Jews, and Paul is not then necessarily saying that *national* Israel will be restored to God. But the "spiritual" Israel view is unlikely, seeing that the other ten times "Israel" is used in Romans 9–11 (9:6 [2x], 27 [2x], 31; 10:19, 21; 11:2, 7, 25) it refers to ethnic Israel. For 11:26 to posit a different meaning is unlikely.

(b) What do the words "and thus all Israel will be saved" mean? Some take the phrase as temporal—"and then"—meaning that after the spiritual hardening of Israel and the fullness of the Gentiles, *then* all Israel will be saved. But a temporal rendering of this Greek phrase is rare in Paul. Most, therefore, take the phrase comparatively—"and so" or "and in this manner"—referring to the immediate context of Romans 11:25. Some of these interpreters go on to suggest that 11:26 refers to the remnant (including both Jew and Gentile; i.e., the church), thereby ruling out any future conversion of national Israel. It is preferable, however, to take the antecedent of 11:26 as the Gentiles coming into the community of faith, which, when completed, turns Israel to Jesus the Messiah. The future tenses "will ... be grafted" (11:24) and "will be saved" (11:26) support this conclusion. On this reading, 11:26 refers to an event that will witness a national turning of Israel to Christ.

(c) What does "all Israel" mean? Three main possibilities surface: (i) Covenantal/Reformed theologians take the phrase to mean *spiritual* Israel, the elect of God including both Jew and Gentile Christians (i.e., the church) (see COVENANT THEOLOGY). To say that the church will be saved, however, seems redundant. (ii) Dispensationalists take the word to refer to *national* Israel, Israel as a whole, though not necessarily every individual Israelite (see DISPENSATIONALISM, CLASSICAL). The phrase "all Israel" is used elsewhere to refer to the nation but without necessarily including every Jew (1 Sam. 7:2–5; 25:1; 1 Kings 12:1; 2 Chron. 12:1–5; Dan. 9:11). (iii) The most recent theory is the unified Israel interpretation proposed by Bruce Longenecker, which builds on the second possibility. He writes:

> Instead, in 11:26 Paul is thinking exclusively of an ethnic entity, and moreover, of that entity as a whole. Throughout 9–11, Paul draws out the disparate courses of two groups—believing and unbelieving—within ethnic Israel. By the inclusive "all" in 11:26, he joins both groups together. Thus Paul looks forward to the time when not only the remnant of Israel who have believed but also those of Israel who have strayed from the course of their belief will be saved. When Paul speaks of "all Israel" in 11:26, what he has in mind is an ethnic group whose members at present are schismatically divided. In this sense, his point is not so much that all *Israel* will be, but that *all* Israel will be saved.[25]

In other words, "all Israel" in Romans 11:26 refers to the future event of the nation of Israel's conversion to Jesus as Messiah, which will unite it with those Jewish Christians (spiritual Israel) throughout the period of the church. Truly, all Israel, united Israel, will for the first time be saved, thus ending the "callousness of Israel."

Chaldea/Chaldeans

In numerous verses of the Bible some English translations speak of Chaldeans while other translations refer to Babylonians. For example, the KJV frequently reads *Chaldea* or *Chaldean* while the NIV reads *Babylonia* or *Babylonian* in the same verses. The variation can be confusing, but the explanation is simple. Chaldea refers to a small region just to the south of Babylonia. The Chaldeans formed a critical element of the power base that propelled the Neo-Babylonian empire to world dominance. In fact, the dynasty that produced Nebuchadnezzar and brought Babylonia to the world stage was Chaldean.

Thus, the people ruling the Neo-Babylonian empire can be called either Babylonians or Chaldeans. During much of the biblical period these two terms were interchangeable. For the sake of clarity, translations such as the NIV have translated the Hebrew term *Chaldea* by the better-known term *Babylonia* (see BABYLON/BABYLONIANS).

Chaoskampf

Chaoskampf is a German word that means the "fight with chaos" or the "struggle with chaos." Some scholars consider this an important theme throughout the Bible. They suggest that the creation account does not stress that God created the world out of nothing as much as it stresses that God brought order and life out of the watery chaos. Chaos is often represented by the sea. Thus the description in Genesis 1:2 of the initial situation is one of chaos. The earth is described as "formless and empty," dark, and covered with water. God brings land, life, and order out of this chaos. Likewise, in Noah and the flood (Gen. 6–9), the waters return to cover the earth and it resorts back to chaos until God intervenes again. Other scholars, however, point out that God doesn't really struggle in Genesis 1 as he creates the world. He merely speaks and the order emerges out of the chaos.

Those who advocate this theme of *chaoskampf* point to the many times that the "waters" are used—especially in Psalms, but also in the prophets—to symbolize opposition to God (e.g., Ps. 29:3; 32:6; 46:3; 74:13; 77:16; Isa. 27:1). They also note that in Jeremiah 4:23–25, the prophet describes the coming judgment as a reversal and return to the chaos of Genesis: "I looked at the earth, and it was formless and empty" (the identical phrase as found in Gen. 1:2). In addition, the four beasts of Daniel 7 originate from the sea (7:2–3) (see FOUR BEASTS OF DANIEL).

Moreover, the "opponent" of God, while vague in the Old Testament, is clearly identified in the New Testament as Satan, but the close connection between this "opponent" and the raging sea remains. Thus, many see the storm of Mark 4:35–41 as sent by the demons of 5:1–20 and thus continuing the *chaoskampf*. Satan and the raging sea are thus related symbolically.

This theme finds its climactic end in Revelation. Before the Lamb's throne in heaven is not a raging sea but a sea of glass (Rev. 4:6). Back on earth, similar to Daniel 7:2–3, the beast of Revelation 13 comes up out of the sea, this time to wage war against the saints (13:1–8), underscoring the connection between satanic opposition and the sea (see BEASTS OF REVELATION). Finally, at the climax of this theme, when John describes the new heavens and the new earth, he specifically states that "there was no longer any sea" (Rev. 21:1), symbolizing the final end of opposition from Satan and chaos (see DRAGON; SEA).

Cherubim

Cherubim is the Hebrew plural form of the word *cherub*. The original meaning of the word is uncertain, but it is probably related to a word meaning either "gatekeeper" or "intercessor." In the Bible cherubim are winged heavenly creatures, usually associated with the throne or the presence of God.

In Ezekiel 1:4–21 the prophet describes "four living creatures" around the throne of God. In 10:1–22, he mentions the throne and the same creatures, but this time he identifies them as cherubim. From these two chapters a significant description of the cherubim is provided. They have the form of a man, but each has four wings and four faces—that of a man, a lion, an ox, and an eagle. Their four wings and four faces allow them to fly in any direction without turning (10:11). Their entire body is also covered with eyes (10:12), probably stressing how completely God sees the world. These cherubim are also closely associated with bright fire and lightning (1:5, 7, 13, 14; 10:2, 6, 7).

In Genesis 3:24 God stations cherubim at the entrance to the Garden of Eden to prevent the banished couple from returning to the Tree of Life (see GARDEN; TREE OF LIFE). Here the Garden is an archetypal Temple. God is present there; it is the meeting place between him and people (see PRESENCE OF GOD). Guarding the meeting place between God and people appears to be one of the functions of cherubim. Thus in Exodus 25:18–22 God orders that golden cherubim be constructed and placed on either side of the mercy seat on the ark, the place where God declares, "I will meet with you [Moses] and give you all my commands for the Israelites" (25:22).

Pictures and images of cherubim are likewise incorporated into the decorations of the Tabernacle and, later, Solomon's Temple (Ex. 26:1, 31; 1 Kings 6:23–29; 7:29, 36; 8:6–7; 2 Chron. 3:14). Several times in the Old Testament God is described as sitting between the cherubim (Isa. 37:16) or as flying on the wings of the cherubim (Ps. 18:10).

The *seraphim* (lit., "burning ones") that fly around the throne in Isaiah's vision of God in Isaiah 6 are similar to the cherubim, though they have six wings instead of four (see SERAPHIM). Likewise, the "four living creatures" around the throne in Revelation 4:6–8; 5:8 are similar both to the cherubim in Ezekiel 1 and 10 and the seraphim in Isaiah 6 (see FOUR LIVING CREATURES).

Chiliasm

The term *chiliasm* comes from the Greek word *chilioi*, meaning "thousand" (see Rev. 20:2, 3, 4, 5, 6, 7). Chiliasm represents an interpretation of 20:1 – 10 that sees Christ returning to earth and reigning for a thousand years before the eternal state. For instance, one often reads that the views of early church fathers such as Justin Martyr or Irenaeus were chiliastic, meaning that they held to a thousand-year reign of Christ on earth.

Today, the more familiar term used to describe this view is the Latin word *millennium* (a thousand-year period). Of the three schools of interpretation related to the millennium—amillennialism, postmillennialism, and premillennialism—the chiliastic view is associated with premillennialism. As a result, "chiliastic" and "premillennial" are usually considered synonymous. (See MILLENNIAL KINGDOM; MILLENNIALISM; MILLENNIUM; PREMILLENNIALISM, DISPENSATIONAL; PREMILLENNIALISM, HISTORIC.)

Christ

See MESSIAH.

Church, Church Age

The New Testament word for "church" is *ekklēsia*, which means "the called-out ones." In classical Greek, the term was used almost exclusively for political gatherings. In Athens, for example, the word signified the assembling of citizens in order to conduct the affairs of the city. Moreover, *ekklēsia* referred only to the actual meeting, not to the citizens themselves. When the people were not assembled, they were not considered to be the *ekklēsia*. The New Testament records three instances of this secular usage of the term (Acts 19:32, 41).

The most important background of the term *ekklēsia* is the Septuagint (the Greek translation of the Hebrew Scriptures produced about 250 B.C.), which uses the word in a religious sense about one hundred times, almost always as a translation of the Hebrew word *qāhal*. While *qāhal* sometimes indicates a secular gathering (in contrast to ʿêdâ, the typical Hebrew word for Israel's religious gathering, translated by the Greek, *synagōgē*), it can denote Israel's sacred meetings. This is especially the case in Deuteronomy, where *qāhal* is linked with the covenant.

In the NT, *ekklēsia* is used to refer to the community of God's people 109 times (out of 114 occurrences of the term). Although the word only occurs in two Gospel passages (Matt. 16:18; 18:17), it is of special importance in Acts (23x) and Paul's writings (46x). It is found twenty times in Revelation and in isolated instances in James and Hebrews.

We can draw three general conclusions from this usage. (1) *Ekklēsia* (both in the singular and plural) applies predominantly to a local assembly of those who profess faith in and allegiance to Christ. (2) *Ekklēsia* also designates the universal church (Acts 8:3; 9:31; 1 Cor. 12:28; 15:9; esp. in the later Pauline letters, Eph. 1:22–23; Col. 1:18). (3) The *ekklēsia* is *God's* congregation (e.g., 1 Cor. 1:2; 2 Cor. 1:1).

The nature of the church is too broad to be exhausted in the meaning of the one word. To capture its significance the New Testament authors use a rich array of metaphorical descriptions, five of which call for comment: the people of God, the kingdom of God, the temple of God, the bride of Christ, and the body of Christ.

The People of God

The concept of the people of God can be summed up in the covenantal phrase: "I will be their God and they will be my people" (see Ex. 6:6–7; 19:5; Lev. 26:9–14; Jer. 7:23; 30:22; 32:37–40; Ezek. 11:19–20; 36:22–28; Acts 15:14; 2 Cor. 6:16; Heb. 8:10–12; Rev. 21:3). Thus, God's people are those in both the Old and New Testament eras who respond to God by faith and whose spiritual origin rests exclusively in God's grace.

To speak of the one people of God transcending the eras of the Old and New Testament necessarily raises the question of the relationship between the church and Israel. Modern interpreters prefer not to polarize the matter into an either/or issue. Rather, they talk about the church and Israel in terms of there being *both* continuity and discontinuity between them.

Continuity between the church and Israel. Two ideas establish the fact that the church and Israel are portrayed in the Bible as being in a continuous relationship. (1) The church was present in some sense in Israel in the Old Testament. Acts 7:38 makes this connection explicit when, alluding to Deuteronomy 9:10, it speaks of the church (*ekklēsia*) in the wilderness. The same idea is probably to be inferred from the intimate association noted earlier between the words *ekklēsia* and *qāhal*, especially when the latter is qualified by the phrase "of God." Furthermore, if the church is viewed in some New Testament passages as preexistent, then one finds therein the prototype of the creation of Israel (see Ex. 25:40; Acts 7:44; Gal. 4:26; Heb. 12:22; Rev. 21:11; cf. Eph. 1:3–14).

(2) Israel in some sense is present in the church in the New Testament. The many Old Testament names for Israel applied to the church establish that fact. Some of those are:

- Israel (Gal. 6:15–16; Eph. 2:12; Heb. 8:8–10; Rev. 2:14)
- a chosen people (1 Peter 2:9)
- the true circumcision (Rom. 2:28–29; Phil. 3:3; Col. 2:11)
- Abraham's seed (Rom. 4:16; Gal. 3:29)
- the remnant (Rom. 9:27; 11:5–7)
- the elect (Rom. 11:28; Eph. 1:4)
- the flock (Acts 20:28; Heb. 13:20; 1 Peter 5:2)
- priesthood (1 Peter 2:9; Rev. 1:6; 5:10).

Discontinuity between the church and Israel. The church, however, is not totally identical with Israel; discontinuity also characterizes the relationship. The church is the eschatological (end-time) Israel incorporated in Jesus Christ and, as such, is a progression beyond historical Israel (1 Cor. 10:11; 2 Cor. 5:14–21). However, a caveat must be issued at this point. Although the church is a progression beyond Israel, it does not seem to be the permanent replacement of Israel (see Rom. 9–11, esp. 11:25–27).

The Kingdom of God

Many scholars have maintained that the life, death, and resurrection of Jesus inaugurated the kingdom of God, producing the overlapping of the two ages. The kingdom has "already" dawned but is "not yet" complete (see ALREADY–NOT YET). The first aspect pertains to Jesus' first coming and the second relates to his second coming. In other words, the age to come has broken into this age and now the two exist simultaneously.

This background is crucial in ascertaining the relationship between the church and the kingdom of God, because the church also exists in the tension that results from the overlapping of the two ages. Accordingly, one may define the church as the foreshadowing of the kingdom. Two ideas flow from this definition: the church is related to the kingdom of God, but the church is not equal to the kingdom of God.

The church and the kingdom of God are related. Not until after the resurrection of Jesus does the New Testament speak with regularity about the church. However, there are early signs of the church in the teaching and ministry of Jesus, in both general and specific ways. In general, Jesus anticipated the later official formation of the church in that he gathered to himself twelve disciples, who constituted the beginnings of eschatological Israel—in effect, the remnant.

More specifically, Jesus explicitly refers to the church in two passages: Matthew 16:18–19 and 18:17. In the first, Jesus promised to build his church despite satanic opposition, thus assuring the ultimate success of his mission. The notion of the church overcoming the forces of evil coincides with the idea that the kingdom of God will prevail over its enemies and bespeaks the intimate association between the church and the kingdom. The second passage relates to the future organization of the church, not unlike the Jewish synagogue practices of Jesus' day.

The church and the kingdom of God are not identical. As intimately related as the church and the kingdom of God are, the New Testament does not equate them; note how the early Christians preached the kingdom, not the church (Acts 8:12; 19:8; 20:25; 28:23, 31). The New Testament identifies the church as the people of the kingdom (Rev. 5:10), not the kingdom itself. Moreover, the church is the instrument of the kingdom. This is especially clear from Matthew 16:18–19, where the preaching of Peter and the church become the keys to opening up the kingdom of God to all who would enter.

The Eschatological Temple of God

Both the Old Testament and Judaism anticipated the rebuilding of the Temple in the future kingdom of God (Ezek. 40–48; Hag. 2:1–9; 1 En. 90:29; 91:3; Jub. 1:17, 29). Jesus hinted he would build such a structure (Matt. 16:18; Mark 14:58; John 2:19–22). Pentecost witnessed to the beginning of the fulfillment of that dream in that when the Spirit inhabited the church, the eschatological Temple was formed (Acts 2:16–36). Other New Testament writers also perceived that the presence of the Spirit in the Christian community constituted the new Temple of God (see 1 Cor. 3:16–17; 2 Cor. 6:14–7:1; Eph. 2:19–22; cf. also Gal. 4:21–31; 1 Peter 2:4–10).

However, that the eschatological Temple is not yet complete is evident in the preceding passages, especially in their emphasis on the need for the church to grow toward maturity in Christ, which will only be fully accomplished at the Parousia (second coming of Christ). In the meantime, Christians, as priests of God, are to perform their sacrificial service to the glory of God (Rom. 12:1–2; Heb. 13:15; 1 Peter 2:4–10).

The Bride

The image of marriage is applied to God and Israel in the Old Testament (see Isa. 54:5–6; 62:5; Hos. 2:7). Similar imagery is applied to Christ and the church in the New Testament. Christ, the bridegroom, has sacrificially and lovingly chosen the church to be his bride (Eph. 5:25–27). Her responsibility during the betrothal period is to be faithful to him (2 Cor. 11:2; Eph. 5:24). At the Parousia, the official wedding ceremony will take place and, with it, the eternal union of Christ and his wife will be actualized (Rev. 19:7–9; 21:1–2) (see BRIDE OF THE LAMB; BRIDEGROOM).

The Body of Christ

The body of Christ as a metaphor for the church is unique to Paul's letters and constitutes one of his most significant concepts (Rom. 12:4–5; 1 Cor. 12:12–27; Eph. 4:7–16; Col. 1:18). The primary purpose of the metaphor is to demonstrate the interrelatedness of diversity and unity within the church, especially with reference to spiritual gifts. The body of Christ is the last Adam (1 Cor. 15:45), the new humanity of the end times that has appeared in history. However, Paul's use of the image, like the metaphor of the new Temple, indicates that the church, as the body of Christ, still has a long way to go spiritually. It is "not yet" complete.

City of God

"City of God" is a name often associated with the new Jerusalem, the holy city that descends from heaven to earth (see Rev. 21:9–22:9). Three comments can be made about this future celestial home of believers. (1) There is a twofold background informing John's vision of the city of God. It is connected thematically to Genesis 1–3. In fact, there are numerous parallels between Genesis 1–3 and Revelation 21–22 (for a detailed chart listing these parallels, see GENESIS, BOOK OF). The message conveyed by these similarities is that the future city of God constitutes paradise regained (see GARDEN).

In addition, noncanonical Jewish eschatological texts envisioned the descent of the heavenly Jerusalem to earth in a way not unlike Revelation 21:9–22:9. One of these texts (4 Ezra 13:35–36) speaks of the Messiah, who "will stand on the top of Mount Zion. And Zion will come and be made manifest to all people, prepared and built, as you saw the mountain carved out without hands." In other words, John's apocalyptic vision of the holy city coming down would have sounded familiar to those of his day who were knowledgeable of Jewish literature.

(2) The immediate context of Revelation 21:9–22:9 is 17:1–18. In the latter, the harlot aligned with the Antichrist is labeled "Babylon," the city of sin, which is a foil to the city of God, the holy bride of Christ. Regardless of whether Babylon refers to a future end-time rebuilt city of Babylon in

modern-day Iraq or to ancient Rome (see BABYLON/BABYLONIANS), clearly "Babylon" itself is contrasted with the new Jerusalem, the city of God.

(3) We must grasp the concept of the eschatological city of God mentioned in Revelation 21:9–22:9. Will a literal, heavenly city descend to earth after the millennium, or is this portrait simply a symbolic description of God's presence currently in his church? Premillennialists usually opt for the first view, while amillennialists and postmillennialists tend to agree with the second perspective (see AMILLENNIALISM; POSTMILLENNIALISM; PREMILLENNIALISM, DISPENSATIONAL; PREMILLENNIALISM, HISTORICAL).

Club of Rome Conference

The website for the Club of Rome states the following:

> The Club of Rome is a global think tank and centre of innovation and initiative. As a non-governmental organization (NGO), it brings together scientists, economists, businessmen, high-ranking civil servants, heads of state and former heads of state from all five continents who are convinced that the future of humankind is not determined once and for all and that each human being can contribute to the improvement of our societies.

Some popular end-time writers state that the Club of Rome is advocating a one world government, with the world divided into ten administrative regions with representation at the United Nations. Thus, they see the Club of Rome as being one of the signs that the end times are near. However, there seems to be little evidence to substantiate such a claim.

Common Market

See EUROPEAN UNION.

Company of the Prophets

See SONS OF THE PROPHETS.

Conditional Prophecy

Some biblical prophecies have aspects of conditionality attached to their fulfillment. God himself states this clearly in Jeremiah 18:7–10:

> If at any time I announce that a nation or kingdom is to be uprooted, torn down and destroyed, and if that nation I warned repents of its evil, then I will relent and not inflict on it the disaster I had planned. And if at another time I announce that a nation or kingdom is to be built up and planted, and if it does evil in my sight and does not obey me, then I will reconsider the good I had intended to do for it.

God seems to be saying here that in many cases the outcome of a prophecy is conditioned by the response of people to the prophetic word. This does not indicate any kind of failure on the part of God's Word; indeed, God indicates in Jeremiah 18 that this conditionality is part of his sovereign will and related to his sovereign right to decide such things (Jer. 18:6).

Another good illustration of conditional biblical prophecy can be found in the book of Jonah. In Jonah 3:4 the prophet declares, "Forty more days and Nineveh will be destroyed." The people of Nineveh respond to Jonah by believing him, repenting of their deeds, putting on sackcloth, and fasting. God then responds to the actions of the Ninevites with compassion, canceling the prophesied imminent destruction (Jonah 3:10).

A third example of a conditional prophecy occurs in 2 Kings 20:1 – 6 (see also Isa. 38:1 – 6). In 2 Kings 20:1 Isaiah informs the deathly ill King Hezekiah, "This is what the LORD says, 'Put your house in order, because you will die; you will not recover.'" The king responds with prayer and weeping (2 Kings 20:2 – 3). Before Isaiah even leaves the premises, God comes to him again and says: "Go back and tell Hezekiah, the leader of my people, 'This is what the LORD, the God of your father David, says: I have heard your prayer and seen your tears; I will heal you.'" God then gives Hezekiah another fifteen years to live.

In other words, God is free to exercise his sovereign choice and modify the fulfillment of a prophetic word as a consequence of his great compassion and the repentance and prayer of the people under judgment.

Consistent Eschatology

Consistent eschatology is a label applied by New Testament scholars to the works of Albert Schweitzer, a late nineteenth-century biblical scholar. "Consistent" means futurist, with reference to how Schweitzer interpreted the message of Jesus. Judaism at the time of Christ divided history into two periods: this age, when sin rules, and the age to come, when the Messiah is expected to bring the kingdom of God to earth. Schweitzer concluded that an apocalyptic understanding of the kingdom was not only foundational for Christ's teaching, but also to understanding his life.

Thus Schweitzer maintained that Jesus believed it was his vocation to become the coming Son of Man. Initially Jesus revealed this messianic secret only to Peter, James, and John. Later, Peter told it to the rest of the twelve. Judas told the secret to the high priest, who used it as the basis for Jesus' execution (Mark 14:61–64; cf. Dan. 7:13).

According to Schweitzer's interpretation, when Jesus sent out the Twelve on a mission to proclaim the coming kingdom of God, he did not expect them to return. The Twelve were the "men of violence" (Matt. 11:12), who would provoke the messianic tribulation that would herald the kingdom. Whereas some earlier scholars believed that one could only wait passively for the kingdom, Schweitzer believed that Jesus' mission was designed to provoke its coming. When this did not happen, Jesus determined to give his own life as a ransom for many (Mark 10:45) and so cause the kingdom to come.

According to Schweitzer, Jesus took matters into his own hands by precipitating his death, hoping that would be the catalyst for causing God to make the wheel of history turn to its climax—the arrival of the kingdom of God. But, said Schweitzer, Jesus was wrong again, and he died in despair. So, for Schweitzer, Jesus never witnessed the dawning of the age to come; it lay in the distant future, separated from this present age.

The apostle Paul, however, put a new spin on the message of the historical Jesus. In his book *The Mysticism of Paul the Apostle*, Schweitzer argued that Paul's teaching rested on Jesus' proclamation that the kingdom of God was at hand. While for Jesus this kingdom was still future, Paul faced a new situation: if Christ's resurrection was the beginning of the age to come, why had the other events associated with the end of history (resurrection of righteous believers, judgment of the wicked, etc.) not also happened?

Schweitzer's proposed solution to this quandary was Christ-mysticism. He argued that the Pauline phrase "in Christ" signifies that the kingdom of God or age to come has begun—but for Christians only because, through union with the Spirit, they have died and been raised with Christ. Schweitzer writes that through Christ we are moved out of this world and transferred into a state of existence proper to the kingdom of God, notwithstanding the fact that it has not yet appeared. In other words, Paul's Christ-mysticism was a makeshift attempt to explain how it was that, despite Jesus' resurrection, the kingdom of God had not yet appeared on earth.

Evangelical New Testament scholars today generally reject most of Schweitzer's conclusions regarding his "consistent eschatology," especially his disregard for the reliability of the Gospels. On the positive side, he did call attention to the fact that the message of Jesus is rooted in the concept of the kingdom of God, a connection that is still foundational to a proper understanding of biblical prophecy and the Gospels, even though most New Testament scholars today interpret that connection quite differently than Schweitzer did (see ALREADY – NOT YET; KINGDOM OF GOD).

Covenant of Peace

Jeremiah declares that the coming glorious messianic age will be based on a New Covenant. Isaiah describes this coming time as a new Exodus. Ezekiel, by contrast, uses the phrase "covenant of peace" to describe the new relationship that the coming Messiah will bring.

In Ezekiel 34, God describes the terrible past and present leaders of Judah as bad "shepherds" who do not take care of their "sheep." In contrast, God reveals through the prophet that he (God) himself will come and shepherd the sheep. Without doubt Jesus draws from Ezekiel 34 when he declares himself to be the "good shepherd" (John 10:11). In Ezekiel 34 God states that he will rescue and save the sheep and shepherd the flock with justice.

In Ezekiel 34:23 – 24 the prophet focuses the coming shepherd imagery onto the promise of a Davidic messianic ruler, obviously fulfilled by the coming of Christ. Immediately after the Davidic connection, God promises to establish the "covenant of peace." The critical role of the coming Davidic shepherd (king) in establishing this Covenant of Peace is strongly implied. Although the Covenant of Peace appears to draw from the covenant blessings of Leviticus 26:4 – 13 and may perhaps allude to Numbers 25:12, the Covenant of Peace is connected to the coming, new messianic time.

God presents this covenant as an unconditional covenant without any of the stipulations of the Mosaic Covenant. The Covenant of Peace in Ezekiel 34:25 – 31 contains three aspects of peace: peace with the wild animals, peace with vegetation (e.g., the end of famine), and peace from oppression. Famine and dangerous animals are probably used here to symbolize disaster and calamity (see WILD ANIMALS).[26] But this could also refer to the future time when nature itself will be transformed, eliminating the hostility between people and nature that resulted from the fall in Genesis 3 (see TRANSFORMATION OF NATURE).

Thus, inherent in the promise of the coming "good shepherd" is the promise that this great shepherd will bring true peace to his flock.

Covenant Theology

Covenant Theology and its counterpart (Dispensational Theology) constitute the foundation of much of the thinking of American evangelicalism. By way of definition, Covenant Theology is the system of theology that places God's covenant with his people at the center of the Bible. Such an approach posits that God unfolded his relationship with his people in two stages: through the Covenant of Works, and then through the Covenant of Grace.

The Covenant of Works was made with Adam prior to the fall. Because the first man was innocent, his relationship to God was based on works. But, after Adam's disobedience and the subsequent entrance of sin into the human race, God replaced the Covenant of Works with the Covenant of Grace, which ultimately was based on the second Adam, Jesus Christ, and his offer of salvation based on faith.

The origin of Covenant Theology, at least in its systematic form, can be traced to the work of Johannes Cocceius (A.D. 1603–69) and to the Westminster Confession. Consequently, this system of thought came to America with the Puritans through the writings of Francis Turretin. It later flourished under two Princeton theologians: Charles and A. A. Hodge. Covenant Theology is an integral part of Reformed Theology.

Three tenets characterize Covenant Theology. (1) It elevates the concept of covenant to the central place in the Bible. (2) It interprets Old Testament prophecy figuratively, resulting in the replacement of Israel with the church in the plan of God. (3) It is amillennial in its approach to Revelation 20:1–6 (see AMILLENNIALISM).

(1) As its name suggests, Covenant Theology centers its approach to the Bible in the covenant. Reformed theologians believe that after the fall of Adam and Eve, the Covenant of Grace became the chief way God manifested himself in the Scriptures (Gen. 3:15). They maintain that all of the other various covenants of the Bible are to be subsumed under the one Covenant of Grace. Thus the covenants with Noah (Gen.6:8), Abraham (15:6), Moses (Deut. 9:4–6), and David (2 Sam. 7:13–17), along with the New Covenant in Jesus Christ (Jer. 31:31–34), are all expressions of the Covenant of Grace.

(2) Covenant Theology interprets Old Testament prophecy figuratively rather than in a strictly literal fashion (see FIGURES OF SPEECH). More particularly, the promises made to Israel about that nation's ultimate restoration during the millennium are reapplied to the church. This pertains to key texts like Genesis 15:18–19, with its promise of the future boundaries of Israel as a part of the Abrahamic Covenant (see ABRAHAMIC COVENANT),

and Isaiah 40–66, with its predictions of a final return to the land of Israel by Jews. This interpretation is furthered in the New Testament, where a number of texts declare that the church has now inherited the promises once made to Israel (see Rom. 11:25–27; Gal. 6:16; Eph. 2:11–22; 1 Peter 2:9–10; Rev. 7; 14).

(3) Because of its figurative reading of Old Testament prophecy, especially with regard to Israel, Reformed Theology interprets the millennium in a symbolic manner. Thus, whereas Dispensational Theology interprets Revelation 20:1–6 to say that the second coming of Christ will bring about his establishment of the kingdom of God on earth for one thousand years, the covenantal perspective is that the kingdom is here and now. It is the church through which God advances his kingdom on earth, not (as dispensationalists say) Israel. So, according to Reformed thinking, there will be no future literal millennium centered on Israel's restoration to God through Christ. Rather, the millennium is here and now, regardless of how many years pass before the return of Christ, and the church has replaced Israel in the plan of God.

Dispensationalism, by contrast, has its own marks of distinction. (1) There is more to the Bible than one Covenant of Grace; the Scriptures unfold the message of salvation in various dispensations (e.g., innocence, law, grace, tribulation, millennium). (2) Old Testament texts are not revoked in the New Testament. (3) Therefore, Israel will be at the center of God's plan when Christ rules the earth in his future millennial reign (see MILLENNIUM).

Having said all that, today many biblical scholars no longer polarize Covenant Theology and Dispensational Theology. Rather, they contend, the Scriptures offer a mediating position between the two (see ALREADY–NOT YET; DISPENSATIONALISM, CLASSICAL; PREMILLENNIALISM, DISPENSATIONAL; DISPENSATIONALISM, PROGRESSIVE; ECLECTIC VIEW OF REVELATION).

Cross and the Messianic Woes

Some scholars suggest that there is a connection between Jesus' death and the messianic woes (i.e., the signs of the times). They maintain that Jesus' death on the cross is portrayed in the Gospels (especially in Mark) as an eschatological event. In other words, the cross was the place where the Great Tribulation was poured out (see GREAT TRIBULATION).

It is generally accepted that Mark 13, Jesus' Olivet Discourse, predicts that the earth and its inhabitants will undergo the messianic woes of the

Great Tribulation (see OLIVET DISCOURSE). But a careful comparison of Mark 13 and Jesus' suffering and death as described in Mark 14–15 reveals a close connection between the two (the Great Tribulation and the cross of Christ). R. H. Lightfoot has identified a number of parallels between the two:[27]

- Both Jesus and his disciples are described as being "handed over" to the authorities (cf. 14:11ff. with 13:9, 11–12).
- Both are associated with the hour of God's timing (cf. 14:32–42 with 13:32–33).
- Hence both must be watchful (cf. 14:34, 37–38 with 13:32–33).
- Both settings predict the glory of the coming Son of Man (cf. 14:62 and 13:26).
- Both use the same chronological references (cf. 14:17, 72; 15:1 with 13:35).

Dale C. Allison adds the following to the list of parallels between Mark 14–15 (the trial and crucifixion of Christ) and Mark 13 (the Great Tribulation):[28]

1. *Darkness.* Mark 15:33 states that as Jesus hangs on the cross, just prior to his death, darkness comes over the whole land. In 13:24, one of the signs of the Great Tribulation will be the darkening of the sun.
2. *Destruction in the Temple.* In Mark 15:38, when Jesus dies, the veil of the Temple is torn from top to bottom, perhaps signifying the end of the Temple. In 13:2, the Temple will be destroyed before the end comes.
3. *Betrayal by those closest.* In Mark 14:18–20, Jesus indicates that "one of the twelve" (i.e., one close to Jesus) will betray him. Mark 13:12–13 warns that in the last times believers will be betrayed by those who are closest, "Brother will betray brother to death, and a father his child."
4. *A time of fleeing.* In Mark 14:50–52 the disciples of Jesus and an unnamed naked young man flee when Jesus is arrested. Likewise, the end times will bring a time of flight (13:14–16): "then let those who are in Judea flee to the mountains."
5. *Coming, finding, sleeping.* "In Mark 14:40 Jesus comes (*elthōn*) to his disciples and finds (*heuren*) them sleeping (*katheudontas*). The same construction occurs in 14:37: *erchetai-heuriskei-katheudontas.* According to Mark 13:36, true servants should be on guard,

lest, at the end, their master come (*elthōn*) and find (*heure*) them sleeping (*katheudontas*)."

Allison concludes that these similarities are not coincidental and that they carry significance, especially for the meaning of Mark. He writes:

> For Mark, the time of the end has begun. The church is already suffering the tribulation attendant upon the turning of the ages. The events of the present time are the beginning of the birth pangs (13:8). If the Markan church suffers the "Messianic Woes," then it may be proposed that the time of eschatological tribulation extends from the time of Jesus to the consummation, for the parallels between Mark 13 and the passion narrative suggest that the sufferings of Jesus himself belong to the Great Tribulation.[29]

Cryptogram

See ATBASH.

Curse

In Genesis 3, we read of the divine curses that come as a result of the disobedience of Adam and Eve. The serpent is cursed to crawl on its belly for allowing Satan entrance into the human world (3:14). God also declares that, although the serpent might strike the heel of the seed of the woman, the woman's seed will strike the head of the serpent (3:15) (see SEED OF THE WOMAN). This may well be the first allusion to the gospel, especially Jesus Christ's victory over Satan at the cross; a triumph that will become complete at the second coming of Christ (see Rom. 16:20; Rev. 12:1 – 17). Next, Eve is cursed for her role in the fall; God warns that she will endure labor pains at childbirth (Gen. 3:16). Finally, the earth itself is cursed, transforming work into hard labor for Adam and his descendants (3:17 – 19).

The careful reader will notice, however, that the story in the opening chapters of the Pentateuch — sin (disobedience), exile (eviction from the Garden of Eden along with the pronounced curses), and restoration (the promised seed of the woman) — is also the story of the closing chapters of the Pentateuch. Thus Deuteronomy 27 – 34 predicts that Israel, like Adam and Eve, will sin against God, be cursed and exiled from her land, but will one day be restored.

It is this backdrop against which the New Testament should be read. As N. T. Wright has eloquently argued, the Gospels portray Jesus as taking on himself at the cross the covenantal curses so that the covenantal blessings can now be dispersed to Israel—if, that is, the nation accepts him as the Messiah.[30]

Paul takes matters a step further. He contends that those who attempt to be justified by the works of the law will ironically bring on themselves the curses of the covenant. Those who place their faith in Christ, apart from the Mosaic Law, however, will experience the covenantal blessings intended for Israel. This pertains to both Jews and Gentiles (see esp. Gal. 3:13–14).

Finally, in the grand finale of the biblical story, Revelation 21–22 depicts the presence of God as dwelling with believers in the new Jerusalem, the true Temple. They will thereby experience paradise regained and true Israel restored (Rev. 21:1–4; 22:1–5). Thus the story of creation becoming the story of Israel is resolved by the story of Christ. In light of all of this, it is little wonder that Revelation 22:3 proclaims of that day, "No longer will there be any curse."

Cush/Ethiopia

The Hebrew term *Cush/Cushite* occurs over fifty times in the Old Testament. This term refers to an African kingdom on the southern border of Egypt, along the Upper Nile River, in what is now the country of Sudan. There was a continuous civilization in this region for over two thousand years, and the Cushites appear throughout the literature of the peoples of the ancient Near East. The people of Cush were black Africans, and it was through contact with Cush that the ancient world was familiar with black Africa.

While the Old Testament world knew this area as Cush, the Greeks labeled everything south of Egypt—i.e., all of black Africa—as Ethiopia. Thus in the New Testament when the writers refer to the region of Cush, they call it Ethiopia (Acts 8:27, the Ethiopian eunuch). This creates some confusion today because there is a modern country called Ethiopia that is a different country, located to the east of ancient Cush. Confusing the matter further, the Romans called the region Nubia, and many historians today refer to the region of Cush by that term. Most modern Bible translations are inconsistent with how they translate the Hebrew word Cush—sometimes they render it as Cush, sometimes as Ethiopia or Nubia.

The Cushites play an important historical role in the Bible and appear frequently. Tirhakah the Cushite pharaoh marched out against the Assyrians to help Jerusalem when it was under siege (2 Kings 19:9; Isa. 37:9).

Ebed-Melech the Cushite was the one who rescued Jeremiah when all of Jerusalem had turned against the prophet (Jer. 38:1–13).

The Cushites also play an important theological and prophetic role in the Bible, especially in the Old Testament prophets, but also in the book of Acts. The Old Testament prophets proclaim that in the coming future messianic age, all peoples of all nationalities will be gathered together as the people of God in fulfillment of Genesis 12:3. The prophets often use the Cushites as symbolic representatives of this event. That is, they use the Cushites to represent all the other nations of the world.

Acts 8 reflects this kind of prophetic understanding. A Greek-speaking Semitic Jew (Philip) leads a black African eunuch to Christ in one of the first evangelistic encounters recorded in Christian history, thus setting the stage for the explosion of the gospel into the world that took place over the next thirty years and giving a foretaste of the mixed composition of the new people of God that will fill the kingdom of Christ.[31]

Cyrus

Cyrus (Heb., *Koresh*), the son of Cambyses, king of Anshan, rose to power in the realm of Persia (modern day Iran) when he defeated the Medes and their king, Astyages, in 550 B.C. Meanwhile in nearby Babylonia (modern day Iraq) Nabonidus had succeeded Nebuchadnezzar (555 B.C.). Nabonidus's rule was marked by a decrease in Babylonian strength. In fact, for seven years he was absent from the court in Babylonia, residing instead at Tema in Arabia, attending to religious matters rather than geopolitical ones. His son, Belshazzar, ruled as crown prince in Babylon (see Dan. 5) (see BELSHAZZAR).

In 539 B.C. Darius, Cyrus's vice-regent, walked into Babylon unhindered, capturing the Babylonian capital for Persia. The Neo-Babylonian empire was no match against the advance of Cyrus and fell easily into the hands of the Persians. The account is recorded in the famous Cylinder of Cyrus.

Cyrus appears numerous times in the Old Testament, especially in the book of Ezra. Soon after conquering Babylon, Cyrus reverses the exile policy of the Babylonians and allows the Jews to return to their land and to rebuild Jerusalem and the Temple. Furthermore, he gives back to them some of the items that Nebuchadnezzar had plundered from the Temple (2 Chron. 36:22–23; Ezra 1:1–11; 2:64–65; 6:4–5).

An interesting aspect of biblical prophecy, however, is the role of Cyrus in the book of Isaiah. The prophet Isaiah lived 150 years before Cyrus, yet his book mentions Cyrus by name three times (Isa. 44:28; 45:1, 13). In 45:1 God refers to Cyrus as the LORD's "anointed." In essence the book of Isaiah is prophesying that God will raise up Cyrus as the means for returning the Jewish exiles back to Israel.

Because Isaiah mentions Cyrus specifically by name approximately 150 years before he comes to power, some scholars propose that the latter portion of the book of Isaiah (Isa. 40–66) must have been written by someone other than the prophet Isaiah at a much later time (i.e., during or after the reign of Cyrus). Many conservative scholars, however, note that in light of the many, many fulfilled prophecies of the Old Testament, it should not be difficult to accept the fact that Isaiah could prophesy about Cyrus by his specific name in advance.

On April 19, 1993, some eighty-five members of the Branch Davidian cult perished as their compound was engulfed in flames, ending a long stand-off with federal agents. The leader of the compound, Vernon Howell, had renamed himself "David Koresh." He did so believing that he, like Cyrus (*Koresh*) of old, was God's anointed (Isa. 45:1). Thus Howell combined in himself the names of King David and King Cyrus, deliverers of ancient Jews (modern-day Branch Davidians).

Daniel, Book of

Daniel is an important book in the study of biblical prophecy. Its interpretation, however, has been characterized by sharp disagreement and controversy. Nevertheless, Daniel provides valuable insight into the eschatological future, and his book contains critical background for understanding the book of Revelation. The theme of Daniel is reflected in the meaning of the name Daniel, "God is my judge," with reference to God's sovereign judgment of the enemies of ancient Israel and his deliverance of his covenant people, the Jews.

Authorship and Date

One of the key issues regarding Daniel is its authorship and date, both of which are related and important for interpreting its prophecies. Until the modern period, the church accepted the traditional authorship of Daniel —namely, Daniel the Jew—who wrote the book while in Babylonian captivity (ca. 605–539 B.C.). While some of it pertains to his experiences with three ancient Near Eastern kings—Nebuchadnezzar (Dan. 1; 3; 4), Belshazzar (Dan. 5), and Darius (Dan. 6)—over half records futuristic visions revealed to him by God (Dan. 2; 7–12).

Historical issues. Beginning with Porphyry (died A.D. 303), however, and gaining momentum from the Enlightenment on, critical scholars have raised serious questions about the traditional perspective. From a historical perspective, liberal theologians think that Daniel did not write this book; rather, it was penned by a pseudonymous author somewhere around 165–164 B.C., hundreds of years after the life and death of the man Daniel. They argue this way because of alleged historical inaccuracies, suggesting that the author lived much later than the Babylonian exile, during the days when Antiochus Epiphanes persecuted Israel (see ANTIOCHUS EPIPHANES).

The most repeated supposed historical inaccuracies are: (1) Daniel 1:1 says that Nebuchadnezzar invaded Palestine in the third year of King Jehoiakim's reign while Jeremiah 46:2 states that that invasion occurred in the fourth year of Jehoiakim's reign. (2) There is no Babylonian record of King Belshazzar (Dan. 5). (3) Neither can Darius the Mede (Dan. 6) be verified in history.

In response to these accusations, conservative scholars note the following: (1) Two differing ancient Near Eastern methods of counting royal reigns existed, which can explain the first objection. Jeremiah 46:2 follows the Jewish practice of counting the accession year of a king's reign, while Daniel 1:1 naturally follows the Babylonian dating by counting after the accession year. On this reading, there is no real conflict in years. (2) Even though the king lists of Babylon do not mention the name Belshazzar, those records do refer to "Belsarusur" as the son of the last king of Babylon, Nabonidus. He was crown prince of that capital city while his father campaigned in Arabia for some seven years (see BELSHAZZAR). (3) Darius the Mede is either Gubaru the governor of Babylonia, one of Cyrus's right-hand men, or he is none other than Cyrus himself (Dan. 6:1; 6:28) (see DARIUS THE MEDE).

Linguistic issues. The second attack on Daniel's authorship is linguistic in nature. Daniel 1, along with Daniel 8–12, is in Hebrew, the language of the Jews, while Daniel 2–7 is in Aramaic, the language of ancient Babylonia. Liberals claim that the Aramaic of Daniel dates to the third century B.C., not to the sixth century B.C., the traditional date of Daniel. However, the Aramaic Elephantine papyri discovered in southern Egypt give evidence that the Aramaic of Daniel 2–7 indeed matches the Aramaic of the sixth century B.C.

Prophetic issues. Critics argue that the author of Daniel must have lived just after the time when Antiochus Epiphanes polluted the Jerusalem Temple (167 B.C.) since the book of Daniel describes that event. Conservative scholars disagree, noting that most of these types of objections stem from the reluctance of some scholars to accept the ability of the biblical prophets to predict the future. The last two of the four kingdoms of Daniel are long-range predictions (Greece, 330 to 167 B.C.; Rome, either 33 A.D. or an end-time revived Roman empire). Moreover, this view asserts that 11:40–45 as well as chapter 12 predict the eschatological persecution of Israel by the future Antichrist.

Outline of Daniel

Of the various outlines proposed for Daniel, the following parallel structure nicely correlates the chapters of the book:

A. Ch. 1—Daniel faithful among the Babylonians
  B. Ch. 2—Four kingdoms
    C. Ch. 3—Nebuchadnezzar's decree
      D. Ch. 4—Judgment on Nebuchadnezzar
        E. Ch. 5—Judgment on Belshazzar
A'. Ch. 6—Daniel faithful among the Medes and Persians
  B'. Ch. 7—Four kingdoms
    C'. Ch. 8—Antiochus's decree
      D'. Ch. 9—Judgment on Jerusalem
        E'. Chs. 10–12—Judgment on Antichrist

According to this outline, chapters 1 and 6 portray Daniel as faithful to God, first during the Babylonian era (605–539 B.C.) and then during the Medo-Persian period (beginning in 539 B.C.). Chapters 2 and 7 predict the rise of the four kingdoms as well as the triumphant kingdom of God. Chapter 3 recounts Nebuchadnezzar's decree that all should worship him, which foreshadows Antiochus's later demand for Jews to reverence him in chapter 8. According to chapters 4 and 9, God's judgment and restoration fall on Nebuchadnezzar and Israel, respectively. Finally, according to chapters 5 and 10–12, God's judgment falls on Belshazzar just as it will fall on the future Antichrist.

Daniel in the New Testament

Much of New Testament prophecy has its roots in Daniel. The Olivet Discourse (Mark 13), for example, draws much from Daniel 9:24–27 and 11:40–12:13 regarding the predictions of the fall of Jerusalem in A.D. 70 and also, perhaps, of the Great Tribulation to come. Determining whether this Great Tribulation will come on future Israel or on the church depends on one's view of the Tribulation. The pretribulation view believes that Israel will go through the Great Tribulation; the posttribulation view, however, argues that the church will undergo those messianic woes.

Daniel 7:9–14, with its description of the coming heavenly Son of Man to receive the kingdom of God, also provides the background for understanding Jesus' second coming in the clouds as described in Matthew 24:30–31; Mark 13:26–27; and Luke 21:27–28. The same texts from Daniel provide critical background for the book of Revelation, beginning with the promise of the return of the Son of Man in Revelation 1:7, 12–18, continuing with a description of the Great Tribulation in chapters 6–18, and culminating with the return of Christ and the establishment of God's kingdom in chapters 19–22. Second Thessalonians 2, which contains a shorter apocalyptic piece, is also influenced by these texts from Daniel, especially concerning the themes of the Antichrist and the Great Tribulation.

Darius the Mede

Darius was a common name for Medo-Persian rulers and, consequently, is well attested in Persian sources. Especially well documented is Darius Hystapes, who died in 486 B.C. However, the identification of Darius the Mede in Daniel 5:31 and 6:1 is contested, yielding three competing interpretations. (1) Darius the Mede may be Gubaru, an officer in Cyrus's army who became governor of northern Babylon. (2) Daniel 5:31 and 6:1 place Darius the Mede in apposition to Cyrus the Persian. That is, the two are the same. (3) The third approach, one not embraced by most evangelicals, is that the author of the book of Daniel has confused Darius the Mede with Darius Hystapes, one of the greatest of the Persian kings.

Of the three possible interpretations, the first has the most to commend it.[32] Between the reign of Cyrus and that of Darius Hystapes, the Jews back in Israel had been mistreated, thus bringing the rebuilding of Jerusalem to a halt (Ezra 4:1–6). An appeal was made to Darius, who searched and found the original decree of Cyrus permitting the Jews to return to their homeland (536 B.C.). Darius followed the lenient policy of Cyrus, which resulted in the restoration of the walls of Jerusalem and its Temple (Ezra 6:1–15).

Daughters of Philip

Philip the evangelist was one of the first deacons of the early church in Jerusalem (Acts 6:5), who later preached to the Samaritans (8:9–13) and the Ethiopian eunuch (8:26–40). In Acts 21, as Paul travels on his final trip to Jerusalem, he stops at Caesarea and stays with Philip. There we read that Philip "had four unmarried daughters who prophesied" (21:9). Although Luke does not comment on the significance of these four women, it is interesting that he mentions them.

Perhaps this text provides some insight into the importance that prophecy played in the early church. Prophets and prophetesses in the New Testament church seemed to have two basic roles. Often, by the Spirit's insight, they were able to identify fulfillment of Old Testament prophecies in the events of the New Testament. Also, occasionally they gave new predictive prophecies (see PROPHECY IN EARLY CHRISTIANITY; WOMEN PROPHETS). It is also possible that the reference to Philip's daughters as prophets indicates that the power of that first generation of believers (like Philip the evangelist) was being transmitted faithfully to the next generation, even as the apostle Paul was headed for imprisonment and, ultimately, death.

David

David was the second king of Israel, ruling from about 1010 B.C. to 970 B.C. He is the central character in 1–2 Samuel and was succeeded by his son Solomon.

David plays an important prophetic role in the Bible. The nation of Israel moves into the Promised Land in the book Joshua, but soon turns away from God and begins a terrible theological and moral slide that continues throughout the book of Judges and hits the bottom at the end of Judges, leaving the nation in a theological crisis. Who will deliver Israel from the terrible situation found at the end of Judges?

The answer is David, first introduced in the book of Ruth and then exploding onto the stage in 1 Samuel. David is the larger-than-life hero, the "man after God's own heart," who takes over the monarchy and finally finishes the conquest, bringing practically all of the Promised Land under Israelite control for the first time. He also returns Israel to the worship of God, who blesses David tremendously, climaxing that blessing by establishing the Davidic Covenant (see DAVIDIC COVENANT).

In this sense David functions as a prophetic "type" of Messiah (see TYPOLOGY). He is the deliverer chosen by God to restore Israel. Numerous events in his life and in his Psalms appear to have prophetic or typological connections to the life of Christ. At the very least, it is clear that the New Testament writers frequently connect Christ with David. For example, as David marches to attack Jerusalem, the enemies state: "You will not get in here; even the blind and the lame can ward you off" (2 Sam. 5:6). The narrator, however, notes in 5:7: "Nevertheless, David captured the fortress of Zion, the City of David" (i.e., Jerusalem). It is probably no coincidence, therefore, that both Matthew and Mark describe in some detail how Jesus heals the blind right as he is going to Jerusalem for the Passion (Matt. 20:29–34; Mark 10:52).

However, 2 Samuel underscores that although David may be a picture or type of Messiah, in reality he is but a mere man with feet of clay. In chapter 11 David commits a great sin by sleeping with Bathsheba and killing her husband, Uriah. All of David's success and temporal blessing come crashing down and slip away because of his disobedience with Bathsheba. David is not the Messiah, and the story points readers forward, beyond David, to expect the true Messiah, who, unlike David, will not stumble and fall into temptation, but will be a true, righteous, and just king.

Davidic Covenant

The Davidic Covenant is one of the main Old Testament covenants. It plays a central role not only in the unfolding Old Testament story, but in messianic prophecy as well.

God makes this covenant with David in 2 Samuel 7:1–17. David has just recently become king over Israel. He has conquered Jerusalem and has brought the Ark of the Covenant to Jerusalem. In 7:1–2 David bemoans the fact that he himself lives in a fine house while the ark of God remains in a tent. In essence David proposes to build God a "house" (i.e., temple).

God, however, has other plans, and in 2 Samuel 7:5–16 he declares those plans to David through Nathan the prophet. These plans comprise the Davidic Covenant or Davidic promise. At the heart of this covenantal promise is a wordplay on the Hebrew word for "house." The Hebrew word used in 2 Samuel 7 (*bēt*) does mean "house," but it can also mean "Temple" as well as "royal dynasty." Thus David wants to build a "house" (i.e., Temple) for God, but God replies that he has never asked for a "house" (Temple) and that he does not need a "house." Rather, he declares that *he* (God) will build a "house" (i.e., royal dynasty) for David.

The promise God gives to David in 2 Samuel 7:5–16 breaks down into three parts. In 7:5–7 God reminds David that he (God) has never asked for a house. In 7:8–11a, God promises to make David's name great and to provide a secure place for his (God's) people. In 7:11b–16 God promises to establish a future "house" (i.e., dynasty) for David, promising that an offspring of his will rule on this throne forever. Furthermore, God adds, this offspring of David will be the one to build God's "house" rather than David.

The promises God made in the Davidic Covenant have both immediate and future aspects. Solomon, the son of David, does indeed build a "house" (i.e., the Temple) for God. But Solomon hardly fulfills the extent of the promise, and this promise to David becomes foundational to the messianic hope for a great deliverer who is to come from the line of David.

The Davidic Covenant in the Old Testament

The Davidic Covenant plays a critical role throughout the Old Testament. Numerous passages refer back to God's covenant with David. For example, this covenant is enshrined into Israel's worship through the Psalms. Psalm 89:3–4 cites the Davidic Covenant as an example of God's great love and faithfulness, and Psalm 132 deals at length with the Davidic Covenant.

In addition, as the Israelites rebel against God and continually break the Mosaic Covenant (as expressed in Deuteronomy), God frequently states that his judgment is tempered or restrained because of his promise/covenant to David. For example, although God's anger burns against Solomon because of Solomon's apostasy, God declares that he will not take away the kingdom from Solomon during his lifetime "for the sake of David" (1 Kings 11:9–13).

The kings who follow Solomon frequently turn away from God and worship pagan gods. The law in Deuteronomy promises judgment for such blatant unfaithful disobedience. However, 2 Kings 8:19 explains why God delays such judgment: "Nevertheless, for the sake of his servant David, the LORD was not willing to destroy Judah." Likewise in 20:6 God tells Hezekiah, "I will defend this city for my sake and for the sake of my servant David."

However, Israel/Judah continues on their stubborn, disobedient path into idolatry and total disregard for the justice God required in Deuteronomy. The Old Testament prophets declare that such continued, unrepentant idolatrous defiance of God will result in judgment and exile, and eventually it does. Indeed, throughout most of the prophetic books the theme of imminent judgment is central.

However, as the prophets foresee the destruction of Israel, Judah, and even Jerusalem, they also foresee that the promises in the Davidic Covenant point to a great future time of restoration when a righteous descendant of David will return and establish a righteous rule of God. Jeremiah, for example, proclaims, " 'The days are coming,' declares the LORD, 'when I will raise up to David a righteous Branch, a King who will reign wisely and do what is just and right in the land' " (Jer. 23:5). The Davidic Covenant is integrally intertwined into the Old Testament prophetic message of future hope and restoration, and the prophets frequently reference David and the Covenant as the basis for that hope (Isa. 9:7; 55:3; Jer. 30:9; 33:14–26; Ezek. 34:23–24; 37:24; Hosea 3:5; Amos 9:11).

The Davidic Covenant in the New Testament

In the New Testament one of the main themes of the Gospels is that Jesus Christ fulfills the promises of the Davidic Covenant. That is, Jesus himself is the One to whom the Davidic Covenant pointed and of whom the Old Testament prophets spoke.

Matthew introduces this theme in his first verse: "A record of the genealogy of Jesus Christ the son of David." Likewise throughout the Gospels Jesus is presented as the descendant ("son") of David and as the eternal righteous king whom God promised in the Davidic Covenant (Matt. 1:1; 9:27; 12:23; Mark 10:48; 12:35; Luke 18:38–39; 20:41). The New Testament, however, also stresses that although Jesus comes as the "son of David" in fulfillment of the Davidic Covenant, he is nonetheless superior to David; in fact, he is "Lord" to David (Matt. 22:45; Mark 12:35–37; Luke 20:41–44; Acts 2:25–36; 13:32–40).

The book of Revelation continues this theme. In John's opening vision of the reigning Christ (Rev. 5:5) and in his final climactic vision of the reigning Christ (Rev. 22:16), Christ is described as "the Root" and "the Offspring" of David. Both at his birth (Matt. 1:1) and at his climactic reign over all creation, Jesus Christ is the ultimate fulfillment of the Davidic Covenant.

Day of the LORD

In the Old Testament the word "LORD" (in all caps with large "L") is frequently used in English Bible translations to render the Hebrew word *Yahweh*, the specific covenant name of the God of Israel. Thus the phrase "day of the LORD" is a translation of the Hebrew "day of Yahweh."

This phrase is used frequently in the Old Testament prophets, playing a central thematic role in several important passages (e.g., Joel 2:28–3:21; Zeph. 1–3). The prophets will also use other similar phrases such as "that day" or "the day when" with the same apparent meaning. Throughout the prophetic books the "day of the LORD" and associated phrases refer to the future time of God's decisive action and intervention into human history. Indeed, the prophets frequently telescope all of the multifaceted dramatic aspects of the prophetic future — regardless of how long such events may take — into the phrase "the day of the LORD."

Thus, the prophets use this phrase and its associated combinations to refer to the following:

- future judgment on foreign nations that have conquered or oppressed Israel/Judah (Isa. 13:1–22; Obad. 15)
- future judgment on Israel or Judah for covenant disobedience, especially in reference to the Assyrian and Babylonian invasions and destruction (Isa. 3:18–4:1; Amos 5:18–20)
- future deliverance and blessing for Israel/Judah and the nations (Isa. 11:10–12; Joel 3:14–18), often connected to the messianic promise.

Although the prophets use the phrase to refer to future events, those events are often presented as imminent, especially in passages that warn of judgment. Also, note that Joel prophesies the pouring out of God's Spirit on the Day of the LORD (Joel 2:28–31), an event that was fulfilled in the New Testament on the day of Pentecost (Acts 2:17–21). Thus in regard to messianic prophecies, the term "day of the LORD" in the Old Testament can refer to Christ's first coming (as seen in the New Testament) as well as his future second coming.

The New Testament writers pick up this term from the Old Testament and use it frequently to refer specifically to the second coming of Christ (1 Cor. 5:5; 1 Thess. 5:2; 2 Thess. 2:2; 2 Peter 3:10, 12). As in the Old Testament, the New Testament apparently also uses associated terms such as "that day," "those days," "the great day," or "the day of our Lord Jesus" in a sense synonymous to "the day of the Lord," referring to the time of Christ's return (Mark 13:24; 1 Cor. 1:8; Rev. 6:17; 16:14).

Dea Roma Coin

The interpretation of Revelation 17–18 is hotly contested. Some popular writers argue that these chapters predict the rise and fall of literal Babylon in the end times—that "Babylon" here refers to a literal city. Most New Testament scholars, however, hold that the Babylon of Revelation 17–18 is a symbol for ancient Rome. One important piece of evidence for this latter view is the *Dea Roma* coin, a coin minted in A.D. 71 in Asia Minor (home of the seven churches mentioned in Revelation 2–3). This coin is on exhibit in the British Museum in London.

One side of the coin contains a portrait of the emperor with the Latin inscription IMP CAESAR VESPASIANVS AVG PM TP PP COS III, standard abbreviations for "Emperor Caesar Vespasian Augustus, Pontifex

Maximus [Greatest Priest], Tribunicia Potestas [Tribunal Power], Pater Patriae [Father of the Fatherland], Consul for the Third Time."

The reverse side of the coin depicts Roma, a pagan goddess of Rome, sitting on seven hills. This image of a woman sitting on seven hills was obviously a way of representing Rome in the symbolic art of the day that would have been recognized by people of this time period. John's initial readers would certainly have understood it that way. The goddess Roma wears military dress, and a small sword in her left hand rests on her left knee, symbolizing the military might of Rome. She is flanked on the left and the right by the letters S and C, which stand for *senatus consultum* ("a resolution of the Senate"). The river god Tiber reclines against the seven hills at the right. A group consisting of a miniature she-wolf with the twins Romulus and Remus suckling is located on the left side.

Some scholars believe that Revelation 17 may actually be a detailed description of this particular coin. In other words, they maintain that John's vision of Babylon in Revelation is based on the *Dea Roma* coin, suggesting an ironic and not-so-subtle criticism of Rome and all that she represented. The resemblances between the two are indeed striking:

1. The goddess Roma, the deity who represented and protected Rome, sits on the seven hills of that city. The harlot of Revelation likewise sits on seven hills (Rev. 17:9).
2. In some of the Roman legends, the she-wolf who nursed Romulus and Remus carried the connotation of a harlot. The woman in Revelation 17–18 is likewise called a harlot.
3. On the coin the woman is seated by the waters of the Tiber River. The harlot in Revelation sits "on many waters" (Rev. 17:1, 15).
4. There is a possible connection between the phrase "Mystery, Babylon the Great, the Mother of Prostitutes" (Rev. 17:5) and the label *Roma* on the coin. The city of Rome was itself regarded to be a deity with a concealed name. Yet that "secret" name was widely thought by many Romans to be Amor (the goddess of love and sexuality), which is Roma spelled backward. When John describes the goddess sitting on the seven hills but then calls her the mother of prostitutes, he seems to be consciously dragging the popular matron deity of Rome and even Rome itself down into the dirt. His portrayal is a harsh, critical parody.
5. The vision of Revelation 17 presents the woman as drunk with the blood of the saints, who are witnesses of Jesus (17:6). This may be depicted by Roma holding the Roman sword, which represented the

power of Rome. At the time John wrote this book, the Roman imperial worship system was persecuting and executing Christians.

The *Dea Roma* coin equates Caesar Vespasian (the obverse side) with Roma (the reverse side) and thereby provides John with the basis to identify the harlot of Rome with the imperial cult. This is so because the Roman emperor Augustus (31 B.C.–A.D. 14) initiated the custom of building temples dedicated to both Caesar and Roma (the personification of Rome). Augustus commissioned the building of four temples in honor of himself and Roma, two in Asia (Pergamum and Ephesus) and two in Bithynia (Nicea and Nicomedia). Thereafter, coins portraying the emperor on one side and Roma on the other side indicated that the two went hand in hand in implementing Caesar worship (see IMPERIAL CULT). If the *Dea Roma* coin is indeed the basis for John's vision in Revelation 17–18, then the beast (Caesar) and the harlot (Roma) are one and the same—ancient Rome.

Dead Sea Scrolls

The Dead Sea Scrolls were discovered accidentally in 1947 when a Bedouin shepherd, while tending his sheep, amused himself by throwing rocks at a cave opening in the cliffs to the west of the Dead Sea, on a plateau called Qumran. One of the stones made a crashing sound. Later the Bedouin and his friends entered that cave and found ancient jars that contained scrolls and fragments of scrolls. Scholars have since discovered several other caves in the area that also contained scrolls. Here we can only provide a brief summary of what some have called the greatest archaeological discovery of the twentieth century.

The Dead Sea Scrolls are comprised of 867 documents, written primarily on leather scrolls in Hebrew, Aramaic, and some Greek. These materials date from approximately 170 B.C. to A.D. 68. The Scrolls were published from 1947 to 1991, but not without controversy, mainly because of the lack of Jewish scholars appointed to the scrolls committee. Four types of literature make up the Dead Sea Scrolls: the books of the Old Testament (every book except Esther), apocryphal and pseudepigraphical Jewish works (e.g., *1 Enoch*; Sirach), commentaries on the prophets, and the writings about the community itself (i.e., Community Rule; The Damascus Covenant).

The undergirding theme of the Dead Sea Scrolls is the story of Israel: sin–exile–restoration. According to their authors, all Jews except themselves, and all Gentiles without question, have sinned against God's law and therefore are under exile—God's judgment. But because the community producing the Scrolls scrupulously obeyed the Mosaic Law, they considered themselves to be the restored Israel. When the Messiah comes, the Dead Sea Scrolls people believed they would be vindicated and all others destroyed. The Teacher of Righteousness led the community early on (about 152 B.C.), but years after his death his followers still found no messianic deliverance. Rather Roman soldiers destroyed the camp and its inhabitants in A.D. 68, en route to laying siege to Jerusalem.

The traditional view equates the writers of the Dead Sea Scrolls with a group called the Essenes, who had a resident community at Qumran, near the caves where the Scrolls were found. Four pieces of evidence support that interpretation. (1) Sociologically, the sectarian nature of the Dead Sea Scrolls matches the ancient historian Josephus's descriptions of the Essenes, especially in their emphasis on the sovereignty of God contrasted to the Pharisees' and Sadducees' attempt to balance divine sovereignty with human responsibility; the impurity of oil contrasted to its acceptance by the majority of Jews; the stringent requirements to be met before partaking of the communal meals; with respect to toilet habits; and the prohibition of spitting in the camp.

(2) Pliny the Elder, a first-century A.D. Roman historian, gives a geographical description of the Essenes that corresponds with Qumran.

(3) Historically the period of Qumran existence, which ranged from the mid-second century B.C. to A.D. 68, is in agreement with the time frame mentioned by Josephus in connection with the Essenes.

(4) Archaeologically, the recent discovery of two ostraca at Qumran, one of which has the words, "when he fulfilled his oath to the community," confirms the association of the Dead Sea Scrolls with the Essenes at Qumran (if this particular translation holds up to academic scrutiny).

The significance of the Dead Sea Scrolls is immense. (1) The Scrolls have helped scholars to confirm the Hebrew text of the Old Testament. (2) They enable interpreters to understand better how Judaism evolved in its thinking, especially the growth of messianic expectations, in the period between the Old and New Testaments. (3) While no New Testament writing has been discovered in the Dead Sea Scrolls texts, the apocalyptic outlook of the Essenes is similar in some respects to the New Testament perspective. Some biblical scholars even suggest John the Baptist once belonged to the Essene community, although there is no firm evidence for this.

Deborah

Although usually understood as one of Israel's judges, Deborah is also called a "prophetess" (Judg. 4:4). Thus, she not only functions as a leader (the implication of "judge"), but she also speaks the word of God. This is seen in 4:9, where Deborah foretells the nature of the upcoming victory. "The honor will not be yours," she tells the timid Barak, "for the LORD will hand Sisera [the enemy general] over to a woman." Indeed, as the story unfolds, it is the woman Jael who strikes the fatal blow to Sisera (4:21). Deborah and Barak then sing a song of victory celebration and praise to God. Deborah is thus similar to Miriam the prophetess, who also sang a victory song (Ex. 15:20–21) (see MIRIAM).

Delay of the Parousia

The term *Parousia* refers to the second coming of Christ. The delay of the Parousia refers to the assumption by some New Testament scholars that the first generation of Christians (A.D. 30–70) believed that Christ would return before their deaths. When that didn't happen (i.e., when the Parousia was delayed), the early believers were supposedly thrown into a crisis of faith.

It does seem that the early church's expectation about the immediacy of the Parousia did undergo some development. This is suggested perhaps by the Synoptic Gospels' understanding of Jesus' Olivet Discourse, where Jesus says, "This generation will certainly not pass away until all these things have happened" (Mark 13:30, although it should be noted that scholars interpret this text in various ways). Many scholars think Mark recorded Mark 13 somewhere between A.D. 64 to 68, before Jerusalem fell to the Romans (A.D. 70). Thus, Mark 13:30 seems to equate the coming fall of Jerusalem with the last generation.

Luke, by contrast, written probably after the fall of Jerusalem (A.D. 70–80), omits in Luke 21:20 the statement in Mark 13:19, "those will be days of distress unequaled from the beginning . . . until now — and never to be equaled again" with reference to the fall of Jerusalem. Thus, Luke apparently wishes to disassociate the fall of Jerusalem from the last generation, pushing the latter into the distant future.

Finally, Matthew 24 (written A.D. 80–90), appears to blend the previous two views, distinguishing the fall of Jerusalem from the last generation but without placing them in tension. The key to Matthew's perspective is Matthew 24:3, where the disciples, lamenting Jesus' prediction of the upcoming fall of Jerusalem, ask their Master two related, but different, questions: "When will this happen [the fall of Jerusalem in A.D. 70], and what will be the sign of your coming and of the end of the age [the Parousia]?" In other words, the former is the backdrop and the partial fulfillment of the Olivet Discourse while the latter will be the final, future fulfillment of Jesus' prophecies. If the one happened, then certainly the other will also happen. Note the outline of Matthew 24 in light of the twofold question in verse 3:

Matthew 24:3 and the Twofold Answer to the Disciples' Questions	
Partial Fulfillment (vv. 4–20)	*Final Fulfillment (vv. 21–31)*
A. Tribulation (v. 8)	A. Great Tribulation (vv. 21, 29)
B. Messianic pretenders (vv. 4–5)	B. Messianic pretenders (vv. 23–26)
C. Wars (vv. 6–7)	C. Wars (v. 22)
D. Persecution (vv. 9–10)	D. Persecution (v. 22)
E. Apostasy (vv. 11–13)	E. Apostasy (v. 24)
F. Fall of Jerusalem (vv. 15–20)	F. Parousia (vv. 30–31)

Thus it appears that in both Luke and Matthew Jesus provides strong hints that there could indeed be a delay between some of the immediate, partial fulfillment of his prophecies and the ultimate final fulfillment of his prophecies, particularly in regard to the Parousia.

Finally, the early church developed the already–not yet eschatological perspective in order to deal with the delay of the Parousia. Thus, because the early church interpreted Christ's first coming as eschatological (it inaugurated the signs of the times and the appearance of the kingdom of God (see Acts 2:16–17; 1 Tim. 4:1; 2 Tim. 3:1; Heb. 1:2), it could patiently wait for his second coming, however short or long a time that entailed (see ALREADY–NOT YET).

Destruction of the Jerusalem Temple (A.D. 70)

Although the Olivet Discourse (Matt. 24; Mark 13; Luke 21) records Jesus' prediction of the fall of the Jerusalem Temple to the Romans in A.D. 70, Luke 19:41–44 is perhaps the most detailed description of that event in the New Testament. In these verses, Jesus predicts five hostile actions that will accompany the Roman destruction of Jerusalem. (1) Jerusalem's enemies will throw an embankment against the city. The reference may be to the earthworks constructed by the Roman soldiers of General Titus's army. (2) The enemies will encircle the city, laying siege to it. (3) As a result, Jerusalem will be hemmed in on every side. The Jewish historian Josephus describes these events in his book entitled *Jewish Wars*. (4) Jesus predicts that Jerusalem's enemies, having overrun the city's defenses, will dash both city ("you") and its citizens ("your children within you") to the ground, signifying their utter defeat (Luke 19:44). (5) The destruction will be complete; not one stone will be left on another. Note how Josephus describes the fulfillment of this dire prediction:

> Caesar ordered the whole city and the temple to be razed to the ground, leaving only the loftiest of the towers, Phasael, Hippicus, and the Mariamme, and the portion of the wall enclosing the city on the west: the latter as an encampment for the garrison that was to remain, and the towers to indicate to posterity the nature of the city and of the strong defenses which had yet yielded to Roman prowess. All the rest of the wall encompassing the city was so completely leveled to the ground as to leave future visitors to the spot no ground for believing that it had ever been inhabited. Such was the end to which the frenzy of revolutionaries brought Jerusalem, that splendid city of world-wide renown. (*Jewish Wars* 7.1)

The reason for the calamity that would one day befall Jerusalem is that it did not recognize and take advantage of the time of divine visitation offered to it by Jesus (cf. Ex. 3:16; 1 Sam. 1:19–21; Luke 1:68, 78; 7:16).

The interpretation of Luke 19:41–44 should proceed along the lines of a prophetic approach to Jesus' words concerning the fate of the Temple of Jerusalem. That is, the events of 19:41–44 were predicted by Jesus around A.D. 33 and were supernaturally fulfilled in A.D. 70. However, two other viewpoints of this passage should be documented here.

(1) One theory is that Luke 19:41–44 was not uttered by Jesus but rather created later by the early church, *vaticinium ex eventu* ("pronouncement after the fact"), subsequent to the fall of Jerusalem. However, in addition to its unnecessary skepticism toward the supernatural ability of Jesus to predict the future, such a view overlooks the fact that extrabiblical sources record similar predictions of the fall of Jerusalem to the Romans made by individuals before the actual event occurred. Compare, for example, the Qumran community's commentary on Habakkuk 2:8; 3:5–7, which applied the Old Testament prophet's prediction of the com-

ing fall of Jerusalem to the Babylonians in 587/586 B.C. to the Jerusalem of its day, *before* the Roman destruction. Or compare Josephus's account in *Jewish Wars* 6.288–309 of a man named Jesus, the son of Ananias (not to be confused with the Jesus of the Gospels), who *predicted* the fall of the Temple to Rome before A.D. 70.

(2) A second approach to Luke 19:41–44 is more hospitable to a biblical prophetic view. This approach argues that Luke's passages predicting Jerusalem's destruction (19:42–44; 21:20–24) derive from an early oracle, predating the destruction itself in A.D. 70; they were not written after the destruction. In fact, the language describing the destruction is borrowed from the Greek translation of the Old Testament.

The recognition that Jesus uses Old Testament language in his description of Jerusalem's coming destruction is important. Just as the Old Testament prophets predicted the destruction of Jerusalem and the Temple by the Babylonians in 587/586 B.C., using the same language in Luke 19:41–44, so Jesus predicted a second fall of the city and its Temple, this time to the Romans. The cause in both cases was Israel's disobedience and the people's refusal to listen to God's Word.

Dispensationalism, Classical

Dispensationalism takes its name from the belief that God works with humans in different ways or different administrations (dispensations) through history. The term *dispensation* specifically refers to an administration or management order (a rendering of the Greek word *oikonomia* or "household management").

Dispensationalism is a fairly recent movement historically. John Nelson Darby, an Anglican minister and leader in the Plymouth Brethren movement in England during the nineteenth century, seems to have been the first to articulate this system of interpretation. The movement was popularized in the United States through the publication of the *Scofield Reference Bible* and its dispensational study notes. In the 1960s with Charles Ryrie, classical dispensationalism reemerged with more of a focus on a literalistic interpretive method and less on how God had worked in individual dispensations. Other proponents of classical dispensationalism include Lewis Sperry Chafer, John Walvoord, A. C. Gaebelein, Dwight Pentecost, Gleason Archer, Donald G. Barnhouse, M. R. DeHaan, Norman Geisler, and Robert L. Thomas. The movement has been popularized by Hal Lindsey's *The Late Great Planet Earth* and more recently by Tim LaHaye and Jerry Jenkins's *Left Behind* series.

In the 1980s certain dispensationalist scholars thoroughly revised the system, resulting in *progressive dispensationalism*. Most classical dispensationalists refuse to acknowledge progressive dispensationalism as genuine "dispensationalism" because of the major changes the newer movement introduced (see DISPENSATIONALISM, PROGRESSIVE).

The central characteristic of classical dispensationalism is its literal approach to interpreting the Bible. This approach insists that biblical prophecy should be interpreted according to grammatical-historical or literalistic approach. As a result, Revelation (viewed as prophecy rather than apocalyptic) should be read as all other biblical prophecies are read— literally. For example, the Temple in Revelation 11:1 should be identified not as the church but as a literal Temple in Jerusalem to be rebuilt just prior to Christ's return. For Old Testament prophecies to be fulfilled literally, Israel's national life must be restored, including its worship system connected to the rebuilt Temple.

Along with a literalistic interpretive method, classical dispensationalism rests on a number of other important convictions. Its adherents make a sharp distinction between Israel and the church. God made an unconditional covenant with Israel, and they will always be his special people. Even in the New Testament "Israel" means ethnic, national Israel and should never be spiritualized to refer to the church. The church is a parenthesis in God's plan, coming into existence after Israel rejected the kingdom. When the time of the Gentiles is fulfilled, God will offer the kingdom again to Israel. The purpose of the millennium in Revelation fits into God's plan at this point. During the millennium, God's unconditional promises will be kept and other prophecies will be fulfilled through the restoration of Israel.

Classical dispensationalism favors a futurist reading of Revelation. Revelation 1:19 serves as an outline of the entire book—"Write, therefore, what you have seen [Rev. 1], what is now [Rev. 2–3], and what will take place later [Rev. 4–22]." The seal, trumpet, and bowl judgments "telescope" in a chronological series, rather than simply covering the same ground (recapitulation). Prior to encountering God's wrath as poured out in these judgments, the church will be removed to heaven. Classical dispensationalism contends that the second coming of Christ has two phases: (1) Christ comes *for* his church prior to the seven-year tribulation (the rapture), and (2) Christ comes *with* his church at the conclusion of the tribulation (see 3:10–11). Consistent with a pretribulational view of the rapture, classic dispensationalists insist that Christ can return at any moment (imminence). Thus, the church will not go through any part of the Tribulation.

Typically the first half of the Tribulation equates to the seal and trumpet judgments and the beginning of birth pains (Matt. 24:8), while the second half includes the bowls and is commonly called the Great Tribulation (24:21). The entire seven-year period is equivalent to Daniel's seventieth week (Dan. 9:24–27). During the Tribulation Israel comes to recognize Christ as Messiah largely through the sacrificial witness of 144,000 ethnic Jews (physical descendants of Abraham) who become Christians. Christ's return is followed by resurrection, judgment, millennium, and the eternal state.

Classic dispensationalism has a number of strengths. This approach attempts to be biblical. The movement honestly attempts to wrestle with Old Testament prophetic passages about the restoration of Israel. The Bible is the final authority in matters of eschatology, and specific Scriptures are often referenced when supporting the various arguments. Classic dispensationalism also attempts to construct a theological system that recovers and appreciates the biblical idea of progressive revelation. In addition, the approach acknowledges many future elements in Revelation, something most preterists avoid.

The approach, however, has its share of weaknesses. While highlighting the value of progressive revelation, some have questioned whether classic dispensationalism really allows the New Testament to fulfill the Old Testament. Especially with reference to Israel and the church, some contend that this approach fails to come to grips with New Testament passages (especially in Paul's writings) that many understand to teach that the church is the true Israel. (This is one of the central differences between classical dispensationalism and progressive dispensationalism.)

The attempt to build a theological system can be a two-edged sword. For example, when classic dispensationalists equate tribulation with wrath, they must find a way of removing the church from the Great Tribulation, although they admit that other Christians will be present. The result is a novel suggestion that there are two second comings of Christ, a difficult point to defend exegetically. With a controlling system such as classic dispensationalism comes the danger of trying to force every detail to fit the system.

One of the most serious criticisms facing the movement relates to its literal hermeneutic. By denying that Revelation is both prophetic and apocalyptic literature, classic dispensationalists sometimes draw overly literal conclusions that seem far from the plain meaning of the text (e.g., identifying Babylon as a city on the Euphrates rather than Rome). At times when the absurdity of a literal interpretation becomes obvious, the "literal method" must make concessions. For instance when explaining the new Jerusalem's cube shape (Rev. 21:15–17), Robert Thomas concedes that the description of the city must be "an accommodation to finite minds ... where the tangible aspects of the city's architecture have symbolic meaning."[33] (See AMMILLENNIALISM; DISPENSATIONALISM, PROGRESSIVE; PREMILLENNIALISM, HISTORIC; MILLENNIAL KINGDOM; POSTMILLENNIALISM.)

Dispensationalism, Progressive

In the later part of the twentieth century, certain classic dispensationalists began a major revision of their eschatological system, resulting in a new phase of dispensationalism known as *progressive dispensationalism*. Because the revisions have been substantive, many classic dispensationalists describe the progressive variety as nondispensational. The chief proponents of progressive dispensationalism are Craig Blaising and Darrell Bock[34] and Robert L. Saucy.[35]

Unlike the literal hermeneutic of classic dispensationalism, the central theological concept for the progressive movement is the "already–not yet" framework. At his first coming Christ inaugurated the kingdom of God, and at his second coming he will consummate the kingdom. As a result, believers live in the tension between what God has "already" started and what he has "not yet" completed (see ALREADY–NOT YET). Having a different guiding principle causes progressive dispensationalists to differ at major points from classic dispensationalists.

(1) Progressives believe that the Davidic covenant is being fulfilled in Jesus, the Davidic king of Psalm 110:1, who at his resurrection and ascension entered into heaven and began to reign. (2) This group does not draw as sharp a distinction between Israel and the church as does the classical system. Old Testament promises made to Israel are at least partially fulfilled in the church. They insist, however, in contrast to nondispensationalists, that there remains a future restoration for national Israel in the program of God (Rom. 11). (3) Progressive dispensationalism offers a more nuanced approach to biblical interpretation. While still employing a grammatical-historical method of interpretation that highlights the literal, they pay more attention to the literary genre of books such as Revelation.

Progressive dispensationalists continue to retain elements handed down by their classical forefathers. They agree that God will restore Israel in the future. Most will be classified as pretribulational (the church will be removed prior to the Great Tribulation) and premillennial (Christ will establish his millennial kingdom on earth). These remain the major areas of difference between a progressive dispensationalist and a historic premillennialist.

When it comes to interpreting Revelation, most progressive dispensationalists begin with the historical-cultural context of the first readers, especially those situations made explicit in the letters to the seven churches (e.g., persecution of Christians who refuse to worship the Roman emperor). Following the heavenly vision of Revelation 4–5, progressives tend to see chapters 6–18 through the lens of the already–not yet. Some elements were fulfilled in John's day, but the final fulfillment of those prophecies awaits the period immediately before Christ's return. The seal, trumpet, and bowl judgments are viewed as sequential, intensifying toward the end (more of a spiral toward a future endpoint rather than recapitulation). The tribulation saints are usually identified as national or ethnic Jews converted to Christ during the Great Tribulation. The prophecies given in Revelation 19–22 await fulfillment in the future with the return of Christ, resurrection, judgment, the millennium, and the eternal state.

Since progressive dispensationalists are attempting to modify an existing system, they receive criticism from both sides. Classical dispensationalists have one major complaint with many implications. They fault the progressives for abandoning the literal interpretive method in favor of an eclectic method that combines preterist, futurist, and idealist elements with a greater consideration of literary and rhetorical features. Since the literal approach lies at the heart of the classical system and since the interpretive shift has been significant, most classical dispensationalists have refused to acknowledge progressives as dispensationalists.

From the other side, progressive dispensationalism receives many of the standard objections raised against the classical system by nondispensationalists (e.g., future fulfillment of Old Testament prophecies related to national Israel). (See AMMILLENNIALISM; DISPENSATIONALISM, CLASSICAL; PREMILLENNIALISM, HISTORIC; MILLENNIAL KINGDOM; POSTMILLENNIALISM; PREMILLENNIALISM.)

Divination

Divination is a broad term that encompasses a wide range of magic-related practices that were fairly common and widespread throughout the ancient Near East during the biblical period. In general, it refers to various techniques used to communicate with supernatural forces such as gods and spirits in order to determine the future, ward off evil, or change something for the better.

Numerous means of divination show up in the literary texts of the ancient Near East (especially in Egypt, Assyria, and Babylonia). The most common techniques involved watching birds and the patterns of their flight, observing drops of oil spreading across the surface of water in a bucket, astrology, and removing and observing the entrails of sacrificed animals, especially the liver. From these observations the diviner supposedly could advise the king (or other patron) about what course to follow.

The Old Testament strictly forbade divination and numerous other practices associated with magic and sorcery. Deuteronomy 18:9–14, for example, gives a list of prohibited practices, several of which fall into the broad category of divination (although the precise translation of the Hebrew terms in this text is difficult). Divination and all other related pagan methods of seeing or determining the future are described as "detestable to the LORD" (18:12). In the next passage (18:15–22), God informs Israel about the true way to engage with the supernatural— through the true biblical prophets whom he himself will choose and who will speak in his name.

Dome of the Rock

The Dome of the Rock, a Muslim shrine constructed in A.D. 688–691, is one of the most recognizable landmarks of present-day Jerusalem. It sits in the center of what was the Jewish Temple Mount in the biblical period. According to Muslim tradition, the rock enshrined below the dome is the spot from which Mohammed ascended into the heavens. Jewish tradition holds that this rock was the spot where Abraham almost sacrificed Isaac (Gen. 22). The Dome of the Rock is not technically a mosque, but rather a shrine. However, across the courtyard from the Dome of the Rock is the El-Aksa Mosque, also an impressive work of architecture. These two structures dominate the historical Jewish Temple Mount area.

Domitian

Titus Flavius Domitianus was born on October 24, A.D. 51, and ruled as emperor of Rome from A.D. 81 to 96. He was the second son of Vespasian and the brother of Titus. In spite of little prior leadership training or military experience, he became emperor unexpectedly when his older brother

Titus suddenly died. He was a capable administrator and carried on an extensive building program. He was popular with the military because he increased their salary by a large percentage, but he failed to maintain a good relationship with the Roman senate.

There is clear evidence in Revelation that Christians were being persecuted and that the intensity of the persecution was expected to increase in the near future (e.g., Rev. 2:10, 13; 6:9–11; 12:11; 13:7; 14:13; 16:6; 17:6; 18:24; 20:4). Much of this persecution was related to the increased importance in the Roman empire of the imperial cult and emperor worship.

For most of the first century, Romans recognized that the emperor was a mere human who could only become a god after death. Domitian, however, claimed deity while still alive and welcomed the title *Dominus et Deus noster* ("our Lord and God"). In Asia Minor, people showed their loyalty to Rome by promoting emperor worship, and the cities of Asia Minor competed for the privilege of building the associated temples. Ephesus boasted of a temple to Domitian complete with a statue of the emperor that was nearly twenty-five feet high. In the cities of Asia Minor, the imperial cult combined with local temples and other civic institutions (e.g., the local trade guilds and their deities) to exert an increasing cultural pressure on Christians to participate in pagan worship.

During Domitian's reign Rome became increasingly intolerant toward Christians, who refused to worship Caesar. Both pagan and Christian writers confirm Domitian's hostility toward Christians (e.g., Pliny, Seutonius, Melito of Sardis, Dio Cassius, Eusebius). Revelation itself presupposes that Christians were facing increasing pressure to participate in the imperial cult (e.g., Rev. 13:4–8, 15–16; 14:9–11; 15:2; 16:2; 19:20). Because of the cult of Domitian in Ephesus, the record of his persecution of Christians, and the strong push toward deification, many interpreters identify Domitian with the beast of Revelation 13. For others this background serves as the first-century fulfillment without precluding a climactic "beast" figure at the end of the age. In any case, those unwilling to worship the image of the beast are threatened with death.

After ruling the Roman empire for fifteen years, Domitian was stabbed to death in A.D. 96 at age forty-five. Instead of deifying him, the senate officially banned his memory and ordered that his name be removed from public buildings. While the senate was elated, the people were mostly indifferent, and the military mourned his loss. The Flavian dynasty of emperors came to an end with the death of Domitian. (See IMPERIAL CULT; ROME/ROMAN EMPIRE.)

Dragon

In the Old Testament world, the sea monster or dragon was one of several closely related symbols representing the chaos and evil that threatened God's creation. The biblical emphasis usually falls on God's ability to conquer the mighty dragon (e.g., Ps. 89:10; Isa. 27:1). The Old Testament speaks of Leviathan, Rahab, and the dragon or sea monster. In certain contexts each symbol appears distinct, while in other places two or more of the images coalesce into one. For example, Psalm 74:13–14 records that God has defeated the "monster" (dragon) or Leviathan:

> It was you who split open the sea by your power;
>> you broke the heads of the monster in the waters.
> It was you who crushed the heads of Leviathan
>> and gave him as food to the creatures of the desert.

In Isaiah 51:9 the dragon is parallel to Rahab: "Was it not you who cut Rahab to pieces, who pierced that monster [dragon] through?" Although the images are somewhat interchangeable, the overall effect is to symbolize evil (see CHAOSKAMPF).

The image of the dragon appears in Old Testament scenes where evil powers and rulers threaten God's creation and God's people, Israel. The dragon or sea monster is prominent in Job, a book that deals with evil and suffering (e.g., Job 26:12–13). Egypt, the great power defeated by God in the Exodus, and her ruler Pharaoh are described by Ezekiel as dragons (Ezek. 29:3–5; 32:2–8). The king of Babylon is compared to the dragon in Jeremiah 51:34. Isaiah proclaims that the God who slew the sea dragon Rahab in ages past will also bring deliverance from the Babylonians (Isa. 51:9–11). While the Old Testament describes the sea monster or dragon as an evil power intent on disrupting God's creation, it also emphasizes God's power to defeat it.

The dragon image is developed most extensively in Revelation 12, which describes "an enormous red dragon with seven heads and ten horns and seven crowns on his heads" (12:3). John directly equates the dragon with "that ancient serpent called the devil, or Satan, who leads the whole world astray" (12:9). The seven heads and ten horns likely indicate that Satan is the complete manifestation of the dragon image (cf. the seven horns of the Lamb in 5:6).

The crowns may indicate the dragon's false claims to sovereignty (cf. the many crowns of Christ in Rev. 19:12), and the color red is often linked to oppression and persecution (cf. references to the blood of the saints in

6:4, 9 – 10; 17:3 – 6). He is the "accuser of our brothers, who accuses them before our God day and night" (12:10).

The dragon's evil actions are many. His initial rebellion against God that led to the fall of many angels ("stars" typically represent angels in Revelation) provides the most likely background for the dragon sweeping "a third of the stars out of the sky" (Rev. 12:4; cf. 1 Peter 3:19 – 22; 2 Peter 2:4). The dragon is also poised to devour the "male child" (Jesus), but fails as a result of God's sovereign provision (Rev. 12:4 – 6). The heavenly war between Michael and his angels and the dragon and his angels results in the dragon's defeat (12:7 – 9).

Repeatedly the dragon is said to have been "hurled down" (Rev. 12:9, 10, 13), indicating his defeat. Eventually it will be thrown down into the Abyss (20:3) and later into the lake of fire (20:10). Enraged by his celestial defeat, the earth-bound dragon turns his anger toward the mother of the male child and her offspring (12:12 – 17). While the mother is given refuge and protection from the dragon, her offspring (i.e., "those who obey God's commandments and hold to the testimony of Jesus," 12:17) are said to "overcome him [the dragon] by the blood of the Lamb and by the word of their testimony; they did not love their lives so much as to shrink from death" (12:11).

The dragon represents evil, chaos, and ancient opposition to God. Revelation explicitly identifies the dragon with Satan, the archenemy of God and his people. As God defeated the beast from the sea in Daniel and the dragon of Egypt through the Exodus, so he will defeat Satan (Rev. 20:3, 7 – 10). In the new heaven and new earth there will no longer be a sea (21:1) or an ancient sea dragon to threaten God's new creation (see SATAN; SEA; WILD ANIMALS).

Earthquakes

Earthquakes appear briefly in Jesus' teachings (Matt. 24:7; Mark 13:8; Luke 21:11) and seven times in the book of Revelation (Rev. 6:12; 8:5; 11:13, 13, 19; 16:18, 18). The shaking of the earth in the Gospels occurs at the return of Christ. The other New Testament usages all occur at significant events (Matt. 8:24 to depict a "furious storm" at sea, 27:54 at Jesus' crucifixion, 28:2 at Jesus' resurrection, and Acts 16:26 at the deliverance of Paul and Silas from prison in Philippi).

The use of the image in the Old Testament provides the background for grasping its apocalyptic significance in Revelation. Earthquakes there signal a direct manifestation of God's power and holiness, such as the giving of the law at Sinai (Ex. 19:18) or the deliverance of God's people from slavery in Egypt (Ps. 68:8; 77:18; 114:4–7). Earthquakes may also accompany the coming Day of the LORD, when God will shake the entire cosmos in judgment (Isa. 13:10–13; 24:18–23; Ezek. 38:19–23; Joel 2:10–11; Hag. 2:6–7; Zech. 14:3–5; cf. Heb. 12:26–27) (see DAY OF THE LORD).

In Matthew 24:6, Jesus tells his disciples, "You will hear of wars and rumors of wars, but see to it that you are not alarmed. Such things must happen, but the end is still to come." Jesus then continues, "There will be famines and earthquakes in various places. All these are the beginning of birth pains" (24:7–8). Some of the more sensationalist popular prophecy writers in America at the end of the twentieth century announced that earthquakes had increased with frequency from the 1950s up through the

1990s. This increase in earthquakes, they declared, was a fulfillment of Matthew 24:7–8 and strong proof that the end times were near.

Their documentation for such claims, however, was either missing or sloppily inaccurate. In 1999 New Testament scholar Mark Strauss (a dispensationalist) and geologist Steven A. Austin published an article examining the actual geological data regarding the frequency of earthquakes. Based on their clearly documented analysis of the data, they concluded that earthquakes did not increase in frequency in the latter part of the twentieth century. In fact, they concluded that earthquake frequency has remained fairly constant throughout history.[36]

Furthermore, many scholars (including Strauss and Austin) have noted that the reference to earthquakes in Matthew 24 falls within the unit defined by 24:4–8. Although some dispensational writers maintain that all of the Olivet Discourse (Matt. 24) refers to the Great Tribulation, many other dispensationalists and practically all nondispensationalists hold to the view that Matt. 24:4–14 are general prophecies that find fulfillment in the present age. For these scholars, it is 24:15–30 that looks to the future Great Tribulation. The reference to earthquakes falls in the section describing things that are not signs of the end, things for which believers should not get alarmed about (24:4–14) (see OLIVET DISCOURSE; MESSIANIC WOES).

Earthquakes are connected with judgment in Revelation. Each of the three series of seven judgments (seals, trumpets, bowls) ends with an earthquake—Revelation 6:12; 11:19; 16:18. Many scholars believe that at the end of each series of judgments, the reader is shown the end of history. Part of God's answer to the martyrs' question in 6:10 ("How long, Sovereign Lord, holy and true, until you judge the inhabitants of the earth and avenge our blood?") includes the earthquake in the sixth seal (see 6:12–14):

> I watched as he opened the sixth seal. There was a great earthquake. The sun turned black like sackcloth made of goat hair, the whole moon turned blood red, and the stars in the sky fell to earth, as late figs drop from a fig tree when shaken by a strong wind. The sky receded like a scroll, rolling up, and every mountain and island was removed from its place.

The martyrs asked for justice and vindication, and God answers with cosmic judgment on the forces of evil. Likewise, Revelation 8:2–5 seems to reinforce God's response of judgment in answer to the prayers of his people. Following the ascension to heaven of the two witnesses in chapter 11, a severe earthquake kills seven thousand, leaving the survivors terrified and giving glory to God (11:13). When the seventh angel sounds his trumpet, the reader is once again transported to the final end and the consummation of God's kingdom (11:15–19). The pouring out of the seventh bowl in Revelation 16 also coincides with the last of the four "storm passages" (see 4:5; 8:5; 11:19; 16:18). The finality of this passage is apparent:

> The seventh angel poured out his bowl into the air, and out of the temple came a loud voice from the throne, saying, "It is done!" Then there came flashes of lightning, rumblings, peals of thunder and a severe earthquake. No earthquake like it has ever occurred since man has been on earth, so tremendous was the quake. The great city split into three parts, and the cities of the nations collapsed. God remembered Babylon the Great and gave her the cup filled with the wine of the fury of his wrath. Every island fled away and the mountains could not be found. From the sky huge hailstones of about a hundred pounds each fell upon men. And they cursed God on account of the plague of hail, because the plague was so terrible. (16:17–20)

While the lightning and thunder echo God's glory at Sinai (Ex. 19:16), the earthquake indicates the end of history. God's wrath poured out on Babylon the Great includes dramatic cosmic judgment, including a plague of huge hailstones reminiscent of the plagues against Egypt (Ex. 9:18–34). Earthquake notwithstanding, the unrepentant continue in their sin and curse God (Rev. 16:21).

The original audience of Revelation was not unfamiliar with earthquakes. Most of western Asia Minor (modern Turkey) lies in an earthquake-prone region. Sardis and Philadelphia suffered a devastating earthquake in A.D. 17. The Roman historian Pliny described it as "the greatest disaster in human memory."[37] In addition, Laodicea suffered extensive damage in the earthquake of A.D. 60. The history of the churches of Asia Minor with quakes would have heightened the effect of this particular image to describe divine judgment. (See DAY OF THE LORD; JUDGMENT; WRATH OF GOD.)

Eclectic View of Revelation

There are five main interpretive approaches to Revelation: preterist, historicist, futurist, idealist, and eclectic. The eclectic approach seeks to combine the strengths of several of the other views while avoiding their weaknesses. It agrees with preterists that Revelation must mean something to the first readers. The starting point, then, for grasping the message of the book is to understand what God was saying through John to the churches of Asia Minor. This calls for a careful study of the historical-cultural context of Revelation.

With the futurists, eclectics acknowledge that some portions of Revelation await final fulfillment. Although opinions vary about which elements have been fulfilled and which elements are still future, most agree that Revelation 19–22 awaits fulfillment. God's ultimate victory over the forces of evil will be decisively demonstrated in history.

The eclectic view shares the idealist conviction that Revelation has a relevant spiritual message for the church of every age. For eclectics such as Craig Keener, these spiritual insights and applications grow out of a historical-literary exegesis: "Once we understand what God was saying to the churches of Asia through John, we can begin to draw analogies for how the same message is relevant to our churches today."[38]

Many prominent New Testament evangelical scholars writing on Revelation within recent decades have embraced the eclectic approach, such as Greg Beale (with an idealist emphasis), G. R. Beasley-Murray, Alan Johnson, Dennis E. Johnson, Craig Keener, George E. Ladd, Robert Mounce, and Grant Osborne (with a futurist emphasis). Although the eclectic approach may tempt interpreters to uneven and subjective exegesis, the safeguard of building on the strengths of the other approaches while avoiding their weaknesses makes it a promising approach. Eclecticism tends toward balance by simply recognizing that each approach can be dangerous when taken to an extreme. (See FUTURIST VIEW OF REVELATION; HISTORICIST VIEW OF REVELATION; IDEALIST VIEW OF REVELATION; PRETERIST VIEW OF REVELATION.)

Elijah

Elijah is one of the most significant prophets of the Old Testament appearing in the historical narratives (1 Kings 17–19; 21; 2 Kings 1–2), though he does not produce a written book, as the literary prophets do (e.g., Isaiah, Jeremiah). Thus he is often referred to as a nonliterary prophet. Nonetheless there is much that can be learned about Old Testament prophets from his life. In addition, Elijah is mentioned prophetically in Malachi 4:5 and several times in the New Testament. Thus he appears to play some manner of prophetic/typological role in regard to the announcement and coming of Christ (see TYPOLOGY).

Elijah in the Old Testament

Elijah's ministry takes place in the northern kingdom of Israel during the reign of King Ahab (871–852 B.C.), one of the kings of Israel who was the most blatantly idolatrous and disobedient to God. In the Old Testament, starting with Solomon, many of Israel's and Judah's kings turned from the worship of Israel's true God and followed after other gods, especially Baal. One of the major roles of the true prophets of God was to confront the kings over this issue. They proclaimed to the monarchs that they must repent immediately and turn back to the true worship of God or else face judgment. Much of Elijah's ministry fits in this mold and revolves around his confrontations with Ahab and the false religion that the king followed.

In 1 Kings 18:16–46 Elijah's confrontation with Ahab climaxes in a contest between the prophets and gods on Mount Carmel. The false prophets of Baal (the Canaanite storm/fertility god) and the false prophets of Asherah (a Canaanite goddess) agree to a contest with Elijah (the prophet of the LORD) concerning which god Israel should serve. After the false prophets are unable to call down fire from heaven, Elijah prays and the LORD God sends down fire to consume Elijah's altar and sacrifice, thus demonstrating clearly that the LORD is indeed the true and sovereign God. Indeed, afterwards the people cry out, "The LORD is God! The LORD is God!" (1 Kings 18:39), a declaration similar to the meaning of Elijah's name ("the LORD is my God").

Elijah demonstrates the characteristics of a true prophet of the LORD in several dramatic ways. He begins his public ministry by predicting a severe drought (1 Kings 17:1) and later predicts the end of the drought (18:41–46). God works several miracles through and for Elijah, including the multiplication of flour and oil for the widow who gives the prophet a place to stay. Later Elijah raises this widow's son from the dead (17:17–24). Elijah also foretells the coming judgment on the house of Ahab and the gruesome demise of Queen Jezebel (21:20–24), prophecies fulfilled in 2 Kings 9–10.

Another characteristic of a true prophet that emerges in the story of Elijah is his close connection to "the word of the LORD." The "word of the LORD" comes to Elijah (1 Kings 17:1) and he thus speaks authoritatively on the LORD's behalf. Elijah obeys the "word," commands obedience from others to the "word," and foretells judgment based on the "word." This theme is summarized by the widow, after Elijah raises her son from the dead. She proclaims, "Now I know that you are a man of God and that the word of the LORD from your mouth is true" (17:24).

An interesting aspect of Elijah's life is that he appears to experience times of severe discouragement. Soon after his great victory over the prophets of Baal, the persecution by Queen Jezebel leads Elijah to flee into the desert, where he complains to God about his situation. God rebukes Elijah mildly and sends him back to work in his prophetic role (1 Kings 19:1–18), but also gives him an assistant, Elisha.

Another significant aspect of Elijah's life as a prophet is that he does not die. God takes him up to heaven in a whirlwind accompanied by a chariot of fire and horses of fire (2 Kings 2:1–12). His prophetic role and ministry is then transferred to Elisha.

At the end of the Old Testament period the prophet Malachi brings Elijah back into the picture of prophetic history. Malachi 4:5 states: "See, I will send you the prophet Elijah before that great and dreadful day of the LORD comes." This text connects a "reappearance" of Elijah to the inauguration of the future Day of the LORD (see DAY OF THE LORD; MALACHI, BOOK OF).

Elijah in the New Testament

Elijah is mentioned numerous times in the New Testament. In its canonical location, the reference to the coming of Elijah before the Day of the Lord (Mal. 4:5) falls at the very end of the Old Testament; thus in the Christian Bible it serves as a lead-in to John the Baptist, who is the forerunner and announcer of Christ. Jesus apparently identifies John the Baptist as the one who fulfills the prophecy in Malachi 4:5 about Elijah (Matt. 11:11–14; Mark 9:11–13). John the Baptist, however, denies that he is Elijah (John 1:21). The solution to this difference probably lies in the way Luke 1:17 explains the connection. When an angel of the Lord tells the priest Zechariah about John the Baptist's birth, the angel states, "he will go on before the Lord, in the spirit and power of Elijah ... to make ready a people prepared for the Lord."

Some scholars also note the points of similarity between some of Elijah's miracles and the miracles that Christ performs in the New Testament. For example, Elijah multiples food (1 Kings 17:7–16) as does Christ (Luke 9:10–17). Elijah raises the son of a widow from the dead (1 Kings 17:17–24) as does Christ (Luke 7:11–17). After Elijah raises the widow's son she proclaims, "Now I know that you are a man of God and that the word of the LORD from your mouth is truth" (1 Kings 17:24). After Jesus raises a widow's son, the crowd proclaims, "A great prophet has appeared among us" Luke 7:16).

Some suggest that this similarity indicates that Elijah foreshadowed Christ in a typological manner (see TYPOLOGY). Others understand the connection as pointing rather to the fact that Jesus came in the power and in the tradition of the Old Testament prophets. Jesus comes as king, priest, and *prophet*. The allusions to Elijah's miracles in the Gospels thus underscore that Jesus is to be identified as a great prophet (as part of his messianic identity).

Elijah also appears along with Moses at the transfiguration of Jesus (Matt. 17:1 – 13; Mark 9:2 – 13; Luke 9:28 – 36). One of the clear truths stressed in this event is that Jesus is greater than Moses and Elijah, two of the most significant figures in the Old Testament. The specific significance of Moses and Elijah, however, is not entirely clear. Some suggest that Moses represents the Law and that Elijah represents the Prophets, so that the event demonstrates the superiority of Christ over the Law and the Prophets. Others note that Moses brings strong connotations of the Exodus and that Jesus is seen as the new, greater "Moses," who brings a new, great Exodus of deliverance. Elijah, then, is connected through Malachi 4:5 as pointing to the "great day of the LORD" (see DAY OF THE LORD). His presence gives the event a clear eschatological ("end times") significance.

Elisha

Elisha is an important prophet who ministered in the northern kingdom, Israel. He first serves as the attendant of Elijah; later, after Elijah is taken up to heaven in the chariot of fire, Elisha becomes the primary powerful prophet of God, as Elijah had been (see ELIJAH). Elisha prophesies during the reigns of Jehoram, Jehu, Jehoahaz, and Jehoash (approx. 850 – 800 B.C.). Like Elijah, he does not produce any written books; thus he is not one of the literary prophets. However, he is a central prophetic figure in the Old Testament and, along with Elijah, foreshadows the prophetic ministry of Jesus.

Elisha in the Old Testament

Elisha is introduced in 1 Kings 19:19 – 21 as Elijah selects him to become his successor. After Elijah departs in 2 Kings 2, Elisha becomes the primary prophet of Israel and dominates the narrative story of 2 Kings 2 – 9. His final acts and his death are recorded in 2 Kings 13.

Elijah and Elisha are similar in that both minister at a time when the northern kingdom Israel has fallen into apostasy. The monarchs have turned away from the true God of Israel and are worshiping Baal and other false gods. Elisha and Elijah proclaim judgment on the nation and the monarchy because of this sin, but they also proclaim hope for the individuals who trust in God, no matter how poor or downtrodden these individuals may be.

Both Elijah and Elisha perform miracles, but Elisha's recorded miracles are more numerous than Elijah's. One of the main points proclaimed through their miracles is that miraculous deliverance (whether healing, providing food, or even raising the dead) is not available through the idolatrous king or the corrupt idolatrous religious system officially sanctioned by the king; rather, it is through faith in the true God of Israel and through believing the word of his true prophets. Furthermore, both prophets underscore the fact that individual deliverance/salvation can be found through faith in their message even as the nation as a whole heads toward national judgment.

For example, 2 Kings 4 describes four miracles that Elisha performs. The common theme connecting these four episodes is that of hope out of hopelessness, especially for the downtrodden or poor who come to Elisha for help. In 2 Kings 5 Naaman, a Gentile, is healed, demonstrating that even Gentile individuals can be delivered if they turn from following pagan gods and follow the specific directions of God's true prophet. In 2 Kings 6 Elisha demonstrates that he also has power to defeat the enemy armies that attack Israel, underscoring the fact that if the kings of Israel turn to God and listen to God's prophet, the nation itself can be delivered. However, in spite of clear miraculous evidence provided by Elisha, the kings and the nation continue to defy God, follow pagan gods, and thus bring on themselves God's judgment.

Elisha in the New Testament

Unlike Elijah, the prophet Elisha is only specifically mentioned once in the New Testament. In Luke 4:27 Jesus refers to the healing of the Syrian general Naaman, whose leprosy was healed after he followed Elisha's directions (2 Kings 5). Jesus stresses the parallels between the reaction of the Jews to his ministry and the reaction of Israel to Elisha's ministry. As Israel rejected Elisha, so the Jewish nation rejects Jesus. Furthermore, as the Gentile Naaman found healing and deliverance in the time of Elisha, so will the Gentiles find salvation in the time of Jesus.

In addition, however, it is probable that many of Jesus' miracles allude to the ministry of Elisha. That is, Jesus performs numerous miracles that are similar in nature to Elisha's. In this comparison the main difference between the two is that Jesus' miracles are greater.

- Elisha changes bad water into good water (2 Kings 2:19–22) while Jesus changes water into wine (John 2:1–11).

- Elisha defies the gravity of water by making an axhead float (2 Kings 6:1–7), while Jesus walks on the water himself (Matt. 14:22–33; Mark 6:45–51; John 6:16–21).
- Elisha multiplies food for one widow (2 Kings 4:1–7) while Jesus multiplies food to feed a multitude of people (Matt. 14:13–21; 15:29–39; Mark 6:30–44; 8:1–10; Luke 9:10–17; John 6:1–14).
- Both Elisha and Jesus raise people from the dead. Elisha, however, does this only once (2 Kings 4:8–37), while Jesus performs this miracle several times (Mark 5:21–24, 35–43; Luke 7:11–17; John 11:17–44), and then rises from the dead himself (Matt. 28:1–20; Mark 16:1–8; Luke 24:1–53; John 20:1–30).

The similarities between the works of Elisha (and Elijah) and the works of Jesus point to the fact that Jesus the Messiah is not only the coming King, but also the ultimate powerful prophet.

Emperors

The name "Caesar" goes back to the family of Julius Caesar (100–44 B.C.), who eventually became dictator of the republic of Rome in 48 B.C. and ruled until his assassination in 44 B.C. His murder was followed by a civil war out of which Caesar's nephew Gaius Octavianus (Octavian) emerged victorious in 31 B.C. to become the first official Roman emperor.

Octavian is better known as Caesar Augustus (63 B.C.–A.D. 14). The term "Augustus" (Gk. *sebastos*), meaning "revered one" or "august one," was conferred on Octavian by the Roman senate in 27 B.C. as a designation of the Roman emperor. He reigned as sole *imperator* (emperor) of Rome from 31 B.C. to A.D.14 and appears in Luke 2:1 as the emperor who required a taxation census of the Roman world at the time of Jesus' birth. Augustus accepted worship in association with the worship of the goddess Roma and was deified after his death. A temple was built in Athens in honor of Augustus. He was succeeded by Tiberius.

Tiberius (42 B.C.–A.D. 37) reigned as Caesar from A.D. 14 to 37. He had been adopted into the Augustan family and changed his name to Tiberius Caesar Augustus when he became emperor. He was a humble man who had no interest in being worshiped as a god. He was also an excellent administrator known for promoting peace and security within the empire. He did not have good relations with the Roman senate, however, and ruled the last ten years from the island of Capri. In A.D. 26 he appointed Pontius Pilate as governor of Judea. Tiberius was the emperor during the ministry of Jesus, and although he is only mentioned once by name in the New Testament (Luke 3:1), there are a number of general references to the emperor during his rule (paying taxes to Caesar in Matt. 22:17, 21; Mark 12:16, 17; Luke 20:22, 24, 25; 23:2; being a friend of Caesar in John 19:12, 15).

At Tiberius's death, Gaius (Caligula) became emperor at age twenty-five and ruled from A.D. 37 to 41 (see CALIGULA). He was the son of the famous Roman general Germanicus and as a small child often accompanied his father on military campaigns. The Roman troops nicknamed him Caligula ("Little Boot") because on these campaigns he often dressed as a Roman soldier in child-size military garb, complete with small boots. He gained popularity by appealing to the populace (e.g., recalling exiles, publishing censured writings, making the budget public).

Caligula appointed Herod Agrippa I (Acts 12) as king over a portion of northeast Galilee. He supported the notion of the deity of the emperor and revived the imperial cult. After enduring a serious illness that killed several close relatives and advisors, Caligula's rule turned cruel and unpredictable. He eventually squandered the imperial wealth, murdered or banished competitors, and began to persecute the Jews. After only three years he was assassinated by his own guard.

Claudius, the nephew of Tiberius, became emperor more by default than design and ruled from A.D. 41 to 54. After the death of Caligula, the Praetorian Guard proclaimed him emperor and the senate approved. He had little political experience and faced the daunting task of repairing the damage done by Caligula. For example, Caligula's mismanagement of the grain supplies led to a famine during his reign (Acts 11:28). He continued to centralize power under imperial control, while maintaining the appearances of a traditional republic.

While Claudius exempted Alexandrian Jews from the imperial cult, he was also responsible for exiling certain Jews from Rome who were responsible for causing trouble (see Acts 18:2). The Roman historian Suetonius wrote that "because the Jews of Rome were indulging in constant riots at the instigation of Chrestus [Christus or Christ?] he [Claudius] expelled them from the city." When his third wife was put to death, Claudius married his niece Agrippina, the mother of Nero by a former marriage. When Claudius decided that Britannicus (his son from his third wife) should succeed him as emperor, Agrippina poisoned him so that Nero became emperor (A.D. 54).

Nero (A.D. 37–68), the son of Agrippina (Germanicus's daughter), was proclaimed emperor without opposition (see NERO). After a good beginning (e.g., reforming the treasury, providing tax relief, improving grain distribution, appointing competent governors), he murdered his control-ling mother and his wife Octavia. During the early years of his reign, Nero was advised by Burrus (a leading member of the Praetorian Guard) and Seneca (a prominent senator and philosopher). After Burrus died and Seneca retired, Nero's vices went unchecked.

He spent enormous amounts of money on his love of entertainment, especially the theater and the chariot races. Toward the end of his reign (A.D. 54–68), a major fire broke out in Rome and devastated a large por-tion of the city. While most people blamed Nero, Nero blamed the Chris-tians, leading to the persecution of many believers. Possibly both Peter and Paul were martyred during this period. In the latter part of Acts, the Caesar was Nero (Acts 25:11, 12, 21; 26:32; 27:24; 28:19). His lust for power, paranoia leading to multiple murders, mental instability, exhi-bitionism in the arts, lack of interest in the affairs of the empire, and overall viciousness led to his suicide in A.D. 68. Since he was the last in the Julio-Claudian dynasty of emperors, the competition to replace him led to civil unrest.

The year following Nero's death (A.D. 69) became the year of the four emperors. The Praetorian Guard selected Galba as emperor because he had been a successful governor. Because of Galba's unpopularity with the army and his other administrative failures, however, Otho plotted with the same Guard to have Galba murdered and himself proclaimed emperor. Otho only ruled for ninety-five days before committing suicide after he was defeated by Vitellius's army. Vitellius was proclaimed emperor by the Roman armies in the west and marched into Rome as a triumphant con-queror. The Roman armies in the east, however, were loyal to Vespasian, who soon declared war on Vitellius. As Vespasian marched on Rome, his advance guard killed Vitellius, leaving Vespasian as the sole emperor.

Vespasian (A.D. 69–79) became emperor in the fall of A.D. 69 and again brought peace and stability to the Roman empire. He managed the finances well, ruled justly, reorganized the military, and brought a sense of order to the old republic. He repaired much of the infrastructure of Rome and other cities of the empire. Vespasian began the Flavian dynasty of emperors, and his sons Titus and Domitian succeeded him.

Titus (A.D. 41–81) was the general of the Roman army in Palestine when his forces captured the Temple in Jerusalem, killing many Jews (A.D. 70). He returned to Rome with Jewish captives and other spoils of war, depicted in the Arch of Titus erected in Rome to celebrate his conquest. His reign as emperor from A.D. 79 to 81 was marked by his exemplary response to the catastrophic eruption of Mount Vesuvius and another fire in Rome (A.D. 80). When he died unexpectedly of a fever in A.D. 81, Rome mourned a competent leader.

Titus's brother Domitian (A.D. 51–96) waited bitterly for Titus to relinquish the empire so that he could gain power (see DOMITIAN). Domitian reverted to the less benevolent and more autocratic style of earlier emperors. In spite of being a capable administrator, he proclaimed himself divine ("Lord and God"), revived the imperial cult, increased religious persecution, murdered many who opposed him, collected additional taxes, and developed a deserving reputation as a cruel and brutal leader. Most likely he was emperor when the book of Revelation was written, and many equate him with the beast of Revelation 13.

Domitian ruled oppressively from A.D. 81 to 96, when he was murdered. His death ended the Flavian dynasty of emperors and began the era of the three "good emperors": Nerva (A.D. 96–98), Trajan (A.D. 98–117), and Hadrian (A.D. 117–138). The dates for the reigns of the Roman emperors during the New Testament era are presented below. (See ALREADY–NOT YET; LAST DAYS; ROME/ROMAN EMPIRE.)

Julio-Claudian Dynasty	Julius Caesar	100 B.C.–44 B.C.
	Augustus	27 B.C.–A.D. 14
	Tiberius	A.D. 14–37
	Gaius (Caligula)	A.D. 37–41
	Claudius	A.D. 41–54
	Nero	A.D. 54–68
No dynasty	Galba	June A.D. 68–Jan. 69
	Otho	A.D. 69
	Vitellius	A.D. 69
Flavian Dynasty	Vespasian	A.D. 69–79
	Titus	A.D. 79–81
	Domitian	A.D. 81–96
	Nerva	A.D. 96–98
	Trajan	A.D. 98–117
	Hadrian	A.D. 117–138

Ephesus

Ephesus was the largest city in Asia Minor, a center of commerce, religion, and government. Believers at Ephesus were thus surrounded by religious and civic powers and their respective images. The city was the center for the worship of Artemis, the mother goddess, with a massive temple complex, thousands of priests and priestesses, and a thriving business related to goddess worship (see Acts 19:23–40). Emperor worship was also prominent in Ephesus, featuring a new temple to Domitian (likely the emperor when Revelation was written), which contained a colossal statue of the emperor standing twenty-five feet tall (see DOMITIAN).

The church at Ephesus is one of the seven churches of Revelation 2–3. In spite of its difficult environment, Jesus commends it for its hard work, perseverance, and doctrinal discernment. Yet, although they have tested the so-called apostles and found them false (2:2) and they "hate the practices of the Nicolaitans" (2:6), he faults the Ephesian Christians for forsaking their first love (likely meaning both a love for God and a love for each other).

Jesus warns the church in Ephesus to repent and return to their original commitments (Rev. 2:5), or else he will remove their lampstand. Those who overcome are promised the right "to eat from the tree of life, which is in the paradise of God" (2:7), an image that stands in contrast to the tree-shrine featured in the holy place of Artemis. Jesus' prophetic message to the church at Ephesus (and to the contemporary church) integrates truth and love. An emphasis on truth is essential in resisting syncretism and relativism, whereas the centrality of love stands at the heart of the Christian faith. As Craig Keener puts it, "a church where love ceases can no longer function properly as a local expression of Christ's many-membered body"[39] (see SEVEN CHURCHES OF REVELATION).

Epiphany

Epiphany (Gk. *epiphaneia*) in ancient Greek mythology meant "appearing" or "appearance," usually with reference to the gods, pertaining to their births, their miracles, their accession to Mount Olympus to be with the Greek pantheon, or to their return to earth. In Christian tradition, this term is usually used in connection with Christmas, in celebration of Jesus Christ's birth.

Ironically, however, *epiphaneia* as used in the New Testament refers to Christ's second coming (used only by Paul; see 2 Thess. 2:8; 2 Tim. 1:10;

4:1, 8; Titus 2:13). Thus, 2 Thessalonians 2:8 predicts Christ's epiphany will result in the destruction of the lawless one (probably the Antichrist). Titus 2:13 asserts that Christ's return will be accompanied by brilliant glory, while 2 Timothy 4:1, 8 predict that Christ's return will bring judgment on the living and the dead.

The sole exception is 2 Timothy 1:10, where *epiphaneia* describes the first coming of Christ, whose death and resurrection have made more clear the reality of the immortality of the Christian. Analyzing the preceding usages of this term permits one to say that it reflects the already–not yet understanding of the kingdom—at Christ's first coming the age to come or the kingdom of God was partially manifested, but its full appearance awaits the second coming of Christ (see ALREADY–NOT YET; SECOND COMING).

Eschatology

Eschatology (from the Greek word *eschaton*, "last") refers to the study of last things, but it extends also to a broader biblical perspective on God's purpose and direction for history. In contrast to a cyclical view of history, Scripture reveals that God is moving history toward a future goal. As a result, eschatology deals not only with the end of history, but also with the outworking of God's good and sovereign purposes for his creation. The biblical hope rests on God's covenant faithfulness to destroy evil, rescue his people, and restore his creation.

Biblical eschatology begins with God's original purposes for his creation. Humans were made in God's image to live in community with him and exercise stewardship over creation. God's opponent, Satan, deceived humans, who then suffered the disruptive and deadly consequences of sin. Humans continued to rebel against God and his plans as evil was unleashed on creation. Eventually God called Abraham to become the father of a people through whom he would restore creation.

In spite of God's deliverance of his people from slavery in Egypt, the conquest of the Promised Land, the golden age of King David's reign, and the building of the Temple in Jerusalem, Israel's story ends in disaster. The prophets had warned God's people that judgment would come unless they repented. Israel's continued disobedience resulted in the destruction of Jerusalem and exile from the land.

The prophets, however, also sounded a note of hope that God would one day restore his people under terms of a New Covenant (Jer. 31:33; Ezek. 36:26–28; 37:13–14; Joel 2:28–29). One day a Davidic king would arise in whom the promises made to David would be fulfilled (Isa. 9:6–7; 11:1–10;

32:1–8; Jer. 23:5–6; 33:14–22; Amos 9:11–12; Mic. 5:2–4). Daniel speaks of "one like a son of man" who would establish a universal reign at the end of time.

The promises of the Old Testament begin to be fulfilled in the New Testament. Jesus began his ministry by announcing the arrival of the kingdom of God (Mark 1:14–15). By healing the sick, casting out demons, teaching and feeding multitudes, forgiving sins, and raising the dead, Jesus inaugurated the kingdom. God's purposes for history involved a new kingdom breaking into the old world of Satan, sin, and death. The last days had arrived with Christ's coming. The restoration of Israel had begun.

At the heart of this restoration stands the cross and resurrection of Jesus. On the cross God's judgment is executed against his enemies and the New Covenant is constituted in Jesus' shed blood. With the resurrection, the curse of sin and death is reversed. Christ has secured a future for God's people, since his resurrection guarantees their future resurrection. The promises of God to destroy evil, rescue his people, and restore his creation find their fulfillment in Christ.

In the twentieth century there have been three basic forms of eschatology: thoroughgoing or consistent, realized, and inaugurated.

- *Thoroughgoing eschatology* (advocated by Albert Schweitzer; see CONSISTENT ESCHATOLOGY) is the view that Jesus and his followers proclaimed the imminent end of history. Since the end did not come when they expected, Jesus submitted to death as a way of forcing the full arrival of the kingdom.
- *Realized eschatology* (Rudolf Otto and C. H. Dodd; see REALIZED ESCHATOLOGY) takes the position that the first coming of Christ represents the full presence of the kingdom of God.
- *Inaugurated eschatology* (Oscar Cullmann and George E. Ladd; see INAUGURATED ESCHATOLOGY) views the first coming of Christ as the beginning of the kingdom that will be consummated at his second coming. As a result, believers live between the overlap of the "already" and the "not yet." The last view most adequately represents the evangelical understanding of the biblical material.

Although the new age of God's rule in Christ has begun, the old age has not yet come to an end. Biblical eschatology expects a future consummation of the kingdom. Christians await a final day when God's purposes will be fully realized. Consequently, there is a tension between what is "already" experienced because Christ has come and the kingdom has arrived, and what is "not yet" experienced because Christ has not yet returned in all his glory to finalize God's purposes. The consummation of the kingdom includes the return of Christ, the resurrection of the dead, the last judgment, and the new heaven and new earth. As Christians anticipate the consummation of the kingdom, they seek to live by the Spirit, who empowers their mission and guarantees their future.

Jesus came the first time in weakness and humility to bring salvation. He will come a second time in power and glory to defeat evil, vindicate God's people, and establish God's perfect rule (e.g., Rom. 8:38–39; Phil. 2:10–11; 1 Thess. 4:16). At Christ's return believers will be resurrected and transformed (1 Cor. 15:35–57; 1 Thess. 4:13–18). At the last judgment God will pronounce a verdict already reached, based on a person's response to Christ. Those in Christ will experience salvation (John 5:24; Rom. 8:1–3). Those who refuse to embrace God's purposes in Christ will be eternally excluded from his presence and suffer the second death (also referred to as "hell"). The ultimate destination of God's people is a new heaven and new earth, where God will live with them in intimate fellowship (Rev. 21–22). God's original plan for human beings to experience divine community will be fully realized.

Although there is much in the area of biblical eschatology that is open to debate (e.g., the rapture, the millennium), this much is certain: Christ has died, Christ is risen, Christ will come again, and Christ will fulfill God's good purposes for his creation. Between the "already" and the "not yet," the Holy Spirit provides believers a foretaste of God's ultimate purposes (Rom. 8:23; 2 Cor. 1:22; 5:5; Eph. 1:13–14). Through the presence of the Spirit the future touches the present, and believers are empowered to experience the hope already secured in Christ. (See ALREADY – NOT YET; LAST DAYS.)

Eschaton

The Greek word *eschaton* means "last" and often refers to the climax or end of history, which includes the second coming of Christ, the millennium, the last judgment, and the eternal state in the new heaven and new earth. The Old Testament prophets spoke of the last days when God would destroy his enemies (Jer. 23:20; 30:24) and bring salvation to his people (Isa. 48:20; 49:6; Hos. 3:5). The New Testament writers clearly saw the last days as having arrived in Jesus (Heb. 1:1–2; 1 Peter 1:20). The outpouring of the Spirit at Pentecost has only confirmed the dawning of the final days (Acts 2:17; cf. Joel 2:28–32). The final consummation of

God's saving activity awaits Christ's second coming and all that will follow (see ESCHATOLOGY; LAST DAYS).

Euphrates River

The word "Mesopotamia" means "between the rivers." The Tigris River forms the northern boundary and the Euphrates River forms the southern boundary. The Euphrates, however, is much longer than the Tigris. Approximately 1,750 miles (2,800 km) in length, it starts in northeastern modern Turkey, flows south into modern Syria, and then flows east across modern Iraq to meet up with the Tigris and empty into the Persian/Arabian Gulf.

In the Bible the Euphrates is often referred to as "the River," "the great River," or "the River Euphrates." In Bible prophecy the Euphrates River is used in several different contexts. For example, in God's covenant with Abraham, God promises to give Abraham's descendants a land that extends from the River of Egypt to the Euphrates River (see ABRAHAMIC COVENANT). Thus, the Euphrates formed the northern boundary of the description of the Promised Land.

This "river-to-river" description is repeated several times in Scripture (Deut. 1:7; 11:24; Josh. 1:4). Indeed, for a brief time during the reign of Solomon, Israelite control and influence was extended north as far as the Euphrates River. Because Israel soon lost control of this area and even lost the Promised Land itself, the river-to-river description is also used metaphorically, even ironically, as the region from which God will regather his people (Isa. 27:12; Mic. 7:12).

Also, because the city of Babylon was located on the banks of the Euphrates, Jeremiah orders that a stone be tied to the scroll of judgment against Babylon and cast into the Euphrates to symbolize that Babylon will sink and never rise again (Jer. 51:60–64). Included in several Old Testament prophecies regarding judgment on Babylon and restoration of Israel is an image of God drying up the Euphrates (sometimes called the "sea of Babylon") to allow enemies to cross over easily or to allow the regathering of his people (Isa. 11:15; Jer. 50:38; 51:36). This use, of course, is similar to the parting and crossing of the Red Sea in Exodus and demonstrates that God will act as powerfully in the future as he has in the past.

In a literal sense, this prophecy was perhaps fulfilled by Cyrus the Persian in 539/538 B.C. The Euphrates River was a critical component in the defenses of Babylon, but according to the ancient Greek historian Herodotus, Cyrus diverted the Euphrates River and entered into Babylon on the dry riverbed, capturing the city without a fight. Cyrus was the king who then decreed that the Jewish exiles could return home to Israel, in fulfillment of several prophecies in Isaiah (see CYRUS). It is possible that Isaiah 44:27–28 refers to these events, although there is no scholarly consensus on these verses.

Revelation 16:12 appears to draw from the imagery and prophecy of Isaiah. John seems to use Isaiah's imagery in pronouncing a similar judgment on future Babylon, which for John probably represents the world system (see BABYLON/BABYLONIANS), although some take Babylon as referring to the literal resurrected city. Revelation 16:12 states that "the sixth angel poured out his bowl on the great river Euphrates, and its water was dried up to prepare the way for the kings from the East" (see also BOWL JUDGMENTS).

European Union

The European Union (often in past popular literature referred to as the European Common Market) is a group of European nations that have committed to work together for the peace and prosperity of their member nations. Started in the 1950s, it initially had six members: Belgium, West Germany, France, Italy, the Netherlands, and Luxembourg. Current membership now stands at twenty-five nations. It focuses primarily at facilitating economic cooperation between member nations. Over the past forty years or so, many writers of books on biblical prophecy have viewed the rise of the European Union as a movement toward the fulfillment of the prophecy in Daniel 7:7. For a discussion of this view see TEN-HORNED BEAST.

Exile

In theological and prophetic terms, exile "is the experience of pain and suffering that results from the knowledge that there is a home where one belongs, yet for the present one is unable to return there. This existential sense of deep loss may be compounded by a sense of guilt or remorse stemming from the knowledge that the cause of exile is sin."[40] Another feature of exile is that it usually involves being away from God's presence. Moreover, part of being exiled frequently means being scattered and carries connotations of oppression and servitude.

One of the central unifying themes of the Bible that ties the Scriptures together as a coherent story is the pattern of sin–exile–restoration.

People sin against God and are thus driven away into exile as a punishment for sin. But God, in his love and mercy, restores to his presence and fellowship those who believe.

Exile in the Old Testament

This pattern (sin–exile–restoration) begins in Genesis, and the first "exile" occurs when Adam and Eve are driven out of the Garden of Eden because of their disobedience. This sets the pattern for an exile away from a physical home (driven out of the physical garden) and a spiritual exile away from the presence of God (Adam and Eve no longer walk with God in the garden).

Exile is included as one of the curses that God presents to Israel in Deuteronomy 28. God gives Deuteronomy to Israel right before they enter the Promised Land, which presents the rules and standards that Israel must live by if they are to dwell in the land with God among them, blessing them. Deuteronomy 28:1–14 first presents the blessings that Israel will receive if they keep God's laws. However, 28:15–68 presents the terrible curses and punishment that Israel will receive if they fail to keep the law and turn away from God. One of the central climaxing curses within this warning is that of exile (28:64–68).

In Old Testament history, Israel does not keep God's laws and they do turn away to worship other gods. Thus, God sends them prophets to call them to repentance and to get them to return to obeying God's law. A major component in the message of the Old Testament prophets is a strong warning about the coming judgment. If Israel and Judah do not return to God, the prophets warn, they will be overrun and destroyed—first by the Assyrians, who destroy Israel, the northern kingdom, in 722 B.C., and then by the Babylonians, who overrun the southern kingdom, Judah, first in 598 B.C. and then again with terrible destruction in 587/586 B.C. Part of these terrible invasions, the prophets declare soberly, will be the exile of the people away from their land (Isa. 5:13; Jer. 13:19; 20:6; Ezek. 12:3–11; Amos 7:17).

However, the prophets also proclaim that the terrible exile and scattering will be followed by a glorious regathering of God's scattered people. A central component of the prophetic message is that in the coming new program that the Messiah will bring, there will be an end to the exile (and a reversal of all of the other curses as well). God will regather his people back in the Promised Land and bless them tremendously (Isa. 43:5–7; 49:8–12; Jer. 30:3; 31:8–9, 23–25; 32:37–41; 33:7–9; Ezek. 11:17; 36:24; 37:21).

Yet the prophets broaden the concept of regathering and exile reversal for they proclaim that the nations (i.e., non-Jewish peoples) will be included in this messianic regathering. In a sense the nations themselves were scattered and "exiled" away from God in Genesis 10, as a result of the Tower of Babel rebellion in Genesis 11. However, the Old Testament prophets declare that as part of the great and glorious future restoration, God will gather the Gentile nations to worship him alongside of regathered Israel (Isa. 2:2–4; 11:10–12; 49:6; 66:18–24).

As described by Ezra and Nehemiah, a small group of Jews did return from the exile in Babylon back to the land of Israel. Although this perhaps constituted a partial fulfillment of the restoration that the prophets predicted, it fell short of fulfilling these prophecies completely. In addition, the presence of God, a central and critical aspect of the restoration, did not return to Israel during the time of Ezra and Nehemiah. Thus, even though some Jews were physically back in the land God promised, in a theological sense they were still in exile from God.

Exile in the New Testament

The New Testament clarifies that the Old Testament prophecies regarding the end of the exile and the glorious restoration find complete and final fulfillment in Jesus Christ. Through Christ the true people of God—both Jewish believers and Gentile believers—experience the presence of God through the indwelling Spirit and are brought together in unity. Interpreters debate whether this spiritual regathering involves the land of Israel. Yet although Gentile believers are viewed as the true "seed of Abraham" Paul still appears to envision a time when Israel herself will turn to Christ and be restored (Rom. 11).

Still, the New Testament does not see the restoration and the end of exile as being totally complete. Believers in Christ live in the "already–not yet" time of the kingdom (see ALREADY–NOT YET; KINGDOM OF GOD). Some New Testament writers imply that, in the meantime, believers are in an exile of sorts, foreigners in a foreign land, looking forward to the actual consummation of history when they will return home to be with Christ (Heb. 11:1, 13 ; 1 Peter 1:1; 2:11).

The final, consummate, and glorious restoration that fulfills completely the Old Testament prophecies regarding the end of the exile is described in Revelation. In Revelation 7:9 John describes a scene of "a great multitude that no one could count, from every nation, tribe, people and language, standing before the throne and in front of the Lamb." Likewise, chapter 22 portrays the climax of history in terms that connect back to the expulsion from the Garden of Eden in Genesis. In Revelation 22 humanity is back in the garden in the very presence of God. Indeed, 22:3 declares that "no longer will there be any curse." The exile begun in Genesis 3 will end.

Ezekiel, Book of

The book of Ezekiel is one of the four Major Prophets (Isaiah, Jeremiah, Ezekiel, Daniel), a designation based on the length of the book (see MAJOR PROPHETS). It is a large book (48 chapters) and thus makes a major contribution to biblical prophecy.

The prophet Ezekiel is also a priest, born into a priestly family. He is a contemporary of Jeremiah, but while Jeremiah preaches in Jerusalem, Ezekiel preaches in Babylonia. In 598 B.C. the Babylonians invade Judah, and Jerusalem surrenders. The Babylonians collect tribute and take the royal court, the nobles, the artisans, the military officers, and the fighting men with them back to Babylonia. A total of ten thousand Jews are in this first exile, one of which is Ezekiel.

Back in Jerusalem the Babylonians appoint a puppet king, Zedekiah, to the throne. Zedekiah, however, rebels against the Babylonians. With a vengeance the Babylonians return to Jerusalem in 587/586 B.C., and this time, as Jeremiah and Ezekiel predict, they completely destroy the city and carry off practically the entire nation into exile. Ezekiel prophesies primarily during the time period between the first exile (598 B.C.) and the second, final, and destructive exile (587/586 B.C.), although his prophecies continue even after the fall of Jerusalem.

Ezekiel is a priest, and his concern with priestly issues is apparent throughout the book. Likewise, although Jeremiah and most of the other prophets draw heavily from Deuteronomy in their criticism of Israel/Judah, Ezekiel draws from Leviticus (i.e., the book most concerned with priestly things). But his basic message is similar to that of the other prophets. He accuses the Israelites (i.e., Judahites) of breaking the Mosaic Covenant and turning to idols. Because of this, Ezekiel and the prophets proclaim, and because the people refuse to repent, judgment is coming. The nations will also be judged because of their rebellion against God. However, Ezekiel and the prophets proclaim that after the judgment there will be a future time of spectacular restoration and blessing, newer and even better than before.

Several specific chapters in Ezekiel play particularly significant roles in biblical prophecy. In Ezekiel 1, for example, God appears to the prophet

Ezekiel, who is living in Babylonia. God is seated on his glorious throne, which rests on a wagonlike vehicle. This vehicle has four intersecting wheels that can move in any direction. It is also supported by four living creatures who have four wings, allowing them to move in any direction. In 10:1–22 the prophet sees these creatures again, where they are identified as cherubim. The point of this revelation is that God is mobile and is not restricted to the Temple in Jerusalem. Likewise this appearance of God stresses his sovereignty and his omniscience (he sees all and knows all). John's vision of the throne of God in Revelation 4 has several similarities (see FOUR LIVING CREATURES; CHERUBIM).

Another important series of events occurs in Ezekiel 8–10. In Ezekiel 8 God takes the prophet back to Jerusalem in a vision and shows him four startling examples of terrible, flagrant idolatry taking place right before God's presence in the Temple of Jerusalem. After years of prophetic warning, threatening, and ignored calls for repentance, these flagrant acts of idolatry and rejection finally lead God to depart from the Temple. Thus, Ezekiel 10 describes the departure of God's presence from the Temple (see PRESENCE OF GOD).

This is a significant event. Many scholars believe that this departure of God's presence signals the end of the Mosaic Covenant. Remember that at the core of the covenant relationship was the formula statement, "I will be with you." At any rate, it is important to note that God's presence is never described as returning to the Temple in Jerusalem—until Jesus walks in through its gates. Likewise the departure of God's presence underscores the significance of the culmination of prophecy foreshadowed in Ezekiel 40–48 and ultimately fulfilled in Revelation 21–22.

Ezekiel 34 is another particularly significant chapter, one that presents God as the ultimate shepherd caring for his people. Even though God departed from the Temple in Ezekiel 10, thus removing his presence from Israel, in Ezekiel 34 he promises that in the future he will return to shepherd his flock with justice and compassion and will once again dwell in their midst. God declares, "I myself will search for my sheep and look after them. As a shepherd looks after his scattered flock when he is with them, so I will look after my sheep" (34:11–12). Yet God also states that he will place over them one shepherd from the line of David, a clear messianic prophecy pointing to Jesus Christ (34:23–24). When Jesus declares, "I am the good shepherd" (John 10:11–14), he is identifying with the prophecy in Ezekiel 34 (see SHEPHERDS).

It is within the context of the compassionate yet powerful care of the shepherd that God promises a Covenant of Peace (Ezek. 34:25–31) (see COVENANT OF PEACE). Just as Jeremiah uses the terminology "new covenant" to refer to the coming messianic age, so Ezekiel appears to use the phrase "covenant of peace" to describe what the great shepherd will bring to his people in the messianic age.

Equally significant is God's promise of the Spirit in Ezekiel 36:26–27: "I will give you a new heart and put a new spirit in you; I will remove from you your heart of stone and give you a heart of flesh. And I will put my Spirit in you and move you to follow my decrees and be careful to keep my laws." Ezekiel and Joel are the only two prophets to foretell the coming of the Spirit to indwell God's people, an event fulfilled on the Day of Pentecost and throughout Acts.

Ezekiel 37 presents the familiar story of the valley of dry bones. The point of this episode is that no matter how hopeless the situation is (the people/skeletons in the valley are really, really dead), God can restore life and wholeness. No matter how destroyed and scattered Israel is, God demonstrates that he can restore her. Within this chapter focusing on miraculous restoration, Ezekiel restates the promise of a Covenant of Peace (37:26–27).

Ezekiel 38–39 plays an important role in the end-time events as understood by many popular prophecy writers. They argue that these chapters describe an imminent (from today's point of view) invasion of Israel that will be carried out by modern Russia and her Muslim allies. Although these chapters have several interpretive difficulties, most Old Testament scholars maintain that this passage has nothing to do with modern Russia (or Islam). Most tend to lean toward a view that understands this chapter as a symbolic, figurative picture of hostility by Israel's worldwide enemies (i.e., attacks by seven nations from the four corners of the earth symbolize a worldwide opposition; see GOG AND MAGOG; ISLAM; MESHECH AND TUBAL; ROSH; TURKEY).

In Ezekiel 40–48 Ezekiel brings his book to a climactic closing by describing in detail the new Temple of the future. Because of sin and covenant disobedience, the relationship between God and his people was destroyed, causing God's presence to depart from the Temple in Jerusalem (Ezek. 8–10), which was subsequently totally destroyed. Yet, in contrast, Ezekiel 40–48 describes a new and spectacular Temple, along with the personnel, supplies, storerooms, and the like to operate it. Flowing out of the Temple is a river that gives life to everything along its banks (47:1–12). Ezekiel ends on the most important note—the presence of God: "And the name of the city from that time on will be: THE LORD IS THERE."

As with many other portions of prophetic literature that use language referring to Israel's restoration, interpreters take differing views on Ezekiel 40–48 (see AMILLENNIALISM; PREMILLENNIALISM, HISTORIC; RESTORATION OF ISRAEL).

- Some argue that Ezekiel 40–48 describes a new literal Temple that will be built in Jerusalem and used during a literal one-thousand-year (millennial) reign of Christ.
- Others suggest that while the passage may focus on that future millennial Temple, it also has allusions and connections to the final new city of Jerusalem in Revelation 21–22. They underscore the prophets' tendency to merge future pictures from differing time periods together into one vision (see NEAR VIEW–FAR VIEW).
- Still others maintain that Ezekiel 40–48 is almost totally symbolic and is thus fulfilled primarily in Christ (the new Temple) and yet perhaps also pointing to the heavenly city in Revelation 21–22.

(See also GARDEN; NEW HEAVEN AND NEW EARTH; NEW JERUSALEM; NEW TEMPLE.)

False Prophecy

False prophets and their false prophecies are fairly common throughout both the Old and New Testament.

False Prophecy in the Old Testament

In Deuteronomy 18, as the Israelites are preparing to enter the land of Canaan, God warns them of the false prophetic practices they will encounter (Deut. 18:9–22). He tells his people that the pagan inhabitants of the land practice sorcery and divination, but the Israelites are strictly forbidden to do so (18:9–14) (see DIVINATION). On the contrary, God himself will raise a prophet from Israel and they must listen to him (18:15–16). God then declares that any prophet who only pretends to speak in God's name or any prophet who speaks in the name of other gods must be put to death (18:20). Finally, God explains the way to distinguish between the true prophet and the false prophet—by whether the prophecy spoken comes true (18:21–22).

However, after Israel settles in the Promised Land and God establishes the monarchy, the kings of Israel and Judah frequently sponsor and listen to the prophets of other gods. At the time of Elijah, for example, the king and queen sponsor 450 prophets of Baal and 400 prophets of Asherah (1 Kings 18:19). After Elijah defeats these false prophets on Mount Carmel, he has the Israelites put them to death.

False prophets who prophesied by other gods were easily recognizable by Israel's true prophets. However, there were also many false prophets who prophesied in the name of the LORD, the God of Israel. These prophets were much more difficult to contend with. In fact, throughout the book of Jeremiah, God's true prophet (Jeremiah) is continually plagued by false prophets who undermine and contradict his message, thus leading the people astray (Jer. 5:13, 31; 6:13; 8:10–11; 14:14–16; 23:9–40; 27:9).

Frequently God pronounces judgment on these false prophets. In Jeremiah 28, the false prophet Hananiah contradicts Jeremiah and tells all the people that Jeremiah is mistaken. Hananiah breaks the yoke that Jeremiah used to represent Babylonian domination (i.e., judgment from God) and declares that all of the exiles currently in Babylon will return in two years. This counter-prophecy confuses Jeremiah (28:5–11), but God soon clarifies the situation. Jeremiah then prophesies the death of Hananiah, who dies within two months in fulfillment of Jeremiah's prediction. Ezekiel, too, presents an extensive condemnation on the false prophets of his day (Ezek. 13).

False Prophecy in the New Testament

False prophets and false prophecy are present in the New Testament as well. Jesus warns against false prophets in Matthew 7:15–23, pointing out that they can be recognized by their fruit. Likewise 1 John 4:1–3 cautions believers about false prophets, noting that "spirits" that deny the reality of the incarnation are false and not from God. In Acts 13:4–12 a false prophet named Bar-Jesus opposes Paul and Barnabas. Paul calls the false prophet a "child of the devil" and someone who is "full of all kinds of deceit and trickery" (13:10). God then strikes the false prophet with blindness.

False prophets in the New Testament are often associated with the end times. Mark 13:22, for example, states that "false Christs and false prophets will appear and perform signs and miracles to deceive the elect." The theme of deceit connects the work of false prophets with the work of Satan, who is known for his deceiving character and work (cf. Gen. 3). That is why Paul can call the false prophet in Acts 13 a "child of the devil."

In Revelation 19:20 "the false prophet" who serves the evil beast is destroyed. This false prophet appears to be the same character as the beast described in 13:12–17, who is able to deceive many people because of his miraculous works (see BEASTS OF REVELATION; FALSE PROPHET). But both the beast and his false prophet are thrown into the lake of fire (19:20), signifying God's ultimate triumph over Satan and those who serve him through deceitful false prophecies.

False Prophet

The second beast of Revelation 13 appears as the "false prophet" elsewhere in Revelation (16:13; 19:20; 20:10), a description that implies some religious role. This beast has two horns like a lamb, but he speaks like a dragon (13:11). His dragonlike speech suggests a strong alliance with the devil and the beast from the sea. Consequently, many interpreters understand the second beast to represent the religious powers in support of the Roman state, specifically, the priesthood of the imperial cult. Such a beast will pressure believers not only to worship the emperor as a god (e.g., Domitian), but also to sacrifice to the pagan gods (e.g., to Artemis). By the end of the first century, all seven cities mentioned in Revelation 2–3 had temples dedicated to Caesar as a god. The symbolism of the second beast can also be extended to represent pagan religious power (perhaps personified in an individual) allied with the Antichrist at the end of the age.

Imitating Satan, the master deceiver (Rev. 12:9; 20:10), this false prophet carries on a ministry of deception by promoting the worship of the first beast (13:14). John uses the term *deceive* to describe false teachers who lead people to worship other gods (2:20; 12:9; 18:23; 19:20; 20:3, 8, 10). Religious miracles (19:20) are manufactured for political and economic reasons. His "gospel" is the Antichrist's "resurrection" or the healing of the fatal wound (13:12, 14). The false prophet's signs of persuasion include calling fire down from heaven (13:13), perhaps standing in direct contrast to the fire coming out of the mouths of the two godly witnesses of Revelation 11. The land beast also sets up an image in honor of the first beast and empowers the image with breath so that it can speak (13:14–15).

Although these phenomena may include the use of magic, demonic activity may also be involved. In Revelation 16:13 the false prophet is one source of evil spirits who perform miracles (16:14), indicating the demonic source of his miraculous signs. Scripture elsewhere supports the ability of Satan-inspired prophets to perform miraculous signs (19:20; cf. Matt. 7:22; 24:24; Mark 13:22; 2 Thess. 2:9).

The beast from the earth causes all who refuse to worship the image of the first beast to be killed (Rev. 13:15). He also forces everyone to receive the mark of the beast so that they cannot buy or sell without the mark (13:16–17). The worship of the first beast, the "image," and the "mark" are interconnected (14:9, 11; 15:2; 16:2; 19:20; 20:4). Also, the close tie between economics, religion, and politics suggests the use of trade guilds in promoting false worship. Trade guilds were social and economic organizations where membership entailed participation in worship rituals, a practice that put enormous pressure on Christians to compromise their faith.

The false prophet of Revelation 13 partially fulfills what Christ prophesied about false prophets appearing with the intent to deceive many through signs and wonders (see Matt. 7:15; 24:11, 24; Mark 13:22; cf. 2 Thess. 2:9; 1 John 4:1). This land beast is the complete antithesis to all true prophets of Christ. He personifies the power of idolatrous religion to deceive and persecute those who stay loyal to Christ. (See ANTICHRIST; BEASTS OF REVELATION; DOMITIAN; FALSE PROPHECY; IMPERIAL CULT; MARK OF THE BEAST.)

Fig Tree

The parable of the fig tree occurs in the Olivet Discourse (Matt. 24:32–35; Mark 13:28–31; Luke 21:29–33; see OLIVET DISCOURSE). The parable itself is straightforward: as soon as the fig tree's green buds form and begin to sprout leaves, one knows that summer is on its way. But the interpretation of this parable is debated. (1) A popular view is that the fig tree illustrates Israel. Accordingly, Israel's regathering to the land in 1948 began the last generation before the return of Christ, with the signs of the times culminating in that event (see SIGNS OF THE TIMES). But the fact that over a generation has come and gone without seeing the Parousia (second coming of Christ) has called this perspective into question.

(2) Another view is that the budding of the fig tree referred to Jesus' generation, such that his audience expected him to return during their lifetime.

(3) A related approach applies the budding of the fig tree and the signs of the times to the imminent fall of Jerusalem in A.D. 70 (see DESTRUCTION OF THE JERUSALEM TEMPLE [A.D. 70]). The problem with the last two views, however, is that the first generation did not seem to witness the full unfolding of the events predicted in the Olivet Discourse.

(4) A fourth perspective seems more accurate, namely, that the budding of the fig tree and the unfolding of the signs of the times refer to the last generation before the Parousia (second coming of Christ), whenever that may occur.

Figures of Speech

Much of Old Testament prophecy is written in Hebrew poetry and should be interpreted with that in mind. A central feature of Hebrew poetry is the extensive use of *figures of speech*. These figures of speech are some of the main weapons in the literary arsenal of the prophets. Their use of figurative language is what makes the prophetic books so colorful and fascinating.

- Amos does not simply say "God is mad." Rather, he proclaims, "the lion has roared" (Amos 3:8).
- Isaiah does not analytically discuss the contrast between how terrible sin is and how wonderful forgiveness is; he uses figurative language: "Though your sins are like scarlet, they shall be as white as snow" (Isa. 1:18).
- Jeremiah is disgusted with Judah's unfaithful attitude toward God, and the prophet wants to convey some of the pain the LORD feels because Judah has left him for idols. Thus, throughout his book Jeremiah compares Judah to an unfaithful wife who has become a prostitute. "You have lived as a prostitute with many lovers," he proclaims (Jer. 3:1), referring figuratively to Judah's idolatry.

The Old Testament prophets do not write essays; they paint pictures. The colors with which they paint these pictures are figures of speech and wordplays. We are not strangers to this type of language. English is rich in figurative language. Indeed, we use figures of speech all the time. People who do not speak English as their first language can easily misinterpret our meaning since they often do not understand the meaning of such figures of speech. For example, international visitors to the United States might know the grammar and word meanings of English quite well, but still be confused when someone tells them that "it is raining cats and dogs outside."

We come to the Bible in a similar manner, from outside the literary world of the immediate audience. If we take the figures of speech literally, we will misunderstand the text as badly as international visitors misunderstand us. If we want to understand the authors of the Old Testament, it is critical to recognize figures of speech when they are used and to interpret them as figures of speech, not as literal realities.

Keep in mind that this does not deny the literal reality behind the figure of speech. The prophets are conveying real thoughts, events, and emotions to us—that is, *literal* truth—but they express this truth figuratively. Our job as readers is to grapple with the figures and to strive to grasp the reality and the emotion the poets are conveying by their figurative language.

Types of Figures of Speech

Some figures of speech can be subtle and complex. However, most are readily recognized and interpreted. In general, figures of speech in the

Old Testament prophets can be placed into two major categories: figures involving analogy and figures involving substitution. A few figures of speech, however, do not really fall into either category and we will discuss them as a separate, miscellaneous category.

Figures of speech involving analogy. Many figures of speech involve drawing analogies between two different items. However, such analogies themselves fall into several distinct sub-classifications. That is, there are numerous ways of making figurative analogies. The Old Testament employs a wide range of these analogies as figures of speech. The most common ones are *simile, metaphor, indirect analogy, hyperbole*, and *personification/anthropomorphism/ zoomorphism.*

Similes make comparisons by using the words *like* or *as* to explicitly state that one thing resembles another. This is a common figure of speech, both in English and in Old Testament prophecy. For example, Isaiah writes, "Though your sins are *like* scarlet, they shall be as white *as* snow" (Isa. 1:18, italics added).

Metaphors are also common. They make the analogy between items by direct statement without the use of *like* or *as*. For example, God tells Jeremiah, "Today I have made you a fortified city, an iron pillar and a bronze wall to stand against the whole land" (Jer. 1:18).

A more complicated figure of speech is *indirect analogy* (sometimes referred to as *hypocatastasis*). This literary device uses the analogous item without directly stating the comparison. It assumes that the reader can make the comparison without it being explicitly stated. Suppose, for example, that the writers wish to make an analogy between the Lord's wrath and a storm. A simile would say, "The wrath of the LORD is like a storm." A metaphor would express the analogy by saying, "the wrath of the LORD is a storm." Indirect analogy skips the identification of the analogy and states, "the storm of the LORD will burst out in wrath, a driving wind swirling down on the heads of the wicked" (Jer. 30:23).

Another tricky figure of speech is *hyperbole*. Leland Ryken defines hyperbole as a "conscious exaggeration for the sake of effect."[41] As an expression of strong feeling, hyperbole intentionally exaggerates. "It advertises its lack of literal truth." Indeed, as Ryken notes, it makes no pretense of being factual. A struggling student, for example could use hyperbole and say, "The professor gave us the *hardest* test in the world ... I studied *forever* ... it was the *most ridiculous* thing in the world ... *everybody* bombed on it." None of these statements would be literally true. To make an emotional point, the student overstates his case, poetically exaggerating the details.

This is allowed in figures of speech. It does not reflect on the honesty of the speaker. When the student says that he studied forever, the meaning is simply that he studied for a long time and that it seemed like forever. The Old Testament prophets likewise use hyperbole frequently. They will consciously exaggerate in order to express deep emotion. For example, Jeremiah states, "Let my eyes overflow with tears night and day without ceasing" (Jer. 14:17).

Personification, anthropomorphism, and *zoomorphism* are three similar figures of speech in that they attribute to one entity the characteristics of a totally different kind of entity. *Personification* involves attributing human features or human characteristics to nonhuman entities, such as in Isaiah 44:23: "Burst into song, you mountains, you forests and all your trees." *Anthropomorphism* is the representation of God with human features or human characteristics. In the Old Testament God is described as having hands, arms, feet, a nose, breath, a voice, and ears. He walks, sits, hears, looks down, thinks, talks, remembers, gets angry, shouts, lives in a palace, prepares tables, anoints heads, builds houses, and pitches tents. He has a rod, staff, scepter, banner, garment, tent, throne, footstool, vineyard, field, chariot, shield, and sword. He is called a father, husband, king, and shepherd. Nonhuman images for God are also used. When animal imagery is used, the figure is called *zoomorphism.*

Figures of speech involving substitution. Often the prophets use figures of speech that employ substituting the "effect" for the "cause" or vice versa (this figure of speech is also known as *metonymy*). For example, the prophet Jeremiah declares, "Let my eyes overflow with tears" (Jer. 14:17). His tears are the *effect.* What he is really talking about is the coming Babylonian invasion (the *cause*). Rather than say, "The Babylonians are coming and it will be awful," Jeremiah states the emotional *effect* the invasion will have on him: "Let my eyes overflow with tears." This figure can be used in reverse as well—the *cause* can be stated when the *effect* is intended—but this usage is not common.

Another substitution type figure of speech is representation (also know as *synecdoche*). Often the prophets substitute a representative part of an entity instead of the entity itself. We do this in English if we use the city of Washington, D.C., to represent the entire United States. For example, a newscaster could say, "If Washington and Tokyo cannot work out these trade differences, there may be difficult times ahead." Both Washington and Tokyo are used figuratively to represent their respective nations.

In similar fashion the Old Testament prophets use cities and/or individual tribes to represent entire nations. Thus Ephraim (the largest northern tribe) and Samaria (the capital city) can refer to the northern kingdom Israel while Judah (the main southern tribe) and Jerusalem (the capital city) can refer to the southern kingdom of Judah. Numerous other representative figures of speech occur. The words "bow," "sword," and "chariot" are used to represent weapons of war in general. Citing only one or two of them as figures brings into mind the entire category of weapons or military power. "Feet" and "bones," likewise, can represent the entire person.

Miscellaneous figures of speech. Since figures of speech are artistic and fluid, it is sometimes difficult to categorize all of them into nice, neat packages. Although most figures fall into the broad categories of analogy or substitution, a few fall outside of those categories. One of the most significant miscellaneous figures of speech is irony/sarcasm.

When using *irony*, the writer says the exact opposite of what he really means. For example, suppose a student stops his friend Fred in the hall to tell him that a garbage truck just backed into Fred's new candy-apple-colored Corvette. In despair Fred replies, "Oh, that's just *great!*" Obviously the situation is not *great*. Fred states the opposite of the real situation to underscore how bad the news really is.

Sometimes irony is also used in *sarcasm*, as when Fred tells the driver of the truck, "Mister, backing into my car was really smart! You are a great driver if ever I saw one." Old Testament prophecy likewise often combines irony with sarcasm. Note God's use of sarcastic irony in Amos 4:4, where God in essence tells Israel to "go ahead and sin." Likewise, catch the sarcasm in Isaiah 41:22–23 as God speaks with irony of the idols that Israel worships:

> Bring in your idols to tell us
> what is going to happen.
> Tell us what the former things were,
> so that we may consider them
> and know the final outcome.
> Or declare to us the things to come,
> tell us what the future holds,
> so we may know that you are gods.
> Do something, whether good or bad,
> so that we may be dismayed and filled with fear.

Fishermen

Jeremiah 16:16 and Amos 4:2 use the fishermen image as a picture of judgment on Judah and Israel. Amos specifically mentions the use of fishhooks, a graphic and terrible image of judgment. As fishermen pull fish from the water, so the coming invaders will "catch" the Israelites with hooks and pull them away.

In the Gospels, by contrast, Jesus frequently takes the judgment images of the Old Testament prophets and reverses them into promises of blessing, often changing figurative language into literal (figurative sickness in the prophets reversed into literal healing by Jesus, for example). Jesus reverses the fishermen image in similar fashion. The Old Testament prophets used fishermen figuratively to represent judgment, but Jesus calls real fishermen to be his disciples. Then in a figurative sense, but in reversal of the prophet's judgment image, Jesus tells his fishermen disciples that they will be catching people for salvation (Matt. 4:19; Mark 1:16–17), using nets instead of fishhooks, a much more pleasant imagery.

Foe from the North

Several Old Testament prophets mention an attack on Israel or Judah "from the north." This is a prominent theme in the early chapters of Jeremiah, where the prophet repeatedly warns Judah of a coming judgmental invasion by a foe to the north (Jer. 1:13–16; 4:5–8, 13–22, 27–31; 5:15–17; 6:1–8, 22–26; 8:14–17; cf. also 13:20; 25:9). In Jeremiah the foe to the north refers to the Babylonians, and the prophecies of Jeremiah regarding the foe to the north are fulfilled by the Babylonian invasions that take place in Jeremiah's lifetime (598/586 B.C.).

Other prophets also refer to enemy invasions from the north. However, keep in mind that Israel and Judah were bounded by the Mediterranean Sea on the west and by a desert on the other side of Ammon to the east. So the basic way for any enemy other than Egypt to attack ancient Israel or Judah, which lay at the bottom of the Fertile Crescent, was from the north, regardless of where the foe resided. In fact the Bible identifies the following ancient enemies of Israel as from the north, even though they were located in the east: Assyrians (Zeph. 2:13), Babylonians (Jer. 1:13–15; 6:22; Zech. 2:6–7), Persians (Isa. 41:25; Jer. 50:3).[42]

Former Prophets

The books of the Old Testament are arranged slightly differently in the Hebrew Bible than in English Bibles. The Hebrew Bible has three main divisions: Torah (i.e., the Pentateuch), Prophets, and Writings. The Prophets are further divided into two parts: the Former Prophets and the Latter Prophets. The Latter Prophets include all of what are generally called the literary prophets (Isaiah, Jeremiah, etc.). The Former Prophets include books that Christians generally call "the historical books," that is, Joshua, Judges, 1–2 Samuel, 1–2 Kings. In the Hebrew Bible, 1–2 Chronicles is included in the section called "Writings."

Four Beasts of Daniel

Although Daniel 2 and 7 record two separate dreams (Dan. 2, Nebuchadnezzar's dream; Dan. 7, Daniel's dream), they deal with the same scenario —the unfolding in history of four powerful kingdoms, beginning with Daniel's day. There are two basic approaches today toward identifying these four kingdoms. Many interpreters argue for the following:

Kingdom	Leader	Date
Babylonian	Nebuchadnezzar	ca. 570 B.C.
Medo-Persian	Cyrus	ca. 539 B.C.
Greek	Alexander the Great	ca. 330 B.C.
Revived Roman empire	Antichrist	In the end time

However, another widely accepted interpretation of the four kingdoms exists. While liberal theologians in general opt for this view, this perspective need not be limited to that tradition. This interpretation identifies the four kingdoms as follows:

Kingdom	Leader	Date
Babylonian	Nebuchadnezzar	ca. 570 B.C.
Media	Astyages	ca. 550 B.C.
Persian	Cyrus	ca. 539 B.C.
Greek	Alexander the Great	ca. 330 B.C.

According to this interpretation, the fourth kingdom is Greece, not a revived Roman empire. Moreover, this kingdom already occurred in history and therefore does not call for an exclusively futuristic interpretation. In what follows, we will summarize the evangelical expression of the second approach, briefly correlating the biblical descriptions of the four kingdoms with the historical data.

Concerning the identification of the first kingdom in Daniel 2 and 7 there is no debate. The head of the statue made of fine gold, the most valuable of metals (Dan. 2:32, 37–38), and the lion with the wings of an eagle, an ancient symbol for Babylon (Dan. 7:4), by consensus represent the Babylonian kingdom under King Nebuchadnezzar (see BABYLON/BABYLONIANS).

It is with the second kingdom that the problem of identification surfaces. A large number of conservative scholars interpret the chest and arms of silver on the human statue (Dan. 2:32) and the bear with three ribs in its mouth (Dan. 7:5) as the Medo-Persian empire led by Cyrus, who conquered Babylon in 539 B.C. (see CYRUS). This is understandable since that empire came to rule over three nations: Lydia, Babylon, and Egypt (the three ribs). However, other conservatives make a plausible case for identifying the second kingdom with the Median empire alone. That kingdom, under the leadership of the likes of Astyages (550 B.C.) and Cyaxares II, also defeated three nations—Urartu, Mannaea, and the Scythians.

For many, two pieces of evidence tip the scales in favor of the latter interpretation. (1) Identifying the three ribs in the bear's mouth with Urartu, Mannaea, and the Scythians corresponds with Jeremiah 51:27–29. That passage speaks of three nations joining the Medes against Babylon—Ararat, Minni, and Ashkenaz, which respectively represent Urartu, Mannaea, and the Scythians. These three groups were defeated by the Medes and were incorporated into its empire. (2) The other piece of evidence is the inferiority of the second empire when compared to the first (Babylonia, Dan. 2:39), which fits Media much more readily than Medo-Persia.

The only real problem with this view is that little is known about the Median empire. However, John Walton aptly responds to this difficulty:

> One of the difficulties here is that we know so little of the Median empire. Its territory was roughly similar to the size of the Neo-Babylonian empire. During the rule of Nebuchadnezzar's successors the Median monarch was Astyages (585–550 B.C.). There can be little question of Astyages' influence, for he married one of his daughters to Nebuchadnezzar, while the other was married to Cambyses I of Persia and became the mother of Cyrus. Even Nebuchadnezzar's fear of Median power is evidenced in the

fortifications he built along the northern frontier. Both Elam and Susa seem to have fallen prey to Astyages' expansion after the death of Nebuchadnezzar. All of this would give historical support to the view that Media may have been considered a world empire that succeeded Babylon after the death of Nebuchadnezzar, though the city of Babylon had not yet fallen.[43]

The third kingdom, the belly and thighs of bronze in the human statue (Dan. 2:32, 39) and the leopard with four wings and four heads (7:6), is equated by many evangelical interpreters with Alexander the Great (the leopard) and the four generals who divided his kingdom among themselves after his death (323 B.C.) Those four generals were Cassander (the west, i.e., Greece), Lysimachus (the north, i.e., Asia), Seleucus (the east, i.e., Babylonia and Syria), and Ptolemy (the south, i.e., Egypt).

This view is reasonable, but an alternate approach, and one that is just as viable, is that the third kingdom represents the Persian empire. On this reading, the leopard represents Persia, which, with the brilliant, swift-moving armies of Cyrus, defeated the ponderous, bearlike Median empire. The four wings and four heads could signify the four corners of the universe, corresponding to Persia's world domination (contrasted to Media's more limited influence). Or perhaps they symbolize the four Persian kings known to Scripture: Cyrus, Artaxerxes, Xerxes and Darius III Codomannus (who was defeated by Alexander the Great).

Furthermore, the marked superiority of the third kingdom over the second (Dan. 2:39; 7:6) better fits Persian supremacy over the inferior Median empire than Greece's relationship to Persia, since both of the latter were world powers. Moreover, the four successors to Alexander, both in history and in Daniel 8, represent diluted strength, whereas in Daniel 7 the four heads/wings seem to represent the strength itself.

The identification of the fourth kingdom in Daniel 2 and 7 as the Roman empire has a long history, going back to New Testament times. It is understood in this manner by several early nonbiblical writers: *2 Apocalypse of Baruch* 39:1–18 (A.D. 90); *4 Ezra* 12:10–12 (A.D. 80); Josephus (*Antiquities* 10.11.7); the Talmud (second to fifth centuries A.D.); Irenaeus; Hippolytus; and Origen. Many current popular writers follow this interpretation and argue that there will be a revived Roman empire in the end time. However, the identification of Daniel's fourth kingdom with Greece, as led by Alexander the Great (see ALEXANDER THE GREAT), also has a venerable history of interpretation, going back even *before* New Testament times to Herodotus (1.95.130; 300 B.C.) and the *Sibylline Oracles*, book 4 (140 B.C.).

Thus, there are two different options for interpreting the fourth kingdom in Daniel's visions (Dan. 2:40–43; 7:19–24). Many conservatives apply these passages to Rome, appealing to the following pieces of evidence: (1) The Roman empire fits the description of a being like a beast, unlike the three earlier empires, primarily because of its unsurpassed power (it was like iron — 2:40; cf. 7:19). According to this approach, this was the first stage of the Roman empire, occurring in approximately 167 B.C. (2) Accordingly, 7:20 catapults the reader forward in time to, in effect, the twenty-first century A.D., with its description of the ten horns and the one horn that emerges out of the ten with uncontested power. This is the second phase of the Roman empire, namely, the revival of the Roman empire. Some understand this revived Roman empire to be the present day European Union (or the United Nations), which will eventually be led by the Antichrist (see TEN-HORNED BEAST).

This viewpoint is extremely popular among contemporary Christians, but it has been questioned by some scholars. Two problems argue against equating the fourth kingdom with the revived Roman empire. (1) This interpretation means that without explanation, Daniel 7:20 suddenly jumps ahead in time from Daniel's day to the twenty-first century, even though there is no indication of this in the text.

(2) This interpretation departs from the interpretive principles long cherished by evangelicals since the Reformation by failing to root the biblical text in its historical-cultural environment. Those who favor Greece as the fourth empire argue that this interpretation fits the historical context of Daniel 2 and 7 much better. The following summary uses that background. Daniel 2:40; 7:7, 19 declare that the fourth kingdom will be like iron, crushing all its opponents, a fitting description of Alexander the Great's army, which was totally invincible in the face of its foes, whereas Rome was stopped by Parthia in its attempted expansion.

Daniel 7:23 tells us that the fourth kingdom will be unlike the previous three kingdoms. The Western civilization of Greece was very different from the three Oriental empires of Babylonia, Media, and Persia, whereas Rome was in many ways similar to Greece. Daniel 2:40–43 asserts that the fourth kingdom will be divided into two parts, iron and clay, which will not mix well together, a perfect analysis of the Seleucid kingdom (Syria, the strong part, iron) and the Ptolemaic (Egypt, the weaker part, the clay, which was eventually overrun by the Seleucids). The reference to the two substances not mixing together distinctly reminds one of the rupture between the two kingdoms, which occurred despite the intermarriage between them.

We read in Daniel 7:20, 24 that the fourth kingdom will divide into ten horns or kingdoms, which Walton convincingly identifies with the ten independent states (third century B.C.) that eventually replaced the four territories of the four generals who succeeded Alexander the great — Ptolemaic Egypt, Seleucia, Macedon, Pergamum, Pontus, Bithynia, Cappadocia, Armenia, Parthia, and Bactria. Two of these surface in the biblical narrative because of their relevance to Israel in the second century B.C. — Seleucia and Ptolemaic Egypt, as we have seen (2:40–43).

Finally, Daniel 7:8, 20–22, 24–25, with its description of the one horn gaining supremacy over three of the other horns (kings), as John Walton argues, is nicely explained by the defeat of Cappadocia, Armenia, and Parthia by Antiochus the Great (second century B.C.)., whose infamous son, Antiochus IV Epiphanes, continued his father's exploits and severely persecuted the Jews. Walton explains the father-son relationship with regard to Daniel's "little horn":

> While the subduing of the three horns then makes excellent sense in connection with Antiochus the Great, we are faced with the problem that he does not qualify as a convincing little horn with regard to the remainder of the description given in Daniel. That distinction still would seem to suit Antiochus Epiphanes better. A hypothesis that would take advantage of the strengths of each of these elements is one that would see the incorporation of Palestine into the Seleucid state under Antiochus the Great as the beginning of the kingdom of the little horn, which would then be continued and brought to culmination under Antiochus Epiphanes. It is true that Dan. 7:24 speaks of the little horn as a king rather than a kingdom, but we should notice that even in that context (7:17) the two are seen to be interchangeable.[44]

Therefore, although many understand the four kingdoms of Daniel 2 and 7 to be Babylonia, Medo-Persia, Greece, and Rome, there is also a strong case for interpreting the kingdoms as Babylonia, Media, Persia, and Greece.

Four Horsemen of the Apocalypse

The first four seal judgments (Rev. 6:1–8) are better known as the "four horsemen of the Apocalypse." The Lamb opens each seal and John hears one of the four living creatures saying "Come." He then sees a horse of a particular color with a rider who executes the judgment. The presence of the four living creatures indicates that the judgments come from the throne of God. In addition, the verb form "was given" is a "divine passive," meaning that God controls the process, even if he is granting an evil power permission to carry out his work (cf. Rev. 6:2, 4, 5, 8, 11; 7:2; 8:2, 3; 9:1, 3,

5; 11:1, 2; 12:14; 13:5, 7, 14, 15; 16:8). The four riders appear to be angels of judgment, though the text never makes that identification certain.

Overall, the judgments included here closely parallel the "birth pains" Jesus mentions in his end-time teaching—wars, nations rising against nations, earthquakes, famines, and pestilence (Matt. 24:6–8; Mark 13:5–8; Luke 21:8–11). The more specific background appears to be Zechariah 1:7–11 and 6:1–8, where riders on different colored horses (or chariots pulled by horses) are sent by God as instruments of judgment on the enemies of God's people. In 1:8 there are two red horses, a dappled gray horse, and a white horse, while the four horses of 6:1–3 are red, black, white, and dappled gray. In Revelation 6:1–8 the horses are white, red, black, and pale, and the colors seem to correspond to the type of judgment their riders inflict (e.g., red for bloodshed).

(1) The rider of the white horse has a bow and a crown and rides out to "conquer," an indication of military conquest or war. Many see a reference to the Parthians, the mounted archers from the East who defeated the Romans in battle as recently as A.D. 62 (cf. Rev. 9:14; 16:12). They were formidable warriors and their sacred color was white. Even if the Parthians are in the background, the general impact of the image reaffirms the human lust for war and conquest.

(2) The rider on the fiery red horse is given power to rob the earth of peace so that people slaughter each other (on the word "slay," see Rev. 5:6, 9, 12; 6:9; 13:8; 18:24). Each horse leads to the next as warfare results in bloodshed (vividly symbolized by the red horse). The "large sword" also portrays the judgment of violent death that results from human depravity. John's readers may have thought of Nero's slaughter of Christians or of Domitian's persecutions.

(3) The rider on the black horse is holding a pair of scales, indicating rationing because of the scarcity of food caused by the economic disaster connected with warfare. A conquering army often ravaged the land, resulting in famine. An unspecified heavenly voice sets a maximum price for grain. Wheat is more expensive than barley, which is eaten mostly by the poor. The severity of the famine is revealed in prices that are between five and fifteen times the going rate.[45] The voice also commands them not to damage "the oil and the wine"; this has been explained in a variety of ways (e.g., an indication of the social dimension of judgment, a sign of God's mercy in the midst of judgment, and an allusion to the edict of Domitian in A.D. 92 to destroy the vineyards).

(4) As devastating as the famine of the third seal is, the fourth seal intensifies the judgments even more. The fourth horseman rides a "pale"

horse. The color is actually yellowish-green or the color of death (i.e., the color of a corpse). The rider himself is "Death" with "Hades" following closely behind (Rev. 1:18; 20:13, 14). This evil alliance is given power to kill a fourth of the earth's population "by sword, famine and plague, and by the wild beasts of the earth." Lists of judgments like these are not uncommon in the Old Testament (e.g., Jer. 14:12; 24:10; 27:8; Ezek. 6:11; 12:16); John's list most closely resembles Ezekiel 14:21, which also mentions "wild beasts" (see WILD BEASTS).

These four horsemen portray God's general judgments on humanity caused by sin—conquest, war, strife, bloodshed, famine, and death. Again, these closely parallel the "beginning of birth pains" that Jesus describes as a period of false messiahs, wars, nations rising against nations, earthquakes, famines, and pestilence (Matt. 24; Mark 13; Luke 21). For unbelievers, the images of the dreadful horsemen are designed to evoke terror leading to repentance. For believers, who will never experience God's wrath, the horsemen serve as a sober reminder that their faith will be tested (and hopefully strengthened) during these difficult times. After mentioning the birth pains, Jesus warns his first disciples to expect testing (Matt. 24:9–13):

> Then you will be handed over to be persecuted and put to death, and you will be hated by all nations because of me. At that time many will turn away from the faith and will betray and hate each other, and many false prophets will appear and deceive many people. Because of the increase of wickedness, the love of most will grow cold, but he who stands firm to the end will be saved.

Some in the churches of Asia Minor are already passing through these pains (Rev. 1:9; 2:9–10, 22). These first four seal judgments represent preliminary judgments operating throughout history in preparation for the end of the age. Here the sinners seem to destroy themselves under the sovereign judgment of God. With the opening of the fifth seal (martyrdom), the movement accelerates toward the end of history (the sixth seal; see SEAL JUDGMENTS).

Four Living Creatures

In the heavenly throne scene in Revelation 4–5, joining the twenty-four elders around the throne of God are the "four living creatures" (Rev. 4:6–9; 5:6–14; also 6:1–7; 7:11; 14:3; 15:7; 19:4). The description of the creatures is certainly unusual:

> Also before the throne there was what looked like a sea of glass, clear as crystal.
>
> In the center, around the throne, were four living creatures, and they were covered with eyes, in front and in back. The first living creature was like a lion, the second was like an ox, the third had a face like a man, the fourth was like a flying eagle. Each of the four living creatures had six wings and was covered with eyes all around, even under his wings. Day and night they never stop saying:
>
> > "Holy, holy, holy
> > is the Lord God Almighty,
> > who was, and is, and is to come."
>
> Whenever the living creatures give glory, honor and thanks to him who sits on the throne and who lives for ever and ever, the twenty-four elders fall down before him who sits on the throne, and worship him who lives for ever and ever. (Rev. 4:6–10a)

These creatures are located next to the throne as part of the inner circle of the divine presence (Rev. 4:6a; lit., "in the midst of the throne and around the throne").

The four living creatures have been identified as possibly representing: (1) the four quarters of the zodiac according to Babylonian mythology, (2) the four tribes of Israel (Judah, Reuben, Ephraim, Dan) whose standards stood at the four sides of the tabernacle (Num. 2:2), (3) divine attributes or spiritual characteristics, (4) all of God's creation, (5) the four Gospels, or (6) an exalted order of angels. As with the twenty-four elders, however, the role of the four living creatures supports identifying them as an exalted order of angels.

The primary role of the four living creatures is to lead in the worship of God and to execute divine judgment. In their role as worship leaders, they always partner with the twenty-four elders (Rev. 4:6–10a; 5:6–10, 11–14; 7:11–12; 14:1–3; 19:4). An additional role of the four living creatures not played by the twenty-four elders is judgment.

- In 6:1–7, as the Lamb opens each of the first four seals, a living creature issues the command "Come!" to each of the four horsemen.
- In 15:5–8 one of the four living creatures gives the seven golden bowls filled with the wrath of God to the seven angels, who will pour them out.
- Interestingly, the four living creatures may also be connected indirectly to the trumpet judgments. In Revelation 5 they are holding the golden bowls containing the prayers of the saints, most likely prayers

of praise along with requests for vindication and justice (5:8). A similar image surfaces again in Revelation 8 as the beginning of the trumpet judgments:

> And I saw the seven angels who stand before God, and to them were given seven trumpets.
> Another angel, who had a golden censer, came and stood at the altar. He was given much incense to offer, with the prayers of all the saints, on the golden altar before the throne. The smoke of the incense, together with the prayers of the saints, went up before God from the angel's hand. Then the angel took the censer, filled it with fire from the altar, and hurled it on the earth; and there came peals of thunder, rumblings, flashes of lightning and an earthquake. (8:2–5).

The four living creatures serve as heavenly agents of judgment directly in the case of the seal and bowl judgments and indirectly in the case of the trumpet judgments.

Identifying the four living creatures as an exalted order of angels is also supported by the fact that Revelation combines the cherubim of Ezekiel 1 and 10 with the seraphim of Isaiah 6 (see CHERUBIM; SERAPHIM). John has adapted and transformed the Old Testament prophetic images in describing his heavenly vision. The four creatures are "covered with eyes," signifying their awareness and knowledge of all that goes on in God's creation (Rev. 4:6, 8; cf. Ezek. 1:18; 10:12).

Just as the twenty-four elders are angels and yet represent God's people in some way (see TWENTY-FOUR ELDERS), so the four living creatures are angels who represent all of God's creation — they are said to be "like" a lion, ox, man, and eagle (Rev. 4:7; cf. Ezek. 1:10). Each creature has "six wings," enabling them to carry out God's will swiftly (Rev. 4:8; cf. Isa. 6:2). Their chorus of praise no doubt encourages believers facing persecution — God is holy, powerful, and eternal (Rev. 4:8). He is sovereign over all creation and deserving of worship and devotion.

Fourth Ezra

The book of 4 Ezra is historically unrelated to the Old Testament book of Ezra or to the priest Ezra who helped the Jews return to Israel from Babylon and rebuild their religious system. Fourth Ezra is a Jewish apocalyptic book written approximately thirty years after the fall of Jerusalem (A.D. 70). Most of it is Jewish in origin, but chapters 1–2 and 15–16 are probably later Christian additions.

Fourth Ezra is important to New Testament prophecy because of its apocalyptic orientation in general and because of its description of the new Jerusalem in particular (see APOCALYPTIC LITERATURE; NEW JERUSALEM). It was written approximately the same time as the book of Revelation and thus provides helpful background material for understanding Revelation.

One of the central themes in *4 Ezra* relates to the Jewish law, which refers to the Mosaic Law and was God's gift especially to Israel. Alas, however, because of the perpetuation of Adam's evil inclination even in Israel, the Israelites on the whole did not obey the law. Consequently, divine judgment at the hands of the Gentiles descended on the nation. Nevertheless, those few Jews who hear God's law and endure the afflictions of this age will be rewarded with the joys of the age to come. Bruce Metzger pinpoints the issue that arises from all of this for *4 Ezra*:

> It is here that the particular pathos of the book emerges as the author wrestles with the question: Why has God delivered his people into the hands of their enemies? What puzzles the author is that God should permit Israel's oppressors to be in prosperity, while his own people, who are at least no worse than these, he leaves to perish (3:30, 32). It is with this question bearing on divine justice that the seer agonizes, seeking "to justify the ways of God to man."[46]

The resolution of this problem is to be found in the author's claim to have received divine wisdom on the subject. Such apocalyptic insight discloses that God has created two ages — this age and the age to come — and that the former is given over to disobedience and death while only in the latter will there be life for those who follow the law. Wisdom then becomes an apocalyptic reinterpretation of the Mosaic Law. That is to say, for the author of *4 Ezra*, wisdom is to perform the law in this age of suffering in order to inherit the blessings of the age to come.

Fulfillment of Prophecy

One of the critical and foundational issues regarding biblical prophecy is the issue of interpretive method. How should Christians today interpret the prophecies of the Old and New Testaments? In particular, what types of fulfillment should Christians expect to see? At the risk of oversimplification and even unfair labeling, it seems that we can identify three approaches to the interpretation of biblical prophecy. The *fundamentalist* view tends to see biblical prophecy as only predictive. The *liberal* view tends to see it as only historical. The *evangelical* perspective largely interprets biblical prophecy as both historical and predictive of the future.

We will illustrate these three schools of thought by applying them to three key biblical prophecies: Isaiah 7:10–16; Mark 9:1 (cf. Matt. 16:28; Luke 9:27); and the Olivet Discourse (Matthew 24; Mark 13; Luke 21).

Isaiah 7:10–16

The following chart summarizes the preceding three views with reference to the prophecy of Isaiah about the "virgin" (see VIRGIN BIRTH) giving birth to Immanuel (see IMMANUEL), after which we supply a brief explanation.

Isaiah 7:10–16: Near and Far Fulfillments		
	Isa. 7:10–16	*Matt. 1:21*
	(Near fulfillment)	(Far fulfillment)
Fundamentalist	No near fulfillment	Jesus
Liberal	Only past: Syria/ Israelite coalition	Connection made by Matthew but unintended by Isaiah
Evangelical	Hezekiah, or Maher-Shalel-Hash-Baz, or unnamed	Jesus

The fundamentalist view tends to interpret Isaiah's prophecy (Isa. 7:10–16) as being only fulfilled by Jesus (Matt. 1:21), with little regard for the historical setting of Isaiah's day.

The liberal view believes that Isaiah only spoke of God's deliverance from the Syria/Israelite coalition against Judah in 732 B.C. By then, the child born of King Ahaz and the young woman (whomever she may have been in the king's harem) will have been three years old (assuming Isaiah's prophecy was uttered in 735 B.C.). And when Jews in the southern kingdom saw or heard about the child, they proclaimed the son to be "Immanuel," because his presence was proof that God kept his promise to Ahaz to protect his kingdom from Syria and northern Israel. What then of Matthew 1:21? The liberal argues that Matthew has engaged in midrash (commentary) in reading Isaiah 7:10–16 (see MATTHEW, BOOK OF). That is, according to the liberal view, the first Gospel has incorrectly read a prophecy about Jesus back into Isaiah.

The evangelical, however, sees truth in both of the aforementioned positions. With the liberal, the evangelical sees a partial fulfillment of Isaiah 7:10–16 in God's deliverance of Judah from the Syro-Ephraimite coalition. But, with the fundamentalist, the evangelical believes the final, complete fulfillment of the Immanuel prophecy is rightly to be equated with Jesus, as Matthew well notes. Some have identified this method of interpretation as *sensus plenior*—that is, the full meaning of the text develops in time, from partial to final fulfillment.

Mark 9:1 (cf. Matt. 16:28; Luke 9:27)

Mark 9:1 reads, "And he [Jesus] said to them [the twelve disciples], I tell you the truth, some who are standing here will not taste death before the kingdom of God comes with power." In the case of this passage, the fundamentalist and liberal reverse the time frames of the fulfillment of Jesus' prophecy. The fundamentalist interprets Jesus' prediction in this verse as having been fulfilled in the past, namely, at Jesus' transfiguration (Mark 9:2–8 and parallels). That is to say, some of the disciples—the inner three: Peter, James, and John—did witness the glory of Jesus' kingdom at his transfiguration, however temporary that may have been.

The liberal, however, understands the fulfillment of Mark 9:1 to be connected to the previous verse—Mark 8:38 and Jesus' prediction of his second coming. That is, Jesus promised his disciples that they would remain alive until the Parousia (his second coming), at which time they would see the glory of the kingdom of God. That, of course, as the liberals point out, did not happen. Jesus got it wrong.

The evangelical thinks both time frames are important to the interpretation of Mark 9:1: the partial fulfillment of Jesus' prediction occurred at the transfiguration (Mark 9:2–8), which is the backdrop to the ultimate fulfillment, which will occur at the Parousia (Mark 8:38).

The Olivet Discourse (Matt. 24; Mark 13; Luke 21)

Matthew 24, Mark 13, and Luke 21 record Jesus' speech on the Mount of Olives delivered to his disciples about the future (see OLIVET DISCOURSE). The fundamentalist interprets this passage about the signs of the times as being only fulfilled at Christ's second coming.

The liberal, by contrast, tends to see the signs of the times as pointing only to the fall of Jerusalem in A.D. 70 and that generation as the era of the return of Christ.

The evangelical, once again, sees both perspectives as operative in the Olivet Discourse. The fall of Jerusalem (the partial fulfillment of the signs of the times) is the backdrop for the final fulfillment of the signs of the times at Jesus' second coming, which is still future. (See the chart on Matt. 24:3 at DELAY OF THE PAROUSIA as illustrative of the partial/final fulfillment approach to the Olivet Discourse.)

Fullness of the Gentiles

"Fullness of the Gentiles" is the phrase Paul uses in Romans 11:25–26 with reference to Israel and the Gentiles at the end of time. Those verses read, "Israel has experienced a hardening in part until the full number [lit., fullness] of the Gentiles has come in. And so all Israel will be saved." Most likely what Paul has in mind here is the idea that in and around the events of the second coming of Christ, national Israel will be converted to its Messiah. Up until then, Gentiles will largely comprise the people of God (see PEOPLE OF GOD). However, when the predetermined number of Gentiles has become Christian, then large numbers of Jews will also find salvation (see CALLOUSNESS OF ISRAEL).

The inclusion of the Gentiles into the people of God no doubt finds its origin in the future pilgrimage of Gentiles to Zion and their subsequent conversion described in the Old Testament (Isa. 2:2–4; Mic. 4:1–5). Romans 11:25–26, however, stands in contrast to first-century A.D. Jewish expectation by asserting that the salvation of the Gentiles *precedes* that of Israel.

Futurist View of Revelation

There are five main interpretive approaches to the book of Revelation: preterist, historicist, futurist, idealist, and eclectic. The futurist approach contends that Revelation 4–22 relates primarily to a future time just before and after Christ's return at the end of the age. Revelation, say the futurists, is not as concerned with what was happening in John's day as it is with what will happen in the last days. Revelation 1:19 is typically viewed as a key to how the book unfolds: "Write, therefore, what you have seen [Rev. 1], what is now [chs. 2–3], and what will take place later [chs. 4–22]."

Many influential early church leaders held to some form of the futurist view (e.g., Justin Martyr, Irenaeus, Hippolytus, Victorinus). The view faded, however, with the rise of the allegorical method of interpretation of Origen and Clement and the amillennialism of Augustine. As early as the Protestant Reformation and certainly by the nineteenth century, the futurist view began to make a comeback. Today many evangelical interpreters can be classified as futurists, either in its dispensational premillennial form or in historic premillennial form.

Dispensational futurism interprets Revelation as literally as possible and understands God's plan of salvation to consist of a series of stages or dispensations. God elected Israel as his covenant people. The church serves as a parenthesis in his plan, a time for turning to the Gentiles in hopes of restoring ethnic Israel. At the end of the age the church will be raptured into heaven and so avoid the seven-year Great Tribulation, when the Antichrist will come to power. He will assemble the evil nations to war against Jerusalem, but will be defeated when Christ returns to judge the unrighteous and establish his millennial kingdom. Following that millennial reign Satan will be permanently defeated and Christ will begin his eternal reign in the new heaven and new earth.

Historic premillennialism holds to a modified form of futurism. It reads Revelation as prophetic-apocalyptic literature, where the images often represent other realities. It does not interpret Revelation as a strictly chronological sequence (i.e., as a series of dispensations). This view does not see the church as a parenthesis but understands it as the true Israel and the fulfillment of God's plan. The church will endure the Great Tribulation. Christ will return to rescue his people and establish his millennial kingdom. Following the permanent defeat of Satan and the final judgment of God, believers will enjoy eternal life in the new heaven and new earth. While some historic premillennialists view the seal judgments as pertaining to all of church history, most see the trumpet and bowl judgments relating to the end of the age.

The main objection to the futurist view is that it removes Revelation from its original setting so that the book has little meaning for the original readers. A more radical futurist reading eliminates any relevance of Revelation for all except those living at the end of the age. A futurist might respond that Revelation would indeed hold meaning for the original audience since Christ's coming has always been imminent, even for the first readers. This response carries more weight for those futurists who do not insist on a pretribulation rapture of the church.

Some, however, critique the futurist's use of Scripture in relation to prophetic events. Why should modern readers pay attention to issues of historical-cultural background (e.g., emperor worship in the Roman empire) if the book only applies to them? What if Christ comes in the year 5000? Does the book then have no meaning for twenty-first-century readers? Also, unlike the preterist and historicist approaches, the validity of the futurist approach cannot be tested by history since what is predicted has not yet occurred. The futurist can always appeal to what will happen one day.

A futurist approach is certainly correct in claiming that some events in Revelation will occur at the end of the age—events such as the return of Christ, the final judgment, and the new heaven and the new earth. Rather than undermine hope by relegating all of Revelation to the past or to the nonhistorical realm of ideals, the futurist view grounds Christian hope in the certainty that God will one day consummate his kingdom with actual events in history. (See ECLECTIC VIEW OF REVELATION; HISTORICIST VIEW OF REVELATION; IDEALIST VIEW OF REVELATION; PRETERIST VIEW OF REVELATION.)

Gabriel

One of the few named angels in the Bible is Gabriel. Although called an angel in the Bible, Gabriel is classified as an archangel in the noncanonical Jewish book of *1 Enoch* (chs. 9; 20; 40). The name Gabriel means "man of God"; he is mentioned four times in the Bible, each time in connection with a word of prophecy.

- In Daniel 8:16–26, Gabriel tells Daniel of the coming defeat of the Medo-Persians (the ram) by Alexander the Great (the goat).
- In Daniel 9:20–27, Gabriel predicts the murder of the anointed one (either Onias III in 171 B.C., or Jesus Christ in A.D. 30) by the wicked ruler (either Antiochus IV Epiphanes or the Romans, respectively).
- In Luke 1:11–20, Gabriel proclaims the coming birth of John the Baptist.
- In Luke 1:26–38, Gabriel proclaims the coming birth of Jesus to the virgin Mary.

A common theme seems to undergird these four occasions, namely, Gabriel's prophecies announce the upcoming restoration of Israel, which is ultimately accomplished by Jesus Christ.

Gad

Gad is one of Jacob's sons and is also the tribe of Israel that descended from him. But Gad is also the name of a prophet who served David. In

1 Samuel 22, David, who has not yet become king, flees from King Saul and seeks safety in Moab. Gad the prophet appears with no introduction and advises David to leave Moab and return to Judah, which David does.

When David becomes king, Nathan is his primary prophet, and for most of David's reign there is no mention of Gad (see NATHAN). But toward the end of David's life, he takes a census of his fighting men and incurs the anger of God, who speaks once more through the prophet Gad. Indeed, Gad functions as the mediator between God and David to resolve the serious situation (2 Sam. 24:11–25; the parallel passage is in 1 Chron. 21:9–30). Similar to Nathan, Gad also was involved in recording David's court history (1 Chron. 29:29) and in prescribing how the Levite musicians were to function (2 Chron. 29:25).

Garden

The Bible speaks often of the garden as a place of abundance and rest, where plants are richly nourished for human enjoyment (e.g., Num. 24:6; Eccl. 2:5; Isa. 58:11; Jer. 29:5). In the arid climate of much of the biblical world, the key to a lush garden was a plentiful source of fresh water. Occasionally in Scripture, the ordinary garden becomes a metaphor for romantic love (Song 4:12, 15, 16; 5:1; 6:2). The beauty, richness, and intimacy of the garden reflect the pleasures that the two lovers find in each other.

The prophetic image of the garden, however, goes beyond that of the ordinary garden to the "garden framework" for the entire story of the Bible. This framework includes three central gardens: (1) the garden of Eden (or garden of God) in Genesis 2–3, (2) the gardens of Jerusalem associated with Jesus' suffering and resurrection, and (3) the final garden of heavenly paradise highlighted in Revelation 21–22.

The Garden of God

In Genesis 2 God gave Adam a garden with an abundance of fruit trees and a river of fresh water. The garden not only supplied human need ("good for food") but also offered beauty ("pleasing to the eye"). In the Garden of Eden Adam was granted a place of fulfilling work and service (2:15). He was free to eat the fruit of any tree in the garden except one, the "tree of the knowledge of good and evil" (2:16–17). This garden was a place of creation in addition to a place of intimacy without any hint of shame. Above all, the original garden was a place of relational harmony between God and his creation. Sadly, the garden of God became the setting for the temptation and fall of human beings (Gen. 3). The curse of sin reversed many of the original blessings of the garden of God.

The Gardens of Jesus' Passion and Resurrection

After celebrating the Passover during his final week on earth, Jesus and his disciples walked to the Garden of Gethsemane on the Mount of Olives, east of Jerusalem. This was the site of his agonizing prayer related to his upcoming suffering (Matt. 26:36–46), his betrayal by Judas, his arrest by the Temple guards (26:47–56), and his desertion by the rest of his disciples (26:56).

After his crucifixion, Jesus' body was laid in a newly carved tomb in an unnamed garden (John 19:38–42), and this same garden provided the setting for Jesus' first resurrection appearance to Mary Magdalene and to the other women (Matt. 28:8–10; John 20:10–18). These two gardens are the place where Jesus accepted the cross as God's will and God vindicated his Son by raising him from the dead—the central event in history that reversed the curse of the first garden and made possible the final garden.

The Heavenly Garden

The new heaven and new earth in Revelation 21 is described mainly as a city, the new Jerusalem. But this celestial city includes features of a garden. Revelation 22 opens with a description of the heavenly garden where the curse is reversed. The final garden includes a river like the first garden, but in this river flows "the water of life" and its source is "the throne of God and of the Lamb" (Rev. 22:1). Whereas God denied Adam and Eve access to the tree of life in the original garden (Gen. 3:22, 24), the tree of life in the heavenly garden is positioned in the center of the city, where its fruit and leaves continuously provide food and healing for the nations (Rev. 22:2).

As in the original garden, God's people will "serve him" (Rev. 22:3), but now they will also reign forever and ever (22:5). The term *serve* has strong worship connotations. Rather than being banished from an intimate relationship with God, God's people will now "see his face" and have his name "on their foreheads" (22:4). Instead of the curse of sin and darkness, "there will be no more night" since "the Lord God will give them light" (22:5).

The image of the garden evokes a powerful prophetic message. The first garden testified to the beauty and abundance of God's original creation before experiencing the curse of sin. In the final garden the curse of the fall is reversed and God's plan to live among his people is fully realized. The heavenly garden promises to be a place where God will fulfill all human needs—hunger, thirst, and, most of all, harmonious relationships. Without Satan, sin, or any other enemy of God, the deepest human longings will be satisfied by God's personal presence. The ultimate garden paradise is made possible by the gardens of Jesus' passion and resurrection. (See NEW HEAVEN AND NEW EARTH; NEW JERUSALEM; PRESENCE OF GOD.)

Gates

Throughout Scripture gates play a practical role in the biblical story, but they also play a prophetic role as well. Gates were a critical component in the defenses of any ancient city. They were the weak point of most defenses and thus the attack point for most sieges. Therefore, it was important to have strong gates.

But since gates in ancient cities tended to be larger and more elaborate than the regular wall, they also took on decorative significance. That is, not only the size and the strength of the gate, but also its splendor testified to the power and strength of the city. Gates controlled the entrance and the exit to the city. Frequently they were closed at night for protection. In some cases, the Israelites closed their gates for the Sabbath so that merchandise could not be carried in and sold.

The gate area also functioned as the place where legal court was held. For example, in Jerusalem the king apparently held court at the gate (Jer. 38:7). In fact, in Amos 5:12 and 5:15, where Amos cries out for justice in the gates (i.e. at court), the NIV translates the Hebrew word "gate" as "courts." Thus, Amos 5:17 reads, "Hate evil, love good; maintain justice in the courts [lit., *gates*]."

For an enemy to "possess the gate" or to "sit at the gate" implies that they both have captured the city and are currently ruling the city by holding court at the gate. Jeremiah 39:3 describes this situation as Jerusalem falls to the Babylonians: "Then all the officials of the king of Babylon came and took seats in the Middle Gate."

Both of these practical aspects are connected to the prophetic use of the gate image, a theme that starts in Genesis 3 and continues to the end of Revelation. In Genesis 3:24, after God drives Adam and Eve from the garden, God places cherubim to guard the way back in to the tree of life. Although the specific word "gate" is not used in this passage, it seems implied that the cherubim are guarding the "gate" into the garden, a "type" of temple.

In Genesis 22:17–18 God restates several central promises to Abraham (see ABRAHAMIC COVENANT). He promises to bless Abraham and to make his descendants (lit., seed) as numerous as the sand on the shore. God also states that through Abraham's descendants (lit., seed) all the nations of the earth will be blessed, a clear reference to messianic blessings through Christ. In this same messianic context, God states in verse 17 that Abraham's descendants (lit., seed) will possess the "gate" of their enemies (NIV translates "gate" here as "cities"). To possess the gate implies both the capture of the city and ruling over the city.

In Jeremiah 17:19–27, God instructs Jeremiah to stand at the gate of Jerusalem and warn the people that if they continue to violate the Sabbath by bringing products in through the gate, God will judge them by removing their kings from the gate and by burning it.

The book of Nehemiah picks up on this theme from Jeremiah. In Nehemiah 13:19, the people are regularly violating the Sabbath, and Nehemiah orders the gates to be locked on the Sabbath in an attempt to get the disobedient people to obey. Earlier, when Nehemiah completed the walls of Jerusalem, he explicitly orders that the gates be kept locked at night: "The gates of Jerusalem are not to be opened until the sun is hot" (7:3). This is in strong contrast to the earlier prophecy of Isaiah, who proclaimed of the future city, "Your gates will always stand open, they will never be shut, day or night" (Isa. 60:11). When Nehemiah explicitly mentions the regular locking of the gates, it is a reminder that the restoration of Ezra and Nehemiah was not the fulfillment predicted by Isaiah (or the other prophets). Thus the book of Nehemiah joins Isaiah and points the reader forward to the fulfillment by the coming Messiah.

Nehemiah's reconstruction of the walls and gates falls well short of Ezekiel's prophecy as well. Gates play a prominent role in Ezekiel's vision of the future Temple and city of God (Ezek. 40–48). He describes the three gates to the new Temple (40:5–27) and the twelve gates to the new city of God (48:30–35), a city characterized by the presence of God himself (48:35). The new walls and Temple built by the returning exiles clearly fall short of Ezekiel's vision, especially in regard to the presence of God.

Several probable symbolic usages of gates occur in the New Testament. Jesus refers to himself as the gate to the sheep pen, declaring, "I am the gate; whoever enters through me will be saved" (John 10:9). Likewise as Peter miraculously escapes from prison, the iron gate "opened for them by itself" (Acts 12:10), perhaps suggesting symbolically that the locked gates of cities cannot stop the powerful spread of the gospel by the apostles and others.

More clearly symbolic—and probably prophetic—is the mention of the gates to the Temple in Acts 21:30. After once again rejecting the gospel message, the Jews in Jerusalem seize Paul and drag him from the Temple with the intention of killing him. Luke then adds dramatically, "and immediately the gates were shut." This seems to signal that the gospel will not be proclaimed in the Temple any more in Acts and to suggest that the Jewish rejection of Christ at this point is final. Clearly the Gentiles and Paul, the one who proclaimed the gospel to the Gentiles, were to be excluded from the Temple, locked out by the gates. All that awaits the Temple in Jerusalem at that point is judgment, which comes in A.D. 70 (see DESTRUCTION OF THE JERUSALEM TEMPLE [A.D. 70]).

The strands of prophecy regarding gates come together in consummation in Revelation 21, as John describes the new Jerusalem. Gone are the three gates to the Temple described by Ezekiel, because now the ultimate presence of God in the city preempts any need for a Temple (21:22). As in Ezekiel's vision the city itself has twelve gates (21:12–13). In fulfillment of Isaiah 60:11 and in contrast to the shortcomings of Nehemiah's city, the new Jerusalem that John describes never closes its gates (Rev. 21:25). They remain perpetually open.

Like the garden in Genesis 3, this new city likewise has angels guarding each gate (Rev. 21:12), but unlike the cherubim of Genesis 3, these angels are not there to keep everyone out. Indeed, in the new Jerusalem "the kings of the earth will bring their splendor into it ... The glory and honor of the nations [i.e. Gentiles] will be brought into it" (Rev. 21:24, 26). Unlike the gates of the Temple that were locked to keep Paul and the Gentiles out, these gates are perpetually open to anyone, including Gentiles, whose names are written in the Lamb's book of life (Rev. 21:27; see BOOK OF LIFE).

Gematria

Gematria is a mathematical-based "Bible code" that has been explored and expounded within the mystical branch of Judaism referred to as Kaballah since the Middle Ages. The "code" works by correlating Hebrew letters with numbers. The Hebrew language can use the normal letters of the alphabet not only to represent the sounds of words (as in English) but also to represent numbers. Thus the first letter, *aleph*, can be used as a letter for spelling words, or it can stand for the number 1. Likewise, *beth*, the second letter of the alphabet, can also stand for 2, and so forth through the alphabet up to the number 9. Then the consecutive letters represent 10, 20, 30, and so on, up to 90, followed by letters representing 100 to 900, and so forth.

In Gematria, the letters in certain words are analyzed for their mathematical value and then equated with other words that have the same value. For example, the Hebrew word for *father* is comprised of the two letters *aleph* and *beth*. *Aleph* stands for 1 and *beth* stands for 2, so the sum of the word is 3. *Mother* is comprised by the letters *aleph* (1) and *mem* (40), so the sum of the word equals 41. The word for *child* has three letters —*yod* (10), *lamed* (30), and *dalet* (4), which equals 44. So *father* (3) plus *mother* (41) equals *child* (44).

This example illustrates a simple type of analysis with Gematria. The mechanics of Gematria, however, can be extremely complicated, employing various types of addition, subtraction, multiplication, and division.

How should we evaluate Gematria in regard to prophecy? First of all, even though the proponents of Gematria sometimes develop some pretty far-fetched and fanciful connections, the notion that the authors of the Old Testament used the Hebrew number values of letters to make intentional word connections is at least plausible. Numbers are often symbolic in biblical Hebrew. Furthermore, the literature of other ancient Near Eastern cultures occasionally used number cryptograms to refer to their gods or kings. Also, the authors of the Old Testament frequently used other sophisticated literary devices. So it is not out of the realm of possibility that the biblical authors played some number games as well.

However, this is probably not the case with Gematria, and it is doubtful whether these number connections were placed in the text intentionally by either the divine or the human authors. John Davis points out that there is no evidence that Hebrew letters were used to represent numbers until several hundred years after the Old Testament era was over. In other words, not only in the Hebrew Scriptures, but also in the Dead Sea Scrolls and in early Hebrew inscriptions, numbers are always written out in full text and are never represented by letters.[47]

In all likelihood, therefore, Gematria is a result of coincidence, made possible by the shear volume of number possibilities in the Hebrew text of the Old Testament. Thus Christians should probably reject this approach for interpreting the Old Testament, but reject it cautiously, remaining open to the possibility that some Old Testament writers may have used some aspect of number symbology as another sophisticated literary device (see NUMBERS, NUMEROLOGY).

In the New Testament the possibility of Gematria is much more plausible, because by that time, individual alphabet letters were being used to represent numbers. Thus it is possible, for example, to interpret 666, the number of the beast in Revelation 13:18, as being a number developed by adding up the number values of an individual's name. Some writers suggest that the total number sum of the Hebrew equivalent letters for Nero Caesar produces the number 666 (see NERO; SIX HUNDRED SIXTY-SIX). A symbolic representation like this based on number values of letters is a form of Gematria.

Gematria has been used by branches of mystical Judaism for hundreds of years. While it is doubtful that it contains predictive or prophetic elements in the Old Testament, it is nonetheless fascinating and it may even be present in the New Testament. But it should not be confused with the modern ELS type so-called "Bible Code," which has no validity or credibility (see BIBLE CODES).

Genesis, Book of

Genesis introduces many of the major themes of biblical prophecy. This is especially true in regard to the big picture of the biblical story and how it unfolds prophetically. One of the major thematic plots or sequences running throughout Scripture is the following paradigm: (1) creation/blessing; (2) sin; (3) exile/separation; and (4) restoration/blessing/redemption. This sequence is played out several times in the life of the nation Israel, but it is also part of the big picture of the Bible and is a critical element in biblical prophecy (see REVELATION, BOOK OF).

Genesis introduces this "big picture" in the first twelve chapters. Genesis 1–2 describes the wonderful "creation" of God and the tremendous "blessings" associated with it. Genesis 3 presents the disobedience of Adam and Eve ("sin") and their expulsion from the garden of blessing and the associated loss of the presence of God ("exile"). Likewise Genesis 4–11 shows how this pattern of disobedience and exile is typical for humanity in general. In these few chapters three terrible events occur. Cain kills his brother Abel, humanity sins so badly that God destroys all but a remnant in the flood (see REMNANT), and the people of the world unite to rebel against God at the Tower of Babel, only to be scattered across the world. The human race is not off to a good start.

Genesis 12, however, introduces Abraham and the Abrahamic Covenant, and with it the story of God's redemption/restoration begins to unfold. The promises made to Abraham in Genesis 12–22 are foundational for much of biblical prophecy. The fulfillment of these promises drives the biblical story throughout the rest of the Old Testament and into the New Testament (see ABRAHAMIC COVENANT).

God's call of Abraham in Genesis 12 is in direct response to the disastrous human situation described in Genesis 3–11. More specifically, Genesis 10–11 (the Table of Nations and the Tower of Babel) stand as the prologue to 12:1–3. God calls Abraham out of his concern for those nations described in Genesis 10.

Genesis 10 describes the division of the world according to family/tribe/clan (*mishpāchāh*), language (*lāshōn*), land/country/territory (*'eretz*), and nation (*gôy*) (10:5, 20, 31). The call of Abraham picks up on three of these terms: "Go from your country [*'eretz*]" (12:1); "I will make you a great nation [*gôy*]" (12:2); and "in you all the families [*mishpāchāh*] of the earth will be blessed" (12:3) (NRSV). The term "families" (*mishpāchāh*) in 12:3 provides a tight connection back to Genesis 10, for this term occurs not only in the summary statements (10:5, 20, 31) but also in 10:18 and 32. Thus the promise in 12:3 clearly connects back to Genesis 10. The promise to Abraham is the answer to the sin and the scattering of Genesis 3–11.

The call and promise to Abraham in Genesis 12:1–3 introduces God's spectacular redemptive plan, one that culminates in Jesus Christ himself. But from the beginning God has the diverse peoples of the world in mind. He focuses on Abraham, not to be exclusive but to use this individual and his descendants to bless and deliver the entire world. This is a critical aspect of Genesis 12 and the unfolding presentation of God's redemptive plan.

The theme introduced here—that sin scatters the peoples of the world but that God's blessing reunites them—runs throughout the Scriptures. The prophets frequently paint a future picture of all peoples uniting together to worship God, a direct reversal of Genesis 10–11 and a fulfillment of 12:1–3. Luke presents Christ as the fulfillment of the promise to Abraham (Luke 1:54–55, 68-73). Likewise, the power of the Spirit seen at Pentecost (Acts 2) to overcome language is a reversal of Genesis 10–11 (see SPIRIT). Paul identifies the inclusion of the Gentiles and salvation by faith through grace with the promise made to Abraham. Finally, the ultimate picture in Revelation of "every tribe and language and people and nation" (Rev. 5:9; 7:9; 14:6) united as God's people saved by Christ is a direct climactic fulfillment of the promise made to Abraham.

The relationship between Genesis and Revelation is thus close. Genesis serves as a prophetic introduction to the biblical story, and Revelation brings the story to its climactic conclusion. In this sense Genesis and Revelation serve as "prophetic bookends" for the Bible. The story starts in the garden (Gen. 1–2) and it ends in the garden (Rev. 21–22; see GARDEN).

In fact, as Scott Duvall observes, there are numerous points of connection between Genesis and Revelation—themes that are introduced in Genesis and brought to culmination in Revelation.[48] The chart below lists many of those connections.

Genesis	Restoration in Revelation	
Sinful people scattered	God's people unite to sing his praises	19:6–7
"Marriage" of Adam and Eve	Marriage of Last Adam and his bride, the church	19:7; 21:2, 9
God abandoned by sinful people	God's people (new Jerusalem, bride of Christ) made ready for God; marriage of Lamb	19:7–8; 21:2, 9–21
Exclusion from bounty of Eden	Invitation to marriage supper of Lamb	19:9
Satan introduces sin into world	Satan and sin are judged	19:11–21; 20:7–10
The serpent deceives humanity	The ancient serpent is bound "to keep him from deceiving the nations"	20:2–3
God gives humans dominion over the earth	God's people will reign with him forever	20:4, 6; 22:5
People rebel against the true God, resulting in physical and spiritual death	God's people risk death to worship the true God and thus experience life	20:4–6
Sinful people sent away from life	God's people have their names written in the book of life	20:4–6, 15; 21:6, 27
Death enters the world	Death is put to death	20:14; 21:4
God creates first heaven and earth, eventually cursed by sin	God creates a new heaven and earth where sin is nowhere to be found	21:1
Water symbolizes unordered chaos	There is no longer any sea	21:1
Sin brings pain and tears	God comforts his people and removes crying and pain	21:4

Genesis	Restoration in Revelation	
Sinful humanity cursed with wandering (exile)	God's people given a permanent home	21:3
Community forfeited	Community experienced	21:3, 7
Sinful people banished from God's presence	God lives among his people	21:3, 7, 22; 22:4
Creation begins to grow old and die	All things are made new	21:5
Water used to destroy wicked humanity	God quenches thirst with water from spring of life	21:6; 22:1
"In the beginning, God ..."	"I am the Alpha and the Omega, the beginning and the end."	21:6
Sinful humanity suffers a wandering exile in the land	God gives his children an inheritance	21:7
Sin enters the world	Sin banished from God's city	21:8, 27; 22:15
Sinful humanity separated from presence of holy God	God's people experience God's holiness	21:15–21
God creates light and separates it from darkness	No more night or natural light; God himself is the source of light	21:23; 22:5
Languages of sinful humanity confused	God's people is a multicultural people	21:24, 26; 22:2
Sinful people sent away from the garden	New heaven/earth includes a garden	22:2
Sinful people forbidden to eat from tree of life	God's people may eat freely from the tree of life	22:2, 14
Sin results in spiritual sickness	God heals the nations	22:2
Sinful people cursed	The curse removed from redeemed humanity and they become a blessing	22:3
Sinful people refuse to serve/obey God	God's people serve him	22:3
Sinful people ashamed in God's presence	God's people will "see his face"	22:4

Another important prophetic passage is Genesis 3:15, where, as part of the curse God pronounces on the serpent, God states, "I will put enmity between you and the woman and between your offspring [seed] and hers; he will crush your head, and you will strike his heel." Christians have traditionally understood the serpent in Genesis 3 to represent Satan. In a corporate sense, the verse points to the continuous enmity and warfare that occurs throughout history between those of Satan and those of God. In an individual sense, the verse refers to Christ, who ultimately crushes the head of Satan, the great serpent. Often this verse is called the *protoevangelion* ("the first good news") — that is, the first prophetic proclamation of the gospel. Many see fulfillment of this verse in Revelation 12 (cf. also Rom. 16:20; see DRAGON; SEED OF THE WOMAN; WOMAN OF REVELATION 12).

Glory of the LORD

Old Testament Prophecies

In the Old Testament the term glory is connected to concepts of honor and worth. Glory is that which sets someone or something apart as special, valuable, unique, and extraordinary in a positive way. Thus the glory of the Lord, in its basic meaning, alludes to all of the great acts of the Lord (creation, deliverance, etc.) as well as all of the amazing qualities of his character (his love, knowledge, justice, etc.). Throughout Psalms, God is praised repeatedly for his glory.

This abstract quality of glory (what God is and does) also finds a more concrete expression in association with the LORD's presence. That presence is a central theme that ties the Bible together (see PRESENCE OF GOD). Yet when God's presence literally appears on the earth, it is usually described as the "glory of the LORD." Thus, for example, when the presence of God comes and fills the Tabernacle, it is called the "glory of the LORD" (Ex. 40:34–35). Likewise when the Ark of the Covenant is lost, the Israelites declare, "The glory has departed" (1 Sam. 4:21). After Solomon completes the construction of the Temple, "the glory of the LORD filled his temple" (1 Kings 8:11; 2 Chron. 5:13–14). Thus, the "glory of the LORD" refers to God's indwelling presence in the midst of his people, a critical component of the Mosaic Covenant.

In spite of numerous warnings from the prophets, however, Israel continues to disobey God, turning to foreign idols and abandoning the biblical call in Deuteronomy for justice in society. Eventually, these sins lead to the shattering of the Mosaic Covenant and God's departure from Israel.

Ezekiel 8–11 describes this event in some detail. In Ezekiel 8, God shows Ezekiel the many sinful and idolatrous things occurring in the Temple. Then Ezekiel sees the glory of the LORD in the Temple move up away from the ark to the threshold (9:3; 10:4), and then it departs from the Temple altogether, moving toward the east (11:23).

The loss of the glory of the LORD (God's presence) from Jerusalem is devastating to Israel. Yet the prophets (especially Isaiah and Ezekiel) proclaim that one of the bright promises associated with the coming Messiah will be the restoration of the glory of the LORD to his people. Thus in reference to the coming Messiah, Isaiah 40:5 proclaims that the "glory of the LORD will be revealed ... to all people" (see also Isa. 60 and 66). Likewise, when Ezekiel turns to the future and describes the future restored Temple, he underscores the return of the glory of the LORD to fill the Temple (Ezek. 43:2–5; 44:4).

Significantly, when the Jews return to Jerusalem after the exile and rebuild the Temple and city, there is no mention of the return of the glory of the LORD to the Temple. Thus, both in Ezra–Nehemiah and in the postexilic prophet Haggai, the return of the glory of God is conspicuously absent, underscoring the fact that the great restoration promised by Isaiah and Ezekiel had not yet occurred and still awaited future messianic fulfillment. Indeed, after the glory of the LORD departs from the Temple in Ezekiel 9–11, God's Presence does not return to the Temple until Jesus walks in through the gates.

The New Testament Fulfillment

Jesus Christ pulls together all of the strands of Old Testament prophecy regarding the glory of the Lord and brings them to fulfillment. He embodies and reveals the very glory of God (John 1:14). As the acts and character of God in the Old Testament reflected and demonstrated God's glory, so in the New Testament the acts and character of Jesus reflect and demonstrate even more the divine glory of the Father, the Son, and the Spirit.

As in the Old Testament, the glory that Jesus brings is part of the prophesied restored presence of God. Jesus reveals this glory over and over again (John 1:14; 2:11). In the New Covenant that he brings, the glory of God is mediated to his people through the Holy Spirit (2 Cor. 3:3–4:6). Indeed, while the glory of God was seen through Jesus in his earthly ministry, it was revealed even more through his resurrection and awaits a final spectacular revelation at his future coming. Yet the New Testament stresses that the glory of Jesus is not just for himself, but for others as well. Believers in Christ will share in the future glory (Phil. 3:20–21; Col. 3:4).

In Revelation the interconnected themes of glory and presence come to their climactic conclusion. In the new Jerusalem, God's presence is once again equated with the glory of God, eliminating the need for a Temple (Rev. 21:22) or for sunlight, because the glory of God shines with such brightness (21:11, 23; see PRESENCE OF GOD).

Goat

Daniel 8:5–14, 21–26 prophesy that Alexander the Great (symbolized as a goat) will destroy the Medo-Persian empire (symbolized as a two-horned ram), which indeed took place in 334–331 B.C., thanks to the Greek king's swift, phalanx-style army. Daniel 8 alludes to the fact that after Alexander's death in 331 B.C., his empire would be divided up among his four generals (symbolized as four horns on the goat): Cassander (who controlled Macedonia), Lysimachus (who ruled Thrace), Ptolemy I (who secured Egypt), and Seleucid I (who eventually reigned over Syria). The last two-mentioned generals factor heavily in Daniel's prophecies because of their influence on ancient Israel in times leading up to and including the Maccabean revolt (167 B.C.)

Daniel 8:9–14, 23–26 also mention that one horn would arise out of the four horns on the goat, probably referring to Antiochus IV Epiphanes, the Seleucid ruler who caused such affliction for Israel from 171 to 164 B.C. (see ANTIOCHUS EPIPHANES). Some interpreters see a contradiction between Daniel 2/7 and Daniel 8. The former is thought to present the Medo-Persian kingdom as two separate entities whereas the latter presents them as one. However, the contradiction is only apparent, because Daniel 8, in mentioning the two horns on the ram, alludes to the two nations of Media and Persia, but now as combined. (See FOUR BEASTS OF DANIEL.)

God of Heaven

"God of Heaven" is the title used of God in Daniel 2:18, 19: cf. 2:28, 36, 44. It is also used several times in Ezra and Nehemiah. Thus the title is used only by Jews in the exile, suggesting that the name has connotations that are specific to the exile situation. In most of the other Old Testament books, one of the major names used for God is *Yahweh* (i.e., the LORD). This is the personal name of the God of Israel, and it is used primarily in covenant contexts. The more general name for God is *Elohim*, a name that implies more of a universal, aspect of God.

Thus when the Jews of the exile, and Daniel in particular, use "God [*Elohim*] of heaven" rather than the personal, covenant keeping name (*Yahweh*), the suggested implication is that the old Mosaic Covenant is not operational. Moreover, the title may reflect the reality that God is in control of the destinies of all of the kingdoms of world history, not just Israel's destiny.

Gog and Magog

Gog is the leader of a future coalition that will attack Israel, an event described in Ezekiel 38: "Gog, of the land of Magog, the chief prince of Meshech and Tubal" (38:2). The additional allies of Persia, Cush, Put, Gomer, and Beth Togarmah are included in 38:5–6. In Ezekiel's day, the names Gog and Magog were both probably associated with the land of Lydia, in Anatolia (modern Turkey), although the evidence is meager. Meshech and Tubal, by contrast, the regions or peoples that Gog rules over, can be identified with some certainty. They show up several times in ancient Assyrian literature and can be identified with groups in Anatolia (modern Turkey). This seven-nation eschatological alliance that Gog leads comes from north, south, east, and west, and appears to represent a worldwide alliance against Israel.

Gog and Magog seem to carry this same idea in the book of Revelation: "When the thousand years are over, Satan will be released from his prison and will go out to deceive the nations in the four corners of the earth—Gog and Magog—to gather them for battle" (Rev. 20:7–8). Here Gog and Magog seem to symbolize nations from around the world. Gog and his alliance in Ezekiel 38 should probably be understood in the same fashion.

Because Gog's identity is not overly clear, writers throughout church history have identified Gog with numerous different people and places, usually trying to connect Gog to some person or group that was contemporary at that time. Thus at one time or another, writers have identified Gog with the Goths (fourth century), the Arabs (seventh century), or the Mongols (thirteenth century). From time to time Gog has also been identified with Roman emperors, Popes, or the Turks.[49]

In the early twentieth century, the Scofield Reference Bible connected Gog with Russia (see ROSH), assuming that Meshech and Tubal referred to the Russian cities of Moscow and Tobolsk. This understanding is still being circulated today by some popular prophecy writers. However, most Old Testament scholars today reject this view, pointing out that *Rosh* has nothing to do with Russia. Likewise Meshech and Tubal are not related in any way to the modern cities of Moscow and Tobolsk.

Golden Censor

The golden censor or bowl is mentioned in Revelation 5:8; 15:7; 16:1–4, 8, 10, 12, 17; 17:1; 21:9. All these references draw on the background of the Old Testament liturgy of the Temple with its altars, menorah, bowls of incense, and the like. The background of the gold censor may also derive from the early Jewish notion that angels functioned as heavenly priests of God. But Revelation combines these backgrounds to give a negative twist to the usage of golden censors by angels, for they represent God's wrath to be poured out on unbelievers during the Great Tribulation as part of the answer to the prayers of persecuted Christians (see GREAT TRIBULATION).

Gomer

Gomer is one of the nations allied against Israel in the future invasion described in Ezekiel 38. Most scholars identify Gomer with the Cimmerians, a people originally from north of Assyria who migrated south into Asia Minor (modern Turkey) during the eighth to seventh centuries B.C. to flee the invasion of another tribe, the Scythians. The Cimmerians were defeated by the Assyrians and then assimilated into the surrounding peoples through intermarriage; thus they disappear from history around the sixth century B.C. Ezekiel appears to use Gomer and the other six nations listed in Ezek. 38:1–6 to symbolize the worldwide nature of the alliance that opposes Israel in the eschatological (end-time) battle he describes (see GOG AND MAGOG).

Great Prostitute

Revelation contrasts two women who are also represented as cities: God's people as the faithful bride of Christ (the new Jerusalem) and the great prostitute (Babylon). In the Old Testament, Israel herself could appear either as a pure bride (e.g., Isa. 54:5–6; 62:5; Hos. 2:19–20) or as a disobedient prostitute or adulteress (e.g., Jer. 3:6–10; Ezek. 16:15–22; 23:1–49; Hos. 4:12–13; 5:3), depending on her relationship with God at the time.

Occasionally the harlot is not Israel, but foreign evil empires such as Nineveh (Nah. 3:4) or Tyre (Isa. 23:17). Along with the prostitute background in the Old Testament, the ancient Mesopotamian city of Babylon adds another dimension to the harlot image in Revelation. As the political and religious center of a world empire, Babylon was well known for materialism and immorality. She conquered Jerusalem in 587/586 B.C., establishing her fame as a powerful enemy of God's people. Revelation combines the images of the great city Babylon with that of a harlot or prostitute to describe a corrupting center of pagan power. The image appears in Revelation as the "prostitute" (Rev. 17:1, 5, 15, 16; 19:2), the "great city" (Rev. 16:19; 17:18; 18:10, 16, 18, 19, 21), and "Babylon" (Rev. 14:8; 16:19; 17:5; 18:2, 10, 21).

Revelation focuses on the prostitute as the recipient of God's judgment, and deservedly so. She has allied herself with the beast from the sea (Rev. 17:3, 7) as well as demonic spirits (18:2, 23). Babylon's widespread influence (17:1, 15, 18) on the nations is corrupting because of her own idolatry and immorality (17:4–5). On several occasions she is said to make the nations drunk with the "maddening wine of her adulteries" (14:8; 17:2; 18:3, 9), indicating how she seduces the nations with her idolatry and immorality.

Babylon's corrupting influence spreads easily because of her affluence and materialism. She dresses in purple and scarlet (symbolic of luxury and royalty) and adorns herself with gold and precious stones (Rev. 17:4). The merchants grow rich from "her excessive luxuries" (18:3; cf. 18:7). Revelation 18 goes into detail about the prostitute's wealth and economic influence. Even in this extended description of her prosperity, the focus stays on her downfall as kings, merchants, and mariners lament her demise.

Although self-sufficient and independent (Rev. 18:7), Babylon's downfall will be sudden and dramatic (18:8, 10, 21). Those who profited from her wealth will mourn and weep as they observe her "torment" (18:15) and "ruin" (18:19). God even uses the beast to bring judgment on the prostitute (17:16–17). All the normal routines of work and family life cease as the great city faces God's judgment (18:21–23). Revelation leaves no doubt that the almighty God has made the prostitute to drink from the "cup filled with the wine of the fury of his wrath" (16:19; cf. 18:6, 8).

Babylon, the great prostitute, faces God's judgment chiefly because she has persecuted the followers of Jesus Christ. John saw "the woman drunk with the blood of the saints, the blood of those who bore testimony to Jesus" (Rev. 17:6). He adds that in the "great city" was found "the blood of prophets and of the saints, and of all who have been killed on the earth" (18:24). God's judgment on the prostitute is severe because "her sins are piled up to heaven, and God has remembered her crimes" (18:5). The angel calls for rejoicing as God vindicates his people by destroying Babylon: "Rejoice over her, O heaven! Rejoice, saints and apostles and prophets! God has judged her for the way she treated you" (18:20). But believers are also commanded to "come out of her, my people, so that you will not share in her sins, so that you will not receive any of her plagues" (18:4).

Historically, the great prostitute has been identified as Rome, the secular center of political, economic, religious, and military power of the first-century world that opposed God and persecuted his people. But even if ancient Rome lies behind the image, it does not exhaust its meaning. By extension, every age boasts of great centers of materialism, pagan power, and corruption that draw people away from God and threaten his people. But, as Stephen Smalley reminds us, "in the end, the powers of evil serve the purposes of the sovereign God, in addition to being condemned by him."[50] (See BABYLON/BABYLONIANS; BRIDE OF THE LAMB; NEW JERUSALEM; ROME/ROMAN EMPIRE.)

Great Tribulation

The Bible uses the term "tribulation" to refer to the distress, trouble, persecution, and suffering experienced by believers as a result of living faithfully in a world opposed to God (see TRIBULATION). When the world encounters the truth of God in the gospel, it responds with tribulation and persecution for those who bear witness. The expression "the Great Tribulation" is taken by most scholars to refer to an unprecedented period of intense suffering that will characterize the time just prior to Christ's return.

Matt. 24:21	For then there will be *great distress*, unequaled from the beginning of the world until now—and never to be equaled again.
Acts 7:11	Then a famine struck all Egypt and Canaan, bringing *great suffering*, and our fathers could not find food.
Rev. 2:22	So I will cast her on a bed of suffering, and I will make those who commit adultery with her *suffer intensely*, unless they repent of her ways.
Rev. 7:14	I answered, "Sir, you know." And he said, "These are they who have come out of the *great tribulation*; they have washed their robes and made them white in the blood of the Lamb."

The phrase "Great Tribulation" (*thlipsis megas*) only occurs four times in the New Testament: Matthew 24:21; Acts 7:11; Revelation 2:22 and 7:14 (see chart). The reference in Acts describes a time of intense suffering caused by a famine during the time of the patriarchs. In Revelation 2:22 Jesus warns the followers of Jezebel, the false prophetess who is promoting immorality and idolatry, that he will make them "suffer intensely" (see JEZEBEL). Here the expression refers to Jesus' judgment on the unrepentant followers of a false teacher.

Matthew 24:21 occurs in the context of Jesus' Olivet Discourse in Matthew 24–25. The immediate context (24:4–31) may be divided into four parts: (1) 24:4–14 describes the "birth pains" that will occur throughout the entire age of the church (e.g., wars, famines, earthquakes, persecution, apostasy, false prophets); (2) 24:15–20 portrays the horrifying destruction of the Jerusalem Temple in A.D. 70 (cf. Luke 21:20–24; Dan. 9:27; 11:31; 12:11); (3) Matt. 24:21–28 spells out the period known as the "great distress" that immediately precedes Jesus' return (Mark 13:19; cf. Dan. 12:1); and (4) Matt. 24:29–31 depicts the return of Christ.

Some see all of Matthew 24:15–28 as describing the "Great Tribulation" rather than dividing the unit into two sections. They understand Jesus to be interweaving prophetic elements throughout 24:15–28 that relate both to his generation and to the end times. Others see the entire period from A.D. 70 to Jesus' return as the time of "great distress." The parallel passage in Luke 21:20–24 suggests that the destruction of Jerusalem would be followed by a long period of Gentile domination. In summary, the "great distress" of Matthew 24:21 refers to a period of intense tribulation and persecution at the end of the age just prior to Jesus' return.

Assuming that believers will be present during that time, Jesus assures his disciples that those days will be shortened "for the sake of the elect" (24:22). He appears to be using the near event of the destruction of the Temple in Jerusalem in A.D. 70 to predict the far event of the Great Tribulation that immediately precedes his return.

Following the sealing of the 144,000 in Revelation 7:1–8, John sees a "great multitude that no one can count, from every nation, tribe, people and language, standing before the throne and in front of the Lamb" (7:9). They are wearing white robes, holding palm branches, and crying out praises to God and the Lamb (7:10). The angels, elders, and four living creatures join the great multitude in praising God (7:11–12).

Then one of the elders asks John, "These in white robes—who are they, and where did they come from?" (Rev. 7:13). After John pleads ignorance, the elder provides the answer: "These are they who have come out of the great tribulation; they have washed their robes and made them white in the blood of the Lamb" (7:14). Who are these people and what does it mean that they have come out of "the great tribulation"?

The immediate context demonstrates that the entire episode refers to an event that has already occurred rather than one in the process of occurring. Because of the past-tense verbs in Revelation 7:13 ("did ... come") and in 7:14 ("washed" and "made white"), the present-tense participle is properly translated as a past tense ("those who have come out of") rather than as a present tense ("those who are in the process of coming out of"). Their identification as those who have "washed their robes and made them white in the blood of the Lamb" probably alludes to the testing and purifying process explained in Daniel 11:35 and 12:10.

In those passages the "wise" will for a time fall by the sword or be burned or captured or plundered, and even stumble, but will eventually be "refined, purified, and made spotless until the time of the end." Thus, washing their robes white in Christ's blood in Revelation 7:14 likely refers to their perseverance through tribulation made possible by their reliance on and faithful witness to the atoning death of Christ—the "blood of the Lamb" (cf. 3:18; 6:9–11; 12:11; 22:14). Consequently, the people described in 7:14 are believers who have faithfully persevered times of terrible persecution and tribulation.

There is disagreement about whether this group of believers is to be identified with the church or (for those holding to a pretribulation rapture) with other saints who have become Christians during the Tribulation. While all these believers have persevered faithfully, scholars also disagree about whether all have been martyred. Some interpret the metaphor of washing white robes in blood as necessitating martyrdom (Aune, Bauckham, Walvoord), while others see the metaphor as a reference to persevering faith that may result in martyrdom, but doesn't always (Beale, Smalley).

What is this great ordeal that these people have survived? Daniel 12:1 supplies the likely background for the phrase "the Great Tribulation":

> At that time Michael, the great prince who protects your people, will arise. There will be a time of distress such as has not happened from the beginning of nations until then. But at that time your people—everyone whose name is found written in the book—will be delivered.

In Daniel, God's people are persecuted because of their covenant relationship with God (Dan. 11:30, 32), so that some even turn away from the faith. Yet those who trust in the Lord (i.e., "everyone whose name is found written in the book") will ultimately be delivered. Some will be "delivered" through resurrection from the dead (Dan. 12:2).

The same emphasis continues in Revelation 7:14. God will deliver believers of every nation, tribe, people, and language through a time of great distress that includes temptation to succumb to false teaching, pressure to compromise and worship other gods, and intense persecution for those remaining faithful. Although their faithfulness may cost them their physical lives, God will give them resurrection life. With no more hunger, thirst, scorching heat, or tears, they will worship God and the Lamb forever (7:15–17). (See CROSS AND THE MESSIANIC WOES; MESSIANIC WOES; NEAR VIEW–FAR VIEW; PRETRIBULATION RAPTURE; POSTTRIBULIONAL RAPTURE; TRIBULATION; WRATH OF GOD.)

Great White Throne Judgment

God's final judgment on evil takes its name from the opening line of the scene in Revelation 20:11–15:

> Then I saw a great white throne and him who was seated on it. Earth and sky fled from his presence, and there was no place for them. And I saw the dead, great and small, standing before the throne, and books were opened. Another book was opened, which is the book of life. The dead were judged according to what they had done as recorded in the books. The sea gave up the dead that were in it, and death and Hades gave up the dead that were in them, and each person was judged according to what he had done. Then death and Hades were thrown into the lake of fire. The lake of fire is the second death. If anyone's name was not found written in the book of life, he was thrown into the lake of fire.

The Old Testament background appears to be Daniel 7:9–10, where the Ancient of Days, adorned in white and seated on a throne, opens the books to judge those standing before him. In Revelation "white" often symbolizes holiness and purity (Rev. 1:14; 3:4–5; 4:4; 6:11; 7:9, 13–14; 14:14; 19:11, 14). The one seated on the throne in Revelation 20 could be Christ (cf. 5:6; 22:1), but the Father seems more likely because he is normally the one seated on the throne in this book (4:2, 9: 5:1, 7, 13; 6:16; 7:10, 15; 19:4; 21:5). As in 6:14 and 16:20 when the end comes, heaven and earth flee in fear from the presence of God. There is no place left to hide for those standing before the great white throne of God Almighty.

The "dead, great and small" are being judged, but who are these people? The expression "small and great" or "great and small" can be used in Revelation to describe both the righteous (Rev. 11:18; 19:5) and the unrighteous (13:16; 19:18). The identity of those being judged depends on how one understands 20:4–5: "They came to life and reigned with Christ a thousand years. (The rest of the dead did not come to life until the thousand years were ended.) This is the first resurrection." If the first resurrection of 20:5 is limited to the martyrs, then the great white throne likely involves both righteous and unrighteous. If the first resurrection includes all believers, then the second resurrection of 20:13 includes only the wicked.

Some see Revelation 20:12 as describing the judgment of believers and 20:13–15 the judgment of unbelievers.[51] Most scholars see the Great White Throne Judgment as a general judgment of the entire human race, righteous and unrighteous alike. The statement in 20:13 that the sea, death, and Hades give up their dead for judgment appears to affirm the idea of a universal judgment. No one will escape resurrection and judgment.

Judgment is based on the evidence in "the books," probably referring to a person's words and actions during their lifetime (Rev. 20:12; cf. Dan. 7:10). People are "judged according to what they had done as recorded in the books" (Rev. 20:12–13). The theme of judgment by works appears throughout Revelation (2:23; 11:18; 14:13; 18:16; 22:12), as well as the rest of the New Testament (e.g., Matt. 16:27; Rom. 14:12; 1 Cor. 3:12–15; 2 Cor. 5:10; 1 Peter 1:17). Although the exact nature of this judgment is not specified here, in other contexts the recompense may include positive aspects of reward as well as negative aspects of punishment (see REWARDS).

Along with "the books," another book is opened—the "book of life" (Rev. 20:12, 15). The book of life image appears in 3:5; 13:8; 17:8; 20:12, 15; 21:27, always as a record of salvation or redemption. Those whose names are written in the book of life will be given eternal life, while those whose names are not included will suffer condemnation (see BOOK OF LIFE). If Christians do appear before the great white throne (a matter of debate), they can take comfort in knowing that their names are written in the book of life. The final judgment concludes with death and Hades, and anyone whose name is not found in the book of life is "thrown into the lake of fire" (20:14), where the beast, false prophet, and Satan are already suffering torment (19:20; 20:10). The lake of fire is "the second death" (20:15).

This age concludes with God's righteous and holy judgment of sin and sinners. The last enemy (death) is decisively eliminated. Now the new age may begin in full (Rev. 21). (See JUDGMENT; JUDGMENT SEAT OF CHRIST; LAST JUDGMENT.)

Greece

Greece occurs in connection with biblical prophecy in Daniel 2, 7, 8, and 11. The first two references are debated. Some equate Greece with the third empire mentioned in 2:39b (the kingdom of bronze) and in 7:6 (the leopard). Others equate Greece with the fourth empire in 2:40–43 (iron and clay) and in 7:7–8, 19–25 (the hideous beast). The latter reading believes, therefore, that the fulfillment of Daniel's prophecy of the four kingdoms concluded with ancient Greece. The former interpretation identifies Daniel's fourth kingdom with a future, revived Roman empire. (See ALEXANDER THE GREAT; FOUR BEASTS OF DANIEL.)

But concerning Daniel 8:21–22 and 11:2–4, all agree that Greece is the object of Daniel's prophecy and, in particular, the conquest of Alexander the Great over the Persian empire as well as the subsequent fourfold division of the Greek empire after Alexander's death in 323 B.C.

Habakkuk, Book of

The book of Habakkuk is different than many of the other Old Testament prophetic books. It is not a collection of preached oracles and messages, but rather a dialogue between Habakkuk and the LORD. In Habakkuk 1:1–4 the prophet points to injustice in Judah, asking how long it will be until God corrects the situation and brings justice. God answers in 1:5–11, that he is raising up the Babylonians to judge and destroy Judah. This answer is apparently not what Habakkuk is hoping for, and in 1:12–2:1 he voices his disagreement. God, however, responds in 2:2–20 that the Babylonian invasion is, nonetheless, inevitable, and that Habakkuk should remain faithful. Habakkuk replies in a song, declaring in 3:1–19 that he will wait patiently for the coming terrible invasion, but will still rejoice in God.

In God's answer in Habakkuk 2:2–20, God tells the prophet that "the righteous will live by his faith" (2:4). In the New Testament, the apostle Paul uses this verse as a foundational text for explaining justification by faith (Gal. 3:11).

Hadēs

The Greek word *Hadēs* originated in Greek mythology. *Hadēs* was the god of the lower regions (death). Although the King James Version often translates the term as "hell" (with reference to the final destiny of the wicked), *Hadēs* rather should be translated as "death" (with reference to the general abode of the deceased). In terms of biblical prophecy, the book of Revelation uses *Hadēs* four times, in each case as a synonym for death.

- 1:18 asserts that Jesus' resurrection made him Lord over "death and *Hadēs*."
- 6:8 equates the fourth horseman as "death and *Hadēs*."
- 20:13 says "death and *Hadēs*" will give up their victims after the return of Christ.
- 20:14 predicts that "death and *Hadēs*" will be cast into the lake of fire after the millennium.

Haggai, Book of

The three prophets Haggai, Zechariah, and Malachi are called the Postexilic Prophets because they ministered after the exile of the Jews to Babylon is officially over. In 538 B.C. the Persian king Cyrus decrees that the Jews can return from exile in Babylon to their homeland.

The prophecies of Haggai date to the year 520 B.C. A critical component in rebuilding the nation of Israel is the construction of the temple. In Haggai 1:4 the prophet rebukes the people because they are living in fine homes while the Temple of God still lies in ruins. Progress is apparently made on the Temple, but the returning exiles do not have nearly the amount of resources that King Solomon had when he first built the Temple, and the Temple they reconstruct is shabby by comparison and disappointing to many. Furthermore, there is no mention in Haggai or in Ezra-Nehemiah of the glorious presence of God coming to dwell in this Second Temple as God had dwelt in the Most Holy Place of the First Temple.

But through Haggai, the LORD proclaims that "the glory of this present house will be greater than the glory of the former house" (Hag. 2:9). This prophecy is fulfilled as Jesus himself enters the gates of the Second Temple, bringing the glory and presence of God back to the Temple for the first time since God departed from it in 587/586 B.C. (see EZEKIEL, BOOK OF; PRESENCE OF GOD; TEMPLE).

Healing

Jeremiah, along with the other Old Testament prophets, uses the image of sickness and injury to describe the deplorable spiritual situation of Israel and Judah. In Jeremiah 1–29, the prophet proclaims that since the people will not repent, judgment is inevitable. In these chapters he uses the sickness imagery frequently, stating that Israel/Judah is wounded and/or sick, but that there is no healing for them, only judgment. Thus in 8:22 the prophet declares, "Is there no balm in Gilead? Is there no physician there? Why then is there no healing for the wound of my people?" (see BALM OF GILEAD). This theme is repeated in 8:15; 10:19; 14:19; and 15:18.

In Jeremiah 30–33, however, as the prophet looks to the messianic future, he proclaims healing as part of the future salvation that the messianic age brings. Thus in chapter 30, God first recounts the terrible existing situation in Jerusalem and in Judah, using physical wounds and sickness as figures or images to represent serious, incurable spiritual sickness:

> Your wound is incurable,
>   your injury beyond healing.
> There is ... no remedy for your sore,
>   no healing for you ...
> Why do you cry out over your wound,
>   your pain that has no cure?
> Because of your great guilt and many sins
>   I have done these things to you. (Jer. 30:12–15)

However, in stark contrast to the earlier impending inevitable judgment, God now looks to the messianic future and proclaims, "But I will restore you to health and heal your wounds" (Jer. 30:17). This theme of messianic healing for the spiritual sickness and wounds of the nation resurfaces in 33:6. Isaiah adds that it will be precisely by the suffering and the wounds (i.e., the death) of the coming Messiah that people will ultimately be healed (Isa. 53:4–5).

Although the prophets use sickness and healing metaphorically to represent the spiritual situation of Israel, Jesus fulfills these prophecies in both the figurative and the literal sense. He does indeed "heal" the people spiritually, providing forgiveness and restoring to wholeness. But he also literally heals a great number of people (the blind, lame, etc.), ironically fulfilling a figurative prophecy in a literal manner. Thus Jesus fulfills Jeremiah's prophecies in both a literal and a figurative sense.

This dual literal/figurative nature of Jesus' healing is underscored by the dual meanings possible in the Greek word *sōzō*. This word can mean either "to be saved spiritually" or "to be healed physically." When Jesus turns to the bleeding woman who touches him in faith, he declares to her, "Your faith has saved/healed [*sōzō*] you" (Mark 5:34). Does he mean physical healing only (her bleeding had stopped), or does he include spiritual healing as well (forgiveness of sins and deliverance from judgment, as *sōzō* normally means)? Both types of healing have occurred.

Healing plays a central role in the ministry of Jesus. Not only does it demonstrate the fulfillment of specific Old Testament prophecies, but it characterizes and represents the in-breaking of the kingdom of God, highlighting that in the ultimate consummation of the kingdom there will be no sickness (or blindness, leprosy, lameness, etc.). Jesus' healing miracles also serve to authenticate his ministry in a powerful way, witnessing to the fact that he comes with power from God and is to be identified with the LORD, the great healer of the Old Testament.

As with so many other biblical themes, the theme of healing reappears at the end of Revelation. In Revelation 22:1–2 John describes the tree of life on both sides of the river of the water of life. The leaves from the tree of life, John explains, "are for the healing of the nations" (see TREE OF LIFE).

Heaven

The concept of heaven in the Bible carries several meanings. (1) Scripture speaks of a physical heaven or sky above the earth as in the expression, "In the beginning God created the heavens and the earth" (Gen. 1:1), or in Jesus' statement, "I tell you the truth, until heaven and earth disappear ..." (Matt. 5:18). In this sense heaven refers to the physical sky of birds, clouds, wind, and rain. The Hebrew idea of the physical heavens also embraced the heavenly bodies such as the sun, moon, stars, and planets (Gen. 1:14; 15:5). The physical universe is part of God's creation and gives testimony to his power and glory (Ps. 8; 19:1–6).

(2) The Bible refers to "heaven" as the dwelling place of God and his angels (e.g., Deut. 26:15; Neh. 9:6; Matt. 5:45; 16:17; 23:22). Jesus descended from heaven and returned to heaven (Luke 9:51; John 6:33–51; Acts 1:11; Eph. 4:7–16). The Spirit also descended from heaven (Matt. 3:16; 1 Peter 1:12). The New Testament clearly teaches that Jesus will one day return from heaven (John 14:2–3; Acts 1:6–11; Phil. 3:20; 1 Thess. 1:10; 4:16–17; Rev. 19:11–14). As the true Tabernacle of God (Heb. 8:1–5), heaven is sometimes used as a synonym for God himself, as in the parable of the prodigal son: "I will set out and go back to my father and say to him: Father, I have sinned against heaven and against you" (Luke 15:18; cf. Dan. 4:26; Matt. 23:22; John 3:27; 2 Cor. 12:2). In Revelation, heaven appears like a temple (e.g., Rev. 7:15; 11:19; 16:17), and the throne of God serves as the center of all reality (4:2).

(3) Finally, heaven is used in a variety of ways to refer to the believer's hope for deliverance from evil and a permanent home in God's presence. Christians are promised heavenly rewards (Matt. 5:12; 6:1), an inheritance (1 Peter 1:4), and treasure (Matt. 6:20; 19:21). God's children have their names written in heaven (Luke 10:20; Heb. 12:23; Rev. 21:27), the place of their true citizenship (Phil. 3:20).

God's judgment on evil originates in heaven (Rom. 1:18; Rev. 15:1; 16:1). Jesus will return from heaven to conquer evil, raise the dead, and give believers resurrection bodies fit for a new creation (Phil. 3:21; 1 Cor. 15:51–58; 1 Thess. 4:16–17). The eternal home of believers is more precisely described in Revelation 21:1 as "a new heaven and a new earth." Having banished evil from the new creation, God's dwelling place descends to a new earth, where he lives among his people in the city-garden of the new Jerusalem (21:1–22:5).

The fact that Christians have an eternal home awaiting them encourages them to persevere in the face of persecution, ridicule, and injustice. Many of those initially receiving the message of Revelation were facing rejection from the Jewish synagogue and were themselves rejecting the pagan gods and goddesses of Greco-Roman society. From a human perspective, they were left spiritually homeless in this world. The window into heavenly reality provided by Revelation renewed their perspective and bolstered their faith. Jesus, rather than Caesar, is Lord, and God's throne, rather than Rome, is the center of all reality. With a renewed heavenly vision, Christians can continue to overcome. (See NEW HEAVEN AND NEW EARTH; NEW JERUSALEM.)

Historicist View of Revelation

There are five main interpretive approaches to the book of Revelation: preterist, historicist, futurist, idealist, and eclectic. The historicist approach argues that Revelation supplies a prophetic overview of church history from the first century until the return of Christ. Although there have been many esteemed advocates of this approach in the past (e.g., Wycliffe, Knox, Tyndale, Luther, Calvin, Zwingli, Wesley, Edwards, Finney, Spurgeon), there are few today. Historicism was popular during the Protestant Reformation as Reformers identified the Antichrist and Babylon with the pope and Roman Catholicism of their day. This "newspaper approach" to prophecy has led historicist interpreters to identify the Antichrist with figures like Charlemagne, Napoleon, Mussolini, and Hitler, to name just a few.

Classical dispensationalists have generally interpreted the letters of Revelation 2–3 using a modified historicist approach. John Walvoord writes:

> Many expositors believe that in addition to the obvious implications of these messages the seven churches represent the chronological development of church history viewed spiritually. They note that Ephesus seems to be characteristic of the Apostolic Period in general and that the progression of evil climaxing in Laodicea seems to indicate the final state of apostasy in the church ... It would seem almost incredible that such a progression should be a pure accident, and the order of the messages to the churches seems to be divinely selected to give prophetically the main movement of church history.[52]

The primary strength of this view lies in its attempt to make sense of Revelation for the interpreter. The vast majority of scholars agree, however, that this single strength is far outweighed by its many weaknesses. The historicist outline only applies to Western church history, ignoring the spread of Christianity throughout the rest of the world. Since images such as the beast of Revelation 13 are always identified with people and events contemporary to the interpreter, the historicist reading of Revelation is constantly being revised as new events occur and new figures emerge.

Most problematic for historicism is the complete lack of agreement about the various outlines of church history. History is like a moving target for those who want to read Revelation in this way, and there is no consensus about what the book means, even among interpreters within the same school of interpretation. Rather, inconsistency, conjecture, and speculation abound. The historicist approach to Revelation also holds little relevance for the first readers and assumes that the interpreter in question must be living at the end of the age. (See ECLECTIC VIEW OF REVELATION; FUTURIST VIEW OF REVELATION; IDEALIST VIEW OF REVELATION; PRETERIST VIEW OF REVELATION.)

Hosea, Book of

Hosea was a prophet who preached to the northern kingdom Israel during the mid-eighth century B.C., prior to the Assyrian invasion and destruction of Israel in 722 B.C. His message is similar to that of most of the other Old Testament prophets. He proclaims to Israel that they have broken the Mosaic Covenant. In this proclamation of covenant violation, Hosea draws primarily from Deuteronomy, as do most of the other prophets.

Hosea calls on the people to repent, but he holds little hope that they will. Therefore, he pronounces serious and severe judgment on Israel. Finally, he mentions hope for a future time of restoration and blessing. Yet as in the book of Amos, Hosea focuses primarily on sin (covenant violation) and judgment. The message of hope is there, but it is not featured prominently.

Hosea 1–3 is the best-known section. God instructs Hosea to marry a prostitute. He carries out the LORD's command and marries Gomer. Over the years his wife bears three children. God gives names to all three children to symbolize the theological situation and coming events. The first is named "Jezreel," after the location of the massacre of the previous ruling dynasty (2 Kings 9:30–10:17), indicating that the current dynasty will end in a similar fashion (Hos. 1:4–5).

The second child is named "Lo-Ruhamah," meaning "not loved" and indicating that Israel will soon be destroyed by the Assyrians; God will not protect them.

The third child is named "Lo-Ammi," which means "not my people." This name has tremendous significance, because at the heart of the covenant relationship that God had with Israel was the statement, "I will be your God; you will be my people." To name the child "not my people" implies that the Mosaic Covenant with Israel is ending.

Hosea's wife plays the harlot and leaves him. However, God commands Hosea to find her and to restore the relationship (Hos. 2–3). Throughout the prophets, God frequently uses the marriage analogy to illustrate his relationship with his people Israel. He loves his bride Israel/Judah, but his wife betrays him and leaves him for other men (idols). Several prophets (Isaiah, Jeremiah, Ezekiel) use this analogy, underscoring the pain God feels when his people reject him. The command to restore Hosea's wife and love her again is a beautiful picture of how God will forgive and restore his people. Hosea 2:23 declares, "I will say to those called 'Not my people,' 'You are my people,'" thus indicating a renewed covenant relationship. The New Testament continues to use the husband/wife theme, describing the church as the bride of Christ (see BRIDE OF THE LAMB).

Huldah

In 2 Kings 22 Josiah the king commands that the Temple be cleaned out and repaired. During the repair process the book of Deuteronomy is discovered. Josiah's advisers take the book to the king and read it to him. Josiah, apparently hearing the word of the LORD in Deuteronomy for the first time, realizes that the nation is guilty of violating many of God's laws. He then instructs his advisers to go and inquire of the LORD as to what will happen in regard to the judgment described in Deuteronomy.

The advisers go to a woman named Huldah, identified as a prophetess. She was the wife of Shallum, the "keeper of the wardrobe." It is unclear whether Shallum was part of the Temple organization (i.e., keeper of the priest's wardrobe) or part of the royal court (i.e., keeper of the king's wardrobe). At any rate, the advisers seem to know that Huldah is a true and trusted prophetess.

Huldah informs her visitors that the judgments in Deuteronomy will indeed come to pass and that Judah and Jerusalem will indeed be totally destroyed. However, she declares that since Josiah has repented and is humble before God, he will not see the terrible destruction; it will happen after his death. Huldah is the only woman identified as a prophetess in 1–2 Kings, but there are several other women called prophets/prophetesses in the Bible (see WOMEN PROPHETS).

Iddo

Iddo is called both a seer (2 Chron. 9:29; 12:15; see SEER) and a prophet (13:22). In 2 Chronicles he is identified as the prophetic author of additional (nonbiblical) histories of the reigns of Jeroboam (9:29), Rehoboam (12:15), and Abijah (13:22). These histories were lost long ago and are not available to us, but the fact that the authors of these histories were prophets/seers suggests that prophets were also probably responsible for writing 1–2 Samuel, 1–2 Kings, and 1–2 Chronicles. Note also that in the Hebrew canon the books of Joshua, Judges, 1–2 Samuel, and 1–2 Kings are called "Former Prophets." Perhaps that terminology developed because of the connection between prophets like Iddo and historical records (see FORMER PROPHETS).

Idealist View of Revelation

There are five main interpretive approaches to the book of Revelation: preterist, historicist, futurist, idealist, and eclectic. The idealist approach sees Revelation as a symbolic description of the ongoing battle between God and evil. Rather than predicting future events, Revelation offers timeless spiritual truths to inspire Christians of all times as they endure persecution, suffering, and injustice at the hands of God's enemies.

This view gained ground through the allegorical method of interpretation promoted by church fathers such as Origen and Clement. Coupled with the amillennialism of Augustine, the idealist view became the dominant approach to Revelation from several hundred years after Christ until the Protestant Reformation. The view has also become popular today among interpreters who locate Revelation's meaning not in the first-century history, nor in future events surrounding the end times, but in the ongoing struggle against the forces of evil.

The idealist view pays particular attention to Revelation's use of symbolic language. John uses images and symbols to creatively describe God's victory and thus inspire Christians of every age to persevere. The seals, trumpets, and bowls are judgments that fall on unbelievers of every age. Antichristian powers and rulers are depicted through images such as the beast, false prophet, and Babylon. The millennium describes the present church age. Consequently, the prophecies of Revelation are only predictive in the general sense that God will conquer evil.

In terms of strengths, the idealist position may be connected with other views to bring spiritual relevance. Even if preterists identify the beast as Nero or Domitian, they often add an idealist application, warning Christians to beware of secular powers that demand worship. In addition, the idealist view appreciates the prophetic-apocalyptic genre of Revelation, highlights the theological importance of the book, and focuses on its spiritual relevance for Christians of all times and places. Unlike the other views, idealism has no need to worry about harmonizing prophecy and fulfillment since the fulfillment is often supplied by the contemporary reader.

The idealist view affirms much that is true about Revelation, but it has been criticized for failing to identify any of the book's symbols with historical events. If there is no particular historical fulfillment of the prophecies of Revelation, in what sense are its ideals really relevant?

In contrast to the preterist and historicist, who locate the meaning of the book concretely in history, and the futurist, who anticipates a historical fulfillment at some point, the idealist struggles to answer the question of how the theology of Revelation relates to history. Along the same lines, idealism provides little hope that God's kingdom will ever be consummated in the return of Christ, the last judgment, and the new heaven and new earth. (See ECLECTIC VIEW OF REVELATION; FUTURIST VIEW OF REVELATION; HISTORICIST VIEW OF REVELATION; PRETERIST VIEW OF REVELATION.)

Immanuel

Immanuel is a Hebrew word with three components: the preposition *im* ("with"), the pronoun suffix *anu* ("us"), and the divine appellation *el*

("God"). Thus, Immanuel means "God is with us." This particular name occurs only four times in the Bible (Isa. 7:14; 8:8, 10; Matt. 1:23), but the concept of God's presence runs throughout the Bible (see PRESENCE OF GOD).

In Isaiah 7 King Ahaz of Judah is attacked and terrified by the king of Israel and the king of Aram. Isaiah, however, tells him not to fear but to trust in the LORD. In fact, Isaiah proclaims, the LORD will give a sign to Ahaz: An unnamed "virgin" will conceive and give birth to a child, whose name will be Immanuel. Before this child grows old enough to know right from wrong, Isaiah continues, God will destroy both of the kings threatening Ahaz (Isa. 7:14–16). At this point the sign of Immanuel appears to refer to a child born during the time of Ahaz as a sign to him of God's power and his ability to deliver.

The Hebrew word used in Isaiah 7:14 for "virgin" can indeed refer to a "virgin," but it normally references a "young unmarried woman." Hebrew has another explicitly clear word that means "virgin." So Isaiah 7:14 does not necessarily predict a virgin birth during the time of Ahaz, but it does predict the birth of a child who will be a sign to Ahaz.

However, even here in the Old Testament this text seems to be pointing to something beyond the sign to Ahaz. Although the text could be referring to a young woman in the time of Ahaz with no specific reference to her virginity, it is interesting to note that no father is mentioned. In Isaiah 8:8 the LORD states, "Its outspread wings will cover the breadth of your land, O Immanuel." This implies that Immanuel owns the land of Judah, suggesting that he is no mere unknown or obscure child. Likewise, 8:10 proclaims that Judah's enemies will be defeated because "God is with us," an apparent wordplay on this name and a suggestion perhaps that the prediction of Immanuel points beyond a child just in Ahaz's time (although there undoubtedly was also a child named Immanuel born in Ahaz's time who was a sign to him).

When the Hebrew Bible was translated into Greek, the Hebrew word for "young unmarried woman" in Isaiah 7:14 was translated with a Greek word that explicitly means "virgin." Thus, Matthew connects this verse to the virgin birth of Jesus and declares that the virgin birth was a fulfillment of Isaiah 7:14. Apparently this Isaiah prophecy was fulfilled in a dual sense—once during the reign of Ahaz and then ultimately by the virgin birth of Jesus.

The proclamation of Matthew 1:23 that Jesus carried the prophetic identification as Immanuel, "God is with us," introduces a theology of God's presence that runs throughout the New Testament. The book of

Matthew, for example, which has "God with us" at its beginning, ends with the same theme when Jesus proclaims, "I will be with you always" (28:20). So Matthew opens and ends with the theology of Jesus as the presence of God. John declares the same theme in John 1:14, "The Word became flesh and made his dwelling among us."

Thus, the New Testament associates Jesus with God's presence, thus underscoring the appropriateness of his name Immanuel. At the climactic end of the biblical story, Revelation 21–22 proclaims that the "Lord God Almighty and the Lamb" will themselves be the Temple in the new Jerusalem, and they will dwell once again with God's people in the garden.

Imminence

"Imminence" means different things to different interpreters of New Testament prophecy. The key passages are: Matthew 16:27–28; 24:3, 34; Mark 13:30; Luke 21:28–31; John 14:1–4; Romans 13:11–12; 1 Corinthians 7:29–31; 15:51–58; 1 Thessalonians 4:13–18; Hebrews 10:25, 37; James 5:7–9; 1 Peter 4:7; Revelation 1:1; 22:6, 7, 10, 12, 20. All of these texts have to do with the nearness of the end of history in general and the return of Christ in particular, but interpreters differ on how to understand these texts. There are four main views.

(1) Liberals argue that these prophecies by Jesus and the writers of the New Testament refer to their belief that Jesus' second coming was expected to take place in the first generation of Christians, a hope and belief that never materialized.

(2) Conservative Christians of the preterist position argue that the above predictions all occurred in conjunction with the fall of Jerusalem to the Romans in A.D. 70 (see PRETERIST VIEW OF REVELATION). Thus they maintain that the Parousia, or second coming of Christ, was fulfilled in his return to judge Israel at their defeat at the hands of the Romans in A.D. 70.

(3) Advocates of the pretribulation perspective hold that some of the passages (John 14:1–14; Rom. 13:11–12; 1 Cor. 7:29–31; 15:51–58; 1 Thess. 4:13–18) refer to the rapture (the secret coming of Christ to snatch his church away to heaven before the arrival of the Great Tribulation). The other texts refer to the second coming of Christ in visible power and glory after the Great Tribulation. Therefore, because the sign of the Great Tribulation pertain to Jesus' second coming and not the rapture, the latter can happen at any moment.

(4) Posttribulationists (those who equate the rapture with the second coming, placing it after the Great Tribulation) believe the signs of the

times began at the first coming of Christ and will intensify before his return. Therefore, since these signs have already been set in motion, the second coming can occur at any time and is thus imminent.

Imperial Cult

"Imperial cult" refers to the worship system surrounding various Roman emperors from Augustus to Constantine (thirty-six of them) who were proclaimed to be divine. This reality is an important part of the background of Revelation (see esp. Rev. 2–3; 13:1–18; 17:8–13). These passages underscore the conflict between Christianity and the imperial cult.

The influence of the imperial cult in Asia Minor provides a critical background for understanding the letters to the seven churches in Revelation 2–3. Regarding this connection, Colin J. Hemer makes several points.[53] (1) With Domitian (A.D. 81–96), the cult of Caesar worship reached its pinnacle in the first century. Numismatic (coins) evidence provides us with illustrations of his claim to deity; for example, coins bear his title "lord and god" and the image of his deified son, seated on a globe with his hands stretched out to seven stars (cf. Rev. 1:20).

(2) Jews, ironically, were exempt from imperial worship, a privilege extending back to Julius Caesar.

(3) The ensuing resentment of Jews toward Christians in the aftermath of the fall of Jerusalem in A.D. 70 did not bode well for Jewish Christians. The synagogues devised a way to expel the latter from their midst by introducing the curse of the "*minim*" (lit., "heretics," meaning "the Nazarenes" [followers of Jesus]) into the Eighteen Benedictions, which were recited in the synagogues (ca. A.D. 90). That "benediction" reads, "For the renegades let there be no hope, and may the arrogant kingdom soon be rooted out in our days, and may the Nazarenes and the *minim* [heretics] perish as in a moment and be blotted out from the book of life, and with the righteous may they not be inscribed. Blessed art thou, O Lord, who humblest the arrogant."[54]

The Nazarenes are the *minim* and are probably to be identified as Jewish Christians. Thus exposed and excommunicated, Jewish Christians were no longer perceived by the Roman government as under the umbrella of Judaism and, therefore, faced the cruel dilemma of either forsaking Christ (if they were to be readmitted to the synagogues) or denying Caesar. The problem seems to have been exacerbated by those Jews who provided local Roman officials with lists of Christians who were no longer associated with their synagogues.

This politico-historical background sheds light on the theological problem that John addresses in the seven letters. In effect, these prophetic oracles can be seen as praise or warnings to the churches for resisting or not withstanding, respectively, the temptation to succumb to Caesar worship. The Nicolaitans (2:6, 15) and the teaching of Balaam (2:14) seem to allude to those in the churches who said it was permissible to worship Caesar. The teachings of Jezebel (2:20–22) may well be included in this category, especially against the backdrop of the union of Caesar worship and pagan idolatry, which permeated the trade guilds of that day (see JEZEBEL).

It is in the face of such temptation that the risen Jesus challenges the churches to be faithful to him (Rev. 2:4–6, 8–10, 12–16, 20–25; 3:1–5, 7–12, 14–21). Special praise is offered to those who suffered to the point of death for obeying Christ (2:8–10, 12–13), while judgment is pronounced on those Jews who expelled Jewish Christians out of their synagogues, thus exposing them to the imperial cult (2:9; 3:5, 9).

Many New Testament scholars suggest that examining Revelation 13:1–18 through the imperial cult backdrop provides a clearer perspective on these otherwise baffling verses. Nero's infamous character merits the title of "beast" (13:1). Verses 1–6 give the generic background of the beast, which is the Roman empire of the first century. The seven heads correspond to the seven hills of Rome, while the ten horns allude to the Caesars of the first century, however one may number them (see TEN-HORNED BEAST). The blasphemous worship demanded by the beast reminds one of the imperial cult of the first century, and the war the beast wages on the saints cannot help but recall the intense persecutions that Nero, and later Domitian, inflicted on Christians because they did not worship Caesar.

Besides this generic background, there may also be specific allusions in Revelation 13:1–18 to Nero himself. To a beastly character (13:1) can be added his alleged recovery (13:3). Nero's persecution of Christians from November 64 to June 68 may account, in part, for the forty-two months (or three and one-half years) of oppression mentioned in 13:5. The reference in 13:10 to those who kill with the sword being killed by the sword reminds one simultaneously of Nero's persecution of Christians and his own apparent suicide by the sword. The reference in 13:11–15 to the beast of the land securing worship for the beast from the sea (Rome was across the sea from where the Apocalypse was written [Asia Minor]) reminds one of the local priests of the imperial cult in Asia Minor, whose task was to compel the people to offer a sacrifice to Caesar and proclaim him as lord.

Megalomaniac that he was, Nero had coins minted on which he was called "almighty god" and "savior." Nero's portrait also appears on coins as the god Apollo playing a lyre. While earlier emperors were proclaimed deities upon their deaths, Nero abandoned all reserve and demanded divine honors while still alive (as did also Caligula before him, A.D. 37–41). Those who worshiped the emperor received a certificate or mark of approval (Gk. *charagma*, the same word used in Rev. 13:16).

Related to this, in the later reign of Decius (A.D. 249–251), those who did not possess the certificate of sacrifice to Caesar could not pursue trades, a prohibition that conceivably goes back to Nero (cf. Rev. 13:17). Finally, in the number 666 (13:18) one can perhaps detect John's usage of *Gematria*, a mathematic cryptogram that assigns numerical values to letters of the alphabet (see GEMATRIA). More than one scholar has seen a possible referent of this number in *Neron Kaiser*. The Hebrew numerical valuation for *NRWN QSR* is as follows: N=50, R=200, W=6, N=50, Q=100, S=60, and R=200, all of which add up to 666 (see SIX HUNDRED SIXTY-SIX).

The Neronian background also throws light on Revelation 17:8–13. The same metaphors rooted in the Roman empire occur here: seven heads, seven hills, ten horns, Caesars with blasphemous names demanding worship. The added detail concerns the identification of the beast "who was and is not, and is about to come up out of the abyss" (17:8, NASB; see BEASTS OF REVELATION). More specific information about this personage is supplied in 17:10–11. Probably the fifth king "who was and is not" is Nero (in particular, the story of Nero *redivivus*; see NERO REDIVIVUS). Moreover, the king "who is," is Vespasian (A.D. 69–79, discounting the short and ineffective reigns of Galba (A.D. 68–69), Otho (A.D. 69) and Vitellius (A.D. 69). The other king who has not yet come, and when he comes, must remain a little while is then Titus (A.D. 79–81), who died after a short reign (see EMPERORS).

Using this historical framework also helps to uncover the meaning of Revelation 17:1–7. The apostle John describes there a harlot, full of blasphemous names, sitting on the beast (see HARLOT). A number of commentators identify the harlot with unfaithful Israel, especially Jerusalem (although others equate the harlot with Babylon and Rome). The description in 17:6 of the harlot's killing of the martyrs is distinctly reminiscent of Jesus' accusations against Jerusalem (Matt. 23:29–39). The city's idolatry also recalls Israel's past unfaithfulness to God, in this instance probably manifested in first-century Judaism's privileged status before Rome.

Early Jewish Christians, however, did not share this status. Expelled from the synagogues, they had to face Caesar worship. When John speaks of the beast turning on the harlot and destroying her (Rev. 17:16–18), he in all probability alludes to the divine judgment that befell Jerusalem for cooperating with the imperial cult. The destruction of Jerusalem in A.D. 70 also seems to be drawn upon in 11:2, where it is said that the outer court of the Temple "has been given to the Gentiles. They will trample on the holy city" (cf. Luke 21:24).

We must recall here Revelation 13:15–18 and the mark of the beast on the worshiper's right hand and/or forehead. Some scholars suggest that this may well be a parody of Jewish custom of wearing phylacteries. Based on Deuteronomy 6:8, Jewish males often tied leather boxes (called phylacteries) containing portions of the Ten Commandments to their arms and heads during their times of prayer. Seen against this backdrop, the exposure of the mark of the beast could perhaps be understood as pointing a guilty finger at those Jews in the first century who belied their commitment to monotheism by cooperating with imperial Rome.

This poignantly explains why Revelation refers to such people as those "who say they are Jews and are not, but are a synagogue of Satan" (Rev. 2:9, 24; cf. 1:7; 17:3). Their rejection of Jesus and his followers on the one hand, and their acceptance, or at least condoning, of Caesar worship on the other, were nothing less than eschatological apostasy. Nevertheless, although this explanation is plausible and has merit, it is not held by all New Testament scholars.

Inaugurated Eschatology

Inaugurated eschatology is a concept usually connected with the twentieth-century Swiss theologian Oscar Cullmann. Like others before him, Cullmann realized that the Jewish notion of two ages formed an important background for understanding the message of Jesus. According to Judaism, history is divided into two periods: this age of sin and the age to come (i.e., the kingdom of God). For Jews, the advent of the Messiah would bring about the shift from the former to the latter. In other words, Judaism viewed the two ages as consecutive.

According to Cullmann, Jesus Christ announced that the end of time, the kingdom of God, had arrived in history (see Mark 1:15 and parallels; Luke 4:43; 6:20; 7:28; 8:1, 10; 9:2, 11, 27, 60, 62; 10:9, 11; 11:20; 13:18; 20; 16:16; 17:20, 21; 18:16, 17, 24, 25, 29; Acts 28:31). Yet other passages suggest that, although the age to come had *already* dawned, it *was not* yet complete. It awaited Jesus' second coming for its full realization (Luke 13:28, 29; 14:15; 19:11; 21:31; 22:16, 18; 23:51; Acts 1:6). Hence the name "inaugurated" eschatology.

Such a view is pervasive in the New Testament besides the Gospels (see, e.g., Acts 2:17–21; 3:18, 24; 1 Cor. 15:24; 1 Tim. 4:1; 2 Tim. 3:1; Heb. 1:2; 1 John 2:18). So, for inaugurated eschatology, the two ages are simultaneous: the age to come exists in the midst of this present age. Christians therefore live in between the two ages until the Parousia (see ALREADY–NOT YET).

Iran

See PERSIA.

Iraq

See BABYLON/BABYLONIANS.

Isaiah, Book of

The book of Isaiah is one of the most significant books of Old Testament prophecy. The New Testament quotes directly from Isaiah fifty-eight times, and indirect allusions number well over a hundred. Like Jeremiah, Isaiah epitomizes Old Testament prophecy, focusing on the three main themes of Old Testament prophecy: (1) You (Israel/Judah) have broken the Mosaic Covenant (see MOSES); repent immediately! (2) Since you won't repent, judgment is coming. (3) Beyond the judgment is coming a wonderful time of restoration and blessing through the coming Messiah.

In general, Isaiah 1–39 focuses on judgment and Isaiah 40–66 focuses on the future restoration, but this is only a broad generalization. Sprinkled throughout Isaiah 1–39 are passages describing the future blessings and the Messiah; likewise, Isaiah 40–66 still includes passages that warn Judah of coming judgment.

Ironically, the most quoted passage from Isaiah in the New Testament is Isaiah 6:9–10. In 6:1–8 the prophet encounters the living God seated on his throne, surrounded by the seraphim (see SERAPHIM). This is the scene in which God calls Isaiah to be a prophet. However, in 6:9–10 God informs Isaiah that Israel will not listen and that they will reject his prophetic message. This passage is quoted in the New Testament five times (Matt. 13:14–15; Mark 4:12; Luke 8:10; John 12:40; Acts 28:26–27) because by and large the people of Israel in the New Testament times did not listen to Isaiah either, and they rejected Jesus as the Messiah.

Isaiah has numerous other prophetic and messianic passages. In Isaiah 7:14 the prophet states that the Coming One will be born of a virgin and called Immanuel (see IMMANUEL). Matthew 1:23 states that Jesus fulfilled this prophecy. Isaiah 9:2–7 also refers to the birth of the Coming One; here Isaiah begins to reveal complicated aspects of the Coming One. He will be a child and a son (9:6), but he will also be a powerful righteous king on the throne of David (Isa. 9:7; see DAVIDIC COVENANT). Yet Isaiah takes the prophecy beyond the mere promise of a human Davidic king. As is implied in the name Immanuel ("God with us"), Isaiah suggests the Coming One will be more than a mere man (9:6). Indeed, Isaiah calls him "Wonderful Counselor, Mighty God, Everlasting Father, Prince of Peace."

Isaiah 11 also connects the Messiah to the Davidic Covenant, declaring that the Coming One will be a branch (see BRANCH) from the stump of Jesse (David's father) (11:1, 10). This Coming One will have the Spirit of the LORD (see SPIRIT) and will thus have great wisdom and power (11:2). In 11:4–5 Isaiah proclaims that the Messiah will be characterized by righteousness and justice, especially in regard to defending the poor and needy. Throughout the Old Testament prophets these two qualities— righteousness and justice—are repeatedly associated with the Messiah, in stark contrast to the terrible injustice and unrighteousness that frequently characterized the human kings of Israel's history.

Isaiah also frequently states that the reign of the coming Messiah will be a time of peace. Isaiah 11:6–9 presents an image of wild animals and domestic animals living together in peace, led by a small child. Scholars are divided over how to interpret these verses. Some argue that this passage is merely a figurative reference to a time of peace and that the wild animals may be symbolic references to hostile nations. Others connect this passage to the theme of the transformation of nature (see TRANSFORMATION OF NATURE), understanding it as a time in the millennial kingdom, when nature will be so transformed that animals (and people) will no longer hunt and kill each other.

Isaiah 11:10–16 discusses several other major prophetic themes. The coming Messiah will regather and restore Israel (for differing views on this, see RESTORATION OF ISRAEL), bringing the remnant back to the land (see REMNANT). Yet in 11:10–16 the prophet states that Israel will not be alone in this regathering, for the Messiah will also gather the Gentile nations to himself from around the world (11:10, 12). This theme continues throughout Isaiah. For example, a vivid picture of Gentile inclusion is presented in 19:19–25, where Egypt and Assyria—traditional enemies of Israel—are described as worshiping the LORD together with Israel. Isaiah declares, "The LORD Almighty will bless them, saying, 'Blessed be Egypt my people, Assyria my handiwork, and Israel my inheritance'" (19:25).

Isaiah 40–66 has numerous significant prophetic passages that encompass several prophetic themes. All four Gospels cite Isaiah 40:3–5 ("the voice of one calling in the desert"), identifying John the Baptist as the "voice in the desert" and Jesus as the Coming One prophesied by Isaiah here (Matt. 3:3; Mark 1:3; Luke 3:4–6; John 1:23).

Isaiah 40–66 also declares that the Coming One will be a Davidic king who will restore Israel. He will be a light to the Gentiles, and part of his kingdom will involve the inclusion of the Gentiles. He will be characterized by righteousness, justice, and holiness. He will be both a king and a servant.

In fact, at the heart of Isaiah's messianic prophecies are four texts that refer to the Coming One as "the servant of the LORD" (Isa. 42:1–7; 49:1–6; 50:4–10; 52:13–53:12). These important passages are often called the Servant Songs, and they contain some of the most important prophetic theology of the Old Testament (see SERVANT SONGS). Isaiah 52:13–53:12 describes the suffering of the Messiah that Jesus fulfilled on the cross as well as the substitutionary aspect of his death.

Another significant messianic text is Isaiah 61:1–3. At the beginning of his ministry, Jesus quotes directly from this passage, identifying himself clearly with the Coming One whom Isaiah described (Luke 4:18–19). As in numerous other passages in Isaiah, this text stresses the comfort that the Messiah will bring, especially to the poor and brokenhearted. Likewise, when John the Baptist sends messengers to Jesus to ask if he was indeed the Messiah (Luke 7:18–20), Jesus answers by pointing to the deeds he was doing: "The blind receive sight, the lame walk, those who have leprosy are cured, the deaf hear, the dead are raised, and the good news is preached to the poor" (7:22). In this answer Jesus pulls together numerous prophecies from Isaiah (Isa. 29:18–19; 35:5–6; 42:18; 43:8; 61:1) that find fulfillment in his activity, pointing out clearly that Jesus was the Messiah whom Isaiah promised.

Several other prophetic themes occur in Isaiah and especially in Isaiah 40–66. Isaiah frequently compares the wonderful blessings of the coming messianic age to the exodus from Egypt. He points out that the coming "new exodus" will be better and even more fantastic than the old one (see NEW EXODUS). Another important theme is God's role as Creator. Isaiah stresses the creative power and activity of God. Indeed, since God is the all-powerful Creator, he is also able to bring about his plan for the future. Thus Isaiah underscores that the LORD is the Lord and master of history. Foreign kings do not control Israel's destiny, but rather the God of Abraham does. Thus, God is the One who brought judgment on Israel, but also the One who will bring about the glorious future restoration.

Part of the glorious restoration that the Creator of the world will bring about, Isaiah 65:17–25 proclaims, is the creation of a "new heavens and a new earth." This prophecy is further explained and expanded in Revelation 21–22 (see NEW HEAVEN AND NEW EARTH).

Islam

Islam is one of the three major monotheistic religions (i.e., belief in one God) in the world today, along with Christianity and Judaism. Islam is the major religion in many countries of the Middle East (Jordan, Syria, Turkey, Iraq, Iran, etc.), North Africa (Libya, Egypt, Algeria, northern Nigeria, etc.), Central Asia (Uzbekistan, Pakistan, Afghanistan, etc.), and South Asia (Indonesia, Malaysia). The two largest predominately Islamic countries in the world are Indonesia and Pakistan.

The Islamic religion developed hundreds of years after Christianity, so it is not surprising to note that the Bible makes no explicit reference to Islam or to Muslims. But the biblical story takes place in the Middle East, and Israel had frequent contact with such countries as Egypt, Assyria (now Iraq), Babylon (now Iraq), Syria, Ammon (now Jordan), Libya, Cush (now Sudan), and Persia (now Iran). These countries frequently show up in biblical prophecy, both in regard to judgment (e.g., for what they did to Israel) and in regard to future salvation.

For example, in Isaiah 19:1–18 the prophet announces judgment on the nation of Egypt. But in 19:19–25 he paints a future picture in which Egypt turns to God (the God of the Bible) and worships him. As part of that future God declares, "Blessed be Egypt, my people" (19:25).

At the time of Isaiah, the two most powerful nations in the world were Assyria to the north and Egypt to the south. Israel was caught between these two geopolitical superpowers. But as Isaiah looks to the future time of restoration and the coming of the Messiah, he declares that a road will be built connecting Egypt and Assyria so that they can worship the LORD together (Isa. 19:25).

Likewise, when Isaiah refers to the Messiah as the light to the nations, without doubt many of the nations that he had in mind were those of the Old Testament world, such as Egypt, Assyria, Libya, and so on. So while Islam is not mentioned in the Bible, numerous regions and countries are mentioned that are now Islamic. One of the clear future pictures of these areas that the prophets portray is that there will be a turning to the LORD and that these lands will be part of those nations that stream to Jerusalem to worship God.

Moreover, for much of the latter half of the twentieth century and even up to today, many popular writers have maintained that there is an Islamic connection in Ezekiel 38. Some of these writers argue that Gog in Ezekiel 38 represents Russia and that all of Gog's allies are Islamic countries. Thus these writers conclude that Ezekiel 38 describes an imminent invasion of Israel to be carried out by Russia with Islamic allies (Turkey, Sudan, Libya, Iran). However, most Old Testament scholars note that the terms Gog or Magog have nothing to do with Russia (see GOG AND MAGOG).

Furthermore, from the second half of the twentieth century up until today, Turkey has been part of NATO, not an ally of Russia (see TURKEY). At the present time Turkey is trying to join the European Union and thus is seeking tighter alliances with the West, not with the Russians. Things can change radically, of course, but for the present, the current world situation does not seem to correlate with the interpretation that sees Ezekiel 38 as describing an imminent attack against Israel by a Russian-led Muslim coalition that includes Turkey.

Israel, Modern State of

The modern state of Israel came into existence in 1948. This reemergence of Israel as a political entity has had a huge impact on the interpretation of biblical prophecy. For nearly two thousand years there was no political state known as Israel in the land of Palestine. During that time, most Christians assumed that the Old Testament prophecies about a restored Israel in their traditional land were to be understood figuratively or symbolically. That is, those prophecies were either fulfilled through the church (the new Israel; see AMILLENNIALISM) or through the return of the exiles under Ezra and Nehemiah.

However, when a literal state of Israel was established in 1948, many Christians began to reconsider the Old Testament prophecies about Israel and concluded that these prophecies would be fulfilled literally in a political state of Israel. This event provided a tremendous impetus to the rising popularity of premillennialism in general and dispensationalism in particular (see DISPENSATIONALISM, CLASSIC; PREMILLENNIALISM, HISTORIC).

History

Soon after the death of Solomon (922 B.C.), a civil war broke out and the nation of Israel split along tribal lines into two countries: Israel in the north and Judah in the south. Because of apostasy and flagrant covenant disobedience, the northern kingdom of Israel fell to the Assyrians in 722 B.C. and the southern kingdom of Judah fell to the Babylonians in 587/586 B.C. Both of these defeats resulted in forced, large-scale exiles of the Jewish population.

Later during the time of Ezra and Nehemiah, a significant number of Jews migrated back to Palestine, but they continued to remain under foreign domination. Moreover, the vast majority of Jews stayed in other countries. At the time of Christ, the Jews in Palestine were living in a province called Judea that was ruled by Rome. There were approximately 2.5 million Jews living in Palestine at that time, while approximately four to six million lived in other countries throughout the Mediterranean and the Mesopotamian areas.

In A.D. 66 the Jews in Judea rebelled against Rome. The rebellion was crushed ruthlessly and over 600,000 Jews were killed. Most of Jerusalem was destroyed in A.D. 70. Hundreds of thousands fled the country. Just as the Jews were recovering from this, they rebelled against Rome again (A.D. 135). Once more the Romans responded with brutal force, killing over 850,000 Jews and totally destroying Jerusalem, which the Romans then rebuilt as a Hellenized (Greek culture) city, complete with pagan temples. Thousands of Jews fled and any kind of Jewish political entity in Palestine disappeared.

Seventeen hundred years later, toward the end of the eighteenth century, several prominent Jews began writing and organizing with the goal of implementing a mass migration of Jews back to Palestine and the consequent creation of a Jewish state (Israel). This movement was called Zionism (see ZIONISM). In 1917 this movement convinced the British government to write the Balfour Declaration (see BALFOUR DECLARATION), which favored the establishment of a national home for the Jews in Palestine. This document also stated that such an establishment was to be done without infringing on the civil rights of the current inhabitants, the Arab majority who lived in Palestine at that time. Keep in mind that during World War I the British also promised their Arab allies an Arab state in Palestine.

Throughout the first half of the twentieth century Jews immigrated to Palestine by the thousands, often illegally. This immigration was fueled by rising anti-Semitism in Russia and in Europe. The Russian pogroms of the early twentieth century and the rise of Nazism to power in Europe sent hundreds of thousands of Russian and European Jews to Palestine. By the 1920s the Arabs, who still constituted over 85 percent of the population in Palestine, became increasingly alarmed and began vigorously opposing the immigration. Serious violence broke out in 1936.

At the end of World War II the British were in control of Palestine. They quickly passed the responsibility for what to do with the troubled area to the newly formed United Nations. The U.N. made Palestine into a temporary British Mandate, which was to end on May 14, 1948. In part because of the sympathy toward the Jews because of the Holocaust, the movement to create a Jewish state in Palestine began to gain momentum. In 1947 the U.N. decided to partition Palestine into a Jewish state and an Arab state. At the time the U.N. partition plan was proposed, the Arabs in Palestine outnumbered the Jews two to one, and they owned 90 percent of the land. Under the partition plan, however, the Jews were to be given 55 percent of the land. The Arabs, therefore, viewed the U.N. partition plan as unfair, and they refused to accept it.[55]

Although there were many Arabs and Jews who tried to work out a compromise that would create a country where both Jews and Arabs could live and work together peacefully, those with more radical and separatist views prevailed. Unable to work out a compromise, and under frequent terrorist attacks, particularly from radical Jewish Zionists, the British withdrew their military forces when the Mandate ended, without having worked out any kind of solution. Thus on May 15, 1948, the Jews proclaimed the formation of the new state of Israel, and war immediately broke out between the Arabs and Jews. Hundreds of thousands of Arab villagers fled Palestine. The U.N. Partition Plan was abandoned, and when the war ended in an uneasy ceasefire, the Jews controlled considerably more territory that the U.N. Partition Plan had delineated. This area has been in constant turmoil ever since.

Views Regarding the Modern State of Israel in Biblical Prophecy

One of the more popular views among Christians in the United States and Canada is that the creation of the modern state of Israel is a literal fulfillment of Old Testament prophecy. In this view, a literal understanding of the Old Testament prophecies of the end times demands a physical state of Israel in Palestine; thus the creation of this state after hundreds of years is seen not only as a fulfillment, but as a sign that the end times are drawing near.

Many writers, primarily classic dispensationalists, state that with the formation of modern Israel, the world political stage is set for the unfolding of end-time events (see DISPENSATIONALISM, CLASSICAL). Some early writers went so far as to argue that when Israel was created in 1948, an end-times "time clock" began that would be fulfilled within one generation. They derived this understanding primarily from Mark 13:30, where after speaking of the end times, Jesus stated that "this generation will not pass away until all these things have happened." Some writers believed that the end would come before 1988, or forty years (i.e., one generation) after 1948.

However, not all dispensationalists took this view, and as time passes, more and more writers are backing off from connecting the literal generation of Mark 13:30 to the 1948 creation of Israel. Yet many still believe strongly that the current state of Israel will play a significant role in the fulfillment of end-times prophecy, and that the creation of a modern Israel does still signal that the stage is set and that the other end-time events may begin unfolding at any time.

Another view of how modern Israel fits into biblical prophecy urges caution in jumping to end-time conclusions regarding the events of 1948. Some dispensationalists and other premillennialists note that the present state of Israel *may or may not* play a role in the end times or be a sign that the end times are imminent. They note that Israel was disobedient to God in the Old Testament and thus lost the land. Moreover, Israel rejected Jesus the Messiah in the first century, and thus once again the Jews were scattered and exiled, losing the land. The modern state of Israel, they point out, is one of the most hostile countries to the gospel message in the world today. The Jews in Israel today continue to reject God's Messiah. Thus, these Christian writers urge caution regarding the role of modern Israel in prophecy fulfillment. Who is to say that God can't remove the Jews from the Promised Land for disobedience in the future just as he did in the past? Who is to say that God won't judge their lack of justice and righteousness just as he did during the time of Jeremiah?

A third popular view regarding the modern state of Israel is that of amillennialism (see AMILLENNIALISM). Those who hold this view understand the church today to be the "new Israel" and thus maintain that the church fulfills the Old Testament prophecies regarding the regathering and restoration of Israel. Those holding this viewpoint argue that the formation of the modern state of Israel has no bearing at all on the Christian understanding of biblical prophecy.

Jeremiah, Book of

Jeremiah, one of the Major Prophets (see MAJOR PROPHETS), is a large book that makes a huge contribution to biblical prophecy. Indeed, Jeremiah is often regarded as the classic and typical prophetic book. That is, Jeremiah presents the central, basic prophetic themes of the Old Testament. These themes revolve around three main points that God declares to Israel/Judah through the prophets:

1. You have broken the Mosaic Covenant (see MOSES); repent immediately!
2. Since you won't repent, judgment is coming.
3. Beyond the judgment, there is coming a wonderful time of restoration and blessing through the coming Messiah.

Much of Jeremiah deals with points 1 and 2. The prophet illustrates how seriously Judah has violated the Mosaic Covenant. He also pleads repeatedly for the people to repent. However, since they ignore the calls for repentance and stubbornly continue to sin (idolatry and social injustice), Jeremiah describes the terrible coming judgment (the Babylonian invasion). Yet he also includes an extended prophetic picture of the future messianic age. His prophecies of this time can be found in three central passages: Jeremiah 3:14–18; 23:1–8; and chapters 30–33.

Jeremiah 3:14–18
In the middle of a call to repentance (Jer. 3), Jeremiah inserts a radical picture of future restoration. The most remarkable aspect of this prophecy

regards the Ark of the Covenant (see ARK OF THE COVENANT). Jeremiah proclaims that the ark will be gone and forgotten (3:16–17), reflecting a remarkable change. Two strands of thought come together here, for the Ark of the Covenant carried two major nuances. (1) It was the container for the Decalogue (the Ten Commandments) and thus represented the Mosaic Covenant. (2) The ark represented God's presence and the throne of the Lord—the place where the Lord sat and reigned.

In regard to the Old Covenant nuance, this passage foreshadows the replacement of the Old Covenant by the New Covenant of Jeremiah 31. Compare, for example, the statement in 3:16 ("it will never enter their minds") with 31:33: "I will put my law in their minds and write it on their hearts." The second element lost with the ark concerns the LORD's throne, and this is addressed in 3:17, where Jeremiah declares that Jerusalem herself will become the throne of the LORD. The ark, a mere symbol of that throne, will not even be missed when the LORD himself actually reigns in the city. This theme is picked up and brought to its ultimate fulfillment in Revelation 21–22. (See NEW TEMPLE; PRESENCE OF GOD; REVELATION, BOOK OF.)

In a manner similar to Isaiah, Jeremiah presents a picture of the messianic age that places Jerusalem squarely at center stage. Isaiah combines the Davidic promise, a holy mountain theology, and a remnant theology that includes the Gentiles (see ISAIAH, BOOK OF; REMNANT). Jeremiah does not include the Davidic promise until Jeremiah 23 and 33, but he does present the other two concepts in Jeremiah 3. In contrast to the Davidic promise, however, in 3:17 the prophet portrays the LORD himself as the king and the entire city of Jerusalem as his throne. Not only do the Gentiles journey to the city to worship the LORD, but Israel and Judah are reunited and living in the land.

Another element that Jeremiah incorporates into his messianic picture is the concept of the LORD's name. Jeremiah declares that the nations will honor the name of the LORD (Jer. 3:17). The ark was closely related to the presence of the LORD and to his name. Jeremiah frequently uses the concept of the LORD's name in relationship to the revelation of the LORD. Jeremiah uses the phrase "the name of the LORD" fifty-one times in a variety of ways, but the majority of his usages carry revelatory connotations —that is, the LORD as he is known to people.

The significance of Jeremiah's usage of this theme in Jeremiah 3 is that he connects the name of the LORD with worship by the Gentiles. Thus, Jeremiah declares that the revelatory aspect of the LORD—his name— will dwell on earth, reigning from Jerusalem, and that Gentiles from all over the world will come to honor him. This same new revelatory aspect is also reflected in the New Covenant, where Jeremiah states that "they will all know [the LORD]" (Jer. 31:34).

Jeremiah 23:1–8

Jeremiah 23:1–8 is the second central passage that describes the coming messianic age. The passage begins with a cry of woe to the bad "shepherds" (i.e., leaders) who were scattering the Lord's flock (see SHEPHERDS). In 23:3 the remnant theme is introduced, along with a subtle change in imagery. Now the Lord is the one who has scattered the sheep, a reference to the judgment of exile. But Jeremiah then describes the Lord as the one gathering the remnant of his flock. While the term "shepherd" is not used here directly of the Lord, his actions of gathering the flock and leading them to pasture certainly reflect a shepherding imagery. As in 3:15, the Lord promises to place good shepherds over the people. The reference to shepherds is plural and perhaps refers to a godly leadership rather than messianic figures. Yet these shepherds appear to minister in a messianic-style age, one characterized by the regathering of the remnant and by peace, prosperity, and fruitfulness.

The reference to the "coming days" in Jeremiah 23:5 is a general reference to the future eschatological time and probably stresses the importance of the proclamation. The reference to a future Davidic king clearly establishes the messianic nature of this passage. This reference also brings together the images of shepherd, king, and deliverer (see DAVIDIC COVENANT).

The new image introduced at this point in Jeremiah 23:5 is that of a shoot or branch, an image that probably has Isaiah 11:1–9 as a background (see BRANCH). The picture is that of a tree cut down, but which, because of its living roots, sprouts a new shoot and begins growing again. The word used probably carried the connotations of both the vegetative sense of shoot or branch and the human sense of descendants.

The coming Davidic deliverer is given the name "the LORD Our Righteousness," which is a wordplay on the name of King Zedekiah, the unfaithful king ruling over Judah at that time. The sense of the phrase is probably that, in contrast to the prior kings, including Zedekiah, who did not rule righteously, the Messiah will be a true reflection of the LORD's righteousness.

Jeremiah 30–33

Jeremiah 30–33, often referred to as "the Book of Consolation," deals extensively with Jeremiah's prophecies regarding the coming blessings of the messianic age (see BOOK OF CONSOLATION). These chapters are characterized by several other general features. The verbal authority of God is invoked fifty-nine times ("the word of the Lord," "declares the Lord," "the Lord spoke," etc.). While this feature is present throughout Jeremiah, particularly in the poetic sections, the frequency and intensity of these references appears to increase in the Book of Consolation, stressing the authority and emphasis of this section.

Several themes relating to the messianic age run throughout the Book of Consolation. A prominent theme in the opening verses and continued throughout is the promise of restoration for both Judah and Israel in a reunified nation (Jer. 30:3, 10; 31:5–6, 8–9, 20, 27; 32:27; 33:7). The northern kingdom is referred to as Israel, Samaria, and Ephraim. The term *Israel*, while sometimes used in reference to the northern kingdom, can also refer to the united nation (30:10; 31:1–2), thus reflecting a future time of unity. This regathering theme is a continuation of the concept introduced in 3:18 and 23:8.

Closely related to the regathering motif is the theme of the restored land. Jeremiah strongly implies that Israel and Judah lost their right to the Promised Land because of disobedience. Thus the exile, as judgment, carries a special theological significance. The tradition of the land was deeply rooted in the patriarchal traditions, and Jeremiah makes many allusions to the Abrahamic promises in association with the land. The future, glorious return will thus be to "the land I gave their forefathers" (Jer. 30:3), and it will be characterized by prosperity (31:12; 32:42) and an increase of descendants (30:19; 33:22).

The land in a general sense focuses on a specific picture of Zion, the city built on the hill (see ZION). The city will be rebuilt and will honor the LORD (Jer. 30:18; 31:12, 23; 33:9). In contrast to other prophetic references, Jeremiah does not portray the city as the center of Gentile pilgrimage, nor does he allude to any rebuilding of the Temple. This time of restoration will be further characterized by joy and joyful gatherings, in contrast to the times of judgment presented earlier, in which the absence of joy and joyful gatherings such as weddings were specifically excluded. The new era will be characterized by songs of thanksgiving and the sound of rejoicing (30:19), the dancing of maidens (31:13), and the sound of the wedding feast (33:11).

Perhaps the most significant contribution that Jeremiah makes to the study of Old Testament prophecy is his description of the New Covenant. Nowhere else in the Old Testament is a "new covenant" specifically mentioned. The New Testament, in both the Gospels and the letters, clearly identifies the new era inaugurated by Christ with the New Covenant of Jeremiah 31:31–33 (see Matt. 26:28; Mark 14:24; Luke 22:20; Heb. 8–10).

This prophecy announces that the messianic age will not be limited to political and physical restoration, but will incorporate spiritual restoration as well. In so doing, however, the LORD presents something "new"—a theme also proclaimed by Isaiah. The concept of a New Covenant adds an additional parallel between the biblical story of the exodus and the future restoration. The old exodus climaxed in the giving of the Old Covenant. The "new" exodus likewise climaxes in the giving of the New Covenant (see NEW EXODUS).

That the Old Covenant was passing away was implied in Jeremiah 3:16, where the ark is described as "it will not be missed." In addition, 11:10 and 31:32 refer to the Old Covenant as "broken" (i.e., annulled). Part of the messianic picture Jeremiah presents is a time when the Old Covenant that Israel/Judah broke will be replaced with the New Covenant. Hebrews 8–10 expounds at length on this same theme, quoting directly from Jeremiah 31.

At the heart of the Old Covenant relationship was the concept embodied in the formula, "I will ... be your God, and you will be my people" (Lev. 26:12; Deut. 27:9; cf. Ex. 6:7). Jeremiah's New Covenant reflects continuity with the Old Covenant by using the same formula (Jer. 31:33). The relationship between the LORD and his people will be reestablished using the most basic of definitions. Jeremiah makes similar statements throughout the book (7:23; 11:4; 30:22; 31:1).

However, Jeremiah's New Covenant presents a striking contrast to the old one in several respects. The Old Covenant was written in stone, but the New Covenant will be written on the people's hearts (Jer. 31:33). Thus Jeremiah presents a theological change from focusing on external law and external obedience to focusing on internal law and internal obedience. Likewise, knowing the LORD—a concept with strong soteriological associations—will be the characterizing feature of all people under the New Covenant.

Jerusalem

The first reference to Jerusalem is probably in Genesis 14:18. After Abraham defeats four kings and recovers Lot and the people of Sodom, Melchizedek, a priest of the Most High, comes out and blesses Abraham. Melchizedek is called the "king of Salem," which is probably an early reference to the city of Jerusalem. Because Melchizedek's name means "king of righteousness," because he is said to be both priest and king, and because he apparently comes from Jerusalem, some interpreters view him as a prophetic "type" of Messiah (see MELCHIZEDEK; TYPOLOGY).

After this event Jerusalem does not play a significant role in the Old Testament story until David captures it from the Jebusites in 2 Samuel 5. David captures the "fortress of Zion," apparently a reference to the fortress built on the southernmost point of the ridge that later becomes the Temple Mount. The area around this fortress then becomes known as "the City of David." Later, when Solomon expands the city and builds the Temple just to the north of the "City of David," Zion is applied to both the Temple Mount and to the city of Jerusalem. Thus "Zion" and "Jerusalem" are often used interchangeably (see ZION).

In 2 Samuel 6 David brings the Ark of the Covenant to Jerusalem and establishes the capital of the new monarchy there. In 2 Samuel 7, God speaks to David through the prophet Nathan and establishes the Davidic Covenant with him (see DAVIDIC COVENANT). Connected to the establishment of the Davidic dynasty is the promise that God's Name will be associated with the Temple to be built in Jerusalem.

After Solomon builds the Temple (1 Kings 6–8), the glory of the LORD comes and fills it in order to dwell there (1 Kings 8:11). Although Jerusalem was the capital of Israel/Judah and thus plays an important historical role in the history of Israel, it is the dwelling presence of God in the Temple in Jerusalem that gives the city prophetic significance. Thus in much of the Old Testament prophetic literature, Jerusalem is closely associated with the Temple, the Davidic dynasty, and the presence of God (see PRESENCE OF GOD).

But by the time of Jeremiah, the leaders and people of Jerusalem have turned away from God and have shattered the Mosaic Covenant that God had given them to live by (see MOSES). Apparently some people thought God would always protect Jerusalem because of the Temple, in spite of their disobedience. The prophets, however, correct this gross misunderstanding and proclaim clearly that because of disobedience and covenant violation, God will actually become the enemy of Jerusalem (Jer. 21:4–7) and the city will be violently destroyed by the Babylonians (26:18).

In fact, messages of judgment directed against Jerusalem are a major theme in the prophets. Micah 3 is typical. The prophet indicts the unjust and unfaithful leaders of Israel and then proclaims judgment on Jerusalem: "Therefore because of you, Zion will be plowed like a field, Jerusalem will become a heap of rubble, the temple hill a mound overgrown with thickets" (Mic. 3:12). Eventually the sin of those living in Jerusalem drives God away, and Ezekiel 10 describes the departure of God from Jerusalem and the Temple. Soon afterward, as the prophets predicted, the Babylonians capture Jerusalem and destroy it (2 Kings 25; Jer. 52).

However, when the prophets look beyond judgment and the Babylonian invasion to the future time of restoration and the establishment of a just and righteous reign of God in the messianic age, they frequently include references to Jerusalem in their descriptions of that glorious future age (Isa. 44:26–28; 52:1–10; Joel 2:28–3:21). In Zechariah 8:3, for example, the LORD declares, "I will return to Zion and dwell in Jerusalem. Then Jerusalem will be called the City of Truth, and the mountains of the LORD Almighty will be called the Holy Mountain."

Yet as the prophets declare the future glorious reign of God in Jerusalem, new elements begin to emerge. Things will be different. The restoration of Jerusalem will not be a return to the way things were. Everything, including the city and especially the Temple, will be different—and better. For example, the prophets refer to a stream of water flowing out of the future Temple in Jerusalem, giving life (Ezek. 47:1–12; Joel 3:18; Zech. 14:8). Likewise, a central feature of this new Jerusalem is the powerful presence of God.

Ezekiel 40–48 describes this eschatological new Temple in the new Jerusalem. In these chapters, however, the prophet is careful not to call the city Jerusalem. He keeps the name of the city in suspense until the very end. The last verse of Ezekiel reads, "And the name of the city from that time on will be, 'The LORD is there.'" Once again, the presence of God is one of the main stressed features of the future city (see PRESENCE OF GOD).

The New Testament connects integrally into the Old Testament message regarding Jerusalem. In the Gospels Jerusalem and her leaders are the representative symbol of Israel's hostile opposition to and rejection of the Messiah. As Jeremiah mourned over the coming judgment on Jerusalem because of her rejection of God, so Jesus cries out in similar fashion, "O Jerusalem, Jerusalem, you who kill the prophets and stone those sent to you, how often I have longed to gather your children together, as a hen gathers her chicks under her wings, but you were not willing! Look, your house is left to you desolate" (Luke 13:34–35).

In fact, Jesus declares judgment on Jerusalem several times (Luke 19:41–44; 21:20–24). Sounding much like the Old Testament prophets, Jesus describes the coming violent destruction of the city: "They will dash you to the ground, you and your children within your walls. They will not leave one stone on another, because you did not recognize the time of

God's coming to you" (19:44). Indeed, in fulfillment of these prophecies the Romans destroy Jerusalem and the Temple in A.D. 70 (see DESTRUCTION OF THE JERUSALEM TEMPLE [A.D. 70]).

Keep in mind that Jerusalem had become a special blessed place in the Old Testament because of its connection to the Davidic Covenant and its role as the place of God's special presence. There was nothing inherently worthy or special about the physical city apart from its connection to God's rule (through a righteous, Davidic king) and God's presence. Thus, numerous theological ironies surface when Jesus is rejected and killed by "Jerusalem."

Jerusalem was "the city of the king," where the descendants of David were to rule, but Jesus was the true Davidic King. Jerusalem was the place of God's presence, but Jesus was Immanuel, the true presence of God. Jerusalem was the place of sacrifice to God, but Jesus was the ultimate final sacrifice, who ended the entire sacrificial system, and indeed, the relevance of the existing physical Temple. Thus in all aspects, everything that made Jerusalem theologically and prophetically significant was epitomized in Jesus.

Yet the idea of a future, glorious "Jerusalem" continued. Confirming what the Old Testament prophets had declared, the New Testament writers underscore that the coming Jerusalem will be new and better. Scholars today disagree as to the nature of this new Jerusalem (see NEW JERUSALEM). Will a new, literal, physical Temple of mortar and stone be built on the current Temple Mount location in the historical city of Jerusalem? Or are the references to the New Jerusalem figurative and/or symbolic? Scholars remain divided on this issue.

The writer of Hebrews tells readers that just as Jesus went outside the city (Jerusalem) to be killed, so we must go outside the city to him. Then the writer explains, "For here we do not have an enduring city, but we are looking for the city that is to come" (Heb. 13:12–14).

Ultimately, the many prophecies about the future Jerusalem find fulfillment in Revelation 21–22. "I saw the Holy City, the new Jerusalem, coming down out of heaven from God, prepared as a bride beautifully dressed for her husband. And I heard a loud voice from the throne saying, 'Now the dwelling of God is with men ...'" (21:2–3). John's description of the new Jerusalem is similar to that of Ezekiel 40–48. As in the Old Testament prophecies, in Revelation 21–22 there is a river of life flowing out of the throne. In this new city, however, there is no Temple, because "the Lord God Almighty and the Lamb are its temple" (21:22; see NEW JERUSALEM).

Jesse, Root of

Jesse was the father of David and is mentioned numerous times in 1 Samuel 16–17. Thus, prophecies regarding the "root," "branch," or "shoot" of Jesse refer to a descendant of David as well. All three words, used in Isaiah 11:1 and 10, are figures of speech referring to descendants.

Isaiah 11:1 refers to the coming deliverer (the Messiah) as a "shoot from the stump of Jesse; from his roots a Branch." This prophecy emphasizes that the Messiah will be a righteous and just king who will be concerned for the weak and weary, the needy and the poor (11:1–9). Isaiah 11:10 declares that the "Root of Jesse will stand as a banner for the peoples; the nations will rally to him." The Messiah will be the one who gathers both Israel and the Gentile nations to God. Isaiah's strong identification of the Messiah with the lineage of David demonstrates how clearly he understands that the Messiah will come in fulfillment of the Davidic Covenant in 2 Samuel 7 (see DAVIDIC COVENANT).

The book of Revelation uses similar terminology, twice referring to Jesus as "the Root of David" (Rev. 5:5; cf. 22:16).

Jezebel

Jezebel was the daughter of Ethbaal, the priest king of the Sidonians (1 Kings 16:31) and wife of King Ahab of Israel, who ruled from approximately 874 to 853 B.C. She had a negative influence on Israel because of her commitment to Baal worship. She convinced Ahab to build a temple to Baal in Samaria (1 Kings 16:32). Four hundred and fifty prophets of Baal and four hundred prophets of Asherah ate at "Jezebel's table" (18:19), and she aggressively opposed the Lord's prophets, killing a number of them (18:4, 13).

After God gave Elijah the victory over these prophets and prophetesses on Mount Carmel, Jezebel threatened his life and caused him to flee (1 Kings 19). In one incident recorded in 1 Kings 21, Jezebel had a man named Naboth unjustly put to death in order to obtain his vineyard for her husband, Ahab. Later King Jehu of Judah had Jezebel thrown down from the palace window, and he drove over her body with his chariot (2 Kings 9:30–37). This incident fulfilled the earlier prophecies that dogs would devour Jezebel's body at Jezreel (1 Kings 21:23; 2 Kings 9:10).

The book of Revelation draws on this Old Testament background. In the message to the church of Thyatira, the self-proclaimed "prophetess" Jezebel was misleading Christians "into sexual immorality and the eating of food sacrificed to idols" (Rev. 2:20). Jesus promises to "cast her on a bed of suffering" and "strike her children dead," a fitting judgment for leading God's people into spiritual adultery (Rev. 2:22–23). Also, the way Revelation portrays Babylon the prostitute is reminiscent of the original harlotry of Jezebel. (See BABYLON/BABYLONIANS; EPHESUS; NICOLAITANS; PERGAMUM; THYATIRA.)

Joel, Book of

The prophet Joel is not mentioned anywhere else in the Old Testament outside the book of Joel, and thus little is known about him. Likewise, the book has no indication of the time period in which it was written. Unlike many of the other prophetic books, no Israelite or Judahite kings are mentioned that allow scholars to date the book with precision. Based only on the content of the book, most scholars assume that the book was written just prior to either the Assyrian invasion of Israel (late eighth century B.C.) or to the Babylonian invasion of Judah (late seventh to early sixth century B.C.).

Twice Joel describes a terrible locust plague (Joel 1:2–20; 2:1–17). Scholars are divided over how to interpret the two descriptions. However, one of the more plausible understandings is to view the first description (1:2–20) as that of a literal locust plague that was coming (in the near future?), and the second description (2:1–17) as a figurative description using locusts to represent either the Assyrians or the Babylonians coming later. Note that locust plagues were one of the curses God warned Israel about in Deuteronomy 28:38, 42.

One of the most remarkable themes in Joel is that he prophesies the outpouring of God's Spirit on all of God's people. Only Joel and Ezekiel make this prophecy. In the Old Testament era, the Spirit of God was only given to a few special people on a few special occasions. In general, in the Old Testament the presence of God was experienced through God's dwelling in the Tabernacle or Temple (see PRESENCE OF GOD).

People in the Old Testament did not normally experience the indwelling Spirit. In Joel 2:28–32 the prophet makes a radical new prophecy, stating that in the coming Day of the LORD, God will pour out his Spirit on all of his people, young and old, men and women alike (see DAY OF THE LORD). This prophecy was fulfilled on the Day of Pentecost, when the Holy Spirit fell on the disciples in Jerusalem. In Acts 2:14–21 Peter states explicitly that the outpouring of the Spirit the disciples had just experienced at Pentecost was a fulfillment of Joel 2:28–32 (see SPIRIT).

Joel also describes spectacular astronomical signs in 2:30–31, probably to be associated with judgment on the Day of the LORD (see ASTRONOMICAL SIGNS). Then Joel declares, "And everyone who calls on the name of the LORD will be saved" (Joel 2:32). In Romans 10:13 Paul cites this verse to demonstrate that both Jew and Gentile will experience God's salvation.

John, Book of

In general, Jesus' teachings on the kingdom of God and the end times can best be understood through the concept of "already-not yet." That is, with the first coming of Christ many aspects of the "kingdom of God" came into reality. Yet the total and complete fulfillment still lay in the future, to be brought to completion through the second coming of Christ (see ALREADY-NOT YET).

Although the Gospel of John contains both the present ("already") aspect and the future ("not yet") aspect, John's clear focus is on the present ("already"). This emphasis on the "already" can be seen in several areas:

(1) Eternal life, or entrance into the kingdom of God, is a present possession (John 3:5–6, 36; 6:47, 51, 58; 8:51; 10:28; 11:24–26).

(2) The eschatological promise of sonship is granted to the believer in Jesus now (John 1:12–13; 3:3–8; 4:14).

(3) The general resurrection has already begun (John 5:25).

(4) The Spirit, the gift of the end times, currently indwells believers (John 7:37–39; 14:15–31; 15:26–27; 16:5–16; 20:22–23).

(5) The Judgment Day is determined by one's present response to Jesus (John 3:19; 5:22–24, 27, 30–38; 9:38; 12:31–33).

(6) The spirit of anti-Christ has already entered the world scene to oppose Christ (John 6:70; 13:2, 27; 14:13).

(7) Jesus' death on the cross seems to absorb some elements of the messianic woes or aspects of tribulation. In other words, Jesus' passion is where the end-time holy war was raged, and his death and resurrection begins the end of the forces of evil (John 15:18–16:11) (see CROSS AND THE MESSIANIC WOES).

But the Gospel of John also includes some typical future ("not yet") aspects of eschatology. For example, within this Gospel the future resurrection is still expected (John 5:26–30). Likewise, the second coming of Christ is alluded to (14:1–4; 21:22).

Another interesting aspect of eschatology in the Gospel of John is that it focuses more on the spatial/vertical movement between heaven and earth than on historical/linear movement through time. Raymond Brown summarizes the frequent reference to the spatial/vertical movement in John:

> In many ways this Gospel betrays a vertical approach to salvation. The Son of Man has come down from heaven (3:13), the Word has become flesh (1:14), with the purpose of offering salvation to men. The culmination of his career is when he is lifted up toward heaven in death and resurrection to draw all men to himself (12:32). There is a constant contrast in John between two worlds: one above, the other below (3:3, 31, 8:23); a sphere that belongs to Spirit, and a sphere that belongs to flesh (3:6, 6:63). Jesus brings the life of the other world, "eternal life," to the men of this world; and death has no power over this life (11:25). His gifts are "real" gifts, that is, heavenly gifts: the real water of life, as contrasted with ordinary water (4:10–14); the real bread of life, as contrasted with perishable bread (6:27); he is the real light that has come into the world (3:19).[56]

But, as Brown goes on to point out, the historical/linear movement of eschatology through time is not missing in John. Thus the Prologue (John 1:1–18) proclaims Jesus' incarnation to be God's climactic intervention in history. At the other end of the spectrum, the "hour" appointed for Jesus' death (e.g., 2:4; 8:20; 12:23) represents the culmination of God's plan of salvation history. This end of history is accompanied by the time of the church, whose persecution (15:18–16:4) and evangelistic mission (4:35–38; 20:20) hasten the return of Christ.

John the Baptist

John the Baptist was the forerunner of Jesus the Messiah, on the analogy of Elijah the prophet (Mal. 3:4) (see ELIJAH). John was of priestly descent (Luke 1:6), and some scholars suggest that he may have been raised by the Essenes, the people who produced most of the Dead Sea Scrolls (see DEAD SEA SCROLLS). John was filled with the Spirit while still in his mother's womb (1:15), thus signaling his prophetic vocation.

John began his public ministry in about A.D. 26 or 27, preaching near the Jordan River and calling Jews to repentance in order to prepare themselves for the coming kingdom of God and the outpouring of the Holy Spirit (Mark 1:2–8; see KINGDOM OF GOD). To that end, John baptized Jesus in the Jordan and witnessed the descent of the Spirit on him (Mark 1:9–11). This prompted John to identify his cousin Jesus with the Lamb of God (John 1:29). John was soon thereafter imprisoned and beheaded for confronting Herod Antipas for marrying Herodias, his brother's wife

(Mark 6:14–28). Even during the time of Paul's missionary journeys, John still had a following (Acts 19:1–7).

John was a transitional figure, tying the Old and New Testament together. He came in the tradition of the Old Testament prophets; yet after identifying Jesus as the Christ, he recedes into the background.

Jonah, Book of

The book of Jonah does not provide any connections to ruling kings that help to date it. However, 2 Kings 14:25 refers to a prophet named Jonah who prophesied at the approximate time of Jeroboam II (793–753 B.C.). It is probable that this Jonah is the same prophet who features as the main character in the book of Jonah.

The story of Jonah is well known. God tells Jonah to go to Nineveh, the capital of Assyria, and to preach judgment against the people living there. Jonah refuses at first, but after trying to flee and after being swallowed by a great fish, he eventually goes to Nineveh and briefly proclaims judgment on them. Remarkably, the Ninevites, from the king to the lowliest person, humble themselves and repent. God therefore relents from the judgment that Jonah has preached (see CONDITIONAL PROPHECY). Jonah gets upset over God's forgiveness of Nineveh and the book ends with God rebuking Jonah over the prophet's lack of compassion.

This book differs from many of the other prophetic books of the Old Testament in that Jonah preaches to foreigners (the Assyrians), not to the Israelites. Thus there are allusions in this book to the Gentile inclusion prophesied by other prophets such as Isaiah (see ISAIAH, BOOK OF). However, the major function of this book is to highlight the obstinacy and hardheadedness of Israel in their refusal to repent. That is, the other prophets preach repeatedly to Israel and get no response. No one listens and no one repents. Jeremiah, for example, preaches for years and years in Jerusalem, but both the king and the people reject his message. The Assyrians in Nineveh, by contrast, hear Jonah's brief, half-hearted message, and all of them repent. The point is that if the people of Nineveh (the Assyrians) can hear God's word and respond with repentance, why then can't Israel? Thus Jonah further underscores the guilt and culpability of Israel, who, because of repeated idolatry and the refusal to repent, are conquered and exiled by these same Assyrians.

In the New Testament, when the Pharisees and teachers of the law ask Jesus for a sign, he rebukes them and tells them that the only sign given to them will be "the sign of the prophet Jonah" (Matt. 12:38–41; 16:4; Luke

11:29–32). Jesus then connects with the story of Jonah in two respects. (1) Jesus states that just as Jonah was in the fish three days and three nights, so the Son of Man will be in the earth three days and three nights (Matt. 12:40). In other words, Jesus sees the book of Jonah as prophetic of his resurrection.

(2) Jesus points to the testimony of the people of Nineveh, who repented when they heard Jonah's message (Matt. 12:41; Luke 11:32). Jesus is a greater prophet than Jonah; thus, the Israelites of Jesus' day should certainly listen to him and repent. As in Jonah's day, however, Israel refuses to hear God's prophet and repent. Just as the repentance of the Ninevites highlighted the obstinacy of the Israelites in Jonah's day, leading to judgment, so that same repentance highlights the obstinacy of Israel in Jesus' day, likewise leading to judgment.

Judgment

Judgment is God's evaluation of human beings according to the standard of his own holy and righteous character. More specifically, judgment may refer to the Judgment Day when God through Christ will judge every person, believer and unbeliever, according to their behavior (including their response to Jesus Christ), and then will assign their destinies.

Judgment flows from the nature of God. Because God is holy and just, he must condemn evil. Because he is love, he gives people the freedom to make choices, all of which he treats as significant, especially the decision to accept or reject his love demonstrated in Christ. Since God created the world, he has the right to carry out his original purposes in creation. Judgment is God's way of redeeming creation and setting things right once again.

For instance, one of the central symbols in Revelation is God's throne (Rev. 4:9; 5:1, 7, 13; 6:16; 7:15; 21:5; cf. 4:2–3; 7:10; 19:4; 20:11), which signifies God's sovereignty. The great white throne of God appears as the central image in the final judgment of 20:11–15. As the ultimate authority, God is the standard of all true justice. (See GREAT WHITE THRONE JUDGMENT.)

The judgments of God appear both within history and at the end of this age. Throughout this age God has judged cities and nations (e.g., Sodom and Gomorrah, Egypt, Judah, Jerusalem) as well as individuals (e.g., Pharaoh in Egypt, King Saul, Queen Jezebel, Ananias and Sapphira). His partial judgments throughout history are often seen as merciful warnings for people to renounce idolatry and worship God (e.g., Amos

4:6–13; Rom. 1:18–2:4). The present judgment of God also anticipates a final judgment, when he will destroy his enemies and vindicate his people (Rev. 19:1–2).

The basis of judgment is a person's relationship with God reflected in his or her deeds, actions, or works (see Matt. 16:27; 25:34–36; John 5:28–29; Rom. 2:6; 2 Cor. 5:10; Rev. 20:12–13). What a person thinks, speaks, and does over time reflects one's basic direction in life. Chief among these actions is a person's decision regarding Jesus Christ. An allegiance to Jesus determines a person's ultimate destiny with God and transforms a person's way of life. This does not mean, as Leon Morris puts it, "that there are some people whose good deeds merit salvation, but that there are some whose good deeds are evidence of their salvation."[57]

Overall, the theme of judgment found throughout the Scriptures calls for spiritual preparedness. In Jesus' Olivet Discourse (Matt. 24–25; Mark 13; Luke 12, 17, 21), he frequently warns his hearers to "be ready," "watch out," or "be on your guard" (e.g., Matt. 24:4, 44; Mark 13:23, 33; Luke 12:40; 21:8). To be ready for the last judgment means to live in submission to Christ's lordship now. As Jesus says to the seven churches of Revelation, "He who has an ear, let him hear what the Spirit says to the churches." Following Christ and walking by the Spirit now are the best preparation for standing before the Father on the last day. (See BOOK OF LIFE; JUDGMENT SEAT OF CHRIST; LAST JUDGMENT.)

Judgment Seat of Christ

The expression "judgment seat of Christ" occurs only in 2 Corinthians 5:10: "For we must all appear before the judgment seat of Christ, that each one may receive what is due him for the things done while in the body, whether good or bad." Paul does, however, refer to "God's judgment seat" in Romans 14:10: "You, then, why do you judge your brother? Or why do you look down on your brother? For we will all stand before God's judgment seat." In both instances, Paul uses final accountability before Christ (or God) to motivate believers to renounce ungodliness (e.g., judging other believers) and to live to please their Lord.

The judgment seat itself refers to the *bēma* — the bench or platform from which public proclamations and judicial pronouncements were made. For instance, Pilate sat on the judge's seat (Matt. 27:19; John 19:13), as did Herod (Acts 12:21) and Gallio (18:12, 16–17). Archaeologists have identified the *bēma* in Corinth where Paul himself appeared several years before writing 2 Corinthians.

Since Paul is writing to Christians in both 2 Corinthians and Romans, the phrase "we all" (including Paul himself) suggests that believers will appear before Christ's judgment seat. Whether it will only be believers is a matter of debate, but most scholars draw this conclusion.

The idea of "appear" indicates an experience of full disclosure before God rather than just showing up for a casual conversation. As Paul says clearly in 1 Corinthians 4:5, the Lord "will bring to light what is hidden in darkness and will expose the motives of men's hearts." We will not be able to disguise ourselves since Christ will see us for who we really are.

The purpose of the judgment is "that each one may receive what is due him for things done while in the body, whether good or bad." The judgment will be individualistic, with "each one" receiving back or reaping what is due him or her. The basis of judgment will be "things done while in the body," including not only actions but also speech. Paul is likely referring to the sum of a person's deeds rather than to isolated deeds — that is, to a person's character as established by their habitual action. Christ will reward a person for good deeds as well as repay them for bad deeds (see REWARDS).

The word for "bad" denotes something worthless or of no value. The parallel passage of 1 Corinthians 3:10–15 suggests that a person will be rewarded for quality workmanship (i.e., building one's life with gold, silver, and costly stones), while poor workmanship (i.e., building with materials such as wood, hay, or straw) will be destroyed even though the workman will survive "as one escaping through the flames" (3:15). The loss of reward may further define what is involved in being recompensed for bad deeds.

Paul does not specify the exact time of this judgment. The main options include: (1) immediately after the believer's death, (2) following the rapture of the church, and (3) at the return of Christ. Only one thing can be said for sure: believers will be judged when they appear before Christ.

The judgment seat of Christ focuses on the assessment of a Christian's deeds or lifestyle rather than the determination of their eternal destiny. Having been saved by grace through faith (Eph. 2:8–9), Christians are nevertheless committed to working out their faith through deeds (e.g., Gal. 5:6; Eph. 2:10; Phil. 2:12–13; 1 Thess. 1:3). Believers are accountable for individual actions and are not exempt from doing good. Eschatology and ethics are bound tightly together.

The judgment seat of Christ fulfills God's impartial justice, since not all believers live with the same degree of devotion to Christ. Christians are individually accountable for what they do in this mortal body. One day all believers will stand before their Lord, who will impartially evaluate their lives and reward them accordingly (see REWARDS). Paul knows that he too will have to stand before Christ with nothing to hide, and he will have to explain his life. This "fear of the Lord" (2 Cor. 5:11) motivates him (as it should motivate all Christians) to intensify his devotion to pleasing Christ. (See JUDGMENT; LAST JUDGMENT.)

Justice/Justification/Righteousness

The Hebrew term for "righteous" is *tsaddiq*. Its Greek counterparts are *dikaios*, which means "righteous" or "just," and *diakaioō*, which means to "justify." The fact that the same root word informs *righteousness* and *justification* is obscured in the English translation.

The meaning of the phrase "the righteousness of God" is a controversy-laden issue. There are four interpretations of this phrase:

(1) "The righteousness of God" is a possessive genitive, "God's own righteousness," with reference to divine distributive justice. This was the pre-Reformation understanding of the idea, which lent itself to the possibility that human works could merit one's standing before God.

(2) Martin Luther came to disagree strongly with the first perspective, claiming instead that the phrase is a genitive of origin: God's righteous standing is imputed to sinners through Christ. In his classic statement on the subject, Luther writes of Romans 1:17:

> For, however irreproachably I lived as a monk, I felt myself before God to be a sinner with a most unquiet conscience, nor could I be confident that I had pleased him with my satisfaction. I did not love, nay, rather I hated this righteous God who punished sinners ... At last, God being merciful ... I began to understand the justice of God as that by which the righteous man lives by the gift of God, namely by faith ... This straightway made me feel as though reborn and, as though I had entered through open gates into Paradise itself ... And now, as much as I hated the word "justice of God" before, so much the more sweetly I extolled this word to myself.[58]

3. "The righteousness of God" is a subjective genitive that encompasses both God's gift of righteousness and his power. This was the novel view offered by Ernst Käsemann, who claimed that "righteousness of God" was a technical term of late-Jewish apocalypticism for God's saving justice. As such, it reveals God's sovereign faithfulness to his covenant with Israel and to his creation, by which he brings Jews back to himself in obedience.

Thus the righteousness of God expresses both his gift of forgiveness and his power for obedience to his people, the new creation. Käsemann claimed that Paul inherited this conceptual background of the phrase and redefines it in terms of God's present reign over the world through Jesus.[59] But N. T. Wright criticizes this view as failing to note the covenantal nuance of righteousness in Second Temple Judaism.[60]

4. Wright's view is that "the righteousness of God" is a possessive genitive but with reference to God's faithfulness to his covenant with Israel. More specifically, Paul's understanding of the righteousness of God is that God has brought Israel's sin and exile to a close at the cross of Christ so that through his resurrection the covenantal blessings can now be appropriated by Jews and Gentiles alike.[61]

It is clear in the New Testament, especially in Paul and John, that one's response to Jesus in this age determines one's destiny in the age to come. Even more so, justification or condemnation has already broken into this present age for Christians and non-Christians, respectively (see, e.g., John 3:19; 5:22–24, 27, 30–38; 9:38; 12:31–33; Rom. 1:17–18; 2:5; 5:1; 8:1; 1 John 2:1–2; 3:21–24; 4:10, 13–18; 5:16).

The preceding remarks combine to show that justice/justification/righteousness are thoroughly eschatological concepts; that which Judaism expected would happen at the end of history is now occurring in history according to one's present response to Christ.

King, Messianic

One of the dominant portraits of the coming Messiah forecast in the Old Testament is that he will be a Davidic-like king (2 Sam. 7:1–17; Ps. 2:6–8; 89:26–27; Isa. 9:6–7; 11:1; Jer. 23:5–6; Ezek. 17:22; 34:23–24; 37:22–25; Mic. 5:2–5; Zech. 3:8; 6:12; 9:9–10; 12:10). That theme continues in the nonbiblical literature of Second Temple Judaism (539 B.C. to A.D. 70).

In the New Testament, especially in the Gospels, one finds the climax of prophecy regarding the coming Davidic Messiah. N. T. Wright insightfully points out three key aspects of the Gospels' presentation of Jesus as the Davidic Messiah: the anointing of Jesus as the Davidic Messiah, the confession of Jesus as the Davidic Messiah, and the presence of the kingdom of God through the words and works of Jesus, the Davidic Messiah (see KINGDOM OF GOD).

(1) All four Gospels root Jesus' prophetic ministry in his baptism (Matt. 3:13–17; Mark 1:9–11; Luke 3:21–22; John 1:29–34). It is commonly recognized that Psalm 2:7 ("you are my Son") and Isaiah 42:1 ("my chosen one in whom I delight") stand behind the voice heard at Jesus' baptism, thus attributing to him a messianic role. Beyond this, Wright makes the case, two other Old Testament passages inform Jesus' baptism — Isaiah 11:2 (the Davidic Messiah's anointing with God's Spirit) and 1 Samuel 16:13 (where the divine Spirit comes powerfully on David after being anointed by Samuel). Taken together, the preceding four Old Testament passages give the impression that the Gospels portray Jesus' baptism as his anointing as the Davidic Messiah.

(2) The Synoptic Gospels (Matthew, Mark, Luke) report that early in his ministry at Caesarea Philippi, Jesus was perceived to be the Messiah and that, although he redefined the concept (see below), Jesus accepted the title (Matt. 16:13–20; Mark 8:27–30; Luke 9:18–21). Moreover, Peter's confession of Jesus as Messiah precipitated the ensuing journey to Jerusalem. Wright draws two important conclusions from this. (a) Like David of old, Jesus was understood by his disciples to be the king-in-waiting; that is, he was anointed as the Davidic king (baptism and confession), but he was not yet enthroned as such. (b) Related to this, Jesus' journey to Jerusalem was initially interpreted by his followers as the goal of Jesus' ministry, at which point he was expected to be crowned as the Davidic Messiah.

(3) Jesus' words and works also bespeak the inauguration of the kingdom of God through him, both aspects of which are Davidic in orientation. Under the category of Jesus' words are those sayings portraying him, like King David, as Israel's shepherd (cf. Matt. 9:36; 18:12–14; 26:30; 10:6; Mark 6:34; Mark 14:27; Luke 10:3; 12:32; 15:3–7; John 10; with 2 Sam. 24:17; 1 Kings 22:17; Isa. 44:28; Ezek. 34:23–24; Zech. 11:4–17; 13:7; see SHEPHERDS).

Moreover, the claim that in Jesus one greater than Solomon was present (Matt. 12:41–42; Luke 11:31) signified that he was the Messiah who would build the eschatological Temple and establish the Davidic kingdom (see DAVIDIC COVENANT). Furthermore, Jesus' appeal to David's example of feeding his followers as an analog for Jesus' doing the same on the Sabbath (Matt. 12:3–4; Mark 2:25–28; Luke 6:3–5) conveyed his sense of Davidic royalty. Added to this is Jesus' application of Psalm 110, a hymn associated with David, to himself (Matt. 22:41–45; Mark 12:35–37; Luke 20:41–44).

The second aspect of Jesus' ministry that displayed the kingdom of God was his works, which are programmatically set forth in Luke 4:18–21, a quotation of Isaiah 61:1–3.

> "The Spirit of the Lord is on me,
> because he has anointed me
> to preach good news to the poor.
> He has sent me to proclaim release to the prisoners
> and recovery of sight for the blind,
> to release the oppressed,
> to proclaim the year of the Lord's favor."

Then he rolled up the scroll, gave it back to the attendant, and sat down. The eyes of everyone in the synagogue were fastened on him, and he began by saying to them, "Today this scripture is fulfilled in your hearing."

Wright is quite correct to argue that Isaiah 61 is an echo of Isaiah 11:1–10, a prophecy of the works of the coming Davidic king. Thus Luke 4:18–21 should be understood to present Jesus as the Davidic Messiah, who was anointed by God's Spirit to accomplish the supernatural purpose of restoring Israel from her exile.

In summation, then, Jesus' anointing at his baptism, the disciple's confession of him as Messiah, and the purported arrival of the kingdom of God through Jesus' words and works indicate that the Gospels perceived him to be the Davidic king who had come to restore Israel (see also Matt. 1:1; 9:27; 12:23; 15:22; 20:30–34; 21:9, 15; Mark 12:35–37; Acts 2:29–31; 13:23; Rom. 1:3–4; 2 Tim. 2:8; Rev. 5:5; 22:16). Jesus' presentation of himself as the Davidic Messiah took an unfamiliar turn, however, which ultimately subverted the story of Israel's restoration.

(1) Returning to the subject of the inauguration of the kingdom of God through Jesus' words and works, it is noteworthy that both categories redefine the true Israel. Thus the parables about the restoration of Israel (Matt. 13; Mark 4) invite sinners and outcasts to join the ranks of the remnant, because they follow Jesus (e.g., Luke 15). Such a message certainly sounded strange to that nation, which, at least since the Maccabean revolt, prided itself in obeying the Torah and thus separating itself from the ritually and morally unclean. The maimed, blind, lame, deaf, and dumb were not recognized as full Israelites. Wright observes that for a first-century Jew, Jesus' healing would be viewed as restoring to membership in Israel those who, because of their physical illnesses, were thought to be ritually unclean. Jesus' miracles reinforced his redefinition of those who constituted the true people of God. His healings in these categories, therefore, served not only a physical purpose but also a spiritual one. They reintegrated the marginalized into the worshiping community.

(2) Jesus' retelling of Israel's story of sin–exile–restoration involved redefining the enemy. Israel's nemesis was not Rome, but Satan. Three passages highlight this reality, as Wright points out.

(a) The Beelzebub controversy (Matt. 12:22–32; Mark 3:20–30; Luke 11:14–23) reflects the fact that the Jewish leadership, in attributing to Jesus' miracles the power of Satan, accused him of dishonoring the covenant with Yahweh (the LORD), particularly in his dismissal of the boundary markers of the Torah (Sabbath-keeping, dietary laws, circumcision) and later with his cleansing of the Temple. This was perceived as nothing less than being in league with Israel's enemies, now personified in Rome—tantamount to being in cahoots with Satan. In effect, Jesus' refutation of such an accusation redefined Israel's real enemy; his miracles were by the power of God, not Beelzebub, and in actuality were defeating the evil one, the ultimate source of Israel's struggles. To miss this was to invite natural disaster because such a misperception would inexorably lead Israel into battle with Rome, the wrong opponent.

(b) Similarly, Luke 12:4–7 (cf. Matt. 10:28–31) suggests that Israel's enemy was not Rome (the one who had the power to kill the body) but rather Satan (the one who had the power to cast the nation into Gehenna).

(c) So also the story of the attempted exorcism and the returning of seven demons (Matt. 12:43–45; Luke 11:24–26) makes the point that Israel's deliverance needed to be from Satan. That is, the nation's restoration would not come about by revolting against her physical enemies, something regrettably attempted since the Maccabeans, but rather by the expulsion of Satan.

(3) The final aspect of Jesus' retelling of the story of Israel reaches the heart of the matter: Jesus came as the *suffering* Davidic Messiah (e.g., Mark 8:31; 9:31–32; 10:32–34; see MESSIAH, SERVANT SONGS). That such a portrayal amounted to a *reversal* of messianic Jewish expectation in Second Temple Judaism is indicated not only by the disciples' shock at Jesus' prediction of his affliction but also by the fact that there was no clear concept of a suffering Messiah in pre-Christian Jewish thinking, in spite of the presence of that theme in the Old Testament prophets (see DAVID; DAVIDIC COVENANT; MESSIAH).[62]

King of the North

The "king of the north" is a title that occurs in Daniel 11 with reference to the Seleucid kings' various attempts to control Egypt and Israel from 246 B.C. to 164 B.C. The Seleucid kings mentioned in Daniel 11 follow their chronological order of appearance:

- 11:6 (Antiochus II, 261–246 B.C.)
- 11:9 (Seleucus II Callinicus, 246–226 B.C.)
- 11:10 (Seleucus III, 226–223 B.C.)
- 11:10 (Antiochus III [the Great], 223–187 B.C.)
- 11:20 (Seleucus IV Philopater, 187–175 B.C.)
- 11:21–45 (Antiochus IV Epiphanes, 175 B.C.–163 B.C.)

Scholars debate about the last-mentioned king; does Daniel 11:33–45 continue to talk about the historical Antiochus Epiphanes, or does it speak of the future Antichrist? The reason some choose the latter alternative is because the details of 11:33–45 do not fit with what is known of Antiochus Epiphanes (see ANTICHRIST; ANTIOCHUS EPIPHANES).

King of the South

Many New Testament scholars propose that the title "king of the south" in Daniel 11:5 probably refers to Ptolemy I Soter (323–285 B.C.), one of the four generals who took over a portion of Alexander the Great's empire after his death. Ptolemy became the founder of the Ptolemaic dynasty in Egypt (see ALEXANDER THE GREAT).

Several of the descendant Ptolemy rulers are apparently prophesied about in Daniel 11:6–8 as well, including the failed attempt at establishing peace between the Ptolemies and their Seleucid rivals in Syria through the marriage of Ptolemy II's daughter Berenice and King Antiochus II Theos (261–246 B.C.). Antiochus's former wife, Laodice, conspires to have the couple murdered. Ptolemy III Euergetes of Egypt (246–221 B.C.) retaliates against Laodice by doing away with her. Thus, the hostility between the Ptolemies and the Seleucids remains, and Ptolemy III attacks Syria (home of the Seleucids).

Likewise Daniel 11:9–12 appears to point prophetically to the defeat of the Seleucid King Antiochus III by Ptolemy IV Philopator (221–203 B.C.) in 217 B.C. Daniel 11:13–18 points to Antiochus III, who later regroups his army and exacts revenge against Egypt (197 B.C.). Daniel 11:19–28 alludes to the time after Antiochus III's death, when Egypt had to deal with Antiochus the Great's infamous son, Antiochus IV Epiphanes (175–164 B.C.). Finally, some suggest that 11:29–35 refers to the intervention of Roman vessels under the command of Popilius Laenas, which turned Antiochus Epiphanes back from invading Egypt, who then unleashed his frustration on Israel.

Kingdom of God

The kingdom of God is a major theme in the Bible. Its origin is the Old Testament, where the emphasis falls on God's kingship. God is king of Israel (Ex. 15:18; Num. 23:21; Deut. 33:5; Isa. 43:15) and of all the earth (2 Kings 19:15; Ps. 29:10; 99:1–4; Isa. 6:5; Jer. 46:18). Juxtaposed to the concept of God's *present* reign as king are references to a day when God will *become* king over his people (Isa. 24:23; 33:22; 52:7; Zeph. 3:15; Zech. 14:9). This emphasis on God's kingship continues throughout Judaism and takes on special significance in Jewish apocalypticism, which abandoned any hope for present history (see APOCALYPTIC LITERATURE). Only at the end of the age would the kingdom of God come.

"The kingdom of God" is a major theme throughout the New Testament. This expression occurs over a hundred times in Mark, Luke, and Matthew (where "kingdom of heaven" is a synonym for "kingdom of God"). Mark, perhaps the first Gospel to be written, records Jesus' programmatic statement in 1:15, "The time has come ... The kingdom of God is near." That Gospel, along with Luke and Matthew, then goes on to demonstrate that Jesus' miracles, teachings, death, and resurrection inaugurated the kingdom of God.

Yet, it is also clear from Matthew, Mark, and Luke that the final manifestation of the kingdom has not yet happened. Luke indicates that the kingdom was present in Jesus (Luke 7:28; 8:10; 10:9–11; 11:20; 16:16; 17:20–21), but it also awaited the return of Christ for its completion (6:20–26; 11:2; 12:49–50, 51–53; 13:24–30; 21:25–29; 22:15–18, 30). The same dual aspect of the kingdom pertains to Luke's second volume, Acts. The kingdom was present in Jesus' ministry and, now, through his disciples (Acts 1:3; 8:12; 19:8; 20:25; 28:23–31); but it will not be completed until Christ comes again (1:6; 14:22).

There are only three references to the "kingdom of God" in John's Gospel. Nicodemus is told by Jesus that he needs to be born again to enter the kingdom of God (John 3:3–5). Yet Jesus' kingdom was not worldly in nature, but spiritual—one of the heart (18:36). John's emphasis on the present aspect of the kingdom of God is portrayed as the gift of eternal life, which believers already possess (3:15–16, 36; 6:47, 51, 58; 8:51–52; 10:28; 11:24–26; cf. 1 John 2:25; 3:14; 5:11–13).

The term "kingdom of God" and/or "kingdom of Christ" occurs twelve times in Paul's writings. These are listed below:

Text	Kingdom description	Verb tense
Rom. 14:17	Kingdom of God	Present tense
1 Cor. 4:20	Kingdom of God	Present tense
1 Cor. 6:9–10	Kingdom of God (twice)	Future tense
1 Cor. 15:24	Kingdom of Christ/ God	Present and future tense

Text	Kingdom description	Verb tense
1 Cor. 15:50	Kingdom of God	Future tense
Gal. 5:21	Kingdom of God	Future tense
Eph. 5:5	Kingdom of Christ/ God	Future tense
Col. 1:13	Kingdom of Christ	Present tense
Col. 4:11	Kingdom of God	Present tense
1 Thess. 2:12	Kingdom of God	Future tense
2 Thess. 1:5	Kingdom of God	Future tense

Three observations emerge from the chart: (1) The kingdom of Christ/ God is both present and future, already here and not yet complete. This is consistent with what is in the Gospels and Acts. (2) Christ and God are, in at least two instances, interchanged, suggesting equality of status between them (cf. Eph. 5:5; Rev. 11:15; 12:10). (3) In 1 Corinthians 15:24 Paul gives the most precise description of the exact relationship between the kingdoms of Christ and God—the interim messianic kingdom begun at the resurrection of Christ will one day give way to the eternal kingdom of God. Such a temporary kingdom is attested to in apocalyptic Judaism and may be behind Revelation 20:1–6. For Paul, then, the order of history is as follows:

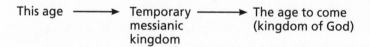

This age ⟶ Temporary messianic kingdom ⟶ The age to come (kingdom of God)

Christians therefore live in between the two ages, in the messianic kingdom.

The General Epistles and Revelation continue the theme of the already–not yet aspect of the kingdom. It is here through Christ and his followers (Heb. 1:8; Rev. 1:6, 9; 5:10; 11:15; 12:10), but only at his second coming will that kingdom be fully manifest (James 2:5; 2 Peter 1:11).

Lake of Fire

Revelation uses the expression "lake of fire" (Rev. 20:14–15) or "lake of burning sulfur" (19:20; 20:10; 21:8) to describe the final destiny of the enemies of God:

- the beast and the false prophet (19:20)
- the devil (20:10)
- death and Hades (20:14)
- anyone whose name was not written in the book of life (20:15)
- the cowardly, the unbelieving, the vile, the murderers, the sexually immoral, those who practice magic arts, the idolaters, and all liars (21:8)

The background of this image may be God's destruction of Sodom (Gen. 19:24) or Ezekiel's prophecy against Gog and Magog (Ezek. 38:22; 39:6). The image parallels Jesus' teachings related to hell (Matt. 10:28; Mark 9:43; Luke 12:5), "darkness" (Matt. 8:12; 22:13; 25:30), the "fiery furnace" (13:42), and "the eternal fire prepared for the devil and his angels" (25:41).

The "lake of fire" portrays eternal punishment and suffering (Rev. 14:10–11; 20:10) and is most vividly described as the "second death" (20:14, 15; 21:8). With the first death being physical death, the second death represents ultimate separation from the presence of God, the new creation, and the people of God. While the theme of the "lake of fire" assures persecuted believers that God will judge evil decisively, the prophetic warnings in 21:8, 27 and 22:15 confront the complacent and rebellious with the damning consequences of unrighteousness.

Lamb

The Bible uses "lamb" in both a literal and figurative sense. As a symbol of innocence, docility, and gentleness (cf. Luke 10:3), lambs were the main animals used in the Old Testament sacrificial system (e.g., Num. 28:16–27; 29:7–8, 13–28). When God delivered Israel from captivity in Egypt, the blood of an unblemished lamb spread on the doorframe protected those who lived in the house (Ex. 12:1–13). When the Lord passed over, no destructive plague harmed those protected by the blood of the lamb.

The symbolic use of the word "lamb" in the New Testament concentrates on Jesus, the "Lamb of God" (John 1:29, 36). The primary background for this image of Jesus as the Lamb was the Passover lamb, although some see a connection to the Suffering Servant as a lamb in Isaiah 53 (Acts 8:32).

The image of Jesus as the Lamb is developed most fully in Revelation, where the term occurs twenty-nine of thirty-five times in the New Testament. The Lamb is worthy to open the scroll and execute God's plan because, while very much alive, the Lamb has been slain—a clear reference to the sacrificial death of Christ (Rev. 5:6, 9, 12; 7:14; 13:8). The sacrifice of Christ provides the source for the spiritual defeat of Satan: "They overcame him by the blood of the Lamb and by the word of their testimony; they did not love their lives so much as to shrink from death" (12:11). In a later vision just before the bowl judgments are poured out, the victorious followers of the Lamb sing the song of Moses, that is, the "song of [or about] the Lamb" (15:3). Again, spiritual victory flows from the sacrificial death of Christ.

The Lamb, however, is much more than a sacrificial victim. The slain (but now resurrected) Lamb shares the throne with God and receives worship from humans and heavenly hosts alike (Rev. 5:6, 8–9, 12–13; 7:9–10, 17; 22:1, 3). Both descriptions affirm the deity of Christ. The exalted Lamb also serves as judge. At the opening of the sixth seal with the end of the world in view, all who have not followed the Lamb will face his terrifying wrath (6:15–16). The Lamb is one with him who sits on the throne as judge of God's opponents (cf. 14:10). Only those who have been sealed can withstand his wrath (7:1–8).

In the later scene of the ten kings who "make war against the Lamb," the battle is barely mentioned and not even described, "but the Lamb will overcome them because he is Lord of lords and King of kings" (Rev. 17:14; cf. 19:16). Whereas the Roman emperor saw himself as the ruler of all rulers on the earth (17:18), the real Warrior-King is Jesus. Those first hearing Revelation would have taken courage to hear that the One who sacrificed himself for them was also the Judge and King of the universe.

In Revelation 13 the ten-horned beast that emerges out of the sea contrasts with the seven-horned Lamb (5:6). Empowered by Satan, this beast makes war against the saints and conquers them (13:7). All will follow the beast except those whose names have been written in the Lamb's book of life (13:8). Then another beast emerges with "two horns like a lamb" (13:11), again in contrast to the seven-horned Lamb (5:6). Rather than speaking like a dragon and deceptively promoting the worship of the first beast, the true Lamb has "seven horns" (symbolizing power and strength) and "seven eyes, which are the seven spirits of God" (representing the Holy Spirit and his perfect ability to know and see). The exalted Jesus is one with Almighty God and with the Spirit of truth. He is the rightful owner of the book of life.

The Lamb is also closely connected to his people. Following the dreadful vision of the two beasts in Revelation 13, the next chapter opens with a heavenly vision of the Lamb standing on Mount Zion (the new Jerusalem) with an army of 144,000 followers who have been redeemed (14:1–3). The Lamb's people follow him faithfully and have been "purchased" and "offered as firstfruits to God and the Lamb" (14:4).

At the end of Revelation, the Lamb is portrayed as the bridegroom who has returned for his bride, the church (Rev. 19:7; 21:9), and those who are invited to the wedding supper of the Lamb are blessed (19:9; see BRIDE OF THE LAMB). The bride is also pictured as a city at the end of the book. The walls of the city have twelve foundations, and on them are written the names of the twelve apostles of the Lamb (21:14). This reference to the twelve apostles affirms the humanity of Jesus. Along with the Lord God Almighty, the Lamb becomes the Temple in the new Jerusalem (21:22), and the glory of God and the Lamb serve as the source of light for the heavenly city (21:23). These images communicate that the Lamb will live among his people. (See BEASTS OF REVELATION; MARRIAGE SUPPER OF THE LAMB; ONE HUNDRED FORTY-FOUR THOUSAND.)

Lampstand

In the opening vision of Revelation, John hears a clear voice commanding him to write on a scroll what he sees and send it to the seven churches.

When he turns to look, he sees "seven golden lampstands" (Rev. 1:12). The Old Testament background is the use of oil lamps on lampstands in connection with the Tabernacle and the Temple.

Moses is commanded to "make a lampstand of pure gold" with places for seven lamps (Ex. 25:31–40; 37:17–24; Num. 8:1–4). Solomon's Temple also featured lampstands (1 Kings 7:48–49; 1 Chron. 28:15). But it is Zechariah's vision of a lampstand that most scholars see as the primary background to Revelation:

> Then the angel who talked with me returned and wakened me, as a man is wakened from his sleep. He asked me, "What do you see?"
>
> I answered, "I see a solid gold lampstand with a bowl at the top and seven lights on it, with seven channels to the lights. Also there are two olive trees by it, one on the right of the bowl and the other on its left."
>
> I asked the angel who talked with me, "What are these, my lord?"
>
> He answered, "Do you not know what these are?"
>
> "No, my lord," I replied.
>
> So he said to me, "This is the word of the LORD to Zerubbabel: 'Not by might nor by power, but by my Spirit,' says the LORD Almighty....
>
> "(These seven are the eyes of the LORD, which range throughout the earth.)"
>
> Then I asked the angel, "What are these two olive trees on the right and the left of the lampstand?"
>
> Again I asked him, "What are these two olive branches beside the two gold pipes that pour out golden oil?"
>
> He replied, "Do you not know what these are?"
>
> "No, my lord," I said.
>
> So he said, "These are the two who are anointed to serve the Lord of all the earth." (Zech. 4:1–6, 10b–14).

John then sees Jesus ("someone like a son of man") in all his glory standing among the lampstands (Rev. 1:13; 2:1), which are identified in 1:20 as the "seven churches" (cf. 2:5).

The image of a lampstand represents a powerful message of God's presence among his people throughout the rest of Revelation. Just as the lampstands in both the Tabernacle and the Temple stood in the presence of God and their light represented God's presence (Heb. 9:2), so Jesus walks among his churches, and their faithful witness, empowered by his Spirit, reflects his presence (cf. Jesus' use of the image Matt. 5:15; Mark 4:21; Luke 8:16; 11:33).[63] The change from one lampstand in Zechariah to seven in Revelation probably signifies Jesus' full presence among the totality of his people and not just among the seven churches of Asia Minor.

In Revelation 11:4 the two lampstands "stand before the Lord of the earth." The number two in this context probably represents the prophetic commission to bear witness. The ultimate fulfillment of the lamp/lampstand image occurs at the end of Revelation. The new Jerusalem is said to be a city that does not need the sun or moon, "for the glory of God gives it light, and the Lamb is its lamp" (21:23). Then again in 22:5: "They will not need the light of a lamp or the light of the sun, for the Lord God will give them light." At that time there will be no more night as the light of God's personal presence burns brightly among his people. (See NEW JERUSALEM; SEVEN SPIRITS OF GOD; TEMPLE; TWO WITNESSES.)

Land

In Genesis 2–3 God creates Adam and Eve and places them in the garden. There they are blessed with close fellowship with the presence of God and access to the tree of life (see PRESENCE OF GOD; TREE OF LIFE). Thus, at the beginning of the biblical story humanity is in a place where God himself dwells. This "place" is special and is tightly interconnected to the multitude of blessings that Adam and Eve enjoy.

However, by the end of Genesis 3, Adam and Eve have sinned and been banished from the garden, from the tree of life, and perhaps from even the presence of God. From Genesis 4 to 11 people continue to disobey God and to be scattered across the face of the earth. As a response to the terrible sin of people in the early chapters of Genesis, God appears to Abraham in Genesis 12 and establishes a promise and a covenant with him. Through this promise and covenant, God will bring salvation to people on earth. Through Abraham, God promises that all nations on earth will be blessed. This promise drives the story throughout the rest of the Bible.

Yet God also promises Abraham that he will be the father of a great nation and that millions of descendants will come from him (as numerous as the stars, Gen. 15:5, or the sand on the beach, 22:17). The other central promise that God makes to Abraham is a Promised Land. In fact, throughout the rest of the Pentateuch and into the book of Joshua, the promise of a land for Abraham's descendants is a central theme that drives the story.

In Exodus 1–14 God delivers Israel from Egypt in order to take them to the Promised Land. Throughout Deuteronomy God repeatedly states that he is giving Israel the land, a good land filled with blessing (the word for land occurs in Deuteronomy over 125 times). Central to the blessings associated with this Promised Land is the renewed presence of God. God will dwell in their midst in the Promised Land.

Thus, much of the Mosaic Covenant (Exodus–Deuteronomy) dealt with how Israel should live in the Promised Land with God in their midst (see MOSES). This covenant describes how Israel can receive the many blessings associated with God's presence among them in the land. Furthermore, the land is presented to Israel as their inheritance from God, since they are his people and his children. Indeed, their occupation of the land plays an important role in defining their relationship to God, since he gave it to them as an inheritance.

In Deuteronomy 28 God summarizes the terms of the Mosaic Covenant. If the Israelites obey God's law and stay faithful to God, they will be blessed abundantly in the land. If, however, they turn away from the true God and worship other deities, they will experience judgment and curses. Ultimately, God warns, such disobedience may result in the loss of the land (and the relationship based on God's presence in the land). Unfortunately, as 1–2 Kings and the prophetic books record, Israel and Judah do turn their backs on God and worship other gods. Thus, as the prophets warn, the Israelites lose the land and are exiled.

However, the prophets also prophesy about a time after both judgment and exile when there will be a glorious time of blessing and restoration. Many of their prophecies include descriptions of Israel being back in the land and in Jerusalem. Closely intertwined into the Old Testament prophecies of the messianic age are allusions to life in the Promised Land, under blessing once again. Although some of the Jews returned to Israel after the exile under Ezra and Nehemiah, the Bible makes it clear that this small and cautious return and rebuilding was not the glorious return and restoration to the land that the prophets proclaimed. The postexilic returnees remain under foreign domination and without a Davidic king, struggling both economically and politically, a far cry from the glorious kingdom in the land that the prophets describe.

Scholars today differ on how to interpret the Old Testament prophecies regarding the future restoration of Israel back in the land (see RESTORATION OF ISRAEL). Those who have a dispensational premillennial perspective maintain that the prophecies should be viewed as literal as possible. Thus they believe that during the thousand-year millennial reign of Christ on earth, Israel will once again be established and be blessed in the land (Palestine). The Old Testament prophecies about Israel in the land and in Jerusalem will also be literally fulfilled at that time.

Amillennial scholars, however, disagree. They maintain that the church has replaced Israel as God's people and thus the promises made to Israel, including promises about the land, are to be transferred to the church, the new people of God. Many of the land promises, they argue, should be understood in a spiritual or symbolic sense, not a literal sense. Also they point out that Jesus himself, as the reality to which much typology points, fulfilled at his first coming many Old Testament prophecies regarding Israel and the land (see TYPOLOGY).

Both views have strengths and weaknesses. However, note that although the theme of land is one of the most central themes in the Old Testament, the New Testament drops it as a central theme, without explanation. In contrast, compare the theme of sacrifice in the Old Testament. The New Testament explains clearly how Jesus connects to this Old Testament theme and how the sacrifice of Jesus abrogates the need to continue the sacrifices of the Old Testament. But in regard to land the New Testament almost completely drops the subject, without explaining why.[64] This leaves interpreters today with differing opinions and viewpoints, but with little concrete evidence and without any semblance of a consensus view.

The New Testament is not completely devoid of themes that relate to land. Note that the theme of "the kingdom of God" plays a central role in the New Testament, especially in the Gospels. Some have pointed out that the idea of kingdom implies land, especially with the Old Testament as a background. Likewise, some point to Paul's frequent theme of inheritance, noting that for most people in the biblical world, inheritance was integrally connected to the concept of land. Likewise, some scholars note that any reference to the promise to Abraham cannot be separated from the strong Old Testament land associations. Thus, Paul's discussions of Abraham in Romans 4 and Galatians 3 cannot be totally separated from the land promise.[65]

However, if the land theme is implicit in the promise to Abraham, it is rather strange that Paul omits any mention of it. Rather, Paul sees fulfillment of the Abrahamic Covenant through Christ in regard to the salvation for the Gentiles ("all the nations will be blessed"). Also note that in Galatians 3:14, Paul connects the blessings promised to Abraham with the gift of the Spirit to the Gentiles. Notice that as the land in the Old Testament was connected to the theme of presence and relationship with God, here in Galatians Paul appears to be connecting the fulfillment of the Abrahamic Promise/Covenant with the indwelling of the Spirit, a major New Testament development regarding relationship with God and experiencing his presence.

An interesting, but inconclusive event in the New Testament that relates to the promise of land occurs in Acts 4:36–5:11. Here in the early Jerusalem church, some Jewish Christians are selling their land and contributing the proceeds to the church (or as in Ananias and Sapphira's case, holding back some of the proceeds). Throughout the Old Testament it was never allowable to sell one's land inheritance outside of the family. The land was a gift from God and an essential part of the means by which God would bless his people. It is unusual that the early Jewish church in Israel approved selling of land. Apparently for them it had lost some of its Old Testament significance as their inheritance from God and as the source of continued blessing.

Ultimately, of course, God promises to create a new heaven and a new earth (Rev. 21–22). A new Jerusalem will come down out of heaven, and God's people will be blessed to dwell with him in peace. Although it may not be clear what will happen regarding the land during the millennial period (however it is defined), the land theme and land promises find their final fulfillment in the climax of prophetic prediction described in Revelation 21–22.

Laodicea

Laodicea was a great commercial city in the Lycus Valley (Col. 2:1; 4:13–16), but the church there was the only one of the seven churches of Revelation not to be praised in any way by the risen Christ (Rev. 3:14–22). Because of its wealth, the city (and apparently the church) had become self-sufficient. Laodicea's affluence and independence was exemplified by its refusal of Roman aid following a devastating earthquake. Instead, the proud residents preferred to rebuild on their own.

Besides being a critical trade intersection, Laodicea also featured a banking center, a medical school specializing in the treatment of eye diseases, and a clothing industry famous for producing glossy black sheep wool. The primary predicament of the city related to its contaminated water supply. Without any direct access to the pure, cold water of Colosse (ten miles to the east) or the hot, healing water of Hieropolis (six miles to the north), Laodicea had to pipe its water from the south. By the time the water arrived it was lukewarm and continued to deteriorate with storage.

Jesus' word to the church connects directly to its local situation. Although the church considered itself wealthy and self-sufficient, Jesus, the "true and faithful witness," reveals their actual condition — they are "wretched, pitiful, poor, blind and naked" (Rev. 3:17). He uses the lukewarm water of the city to illustrate the church's sickening spiritual condition (cf. Jer. 24:1–10, where God's people are compared to rotten food). Jesus uses hard-hitting irony to exhort the Laodicean church to buy fire-refined gold (banking center), white clothes to cover their shameful nakedness (the black wool industry), and eye salve to heal their blindness (the medical school).

Yet Jesus' rebuke is motivated by his love for the church. Often a harsh prophetic warning is tempered by a strong word of compassion. Because of earlier Roman misrule[66] and the rich resources of the city, the Laodiceans had become fiercely independent. In many ways the church had followed the same path as the surrounding culture. Jesus, the "ruler of God's creation," stands at the door knocking, calling on them to renounce their self-sufficiency and turn to reliance on the only One who can supply their true needs. An ongoing prophetic message is that God's people should be countercultural and should seek God's kingdom and rule above all. Indeed, Jesus promises the overcomers in Laodicea that they will one day be permitted to reign with him (Rev. 3:21; see SEVEN CHURCHES OF REVELATION).

Last Days

The "last days" refers to the final period of history when the Messiah will come to establish God's kingdom. The Old Testament expects a time when God will fulfill his promises (Jer. 33:14–16), deliver his people from their enemies (Isa. 13:6–12; Ezek. 30:3; Joel 2:11, 30–31; Amos 5:18–20), and shower them with blessings (e.g., Isa. 2:2–4; 25:9; 65:20–25; Jer. 50:4–5; Hos. 3:5; Joel 3:1; Zech. 8:23). The fulfillment of the last days is also tied directly to the coming ruler from David's line (Isa. 9:6–7; 11:1–9; Jer. 30:9; 33:15).

The New Testament writers believe that the period known as the "last days" has begun with the first coming of Jesus, the Messiah. This inaugural event is confirmed by the coming of the Spirit at Pentecost. When Peter explains the events of Pentecost, he quotes from Joel 2:28–32. He changes the opening phrase in Joel 2:28 from "and afterwards" to "in the last days" in light of the new eschatological situation:

> Joel 2:28: And afterward,
>   I will pour out my Spirit on all people.
> Your sons and daughters will prophesy,
>   your old men will dream dreams,
>   your young men will see visions.

> Acts 2:17: In the last days, God says,
> I will pour out my Spirit on all people.
> Your sons and daughters will prophesy,
> your young men will see visions,
> your old men will dream dreams.

Paul tells Timothy that "there will be terrible times in the last days" characterized by rebellion and ungodliness (2 Tim. 3:1–4:5; cf. also 1 Tim. 4:1; Jas. 5:3; 2 Peter 3:3; Jude 18). Paul then instructs Timothy to avoid the ungodly, who pretend to be religious—an instruction that assumes Paul and Timothy are both living in the last days.

The opening reference to "the last days" in Hebrews also indicates that the writer assumed he was living in that period (Heb. 1:1–2): "In the past God spoke to our forefathers through the prophets at many times and in various ways, but in these last days he has spoken to us by his Son, whom he appointed heir of all things, and through whom he made the universe."

In addition, Peter says that Christ was "chosen before the creation of the world, but was revealed in these last times for your sake," thereby connecting his first-century readers to the last days (1 Peter 1:20). John also warns his readers that "this is the last hour; and as you have heard that the antichrist is coming, even now many antichrists have come" (1 John 2:18). While the New Testament unquestionably teaches that the last days began with the first coming of Christ, it also emphasizes the future aspect of the last days.

Jesus promises to raise his followers from the dead on the last day (John 6:39, 40, 44, 54). For those who reject Jesus, there will be condemnation on the last day (12:48). Peter assures his readers that Christ has provided a living hope through his resurrection and that their faith will be protected by God's power "until the coming of the salvation that is ready to be revealed in the last time" (1 Peter 1:3–5). Jesus' second coming will initiate the "day of the Lord" and begin the consummation of all things. The "last days" will come to a close with the return of Christ.

Jesus, the Messiah or Christ, has come and will come again. His first coming initiated the "last days" and his second coming will conclude that period of time. Consequently, Christians are living in the last days and need a mind-set appropriate for their situation. Satan has already been defeated, but he remains a dangerous enemy intent on deceiving, accusing, and persecuting God's people (Rev. 12:7–17). Paul says that the last days will include terrible times:

> People will be lovers of themselves, lovers of money, boastful, proud, abusive, disobedient to their parents, ungrateful, unholy, without love, unforgiving, slanderous, without self-control, brutal, not lovers of the

good, treacherous, rash, conceited, lovers of pleasure rather than lovers of God—having a form of godliness but denying its power … while evil men and impostors will go from bad to worse, deceiving and being deceived … For the time will come when men will not put up with sound doctrine. Instead, to suit their own desires, they will gather around them a great number of teachers to say what their itching ears want to hear. They will turn their ears away from the truth and turn aside to myths. (2 Tim. 3:2–5, 13; 4:3–4)

Paul encourages Timothy to remain faithful in what he knows to be true (2 Tim. 3:10, 14–15), to be prepared to face persecution (3:12), and to persevere in fulfilling his God-given ministry (4:1–2, 5). In light of their situation, Peter also encourages his readers to "live holy and godly lives" (2 Peter 3:11, 14). In light of the attacks by Satan, the defeated but still-dangerous enemy, John says that believers will "overcome him by the blood of the Lamb and by the word of their testimony"; they will not "love their lives so much as to shrink from death" (Rev. 12:11).

Such apostolic advice is reminiscent of Jesus' warnings in the Olivet Discourse that his disciples should be prepared for his return by being faithfully engaged in doing what he has commanded (Matt. 24–25). (See ALREADY–NOT YET; DAY OF THE LORD; ESCHATOLOGY; ESCHATON; LAST JUDGMENT; SECOND COMING.)

Last Judgment

The "last judgment" refers to the climactic event at the end of the age when God will judge all people and hold them accountable for how they have lived. No one can hide from God's presence. All people, both righteous and wicked, must appear before God, the righteous Judge. The last judgment finds support throughout Scripture.

The expression "the day of the LORD" appears in Old Testament prophetic books and normally denotes judgment and condemnation (Isa. 2:12–21; Jer. 46:10; Ezek. 13:5; Hos. 9:5; Joel 1:15; 2:1, 11; Amos 5:18–20; Zeph. 1:7, 14; Zech. 14:1), but occasionally conveys the idea of God's favor and blessing (Hos. 2:16, 18, 21; Joel 3:18; Mal. 3:17). Primarily, the expression points to a time when God intervenes to punish sin, but the prophets also use "day of the LORD" to speak about the climactic future judgment (Joel 3:14–16; Mal. 4:1–5). Sometimes the prophets see a near-future event as overlapping with the last judgment, as in Isaiah's prophecy against Babylon (Isa. 13:5–13) or Joel's against the nations (Joel 3:12–16) (see DAY OF THE LORD).

In the New Testament "the day of the Lord" is clearly identified with the last judgment, expressed in a variety of ways: the day of the Lord (2 Thess. 2:2), the day of judgment (Matt. 10:15; 1 John 4:17), the last day (John 6:39; 12:48), that day (Luke 21:34), the day (Heb. 10:25; 2 Peter 1:19), the day of Christ (Phil. 1:6), the day of God (2 Peter 3:12), the day of judgment (1 John 4:7), the day of God's wrath (Rom. 2:5), the day of their wrath (Rev. 6:17), and the great day of God Almighty (16:14). God and Christ unite in judgment as both are mentioned as Judge on the final day. When compared to the Old Testament, the New Testament intensifies hope for believers as they anticipate the day of their salvation, while maintaining the sense of calamity and doom for unbelievers.

Jesus clearly taught the reality of a final judgment (e.g., Matt. 10:15; 11:22; 12:36–37, 41–42) and placed himself alongside God at the center of the events (Matt. 7:21–23; Luke 17:30–35). Specifically, the last judgment is associated with the appearing of Christ (Matt. 24:29–31; Mark 13:24–27; Rev. 22:12). All will face the Judge to receive either eternal life (Matt. 25:34, 46) or eternal punishment (25:41, 46).

Who will be subject to final judgment? There is little doubt that God will condemn Satan, wicked angels, and unrighteous humans on the last day (Rev. 20:7–10, 15; cf. 2 Peter 2:4–10; Jude 6). But the Bible indicates that judgment will extend to "all the nations" (Matt. 25:32), "all men" (Heb. 12:23), and "the living and the dead" (Acts 10:42; 2 Tim. 4:1; 1 Peter 4:5), which includes Christians. While it is debated about whether believers will appear before the Great White Throne Judgment of Revelation 20, the fact that "the dead, great and small" are judged there (20:12), plus the implication that there will be some whose names *are* found in the book of life (20:15), suggests the distinct possibility.

If Christians do appear at the Great White Throne, the outcome of that judgment will be life (see GREAT WHITE THRONE JUDGMENT). What is beyond debate is that Christians will appear before the judgment seat of Christ (Rom. 14:10; 2 Cor. 5:10; cf. 1 Cor. 3:10–15; Heb. 10:30) to give an account for their deeds. James Garrett insightfully notes Paul's instructions in 1 Corinthians 11:32, where he distinguishes between the disciplining of believers and the condemnation of unbelievers, yet both are termed "judgment."[67] In some sense, both righteous and unrighteous will experience the last judgment.

When will the last judgment occur? Recently Christians have disagreed about whether the last judgment will be a series of judgments or a singular judgment. John Walvoord, representing the more classic form of dispensationalism, contends that there are seven judgments taught in

Scripture:[68] (1) judgment of the church in heaven following the rapture or the judgment seat of Christ (2 Cor. 5:10); (2) reward of saints who endured the tribulation (Rev. 20:4); (3) judgment of Old Testament saints at Christ's return (Dan. 12:2); (4) judgment of Gentiles living on earth at Christ's return (Matt. 25:31–46); (5) judgment of the remnant of Israel (Ezek. 20:33–38); (6) judgment of Satan (Rev. 20:1–3); and (7) the Great White Throne Judgment of the unrighteous dead (20:11–15). Other scholars have argued for one final judgment associated with the resurrection of the dead and the second coming of Christ (e.g., Matt. 12:41–42; 25:19, 31; 2 Thess. 1:7–10; 2 Peter 3:7–13).

The last judgment will be based on human deeds or works (Matt. 7:21; 12:36–37; 16:27; 25:34–36; John 5:28–29; Rom. 2:6; 2 Cor. 5:10; Rev. 20:12–13; 22:12). The primary "work" of a person's life is entering into a relationship with Jesus Christ as Lord and Savior. For example, in Matthew 7:21–23 Jesus teaches that what secures a person's destiny with God is not empty religious rhetoric ("Lord, Lord"), or works detached from personal devotion (he condemned those who prophesied, drove out demons, and performed miracles in his name as evildoers because he never knew them), but works that demonstrate a genuine relationship with Jesus (he truly knows only the one who "does the will of my Father in heaven"). Notice also Luke 12:8–9, where acknowledging Jesus or failing to acknowledge Jesus is the criterion of judgment. The Bible emphasizes judgment according to works as evidence of a person's relationship to God through Christ.

What will be the outcome of the last judgment? (1) God will expose the character of every person as revealed by their deeds — chief among them their relationship with God. A person's destiny (already determined in their lifetime) is then assigned or announced. This explains why out of terror the wicked will seek to hide from God (Isa. 2:19–21; Rev. 6:15–17), while the righteous anticipate "the day" (1 Cor. 1:7; Phil. 3:20–21; 2 Tim. 4:8; Rev. 22:17, 20).

(2) Judgment necessarily involves a separation of the righteous from the unrighteous. Jesus gathers the wheat, but burns up the chaff (Luke 3:17; cf. Matt. 13:29–30). He welcomes the wise virgins to the wedding banquet, yet denies entry to the foolish virgins (Matt. 25:1–13). He separates the sheep and the goats (Matt. 25:31–46). The grain and grape harvests of Revelation 14 assume a separation of the righteous from the wicked. Unbelievers are excluded from God's presence (Rev. 21:27; 22:15), while believers are welcomed (21:3–4; 22:14).

(3) At the last judgment God will vindicate his suffering people by bringing judgment on their enemies (Rev. 6:9–11; 11:15–19; 19:1–2,

11–21).[69] The angel's words at the pouring out of the third bowl in 16:5–7 summarize this last purpose:

> Then I heard the angel in charge of the waters say:
>
> > "You are just in these judgments,
> > you who are and who were, the Holy One,
> > because you have so judged;
> > for they have shed the blood of your saints and prophets,
> > and you have given them blood to drink as they deserve."
>
> And I heard the altar respond:
>
> > "Yes, Lord God Almighty,
> > true and just are your judgments."

Because God has avenged the blood of the saints on their persecutors, his justice stands pure and true in the end. (See DAY OF THE LORD; GREAT WHITE THRONE JUDGMENT; JUDGMENT; JUDGMENT SEAT OF CHRIST.)

Latter Prophets

The books of the Old Testament are arranged differently and are labeled differently in the Hebrew Bible than in Christian Bibles. The Hebrew Bible splits the Old Testament books into three main divisions: Torah (i.e., the Pentateuch), the Prophets, and the Writings. The Prophets are further divided into two parts: the Former Prophets (see FORMER PROPHETS) and the Latter Prophets. The Former Prophets include books that Christians generally call "the historical books" (i.e., Joshua, Judges, 1–2 Samuel, 1–2 Kings). The Latter Prophets include most of what are generally called the literary prophets: Isaiah, Jeremiah, Ezekiel, Hosea, Joel, Amos, Obadiah, Jonah, Micah, Nahum, Habakkuk, Zephaniah, Haggai, Zechariah, and Malachi. Lamentations, located after Jeremiah in the Christian canon, is located in the Writings in the Hebrew Bible. Likewise, Daniel is not included in the Latter Prophets in the Hebrew Bible, but is located instead in the Writings.

Levitical Covenant

The Levites were the tribe of Israel in the Old Testament that God selected to be priests. Frequently in the Old Testament the term *Levite* designates a true priest in contrast to a usurper line of priests. A covenant is an agreement or a binding promise. The expression "Levitical Covenant" refers to the concept of a binding promise that God gives to the Levites, that is, the legitimate priests. Numbers 18:19 perhaps anticipates the broader "priestly" covenant as God declares to Aaron, the Levitical high priest, that he and his descendants have the right to take a portion from the regular offerings to support themselves and that this right is an "everlasting covenant" (see also Ex. 29:9; 40:15).

In Numbers 25:12–13, a "priestly covenant" is made expressly with Phinehas, a Levitical priest. God declares: "Therefore tell him I am making my covenant of peace with him. He and his descendants will have a covenant of a lasting priesthood, because he was zealous for the honor of his God and made atonement for the Israelites" (see COVENANT OF PEACE). This text establishes that the true high priests in Israel will all come from the lineage of Phinehas.

In Jeremiah 33:17–22, the prophet Jeremiah merges the promise of continual and legitimate priestly service to God with the Davidic messianic promise of a righteous King (see DAVIDIC COVENANT). Jeremiah specifically mentions God's "covenant with the Levites," and merges imagery from the Abrahamic Covenant (see ABRAHAMIC COVENANT), stating, "I will make ... the Levites who minister before me as countless as the stars of the sky and as measureless as the sand on the sea shore." Keep in mind that throughout Jeremiah, the prophet criticizes both his contemporary corrupt king and corrupt priesthood. In this passage, as Jeremiah looks forward to the coming of the Messiah, he underscores that when the true, righteous descendant of David comes to rule in justice, there will be numerous, uncountable numbers of faithful priests as well.

This passage regarding the covenant with Levitical priests in Jeremiah 33:17–22, however, is not without its problems. The Septuagint—the Greek translation of the Hebrew Old Testament and the text that the early Christian church used for their Old Testament—does not contain this passage at all, thus raising at least the possibility that these verses (33:17–22) were not in the original copy of Jeremiah. Scholars remain divided over this. Some take these verses as authentic and some don't. Several urge caution about using a questionable text like this as foundational for a specific doctrine or theme such as the Levitical Covenant.

Yet, no matter how one views Jeremiah 33:17–22, Hebrews 7–8 makes it clear that Jesus Christ comes as the new and better high priest, mediator of a new and better covenant. Jesus both fulfills the Levitical Covenant and replaces it with something better. As such the high priestly role of Jesus should probably be viewed as a fulfillment of the high priestly aspects of that covenant.

Thus Jesus as king and high priest fulfills both the Davidic king promise of Jeremiah 33:17–22 and the priestly covenant of Numbers 25:12–13. Furthermore, as Peter points out in 1 Peter 2:5–9, because of what Jesus did on the cross, all believers are now incorporated into the priesthood. Therefore, even as Jesus becomes the new high priest in fulfillment of prophecy, his followers become the broader Levitical (i.e., true) priesthood, indeed fulfilling the promise in Jeremiah 33:22 of priests as numerous as the sands on the shore.

Libya

Libya in the ancient world refers to the same general area that is represented by modern Libya today. This country lies in North Africa along the Mediterranean coast to the immediate west of Egypt. The name Put is also associated with this area and apparently referred to a subregion or subgroup in Libya (see PUT). Thus some translators translate "Put" as "Libya."

Throughout the Old Testament era the history of Libya is closely intertwined with that of Egypt. Sometimes Egypt ruled over Libya and, for a period, a Libyan dynasty ruled over Egypt. Thus in the Old Testament Libya is also mentioned alongside texts that refer to Egypt, especially texts that refer to judgment on Egypt (Ezek. 30:5; Nah. 3:9). In Ezekiel 38:5 Put (Libya) is included as one of the allies of Gog (see GOG AND MAGOG).

Light to the Nations/Gentiles

In the Old Testament the Hebrew word *goyyim* can mean either "Gentiles" (i.e., non-Jewish peoples) or "nations." Likewise, in the New Testament the Greek word *ethnē* carries the same range of meaning; it can refer to "Gentiles" or to "nations." The two meanings are related; all nations other than Israel/Judea were comprised primarily of Gentiles. Yet sometimes it is difficult for Bible translators to determine whether a text using one of these words is focusing on the fact that the people being discussed are non-Jewish (Gentiles) or are focusing on the worldwide collection of nations. Thus readers will notice variations in their translations of these terms. Some translations read "Gentiles" while others read "nations."

"Light" is a major theological theme in the Bible. It can be used in a philosophical sense, referring to knowledge of the truth or to divine enlightenment that allows one to see the truth. In a similar vein, light in the Old Testament is sometimes connected to the concept of true justice or true righteousness. Yet also note that in the story of creation (Gen. 1), light is the first thing that God creates. Indeed, the Bible often connects light to God's powerful presence, especially in regard to his creative activity and his gift of life. In addition, in both the Old and New Testament light is frequently associated with the glory of God. Darkness, by contrast, often refers not only to ignorance and foolishness, but also to judgment, particularly judgment that involves the loss of God's presence and, consequentially, to death itself.

Early on in Isaiah, the prophet introduces the coming Messiah and the coming messianic age in terms of light replacing darkness: "The people walking in darkness have seen a great light" (Isa. 9:2). Then in later chapters Isaiah proclaims that the coming Messiah—whom Isaiah calls the "Servant of the LORD"—will offer salvation to not only Israel but also to all of the nations/Gentiles of the world (see SERVANT OF THE LORD). It is in this context that God declares to the Servant (Messiah), "I will make you a light to the Gentiles [nations], that you may bring my salvation to the ends of the earth" (Isa. 49:6; cf. 42:6).

Thus "light to the nations" involved more than just enlightenment. It included salvation for the nations. This stands in direct fulfillment of the promise given to Abraham that "all nations on earth will be blessed through him" (Gen. 18:18; cf. 12:3). This promise implies the reversal of the scattering of the nations seen in Genesis 10.

The New Testament identifies Jesus as the fulfillment of the "light to the nations/Gentiles" prophecy. Simeon states this when he first sees Jesus in the Temple (Luke 2:32). Paul quotes directly from Isaiah 49:6 as he shifts the focus of his ministry from the Jews to the Gentiles (Acts 13:47). In John 8:12 Jesus himself declares, "I am the light of the world." In addition, John 1 identifies Jesus as the light of all people (John 1:4, 5, 8, 9). Note also that John 1 brings together in Christ many of the Old Testament themes regarding God and light: creative power, enlightenment, presence.

The theme of Jesus as the light of the nations reaches its ultimate conclusion in Revelation, where the climax of all human history is presented as living in the light of God. Revelation 21:23–24 declares, "The city does not need the sun or the moon to shine on it, for the glory of God gives it light, and the Lamb is its lamp. The nations [Gentiles] will walk by its light."

Living Creatures

See FOUR LIVING CREATURES.

Luke, Book of

Luke's two-volume work, Luke-Acts, is best interpreted through the lens of "inaugurated eschatology" (i.e., "already-not yet"). That is to say, already the kingdom of God has arrived in the ministry of Jesus, but it will not reach its consummation until the Parousia (second coming of Jesus Christ) (see ALREADY-NOT YET).

This is seen especially in Luke 1–2. These two chapters are a carefully constructed introduction to the Gospel of Luke in particular and his two volumes in general. The dominant chord struck is that the messianic era has dawned in the personal ministry of Jesus. Various proofs of that reality first appear in Luke 1–2 and then are repeated in the Gospel and in Acts. (1) According to Jewish thinking, prophecy ceased at the close of the Old Testament and its return was expected to occur only with the coming of the Messiah. Luke's emphasis on this renewal of prophecy in the ministries of Jesus and the church signals the in-breaking of the messianic kingdom (e.g., Luke 1:67–79; 2:29–38; 3:3–6; 4:17–24; Acts 2:14–36; 3:11–26).

(2) The forerunner predicted in Malachi 3:1; 4:5–6, whose job it was to prepare the way for the Messiah by effecting repentance within Israel, is fulfilled in John the Baptist (Luke 1:16–17, 76–77; 3:1–20; 7:18–35).

(3) The activity of the Spirit is replete in Luke-Acts, beginning with the infancy narratives (Luke 1:35, 41, 67; 2:25–27) and continuing on in both the Gospel and Acts (3:16, 22; 4:1, 14, 18; 10:21; 11:13; 12:10, 12; Acts 2:1–21; 8:4–24; 10:34–48; 19:1–10); it is proof positive of the dawning of the age of the Messiah (cf. Joel 2:28–32).

(4) One of the attendant blessings prophesied for the coming of the Messiah was joy and good news (Isa. 40:9; 41:27; 52:7; 60:6; 61:1), which resound in Luke-Acts (Luke 1:14, 44, 47, 58; 2:10; 6:23; 10:20; 15:7, 32; 24:52–53; Acts 3:19)

(5) Another occurrence connected with the coming of the Messiah was the concept that God's faithful would undergo suffering, but that such affliction would be replaced with eschatological glory in the reign of the Messiah (see Isa. 52–53; Dan. 12:1–2) These messianic woes, or Great Tribulation (see GREAT TRIBULATION), are in keeping with Luke's understanding that the glory of the age to come is a present possession of Christians, despite the continuing reality of trials (Luke 1:46–55; 2:35; 24:44–46; Acts 14:23; 20:23). These ideas, and more, are convincing proofs that Jesus is the Christ, who inaugurated the kingdom of God.

Magog

See GOG AND MAGOG.

Major Prophets

The prophetic books in the Old Testament are often divided into two groups: the Major Prophets and the Minor Prophets. This classification is based solely on length and not on importance. Thus the Major Prophets are the longest ones (Isaiah, Jeremiah, Ezekiel, Daniel) and they come first in the Christian Bible. The Minor Prophets (Hosea, Joel, Amos, Obadiah, Jonah, Micah, Nahum, Habakkuk, Zephaniah, Haggai, Zechariah, Malachi) are shorter in length and follow the Major Prophets (see also BOOK OF THE TWELVE).

Malachi, Book of

The name Malachi means "my messenger." Scholars are uncertain whether this term is the prophet's proper name or his title. The word is used in the sense of "my messenger" in Malachi 3:1. Malachi is a postexilic prophet (see POSTEXILIC PROPHETS). That is, he lives and prophesies after the exile and after the return to the land under Zerubbabel, Ezra, and Nehemiah. In fact, although the book of Malachi does not contain any references to kings or other events, from which it can be unambiguously dated, most scholars maintain that Malachi is probably a contemporary with Nehemiah.

The postexilic community was led back to Israel by Zerubbabel and Ezra. The prophets Haggai and Zechariah helped to reestablish the Temple and the priesthood. Was this the glorious regathering and restoration of Israel that the preexilic prophets had predicted? Malachi, along with Haggai and Zechariah, answers that question with the negative. The nation is apparently cured of idolatry, but it quickly slides into extreme legalism, embracing religious ritualism while excusing social injustice. The social and theological issues that Malachi struggles against reveal the early forms of Judaism that Jesus encounters in Israel when he appears.

Malachi preaches against the severe corruption of worship that is taking place. Thus he speaks of unacceptable sacrifices, corrupt priests, failure to tithe, and social injustice. Yet like the preexilic prophets, Malachi looks forward to the coming Day of the LORD. He envisions a time when all peoples will be part of the kingdom of God.

Malachi 3:1 points to the preparation for that coming kingdom: "See, I will send my messenger, who will prepare the way before me." This verse is cited in Matthew 11:10; Mark 1:2; and Luke 7:27, all of which identify the "messenger" with John the Baptist. Yet Malachi 4:5 states that the prophet Elijah will also come prior to the Day of the LORD. Is Elijah to be identified with the messenger of 3:1? Is John the Baptist to be identified with Elijah?

When asked if he was Elijah, John the Baptist denies it (John 1:21). However, the connection between the two should probably be understood typologically. John is a type of Elijah, not the actual person Elijah himself (see TYPOLOGY). Thus in Luke 1:17 the angel who speaks to John's father, Zechariah, explains that John will "go on before the Lord, in the spirit and power of Elijah." Also in Matthew 11, after identifying John the Baptist with the messenger of Malachi 3:1, Jesus implies that John the Baptist has fulfilled the prophecy of Malachi concerning Elijah. In Matthew 11:14 Jesus states, "And if you are willing to accept it, he is the Elijah who was to come" (see ELIJAH; JOHN THE BAPTIST).

Man of God

The Old Testament uses three main terms to designate the people who prophesy the word of God: prophet (Heb. *nabi'*), seer, and "man of God." These three terms are nearly synonymous (1 Sam. 9:8–10; see NABI'; SEER). However, the term "man of God" is not used of any of the literary prophets (Isaiah, Jeremiah, etc.), only of those prophets in the historical books.

"Man of God" is used interchangeably with the word "prophet" in 1–2 Samuel and 1–2 Kings. Several prophets are called a "man of God" in these books. An unnamed man of God prophesies against Eli in 1 Samuel 2:27. Samuel himself, identified as a prophet in 3:20, is called "man of God" in 9:6–10. Unnamed men of God prophesy in 1 Kings 13:1–32 and 20:13–34. A prophet named Shemaiah is called a "man of God" in 12:22. Elisha too is called the "man of God" numerous times throughout his career (2 Kings 4–8; 13:19); it is the primary term used of Elisha.

At the end of his life, for the first time in the text the prophet Elijah is called the "man of God" (2 Kings 1:1–18). This term is used here to develop an ironic and clever wordplay. The Hebrew word for "man" is *ish*, and the Hebrew word for "fire" is *esh*. The two words sound similar. Elijah is on top of a hill and the king sends soldiers to capture him. The captain of the guard says, "Man [*ish*] of God, the king says, 'Come down!'" Elijah answers, "If I am a man [*ish*] of God, may fire [*esh*] come down from heaven and consume you" (1:9–14).

In general "man of God" is associated with one who delivers the word of the LORD. Thus it is applied a few times to Moses (1 Chron. 23:14; Ezra 3:2) and David (Neh. 12:24, 36). Unlike the term prophet, "man of God" is only used of true prophets; there do not appear to be any false "men of God."

Mark, Book of

That the second Gospel was written by Mark is the consensus view of New Testament scholarship. Moreover, Mark appears to have written his "biography" of Jesus to recount the life of Christ and to apply for the early church in Rome the twofold theme of Jesus' suffering and glory. This church was reeling from Emperor Nero's persecution of Christians in Rome, Peter and Paul included (ca. A.D. 64; see NERO). Mark wrote his Gospel, therefore, to steel the Roman church's faith by reminding it of the path Christ trod. Even the outline of this Gospel echoes the twofold theme of suffering and glory: Mark 1:1–8:30 concerns Jesus the Messiah; 8:31–16:8 (the most likely ending of Mark) concerns Jesus the suffering and raised Messiah.

Hand in hand with Jesus' suffering and glory is Mark's presentation of the kingdom of God. Seven key passages show that Mark rooted Jesus' message of the kingdom of God in biblical prophecy.

(1) The inauguration of the kingdom. In Mark 1:15 Jesus proclaims the good news that the kingdom of God is at hand. Even if the meaning of the verb *ēngiken* (1:15) is not clear ("arrived" or "at hand"), the parallelism it forms with the phrase "the time has come [is fulfilled]" (1:15) is clear: the kingdom of God has arrived, or dawned. The first half of Mark's Gospel is devoted to demonstrating that the kingdom of God was present in Christ's words and works (1:1–8:21). With the second half of the Gospel (8:22–16:8), however, a shift occurs in the way Jesus presents the kingdom; Jesus is a suffering, not a political, Messiah, and his kingdom is not of this world. Though the kingdom is present, it is hidden until its future manifestation at the end of time. This is especially the case for the Markan community, which is vulnerable to affliction and persecution. This theme of the kingdom of God as present but hidden seems designed to counteract what to that author was a false Christology (Jesus is the glorious, not a suffering, Messiah).

(2) The growth of the kingdom. Mark 4 records the parables of Jesus, the theme of which has to do with the growth of the kingdom of God. In the parable of the sower (4:1–20), only a small portion of the seeds take root and grow, yet it culminates in a bumper crop. Likewise, in the parable of the mustard seed (4:30–34), the mustard tree starts with a small beginning but grows to be a large tree. So it is with the kingdom of God. It starts small and insignificant (with twelve disciples whose message Israel as a whole is rejecting), but it will grow one day to encompass the earth. And it will do so ultimately without the aid of human resources (see the parable of the seed growing secretly, 4:26–29; see PARABLES OF THE KINGDOM).

(3) The paradox of the kingdom of God. The three passion predictions in Mark (8:31; 9:31; 10:33–34) illustrate the same truth about the kingdom of God: it begins with Jesus' suffering, which will result in his resurrection glory. A twofold component, therefore, undergirds each passion prediction: suffering (the Son of Man will be persecuted and killed) and glory (on the third day he will be resurrected).

That this pattern of suffering leading to glory is eschatological in nature is demonstrable on two grounds. (a) The twofold theme of righteous suffering in this age, which results in the glory of the age to come, was a pervasive characteristic of Jewish apocalypticism (see APOCALYPTIC LITERATURE). (b) The concept of the Son of Man dying and rising again is rooted in Daniel 7, obviously an apocalyptic text (see SON OF MAN). In comparing Daniel 7 with Jesus' expression "Son of Man" in his passion predictions, three observations can be made: (i) According to Daniel 7, the Son of Man is a corporate figure—he is identified with the saints of the Most High (7:17–18, 21–22, 26–27). Jesus' application of this concept to himself and his followers seems almost certain. (ii) Jesus, like the Son of Man in Daniel, is a suffering figure in that both are identified with the afflictions of the saints (7:21, 25). (iii) Because the Son of Man/saints suffer the eschatological woes, they are promised triumph over their enemies, the same pattern presumed in the passion predictions.

(4) The foretaste of the kingdom. Mark 9:2–8 records the transfiguration of Jesus before his inner group of three disciples—Peter, James, and John. It is clear from 9:1 (Jesus' prophecy that some of his disciples will not see death until they see the kingdom of God in power) that the transfiguration is the fulfillment of Jesus' prophecy. Furthermore, even though such a glorious moment for the disciples is temporary, it is a foretaste of Jesus' second coming in power and glory (Mark 8:38; see TRANSFIGURATION).

(5) The rejection of the kingdom. The Jewish nation, however, rejects Jesus' offer of the kingdom of God. Mark 12 forecasts this event through a parable illustrating the story of Israel throughout the Old Testament, now climaxing at the time of Christ. Such a story contains four components: (a) Israel sinned against God. (b) God sent his prophets to reclaim the nation for himself. (c) But Israel rejected the divine messengers, and even now they are rejecting their Messiah, the Son of God. (d) Consequently, God will judge his people Israel by allowing the Romans to destroy Jerusalem and the Temple (in A.D. 70), even as he had allowed the Babylonians to do so in 587/586 B.C. This is prophecy come true in the form of punishment.

(6) The consummation of the kingdom. Mark 13 presents the Olivet Discourse—Jesus' most extensive sermon about future things—in terms of the "signs of the times" of the Great Tribulation (also called the messianic woes). These include: false Messiahs (Mark 13:3–6); wars (13:7–8); global calamities (earthquakes, famines, etc.) (13:8b); persecution of God's people (13:9, 11–13); worldwide preaching of the gospel (13:10); the fall of Jerusalem (13:1–3, 14–23); cosmic upheaval (13:24–25); and the Parousia (Jesus' second coming) along with the full arrival of the kingdom of God (13:26–27).

Among conservatives, three views compete for the interpretation of Mark 13. (a) Preterists believe Jesus' words concerning the signs of the times were fulfilled in the first generation of Christians at the fall of Jerusalem to the Romans in A.D. 70. It was then that Christ returned in judgment on those Jews who rejected him (see PRETERIST VIEW OF REVELATION). (b) Many futurists (dispensationalists) believe the signs of the times did not begin to be fulfilled until 1948, when Israel was reconstituted as a nation (see ISRAEL, MODERN STATE OF). Consequently, Christ's return (whether the rapture or his visible second coming) could happen any time now (see DISPENSATIONALISM, CLASSICAL). (c) Most New Testament scholars, however, suspect that the messianic woes began with Jesus and his generation, especially the fall of Jerusalem to the Romans, and will be in effect until his second coming, however soon or far away in time that may be. In other words Mark 13 attests to the conviction that the kingdom of God has already dawned (at the first coming of Jesus), but it will not be completed until Jesus' second coming (see ALREADY – NOT YET).

(7) The triumph of the kingdom. The careful observer might notice that the passion narrative in Mark (Mark 14 – 15) suggests that the messianic woes recorded in Mark 13 were poured out on Jesus on the cross and that his resurrection (Mark 16:1 – 8) signaled his glorious triumph. It is the same fate — first suffering, then glory — that awaits all followers of Jesus.

Mark of the Beast

Revelation includes seven references to the "mark of the beast" (Rev. 13:16, 17; 14:9, 11; 16:2; 19:20; 20:4). In chapter 13, the second beast performs miraculous signs, deceives the "inhabitants of the earth" (a common designation in Revelation for unbelievers), kills all who refuse to worship the image of the first beast, and forces "everyone, small and great, rich and poor, free and slave, to receive a mark on his right hand or on his forehead, so that no one could buy or sell unless he had the mark, which is the name of the beast or the number of his name" (13:16 – 17).

The mark of the beast is directly connected with worship of the beast. Those who refuse to worship the beast and accept his mark will face financial persecution and perhaps death (Rev. 13:7, 10, 15, 17; cf. 2:9; 6:5 – 6). Everyone who accepts the mark of the beast, however, will incur the wrath of God. The references to the "mark" following Revelation 13 spell out the consequences of taking the mark. While those who do not take the mark may die physically as a result of persecution (e.g., 13:15; 14:12 – 13), those who compromise and take the mark will suffer the eternal wrath of God (14:9 – 11; 16:2; 19:20).

John's audience would have been familiar with image worship. Not long before Revelation was written, Emperor Domitian had a statue of himself erected in Ephesus that stood over twenty feet tall. The word for "mark" (*charagma*) was also used of the Roman emperor's seal on business contracts and the impress of his head on Roman coins. More than anything, a mark denoted identification and ownership (see DOMITIAN; EMPERORS; IMPERIAL CULT).

Mark of beast	Name of beast	Seal of God/Lamb (noun)	Seal of God/Lamb (verb)	Name of God/Lamb
13:16, 17; 14:9, 11; 16:2; 19:20; 20:4	13:17; 14:11; 15:2	7:2; 9:4	7:3, 4, 5, 8	2:3, 13, 17; 3:8, 12, 12, 12; 11:18; 14:1; 21:12, 14; 22:4

The "seal of the living God" (Rev. 7:2) stands in direct contrast to the mark of the beast, just as the name of the beast is contrasted with the name of God and the Lamb (see the chart above that summarizes these parallels). The mark, the seal, and the name are all placed on the hand (13:16; 14:9; 20:4) or the forehead (7:3; 9:4; 13:16; 14:1, 9; 20:4; 22:4). In the Old Testament God instructed Israel to observe certain practices as a "sign on your hand and a reminder on your forehead that the law of the LORD is to be on your lips. For the LORD brought you out of Egypt with his mighty hand" (Ex. 13:9; cf. 13:16; Deut. 6:8; 11:18). In Ezekiel 9 the Lord gives instructions to "go throughout the city of Jerusalem and put a mark on the foreheads of those who grieve and lament over all the detestable things that are done in it" (Ezek. 9:4, 6).

Since the mark of the beast and the seal of God are parallel (yet contrasting) stamps of ownership, they should both be understood either literally or figuratively. For the sake of consistency, most biblical scholars lean toward a figurative interpretation. In light of the "marks" and "seals" common at the time when Revelation was written, receiving the "mark of the beast" implied a willingness to ally oneself with the powers that oppose Christ.

Revelation sees two powers at war with no neutral ground between them. People give allegiance either to the beast or to God, and their loyalty is reflected chiefly through their ethical decisions and their worship. The mark is always deliberately received or obtained in Revelation (i.e., it is always the object of some verb such as "receive" or "take"); it is not something a person will receive by accident. People must choose to accept the mark of the beast or choose to reject it out of loyalty to Christ. When pressured to worship an evil power that combines religion, politics, and economics, true followers of Christ will refuse to worship the power and will reject its defining marks of ownership. (See IMPERIAL CULT.)

Marriage Supper of the Lamb

The "marriage supper of the Lamb" refers to the future celebration of God and his people in the new heaven and new earth. In the Old Testament, God as the divine husband of Israel (Isa. 54:5) promises his people a lavish banquet when he will destroy death and wipe away their tears and disgrace:

> On this mountain the LORD Almighty will prepare
>   a feast of rich food for all peoples,
> a banquet of aged wine—
>   the best of meats and the finest of wines.
> On this mountain he will destroy
>   the shroud that enfolds all peoples,
> the sheet that covers all nations;
>   he will swallow up death forever.
> The Sovereign LORD will wipe away the tears
>   from all faces;
> he will remove the disgrace of his people
>   from all the earth.
>   The LORD has spoken. (Isa. 25:6–8)

Jesus also uses the image of a wedding feast to speak about a future celebration in the consummated kingdom. In the story of Jesus' healing the centurion's servant in Matthew 8, he speaks about the "feast with Abraham, Isaac and Jacob in the kingdom of heaven" (8:11). In the parable of the wedding banquet (22:1–14; Luke 14:16–24), Jesus pronounces judgment on the Jewish leaders of his day who reject his invitation; he then announces that the undeserving and unworthy will attend instead (i.e., the "sinners" of Israel and the Gentiles). In the parable of the ten virgins (Matt. 25:1–13), those who are ready and prepared for the bridegroom's coming will accompany him to the wedding feast. Jesus explicitly connects the wedding banquet with events that follow the unexpected second coming of the Son of Man (Luke 12:40).

Revelation also mentions the wedding feast in the fourth of seven beatitudes in the book: "Blessed are those who are invited to the wedding supper of the Lamb" (Rev. 19:9; cf. 1:3; 14:13; 16:15; 20:6; 22:7, 14). The

Lamb's feast stands in bold contrast to the "great supper of God," in which the birds consume the dead bodies of God's enemies (19:17–18, 21). While God's people will enjoy the promised supper of the Lamb, the wicked will actually be the supper for the birds of prey (cf. Ezek. 39:17–20).

The supper or feast element enhances the wedding image by showing the personal and intimate nature of the communion that God and his people will experience. Meals were occasions for close, personal fellowship in the ancient world (cf. Jesus' promise to the Laodicean church to "eat with them" in Rev. 3:20). The Lord's Supper takes on added significance in light of the marriage supper image. The church's celebration of the Lord's Supper becomes a foretaste of the future blessing of eternal fellowship with the heavenly community (1 Cor. 11:17–34). In addition, Jesus' assurance that he will "not drink of this fruit of the vine from now on until that day when I drink it anew with you in my Father's kingdom" (Matt. 26:29) becomes a comforting promise for believers, especially those facing trials. (See BRIDE OF THE LAMB; BRIDEGROOM.)

Martyrdom

A "martyr" is a person who voluntarily chooses death instead of renouncing the faith or, stated more positively, chooses to give one's life out of faithfulness to God. A number of martyrs are mentioned in the Old Testament. The psalmist speaks of those who for God's sake "face death all day long" and who are "considered as sheep to be slaughtered" (Ps. 44:22). The Suffering Servant of Isaiah 40–55 gives his life "like a lamb to the slaughter" (Isa. 53:7). He "poured out his life unto death, and was numbered with the transgressors" (53:12). The book of Daniel describes three young men who choose the fiery furnace rather than worship the king's golden image. Their martyr mentality is summarized in Daniel 3:17–18:

> If we are thrown into the blazing furnace, the God we serve is able to save us from it, and he will rescue us from your hand, O king. But even if he does not, we want you to know, O king, that we will not serve your gods or worship the image of gold you have set up.

Later in the book, Daniel describes a time when a ruler will attack Jerusalem, desecrate the Temple, and set up the "abomination that causes desolation" (Dan. 11:29–31). This king will "exalt and magnify himself above every god and will say unheard-of things against the God of gods" (11:36). Although God's people will resist him, many will "fall by the sword or be burned or captured or plundered" so that they might "be refined, purified, and made spotless until the time of the end" (11:33, 35).

Martyrdom also figures prominently in the New Testament. John the Baptist (Mark 6:14–29), Stephen (Acts 7), the Christians martyred under Paul's preconversion persecution (8:3; 9:1), James (12:1–2), and Antipas (Rev. 3:13) all provide specific examples. Paul occasionally refers to his impending death in the context of martyrdom (Phil. 1:19–26; 2 Tim. 4:16–18). Jesus warns his followers that they should expect the possibility of martyrdom (Matt. 24:9; Luke 21:12–19).

Jesus himself serves as the supreme example of a martyr. He clearly says that "no one takes it [my life] from me, but I lay it down of my own accord. I have authority to lay it down and authority to take it up again. This command I received from my Father" (John 10:18; cf. 12:27). Jesus repeatedly refers to his upcoming death as essential to his mission (e.g., Mark 8:31–32; 9:31; 10:33–34, 45; 14:36).

Jesus as the supreme martyr plays a prominent role in the martyr theology of the book of Revelation. In the opening verses of this book, John describes Jesus Christ as "the faithful witness [*martys*], the firstborn from the dead, and the ruler of the kings of the earth," the one "who loves us and has freed us from our sins by his blood" (Rev. 1:5). Jesus also addresses the church in Laodicea as the "faithful witness [*martys*]" (3:14). Throughout Revelation the chief image used of Jesus is that of a sacrificial Lamb (chs. 5, 6, 7, 12, 13, 14, 15, 17, 19, 21, 22; see LAMB). The Lamb of God is worthy to unfold the plan of God because he was slain, yet lives (5:6, 12; cf. 12:11; 13:8).

Although the words for "witness" (*martys, martyria*) are probably not technical terms in Revelation for "martyr," it is frequently connected to the death of Christians (see 1:9; 2:13; 11:3, 7; 17:6). Many of those who follow the slain Lamb shed their blood in martyrdom. As the fifth seal is opened, the martyrs ask how much longer they must wait for vindication (Rev. 6:9–11):

> When he opened the fifth seal, I saw under the altar the souls of those who had been slain because of the word of God and the testimony [*martyria*] they had maintained. They called out in a loud voice, "How long, Sovereign Lord, holy and true, until you judge the inhabitants of the earth and avenge our blood?" Then each of them was given a white robe, and they were told to wait a little longer, until the number of their fellow servants and brothers who were to be killed as they had been was completed.

The "great multitude" of Revelation 7:9–17 likely refers to believers who "have come out of the great tribulation; they have washed their robes and made them white in the blood of the Lamb" (7:14). As an army of the Messiah, they have conquered the enemy by their own death.

The enemies of God are often identified as those who have shed the blood of God's people (Rev. 16:6; 17:6; 18:24; 19:2). Ironically, what appears to be the martyrs' defeat is in reality their victory, as 12:11 demonstrates: "They overcame him by the blood of the Lamb and by the word of their testimony [*martyria*]; they did not love their lives so much as to shrink from death." When the saints are "conquered" by their enemies (11:7; 13:7), their martyrdom turns out to be the means of victory over their enemies (cf. 2:10–11; 3:9, 12; 15:2). As Richard Bauckham points out, "Revelation portrays the future *as though* all faithful Christians will be martyred ... It is not a literal prediction that every faithful Christian will in fact be put to death. But it does require that every faithful Christian must be prepared to die."[70] (See TRIBULATION.)

Matthew, Book of

Though some doubt that Matthew, one of Jesus' twelve apostles, actually wrote the first Gospel, it looks very much like Matthew's testimony is behind Matthew 9:9–13 (the calling of Levi the tax collector to follow Jesus) and 13:47–52 (the parable of the net, which emphasizes the scribal background of Matthew). Furthermore, the early church fathers were unanimous in holding that Matthew was indeed the author of this Gospel.

The Jewish nature of Matthew's Gospel suggests it was written in Palestine or perhaps in Syrian Antioch. Many scholars believe Matthew was written to counter the emergence of rabbinic Judaism in the A.D. 80s. Above all, the first Gospel wishes to demonstrate that Jesus is the Messiah, drawing heavily on the promise-fulfillment theme (see below). The book, therefore, is steeped in biblical prophecy.

Matthew follows Mark's major points regarding biblical prophecy. Thus, Jesus the Christ inaugurates the kingdom of God (Matt. 4:12–17); the parables record the small beginning but big projected ending of the kingdom (ch. 13); the paradox of the kingdom means that Jesus first suffers and then enters heavenly glory (16:21–28; 17:22; 20:17–19); at the transfiguration, the inner three disciples witness the foretaste of the coming kingdom of God (16:28–17:7); the nation as a whole rejects Jesus (12:1–12, for which Matthew especially blames the Pharisees, the founders of rabbinic Judaism); and Jesus' death and resurrection underscore his triumph over the messianic woes (ch. 28).

But there are added features in Matthew that reveal the depth of influence of biblical prophecy on the first Gospel.

(1) It is clear in Matthew's infancy narratives (Matt. 1 – 2) that Jesus is the Messiah who fulfills Old Testament prophecy in two ways. (a) Jesus is the new Moses who is going to bring about a new exodus, one spiritual in nature (1:21; 2:13 – 15). (b) Jesus is the long-awaited Davidic Messiah (1:23; cf. Isa. 7:14 [the Messiah will be called Immanuel]; Matt. 2:1 – 8; cf. Mic. 5:2 [the prediction of the Messiah's birth in Bethlehem]; Matt. 2:9; cf. Num. 24:17 [the star of the Davidic dynasty rising]).

(2) Matthew announces fourteen times that Jesus is the fulfillment of Old Testament biblical prophecy, especially related to the restoration of Israel. In Matthew 1:22 – 23 and Isaiah 7:14 Jesus is called "Immanuel" because he will save his people from their sins (see IMMANUEL). Matthew equates Jesus with the Messiah who will deliver his people (Matt. 2:5 – 6; cf. Mic. 5:1; also 2 Sam. 5:2). In Matthew 2:14 – 15 Jesus' return to Israel from Egypt after Herod the Great's death is portrayed as a type of exodus that, in light of Matthew 3:3, should be understood as his vocation to deliver Israel from the bondage of sin (cf. Hos. 11:1). Matthew also perceives in Jesus' ministry the fulfillment of Jeremiah's prophecy of Israel's restoration (Matt. 2:17 – 18; cf. Jer. 31:5).

The text of Isaiah 11:1 (cf. Isa. 4:2) envisions the coming of the Davidic deliverer, called the Branch. If "Nazarene" in Matthew 2:23 refers to *nezer* ("Branch"), then this verse can be viewed as equating Jesus with the Davidic Messiah. Isaiah 9:1 – 2 foretells of Israel's future restoration and the Gentiles' conversion, which Matthew sees as resulting from Jesus' miracles (Matt. 4:14 – 16). In both 8:17 and Isaiah 53:4, healing as a metaphor for Israel's restoration is applied to Jesus' dealings with the masses (see HEALING).

Obviously, the first Gospel perceives in Jesus the Suffering Servant who will be the catalyst for Israel's restoration to God (Matt. 12:17 – 21; cf. Isa. 42:1 – 4). In Matthew 13:14 – 15 Israel's rejection of Jesus is interpreted as indicating that the nation's sin and exile persist (cf. Isa. 6:9 – 10). The overriding theme of Psalm 78 is the story of Israel (sin – exile – restoration) and for that reason is drawn on in Matthew 13:35. Isaiah 62:11 and Zechariah 9:9 predict that God will send a messianic deliverer to Israel, which is applied by Matthew to Jesus at his triumphal entry (Matt. 21:4 – 5).

The smiting of the shepherd and the scattering of the nation is applied in 26:56 (cf. v. 31) to Jesus' death and the disciples' subsequent departure, perhaps as an allusion to the continuing exile of Israel (cf. Zech. 13:7). The purchasing of a field by Jeremiah (Jer. 32:6–15) was promissory of the coming restoration of Israel, even though that nation was about to go into exile. Perhaps Matthew (Matt. 27:9–10; cf. Zech. 11:12–13) understands the purchase of the field with Judas's blood, and at the expense of Jesus' death, to have conveyed a divine irony; that which cost Jesus his life (the cross) was the basis for the true restoration of Israel.

The dominant theme, then, in all of these Matthean fulfillment texts is the restoration of Israel inaugurated by Jesus. Not to be overlooked is the historical situation necessitating the writing of Matthew's Gospel, which is commonly thought to have been the post–A.D. 70 debates between the Matthean community and the Pharisees. Both of these groups (along with others) were touting their respective devotees as the true Israel to emerge after the fall of Jerusalem. Matthew portrays the Jesus movement as restored Israel over against the Pharisees—hence, his use of the Old Testament as a witness to the truth of that message.

(3) Matthew 5–7 records Jesus' Sermon on the Mount, which presents the ethics that should characterize the citizens of the kingdom of God. Two modern interpretations of this sermon on this point compete with one another. One school of thought (held by some dispensationalists) argues that because the requirements set forth in Matthew 5–7 are too unrealistic to follow in this present evil age, it will only be in the millennium (the thousand-year reign of Christ on earth after his second coming) that Christians will live up to these noble standards (see DISPENSATIONALISM, CLASSICAL). Most scholars, however, believe that the already–not yet eschatological tension governs this sermon. Because the kingdom of God has already dawned, believers should live by the ethics of the kingdom as detailed in Matthew 5–7. But because the kingdom is not yet complete, the full realization of the standards of this sermon awaits the Parousia (Jesus' second coming).

(4) The content of Matthew 10, which is not found in Mark, describes the mission of the twelve apostles to Israel before the passion of Christ. It is clear that the same language found in Mark 13:9–13 (the Olivet Discourse) is applied to the disciples' mission (see particularly Matt. 10:17–22), thus stamping it with prophetic import. The apostles' struggles and triumphs in preaching the gospel bespeak the presence now of both the messianic woes and the kingdom of God, respectively. This paradoxical circumstance will continue until the Parousia (10:23).

(5) Matthew's record of Jesus' triumphal entry (Matt. 21:1–11) distinguishes itself from its Markan counterpart in that it views Jesus' entrance

into Jerusalem as the fulfillment of Zechariah 9:9–10, a prophecy of the Messiah's arrival in the holy city. But both Matthew and Mark agree that Jesus is the prophesied Davidic king (Matt. 21:9; Mark 11:9–10).

(6) Matthew's account of Jesus' Olivet Discourse (Matt. 24) agrees with Mark 13, except for one critical point. In Mark 13:3, the question of the disciples about the coming fall of Jerusalem to the Romans equates that with the end of the age. But in Matthew 24:3, the disciples' question separates the fall of Jerusalem (see 24:4–20) from the second coming of Christ (24:21–31). The former is the backdrop of the latter. Here again is the already–not yet tension: already Jerusalem has fallen, but not yet has the end of the age come.

(7) Another matter raised in Matthew 24 is the identity of the elect who will be gathered together to be delivered at the second coming of Christ (cf. Matt. 24:31 with Mark 13:27). Those who are pretribulationists think the elect is Israel, who will convert to Jesus the Messiah during the Great Tribulation. Posttribulationists, however, see the reference to be Christians (i.e., the church), who will endure the Great Tribulation. One's interpretation of the elect in Matthew 24:31 governs one's perspective toward the sheep and goats judgment, which is unique to Matthew 25. Pretribulationists think the sheep are Jews while the goats are the nations of the world who mistreat Israel in the Great Tribulation. But posttribulationists believe the sheep are Christians of all ages, who are persecuted by the enemies of God (the goats), and the two will meet with opposite fates at the divine judgment that will conclude the Great Tribulation.

Medes

The Median empire is dealt with in Daniel 2 and 7. Two views compete for the correct interpretation of Daniel's biblical prophecy therein. (1) One view interprets the four kingdoms predicted by Daniel to be Babylonia (550 B.C.), Medo-Persia (539 B.C.), Greece (330 B.C.), and a revived Roman empire at the end of history. There is good evidence to support this view because in 550 B.C. Cyrus the Persian conquered the Medes and incorporated them into his empire. Daniel 8 is appealed to in support of this view, since the ram in Daniel's vision has two horns (Medes and Persians).

(2) The other perspective treats the Medes as a separate entity in Daniel 2 and 7. Thus the four kingdoms are: Babylonia (550 B.C.), Media (550–539 B.C.), Persia (539 B.C.), and ancient Greece (330 B.C.). Two pieces of evidence support this view. (a) According to Daniel 7:5, the second kingdom defeated three nations, which seems to allude to Media's

triumph over Ararat, Minni, and Ashkenaz and their subsequent victory over Babylonia (cf. Jer. 51:27–29). (b) According to Daniel 2:39, the second empire was ultimately inferior to Babylonia, which fits Media more readily than Medo-Persia (see FOUR BEASTS OF DANIEL).

Melchizedek

The name Melchizedek means "king of righteousness." Genesis 14:18 identifies Melchizedek as the king of Salem (probably Jerusalem) and a priest of God Most High. In 14:18–20, after defeating several hostile kings and recapturing his nephew Lot, Abraham is met by the king/priest Melchizedek, who pronounces a blessing on both Abraham and God because of the victory God has given. Acknowledging Melchizedek as a valid priest of God, Abraham then gives Melchizedek one tenth of everything he has just captured.

Melchizedek is not mentioned again until Psalm 110, a messianic psalm quoted frequently in the New Testament (see PSALMS, BOOK OF). In 110:1–3 the LORD establishes the Messiah on a throne at his right hand. In 110:4, however, the LORD declares that this special Coming One (i.e., the Messiah) is also a priest—indeed an eternal priest from the order of Melchizedek. Thus like Melchizedek, the Messiah will be both king and priest.

In the book of Hebrews the events of Genesis 14 and the theological proclamation of Psalm 110 are discussed in light of their typological fulfillment in Jesus Christ (see TYPOLOGY). In Hebrews 7, Melchizedek and the priestly order of Melchizedek are the focus of the entire chapter. The writer of Hebrews points out that in Psalm 110 God proclaimed Jesus Christ to be a priest according to the priestly order of Melchizedek. In contrast to the existing Levitical priestly order, the order of Melchizedek is not an order based on lineage or on law. Furthermore, in contrast to the Levitical order, the order of Melchizedek is eternal. Thus the writer of Hebrews declares that the Levitical priesthood and the law have passed away (Heb. 7:12), to be replaced by Jesus Christ, the superior high priest from a superior and eternal priesthood. Jesus Christ, the ultimate high priest (holy, pure, sinless, exalted), now intercedes for his people instead of weak and sinful human priests (7:26–28).

Merkabah

Merkabah is the Hebrew word for "chariot," used both for literal chariots that people ride in and figurative chariots that God rides in. Based on Old Testament texts that associate the chariot with the heavens and the throne of God (such as 2 Kings 2:11; Isa. 66:15; Jer. 4:13; Ezek. 1), some apocryphal literature of the intertestamental period began to use the word in reference to some type of mystical ascent to the divine throne. The throne vision in the apocryphal book *1 Enoch* 14 (150 B.C.) probably represents the oldest example of such *merkabah* mysticism, but similar descriptions occur in the New Testament as well (2 Cor. 12:1–7; Col. 2). Similar descriptions of mystical ascents continue to appear in Jewish literature after the New Testament era.

The main components of *merkabah* often include: (1) rigorous preparation for the heavenly ascent via prayer and fasting; (2) mystic ascent through the seven "houses" or palaces of heaven; (3) negotiations with the angels assigned to each of the palaces by the use of magical formulae, seals, and so on; (4) danger accompanying the ascent; and (5) vision of the glorious, divine throne-chariot.

Although *merkabah* mysticism and apocalypticism are related, three matters distinguish between them. (1) *Merkabah* texts concentrate more on the mysteries of heaven and on the description of God's throne and less on eschatological themes than does apocalypticism. For example, apocalypticism often focuses on the last judgment, the resurrection of the dead, the messianic kingdom, and the world to come, while *merkabah*-type texts do not. Not that *merkabah* does not contain eschatology (e.g. *1 En.* 14:8–25); rather, the difference between the two is one of emphasis. (2) *Merkabah* is less occupied with cosmology than is apocalyptic. (3) *Merkabah* texts stress more the role of miracles than does apocalyptic material.

It may be that prior to A.D. 70 *merkabah* mysticism and apocalypticism were intermingled traditions, which would account for similarities between the two; but with the dashed hopes of apocalypticism as a result of the events between A.D. 70–135 (i.e., the destruction of Jerusalem and the Temple), *merkabah* emerged as an independent movement.

Meshech and Tubal

Meshech and Tubal were countries or peoples located in Asia Minor (modern Turkey). Ezekiel mentions Meshech and Tubal five times (Ezek. 27:13; 32:26; 38:2; 38:3; 39:1), always in the combination "Meshech and Tubal." Tubal is mentioned without Meshech in Isaiah 66:19, which refers to the widespread places of the world to which God will send messengers to proclaim his glory. In Ezekiel 38:2–3 "Gog ... of Magog" is said to be chief prince of Meshech and Tubal (see GOG AND MAGOG; ROSH). Ninth- and eighth-century B.C. documents of the Assyrians place Meshech and Tubal in Asia Minor, as do the later ancient writers Herodotus and Josephus.

In Ezekiel 38–39, Meshech and Tubal are combined in an alliance with five other nations from widespread areas against Israel in an eschatological (end-time) battle. Ezekiel thus appears to use the reference to Meshech, Tubal, and the other nations to symbolize the many widespread nations of the world in alliance against eschatological Israel. This is also how Revelation 20:7–8 seems to use the associated terms Gog and Magog. There is no credible evidence to connect Meshech with the modern Russian city of Moscow, a speculative view put forth at the beginning of the twentieth century and still propagated by some popular writers.

Messiah

The Hebrew word behind the English word "Messiah" means "to anoint" (usually with oil). Throughout the ancient Near East the custom of anointing people with oil for special occasions was common. Anointing with oil symbolized purification, but it also symbolized the conferring of power, authority, and honor. Thus "Messiah" refers to "the Anointed One" or the "One conferred with power, authority, and honor." The comparable New Testament Greek word is *Christos*, from which we get the English word "Christ." The Greek word carries the same connotations as the Hebrew word—"the Anointed One."

Throughout the prophetic texts of the Old Testament, the promise of future blessings and restoration usually centers on a special person, someone coming to make all things right. Often this Coming One is described in royal terms. He is the coming righteous and just King, the Branch of David, and the Shepherd (royal imagery) who regathers the flock (see BRANCH; DAVIDIC COVENANT; SHEPHERDS). He is often equated with Yahweh (i.e., the LORD), the God of Abraham, Isaac, and Jacob. He is called Immanuel ("God with us"), but he is also identified as the Suffering Servant (see IMMANUEL; SERVANT SONGS). There are also allusions to the Coming One as prophet and priest.

Thus in the Old Testament the picture of the Coming One is rather complex, and there is no one central term used to define him. Surprisingly, the specific term *Messiah* ("Anointed One") is used only a handful of times in regard to the future coming deliverer (Isa. 61:1; Dan. 9:25–26; several times in Psalms), even though the concept is much more common. Thus in the Old Testament, while it is clear that someone special, even divine, was coming to carry out the spectacular works of God, there is no central defining term for what to call him.

It is during the intertestamental period (the time between the close of the Old Testament and the coming of Jesus) that the term *Messiah* became popular among the Jews as the main term for referring to the Coming One predicted by the Old Testament prophets. Unfortunately, however, during this time many of the Jews distorted this term. Often it became tightly associated with Jewish political aspirations of independence from Rome. It also became disassociated with the concept of the Suffering Servant and with the central concepts of justice and righteousness emphasized in the Old Testament. The Jews wanted a powerful king to lead them to military victory over Rome.

When Jesus enters the scene in Palestine, the Greek term *Christos* was being used like the Hebrew term *Messiah* and was likewise associated with numerous misconceptions about a Coming One who was strictly a political, military leader, who would defeat the Romans. Thus when Jesus appears in the New Testament Gospels, he is cautious about using the term *Christ*. Jesus is clear about identifying himself with the Coming One that the Old Testament predicted, and the Gospels have numerous passages where Jesus or the Gospel writers point out how Jesus fulfills the Old Testament prophecies about the coming deliverer (e.g., Matt. 1:22; 2:5–6, 17–18, 23; 4:14–16; 12:17–21; 13:13–15, 35; 21:4–5; 26:31). Yet Jesus uses the term *Christ* sparingly, to avoid furthering the misconceptions associated with the term. The Gospel writers—as well as Jesus—do clearly affirm that Jesus is "the Christ," and they do use the term occasionally, but in general Jesus himself prefers the term *Son of Man* (see SON OF MAN).

However, after the death and resurrection of Jesus, when his ministry could no longer be misunderstood or misconstrued into a political, military rebellion against Rome, the apostles freely use the term *Christ*, proclaiming clearly that Jesus of Nazareth is "the Christ" of the Old Testament. Thus Peter, for example, proclaims in Jerusalem, "Therefore let all Israel be assured of this: God has made this Jesus, whom you crucified, both Lord and Christ" (Acts 2:36). In Acts the apostles proclaim that not only was Jesus the Messiah (Christ) while on earth, but that he is now exalted to the right hand of God and is the reigning messianic King, as prophesied by Psalm 110:1, one of the most quoted Old Testament texts in the New Testament.[71]

The identification of Jesus as "the Christ" became so foundational to the early church that soon "Christ" became attached to the name "Jesus," so that the Savior was frequently simply called "Jesus Christ." Likewise, the early followers of Jesus soon took on the name "Christians" (e.g., Acts 11:26). Paul uses "Christ" over four hundred times in his letters, but most of the time he uses this word as the name of Jesus, without immediate tight "messianic" connections to the Old Testament, other than perhaps a faint allusion to Jesus as the One who rules. As did Jesus and the Gospel writers, Paul does affirm that Jesus Christ is the Coming One predicted by the Old Testament and that he did fulfill all that the Old Testament prophesied, but Paul doesn't often use the term *Christ* ("the Anointed One") to make that point (though cf. Acts 17:3).

Messianic Woes

The "messianic woes" refer to the time of great sorrow and tribulation to come on God's people immediately prior to the coming of the Messiah. In the Old Testament the concept is usually associated with the coming Day of the LORD (Isa. 24:17–23; Dan. 12:1–2; Joel 2:1–11a, 28–32; Amos 5:16–20; Zeph. 1:14–2:3). This concept was further developed in Jewish apocalypticism (see APOCALYPTIC LITERATURE) and is reflected in New Testament prophecy as well. The actual expression "messianic woes" itself, however, does not occur until the writing of the Jewish Talmud, later than the New Testament.

Although Jewish apocalypticism was not completely uniform or consistent in its theology, certain commonalities emerge in its writings, including: the use of symbolism and visions; an emphasis on angelic mediators of revelation; the expectation of divine judgment; a fervent desire for the advent of the kingdom of God, including the arrival of the new heavens and the new earth; and the dualism of the two ages (i.e., the present age of suffering and the coming messianic age of glory). The last of these similarities especially informs the concept of the messianic woes as found in this literature, where the suffering of this present age is portrayed as giving way to the glory of the age to come.

The transition period between these two ages is to be accomplished by an intensification of affliction as perpetrated on godly Jews, which, in turn, gives birth to the messianic age. This aspect of Jewish apocalyptic thinking is similar to the New Testament description of the Great Tribulation, especially regarding the imagery of the birth pains (e.g., Mark 13:8; 1 Thess. 5:3; Rev. 12:2–5). Sometimes these events are called the "signs of the times."

There is striking agreement between the New Testament and Jewish apocalyptic literature regarding the Great Tribulation, especially concerning the appearance of the signs of the times that will culminate in the arrival of the kingdom of God. Five themes occur regularly in both biblical and noncanonical apocalyptic texts: (1) earthquakes (cf. Mark 13:8); (2) intense famine (13:8; Rev. 6:8; 18:8); (3) wars (Mark 13:8; Rev. 6:4); (4) internecine strife (Mark 13:12); and (5) cosmic disturbances (Mark 13:24–25; Rev. 6:12–17; see GREAT TRIBULATION).

Micah, Book of

The name Micah means, "Who is like the LORD?" Micah was a prophet from the southern kingdom Judah, but he preached against both the northern kingdom Israel and the southern kingdom Judah. He was a contemporary of Hosea, Isaiah, and Amos, living in the eighth century B.C. He preached and lived through the fall of Israel to the Assyrians in 722 B.C.

The book of Micah is similar to Isaiah, only much shorter. Indeed, several passages in Micah resemble passages in Isaiah, and Micah 4:1–3 is practically identical to Isaiah 2:1–4. Micah is quoted by Jeremiah (Jer. 26:18 = Mic. 3:12), who lived a hundred years later, demonstrating that the prophets were known and quoted even after their death.

The central message of Micah is the same as many of the other prophets. He accuses the nation of covenant violation and charges them with idolatry, social injustice, and a reliance on religious ritual instead of true relationship with their God. He calls on them to repent, but notes that repentance is unlikely and proclaims judgment. Finally, Micah proclaims that there is hope for future restoration and blessing centered on a Davidic King/Shepherd who is to come.

In contrast to the terrible devastating warfare common in Micah's day, he prophesies that the Coming One will establish peace between nations (Mic. 4:2–5). He declares: "They will beat their swords into plowshares and their spears into pruning hooks. Nation will not take up sword against nation, nor will they train for war anymore."

In Micah 5:2–5 the prophet proclaims that the Coming One will be a shepherd and that he will establish peace. Furthermore, he will come from the town of Bethlehem. The additional designation "Ephrathah" is added to Bethlehem to distinguish this Bethlehem from the two other towns with the same name, thus designating this particular town with precision. This was the town in which David was born, so Micah's prophesy not only identifies the town in which the Messiah will be born, but it also connects the Messiah to the Davidic Covenant (see DAVIDIC COVENANT). In Matthew 2, when the Magi from the east come to Jerusalem looking for the newborn king of the Jews, it is from Micah 5:2 that the location of the baby is determined. Based on this verse, and confirmed by the star they followed, the Magi find the baby Jesus (Matt. 2:3–12). Herod likewise uses the verse to determine where to go to try and kill the newborn king.

Central to Micah's message is the proclamation of Micah 6:8. In the previous verses Micah underscores that God does not really want more sacrifices and that his people cannot appease him or cover their sin with their own sacrifices. Micah then indicates what God does want: "He has showed you, O man, what is good. And what does the LORD require of you? To act justly and to love mercy and to walk humbly with your God."

Michael

The angel Michael is mentioned several times in the Bible, all of which connect him with biblical prophecy (see also ANGELS). Daniel 10:13, 21 tells how it took twenty-one days for Michael to prevail over a demonic force controlling ancient Persia in order to answer Daniel's prayer for illumination of the future. The content of the angel's message pertained to how Alexander the Great's successors impacted Israel's future (Dan. 11) (see ALEXANDER THE GREAT). In 12:1, Michael is called the great prince (archangel) of Israel, who will fight for her in the future against Antiochus Epiphanes (167 B.C.; see ANTIOCHUS EPIPHANES).

Another view of Daniel 12:1 is that Michael will defend Israel in the last days as the nation suffers the Great Tribulation. It may be that Revelation 12:7 refers to that future event, when Michael casts Satan out of heaven to earth. Satan then will persecute Israel, or the church (depending on one's view), in the Great Tribulation. It is also possible that 12:7 alludes to the beginning of the defeat of Satan at the first coming of Christ.

Finally, Jude 9 records an event not mentioned in the Old Testament: the dispute between Michael and Satan over the body of Moses at his death. In the context of Jude's day, the author believed that end-time pseudoprophets had infiltrated the church. These false teachers were enamored with their own spiritual ability to fight Satan. Jude uses the Michael–Satan dispute to demonstrate the need for his audience to distance themselves from the arrogant intruders.

Midtribulation Rapture

The midtribulation rapture view insists that the church will go through the first half of the Great Tribulation, but it will be removed prior to experiencing God's wrath. (For an even more nuanced approach to the timing of the rapture of the church in relation to the wrath of God, see PRE-WRATH RAPTURE.) Like posttribulationism, this view makes a distinction between tribulation and wrath. During the first three and one-half years of Daniel's seventieth week, the church will be present and experience tribulation. Tribulation has always been the lot of God's people. This view sees the "elect" of Jesus' Olivet Discourse referring to the church rather than to the Jews as argued by pretribulationists. According to Matthew 24:21–22, the Great Tribulation will include the elect:

> For then there will be great distress, unequaled from the beginning of the world until now—and never to be equaled again. If those days had not been cut short, no one would survive, but for the sake of the elect those days will be shortened.

In Matthew 24:29 Jesus adds, "Immediately after the distress of those days the sun will be darkened, and the moon will not give its light; the stars will fall from the sky, and the heavenly bodies will be shaken." After the "distress" or Great Tribulation God will pour out his wrath, as indicated by the severe judgments on the cosmos. Since the church will not experience God's wrath (Rom. 5:9; 1 Thess. 1:9–10; 5:9), the rapture of the church will occur at this midpoint of the seven-year Great Tribulation (i.e., just before God begins to pour out his wrath).

In Revelation the rapture corresponds to the sounding of the seventh trumpet (Rev. 11:15, 17–18):

> The seventh angel sounded his trumpet ...
>
> "We give thanks to you, Lord God Almighty,
>   the One who is and who was,
> because you have taken your great power
>   and have begun to reign.
> The nations were angry;
>   and *your wrath has come.*
> The time has come for judging the dead,
>   and for rewarding your servants the prophets
> and your saints and those who reverence your name,
>   both small and great—
> and for destroying those who destroy the earth." (italics added)

The resurrection and catching up of the two witnesses in Revelation 11:11–12 represent the rapture of the church. Also, midtribulationists see the woman's flight into the desert for a time, times, and half a time in 12:14 as evidence for their view.

This halfway point of the Great Tribulation is alluded to in Daniel 7:24–25, where it says that "another king" different from the ten kings will "speak against the Most High and oppress his saints," and they "will be handed over to him for a time, times and half a time." Daniel also reveals that in the middle of the seven-year period (the seventieth week of years or the Great Tribulation), the "abomination that causes desolation" will be set up in the Temple (9:27).

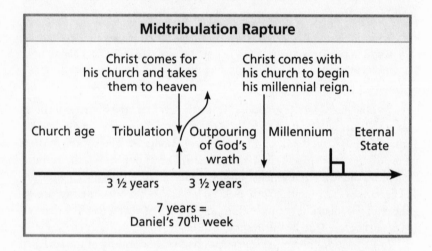

This is also what Paul appears to have in mind when he speaks of the "man of lawlessness" setting himself up in God's Temple (2 Thess. 2:3–9). Just before this time of wrath begins, God will rapture his church. Therefore, the rapture will occur three and one-half years into the Great Tribulation. The midtribulation view agrees with the pretribulation view that there will be two comings of Christ. Midtribulationists locate these two comings at the midpoint of the Great Tribulation (for the church) and at the end of the outpouring of God's wrath (with the church).

The midtribulation rapture view attempts to take advantage of both the pretribulation and posttribulation views. With pretribulationism it argues for two second comings of Christ and for the rapture as physical removal from God's wrath. With posttribulationism it prefers the more natural reading of "elect" along with the admission that the church always has and always will endure tribulation. The weakness of the midtribulation view is the questionable restriction of God's wrath to the last half of the Great Tribulation as well as the absence of direct biblical evidence for the rapture occurring in the middle of this period. (See PARTIAL RAPTURE;

POSTTRIBULATION RAPTURE; PRETRIBULATION RAPTURE; PREWRATH RAP-
TURE; RAPTURE; WRATH OF GOD.)

Millennial Kingdom

The "millennial kingdom" is usually considered to be another way of describing the literal one-thousand year reign of Christ on earth immediately after his second coming in glory. In other words, the term is an affirmation of the millennial school of thought. Thus, amillennialism and postmillennialism (which reject the notion that Christ will return to establish his earthly kingdom) are not attracted to the concept of a millennial kingdom.

Advocates of the idea of the millennial kingdom often put forth four arguments in their defense of this position. (1) They interpret the Abrahamic Covenant literally and unconditionally (Gen. 12:1–3; 15:18–21; 17:7–8). That is, God's promise to Abraham that his seed would inherit the land of Israel has never been revoked (cf. Isa. 40ff.; Jer. 29:1–14; Dan. 9:2; etc.). In other words, the church has not permanently replaced Israel in God's plan. The day is coming when Israel will convert to Jesus as their Messiah. When Jesus returns from heaven to establish the millennium, Jerusalem will serve as his base and Jewish Christians will play a leading role (Rom. 11:25–27; Rev. 7; 14).

(2) The idea of a millennial kingdom is attested in at least three Jewish apocalyptic works basically contemporaneous with the New Testament: *1 Enoch* 93:3–17 (ca. 167 B.C.); *4 Ezra* 7:26–44/12:31–34 (ca. A.D. 90); and *2 Baruch* 29:3–30:1/40:1–4/72:2–74:3 (ca. A.D. 100). Each of these writings envisions the following scenario: *this age—temporary messianic kingdom—eternal age to come/kingdom of God*. In each instance, the Messiah will come and form a transitional kingdom between this age and the age to come. Some ancient rabbis held to the same belief (Akiba, ca. A.D. 135; Eliezer b. Hyrcanus, ca. A.D. 90; Jehoshua, ca. A.D. 90).

(3) Paul seems to allude to the temporary messianic kingdom in 1 Corinthians 15:20–28. Some scholars have synthesized his view of the sequence of eschatological events in this way: (a) the sudden and unexpected Parousia (second coming, 1 Thess. 5:1–4); (b) the resurrection of deceased believers and the transformation of living believers, all of whom meet the Lord in the air (1 Thess. 4:16–17); (c) the messianic judgment presided over by Christ (2 Cor. 5:10) or God (Rom. 14:10); (d) the dawn of the messianic kingdom (not described by Paul, but perhaps hinted at in Gal. 4:26); (e) during the messianic kingdom the transformation of

all nature from mortality to immortality (Rom. 8:19–22), along with a struggle with angelic powers (Rom. 16:20) until death itself is conquered (1 Cor. 15:23–28); (f) the end of the messianic kingdom (Paul does not mention its duration); and (g) a general resurrection at the end of the messianic kingdom (1 Cor. 6:3); immediately followed by (h) judgment on all men and defeated angels.

According to this proposal, Paul introduces two resurrections—one at the return of Christ and the other at the end of the messianic kingdom. This modification of Jewish eschatology was motivated by the life, death, and resurrection of Jesus the Messiah. The first resurrection enables believers to participate in the messianic kingdom.

(4) The key New Testament passage thought by premillennialists to teach the temporary messianic kingdom is Revelation 20. Christ will return at the end of the Great Tribulation (Rev. 6–18) to defeat Satan, the Antichrist, and their minions and throw them into the bottomless pit for a thousand years. The absence of God's enemies will result in an unprecedented era of peace on the earth as Christ rules from Jerusalem (20:1–3). Along with Christ, Christians will rule in the millennial kingdom (20:4–6). At the end of the thousand years, Satan will be released temporarily for the purpose of deceiving the nations into joining him for one last stand against God and his Christ—the battle of Gog and Magog. Christ, however, will destroy Satan and sin forever, casting them into the lake of fire at the Great White Throne Judgment (Rev. 20:7–15). These events will be followed by the final state or the eternal kingdom of God.

Those who are not premillennialists often raise two objections against the proposal of a millennial kingdom. (1) They argue that only the martyrs of the Great Tribulation are referred to as reigning with Christ (Rev. 20:4). (2) They view the resurrection mentioned as spiritual rather than physical in nature (20:4–6).

Premillennialists counter both of these objections. (1) The resurrection of the martyrs does not occur until later, thus distinguishing them from the general populace of Christians, who also coreign with Christ (Rev. 20:4). In addition, elsewhere in Revelation John promises that the faithful, not just the martyrs, will share Christ's future reign (2:26–28; 3:12, 21; 5:19; cf. 1 Cor. 6:2–3).

(2) A spiritual resurrection can hardly compensate the martyrs mentioned in Revelation 20:4, because they are physically dead but spiritually alive in the presence of the Lord. What they need is a bodily resurrection. Furthermore, the Greek expression translated "they lived" in 20:4 refers to a bodily resurrection, for a number of reasons: (a) the same verb in

20:5 means bodily resurrection; (b) the related root verb *zaō* ("I live") in Revelation frequently refers to bodily resurrection (1:18; 2:8; 13:14; 20:5); (c) in the context of death *zaō* always refers to physical resurrection in the New Testament (John 11:25; Acts 1:3; 9:41); and (d) John clearly equates "live" with resurrection in Revelation 20:5 (*anastasis*, the Greek word used over forty times in the New Testament with reference to physical resurrection). (See AMILLENNIALISM; DISPENSATIONALISM, CLASSICAL; DISPENSATIONALISM, PROGRESSIVE; KINGDOM OF GOD; PREMILLENNIALISM; POSTMILLENNIALISM; THOUSAND-YEAR REIGN.)

Millennialism

There are three major interpretive views related to the millennium. *Premillennialism* ("pre" means "before") is the view that Christ will return *before* establishing an earthly reign with his saints for a thousand years. This may or may not be a literal thousand-year period of time, but it will be a full and complete earthly reign. Many premillennialists understand the millennium to be the fulfillment of Old Testament prophecies portraying the Son of David ruling over a kingdom of righteousness and peace on earth.

Premillennialists tend to take Revelation 19–21 as a sequence of events occurring at the end of the age. Christ will return (ch. 19), Satan will be bound, and the saints resurrected will reign with Christ for a thousand years (20:1–6). Then Satan will be released for a final rebellion before his ultimate defeat (20:7–10). Then comes the last resurrection and the final judgment (20:11–15), followed by the new heaven and new earth (ch. 21). The following chart summarizes the basic types of premillennial0ism.

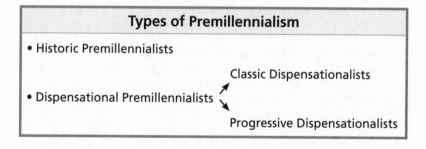

Types of Premillennialism
• Historic Premillennialists
Classic Dispensationalists
• Dispensational Premillennialists
Progressive Dispensationalists

Postmillennialism ("post" means "after") believes that Christ will return *after* the millennium. Postmillennialists maintain that the gospel of Christ will eventually triumph and bring about the millennial age (e.g., wars will cease, peace and righteousness will prevail, most of humanity will convert to Christianity). This view is founded on the notion of progress, since it is the progress of the gospel rather than the return of Christ that ushers in the spiritual reign of Christ known as the millennium. The millennium will be followed by the return of Christ, a general resurrection and judgment, and the eternal kingdom.

Amillennialism ("a" means "not") contends that there will be *no* visible, earthly millennial reign of Christ. This view stresses the symbolic nature of Revelation and interprets Revelation 20:4–6 either as symbolizing (1) the heavenly reign of Christ with Christians who have already died and are now with the Lord, or (2) the spiritual reign of Christ during the present age in the hearts of believers on earth. Satan has been bound by the gospel of Christ. At the end of history and as part of the transition to the eternal state there will be the return of Christ, a general resurrection, and a last judgment. (See AMILLENNIALISM; MILLENNIUM; MILLENNIAL KINGDOM; POSTMILLENNIALISM; PREMILLENNIALISM, DISPENSATIONAL; PREMILLENNIALISM, HISTORIC.)

Millennium

The word "millennium" comes from two Latin words: *mille* ("thousand") and *annus* ("year"), thus meaning "one thousand years." Theologically, the millennium refers to the thousand-year reign of Christ described in Revelation 20:1–7, where the Greek word for "thousand" (*chilioi*) is used six times (Rev. 20:2, 3, 4, 5, 6, 7):

> And I saw an angel coming down out of heaven, having the key to the Abyss and holding in his hand a great chain. [2] He seized the dragon, that ancient serpent, who is the devil, or Satan, and bound him for a *thousand years*. [3] He threw him into the Abyss, and locked and sealed it over him, to keep him from deceiving the nations anymore until the *thousand years* were ended. After that, he must be set free for a short time.
>
> [4] I saw thrones on which were seated those who had been given authority to judge. And I saw the souls of those who had been beheaded because of their testimony for Jesus and because of the word of God. They had not worshiped the beast or his image and had not received his mark on their foreheads or their hands. They came to life and reigned with Christ a *thousand years*. [5] (The rest of the dead did not come to life until the *thousand years* were ended.) This is the first resurrection. [6] Blessed and holy are those who have part in the first resurrection. The

second death has no power over them, but they will be priests of God and of Christ and will reign with him for a *thousand years.*

⁷ When the *thousand years* are over, Satan will be released from his prison. (italics added)

Interpreters have disagreed about how to understand this passage — and Revelation 19–21 in general. There are three main schools of interpretation related to the millennium: premillennialism, postmillennialism, and amillennialism (see MILLENNIALISM). Premillennialists tend to take 20:1–7 more literally and understand the millennium to be an earthly reign of Christ after his return. Postmillennialists also opt for a literal millennium, but they place it before the return of Christ and view it as a time of peace and righteousness resulting from the progress of the gospel. In contrast, amillennialists view the period symbolically as a spiritual reign of Christ in the lives of believers.

While the doctrine of the millennium is explicitly taught only in Revelation 20, some see the idea of a thousand-year reign supported by other Scriptures as well (e.g., Isa. 11:2–9; 65:20; Zech. 14:6–21; Acts 3:19–21; 1 Cor. 15:23–25). (See AMILLENNIALISM; MILLENNIAL KINGDOM; POST-MILLENNIALISM; PREMILLENNIALISM, DISPENSATIONAL; PREMILLENNIAL-ISM, HISTORIC.)

Minor Prophets

The prophetic books in the Old Testament are often divided into two groups: the Major Prophets and the Minor Prophets. This classification is based solely on length, not on importance. The Minor Prophets are Hosea, Joel, Amos, Obadiah, Jonah, Micah, Nahum, Habakkuk, Zephaniah, Haggai, Zechariah, and Malachi. In Jewish tradition and in Hebrew Bibles they are known as "The Book of the Twelve" (see BOOK OF THE TWELVE). These books are shorter in length than the Major Prophets (Isaiah, Jeremiah, Ezekiel, Daniel), and they follow the Major Prophets in the Christian canon.

The twelve Minor Prophets span the entire time of the literary prophets. Thus the date of the books ranges from the eighth century B.C. (Hosea, Amos, Micah) to the sixth and fifth century B.C. (Haggai, Zechariah, and Malachi). There is no scholarly consensus as to the reason for the order of the books. The last three (Haggai, Zechariah, and Malachi) are located chronologically last (i.e., the last to be written). Likewise, Hosea (first), Amos (third), and perhaps Joel (second) are among the earliest. So there appears to be some order based on when the books were written. But this explanation does not explain the rest of the Minor Prophets and their ensuing order.

Miriam

Miriam, the sister of Moses and Aaron (Num. 26:59), is called a "prophetess" in Exodus 15:20. After God delivers the Israelites by parting the Red Sea and then destroying the Egyptian army, Moses and the Israelites sing a song of celebration and praise (15:1–18). Then "Miriam the prophetess," with a tambourine in hand, leads the Israelite women in singing a similar song of celebration and praise. The women also celebrate by dancing (15:20–21). As a prophetess, Miriam apparently functions in some sort of leadership role. In fact, in Micah 6:4 God himself declares, "I brought you up out of Egypt and redeemed you from the land of slavery. I sent Moses to lead you, also Aaron and Miriam."

In Numbers 12:1–15, for some unexplained reason Miriam objects to Moses' marriage to a Cushite woman. God rebukes Miriam for this act and ironically strikes her with leprosy. At God's insistence she is exiled outside the Israelite camp for seven days. After that, it appears that God heals her so that she can return to the Israelite community.

Moon

"Moon" in biblical prophecy proceeds from Joel 2:31, a significant Old Testament text heralding end-times events: "The sun will be turned to darkness and the moon to blood." This characteristic of the moon occurs in the New Testament in connection with prophecies concerning cosmic disturbances brought on by the latter days: Mark 13:24–25 (cf. Matt. 24:29; Luke 21:25) and Revelation 6:12–17.

These New Testament passages generate three competing interpretations as to the timing of their fulfillment. (1) Futurists believe these cosmic appearances will only happen literally at the second coming of Christ. (2) Preterists think these cosmic disturbances have already occurred at the fall of Jerusalem to Rome in A.D. 70 (see PRETERIST VIEW OF REVELATION). (3) Others suspect that what cosmic abnormalities there may have been connected with the fall of Jerusalem in A.D. 70 (eclipse, earthquake) represent only a partial fulfillment of the pertinent biblical prophecies, while their complete realization will transpire at the Parousia (second coming). (See DESTRUCTION OF THE JERUSALEM TEMPLE [A.D. 70]; ASTRONOMICAL SIGNS.)

Moses

The books of Exodus, Leviticus, Numbers, and Deuteronomy are dominated by two central characters — God and Moses. Moses is indeed a unique individual who plays a unique role in the Old Testament. God chooses Moses and empowers him to deliver Israel from the Egyptians. Thus Moses leads in the defeat of Pharaoh and in the exodus out of Egypt. He then continues to lead Israel as they form into a nation and enter into covenant relationship with God.

Throughout Exodus, Leviticus, Numbers, and Deuteronomy Moses is the mediator through whom God gives his law to Israel. So not only does Moses carry out spectacular miracles (such as the parting of the Red Sea) but he also talks directly to God on numerous occasions and relays God's word to God's people. Because he performs powerful miracles and because he mediates the very words of God, several Old Testament passages refer to him as a prophet (Num. 12:6–8; Deut. 18:15–18; 34:10–12).

In Deuteronomy 18:14–22 God promises the Israelites that he will send future prophets "like Moses" to lead the people. This passage also contains a strong warning against false prophets (see FALSE PROPHECY). It also stresses that the true prophet will speak the word given by God, while the false prophet will only presume to speak for God. God declares to Moses, "I will raise up for them a prophet like you from among their brothers; I will put my words in his mouth, and he will tell them everything I command him" (18:18). It is Moses' role as speaking the word of God that identifies him as a prophet.

Because of the powerful miracles that Moses performs and because of the special relationship that Moses has with God, God underscores that Moses is no ordinary prophet. For example, in Numbers 12:6–8a God states:

> When a prophet of the LORD is among you,
>   I reveal myself to him in visions,
>   I speak to him in dreams.
> But this is not true of my servant Moses;
>   he is faithful in all my house.
> With him I speak face to face,
>   clearly and not in riddles;
>   he sees the form of the LORD.

Likewise in Deuteronomy 34:10–11, the epitaph given for Moses declares, "No prophet has risen in Israel like Moses, whom the LORD knew face to face, who did all those miraculous signs and wonders the LORD sent him to do in Egypt."

Throughout the rest of the Old Testament there are prophets like Elijah and Elisha who are known for their spectacular miracles, and there are prophets like Isaiah and Jeremiah, who are known for being spokesmen for God. In his unique role as the powerful leader of God's people and as God's prophetic spokesman who transmits God's word to the people, Moses embodies both of these aspects of prophecy. Likewise, he has an intimacy with God not experienced on the same scale by any of the other prophets. Only Christ, who comes as the ultimate leader and prophet, surpasses Moses in this regard (see Heb. 3:1–6). Indeed, the unique power of Moses and his special revelatory role in mediating the covenant foreshadows the coming Messiah.

In the New Testament, Moses is acknowledged as a special and unique servant of God who mediated the old covenant. Christ, however, is superior to Moses because he is the Son of God (not a servant like Moses) and because he mediated the New Covenant, a superior covenant to the one Moses mediated (2 Cor. 3:7–18; Heb. 3:1–6; 8:1–10:39). It is true that Moses was great and mediated a great covenant. Yet he merely foreshadowed the Messiah, who was even more glorious and who inaugurated an even more glorious covenant (see NEW COVENANT).

Mount of Olives

The Mount of Olives is a flattened, rounded ridge with four identifiable summits adjacent to the southeast side of Jerusalem. It takes its name from the olive groves that covered the ridge in ancient times. The Mount of Olives rises 250 feet above Temple Mount. Running between the Mount of Olives and the southeast wall of Jerusalem is the Kidron Valley. Near the foot of the Mount of Olives, on the western slope above the Kidron, is the likely site of the Garden of Gethsemane.

Two key prophetic biblical events relate to the Mount of Olives. (1) Zechariah 14:1–5 forecasts a coming day when the Lord will descend to the Mount of Olives for the purpose of delivering and restoring his people, the Jews. During this dramatic event the Mount of Olives will "be split in two from east to west, forming a great valley" (14:4). It is commonplace among Christians to interpret that event as being fulfilled at the second coming of Christ (cf. Acts 1:9–11). (2) Jesus' prophetic sermon about the future of Jerusalem, Israel, and the nations was given on the Mount of Olives and is thus often called the Olivet Discourse (cf. Matt. 24:3; Mark 13:3; Luke 21:37).

Muslims

See ISLAM.

Mystery of the Kingdom of God

The mystery, or secret, of the kingdom of God (see KINGDOM OF GOD) is a theme most associated with the Gospel of Mark (see MARK, BOOK OF). In general, a mystery or secret in ancient Jewish apocalyptic writings refers to the plans of God for the world that are now being revealed to his people. In Mark, such a concept centers on the kingdom (i.e., reign) of God, where we learn that the kingdom of God was inaugurated in the works and words of Jesus Christ, though it was perceived only through the eyes of faith. This idea of the veiled kingdom of God is intimately related in Mark to the parables (words) and miracles (works) of Christ.

(1) Mark 4 records several parables of Jesus regarding the kingdom, the most significant of which is the parable of the sower and seed. The emphasis of this parable is on the bumper harvest of the fourth soil. Even though the three other soils (that from which the birds plucked seed, the rocky soil, and the thorny soil) fail to produce, the good soil's hundredfold crop more than compensates for the other responses. In other words, though the offer of the kingdom of God meets initially with only a minimal positive response, it nevertheless will ultimately prevail. It starts small but is destined one day to encompass the earth at the second coming of Christ.

Jesus conveys a similar teaching in the parable of the mustard seed (4:30–34). This message of the veiled presence of the kingdom is passed on by Jesus to the disciples, who, though initially failing their Lord, eventually fulfill their mission of proclaiming the gospel (4:10–12, 21–25).

(2) It is one thing for Jesus to announce the arrival of the kingdom of God, but it is something else for him to prove it indeed has come. Such evidence is to be found in the miracles of Jesus. The first half of Mark's Gospel is devoted to demonstrating that Jesus' miracles of healing, exorcism, power over nature, and resurrection are proof positive that the kingdom or reign of God has indeed broken into this age (Mark 1:1–8:21). In the second half (8:22–16:8), however, a noticeable shift occurs in the way Jesus presents the kingdom in that the miracles for the most part cease. In their place, Jesus redefines himself as the suffering, crucified Messiah, not a political one, whose kingdom is not of this world. Thus, the kingdom

of God has already dawned, but has not yet been completed. This is the mystery of the kingdom of God.

The preceding information helps to explain a curious happening in the Gospel of Mark, that on numerous occasions Jesus strangely commands the people whom he has just healed to be silent about the miracle. They are not to tell anyone (Mark 1:40–44; 5:21–23, 35–43; 7:31–36; cf. 5:19). Liberal scholars a century ago named this phenomenon "the messianic secret." They argued that the historical Jesus did not actually identify himself as the Messiah; rather, the early church made up such a claim. In order to cover up the truth, so liberals argued, the church fabricated those charges Jesus made to silence. But a far more satisfying answer to the "messianic secret" is ready to hand: Jesus did not want people to broadcast his messiahship too early, at least not the wrong kind of Messiah. Jesus came to be a suffering Christ, not a political deliverer (SEE MESSIAH).

Nabiʾ

Nabiʾ is the most common Hebrew word meaning "prophet," designating a person involved in prophecy. Sometimes it is used interchangeably with the terms "man of God" (see MAN OF GOD) and "seer" (see SEER).

Nahum, Book of

The book of Nahum is different from most of the other prophetic books in that the prophet does not prophesy against Israel or Judah, but only against the foreign nation Assyria. The Assyrians conquered the northern kingdom Israel in 722 B.C., carrying off many of the Israelites into exile (2 Kings 17). They also attacked Jerusalem in 701 B.C., but were unsuccessful because of God's direct intervention (chs. 18–19). Because of these attacks Nahum prophesies in his book that Assyria will be totally destroyed. The Assyrian capital of Nineveh fell to the Babylonians in 612 B.C., fulfilling Nahum's prophecy.

Nathan

Nathan is a true prophet of the Lord living during the time of David. Although David had a son named Nathan (2 Sam. 5:14), the name is a common name, and there is no indication that the prophet Nathan is David's son.

Nathan the prophet functions as a spokesman for God and as a member of David's royal court. He plays several important roles in the Old Testament biblical story. In 2 Samuel 7 it is through Nathan that God tells David that he (God) does not need nor want a Temple, but that he (God) will establish the throne of David forever (see DAVIDIC COVENANT). In 2 Samuel 12, after David commits adultery with Bathsheba, it is Nathan the prophet who rebukes David and leads him to confess (see also Ps. 51). Indeed, critique of the king is one of the main roles of the biblical prophets, in this case even of King David. Finally, in 1 Kings 1, Nathan works with Bathsheba to convince the aging, feeble David that he has promised Solomon as his successor.

The Old Testament prophets are frequently associated with music, and this is true of Nathan as well. Note 2 Chronicles 29:25, which states that King Hezekiah "stationed the Levites in the temple of the LORD with cymbals, harps and lyres in the way prescribed by David and Gad the king's seer and Nathan the prophet; this was commanded by the LORD through the prophets."

Finally, Nathan, along with other prophets from his time, appears to have been involved in keeping royal court historical records. Thus "the records of Nathan the prophet" chronicle King David's reign (1 Chron. 29:29–30) as well as King Solomon's reign (2 Chron. 9:29). However, these historical annals never became part of the Bible, and they disappeared long ago.

Nations

In the Old Testament the Hebrew word *goyyim* can mean either "Gentiles" (i.e., non-Jewish peoples) or "nations," but most of the time it refers to "nations." In the New Testament the Greek word *ethnē* carries the same range of meaning, referring to "Gentiles" or to "nations."

Genesis 11 describes the early situation where all people are united by a common language and form one people and nation. However, after the sin committed by this united group at the Tower of Babel, the people of the earth are scattered throughout the world into peoples and nations, each with their own language. This scattering is described in Genesis 10.

Starting in Genesis 12, however, God begins to present his promise/covenant to Abraham as a salvation solution to the human sin and rebellion seen in Genesis 3–11. A critical part of that promise is that all peoples (12:3) and all nations (18:18) will be blessed through Abraham. This reference to peoples and nations alludes back to the scattering of Genesis 10 and points forward prophetically to a time when the scattered nations of the earth will be brought back together in blessing to worship God.

Prophets such as Isaiah make it clear that the nations will be saved and included as the people of God when the Messiah comes. This theme is highlighted by the promise that the Messiah will be a "light to the nations/Gentiles" (see LIGHT TO THE NATIONS/GENTILES; ISAIAH, BOOK OF).

The New Testament presents Christ as the fulfillment of the Abrahamic promise/covenant (see ABRAHAMIC COVENANT). Likewise, the powerful act of the Spirit at Pentecost (Acts 2) in overcoming language barriers is presented as a prophetic reversal of Genesis 10–11 and points to the reuniting of all people/nations in Christ. Finally, the ultimate picture of God's people in the book of Revelation is of "every tribe and language and people and nation" united together in Christ and worshiping God together (Rev. 5:9; 7:9). Thus the reuniting of the scattered nations into the people of God is an important prophetic theme running from Genesis to Revelation.

Nature, Natural World

See TRANSFORMATION OF NATURE.

Near View – Far View

Although most of what the Old Testament prophets prophesied was fulfilled in their own time, some prophecies remain future even for modern readers. These remaining prophecies pose a special problem known as the *near view–far view* problem. Are the prophets referring to events in the near future (e.g., the destruction of Jerusalem by the Babylonians) or to events in the distant or far future (e.g., the Day of the Lord)? When the prophets are describing the restoration of God's people, are they alluding to the return of the Jewish exiles under Zerubbabel and Ezra, to the first coming of Christ, or to the second coming of Christ? The *near view–far view* phenomenon is similar to what a mountain range looks like from a distance. All the mountains appear to be the same distance away, but in reality some mountains are much closer than others, perhaps miles closer. The prophets often appear to describe the future like a distant mountain range, without noting the distances in time between near future events and far future events.

The *near view–far view* reality for interpreters is really about which prophecies have already been fulfilled and which are yet to be fulfilled. For example, the prophets speak of a time following the Babylonian exile when a remnant will return and rebuild Jerusalem. Micah writes, "I will make the lame a remnant, those driven away a strong nation. The LORD will rule over them in Mount Zion from that day and forever" (Mic. 4:7). Jeremiah writes, "I myself will gather the remnant of my flock out of all the countries where I have driven them and will bring them back to their pasture, where they will be fruitful and increase in number" (Jer. 23:3). Again, " 'The days are coming,' declares the LORD, 'when this city will be rebuilt for me from the Tower of Hananel to the Corner Gate' " (31:38).

When the exiles do return under the leadership of Zerubbabel, Ezra, and Nehemiah to rebuild the Temple and the city walls, were these prophecies (and others like them) fulfilled at that time, or will there still be a future fulfillment? Does the "remnant" refer to those who returned from exile, or is there yet a distant future restoration to come? To put it another way, will there be a future restoration of Israel to the land of Palestine?

Likewise, sometimes it is difficult to tell when the prophets are referring to events fulfilled by the first coming of Christ and when they are referring to events of his second coming. The *near view–far view* problem means that contemporary interpreters should be cautious about being too dogmatic about the details of future events. Sometimes modern readers cannot tell if Old Testament prophecies have already been fulfilled or if there remains a future fulfillment. In many cases, the broader biblical, theological, and ethical principles should take precedence over speculation about the specific details of fulfillment. This seems to be what Jesus encourages in his response to the disciples' question about the fulfillment of a particular prophecy (Acts 1:6–8):

> So when they met together, they asked him, "Lord, are you at this time going to restore the kingdom to Israel?"
>
> He said to them: "It is not for you to know the times or dates the Father has set by his own authority. But you will receive power when the Holy Spirit comes on you; and you will be my witnesses in Jerusalem, and in all Judea and Samaria, and to the ends of the earth."

Although this is probably not the answer the disciples wanted to hear, it serves as a reminder that there may not always be clear, obvious, unambiguous answers regarding which prophecies have already been fulfilled and which have not.

Nebuchadnezzar

Nebuchadnezzar was the second king of the Chaldean dynasty, who ruled Babylonia from 605 to 562 B.C. He plays a huge role in the Old Testament, especially in the prophetic books, because he is the one who leads the Babylonian invasion against Judah, destroys Jerusalem and the Temple, and carries off the Jews into exile. He is mentioned ninety times in the Old Testament, primarily in 2 Kings 24–25; 2 Chronicles 36; Jeremiah 21–52; and Daniel 1–5 (see BABYLON/BABYLONIANS).

Necromancy

Necromancy is the practice of divination through consulting the dead. Many of the peoples and nations around Israel in the ancient Near East had a class of individuals also called prophets (see PROPHECY IN THE ANCIENT NEAR EAST). However, often these pagan prophets practiced magic and other forms of divination. One of these practices was necromancy—consulting the dead. Necromancy, along with other forms of magic and sorcery, was strictly prohibited among the Israelites (see Deut. 18:9–13). Note that immediately following this text is the description of what true prophecy in Israel should look like (18:14–22).

An example of apparent necromancy occurs in 1 Samuel 28. The prophet Samuel has died, and disobedient King Saul is bewildered because God has rejected him and no longer gives him any guidance. So Saul seeks out a medium, a woman who can supposedly communicate with the dead. He demands that she bring up the departed Samuel from the dead, and the text suggests that she does indeed do this. Samuel apparently comes back from the dead to issue one final prophecy to King Saul, "Tomorrow you and your sons will be with me" (28:11–19). This story is admittedly strange and puzzling, but not easily dismissed.

Nero

Nero lived from A.D. 37 to 68 and ruled as emperor of Rome from A.D. 54 to 68. He was born into a distinguished family of Roman aristocracy. His father was a senator who died while Nero was young, and his mother, Agrippina, was the great-granddaughter of Augustus and the fourth wife of Emperor Claudius. Nero was renamed as Nero Claudius Caesar Germanicus when he was adopted at age twelve by Claudius. Since Claudius wanted his son Britannicus to become emperor, Agrippina murdered the boy, paving the way for her son Nero to become emperor.

In the early years of his reign, Nero relied on two trusted senators to administer the empire: his tutor, Seneca (the famous philosopher), and the commander of the Praetorian Guard, Burrus. Both senators ruled the empire effectively while Nero spent most of his time on entertainment and pleasure. Within the imperial household, Agrippina desired to reign alongside her young son and this led to her demise. Nero murdered his mother and his wife, Octavia, in order to marry the beautiful Poppea, the wife of Otho, who succeeded Nero as emperor. Nero eventually also put Poppea to death.

In the early 60s after Burrus died and Seneca retired, Nero began to live without restraint in his pursuit of power and glory. Nero's fascination with his own artistic ability (music, poetry, acting) and with chariot races occupied most of his time. Expensive wars in Britain and Armenia along with a new group of greedy advisors caused a financial crisis. He developed a widespread reputation as a brutal, licentious, self-indulgent emperor.

In A.D. 64 a fire broke out in the shops around the Circus Maximus and eventually devastated a large portion of Rome. Nero returned to Rome amidst rumors that he had set the fire himself. Perhaps under the influence of Poppea (very pro-Jewish), he quickly found a scapegoat in the Christians. The persecution of Christians that followed included crucifixions, where the victims were used as human torches to light the emperor's races. Quite possibly both Peter and Paul were martyred during this persecution.

Ironically, Nero was emperor when Paul had earlier appealed to Caesar (Acts 25:20–21) and when he instructed the Christians in Rome to submit to governing authorities (Rom. 13:1–7). The political reality was that Nero blamed a minority that was already disliked or even hated for being exclusive. Nero personally benefited from the fire by using the land to build an opulent palace known as the "Golden House."

After a failed plot on his life in A.D. 65, Nero became more suspicious and paranoid. Many respected citizens lost their lives during several waves of executions designed to destroy the opposition. He behaved in a vicious and sinister manner toward his family and peers. The philosophers, nobility, military, and most of the rest of society came to detest Nero for his cruelty, exhibitionism, self-glorification, lust for power, and total lack of concern for the well-being of the empire.

In A.D. 66 when the Jewish revolt broke out in Palestine, Nero ordered Vespasian to deal with the matter. This revolt led to the destruction of Jerusalem and the Temple in A.D. 70. Nero played no part in the military details and seemed oblivious to the dynamics of the situation. Instead, Nero irresponsibly left Rome in A.D. 66 for an extended artistic tour of Greece, where his ego was flattered by his victorious competition in their games. Nero expressed gratitude to his Greek fans by liberating Greece from Roman control and taxation. Faced with rising opposition not only in Rome but throughout the empire, Nero committed suicide in A.D. 68 in the villa of an ex-slave.

Toward the end of his reign Nero came to embody evil power and brutality. The number 666 is thought by many interpreters of Revelation to form an acronym of his name, and thus they identify him as the beast in Revelation 13. Because his death and burial were shrouded in secrecy, a legend known as the *Nero redivivus* ("Nero revived") circulated widely in the eastern provinces, stating that Nero would return (perhaps with a Parthian army) to recapture Rome and reclaim his imperial throne. (See EMPERORS; NERO REDIVIVUS; SIX HUNDRED SIXTY-SIX.)

Nero Redivivus

In Revelation 13 one of the beast's seven heads is dealt a fatal wound, but the wound is healed and the beast survives. Many scholars interpret the wounded head as representing one of the Roman emperors, most likely Nero. He was the first emperor to declare a state persecution against Christians, although it was probably limited to Rome. In A.D. 68 after being censured by the senate and declared an enemy of Rome, Nero committed suicide.

People had a hard time believing that Nero had actually died. For many years rumors circulated widely that he had not actually died, but had escaped to Rome's enemies to the east, the Parthians. (A variation of the rumor said that he had died and had been resurrected.) Supposedly he was preparing an army and would one day return to invade the Roman Empire and recapture his throne. This legend became known as the *Nero redivivus* ("Nero revived") myth.

Some interpreters also see the myth in connection with Revelation 17:11, which says that "the beast who once was [Nero lived and ruled], and now is not [Nero is now dead], is an eighth king [*Nero redivivus* or the Antichrist]." Nonbiblical Jewish oracles had predicted Nero's return (e.g., *Sib. Or.* 3:63–74; 5:33–34, 137–54, 361–85). Because many Christians had been martyred under Nero, the church feared him and commonly associated Nero with the Antichrist.

Revelation does not predict a literal return of Nero from the dead, but John may have drawn on this popular legend to fashion the vision of the beast. What people had heard as legend would one day become reality as a Nero-like ruler, much worse than Nero himself, would arise to blaspheme God and wage war against his people. (See ANTICHRIST; NERO; SIX HUNDRED SIXTY-SIX.)

New Covenant

The Old Testament prophets proclaim to Israel and Judah that they have broken the Mosaic Covenant (as represented by the books of Exodus, Numbers, Leviticus, and especially Deuteronomy). They plead with the people to repent, to turn away from idols, and to return to keeping the Mosaic Covenant. However, the people refuse, and as the prophets predict, the nations of Israel and Judah are destroyed, respectively, by the Assyrians and the Babylonians. The presence of God departs from the Temple, signaling the end of the Mosaic Covenant (see PRESENCE OF GOD).

All of this is prophesied in advance by the Old Testament prophets. Yet the prophets look beyond the broken Mosaic Covenant and the judgment to a future time of restoration and blessing. One of the central elements in the coming time of blessing that the prophets describe is the New Covenant. Because of the disobedience of Israel, the Old (Mosaic) Covenant had failed. Therefore, the Old Testament prophets, especially Isaiah, Jeremiah, and Ezekiel, point to a new time characterized by a new relationship with God—in essence, a New Covenant.

Isaiah 40–66 calls it a "new exodus" and connects it to the coming Servant of the LORD (Messiah) and the inclusion of the Gentiles. Ezekiel 34, 36–37 calls it a "covenant of peace" (34:25) and describes it as a time when God will cleanse them from all sin, create a new heart within them, and actually put his Spirit within them (37:25–27). However, it is Jeremiah who actually labels this coming new arrangement as the "new covenant." In Jeremiah 31:31–33, God declares that he will make a "new covenant" with Israel. This covenant will not be like the old one that Israel broke. In its place, God will put his law in their minds and in their hearts. All those within the covenant will know God, and once again his people will be in close relationship to him. This New Covenant, God declares, will be characterized by the forgiveness of sin.

The promised New Covenant is formally inaugurated by Jesus at the Last Supper when he states, "This cup is the *new covenant* in my blood, which is poured out for you" (Luke 22:20, italics added); cf. 1 Cor. 11:25). Indeed, the change from the Old Testament (i.e., Old Covenant) to the New Testament (i.e., New Covenant) was brought about by the life, death, and resurrection of Jesus.

Although there are numerous places throughout the New Testament that connect Jesus to the fulfillment of the Old Testament prophetic promise of something new and better, especially with implications of New Covenant fulfillment, the clearest presentation of this theology is in Hebrews

7–10. Here Jesus is explicitly identified as the one who brings the "new" and better covenant to replace the old one, which is said to be "obsolete" and passing away (Heb. 8:13). The specific "new covenant" promise of Jeremiah 31 is quoted twice in Hebrews (Heb. 8:8–12; 10:16–17). This book underscores that the New Covenant is better than the Old Covenant because it is based on better promises, has a better mediator (Christ), offers total and complete forgiveness, and is ratified by superior blood, the very blood of Christ.

New Exodus

In the Old Testament story of the exodus, God delivers his people from slavery in Egypt and leads them through the Red Sea, the desert, and the Jordan River, and then victoriously into the Promised Land. Throughout the Old Testament the exodus event is viewed as the paradigm or the proto-typical picture of salvation. It is to the Old Testament as the cross is to the New Testament.

Thus, when the Old Testament prophets speak about the coming messianic age and all of the new and better features of that coming new relationship with God, they frequently describe it in terms of the exodus. That is, they poetically and figuratively describe the coming deliverance in terms of a new exodus. Several of the prophets speak vividly of a time when God will gather his people out of oppressive situations and bring them once again into the Promised Land.

Yet in all aspects the new exodus is always bigger and better than the old one. The people whom God gathers are not just slaves from Egypt, but now include the lame, the blind, and other weak people (Isa. 40:11; 42:16; Jer. 31:8; Mic. 4:6–7). They will come not just from Egypt, but from the north and south, from the east and west (Isa. 43:5–6). Not only will this Exodus include Israel, but the nations too will be included, including Egypt herself (Isa. 11:10–16; 19:19–25). As God dried up the Red Sea and stopped up the Jordan River to let his people pass through in the old exodus, so he will dry up waters and rivers to allow his people to cross in the imagery of the new exodus (Isa. 11:15; 19:5; 43:2). Isaiah especially uses exodus imagery and exodus-related figures of speech to describe the new and better deliverance that was coming with the Messiah.

Many New Testament writers connect Jesus and his work with the new exodus prophecies of the Old Testament. The book of Mark, in particular, often portrays the events in Jesus' life as parallel (but better and bigger) to the events regarding Moses and the original exodus. Other

New Testament Gospels use new exodus imagery as well, albeit to a lesser extent. Sometimes Jesus is compared to Moses and sometimes to the nation Israel. In each case, Jesus is clearly identified as similar but more obedient and more powerful.

For example, as Israel was tempted in the wilderness for forty years, Jesus is tempted in the wilderness for forty days. Jesus, however, does not fail. Likewise, as God provided manna for the Israelites during the exodus, so Jesus himself feeds five thousand people in the New Testament. Ironically, like Moses, Jesus demonstrates powerful signs, but like the hard-hearted pharaoh of the Exodus, most of the Israelites who hear Jesus reject his new exodus revelation.

New Heaven and New Earth

In the age to come, the place where God will live with his people is identified as "a new heaven and a new earth" (Rev. 21:1). In the Old Testament, God had promised his people that one day he would usher in a new creation: "Behold, I will create new heavens and a new earth. The former things will not be remembered, nor will they come to mind" (Isa. 65:17; cf. 66:22). The goodness of God's original creation described in Genesis 1–2 was marred by Satan, sin, and death. God has been working since to liberate his creation from bondage and to reverse the curse of sin (Rom. 8:18–25).

Consequently, the final home of the righteous will exclude some elements familiar to those living in the present age, including the sea (Rev. 21:1); crying, mourning, pain, or death (21:4); anything impure, including unrighteous or wicked people (21:8, 27; 22:15); a man-made temple (21:22); natural lights (sun and moon) or night (21:23–24; 22:5); and the curse of sin (22:3). Of particular note is the disappearance of the "sea" (21:1)—a symbol of the evil that threatens God's people in the old world.

Although there will be some continuity with the present creation, both New Testament references to the new heaven and new earth seem to indicate a total transformation (cf. Heb. 12:26–27):

> But the day of the Lord will come like a thief. The heavens will disappear with a roar; the elements will be destroyed by fire, and the earth and everything in it will be laid bare.
> ... That day will bring about the destruction of the heavens by fire, and the elements will melt in the heat. But in keeping with his promise we are looking forward to a new heaven and a new earth, the home of righteousness. (2 Peter 3:10–13)

> Then I saw a new heaven and a new earth, for the first heaven and the first earth had passed away, and there was no longer any sea.... for the old order of things has passed away.
> He who was seated on the throne said, "I am making everything new!" (Rev. 21:1, 4–5)

The term "new" used to describe heaven and earth in Revelation 21:1 indicates a completely new form of existence. Most importantly, those who overcome will experience the triune God in a new way—his comforting touch (21:4), his life-giving provision (21:7; 22:1), his glory (21:11, 23), his personal presence (21:22; 22:4), his light (21:23; 22:5), his name (22:4), his reward (22:12), and his life (22:14, 17).

Creation has come full circle. In the untainted garden of Genesis 1–2, God enjoyed fellowship with his creatures. After Adam and Eve abused their freedom by disobeying, God seems to remove himself from the earth except for special occasions (e.g., Tabernacle, Temple, prophets). The incarnation of Jesus Christ is the pivotal manifestation of God's presence, as John declares, "The Word became flesh and made his dwelling among us. We have seen his glory ..." (John 1:14).

Prior to Revelation 21 God's presence is focused on his throne in heaven. When all evil has been destroyed and his kingdom restored, God will move heaven to earth to live once again among his people (21:3). The only use of the verb *skēnoō* ("dwell, live") outside of Revelation in the New Testament is in John 1:14. God's very presence is what is most "new" about the new creation. The response of God's people is worship (Rev. 22:3). (See GARDEN; HEAVEN; NEW JERUSALEM; PRESENCE OF GOD; SEA.)

New Israel

The term "new Israel" takes one to the heart of an ongoing debate: What is the relationship between Old Testament Israel and the New Testament church? Covenantalists (Reformed theologians) argue that Old Testament prophecies made to Israel have permanently been shifted to the church and that, consequently, Israel's place in biblical prophecy is finished. In common parlance this is often called "replacement theology." Dispensationalists, however, argue that God's promises to Israel about possessing her land have not been spiritualized to apply to the church.

Two key Old Testament passages envision Israel as inhabiting Canaan, with reference to the Abrahamic Covenant (see ABRAHAMIC COVENANT): Genesis 15:18 (cf. 2 Chron. 9:26) and Isaiah 40–55. Genesis 15:18 says of God's promise to Abraham, "On that day the LORD made a covenant with

Abram and said, 'To your descendants I give this land, from the River of Egypt to the great river, the Euphrates.'" This text raises two questions: (1) Was the Abraham Covenant conditional or unconditional? (2) Has the Abrahamic Covenant been fulfilled already? Covenantalists' respective answers to these queries are conditional and yes. Thus, Israel failed to be true to God after she entered Canaan and consequently the promise of land was revoked.

Moreover, 2 Chronicles 9:26 (cf. 1 Kings 4:21, 24) seems to say that King Solomon ruled over the geographical dimensions of the Abrahamic Covenant, thus fulfilling the Genesis prophecy. But dispensationalists contend that Genesis 15:18 should be interpreted unconditionally; that is, God's promise to give Israel a land permanently was not dependent on her response to God but on God's faithfulness to his covenant. Nor does 2 Chronicles 9:26 indicate, according to this view, that Solomon's empire actually encompassed the borders of Genesis 15:18.

These two schools of thought also debate the meaning of Isaiah 40–55, chapters filled with prophetic assurances that Israel will return to her land from exile in Babylonia. Covenantalists argue that the return of Israel to Palestine under Cyrus the Persian (536 B.C.) fulfilled God's promise to Abraham. In any event, the church ultimately has replaced Israel in the plan of God. Dispensationalists, however, believe that Isaiah 40–55 was not fulfilled in the New Testament, but rather awaits the end times, perhaps beginning with the return of modern Jews to Israel to form a nation in A.D. 1948.

This discussion in the New Testament centers on Romans 11:25–27; Galatians 6:16; Ephesians 2:11–22; 1 Peter 2:4–10; and Revelation 7. Covenantalists claim that these passages apply the language of Old Testament Israel to the church to indicate that the promises of Israel have now been spiritualized and passed along to the church. Thus, Galatians 6:16 calls the church "the Israel of God." Romans 11:25–27 suggests that the church, the true Israel, will triumph in the future; Ephesians 2:11–22 makes clear that believing Gentiles, along with Christian Jews, are now a part of the one people of God, the church (see PEOPLE OF GOD); 1 Peter 2:4–10 labels the church "a royal priesthood, a holy nation, a people belonging to God," terms distinctly reminiscent of ancient Israel. Likewise Revelation 7 forecasts the victory of the church in the Great Tribulation, using the imagery of the twelve tribes of Israel.

Dispensationalists counter with their own interpretation of the preceding passages. According to their view, Galatians 6:16 most likely refers to Jewish Christians, in contrast to the Judaizers, as the true Israel. Likewise "Israel" in Romans 11:25–27 is consistent with the other ethnic usages of

Israel throughout Romans 9–11; hence Paul's forecasts about "all Israel" being saved is a reference to the Jewish people's future conversion in the end times. Ephesians 2:11–22, in its description of the one people of God, need not be discounting a future for Israel, and the same could be said of 1 Peter 2:4–12. In addition, Revelation 7 speaks of 144,000 *out of* each of the twelve tribes of Israel, thus referring to the future of Jewish Christians in the Tribulation, that is, the remnant, or believing ones, of Israel, not the church.

New Jerusalem

The specific phrase "new Jerusalem" is only used twice in the Bible (Rev. 3:12; 21:2); both times it refers to the final destination of God's people, the heavenly city, where they will experience the presence of God for eternity. The background for these references relates to the historic importance of the earthly Jerusalem. After conquering the Jebusite city, David made it the capital of Israel (2 Sam. 5:6–10), the home of Israel's earthly kings, and the center of God's kingship as signified by the presence of the Ark of the Covenant (6:17).

The prominence of Jerusalem culminated in the construction of Solomon's Temple (2 Chron. 3:1–17), and the city with its Temple came to represent the very heart of the nation of Israel. The later destruction of Jerusalem by the Babylonians represented God's discipline on the nation (2 Kings 23:27).

Following the exile, rebuilding the city and the Temple became crucial to the restoration of Israel itself. The city had to once again become the place where the Davidic king ruled and where God's presence dwelt. This setting helps explain Jesus' close connection to Jerusalem and its Temple (e.g., his triumphal entry signaling the return of the Davidic King to the city). Since the city eventually rejected Jesus as king, however, it again faced God's judgment in A.D. 70, being devastated by the Roman army (see DESTRUCTION OF THE JERUSALEM TEMPLE [A.D. 70]; JERUSALEM).

As the earthly Jerusalem came to represent the soul of the nation of Israel, the New Testament points Christians toward the heavenly Jerusalem as the ultimate realization of God's kingdom promises. The writer of Hebrews makes it clear that the earthly Jerusalem is not "an enduring city," since Christians are still "looking for the city that is to come" (Heb. 13:14; also 12:26–28). He writes that even Abraham looked "forward to the city with foundations, whose architect and builder is God" (11:10).

The people of faith highlighted in Hebrews 11 were longing for a "heavenly" country that included a city prepared by God (11:16). In describing the New Covenant mountain (likely Mount Zion in contrast to Mount Sinai), the writer focuses on the heavenly Jerusalem: "But you have come to Mount Zion, to the heavenly Jerusalem, the city of the living God. You have come to thousands upon thousands of angels in joyful assembly, to the church of the firstborn, whose names are written in heaven" (12:22–23a; cf. the promise to the church in Philadelphia, Rev. 3:12).

The most extensive description of the new Jerusalem is left for the final two chapters of the Bible. In Revelation 21–22 John portrays it as a place where God will live forever among his people. The holy city stands in contrast to Babylon, the representative wicked power that defies God and oppresses his people.[72]

Babylon, the great prostitute	New Jerusalem, the holy city
The harlot with whom the kings of the earth fornicate (17:2)	The chaste bride, the wife of the Lamb (21:2, 9)
Babylon's glory comes from exploiting the empire (17:4; 18:12–13, 16)	New Jerusalem's glory from God's glory (21:11–21)
Her corruption and deception of the nations (17:2; 18:3, 23; 19:2)	The nations walk by her light, which is the glory of God (21:24)
Babylon rules over the kings of the earth (17:18)	The kings of the earth bring their glory into the new Jerusalem as worship and submission to God (21:24)
Babylon's luxurious wealth extorted from the nations (18:12–17)	The nations bring their glory and honor into the new Jerusalem (21:26)
Babylon's abominations, impurities, deceptions (17:4, 5; 18:23)	Uncleanness, abomination, and falsehood are excluded (21:27)
Babylon's wine makes the nations drunk (14:8; 17:2; 18:3)	The water of life and tree of life heal the nations (21:6; 22:1–2)
Babylon contains the blood of slaughter (17:6; 18:24)	New Jerusalem contains life and healing (22:1–2)
God's people are to come out of Babylon (18:4)	God's people are called to enter the new Jerusalem (22:14)

Positively, the holy city that descends from heaven fulfills God's three-part covenant promise to Israel: (1) I will be your God, (2) you will be my people, and (3) I will live among you (Rev. 21:3; cf. Ex. 29:45–46; Lev. 26:12; Ezek. 37:27). God's original promise included a restored Temple (e.g., Ezek. 37), but in Revelation the entire city of the new Jerusalem is a Temple (Rev. 21:22) in the shape of the Holy Place (21:16). The Temple city will know nothing of Satan, sin, sorrow, or death (21:4, 8, 27; 22:3).

The most intimate description of the new Jerusalem draws on Isaiah 61–62 and presents the city as a "bride beautifully dressed for her husband" (Rev. 21:2, 9–10). This marriage relationship is available to all who "overcome," regardless of nationality (21:7, 10–14, 24, 26; 22:2) (see BRIDE OF THE LAMB). In sum, the new Jerusalem represents the unhindered fellowship of the glorious, triune God with his people in the new creation. Finally secure from threats and temptations, God's people reside in his perfect presence and respond in endless worship and service (22:3–5). (See HEAVEN; NEW HEAVEN AND NEW EARTH; TEMPLE; ZION.)

New Temple

The background of the new Temple centers on the Old Testament Tabernacle and Temple. As part of God's covenant with his people, he chose to live or dwell among them (Lev. 26:11–12). The first such dwelling place was the desert Tabernacle (Ex. 25–31). This "tent of meeting" (27:19; 30:16) was the place where God met with his people, where sacrifices were offered, and where atonement was made (29:38–43; 30:7–10). It consisted of a Holy Place and the Most Holy Place, where the Ark of the Covenant was located.

The Temple in Jerusalem in many ways followed the pattern of the Tabernacle as the place where God's presence rested (e.g., 1 Kings 8:1–11). Rather than a city with a Temple, Jerusalem was more like a Temple with a city around it. Above all, the Jerusalem Temple was the place where God dwelt (e.g., 2 Sam. 7:12–17; Ps. 84; 122; 132). The prophets came to see the city of Jerusalem and the Temple as a place of final salvation not only for the nation of Israel, but for all nations (e.g., Isa. 2:2–4; Mic. 4:1–5; Zech. 14:16–19). Consequently, its destruction in 587/586 B.C. signified the loss of God's presence and their future hope (Ezek. 10–11).

God's promise to restore Israel included a new Temple. In an elaborate vision, Ezekiel is shown the new Temple where God's glory will one day reside (Ezek. 40–48). This vision closes as the prophet names the new Jerusalem, "THE LORD IS THERE" (48:35). Other prophets also make reference to a new Temple (Isa. 56:7; 66:18–21; Hag. 2:9; Zech. 14:16–21).

Jesus, the Word, became flesh and made his dwelling (lit., "taberna-cled") among people (John 1:14). Jesus' actions in relation to the Jerusalem Temple play a crucial role in understanding the new Temple. Jesus cleanses the Temple and speaks clearly of its destruction (Mark 11:12–25; 13:1–2). He speaks of replacing the destroyed Temple with one "not made by man" (Mark 14:57–58; John 2:19–22). In addition, at Jesus' death the curtain within the Temple is torn from top to bottom (Mark 15:38). In short, Jesus saw himself replacing the Temple as the locus of God's presence.

In the New Testament the church becomes the new Temple of God's Spirit (Joel 2:28–29; Acts 2:1–4). In 1 Corinthians 3:16 Paul tells the community, "you yourselves are God's temple" since "God's Spirit lives in you." Again, in 2 Corinthians 6:16 he tells the Christian community that they "are the temple of the living God," fulfilling the common Old Testament promise of God's presence: "I will walk among you and be your God, and you will be my people" (see Lev. 26:12; Jer. 32:38; Ezek. 37:27). Paul uses the Temple image for the church again in Ephesians 2:11–22, arguing for one community of both Jews and Gentiles where God manifests his presence (cf. 1 Peter 2:4–8).

The writer of Hebrews says that Christ as high priest has entered the true, heavenly Tabernacle (Heb. 4:14–16; 8:1–6), of which the earthly Tabernacle was merely a copy (8:2, 5; 9:24). Jesus entered the very throne room of God with his own blood (9:11–12; cf. John 2:21). In Christ's priestly act on our behalf, we as believers are provided access to the very presence of God (Heb. 10:19–22). This spiritual experience offers a fore-taste of our final rest in the heavenly Tabernacle (6:19–20).

The New Testament concept of the new Temple plays a significant role in Revelation. Jesus promises the overcomers in the church in Phil-adelphia that he will make them "a pillar in the temple" of his God (Rev. 3:12). The incalculable multitude of Revelation 7 from "every nation, tribe, people and language" who has "come out of the great tribulation" serves God night and day "in his temple" (7:9, 14–15). Interestingly, the language of 7:16–17 parallels the description of the Holy City in 21:1–4:

Rev. 7:16–17	Rev. 21:1–4
Never again will they hunger; never again will they thirst. The sun will not beat upon them, nor any scorching heat. For the Lamb at the center of the throne will be their shepherd; he will lead them to springs of living water. And God will wipe away every tear from their eyes.	Then I saw a new heaven and a new earth, for the first heaven and the first earth had passed away, and there was no longer any sea. I saw the Holy City, the new Jerusalem, coming down out of heaven from God, prepared as a bride beautifully dressed for her husband. And I heard a loud voice from the throne saying, "Now the dwelling of God is with men, and he will live with them. They will be his people, and God himself will be with them and be their God. He will wipe every tear from their eyes. There will be no more death or mourning or crying or pain, for the old order of things has passed away."

The commonly quoted Old Testament promise of the divine presence occurs in Revelation 21:3 (e.g., Ex. 25:8; 29:45–46; Lev. 26:12; 1 Kings 6:13; Ezek. 37:27; 43:7, 9; Zech. 2:10–11).

Regarding Revelation 11:1–2, most dispensationalists believe that a literal Temple will be rebuilt in Jerusalem just prior to Christ's return. This literal Temple will finalize the reconstitution of the nation of Israel and will provide the setting for the desecration of the Temple by the Antichrist (Dan. 9:27; 12:11; 2 Thess. 2:4). Most nondispensationalists favor a more symbolic reading of Revelation 11:1–14, where the image of the Temple represents Christians, both Jewish and Gentile.[73]

As the book closes, John surprisingly reports that he does "not see a temple in the city" (Rev. 21:22). This report does not mean, however, that a restored Temple does not exist. Rather, John explains that the new Temple is not less than hoped for, but much more—"the Lord God Almighty and the Lamb are its temple" (21:22). The hand of God will wipe away their tears (21:4) and "they will see his face" (22:4). In addition, the entire Temple city has the cube shape of the old Most Holy Place (21:16; cf. 1 Kings 6:20). The Temple once represented God's presence; now God has become the Temple as the earthly copy fades. (See NEW JERUSALEM; PRESENCE OF GOD.)

Nicolaitans

The Nicolaitans are a group of false teachers mentioned in Revelation 2:6, 15. Apparently they were teaching Christians that it was permissible to participate in pagan religious culture and still be considered faithful Christians. In the message to the church at Ephesus, they are faulted for claiming to be apostles while practicing wickedness (2:2, 6). In the message to Pergamum they are identified with those who hold to the teaching of Balaam, who taught Balak to entice Israel to sin by "eating food sacrificed to idols and by committing sexual immorality" (2:14). In the message to Thyatira, the group is identified with the "prophetess" Jezebel, who "misleads my servants into sexual immorality and the eating of food sacrificed to idols" (2:20).[74] These false teachers are redefining the apostolic faith to allow Christians to fit in easily (and perhaps profitably) with pagan society.

The prophetic word from the risen Lord commands the church to deal quickly and decisively with these false teachers so that the entire church is not destroyed. False teaching leads to pagan practices, and Christians are called to overcome such teaching by walking in line with God's Word. (See EPHESUS; JEZEBEL; PERGAMUM; SEVEN CHURCHES OF REVELATION; THYATIRA.)

Noadiah

Two people in the Old Testament have the name Noadiah. One is a faithful Levitical priest who works with Ezra (Ezra 8:33). The other is a prophetess who opposes Nehemiah and tries to frighten him into abandoning his plan to rebuild the walls of Jerusalem (Neh. 6:14).

Number Codes

See BIBLE CODES; GEMATRIA; NUMBERS, NUMEROLOGY.

Numbers, Numerology

Numbers appear throughout the Bible and therefore occur frequently in biblical prophecy. They are used in the Bible in several different ways. They can be used in conventional fashion to refer to actual literal numbers, but they can also be used rhetorically and symbolically. Some scholars also suggest that numbers can be used mystically, or with hidden meanings, usually by connecting numbers to letters of the alphabet, although this usage is contested by many.[75]

In biblical prophecy numbers are clearly used in the first three categories. (1) The *conventional* use is common. Literal numbers are used much like people today use literal numbers. Under conventional use, the biblical writers also employ "rounding." That is, sometimes they will cite round numbers (e.g., "forty," a frequently used round number) instead of more detailed specific numbers (e.g., "thirty-seven" or "forty-two"). This does not imply that the number is inaccurate or mistaken. Writers in the ancient world (including biblical writers) felt free to use rounded numbers, just as writers today do.

(2) The *rhetorical* use of numbers in biblical prophecy is more complicated. Several times writers use a sequence of X, X+1. That is, they mention a number and then that number plus one. For example, Amos 2:1 states, "For three sins of Moab, even for four, I will not turn back my wrath." The meaning of this sequence is that there are lots of other examples that could be cited. The sequence X, X+1 is a poetic way of referring to "many." Thus, Moab's sins are not three or even four, but many beyond that.

(3) The *symbolic* use of numbers is also common in biblical prophecy, especially in the book of Revelation. Several numbers in the Bible have symbolic significance. The number *seven*, for instance, symbolizes completeness or totality. God creates the world in *seven* days, representing completeness. Keep in mind that the symbolic significance of a number does not necessarily imply that the number does not have conventional or literal meaning as well; sometimes the symbolic numbers have conventional meaning and sometimes they do not. In Revelation 5:6 the Lamb (Christ) is described as having "seven horns and seven eyes," a symbolic use of the number seven that is unlikely to carry conventional literal meaning. Horns are symbolic of power, so "seven horns" signifies "complete or total power." Likewise, eyes often represent knowledge and insight, so "seven eyes" signifies total knowledge and the ability to see all. The number seventy often carries similar connotations.[76]

Another number frequently used in biblical prophecy with symbolic meaning is *four*. Both the use of this specific number and the literary grouping of items in groups of four carry nuances of universality or "worldwide" reference. Yet this number can also carry the similar connotations of supremacy or completeness. Thus in the prophetic literature one finds references to "four winds," "four corners of the earth," "four living creatures" with "four faces" (see FOUR LIVING CREATURES).[77]

(4) The *mystical* use or "hidden meaning" use of numbers is disputed. Some claim that the Hebrew alphabet letters in the Old Testament Hebrew texts represent numbers and carry significant "hidden" meaning. This is called *gematria* (see GEMATRIA). However, it is doubtful that the practice of using letters to represent numbers developed before the close of the Old Testament canon, so it is unlikely that there are hidden number values to be attached to specific words in the Old Testament.

This practice is much more plausible, although not certain, in New Testament apocalyptic literature, such as the book of Revelation. Some scholars maintain that 666, the number of the beast in Revelation 13:18, refers to Nero because when his name is transliterated into Hebrew and then converted from letters to representative numbers, the sum equals 666; this, however, is disputed (see NERO; SIX HUNDRED SIXTY-SIX).

Obadiah, Book of

Obadiah means "servant of the LORD" and was a common name in Israel and Judah. The prophet who writes the book of Obadiah is a different individual from the official who served in Ahab's court and who secretly hid the LORD's prophets from Jezebel during the time of Elijah (1 Kings 18:3–16; see ELIJAH). The Obadiah in 1 Kings 18 and the literary prophet Obadiah are separated historically by more than 270 years.

Obadiah prophesies against the kingdom of Edom, a small kingdom lying adjacent and to the southeast of Judah. During the Babylonian invasion of Judah in 588–586 B.C., Edom was allied with Babylonia against Judah. While Judah was preoccupied with fighting the powerful Babylonians, Edom annexed portions of Judah. Obadiah writes after this event and predicts an end to Edom, which takes place in the fifth century B.C. when the Nabateans invade and destroy Edom.

Obadiah is thus probably a contemporary with Jeremiah. In fact, the form and message of Obadiah is similar to Jeremiah 49:7–22, which is also a prophecy against Edom. The basic message of both Obadiah and Jeremiah is as follows: (1) The day of the LORD is coming, a day of ultimate judgment and justice; (2) those who oppose the LORD will be judged; and (3) there will be an ultimate restoration of Israel, in contrast to the total destruction and end of Edom (see JEREMIAH, BOOK OF).

The Olivet Discourse

Matthew 24, Mark 13, and Luke 21 contain Jesus' predictions about the future as he teaches his disciples on the Mount of Olives on the eastern side of Jerusalem. Three main interpretations of this sermon are taken in evangelical commentaries: the preterist view, the futurist view, and the already–not yet view.

The Preterist View

The preterist view of the Olivet Discourse interprets Jesus' prophecies given in about A.D. 30 as being completely fulfilled at the fall of Jerusalem to the Romans in A.D. 70. Thus the signs of the times forecasted by Jesus—tribulation, messianic pretenders, wars, persecution, apostasy—accompanied the failed Jewish revolt against the Romans in A.D. 66–73. That war brought on severe tribulation and persecution for the Jews as the Roman legions systematically conquered Palestine, culminating in the destruction of Jerusalem.

Josephus documents these happenings, blaming them on the Zealots' claim that if Jews rebelled against the Roman occupation of their land, God would send his Messiah. Indeed, numerous messianic pretenders appeared in Israel from A.D. 6 to 66, proclaiming just such a message. All of this resulted not in the deliverance of the Jews but their defeat and, in many cases, their subsequent loss of faith (Josephus, *Jewish Wars* 1.10.6/209; *Antiquities* 10.1.3/19).

The preterist view, besides rooting the fulfillment of these prophecies in Josephus' firsthand description of the siege of Jerusalem, appeals to two other key items in the Olivet Discourse. (1) Jesus' promise in the discourse, "this generation will certainly not pass away until all these things have happened" (Matt. 24:34; Mark 13:30; Luke 21:32), is thought by this approach to fit the time period from Jesus (A.D. 30) to Jerusalem's demise (A.D. 70). Since "these things" are the signs of the times that attended the fall of Jerusalem, then the statement about this generation not passing away is to be equated with the first generation of Christians (see DESTRUCTION OF THE JERUSALEM TEMPLE [A.D. 70]; SIGNS OF THE TIMES).

(2) The preterist view interprets the Parousia, or coming of Christ, not as Christ's second coming at the end of history, but as Christ's coming to Jerusalem in A.D. 70 in the form of judgment. Thus the "second coming" of Christ and the "Great Tribulation," as the signs of the times in the Olivet Discourse, have already occurred.

The Futurist View

The second major view of the Olivet Discourse is the futurist school of thought, a popular view in American Christianity today. As its name suggests, this approach equates the signs of the times in Jesus' sermon with the future Great Tribulation. Accordingly, the Olivet Discourse predicts the unfolding of the end of time in three stages. Using Matthew 24, those key time frames are:

(1) Matthew 24:4–14: the first half of the tribulation period. Here is the beginning of God's judgment of the earth, that is, the "birth pains." These judgments of earthquakes, famines, and wars are not referring to events of the present age; rather, they parallel the seal judgments of Revelation 6. Also, during this time there will be a great rise in false prophets, as well as wickedness in general. But this will be countered by a worldwide preaching of the gospel of the kingdom.

(2) Matthew 24:15–28: the second half of the tribulation period. This period begins with the great sign of the "abomination that causes desolation." This terrible desecration of the rebuilt Jerusalem Temple by the Antichrist and the False Prophet will be the unmistakable sign for the Jewish people to flee the land of Israel. It is at this time that terrible persecution will break forth on Jews. Also, a great outpouring of powerful and deceptive miracles will take place at this time. The Lord warns that there will be an unbelievable and massive destruction of humanity. In fact, he declares that if this period of time is not cut short and limited to three and a half years, no flesh will survive (cf. Rev. 8–11, trumpet judgments; chs. 15–18, bowl judgments).

(3) Matthew 24:29–31: the second coming of Christ. This event will be witnessed by all humanity, believers and unbelievers alike. Prior to Christ's return a sign will appear in the heavens, indicating that Jesus Christ is now about to return. This warning will cause the unbelievers of the earth to mourn because they realize that they will face immediate judgment. At this time the nation of Israel will be regathered from all over the world. The judgment that determines entrance into the kingdom will occur at this time (cf. Rev. 19–20).

The Already–Not Yet View

The third major view of the prophecies of the Olivet Discourse is the already–not yet perspective. This approach understands the first half as having been fulfilled at the fall of Jerusalem in A.D. 70 (the "already" aspect), with the second half of the discourse awaiting final completion at the second coming of Christ at the end of history (the "not yet" aspect). According to this view Matthew 24:4–31 is to be understood as follows:

The "already"	The "not yet"
Partial fulfillment (Matt. 24:4–20; cf. Mark 13:5–23; Luke 21:8–24; Rev. 6)	Final fulfillment (Matt. 24:21–31; cf. Mark 13:24–27; Luke 21:25–36; Rev. 8–11, 15–18)
A. Tribulation (Matt. 24:8)	A. Great Tribulation (Matt. 24:21, 29)
B. Messianic pretenders (Matt. 24:4–5)	B. Messianic pretenders (Matt. 24:23–26)
C. Wars (Matt. 24:6–7)	C. Wars (Matt. 24:22)
D. Persecution (Matt. 24:9–10)	D. Persecution (Matt. 24:22)
E. Apostasy (Matt. 24:11–13)	E. Apostasy (Matt. 24:24)
F. Fall of Jerusalem (Matt. 24:15–20)	F. Fall of Jerusalem (Matt. 24:30–31)

According to this view, the fall of Jerusalem in A.D. 70 serves as the backdrop for the future return of Christ. Thus the signs of the times began in Jesus' generation and will continue until the Parousia (second coming of Jesus).

One Hundred Forty-Four Thousand

The figure of 144,000 appears only in Revelation 7:4 and in 14:1, 3. At the opening of the sixth seal in 6:12, the entire cosmos is shaken and wicked humanity attempts to hide from God's wrath. The end has come. Revelation 6 closes with an all-important question, "For the great day of their wrath has come, and who can stand?" As Revelation 7 opens, John sees a vision of the sealing of the servants of God (7:2–4):

> Then I saw another angel coming up from the east, having the seal of the living God. He called out in a loud voice to the four angels who had been given power to harm the land and the sea: "Do not harm the land or the sea or the trees until we put a seal on the foreheads of the servants of our God." Then I heard the number of those who were sealed: 144,000 from all the tribes of Israel.

The 144,000 are the servants of God who have been sealed or protected against God's wrath.

Revelation 13 describes the two satanic beasts, one from the sea (13:1–10) and the other from the earth (13:11–18). While the first beast blasphemes God and makes war against the saints, the second beast deceives the nations and forces them to worship the first beast and his image under penalty of death. Only those who receive the beast's mark on their right hand or forehead can buy and sell. As Revelation 14 opens, John sees a contrasting vision of the Lamb standing on Mount Zion with 144,000 who "had his name and his Father's name written on their foreheads" (14:1).

The judgment scenes of Revelation 6 and 13 are followed by the "parentheses" or interludes of Revelation 7 and 14, where readers are encouraged by a picture of God's protecting the righteous. The primary significance of the 144,000 is that they in some way represent the righteous who are sealed by God, in contrast to the wicked who take the mark of the beast.

What about the specific identity of the 144,000? What information does Revelation itself provide about their identity?

- Sealed with the seal of the living God (Rev. 7:2)
- Servants of God (Rev. 7:3)
- 144,000 from all the tribes of Israel (Rev. 7:4)
- They stand on Mount Zion with the Lamb (Rev. 14:1)
- Have the Lamb's name and the Father's name on their foreheads (Rev. 14:1)
- Sing a new song before the throne and before the four living creatures and elders (Rev. 14:3)
- Redeemed from the earth (Rev. 14:3)
- Did not defile themselves with women (Rev. 14:4)
- Follow the Lamb wherever he goes (Rev. 14:4)
- Purchased from among men and offered as firstfruits to God and the Lamb (Rev. 14:4)
- No lie was found in their mouths (Rev. 14:5)
- They are blameless (Rev. 14:5)

These characteristics have been interpreted in two primary ways. (1) Some take the 144,000 as literal Israel or, more specifically, as a literal number of Jews who become Christians during the Great Tribulation. The expression "144,000 from all the tribes of Israel" (Rev. 7:4) supports a literal interpretation. This group represents the end-time Jewish remnant who will be protected by God during their time of distress. There is biblical support for expecting a large-scale Jewish conversion to faith in Christ at the end of history (e.g., Rom. 11:25–27).

(2) A second interpretive approach understands the 144,000 to represent all true followers of Jesus. The expression "servants of God" throughout Revelation signifies all believers (Rev. 1:1; 2:20; 6:11; 10:7; 11:18; 19:2, 5, 10; 22:3, 6, 9). Taking all of the details in these passages literally becomes problematic (e.g., only 144,000 male virgins from twelve tribes of Israel will be protected; all others must suffer God's wrath). The number 144,000 does not even fit literal Israel, since the tribe of Dan is missing from the list in Revelation 7.

More positively, this view argues that Revelation highlights the Jewish heritage of all true believers (e.g., Rev. 1:20; 2:9). In addition, the seal of God is connected with all believers (7:3–5; 14:1; cf. also 3:12; 22:4), just as unbelievers bear the mark of the beast (13:16–17; 14:9, 11; 16:2; 19:20; 20:4). Since numbers in Revelation are normally taken to be symbolic, the 144,000 represents the true people of God (cf. 21:16–17). The number itself is a result of multiplying numbers that hold significance in Revelation (e.g., $12^2 \times 1000$ or $10^2 \times 12^2 \times 10$; cf. the use of twelve in Rev. 21–22). This figure is another depiction of Christians as the true Israel (see also 1:6; 2:17; 3:9, 12; 5:9–10).

As with other numbers and images in Revelation, the view one supports depends to a large degree on how one interprets prophetic-apocalyptic material in general. What the explicit description in Revelation 7 and 14 makes clear is that the 144,000 should be seen as a group of Christians who have been sealed or protected against the coming wrath of God. Rather than follow the beast, they "follow the Lamb wherever he goes" (14:4). Their defining characteristic is their intimate relationship with God and the Lamb. (See MARK OF THE BEAST; NUMBERS, NUMEROLOGY.)

Oracle

The term *oracle* refers to an "utterance" or "declaration" of God. Many English Bible translations such as the NIV use the English word "oracle" to translate the Hebrew word *maśśaʾ*, a word frequently used by the Old Testament prophets. Several prophets begin their books with this word (Nah. 1:1; Hab. 1:1; Mal. 1:1). This word is also used often at the beginning of new prophetic units (Isa. 13:1; 15:1; 17:1, etc.).

However, numerous times in the Old Testament *maśśaʾ* means "burden" or "load." Usually the context is clear whether the word means "burden" or "oracle." However, the word occurs eight times in Jeremiah 23:33–38, and in this passage both meanings ("oracle" and "burden") can fit the context. Jeremiah loves to use wordplays, and in this passage he is probably playing off of both meanings.

P

Parables of Enoch

The *Parables of Enoch* (sometimes called the *Similitudes of Enoch*) comprise chapters 37–71 of *1 Enoch*, a second-century B.C. nonbiblical Jewish Palestinian work. They consist of three parables (chaps. 38–44; 45–57; 58–69) that reflect a blending of mysticism and apocalypticism (see APOCALYPTIC LITERATURE). Thus in each parable, the seer is caught up to heaven (39:3; 52:12; 71:5), where he is granted visions of the eschatological dwelling places of the righteous and the wicked.

These revelations are the parables themselves, and they contain three main analogies that compare the destiny of the righteous and of the wicked, the holy on earth and the sanctified ones in heaven, and the order of the cosmos and the lot of the righteous. The major emphasis of the *Parables of Enoch* is on the fate of the righteous and their wicked counterparts.

Also important in the *Parables* is the rule of the heavenly Son of Man (see SON OF MAN). The teaching about the Son of Man here can be summarized around three points: (1) He is an individual, though enjoying some sort of representative role on behalf of the elect ones. (2) He is a Messiah. (3) His hiddenness in some fashion is integral to the sufferings of the righteous.

It is through mystic ascent to the heavenly throne that Enoch is granted visions of the true status of the heavenly Son of Man, the elect ones on earth, and their abusers (see MERKABAH). It is in heaven, therefore, that Enoch realizes that the dawning of the age to come has already occurred, despite appearances on earth to the contrary. It is this context that one must keep in mind when interpreting the relationship between the hiddenness motif of the Son of Man and the affliction of the elect ones on earth, namely, that through mysticism the Son of Man suffers through his followers on earth while they currently enjoy his glory in heaven.

While the *Parables of Enoch* is not a canonical book, it does provide helpful background for understanding the Gospels as well as the term *Son of Man*. Jesus the suffering Messiah suffered for his people that they might enjoy his heavenly glory (see SON OF MAN).

Parables of the Kingdom

Gospel scholars agree that the parables of Jesus are intimately connected to his message of the kingdom of God. However, Jesus' offer of the kingdom differed radically from Jewish expectations at that time. Six central aspects pertaining to the kingdom of God are reflected in the parables of Jesus: (1) the inauguration of the kingdom; (2) the recipients of the kingdom; (3) the requirements of the kingdom; (4) the growth of the kingdom; (5) the rejection of the kingdom; and (6) the consummation of the kingdom.

(1) The inauguration of the kingdom of God. One need only to examine the characteristics of the teaching of Jesus to discover that in him the kingdom of God is being inaugurated. One such characteristic is that he taught with authority. He also taught with a compassionate, keen sense of wisdom. Last, but not least, Jesus taught in parables; in fact, one-third of his teachings consists of parables. It is this characteristic alone that should have hinted at his messiahship, for one of the Old Testament prophecies foretold that the Messiah would come as the originator of parables (Ps. 78:2).

The Jewish people, however, for the most part, missed the hints. The kingdom they anticipated lay in the distant future, not in the present. Yet Jesus came teaching his people that the kingdom of God had already come; it came in him! This is implied in several parables, such as the parable of the wineskins and patch (Matt. 9:16–17; Mark 2:21–22; Luke 5:36–38) and the parable of the divided realm (Matt. 12:25–29; Mark 3:23–30; Luke 11:17–28).

In the wineskins and patch parable, Jesus' basic point is that a whole new age has arrived and that the old is finished, having served its purpose. Now someone greater than just another prophet has arrived, namely, the Messiah himself. In the parable of the divided realm, Jesus answers his critics by pointing to his miracles as validation and testimony to his messiahship, and thus to his deity. This is so because, like the man who overcomes the owner of the house, Jesus has invaded and defeated the kingdom of Satan, that is, this world.

(2) The recipients of the kingdom of God. The contrast in the two concepts of the kingdom becomes apparent again relative to the recipients of the kingdom. The Jews at the time of Jesus felt that they would be the exclusive participants in the coming kingdom of God. One can imagine their horror in discovering that the true recipients are sinners and Gentiles! In numerous parables, Jesus makes plain who the true recipients are. In the parable of the lost sheep (Luke 15:3–7) as well as in the parable of the lost son (15:11–32), Jesus identifies nonobservant Jews as being recipients, people despised by the ultra-observant Pharisees. Jesus declares not only that they are recipients, but that God actually delights in their entrance into the kingdom.

In the parable of the two debtors (Luke 7:36–50), Jesus offers the kingdom of God to women, even "sinful" women. In the parable of the great banquet the kingdom is offered to "sinners" (harlots and tax collectors, 13:28–29) and to those who are outcasts from society. Indeed, the Jewish understanding of the recipients of the kingdom of God and Jesus' conception are diametrically opposed.

(3) The requirements of the kingdom of God. Once again, the distinction in the two concepts of the kingdom of God becomes visible through Jesus' parables regarding the requirements of the kingdom. The Jewish people were taught that acceptance into the kingdom of God involves embracing the Shema (the unity of God) and the Torah as a whole. Jesus' requirements, however, go to the heart of the matter. One requirement for entrance is illustrated in the very purpose of Jesus' parables. To those who repent, the parables *reveal* truth, but for those who do not repent, the parables *conceal* truth (Matt. 13:13–15). This need for repentance is illustrated in the parable of the royal wedding (Matt. 22:1–4), where those clothed in the garments of "repentance" are invited in while those who are not so clothed are cast out.

A second requirement is the element of *risk*, as is revealed in the parable of the hidden treasure and the parable of the pearl of great price (13:44–46).

A third requirement is *faith*, as is attested to in the parable of the two debtors, where the woman was "saved because of her faith" (Luke 7:50), and in the parable of the dishonest steward (16:1–15), whose only hope lies in his master's grace.

Another requirement for entrance into the kingdom of God, as Jesus presents it, is *counting the cost*, as is apparent in the parable of the tower builder (14:25–30).

A final requirement is *humility*. In the tax collector in the parable of the Pharisee and the tax collector (18:9–14), humility is redefined by Jesus as an honest assessment of oneself before God.

(4) The growth of the kingdom of God. Jesus' thoughts on the growth of the kingdom are found in various parables. In the parable of the leaven (Matt. 13:33), the leaven is hidden in the three pecks of meal, symbolizing the secret, inward growth of his kingdom. The same truth is portrayed in the parable of the mustard seed (Matt. 13:31–32; Mark 4:30–32; Luke 13:18–19) and the parable of the seed growing secretly (Mark 4:26–29). These parables illustrate the mysterious growth of the kingdom as well as the lack of human work involved in it.

The truth of these parables, however, stands in direct opposition to ancient Jewish thinking on the subject. The Jews (particularly the Zealots) believed that the kingdom of God would come through the use of force — through a revolutionary upheaval of the existing political system. The Zealots sought to bring about the messianic deliverance by forcibly throwing off the Roman yoke. Another parable that illustrates Jesus' thoughts on the growth of the kingdom is the parable of the sower, where, despite the insignificant beginning, a bumper crop is promised. This brings with it great assurance concerning the success of the kingdom.

(5) The rejection of the kingdom of God. Despite the open invitation of Jesus, the Jews (and particularly the religious leaders of his day) reject his kingdom. There are several reasons for this rejection, not the least of which are covetousness and the love of money. Jesus points this out in the parable of the rich fool (Luke 12:16–21) and the parable of the rich man and Lazarus (16:19–31). In addition, there is prejudice against the Gentiles, as the parable of the talents (Matt. 25:14–30) reveals, where the religious leaders had been hoarding the Law for themselves, refusing to share it with the Gentiles.

The logical conclusion of this rejection is emphasized in the parable of the empty house (Luke 11:25–26) and the parable of the wicked farmers (Matt. 21:33–46; Mark 12:1–12; Luke 20:9–19), where judgment is pronounced on the nation of Israel, a pronouncement fulfilled in A.D. 70 when Jerusalem is destroyed (see DESTRUCTION OF THE JERUSALEM TEMPLE [A.D. 70].

(6) The consummation of the kingdom of God. While Jesus announces the inauguration of the kingdom of God at his first coming, he also makes

numerous references to the future consummation of the kingdom. In the parable of the weeds (Matt. 13:24–30), the main thrust is that a day of separation is coming—a separation of the authentic from the inauthentic. But Jesus' primary concern is not with the forceful division of the two kingdoms here and now but with the weeding out that will come at the great eschatological consummation.

In the parable of the persistent widow (Luke 18:1–8), encouragement to continue in prayer is given in light of the return of Christ. The parable of the ten virgins (Matt. 25:1–13) emphasizes the certainty and the suddenness of this consummation. Finally, as noted above, in the parable of the sower the great assurance of this consummation is revealed. Even though the kingdom of God has an insignificant beginning, its ending will be triumphant.

Parousia

See SECOND COMING.

Partial Rapture

The partial rapture view claims that not all believers will be caught up (i.e., raptured) at the same time. Some believers will be removed before the Great Tribulation, others during this period, and still others at its end. The time of a believer's rapture depends on one's spiritual maturity and preparedness. Because of frequent exhortations in Scripture for Christians to be alert, watchful, and prepared for Christ's coming, the time of the rapture rests on a believer's faithfulness. The rapture comes as a reward for obedience. Those who are watchful and prepared will be rewarded with rapture before those who lack maturity. This view requires, of course, that there be multiple resurrections of believers. Again, the time of their resurrection depends on their faithfulness.

This view seeks its support mostly from Jesus' parables and sayings related to his second coming. For instance, in the parable of the ten virgins (Matt. 25:1–13), all ten represent believers. Five are taken earlier, however, because they are awake and ready, while the remaining five are taken later. In 24:40–41, where two men are in the field and two women are grinding, the text implies that the one taken is the one who is watchful, alert, and spiritually ready. The partial rapture view can be summed up by Jesus' advice in Luke 21:36: "Be always on the watch, and pray that you may be able to escape all that is about to happen, and that you may be able to stand before the Son of Man."

While some scholars are convinced of the partial rapture view with its multiple resurrections and raptures based on reward, the majority remains unconvinced. The primary weakness of this view is exegetical. For example, in all these eschatological sayings and parables, Jesus appears to be teaching that "watchfulness" characterizes all true believers. The unprepared are often condemned at the end of these stories (e.g., Matt. 24:50–51; 25:12, 28–30, 41–46), not raptured later. In addition, clear evidence for multiple resurrections and multiple raptures appears lacking in the New Testament. (See MIDTRIBULATION RAPTURE; POST-TRIBULATION RAPTURE; PRETRIBULATION RAPTURE; PREWRATH RAPTURE; RAPTURE; REWARDS.)

People of God

Essentially, the concept of the people of God can be summed up in the covenantal phrase: "I will be their God and they will be my people" (e.g., Ex. 6:6–7; 19:5; Lev. 26:9–14; Jer. 7:23; 30:22; 32:37–40; Ezek. 11:19–20; 36:22–28; Acts 15:14; 2 Cor. 6:16; Heb. 8:10–12; Rev. 21:3). Thus, the people of God are those in both the Old and New Testament eras who have responded to God by faith and whose spiritual origin rests exclusively in God's grace.

To speak of the one people of God transcending the eras of both Testaments necessarily raises the question of the relationship between the church and Israel. Some recent theologians prefer not to polarize the matter into an either/or issue. Rather, they talk about the church and Israel in terms of there being *both* continuity *and* discontinuity between them.

Continuity between the Church and Israel

Two ideas establish the fact that the church and Israel are portrayed in the Bible as being in a continuous relationship. (1) The church was present in some sense in Israel in the Old Testament. Acts 7:38 makes this connection explicit when, alluding to Deuteronomy 9:10, it speaks of the *ekklēsia* ("church, assembly") in the desert. The same idea is probably to be inferred from the intimate association existing between the Greek word *ekklēsia* and the Hebrew word *qāhāl* ("assembly"), especially when the latter is qualified by the phrase "of God." Furthermore, since the church is viewed in some New Testament passages as preexistent, one finds the prototype for the creation of Israel (see Ex. 25:40; Acts 7:44; Gal. 4:26; Heb. 12:22; Rev. 21:11; cf. Eph. 1:3–14).

(2) Israel in some sense is present in the church in the New Testament. The many names for Israel applied to the church establish that fact. Some of those are: "Israel" (Gal. 6:15–16; Eph. 2:12; Heb. 8:8–10; Rev. 2:14), "a chosen people" (1 Peter 2:9), "the true circumcision" (Rom. 2:28–29; Phil. 3:3; Col. 2:11), "Abraham's seed" (Rom. 4:16; Gal. 3:29), "the remnant" (Rom. 9:27; 11:5–7), "the elect" (Rom. 11:28; Eph. 1:4), "the flock" (Acts 20:28; Heb. 13:20; 1 Peter 5:2), and "priesthood" (1 Peter 2:9; Rev. 1:6; 5:10).

Discontinuity between the Church and Israel

The church, however, is not coterminous with Israel; discontinuity also characterizes the relationship. The church, according to the New Testament, is the eschatological Israel incorporated in Jesus the Messiah and, as such, is a progression beyond historical Israel (1 Cor. 10:11; 2 Cor. 5:14–21). What was promised to Israel has now been fulfilled in the church, in Christ, especially through the Spirit and the New Covenant (cf. Ezek. 36:25–27; Joel 2:28–29 with Acts 2; 2 Cor. 3; Rom. 8). However, a caveat must be issued here: Although the church is a progression beyond Israel, it does not seem to be the permanent replacement of Israel (Rom. 11:25–27).

Relating to the discontinuity, Romans 11 makes three points. (1) Israel's rejection of Jesus Messiah is partial, not total (11:1–10). Some Jews indeed have responded in faith to Christ; this is "the remnant" that includes Paul himself. (2) Israel's rejection of Jesus Messiah actually served a merciful purpose. It has paved the way for Gentiles to come to Christ (11:11–24). But that is not the end of the story for Israel because God will use the Gentiles' conversion to stir the Jews to jealousy to receive Jesus as their Messiah. (3) Israel's rejection of Jesus as Messiah is temporary, not permanent (11:25–27). A day is coming when "all Israel will be saved" (11:26).

Pergamum

Pergamum was the religious capital of Asia Minor with temples and altars to Athena, Zeus, Hera, Dionysius, Demeter, Asclepius, and others. In addition, it was a leading center for emperor worship. In fact, inscriptions using divine titles for Roman emperors can still be seen there today.[78] The altar of Zeus was prominent in Pergamum and serves as the most likely historical identification of "Satan's throne" in Revelation 2:13. The church at Pergamum lived in this difficult environment and received Jesus' praise for remaining faithful even to the point of death (Antipas is mentioned as a martyr in 2:13).

As with other messages to the seven churches, obedience in one area — even suffering — does not automatically excuse disobedience in other areas. Jesus reproves this church for compromising with those who "hold to the teaching of Balaam" and "the Nicolaitans" (2:14 – 15) — false teachers within the church who are using their freedom as a license to sin (e.g., eating food offered to idols and indulging in sexual immorality). Participating in the cults of other deities was probably connected with membership in the trade guilds so that Christians who refused to compromise suffered financial persecution. Keener sums up the situation faced by the Christians in Pergamum: "Compromise with the imperial cult to save one's life and compromise with the pagan activities of trade guilds to save one's livelihood are all of one piece (cf. 13:17); they represent accommodation to the world at the expense of one's total devotion to God's standards" (see IMPERIAL CULT).[79]

Jesus' prophetic word to the church at Pergamum relates strongly to its local context. As the holder of the ultimate authority and power (e.g., "the sharp, double-edged sword" in Rev. 2:12), he promises "hidden manna" and a "white stone with a new name" (2:17). For refusing to confess Caesar as Lord and refusing to partake of pagan idol feasts, Jesus promises them membership in the eternal city complete with a heavenly feast. (See BALAAMITES; MARTYRDOM; NICOLAITANS; SEVEN CHURCHES OF REVELATION.)

Persia

The ancient kingdom of Persia comprised the area that is now modern-day Iran. The Persian Empire, beginning with Cyrus, ruled the ancient Near East and Asia Minor after it defeated the Babylonians in 539 B.C. Isaiah 45:1 – 8 hails Cyrus as God's "anointed" because in 536 B.C. he decreed that Jews could return to Israel (see CYRUS). Persia dominated the Western Mediterranean area, including Mesopotamia and Asia Minor, until 330 B.C., when Alexander the Great conquered the area and took control of the Persian Empire (see ALEXANDER THE GREAT).

Ezra, Nehemiah, and Esther were written against the backdrop of the Persian kingdom. Likewise, Daniel lived through the transition from the

Babylonian Empire to the Persian Empire. Persia is one of the kingdoms in Daniel's predictions of the four world kingdoms (Dan. 2; 7) (see FOUR BEASTS OF DANIEL).

Philadelphia

In contrast to the church at Sardis, the believers at Philadelphia are suffering at the hands of the Jewish community, a group described as "the synagogue of Satan" (Rev. 3:9). The church there has "little strength," yet they remain faithful. While these Christians have been rejected by the synagogue community (cf. Matt. 23:13), Jesus reminds them that he "holds the key of David" and has authority to open a door that no one — not even the synagogue officials — can close. The "door" image probably refers to access to God and membership within the true people of God. Knowing their faithfulness, Jesus has placed before the church in Philadelphia "an open door that no one can shut" (Rev. 3:8).

Moreover, because these believers have kept or guarded his Word, Jesus promises to guard them in the hour of trial that is coming on "those who live on the earth" (a standard expression in Revelation for unbelievers; see Rev. 3:10; also John 17:15). Along with Smyrna, the church at Philadelphia receives no rebuke or accusation from Jesus, only praise and encouragement. While these Christians have been rejected by pagan temples and "Satan's synagogue," Jesus promises them a permanent place in God's new Temple (Rev. 3:12; cf. Isa. 56:5). As ancient pillars often featured honorary inscriptions, these "pillars" in God's new Temple will bear the name of God and the new Jerusalem along with Jesus' new name (see SEVEN CHURCHES OF REVELATION).

Poetry

Although the Old Testament prophets occasionally wrote in narrative (prose), their primary literary style was poetry. Likewise, significant portions of the New Testament book of Revelation are in poetry. Poetry is different than prose (narrative or essay), and Christians will interpret it better if they understand those differences.

The Old Testament prophets appeal primarily to our emotions. They do not build complex grammatical arguments as Paul does, but rather use images to get their point across. They paint colorful pictures with words to convey messages loaded with emotional impact. This doesn't mean that they ignore logic or write illogically. It simply means that they focus on emotional aspects more than on logical aspects. Conversely, we should note that Paul does not ignore emotion in his letters, but his primary focus is on reasoning.

Old Testament poetry, by its artistic nature, is not easy to define precisely. Indeed, prose and poetry are not totally separate, and in some Old Testament texts it is not clear whether the text is prose or poetry. We agree with Klein, Blomberg, and Hubbard's suggestion that poetry and prose be viewed as opposite ends of a literary continuum.[80] Poetry is characterized by terseness, a high degree of structure, figurative imagery, and numerous wordplays. The more that a literary work reflects these four elements, the further it moves to the poetry end of the literary spectrum. Here are the central features of Old Testament poetic texts common in Old Testament prophecy.

(1) Terseness. Poetry uses a minimum number of words. The words are chosen carefully for their impact and power. Narrative texts frequently have long, descriptive sentences, but the poetic texts in the Old Testament prophets are usually comprised of short, compact lines of verse with few words.

(2) Structure. One of the most obvious features of poetry in the Old Testament prophets is that the text is structured around poetic lines of verse rather than around sentences and paragraphs. So interpreters should train their eyes to read line by line rather than sentence by sentence. Furthermore, the lines of poetic text are usually grouped in units of two or three. That is, two lines of Old Testament poetry are grouped together to express one thought.

Most poetic verses in the prophets are structured this way. This feature is called *parallelism*, and it is the dominant structural characteristic of Old Testament poetry. Usually one thought will be expressed by two lines of text (although occasionally the prophets will use three or even four lines to convey one thought). Often the verse notations follow this pattern, and each verse consists of two lines of text. Such verse notations help us as we read because we need to interpret the text by reading each parallel construction together. That is, we look for two lines to convey one idea or thought.

(3) Figurative imagery. (See FIGURES OF SPEECH.)

(4) Wordplays. Wordplays are common in English, and many of them are quite clever. For example, as he signed the Declaration of Independence, Ben Franklin is credited with quipping, "Let us all *hang together* or else we may all *hang separately*." Franklin was making a play of two very

different meanings of the word *hang*. Klein, Blomberg, and Hubbard cite another clever English wordplay. A preacher was contrasting the views on self-esteem of the apostle Paul and Norman Vincent Peale (a well-known proponent of positive thinking). The preacher argued in favor of Paul's view and, in conclusion, stated, "That's what makes *Paul* so *appealing* and *Peale* so *appalling*."[81]

Many Hebrew wordplays in the Old Testament prophets follow the patterns of these two examples. They either play off of variant possible meanings of a word, or they play off of sound similarities. Unfortunately, the wordplays rarely translate into English. However, here is an example to enable you to appreciate the rich, literary artistry of the Old Testament prophets.

The prophet Jeremiah employs an extended wordplay throughout his book with his usage of the Hebrew word *shub*. This word basically means "to turn." It can mean "to turn to something" or "to turn away from something." Thus, it can be used of turning to God (repentance) or of turning away from God (backsliding), meanings that are exactly opposite. Jeremiah cannot resist using it in both senses. He outdoes Ben Franklin's use of "hang" by using *shub* eleven times from Jeremiah 3:1 to 4:1 alone. He uses the word three times in a single verse (3:22). In English this verse reads: "*Return*, *faithless* people; I will cure you of *backsliding*." A quick look at a concordance shows that *return*, *faithless*, and *backsliding* are all English renderings of the Hebrew word *shub*. A very literal translation reads: "*Turn*, you sons of *turning*; I will cure your *turning*."

The Old Testament prophets love wordplays and they use them frequently, especially in poetic texts.[82]

Postexilic Prophets

The Postexilic Prophets are those prophets who prophesied after the exile (see EXILE) and after the Hebrews had returned from Babylon/Persia to the land of Israel. These prophets include Haggai, Zechariah, and Malachi.

Postmillennialism

This view on the millennium claims that Jesus will return in glory after ("post" means "after") an era of millennial conditions, as Kenneth Gentry explains:

Postmillennialism expects the proclaiming of the Spirit-blessed gospel of Jesus Christ to win the vast majority of human beings to salvation in the present age. Increasing gospel success will gradually produce a time in history prior to Christ's return in which faith, righteousness, peace, and prosperity will prevail in the affairs of people and of nations. After an extensive era of such conditions the Lord will return visibly, bodily, and in great glory ending history with the general resurrection and the great judgment of all humankind.[83]

As this definition indicates, postmillennialism rests on certain beliefs related to God's ability to work in this world through the good news of Christ. To begin with, postmillennialism emphasizes the present earthly reality of the kingdom of God rather than its future heavenly reality. As Jesus indicates in many of his parables, the kingdom of God (or God's rule in human hearts) will grow gradually and steadily (e.g., the parables of Matt. 13). In addition, postmillennialism relies on Old Testament passages like Psalm 2; 47; 72; 110; Isaiah 2:2–4; 45:22–25; Hosea 2:3, and New Testament passages such as John 12:31–32 and 1 Corinthians 15:20–28 for primary exegetical support.

Postmillennialism places great confidence in the power of the gospel to convert all nations prior to Christ's return. Through the Spirit's power the message of Christ will slowly but surely transform the present world. Jesus claims that "this gospel of the kingdom will be preached in the whole world as a testimony to all nations, and then the end will come" (Matt. 24:14). Christ commissions his disciples to take the gospel to all nations (28:18–20).

The hope of postmillennialism is that the gospel of Christ will cause kingdom growth resulting in a period of earthly peace and prosperity known as the millennium. Most postmillennialists are not literalistic about the length of the millennium or even whether this period should be called the "millennium." Rather, they are confident about the gradual progress of the gospel to the point where conflicts cease, problems are solved, and relationships mended as people experience God's sovereign rule within history. While holding steadfastly to this same notion of progress, some postmillennialists believe that the millennium includes all of church history from the time of Christ until his return.

Since the 1960s there has been a movement within postmillennialism known as Christian Reconstructionism. As a component of this larger movement, "theonomic postmillennialism" attempts to apply God's laws (theonomy) in the Old Testament to New Covenant conditions. Theonomic postmillennialism seeks to promote a "gradual return to biblical norms of civil justice as a consequence of widespread gospel success through preaching, evangelism, missions, and Christian education."[84] Within theonomic postmillennialism the sociopolitical concerns of the older Puritan form of postmillennialism are integrated with the gradualism of the modern form.

At the end of this millennial era, some postmillennialists believe God will allow a temporary surge of evil to demonstrate the necessity of judgment. Then the millennium will officially close with the return of Christ, the resurrection of the dead, the last judgment, and the eternal state. On these final matters, postmillennialism shares with other millennial views.

Although a matter of debate, some claim that postmillennialism began with several prominent church fathers — Origen, Eusebius, Athanasius, and Augustine. Postmillennialism became widespread beginning with the Protestant Reformation and extending through the time of the Puritans, featuring people such as John Calvin, John Owen, John and Charles Wesley, Isaac Watts, and Jonathan Edwards. Others debate whether leaders like John Calvin should be classified as postmillennial. In the latter part of the twentieth century, postmillennialism has declined sharply, so that today only a small minority of scholars adheres to it.

Postmillennialism may be credited for highlighting the present dimension of the kingdom of God and for recognizing the life-changing power of the gospel of Jesus Christ. In addition, this view promotes optimism about God's ability to work in history, which in turn encourages a diligent activism on the part of Christians.

Several challenges are raised against postmillennialism. Aside from the somewhat unrealistic expectation of a worldwide conversion of the nations, it faces many challenges from an exegetical point of view. The present age, according to the New Testament, is a time of tribulation, persecution, and suffering for God's people (e.g., John 16:33; Rom. 8:17–27). Jesus seems to teach that things will get worse in the last days (e.g., Matt. 24:9–14). A glorious future on earth is promised, but only after the return of Christ, not before. God's purpose for his creation is fulfilled in the new creation (2 Peter 3:8–13; Rev. 21:1–7). A believer's hope centers on the return of Christ (1 Thess. 1:9–10; Titus 2:12–13; Heb. 9:28; 1 Peter 1:13).

Perhaps the greatest exegetical challenge for postmillennialism relates to how it treats (or fails to treat) the primary text on the millennium (Rev. 20). Rather than struggle with the details of the passage (e.g., the meaning of the two resurrections), postmillennial interpreters tend to dismiss the significance of the passage altogether or redefine terms and import ideas in a manner completely foreign to the context (e.g., the binding of Satan is gradual, the coming to life is regeneration). (See AMILLENNIALISM; MILLENNIAL KINGDOM; PREMILLENNIALISM, HISTORIC.)

Posttribulation Rapture

On the issue of the rapture of the church (see RAPTURE), the posttribulation view maintains that the church will *not* be removed from the world before the Great Tribulation. Rather, the church will go through the Tribulation but will be protected from God's wrath by his grace. Christ will return at the end of the Great Tribulation, will raise Christians who have died, and will gather all believers (those living at the time and those just raised from the dead) to himself (1 Thess. 4:16–17). As a result, the second coming (or return) of Christ should be understood as a single event rather than as a two-stage event, as in the pretribulation view. The posttribulation view sees two resurrections—one of the righteous at the end of the Tribulation and beginning of the millennium, and a second of the unrighteous at the end of the millennium.

The central passage teaching the rapture of the church is 1 Thessalonians 4:16–17:

> For the Lord himself will come down from heaven, with a loud command, with the voice of the archangel and with the trumpet call of God, and the dead in Christ will rise first. After that, we who are still alive and are left will be caught up [the word sometimes translated "rapture"] together with them in the clouds to meet the Lord in the air. And so we will be with the Lord forever.

Those who hold to the posttribulation rapture point out that rather than a secret, invisible coming of Christ (as found in the pretribulation view), this text describes a loud, visible, public coming. Jesus' glorious return will be witnessed by all, believer and unbeliever alike (Matt. 24:30–31; Rev. 1:7). At his return he will raise to life believers who have died so that all the redeemed will be caught up together to meet the Lord in the air.

This "catching up" refers to the gathering of believers that Jesus speaks about in Matthew 24:31: "And he [the Son of Man] will send his angels with a loud trumpet call, and they will gather his elect from the four winds, from one end of the heavens to the other" (cf. Mark 13:27; 2 Thess. 2:1). The word "meet" in 1 Thessalonians 4:17 is a term used in the ancient world for a delegation going outside the city to meet an arriving dignitary in order to provide an honorable escort back to the city. The word carries this sense in all three of its New Testament occurrences. In Matthew 25:6 the wise virgins go out to meet the bridegroom and accompany him to the wedding banquet; in Acts 28:15 some Christians from Rome go out to meet Paul and escort him back into the city; in 1 Thessalonians 4:17 all believers will form one great welcoming party, escorting Jesus to earth for his millennial reign. Consequently, the posttribulation view fully affirms a rapture of the church, but understands it to occur simultaneously with the return of Christ. The purpose of the rapture, then, is not to rescue the church from tribulation, but to gather the church to Christ for the purpose of welcoming or receiving him at his glorious return.

The posttribulation rapture view does not maintain the sharp distinction between Israel and the church, which is essential to the pretribulation view. When Scripture speaks of the "elect" or "saints" or "servants" enduring the tribulation (e.g., Matt. 24:22; Rev. 7:3), these are all references to Christians (i.e., the church). Since the New Testament clearly teaches that both Jewish and Gentile believers constitute one body in Christ, this distinction between Israel and the church should not be used to determine who will be present during the Great Tribulation (Rom. 2:28–29; 3:29–30; 4:11–12; Gal. 3:26–29; 6:16; Eph. 2:14–22). Even pretribulationists concede that there will be both Jews and Gentiles who become Christians during the Great Tribulation and live through the remainder of that period.

According to the posttribulation view, there is a fundamental difference between the wrath of God and the Tribulation. Christians are assured that they will never experience God's wrath (Rom. 8:1; 1 Thess. 1:9–10; 5:9), but they have never been promised immunity or protection from persecution and suffering at the hands of God's enemies. The Great Tribulation includes both God's wrath and suffering that comes from the evil one. God pours out his wrath on the wicked, while the Tribulation is the wrath of Satan and his followers directed against God's people (Rev. 12:12, 17). Therefore, although believers may be persecuted to death, their relationship with God will be protected. What is far worse than physical death for staying faithful to Jesus is facing the wrath and judgment of Almighty God that leads to eternal death.

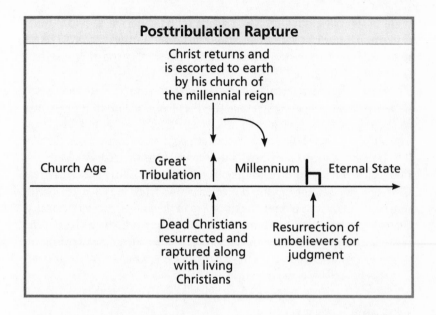

A case in point is Jesus' promise to the Christians at Philadelphia in Revelation 3:10: "Since you have kept my command to endure patiently, I will also keep you from the hour of trial that is going to come upon the whole world to test those who live on the earth." Assuming that a promise to a single, first-century church can apply to the whole church and that the "hour of trial" represents the Great Tribulation — both debatable assumptions — the promise still does not guarantee exemption from tribulation. While the phrase "keep [you] from" (*tēreō ek*) can mean "removal out of" or "preservation through," a parallel in the Gospel of John settles the issue. Jesus' prayer for his disciples in John 17:15 is the only other place where the same verb and preposition are used together: "My prayer is not that you take them out of the world but that you protect them from [*tçreô ek*] the evil one." Jesus assures his followers that in the world they will face tribulation (16:33), but God will protect them spiritually. If there is no distinction between God's wrath and satanic persecution or tribulation, what will happen to those who become followers of Christ during the Great Tribulation? Will they incur the wrath of God?

In summary, the posttribulation rapture view says that Christ will return at the conclusion of the Great Tribulation. He will gather his people to himself and continue his descent to earth to begin his millennial reign. The strengths of the position include its conviction that the church will never experience God's wrath, along with its realistic picture of the costs of discipleship (including the reality of persecution or tribulation throughout history). In addition, this position finds no New Testament support for a secret, silent coming of Christ, advocating instead a single return of Christ.

Perhaps the greatest strength of the posttribulation rapture view lies in its natural treatment and explanation of the biblical material. For instance, in the one passage that speaks of a "catching up" or rapture (1 Thess. 4:16–17), this view honors the immediate context by focusing on the visible, public return of Christ with the rapture playing a secondary, but still important, role. According to the posttribulation rapture view, the great Christian hope is not rapture but resurrection from the dead at Christ's return. Until the rise of pretribulationism in the mid-nineteenth century, the vast majority of Christians throughout church history favored the posttribulation view.[85] (See GREAT TRIBULATION; MIDTRIBULATION RAPTURE; PRETRIBULATION RAPTURE; PRE-WRATH RAPTURE; SECOND COMING; TRIBULATION; WRATH OF GOD.)

Preexilic Prophets

In 598 B.C. the Babylonians invaded Judah. Jerusalem surrendered and the Babylonians took the king, the royal court, and most of the aristocracy back to Babylonia. Later Jerusalem rebelled again against the Babylonians; in 587/586 B.C. the Babylonians again invaded and this time completely destroyed Jerusalem. They deported — or exiled — most of the remaining Israelites to Babylon. This deportation is called the exile (see EXILE). Prophets who prophesied *before* (or during) the exile are called Preexilic Prophets. Those who prophesied after the exile and the return to the land of Israel are called the Postexilic Prophets (see POSTEXILIC PROPHETS).

Those prophets who prophesied before the terrible exile of 587/586 B.C. are Isaiah, Jeremiah, Hosea, Joel, Amos, Obadiah, Jonah, Micah, Nahum, Habakkuk, and Zephaniah. Ezekiel was carried to Babylonia during the 598 B.C. deportation and prophesied both before and after the 587/586 B.C. destruction of Jerusalem and the resulting exile (see EZEKIEL, BOOK OF). However, he is generally included with the Preexilic Prophets.

Sometimes Daniel is not included with the prophets at all. In fact, in the Hebrew Bible Daniel is located in the Writings (with Psalms, etc.) rather than in the Prophets. Sometimes when he is classified as a prophet, he is included with the Preexilic Prophets, although he lived in exile from his youth until his death. Thus Daniel does not fit easily into either category of Preexilic or Postexilic Prophet.

Premillennialism, Dispensational

Premillennialism ("pre" means "before") is the view that Christ will return before the millennium. Prior to the millennium there will be a Great Tribulation on earth. The millennium constitutes Jesus' reign on earth with his saints during a time of peace and righteousness and firm control over the powers of evil. After the millennium there will be a final rebellion of evil followed by God's final victory, including judgment and the eternal state.

There are two major groups within premillennialism, divided over the issue of the timing of Christ's return in relationship to the Tribulation that precedes the millennium. Dispensational premillennialists favor a pretribulation rapture of the church. Thus, Christ will return twice, once for his church in a secret coming and then visibly and publicly with his church at the end of the Tribulation to begin the millennial reign. (Dispensational premillennialists are themselves divided into two main groups: classical dispensationalists and progressive dispensationalists.)

The second main group of premillennialists is known as historic premillennialists. This group believes that Christ will return after the Tribulation (posttribulational) and that the church will endure the Tribulation. (See DISPENSATIONALISM, CLASSICAL; DISPENSATIONALISM, PROGRESSIVE; MILLENNIUM; MILLENNIAL KINGDOM; POSTTRIBULATION RAPTURE; PREMILLENNIALISM, HISTORIC; PRETRIBULATION RAPTURE.)

Premillennialism, Historic

Along with other forms of premillennialism, the historic view shares the conviction that Christ will return to earth prior to the millennium (the time of Christ's literal reign on earth). The name "historic" derives from the connection to early Christianity. Many of the early church fathers from Papias (late first and early second century A.D.) on expected Christ to return and establish a millennial kingdom prior to judgment and the eternal state. Other prominent early Christian premillennialists include Justin Martyr, Irenaeus, Tertullian, Hippolytus, and Lactantius. In recent history, the most prominent proponents of historic premillennialism have been George E. Ladd, G. R. Beasley-Murray, Robert H. Mounce, Millard J. Erickson, J. Barton Payne, R. A. Torrey, W. R. Eerdman, Wayne Grudem, and Theodore Zahn.

Historic premillennialism differs in significant ways from both dispensational premillennialism and amillennialism. (1) Instead of following the strictly literal method of biblical interpretation used by dispensation-alists, they prefer an approach that honors a text's historical and literary context, its structure and grammar, and its theological role in the larger story of salvation. One reason for the different hermeneutic is that historic premillennialists fully accept the "already–not yet" framework advocated by progressive dispensationalists and certain nondispensationalists (see ALREADY–NOT YET).

(2) When it comes to interpreting Revelation, historic premillenni-alists prefer an eclectic approach combining the preterist, futurist, and idealist views rather than the primarily futurist emphasis of dispensation-alism (see ECLECTIC VIEW OF REVELATION).

(3) Unlike dispensationalists, who make a sharp distinction between Israel and the church, historic premillennialists view the church as the ful-fillment of Israel or the "true Israel" (Rom. 2:28–29; 4:11–12; 9:6–8; Gal. 3:16–29; 6:16; Eph. 2:11–22). The multinational church will receive the promises made to national Israel. There remains the likelihood that many Jews will convert to Christ at the end of the age, but the nation itself retains no unique role in God's plan, as is the case with dispensationalism.

(4) In contrast to all pretribulationists, historic premillennialism is posttribulational, insisting that the church will be present on earth dur-ing the Tribulation.

(5) There is one personal, visible, public return of Christ at the end of the Tribulation, rather than two second comings featured in dispensa-tionalism. For historical premillennialists, the great Christian hope is the return of Christ, not the rapture. The rapture is simply the term used to describe Christ's gathering his people to himself when he returns.

(6) Historic premillennialists see the two resurrections in Revelation 20 as both physical, in contrast to amillennialists, who see the first as spiritual and the second as physical.

(7) The millennium may or may not be a literal thousand years, but it will be a complete period of time. Some historic premillennialists limit the millennial experience to martyrs, while others believe it will include all believers.

(8) The second coming of Christ may be near (imminent in a general sense), but other events must occur before he will return (e.g., the appear-ance of the Antichrist). As this summary indicates, historic premillenni-alism has much more in common with progressive dispensationalism and amillennialism than it does with classic dispensationalism.

Historic premillennialists are criticized by amillennialists for putting too much weight on Revelation 20:1–10 in developing an overall eschatological system. They are also charged with a pessimistic view of history, although this is modified by their acceptance of the already–not yet framework. Classic dispensationalists fault the historic view for betraying the literal interpretive method. This difference in interpretive approaches lies at the heart of what separates the two main forms of premillennialism. Progressive dispensationalists criticize historic premillennialists for failing to explain how the Old Testament promises made to national Israel will be fulfilled.

The strengths of historic premillennialism are many. It lays claim to the strongest support from early Christianity. It gives serious attention to all aspects of biblical interpretation (e.g., historical, literary, grammatical, theological) and applies this more nuanced approach to reading Revelation. Because it does not have an overarching theological system driving its exegesis, it makes a strong case for adopting the most natural reading of biblical texts relating to the tribulation, the rapture, Christ's return, and the millennium. On a practical level, historical premillennialism tends to cultivate in believers a mentality appropriate for enduring persecution and suffering, as opposed to the escapist mind-set of some who are focused on a pretribulation rapture. (See AMILLENNIALISM; DISPENSATIONALISM, CLASSICAL; DISPENSATIONALISM, PROGRESSIVE; MILLENNIAL KINGDOM; POSTMILLENNIALISM; PREMILLENNIALISM, HISTORIC.)

Presence of God

The presence of God is one of the most important prophetic themes in the Bible. To have a relationship with God is to know and experience his presence. Throughout the Bible God's presence is not portrayed as something abstract, esoteric, or even merely emotional, but something that is real, concrete, and powerful. Indeed, the power of God and the glory of God are often connected to his presence. Likewise, salvation can only be adequately understood when placed in the context of enjoying God's presence.

The Bible begins with Adam and Eve in the garden, enjoying God's close presence. God even walks with them in the garden. At the end of the story, Revelation 21–22 describes the climax of history; humankind is once again back in the garden, worshiping God, experiencing his close presence, and enjoying the benefits of his presence, such as eternal life.

The Presence of God in the Old Testament

The Old Testament story starts out with the first human couple in the garden fellowshiping with God in close presence. However, Adam and Eve disobey God and are thus driven out of the garden (Gen. 3:22–24). One of the most serious negative consequences of this banishment is that it moves Adam and Eve away from the close, intimate presence of God (and the tree of life). Life is associated with the presence of God, and death is associated with the absence of his presence. Although relationship with God seems to be restored in the early verses of Genesis 4 (through sacrifice perhaps), Cain abuses the sacrifice and then kills Abel. He is thus driven away to the east, away from the presence of God (4:14, 16).

In Genesis 12 God appears to Abraham, and over the next several chapters he establishes a Covenant with him (see ABRAHAMIC COVENANT). Abraham builds an altar to the LORD because the LORD "appeared" to him (12:7). In this sense "appearing" relates to God's presence. Then as part of that relationship, God tells Abraham to "walk before me" (17:1). The Hebrew preposition translated "before" is often used of God's presence. Abraham, therefore, is called to walk "in the presence of" God. The Covenant relationship and God's presence are tightly interconnected.

In Exodus the presence of God becomes even more central to the story. In Exodus 3, after Moses expresses doubt about his ability to lead the Israelites out of Egypt, God declares, "I will be with you" (3:12), indicating that God was entering into a relationship with Moses and the people of Israel. As the Israelites flee Egypt, God guides and protects them by being in a pillar of cloud by day and a pillar of fire by night (13:21–22). Then the Israelites come before the powerful, intense presence of God at Mount Sinai to enter into a formal Covenant (Ex. 19). This Covenant was established on three critically important statements by God: "I will be your God. You will be my people. I will dwell in your midst."

Elements of this formula are stated over and over throughout the Old Testament. In Exodus, after God promises to dwell in their midst, he gives the people explicit instructions on how to build the Tabernacle, the place where he will reside (Ex. 25:8–9). God then explains that his glory is closely related to his presence. That is, coming into God's presence exposes one to the spectacular glory of God as well (33:12–23). After the completion of the Tabernacle, God does indeed come and fill it with his glory (40:34–38).

God's presence continues to be with Israel, "residing" around the Ark of the Covenant in the Tabernacle. In 1 Kings 6–7 Solomon builds the Temple in Jerusalem and places the Ark inside the Most Holy Place in the Temple. As with the Tabernacle, the glory of God now fills the Most Holy Place and God's presence dwells with Israel in the Temple.

Starting with Solomon and continuing for the next four hundred years, however, most of the kings and people of Israel turn away from God and worship idols, shattering the Mosaic Covenant. God waits patiently for Israel to repent and return as prophets warn of judgment and plead with Israel to keep the Covenant and worship him faithfully. Israel and Judah both refuse to repent, and eventually their idolatrous sin and injustices drive God out of their midst.

This tragic turn of events is described in Ezekiel 8–10. In Ezekiel 8, God gives the prophet a tour of the Temple in Jerusalem, pointing out all of the idols and idolatrous worship taking place there right before his very presence. "Son of Man," God asks Ezekiel, "do you see what they are doing—the utterly detestable things the house of Israel is doing here, things that will drive me far from my sanctuary?" (Ezek. 8:6). Then in Ezekiel 10 the glory of God actually departs from the Temple. Soon after the Babylonians capture Jerusalem and destroy both the city and the empty Temple (see EZEKIEL, BOOK OF).

Just as the prophets warn of judgment and of the loss of God's presence in the immediate future, they also look beyond the destruction to the spectacular coming kingdom when the Messiah will come and God will regather his people and rule among them with justice. In this context, as the prophets proclaim the new and better Covenant that is coming, they frequently declare that one of the features of this new and better kingdom is a restored and intensified presence of God.

God promises to once again dwell in the midst of his people. Isaiah declares that the name of the Coming One will be "Immanuel" (Isa. 7:14), which means "God with us" (see IMMANUEL). In addition, Ezekiel 40–48 describes the new Temple in the coming era. One of its most important features is the stress on the presence of God. In fact, the final words of Ezekiel state that "the name of the city from that time on will be: THE LORD IS THERE" (48:35).

One of the new features that the prophets declare regarding God's presence in the coming kingdom is his promise to put his Spirit within his people. In Joel 2:28 God declares, "I will pour out my Spirit on all people." In Ezekiel 36:26–28 God promises, "I will give you a new heart and put a new spirit in you; I will remove from you your heart of stone and give you a heart of flesh. And I will put my Spirit in you and move you to follow my decrees ... you will be my people and I will be your God." This is a spectacular change in the concept of God's presence. No longer will that presence be limited to the Most Holy Place in the Temple, but through the indwelling of his Spirit his presence will be within each of his people.

The Presence of God in the New Testament

It is significant that God's presence does not return to the Temple in Jerusalem until Jesus walks in through its gates. When the Jewish exiles return to Jerusalem under Zerubbabel and Ezra and when the Temple is rebuilt, there is no mention of God's glory coming to fill it. Indeed, as Jeremiah had predicted, the Ark of the Covenant (the symbol of God's presence in Israel's midst) had been lost and had not been returned (see ARK OF THE COVENANT). From God's departure in Ezekiel 10 and the subsequent fall of Jerusalem until the arrival of Jesus, the Jews live without the powerful presence of God in their midst.

Matthew clearly connects Jesus to the promise of Immanuel or "God with us" (Matt. 1:22–23). John declares that "the Word became flesh and made his dwelling [lit., tabernacled] among us" (John 1:14). In the Old Testament the glory of God was closely connected to the presence of God. The presence of Jesus likewise reflects the glory of God. After declaring that Jesus "tabernacled" among us, John states that "we have seen his glory" (1:14). When Jesus arrives in the Temple (2:12–24; cf. Matt. 21:12–17) for the first time in six hundred years the presence of God is back in the Temple. There he finds moneychangers and hypocritical worship; he finds hostility and opposition to the new revelation from God.

After Jesus' death and resurrection, the prophecies of Joel and Ezekiel are fulfilled regarding the Spirit of God. In Acts 2 the Holy Spirit falls on the followers of Jesus, filling them with God's powerful presence. Peter cites Joel 2:28–32 as the explanation of what has just happened. It is important to note that this new presence of God does not come to the Temple and reside in the Most Holy Place. It comes on believers and resides within them. Thus it is much more personal and relational.

Also, as in the Old Testament, in the book of Acts the presence of God (i.e., the Spirit) is associated with power. It is the mighty indwelling Spirit of God that powers the explosive spread of Christianity across the Mediterranean world in Acts. Likewise, throughout Paul's letters, the Spirit plays a powerful role in the lives of those who follow Christ. Moreover, the New Testament teaches that not only do believers have God's presence through the Spirit, but they also have direct access to the very throne and presence of the Father through Jesus Christ. As in the Old Testament, such access is interconnected to the related blessing of eternal life.

At the climax of the biblical story, as history reaches its culmination at the end of Revelation, once again God's presence plays a central role.

As the new Jerusalem comes down out of heaven, a loud voice from the throne of God declares, "Now the dwelling of God is with men, and he will live with them. They will be his people, and God himself will be with them and be their God" (Rev. 21:3).

Also, as throughout the Bible, John proclaims that the presence of God results in a spectacular display of his glory: "I did not see a temple in the city, because the Lord God Almighty and the Lamb are its temple. The city does not need the sun or the moon to shine on it, for the glory of God gives it light, and the Lamb is its lamp" (Rev. 21:22–23). Faithful believers will be able to enter through the gates of this city and go into the garden, where God and the Lamb are on the throne and where the tree of life flourishes on both sides of a river (22:12–21). Thus, humankind has gone full circle and been restored by God back to the garden, where they can enjoy his wonderful presence and have the blessing of eternal life.

Preterist View of Revelation

There are five main interpretive approaches to the book of Revelation: preterist, historicist, futurist, idealist, and eclectic. The preterist approach believes that Revelation relates to the situation in which John lived and should be read the way the original audience in the seven churches of Revelation would have read it (see SEVEN CHURCHES OF REVELATION). John uses symbolic language to communicate to the first-century readers how God will intervene on their behalf to deliver them from the evils of the Roman Empire. Under the preterist view, the prophecies of Revelation are thus fulfilled in the first century A.D.

There are two main forms of the preterist approach to reading Revelation. (1) One type prefers an earlier date for Revelation and sees the book as a prophecy of the fall of Jerusalem to the Romans in A.D. 70. The beast is Rome, and Babylon is unbelieving Israel who cooperates with Rome in oppressing the church. Armageddon is the siege of Jerusalem. Thus, Revelation offers hope to the suffering church (the true Israel) that their Jewish oppressors will be judged.

(2) The second type of preterist reading contends that Revelation predicts the fall of the Roman Empire (Babylon the Great) in A.D. 476. The Roman system will be judged for persecuting Christians, who refuse to worship the emperor as divine. Revelation warns Christians not to compromise with this idolatrous system and comforts them with the assurance that God will judge their enemies.

347

The strength of the preterist approach is that it seeks to understand Revelation in light of its historical-cultural context. In contrast to the purely futurist approach, which virtually ignores the first readers, the preterist approach honors the relevance of Revelation for the seven churches and their life situation. Both the warnings and the promises to these churches take on added urgency in light of their imminent fulfillment. The preterist view rightly contends that Revelation must have made sense to its first audience.

The great weakness of the preterist view is its failure to deal adequately with predictive prophecy. Revelation is self-described as a "prophecy" (Rev. 1:3; 22:7, 10, 18, 19), and most interpreters view at least some of those proclamations as awaiting a future fulfillment. All forms of the preterist view have been unsuccessful in locating historical referents for the return of Christ, the last judgment, and the new heaven and new earth in the first century.

In addition, the A.D. 70 form of this view struggles to admit to Revelation's claim that the last judgment will be a universal judgment rather than one pertaining to disobedient Israel. In its most liberal forms, the preterist view is forced to concede that Revelation has simply erred in its prediction of the end of the age, a conclusion unacceptable to evangelical scholars. (See ECLECTIC VIEW OF REVELATION; FUTURIST VIEW OF REVELATION; HISTORICIST VIEW OF REVELATION; IDEALIST VIEW OF REVELATION.)

Pretribulation Rapture

The various views related to the rapture of the church (pretribulation, midtribulation, posttribulation) center on one question: Will the church endure the Great Tribulation or will it be removed from the earth prior to that time? The pretribulation position holds that God will remove his church from the earth prior to the Great Tribulation so that the church will not be present on earth during the outpouring of God's wrath. Suddenly and unexpectedly Christ will return to just above the earth and will gather the church to himself (the rapture); then they will return together to heaven. The apostle Paul described this event in 1 Thessalonians 4:16–17:

> For the Lord himself will come down from heaven ... and the dead in Christ will rise first. After that, we who are still alive and are left will be caught up together with them in the clouds to meet the Lord in the air. And so we will be with the Lord forever.

The Great Tribulation will occur after Christ and the church have gone to heaven.

Generally, pretribulationists hold to three comings of Christ, three resurrections, and two judgments. The first coming of Christ was at his incarnation as Jesus of Nazareth. The second coming will be the secret rapture, as just noted. The third coming occurs when Christ returns with his church after the Tribulation to reign on earth during the millennium.

The first resurrection includes those righteous dead who are raised at the rapture to accompany Christ to heaven. Then at the end of the Tribulation there will be another resurrection of the righteous who died during the Tribulation. Finally, at the end of the millennium will be a resurrection of the wicked for judgment. The church will be judged at the time of the rapture (the judgment seat of Christ) for the purpose of rewarding their faithfulness. At the end of the millennium the unrighteous will stand before God at the great white throne judgment to be condemned (see GREAT WHITE THRONE JUDGMENT). The church will not participate in this last judgment. The chart below illustrates the pretribulation view.

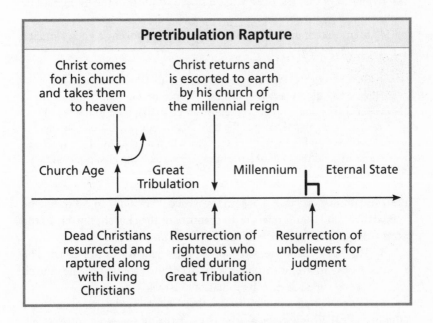

The pretribulation view is closely linked to dispensational premillennialism, which makes a clear distinction between Israel and the church.

Prior to the Tribulation God has been working primarily with the church, but in the Tribulation he will restore his chosen people, Israel. This period will mark the time of the great ingathering of Jews as they turn to Christ as Messiah. The purpose of the pretribulation rapture is to conclude the time of the Gentiles (Luke 21:24), to deliver the church from the Tribulation so that they do not experience the wrath of God, and to prepare for the restoration of national Israel.

Those who support a pretribulation rapture do so for several reasons. (1) This view takes seriously the horrific nature of the Great Tribulation. That time period will be unequaled in human history. Rather than being a time for testing or purifying the church, it will be a time when God pours out his wrath.

(2) Since the church will not experience the condemning wrath of God (see Rom. 5:9; 1 Thess. 1:9–10; 5:9), it cannot be present during the Tribulation. Note too Jesus' words in Revelation 3:10: "I will also keep you from the hour of trial [the Great Tribulation] that is going to come upon the whole world to test those who live on the earth."

(3) The rapture of the church is taught plainly in 1 Thessalonians 4:17, where Paul says that the dead will be raised to life and the living will be raptured to be with the Lord.

(4) Many pretribulationists find additional support in 2 Thessalonians 2:1–3 (italics added):

> Concerning the coming of our Lord Jesus Christ and our being gathered to him, we ask you, brothers, not to become easily unsettled or alarmed by some prophecy, report or letter supposed to have come from us, saying that the day of the Lord has already come. Don't let anyone deceive you in any way, for that day will not come until the *rebellion* occurs and the man of lawlessness is revealed, the man doomed to destruction.

Pretribulationists say that the word translated "rebellion" in 2:3 should be "departure" and that it refers to the rapture of the church; the day of the Lord will not come until the "departure" occurs.

(5) This view takes literally God's prophecies to restore Israel. The promises of God are not to be spiritualized and applied to the church since they were spoken directly to national Israel.

(6) The pretribulation view insists that Christ could come at any time (sometimes called *imminency*), thereby affirming many Scriptures that indicate that since Christ's coming will be sudden and unexpected, believers should be ready and prepared (e.g., Matt. 24:36–25:30).

For the weaknesses of this view see the discussion of the posttribulation rapture position. (See GREAT TRIBULATION; MIDTRIBULATION RAPTURE; POSTTRIBULATION RAPTURE; PREWRATH RAPTURE; RAPTURE.)

Prewrath Rapture

This rapture view attempts to synthesize pre-, mid-, and posttribulational rapture views by refining the actual timing of the rapture in hopes of arriving at a harmonizing position. The prewrath view insists that the truth about the rapture will be some combination of the three established views.

From pretribulationism the prewrath view accepts the truth that all believers will be exempt from God's wrath. They do not, however, follow the pretribulation view in claiming that all seven years of the Great Tribulation include the outpouring of God's wrath.

With midtribulationism, the prewrath view maintains the distinction between the wrath of God poured out on the powers of evil and the wrath of Satan poured out on God's people. Prewrath proponents cite Revelation 12:7–17 as evidence that Satan's wrath arrives during the second half of the seven-year Tribulation (i.e., the forty-two months of Daniel's seventieth week). This means that the wrath of God and of Satan overlap to some degree during this period.

Like posttribulationism, the prewrath view does not equate the Day of the Lord and the Great Tribulation, but rather sees the Day of the Lord coming at the end of the Tribulation. God's wrath will be restricted to the last part of Daniel's seventieth week—that is, the Day of the Lord. Thus believers will be present during the Great Tribulation, but they will not experience God's wrath. The prewrath view does not accept the posttribulational position that believers will be present when God's wrath is poured out. Rather, they will be protected from that wrath.

The prewrath rapture view attempts to combine three elements from the established views along with a fourth element of its own, namely, that the wrath of Satan will be cut short by removing the object of his wrath through the rapture of the church and protection of a remnant of Israel to inhabit the millennial kingdom. This gap between the rapture of the church at the inception of the Day of the Lord and Christ's coming is the time when God's wrath is poured out through the trumpet and bowl judgments of Revelation.

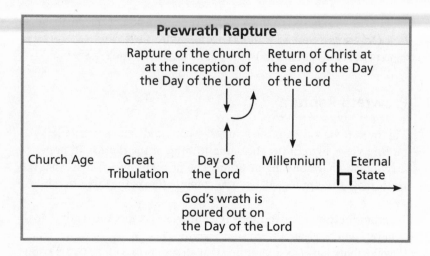

The strengths of the prewrath rapture view lie in its attempt to build on the established views. It is most dependent on posttribulationism, but it stops short of having believers on earth when God's wrath is poured out, in spite of the fact that they would be spiritually protected. Whether this most recent of the rapture views can sustain exegetically its nuanced position without shifting into posttribulationism remains to be seen. (See MIDTRIBULATION RAPTURE; PARTIAL RAPTURE; POSTTRIBULATION RAPTURE; PRETRIBULATION RAPTURE; RAPTURE.)

Prince

The key biblical prophecy concerning a "prince" is found in Daniel 9:25: "Know and understand this: From the issuing of the decree to restore and rebuild Jerusalem until the Anointed One, the ruler [prince], comes, there shall be seven 'sevens' and sixty-two 'sevens.' It will be built with streets and a moat, but in times of trouble" (author's translation).

This text delineates two time units: the first seven weeks of years (forty-nine years) and the next sixty-two weeks of years (434 years). One interpretation is that it refers to Artaxerxes' decree in 445 B.C. to rebuild Jerusalem (before the first week of sevens or forty-nine years), while the prince, the Messiah, is Jesus, whose death in A.D. 33 completed the 434 years (the sixty-two weeks of sevens).

However, there are two major problems with this view. (1) The term used to describe the rebuilding of Jerusalem is not "decree" but "word" (*dabar*) — in particular, a prophetic word. Thus, it is not the decree of the Persian king Artaxerxes, but the predictive word of the Lord through Jeremiah in 587/586 B.C. that Jerusalem will one day be restored (Jer. 30:18–22; 31:38–40) that Daniel refers to here.

(2) This view is inaccurate in translating the Hebrew word as "the Messiah" (Jesus). In fact, the Hebrew has no definite article and should be rendered "an anointed one"—a term that can even be applied to a pagan king such as Cyrus, the Persian (Isa. 45:1). The next word, *nagid*, can refer to a prince (e.g., 1 Sam. 2:10, 35; 9:16; 10:1) or a (high) priest (e.g., Lev. 4:3; Neh. 11:11; Jer. 20:1). Adding forty-nine years to the time of Jeremiah's prophetic word in 587/586 B.C. leaves no doubt about who this "anointed one" is—it is Joshua the high priest, who came to Jerusalem in 538 B.C. with Governor Zerubbabel for the purpose of rebuilding Jerusalem. According to this approach, Daniel's 490 years ran from 605 B.C. (the date of Jeremiah's prophecy about the coming fall of Jerusalem to the Babylonians) to 171 B.C. (the date of the murder of the Jewish high priest, Onias III). (See DISPENSATIONALISM, PROGRESSIVE.)

Prophecy in the Ancient Near East

Both the Bible and nonbiblical historical records from the ancient world indicate that many nations and religions of the ancient Near East during the Old Testament era had prophets or prophet-like individuals who reportedly functioned as intermediaries between the pagan gods and the respective monarchs. For example, in 1 Kings 18:16–46 the prophet Elijah confronts 450 prophets of Baal and 400 prophets of Asherah. These prophets were supported by Queen Jezebel, a Baal worshiper from Sidon who had married Ahab, king of Israel.

Jeremiah likewise indicates that prophecy and other related practices were common in the royal courts of all the nations throughout the region. In Jeremiah 27 the nations of Edom, Moab, Ammon, Tyre, and Sidon were conspiring to rebel against Nebuchadnezzar. Jeremiah sends word to the kings of these countries, warning them against listening to the advice of their court prophets: "So do not listen to your prophets, your diviners, your interpreters of dreams, your mediums or your sorcerers who tell you, 'You will not serve the king of Babylon'" (27:9). In other words, the royal courts of the surrounding countries had official court prophets as well as others who claimed to bring messages to the king from the various gods of the region.

The nonbiblical literature of the ancient Near East likewise contains numerous references to court prophets and other diviners and mediums.

From the Assyrian and Babylonian archaeological sites in Mesopotamia thousands of clay tablets have been recovered, many of which mention court prophets, although a wide range of terminology is used for these individuals and their occupations. In the Old Testament the major terms for the biblical prophets are "seer," "man of God," and "prophet." In Mesopotamia, those involved in bringing oracles and other messages from the gods are given official titles such as "answerer," "cult functionary," "ecstatic," "diviner" (this word is similar to the Hebrew *nabi*ʾ or "prophet"), "proclaimer," "revealer" (this word is similar to the Hebrew term "seer"), and "sent one." There are also numerous individuals who carry out prophet-like activities who are not given official titles.

These prophets appear to have had a fairly high status in the royal courts of the ancient Near East. In general their oracles and dreams supported the king and his political/military policies. On rare occasions they admonished the king, but this was always done mildly and was usually related to the king's failure to follow an earlier utterance of the gods.[86]

Many of the specific practices (such as sorcery, necromancy, etc.) of these prophet-like people in the Old Testament world are explicitly prohibited for Israel in Deuteronomy 18:9–22. Throughout the time of the Israelite and Judahite kings, the backsliding kings often try to copy the pattern of the royal courts in the countries around them. Thus, they try to bring the office of prophet under their direct royal control. The true prophets of God, however, emphasize that they are independent of the king. Indeed, they often bring a critical word of God against the king.

The disobedient kings, however, often respond by appointing their own prophets, who bring messages — supposedly from God — that are more favorable to the king and that do not criticize his behavior. These are the "false prophets" that Deuteronomy 18 warns against and that the true prophets of God — especially Jeremiah — struggle against (see FALSE PROPHECY).

Prophecy in Early Christianity

Prophecy in the New Testament is first and foremost evidence that the age to come, or the kingdom of God, has arrived with its pouring out of the Holy Spirit on the church (Acts 2:1–47). As the New Testament era dawned, Judaism had developed the sense that, with the closing of the Old Testament, the voice of prophecy and the Spirit had ceased. This is reflected in several noncanonical Jewish writings (see, e.g., Sir. 49:10; 1 Macc. 4:49; 9:27; 14:41; *Sib. Or.* 18b). Yet they also believed that at the end of history with the arrival of the Messiah, the voice of prophecy and the Spirit would resume (Joel 2:28–32). The New Testament declares that this expectation is now fulfilled in Jesus.

New Testament prophecy interprets Jesus as the long-awaited Messiah prophesied in the Old Testament. The Gospel of Mark clearly identifies John the Baptist as the forerunner of the Messiah (cf. Mark 1:1–4 with Isa. 40:3). Yet John the Baptist himself came as a prophet, similar in many ways to the prophets of the Old Testament, calling on Israel to repent (Mark 1:4–5; Luke 3:3–9). John also identifies Jesus as the Messiah, acknowledging Jesus' true messianic role by proclaiming, "Look, the Lamb of God, who takes away the sin of the world!" (John 1:29).

There is a sense in which John the Baptist is a transitional character. He comes as an Old Testament prophet, but as he identifies Jesus to be the Christ, he moves the biblical phenomenon of prophecy into the New Testament era. In fact, one of the main prophetic activities in the New Testament is the identification of Jesus as the Messiah and as the One who fulfills the Old Testament messianic prophecies.

In Luke's account of Jesus' birth, key prophetic witnesses under the inspiration of the Spirit reveal Jesus as the Messiah. Thus Elizabeth (Luke 1:39–45), Zechariah (1:67–79), and Anna (2:36–38) all give inspired prophetic witness to that fact (see ANNA). Jesus himself perceives that he, as the Messiah, is fulfilling the role of the predicted Suffering Servant of Isaiah 61 (see Luke 4:18–21). Moreover, Luke 9–19 casts Jesus as the predicted coming prophet (Deut. 18:15, 18–20). Jesus also reminds two of his disciples that he is the suffering and glorious Messiah anticipated throughout the Old Testament (Luke 24:44–47; cf. John 6:14; 7:7, 40, which probably allude to the promise of a prophet in Deut. 18:18; see MOSES).

Several times the New Testament mentions functioning prophets in the early church. These prophets convey oracles, messages, or interpretations to the church from God through the inspiration and initiative of the Holy Spirit. Usually these prophecies are given to strengthen the church and to meet specific needs of the early church. As in the Old Testament, these New Testament prophets speak both to existing situations (often interpreting the Old Testament messianically) and to future situations (i.e. predicting the future), but these prophecies are always for the purpose of strengthening the church. Thus Paul speaks of prophecy as one of the gifts of the Spirit, particularly to be manifested in the worship setting of the churches for the edification of the church (1 Cor. 12:10, 28; 14:1; Eph. 4:11; 1 Thess. 5:19–21).

John 14–16 envisions the Spirit (of prophecy) as teaching the disciples the true meaning of Jesus' words (cf. 1 John 2:20, 27; Rev. 22:6, 9). Some scholars suggest that the apostles themselves are prophets and that the apostolic word functions for the New Testament as the prophetic word functioned in the Old Testament. Likewise some have suggested that Paul himself takes on many of the functions and responsibilities of a prophet (especially in his role of revealing and interpreting the Word of God), even though he is never called a prophet. However, even though the apostles do seem to function like prophets (like Jesus himself), it does appear that the gift of prophecy is also given by the Spirit to others in the early New Testament church.

Some New Testament prophecy focuses on predictions about the second coming of Christ and attendant circumstances. This is so in Jesus' Olivet Discourse (Matthew 24; Mark 13; Luke 21). It is also characteristic of Paul (1 Thess. 4:13–18; 2 Thess. 2:1–12; 1 Tim. 4:1–5; 2 Tim. 3:1–9), Peter (2 Peter 3:1–10), Jude (Jude 5–19), and John (1 John 4:1–6). Likewise, the book of Revelation, from beginning to end, is a prophetic vision of the second coming of Christ and the signs of the times that will herald his return (Rev. 1:3; 22:7, 10–21). (See JOHN THE BAPTIST; KINGDOM OF GOD; MESSIAH, THE; OLIVET DISCOURSE; SECOND COMING.)

Prophecy in the Greco-Roman World

Prophecy was pervasive among the Jews of the Old Testament era. The prophets' messages form a critical part of the Old Testament canon. Likewise the writings of Philo, the Dead Seas Scrolls, Josephus, and the *Sibylline Oracles* demonstrate that the phenomena of prophecy continued into New Testament times and into the era of early Christianity.

Prophecy, however, also flourished in Greco-Roman life. It appears in Hellenistic (Greek) literature as early as Homer (750 B.C.) and continues up until the fourth century A.D., especially in connection with oracular shrines. These sacred places of revelation were widely distributed throughout the Hellenistic world during the Greek period (fourth century B.C. to first century B.C.). Most famous were oracles to Apollo at Delphi, Claros, Didyma, Corope, and Argos, and the sanctuaries for Zeus Dodona, Olympia, and so on.

These oracular places maintained a cult personnel for disclosing to inquiring folk divine guidance regarding the past, present, and future. Most notable was the Pythia, a priestess whose job was to speak on behalf of the gods to inquirers. The Pythia was a prophetess who delivered oracular responses supposedly inspired by Apollos. Scholars continue to debate whether the Pythia responded to inquiries by speaking in an ecstatic trance, which was then interpreted by attendant prophets, or if she spoke in intelligible speech directly to the inquirer.

The oracle questions submitted to the cult personnel were usually in oral form as was the Pythia's responses, but they were apparently later written down. Most of the questions posed to the Pythia required a simple yes or no. A papyrus (ancient written document) from the temple at Delphi contained the following questions for the Pythia: "Shall I be victorious? Shall I marry? Will it be advantageous to sail? Should I farm? Shall I travel?" The divine reply to questions like these could be given through the Pythia or by lot.

By contrast, prophecy in ancient Rome (fourth century B.C. to fourth century A.D.) was connected not with oracular places but with oracular people, most notably the Sibylline prophetesses. "Sibyl" in the fourth century B.C. became a generic term for an inspired prophetess. Varro, the Roman writer, listed ten sibyls whose prophetic writings circulated widely in the Roman world. The written oracles of the Cumaean Sibyl became famous because of their influence in Rome. They were even entrusted to a priestly college, which was asked to interpret the Sibyl's predictions relative to the Roman Senate in times of crises and turmoil. Such a collection was consulted from at least 83 B.C. to A.D. 363. So influential was the Cumaean Sibyl's influence on Rome that Caesar Augustus (13 B.C.) and Tiberius (A.D. 43), unhappy with her prophecies, destroyed her writings; but her influence nevertheless continued.

Prophet

The Hebrew designation for prophet in the Old Testament is *nabi'*, while its Greek correspondence is *prophētēs*. The calling of a prophet in the Old Testament involved a twofold role: forth-telling the word of the Lord concerning Israel and the nations for his own time, and foretelling the future. These two aspects focused on the divine calling of the prophets to be the enforcers of God's covenant with Israel. If his people, the Jews, obeyed the law of Moses, there would be blessings for them in the land; if not, the curses for breaking the covenant would ensue, including their defeat and exile at the hands of enemy nations. But if Israel repented, the nation could be restored to their former fortunes.

Such a twofold message explains the various types of prophetic speech one finds in the Old Testament: announcement of judgment, announcement of salvation, lawsuit, oracle of assurance, and the like. It is customary to divide the prophets of the Old Testament into two categories: the Former Prophets (the nonwriting prophets such as Samuel, Elijah, and Elisha) and the Latter Prophets (the writing prophets, such as Isaiah, Jeremiah, and Ezekiel) (see FORMER PROPHETS; LATTER PROPHETS).

Modern scholars debate whether ancient Judaism believed that the voice of prophecy ceased at the closing of the Old Testament canon. Yet it is clear in the New Testament that for the early church, the prophetic witness was alive and well. In the early days of the New Testament John the Baptist appears, looking and sounding much like an Old Testament prophet. Thus John is dressed like a prophet (Matt. 3:4; Mark 1:6; cf. 1 Kings 19:19; 2 Kings 1:8; 2:13–14; Zech. 13:4). He receives the spirit of prophecy while still in his mother's womb (Luke 1:15). Like the Old Testament prophets, he calls on Israel to repent (Matt. 3:7–10; Luke 3:7–9). Jesus also is identified as a prophet (see especially Jesus' place with the prophets in Luke 9–19).

The phenomenon of prophecy likewise continues in the early church (see Acts as a whole; 1 Thess. 5; Rev. 1:3; 2–3; 22:7, 10, 18–19). Like the Old Testament prophets, it seems that the same twofold proclamation characterized the prophetic tradition of the New Testament: forth-telling what God had done for his people through Jesus the Messiah in fulfillment of Old Testament prophecy and foretelling the future in terms of the second coming of Christ.

Psalms, Book of

In Luke 24:44 Jesus tells his disciples, "Everything must be fulfilled that is written about me in the Law of Moses, the Prophets and the Psalms." Although the Psalms are usually not considered as part of the prophetic literature of the Old Testament, many psalms do, nonetheless, contain prophetic material, especially regarding the coming Messiah. Indeed, as the New Testament writers cite Old Testament texts to demonstrate how Jesus fulfills Old Testament prophecy, Psalms is one of the most frequently quoted books. Citations from Psalms regarding prophecy and fulfillment occur in the Synoptic Gospels (Matthew, Mark, Luke), Acts, the letters of Paul, Hebrews, and Revelation.

One of the main prophetic themes in the Psalms is that of the messianic King. The psalms associated with this theme recall with praise the promises made by God to David regarding a Davidic dynasty (see DAVIDIC COVENANT). Most of these Psalms appear to be describing both present and future situations. Thus, they praise the Davidic king that currently sits on the throne, but they also anticipate a future Davidic king who will be greater.

In Hebrew the main verb tense used in the Psalms can carry either a present tense idea or a future tense idea. Thus when the psalmist proclaims, "The LORD reigns!" the verse can also be translated, "The LORD will reign!" Thus it is difficult for translators and interpreters to distinguish clearly whether the psalmist is celebrating the current rule of God over Israel (and the world) or anticipating (prophetically) the future rule of God on earth. The same is true in psalms of God's Anointed One, the Davidic ruler who makes God's rule visible to his people on earth.

Several other themes are frequently found in the Psalms that deal with the messianic King. One theme relates to suffering. Not only is the Messiah the ruling king, but in some psalms (e.g., Ps. 22) the messianic King is reviled and humiliated as he tries to carry out God's will. In addition, some psalms focus on the messianic King as a shepherd, who shepherds God's people with justice and righteousness. Finally, as the King extends God's rule over the earth, he carries out a twofold role of deliverance and judgment. The coming messianic King is both a judging warrior and a gentle savior.[87]

Although numerous psalms are cited and alluded to in the New Testament in regard to prophetic fulfillment, five psalms in particular (Ps. 2; 22; 69; 110; and 118) have special significance because they are each cited numerous times in several books of the New Testament, much more so than the other psalms.

Psalm 2 is used several ways in the New Testament. (1) It is quoted often, especially in the Synoptic Gospels, in connection with the Lord's baptism and his transfiguration ("You are my Son; today I have become your Father" Ps. 2:7). In Acts 13:33 this verse is even quoted in regard to the resurrection of Christ. Note that Psalm 2:2 uses the term "Anointed One" (i.e., Messiah, see MESSIAH). (2) Psalm 2 describes the installation of the Anointed One as king in Zion. Thus 2:7 is also cited in New Testament passages that expound on the exaltation of Christ into heaven, at the right hand of God (Heb. 1:5; 5:5; 7:28). (3) The New Testament also cites Psalm 2 in regard to the themes concerning the threats by hostile nations against God's Anointed One, and the triumph over these nations and their rulers by the Son of God, his Anointed (Acts 4:25–26; Rev. 12:5).[88]

Psalm 110 likewise plays a significant role in the New Testament. The book of Hebrews stresses that Jesus was made a high priest after the order of Melchizedek (see MELCHIZEDEK). Indeed, Psalm 110 merges the two messianic images of king and priest into one person. In Mark 12:35–36 Jesus quotes Psalm 110:1 to make the point that the Messiah is the Lord of David, not merely the Son of David. In addition, the imagery of the Messiah seated at the right hand of the throne of God (110:1) is alluded to frequently in the New Testament in regard to Jesus' resurrection, ascension, and exaltation.[89]

Psalm 22 is another Psalm quoted numerous times in the New Testament. Jesus quotes verse 1 from the cross, "My God, my God, why have you forsaken me?" (Matt. 27:46; Mark 15:34), thus making an explicit connection between this psalm and his crucifixion. Several other aspects of Psalm 22 find fulfillment in the story of the crucifixion. (1) The forsaken one suffers derision, as the ones passing by shake their heads (Ps. 22:7; Matt. 27:39; Mark 15:29). (2) The bystanders hurl taunting challenges to the one suffering (Ps. 22:8; Matt. 27:43). (2) The manner of suffering ("my bones are out of joint"; "they have pierced my hands and feet") reflects the type of suffering Jesus experienced on the cross (Ps. 22:14–16). Finally, his clothes are divided and lots are cast to determine new ownership (Ps. 22:18; Matt. 27:35; Mark 15:24).[90]

Some scholars suggest that the many psalms of suffering and crying out, such as Psalm 22, express the collective suffering and pain of all of God's people. They note that Jesus vicariously bears this pain and suffering on the cross. Thus he identifies with the psalm that typifies this suffering by citing from it.

However, there seems to be more to Jesus' use of Psalm 22 than that. Psalm 22 is titled as a "psalm of David," so historically this psalm reflects a cry of extreme suffering by David. This suffering and cry probably becomes prophetic, even predictive, through typology (see TYPOLOGY). David is not crucified on a cross, but he does suffer greatly. He describes that suffering in figurative ways. Many of the figures of speech (e.g., "my bones are out of joint") that David uses find literal fulfillment in the crucifixion of Christ. Thus in his suffering and cry, David is a *type* of Christ.

Psalm 69 is another frequently cited psalm. Psalm 69:21 is used in much the same fashion as Psalm 22 in reference to the crucifixion. However, Psalm 69:9 ("zeal for your house consumes me") is cited after Jesus cleanses the temple (John 2:17).

The last psalm that appears numerous times in the New Testament is Psalm 118. This psalm is interpreted Christologically in two different situations. (1) Psalm 118:25 begins with the Hebrew phrase "Hosanna!" which means, "Lord, save us!" The next verse begins, "Blessed is he who comes in the name of the LORD." In Jesus' day, the Jews understood these verses to be referring to the Messiah. Thus as Jesus enters Jerusalem triumphantly accompanied by the people shouting "Hosanna!" and as Jesus then confronts the Temple leaders over his status, the four Gospel writers make the connection to Psalm 118, underscoring that these are messianic events (Matt. 21:9,15; 23:39; Mark 11:9–10; Luke 13:35; 19:38; John 12:13).

(2) Psalm 118:22–23 ("the stone the builders rejected has become the capstone") is cited to explain that the irony between Israel's rejection of Christ followed by his exaltation is indeed a fulfillment of prophecy (see Matt. 21:42; Luke 20:17; Acts 4:11; 1 Peter 2:7).

Put

Put is the name of a country often associated with Egypt and Cush (Gen. 10:6; Jer. 46:9; Ezek. 30:5; Nah. 3:9). The soldiers of Put likewise at one time served the king of Tyre (Ezek. 27:10). In Ezekiel 38:5 Put is mentioned as one of the allies of Gog (see GOG AND MAGOG). A few scholars have suggested that Put may refer to the area of modern Somalia, but most scholars maintain that Put was a nation in North Africa, in the area occupied by the modern country of Libya.

Ram

Daniel 8:3–8, 19–21 records the author's prophecy of a future battle between the Medo-Persian Empire (symbolized as a two-horned ram) and Alexander the Great (symbolized as a goat), which occurred in approximately 330 B.C. The army of the Greek king crushed the Medo-Persian army, thereby asserting itself as the unrivaled empire of the then-known world until Rome made its presence felt in the second century B.C.

Rapture

The English word "rapture" derives from the Latin verb *rapto*, which means "to seize, snatch, carry away." This term is one way to translate the Greek term *harpazō*, a word that occurs fourteen times in the New Testament with three senses: (1) to steal or carry off (Matt. 12:29; John 10:12); (2) to take or lead away by force (Matt. 11:12; 13:19; John 6:15; 10:28, 29; Acts 23:10; Jude 23); and (3) to be carried away by the Spirit (Acts 8:39; 2 Cor. 12:2, 4; 1 Thess. 4:17; Rev. 12:5). This final sense of the word (and 1 Thess. 4:17 in particular) forms the centerpiece of the prophetic discussion related to the rapture.

Some in the church at Thessalonica were concerned about their loved ones who had already died. Would they be left out or disadvantaged in any way? Paul's answer comes in 1 Thessalonians 4:16–17:

> For the Lord himself will come down from heaven, with a loud com-
> mand, with the voice of the archangel and with the trumpet call of God,
> and the dead in Christ will rise first. After that, we who are still alive and
> are left will be caught up together with them in the clouds to meet the
> Lord in the air. And so we will be with the Lord forever.

Paul assures these believers that when Christ returns, the resurrection of those who have died will be first priority. Then those who are still alive will be "caught up" (*harpazō*) with those just resurrected to meet the Lord in the air. The rapture of the church refers to the "catching up" of believers to be united with Christ at his coming. While Paul's words no doubt brought comfort to the Thessalonian believers, they have generated endless theological debates among later generations of Christians.

The primary point of contention is the time of the rapture of the church, resulting in five main positions, all of which are typically associated with premillennialism (see PREMILLENNIALISM, DISPENSATIONAL; PREMILLENNIALISM, HISTORIC). Each position is concerned with how the rapture relates to the Tribulation. (1) The pretribulation rapture view says that Christ will come for his church prior to the seven-year period of Great Tribulation. At this time Jesus will come *for* his church and rescue them from the coming wrath of God. After the Tribulation Christ will come *with* his church to reign on earth during the millennium (see PRE-TRIBULATION RAPTURE).

(2) The midtribulation rapture view claims that the church will go through the first half of the Great Tribulation, but will be raptured prior to the second half, when God pours out his wrath. The church will experience tribulation and persecution but will never experience God's wrath (see MIDTRIBULATION RAPTURE).

(3) The prewrath rapture view also claims that the church will endure much of the Great Tribulation, but it will be raptured prior to God's pouring out his wrath. This view restricts the wrath of God with the Day of the Lord, which it believes will occur at the very end of the Great Tribulation (see PREWRATH RAPTURE).

(4) The posttribulation rapture view believes that the church will endure the Great Tribulation but will be protected from divine wrath. This view distinguishes between the wrath of God poured out on the wicked and the wrath of Satan poured out on believers in the form of persecution and martyrdom. According to this position, the Bible connects the rapture and the second coming of Christ as one event rather than two separate events (see POSTTRIBULATION RAPTURE).

(5) The partial rapture view maintains that not all believers will be taken at the same time. The more faithful believers will be raptured before the less faithful ones (see PARTIAL RAPTURE).

Generally speaking, a person's position on the timing of the rapture is connected with their millennial view. Most dispensational premillennialists prefer a pretribulation rapture, while most historic premillennialists, amillennialists, and postmillennialists favor a posttribulation rapture. All agree that the rapture of the church, whenever it occurs, results in a reunion of believers with their Lord.

Realized Eschatology

In contrast to futurist eschatology, where the kingdom of God awaits a final consummation at the end of history, realized eschatology views the kingdom of God as already realized in the person and mission of Jesus. The futurist aspects of Jesus' teaching are reduced to a minimum and his apocalyptic language is viewed as symbolic of theological truths.

The person most responsible for advocating this position is British scholar C. H. Dodd. In his 1935 book *Parables of the Kingdom* he focused on Jesus' teachings that announced the arrival of the kingdom with his coming. For instance, in Luke 11:20 Jesus says, "But if I drive out demons by the finger of God, then the kingdom of God has come to you" (cf. 17:21; Matthew 13). Eschatology becomes a matter of the present experience rather than any kind of future event. The kingdom has come in the messianic ministry of Jesus.

Most interpreters have criticized Dodd's realized eschatology for ignoring Jesus' teachings that point to a future consummation of the kingdom (e.g., Matt. 24–25; Mark 13). When all of Jesus' teachings are considered, futurist eschatology balances realized eschatology. To be sure, the kingdom arrived with Jesus, but Jesus himself taught that history still awaits a final completion. The kingdom of God is both "already" and "not yet" (see ALREADY – NOT YET; ESCHATOLOGY).

Red Heifer

A heifer is a young female bovine (cow) that has not produced her first calf. According to Numbers 19 ancient Israel was to use a red heifer to purify itself from uncleanness. Numbers 19:2–7 specifies the following of the red heifer: (1) It must be without blemish; (2) it must be without defect; (3) it must never have worn a yoke; (4) it must be sacrificed and then its ashes must be mixed with clear water; that mixture is to be sprinkled over the unclean. Hebrews 9:13–14 seems to allude to this procedure in referring to the death of Christ: "The blood of bulls and goats and the ashes of a heifer sprinkled on those who are ceremonial unclean sanctifies them so that they are outwardly clean. How much more, then, will the blood of Christ ... cleanse our consciences from acts that lead to death."

According to some popular writers, Jewish tradition holds that no flawless red heifer has been born in Israel since the destruction of the Jerusalem temple by the Romans in A.D. 70. For some who believe that in the last days Israel will rebuild a literal Temple on the Temple Mount and begin sacrificing again, such an obstacle must be overcome, for otherwise no Jew will be purified enough to come into contact with God's new dwelling place. Thus there are reports that some fringe groups today are attempting to raise the perfect red heifer.

Remnant

The concept of a remnant or a "remnant theology" runs throughout Scripture. Although appearing in a wide variety of texts and contexts, the central idea of the remnant is that in the midst of seemingly total apostasy and the consequential terrible judgment and/or destruction, God always has a small faithful group whom he delivers and works through to bring blessing.

Early allusions to the idea of a remnant are introduced in Genesis. Noah and his family (Gen. 6–9) are the remnant that is saved during the flood, while all other people are destroyed in judgment. Likewise in 45:6–7 Joseph declares to his brothers, "For two years now there has been famine in the land, and for the next five years there will not be plowing and reaping. But God sent me ahead of you to preserve for you a remnant on earth and to save your lives by a great deliverance."

The remnant theme is also evident when Elijah complains to God that he is the only faithful one left. God corrects him by pointing out that he has maintained a remnant of seven thousand faithful ones in the midst of national apostasy (1 Kings 19:10–18).

However, it is in the Old Testament prophets that the remnant theme flowers into full blossom. The Hebrew word for remnant occurs over a hundred times in the prophetic books. The prophets proclaim that since Israel/Judah has broken the Covenant and since they refuse to repent and turn back to God, judgment is coming. This judgment will take the form of terrible foreign invasions and destruction, followed by exile from the land. Thus, the northern kingdom of Israel is destroyed and exiled by the Assyrians in 722 B.C., and the southern kingdom Judah is destroyed and exiled by the Babylonians in 587/586 B.C.

Yet the prophets also prophesy hope and restoration beyond the judgment. Though many will be destroyed in the judgment, not everyone will; rather, a remnant will survive and God will work through the remnant to bring blessings and restoration. Usually the remnant is identified as those who go into exile but who likewise hope to return to the land of Israel. The reestablishment of the remnant is often connected with the inauguration of the messianic age.

The remnant theme continues into the New Testament, but it is not nearly as prominent as in the Old Testament prophets. The term *remnant* does not occur in the Gospels, although the idea is implied in several texts. Thus in Matthew 7:13–14 Jesus states, "For wide is the gate and broad is the road that leads to destruction, and many enter through it. But small is the gate and narrow the road that leads to life, and only a few find it." Likewise in 22:14 Jesus summarizes his preceding parable by stating, "Many are invited, but few are chosen."

In Romans 11, Paul is much more explicit. Not only does he use the word "remnant" but in 11:2–5 he connects his argument specifically to the remnant idea in 1 Kings 19:18 ("I have reserved for myself seven thousand"). Paul is pointing out the similarities between the apostasy in Israel in 1 Kings 19 and the parallel rejection of the Messiah by Israel during Paul's day. In both cases the nation had rejected God's Word and salvation plan. But in both situations, even though the nation as a whole rejected God, God maintained a faithful remnant. Paul also underscores that the remnant is established by God's grace. Thus in Romans 11:5 he explains, "So, too, at the present time there is a remnant chosen by grace."

Repentance

The theme of repentance occurs frequently throughout many Old Testament prophetic books as well as in the New Testament. The Old Testament prophets accuse Israel/Judah of breaking the Mosaic Covenant and of turning away from God, thus destroying their relationship with God. This disobedience to the Covenant will result in judgment. However, the prophets also state that if Israel/Judah will repent, the relationship with God can be restored and judgment averted. In fact, the prophets in general, and Jeremiah in particular, plead continuously for the Israelites to repent. Even in the context of proclaiming imminent, unavoidable judgment (invasion by the Babylonians), prophets like Jeremiah still beg the people to repent.

The Old Testament Hebrew word frequently used for repenting is *shub*, which has a literal meaning of "to turn." This word can mean to turn back to God ("repent"), but it can also be used of turning away from God ("backslide"). This dual meaning invites colorful wordplays, such as the prophets love to use (see POETRY).

Shub is a favorite word of Jeremiah's, occurring over 110 times in his prophecy. Jeremiah will use it both of backsliding (turning away from God) and for repentance (turning to God), often in the same verse. In Jeremiah 3:22, for example, the prophet uses the word three times in one verse. A literal rendering of this verse is, "*Turn*, you sons of *turning*! I will cure you of your *turnings*." Although Jeremiah and the other prophets use *shub* in numerous colorful wordplays, the emerging meaning is clear. God offers deliverance and salvation instead of judgment and destruction to those who repent (turn from sin and turn to him).

The New Testament word for repentance (*metanoia*) implies a change of one's mind or one's will to the degree that there is a complete reorientation of the person.[91] Obviously this term plays a major role in the salvation message of the Gospels and of the New Testament letters. However, it also plays a major role in the book of Revelation. In fact, the Greek verb translated "repent" (*metanoeō*) occurs more frequently in Revelation than in any other New Testament book. In the letters to the seven churches of Asia Minor (see SEVEN CHURCHES OF REVELATION) in Revelation 2:1–3:22, the word for "repent" occurs eight times. Five of the churches are called upon to repent (Ephesus, Pergamum, Thyatira, Sardis, and Laodicea). Reflecting a prophetic theology similar to that of the Old Testament prophets, John exhorts these churches to repent of their sin and to turn back to God before it is too late and the judgment comes.

Likewise, as Revelation progresses, several times the writer stops to wonder at the lack of repentance by people in spite of God's spectacular and terrible acts of judgment (Rev. 9:20–21; 16:9–11). Thus, the theme of repentance in Revelation is similar to that found in the Old Testament prophets. People are called upon to repent (to turn from their sin and to turn to God) before it is too late and the eschatological judgment arrives. However, many people in Revelation ignore the warnings and the miraculous signs from God. Like so many in ancient Israel, many in Revelation remain obstinate and disobedient, and thus they perish.

Restoration of Israel

The message of most Old Testament prophetic books can be synthesized into three main points, addressed to Israel/Judah:

- You have broken the Mosaic Covenant, so repent.
- Since there is no repentance, judgment is coming (i.e., the Babylonians or Assyrians).
- Beyond the judgment and destruction will come future blessing and restoration.

Much of the Old Testament prophetic message regarding the future involves the restoration of the nation Israel. As the prophets predict, the Babylonians invade, completely destroy Jerusalem and the rest of Judah, and carry off the people into exile. The prophets, however, predict a new exodus (see NEW EXODUS) or a return to Israel. They describe a rebuilt Jerusalem/Zion where a just, righteous Davidic king rules (or often, God himself reigns). Often they also describe a scene where peoples of all nations stream to Jerusalem to worship the true God. At this time there will be peace and prosperity in the land of Israel.

After the exile many of the Jews did return to Israel under Zerubbabel and Ezra, and a nation of sorts was rebuilt. But they remained a small, struggling country under foreign domination. Few of the descriptions that the Old Testament prophets had provided of the restoration were fulfilled in this return (the postexilic return). Thus the strong implication (and the message of the postexilic prophets) was that the people in postexilic Israel were to continue to look forward to a fulfillment of those prophecies regarding restoration.

How are we to understand these prophecies today? Evangelical scholars are sharply divided on how to interpret the prophecies of a restored Israel. Many premillennialists, especially dispensationalists (see DISPENSATIONALISM, CLASSICAL; PREMILLENNIALISM, HISTORIC) tend to take these prophecies as literal as possible. They maintain that these prophecies about the restoration of Israel will be literally fulfilled during the thousand-year millennial reign of Christ on earth. At that time, Jerusalem will be reestablished and Christ will rule from Jerusalem over a literal, restored, believing nation of Israel in the literal land of Israel, and, indeed, over the entire world. This millennial reign will be a time of justice, peace, and prosperity, as described by the Old Testament prophets (see MILLENNIAL KINDGOM). Many premillennialists, especially dispensationalists, point to the reestablishment of modern Israel in 1948 as an indication of a current movement toward the literal fulfillment of these prophecies in the end times.

Other premillennialists are more cautious, noting that the formation of a modern state of Israel does not necessarily indicate that the "time clock" of the end times has started ticking down. They note that just as Israel was disobedient in the past, resulting in judgment and loss of the land, so it is possible that the modern state of Israel, since it rejects Jesus the Messiah and often does not stand for justice, could easily lose its right to the land once again. The restoration of Israel as predicted by the Old Testament prophets may still be well into the future and may not have anything to do with modern Israel today.

The other major view among evangelicals regarding Old Testament prophecies about the restoration of Israel is that of amillennialism (see AMILLENNIALISM). In general, the amillennial view argues that many of those Old Testament prophecies should be interpreted more figuratively, symbolically, or typologically (see TYPOLOGY). They argue that this is the way these prophecies are understood within the New Testament. Amillennialists maintain that the Old Testament prophecies regarding the restoration of Israel (reestablishment of Jerusalem, rule of Davidic king, etc.) are fulfilled by the first coming of Christ, by the church during the time between the two advents of Christ, or by the second, final return of Christ when final judgment is carried out and the new heaven and new earth are inaugurated. In other words, there is no biblically predicted future reestablishment of the literal nation Israel.

Resurrection

A belief in the resurrection from the dead finds some support in the Old Testament (Job 19:26; Ps. 49:15; 73:24; Isa. 26:19; 53:10–12; Dan. 12:2, 13; Ezek. 37:1–4; Hos. 6:2). The references in Ezekiel and Hosea portray a future national restoration after the exile, while Isaiah 26:19 and Daniel 12:2 suggest individual resurrection. In Daniel 12 some are raised "to everlasting life," while others are raised "to shame and everlasting contempt." Yet in general, the Old Testament is vague about the afterlife. It is in the New Testament that the theology of resurrection is truly explained.

There are several types of resurrection mentioned in the New Testament. Some people are raised from the dead or resuscitated with the expectation that they will die again (e.g., Luke 7:14–15; John 11:43–44; Heb. 11:35). The central resurrection in the New Testament is the resurrection of Jesus Christ (1 Cor. 6:14; 15:20, 23, 48–49). Paul can speak figuratively of a believer's past spiritual resurrection with Christ (e.g., Rom. 6:1, 10–11; Eph. 2:6; Col. 2:12; 3:1). The two remaining types of resurrection relate to the end of the age when believers are raised to eternal life (e.g., 1 Cor. 15) and unbelievers are raised to eternal condemnation (John 5:29; Acts 24:15; Rev. 20:4–6).

The resurrection of Jesus provides the foundation for the future resurrection of believers. Paul clearly spells out the centrality of that event in 1 Corinthians 15:20–26:

> But Christ has indeed been raised from the dead, the firstfruits of those who have fallen asleep. For since death came through a man, the resurrection of the dead comes also through a man. For as in Adam all die, so in Christ all will be made alive. But each in his own turn: Christ, the firstfruits; then, when he comes, those who belong to him. Then the end will come, when he hands over the kingdom to God the Father after he has destroyed all dominion, authority and power. For he must reign until he has put all his enemies under his feet. The last enemy to be destroyed is death.

Christ's resurrection is the basis of a believer's faith (Rom. 10:9; 2 Tim. 2:8) and hope (Acts 24:15; 1 Cor. 15:19; 1 Thess. 4:13–14; 1 Peter 1:3, 13). Since Christ has been raised as the "firstfruits," all believers will be raised at the return of Christ. With the gift of his Holy Spirit God has sealed this pledge to raise believers (Rom. 8:10–11; 2 Cor. 5:5; Eph. 1:13–14).

The resurrection of believers will occur at the second coming of Christ (John 6:39–40; 1 Cor. 15:23, 52; 1 Thess. 4:16); it will be a resurrection to eternal life (John 5:24–25; 11:25–26). For believers, resurrection will include the sudden transformation of mortal bodies into imperishable, powerful, glorious bodies fit for heaven (1 Cor. 15:49, 51–54; Phil. 3:20–21; 1 John 3:2). Above all, the resurrection body will be energized and animated by God's Spirit (1 Cor. 15:44, 46) rather than by the human soul.

In his lengthy chapter on the resurrection (1 Cor. 15), Paul concludes with these words: "Therefore, my dear brothers, stand firm. Let nothing move you. Always give yourselves fully to the work of the Lord, because you know that your labor in the Lord is not in vain" (15:58). In other words, the hope of the resurrection should motivate believers to live holy, blameless lives (15:29–35; Phil. 1:20–21; 1 John 3:3). This same hope also provides a perspective on suffering as well as an incentive to endure faithfully (Rom. 8:17; 1 Peter 4:12–13).

The New Testament is also clear that resurrection pertains to both believers and unbelievers (Acts 24:15).The wicked are raised to face God's condemnation (Matt. 25:46). They are "resurrected" only in the sense that they are given mortal life again in order that they may appear before God. Those who "do not know God and do not obey the gospel" will be "punished with everlasting destruction and shut out from the presence of the Lord" (2 Thess. 1:8–9). At the end of Revelation the dead (both "great and small") stand before God, and all whose names are not found in the book of life are thrown into the lake of fire (Rev. 20:15).

Although all agree that the resurrection will occur at the end of the age, the various millennial positions differ among themselves about the timing of the resurrection. The pivotal passage is Revelation 20:4–6 (the debated phrases are in italics):

> I saw thrones on which were seated those who had been given authority to judge. And I saw the souls of those who had been beheaded because of their testimony for Jesus and because of the word of God. They had not worshiped the beast or his image and had not received his mark on their foreheads or their hands. *They came to life* and reigned with Christ a thousand years. (*The rest of the dead did not come to life* until the thousand years were ended.) This is the first resurrection. Blessed and holy are those who have part in the first resurrection. The second death has no power over them, but they will be priests of God and of Christ and will reign with him for a thousand years.

What is the meaning of "they came to life" (*zaō*) in Revelation 20:4? How does this relate to the statement in the next verse relating that "the rest of the dead did not come to life until the thousand years were ended"? There is agreement that the coming to life (*zaō*) of "the rest of the dead" in 20:5 is a resurrection at the end of history (cf. the same verb in Matt. 9:18; John 11:25; Rom. 14:9; Rev. 1:18; 2:8; 13:14).

Premillennialists believe that the expression "come to life" refers to bodily resurrection in both verses. In the first instance, believers (some restrict this group to martyrs) are raised to reign with Christ during the millennium (Rev. 20:4). In the second instance, the unrighteous are raised to face judgment (20:5). In addition, dispensational premillennialists hold to a resurrection of believers at the rapture and a separate resurrection of believers who have died during the tribulation at the return of Christ.

Amillennialists, by contrast, view the first resurrection in Revelation 20:4 as new spiritual life experienced presently through Christ or as a heavenly exaltation with Christ after death during the intermediate state. Regardless of the timing of this "first resurrection," those who participate in this experience will not be affected by the "second death" (i.e., eternal death; cf. 20:14; 21:8). John does not describe the "rest of the dead coming to life" as a second resurrection, since it is likely just a raising to life in order to face judgment. Those who do experience the first resurrection will also "be priests of God and of Christ and will reign with him for a thousand years" (20:6; cf. 1:6; 5:10; 7:15; 22:3; see also Ex. 19:5–6). (See JUDGMENT SEAT OF CHRIST; LAST JUDGMENT; SECOND COMING.)

Revelation, Book of

The last book of the Bible is known as "the revelation of Jesus Christ" (Rev. 1:1). This phrase can denote a "revelation *about* Jesus Christ" (the central character) or a "revelation *from* Jesus Christ" as he reveals a divine message to John. Perhaps Revelation includes some of both.

As the final chapter in the divine story of salvation, God pulls back the curtain to reveal his plans for human history, plans that center around Jesus Christ. Revelation presents in colorful language and powerful imagery the final chapter in God's story, where he defeats the powers of evil, reverses the curse of sin, restores his creation, and lives among his people forever. While the details of this awesome and mysterious book are often debated, the main idea is not. God intends the vision of Revelation to transform his people so that they will live faithfully in a fallen world until Jesus returns.

Many people have trouble understanding Revelation primarily because they are unfamiliar with Old Testament prophetic books, with Jewish apocalyptic writings, and with the historical setting of this particular book. This overview of Revelation will touch on Revelation's literary genre, its historical situation and purpose, the various approaches used to interpret the book, an overview of its content, and the book's purpose and theological message.

Literary Genre

Revelation is a strange book when compared to other biblical books because it combines three different literary types or genres — letter, prophecy, and apocalyptic.

A letter. The opening of the book contains a conventional letter greeting (Rev. 1:4–5) and benediction (22:21). John is commanded to write what he sees and send it to the seven churches (1:11). As a result, the entire book of Revelation (not just chs. 2–3) is a single letter addressed to seven churches in Asia Minor. Because the number seven symbolizes wholeness or completeness in Revelation, a letter to seven churches is in reality a letter to the whole church.

New Testament letters were meant to be read aloud to the gathered congregations, and this is true also of Revelation. In fact, the opening beatitude (Rev. 1:3) pronounces a blessing on the one who reads the book and on those who listen and obey what they hear: "Blessed is the one who reads the words of this prophecy, and blessed are those who hear it and take to heart what is written in it, because the time is near." The book closes with a warning to anyone (reader or listener) who tries to change the book in any way (22:18–19).

Also, New Testament letters were situational, meaning that they addressed the specific situation of the readers. Revelation is no different in that its message is directed to the churches of Asia Minor at the end of the first century. Its message may (and perhaps does) extend beyond the first century, but it does not neglect its original audience. Any approach to Revelation that ignores its message to the seven churches fails to grasp the nature of Revelation as a letter.

A prophetic letter. Both the letter's opening (Rev. 1:3) and closing (22:7, 10, 18–19) describe the book as a "prophecy." John is viewed as a prophet of God commissioned by the Lord to write this prophecy. In 19:10 the angel tells John, "I am a fellow servant with you and with your brothers who hold to the testimony of Jesus ... For the testimony of Jesus is the spirit of prophecy." In 22:9 John is told again by an angel, "I am a fellow servant with you and with your brothers the prophets and of all who keep the words of this book." Revelation is a prophetic book in line with Old Testament prophetic books.

Biblical prophecy includes both *prediction* of the future and *proclamation* of God's truth for the present, with the emphasis falling on the latter. Often in the very places where Revelation is described as a prophecy, the readers are commanded to *obey* the prophecy (Rev. 1:3; 22:7, 18–19). The emphasis falls on proclamation rather than on prediction because it is difficult to imagine someone being commanded to *obey* a prediction. Most interpreters agree that Revelation has something to say about the future, though it is not only about the future; it is also a book about what God wants to see happen in the here and now.

A prophetic-apocalyptic letter. In the phrase "the revelation of Jesus Christ," the term "revelation" is a translation of the Greek term *apocalypsis*, which means "unveiling; revealing what is hidden" (see APOCALYPSE). The term *apocalypse* describes a body of literature that was popular during the time between the Old and New Testament. Most scholars believe that apocalyptic literature grew out of Hebrew prophecy and actually represents an intensified form of prophecy written during a time of crisis.

In apocalyptic there is a divine revelation through a heavenly intermediary to some well-known figure, in which God promises to intervene in human history to overthrow evil and establish his kingdom.

In the Old Testament, apocalyptic is often associated with the books of Daniel and Zechariah as well as select passages in other prophetic books (e.g., Isa. 24–27; 56–66; Ezek. 38–39). Jewish apocalypses became popular during the intertestamental period (e.g., 1 and 2 Enoch, Jubilees, 2 and 3 Baruch, 4 Ezra, and the Apocalypse of Abraham). The genre of apocalyptic continued through the New Testament period. In addition to the book of Revelation, apocalyptic appears in Jesus' Olivet Discourse (Matt. 24–25; Mark 13).

As an apocalypse, Revelation assumes a situation of crisis and growing hopelessness. God's people are facing difficult times as hostile powers threaten to overwhelm them. No matter how bleak the situation, however, God is portrayed as sovereign and trustworthy. There is the clear promise in apocalyptic that God will one day intervene to punish the wicked and destroy evil. The visions included in apocalyptic transport readers to another world in order to give them heavenly perspective, which allows them to persevere. In addition to endurance, the righteous are also called to holy and blameless living as they follow the only God worthy of worship. In the end, God will restore creation and live forever with his people in perfect community.

Apocalyptic literature contains fantastic visions and bizarre characters. In Revelation, for example, we read of four living creatures covered with eyes and wings, a red dragon with seven heads and ten horns, locusts with human faces and tails that sting like scorpions, and so on. Revelation should be interpreted with this in mind. (See APOCALYPTIC LITERATURE.)

Historical Situation and Purpose

Reading Revelation leaves the clear impression that some Christians are suffering for their faith and that many more should expect to suffer as the sporadic persecution intensifies and spreads. John himself has been imprisoned on the island of Patmos "because of the word of God and the testimony of Jesus," and he writes as one who knows "the suffering and kingdom and patient endurance" that are part and parcel of following Jesus (Rev. 1:9). Antipas, a believer in Pergamum, has been put to death (2:13), and the pressure to submit to the Roman system is expected to get worse as Jesus indicates in his message to Smyrna (2:10):

> Do not be afraid of what you are about to suffer. I tell you, the devil will put some of you in prison to test you, and you will suffer persecution for ten days. Be faithful, even to the point of death, and I will give you the crown of life.

There are also numerous references in the book to pagan powers shedding the blood of God's people (Rev. 6:10; 16:6; 17:6; 18:24; 19:2). There is little doubt that many of these early Christians are feeling the effects of war with the dragon (12:17), and some have paid the ultimate price (6:9; 20:4). Revelation addresses a situation in which false religion has formed a partnership with pagan political power. Thus, those who follow Christ face increasing pressure to conform to the system at the expense of faithfulness to Christ (see IMPERIAL CULT).

There are two main possibilities for the time that Revelation was written. Some argue for a time shortly after the death of Nero (A.D. 68–69), while others lean toward a date near the end of Domitian's reign (A.D. 95). There are many factors to consider when dating the book, and the standard commentaries discuss these at length. At present the majority opinion is that the book was written during the reign of Domitian when persecution threatened to spread across the Roman Empire (see NERO; DOMITIAN).

Whether the imperial cult (i.e., the worship of the Roman emperor) was as widespread and pervasive as some have suggested is open to debate, but its growing influence during this period seems certain. Asia Minor enthusiastically embraced emperor worship, complete with temples, priests, festivals, and the like. There was a major temple to Domitian in Ephesus. The imperial cult was a force to be reckoned with precisely because it united political, social, and economic elements into a single, dominating religious force.

Not every Christian in Asia Minor, however, was standing strong. When confronted with the possibility of suffering, some openly denied Christ, others reverted to Judaism (a somewhat protected religion within the Roman Empire), while others fashioned an acceptable compromise (e.g., join a trade guild and participate in pagan worship in order to avoid the economic penalty associated with remaining faithful). The temptation to turn away from Christ and compromise with the world system shows up clearly in the messages to the seven churches.

To summarize, the historical situation of the book is one in which false religion has forged a partnership with pagan political power. As a result, those who claim to follow Christ are facing tremendous pressure to conform to the system at the expense of faithfulness to Christ. Some are standing strong, while others are compromising. Revelation has a powerful message for both groups, and this relates to its purpose.

The purpose of Revelation is to comfort those facing persecution because of their faithfulness to Jesus and to warn those compromising with the world system out of faithlessness to Jesus. Revelation answers the question, "Who is Lord?" During times of oppression and persecution, the righteous suffer and the wicked seem to prosper. This begs the question, "Is God still on his throne?" Revelation says that in spite of how things appear, Caesar is not Lord and Satan is not Lord; rather, Jesus is Lord and he is coming soon to restore his creation and establish his eternal kingdom. Satan, sin, and death will not have the final word.

The main message of this final book of Scripture is "God wins!" Those facing persecution have their hearts and minds immersed in hope and their eyes opened to see God's future. Those who are selling their souls to the pagan powers are shown God's future so as to shock them into repentance. The purpose of Revelation is to transform the audience to live in faithful obedience to Jesus.

Interpretive Approaches

There are five main interpretive approaches to Revelation: preterist, historicist, futurist, idealist, and eclectic. (1) The *preterist* approach believes that Revelation is directed to the situation in which John lived and should be understood the way the original audience in the seven churches of Asia Minor would have understood it. John uses figurative language to communicate to first-century readers how God plans to intervene to deliver them from the evils of the Roman Empire (see PRETERIST VIEW OF REVELATION).

(2) The *historicist* approach argues that Revelation supplies a prophetic overview of church history from the first century until the return of Christ (see HISTORICIST VIEW OF REVELATION).

(3) The *futurist* approach claims that most of Revelation deals with a future time just before the second coming of Christ. Revelation is primarily concerned with what will happen at the end of history (see FUTURIST VIEW OF REVELATION).

(4) The *idealist* approach maintains that Revelation is a symbolic description of the ongoing battle between God and the devil. Rather than focusing on future events, Revelation offers timeless spiritual truths to inspire Christians of all times as they endure persecution, suffering, and injustice (see IDEALIST VIEW OF REVELATION).

(5) The *eclectic* approach seeks to combine the strength of several of the traditional approaches while avoiding their weaknesses. The eclectic approach finds value in the message to the original readers, while also acknowledging that some portions of the book await future fulfillment. The eclectic view also holds that Revelation has a relevant spiritual message for the church of every age (see ECLECTIC VIEW OF REVELATION).

An Overview of Revelation

(1) *Introduction (1:1–20)*. Revelation 1 serves as an introduction to the entire book. The prologue (1:1–8) contains a statement about the origin and nature of the book, a blessing (the first of seven), a greeting from the Triune God, a doxology of praise to Jesus, a promise of Jesus' return, and an affirmation of God's eternality. In 1:9–20 John, the one exiled to Patmos because of the "word of God and the testimony of Jesus" (1:9), receives a commission to write what he sees to seven churches in Asia Minor. John's vision focuses on the risen, glorified Christ and his ongoing presence among the seven lampstands or churches.

(2) *Messages to the seven churches (2:1–3:22)*. Revelation 2–3 contains seven messages to the churches of Asia Minor: Ephesus, Smyrna, Pergamum, Thyatira, Sardis, Philadelphia, and Laodicea. Each message contains Jesus' prophetic word given through the Spirit, who is inspiring John. The seven messages follow a similar literary pattern containing a description of Jesus, a commendation of the church's good works, an accusation against the church because of some sin, an exhortation followed by a warning or an encouragement, an admonition to listen to the Spirit, and a promise to those who overcome.

(3) *A vision of the heavenly throne room (4:1–5:14)*. The seven messages set the scene on earth and clarify the twin dangers that it faces: persecution and compromise. In Revelation 4–5 the scene shifts to heaven where God reigns in majestic power from his throne. All of heaven worships the Creator. Also worthy of ceaseless praise is the Lion-Lamb (Jesus), who alone is able to open the scroll. By his sacrificial death the Lamb has redeemed a people to serve God.

(4) *The opening of the seven seals (6:1–8:1)*. The stage has been set and the unveiling of God's ultimate victory formally begins. This section marks the first of a series of three judgment visions (seals, trumpets, and bowls), each with seven elements. Crucial to understanding the larger story is the question in the opening of the sixth seal: "Who can stand?" (as the Lamb pours out his wrath). The answer comes in Revelation 7 with two visions of people belonging to God—the 144,000 on earth, sealed with divine protection, and the great multitude in heaven standing before God's throne.

(5) *The sounding of the seven trumpets (8:2–11:19)*. The trumpets reveal God's judgment on a wicked world. They are patterned after the plagues of Egypt leading up to the Exodus. In spite of the ever-intensifying judgments, the "earth-dwellers" (a common term in Revelation for unbelievers) refuse to repent (9:20–21). Once again, before the seventh

element in the series, there is an interlude consisting of two visions: the angel and the little scroll (10:1–11) and the two witnesses (11:1–14). These visions once again offer the saints encouragement and instruction as God carries out his purposes in history.

(6) *The people of God versus the powers of evil (12:1–14:20)*. Revelation 12 provides the real reason why God's people face hostility in this world. The root cause is the conflict between God and Satan (the dragon). Although Satan is decisively defeated by Christ's death and resurrection, he vents his anger for a limited time on God's people.

Revelation 13 introduces Satan's two agents for waging war against God's people — the beast out of the sea and the beast out of the earth. The dragon and the two beasts constitute a satanic or unholy trinity resolute on seducing and destroying God's people.

In Revelation 14 the reader is once again given a glimpse of the final future that God has in store for his people. In spite of the persecution they now face in this world, the followers of the Lamb will one day stand with him on Mount Zion and sing a new song of redemption.

(7) *The pouring out of the seven bowls (15:1–16:21)*. Revelation 15 features seven angels with seven golden bowls filled with the wrath of God. The bowls follow the seals and trumpets as the final series of seven. The next chapter describes the pouring out of these seven bowls on the unrepentant world. The plagues are devastating, uninterrupted, universal manifestations of God's anger toward sin and evil. God will make Babylon the Great (probably the first-century Roman Empire) drink the "wine of the fury of his wrath" (16:19). In response the earth-dwellers not only refuse to repent, they go so far as to curse God (16:9, 11, 21).

(8) *The judgment and fall of Babylon (17:1–19:5)*. From this point on in the book John sets before us a "tale of two cities" — the city of humanity (earthly Babylon destined for destruction) and the city of God (heavenly Jerusalem, where God will dwell among his people forever). Revelation 17 and 18 depict the death of Babylon, a pagan power said to be "drunk with the blood of the saints, the blood of those who bore testimony to Jesus" (17:6). This world's dirges for the deceased Babylon of Revelation 18 give way to the explosive celebration in heaven as God's people rejoice over Babylon's downfall (19:1–5).

(9) *God's ultimate victory (19:6–22:5)*. This section of Revelation portrays God's ultimate victory over the forces of evil and the final reward for his people. The scene opens with the announcement of the wedding of the Lamb (19:6–10) and the return of Christ for his bride (19:11–16). The Warrior-Christ returns, captures the two beasts and their allies,

and throws them into the lake of burning sulfur (19:17–21). The dragon (Satan) is bound (20:1–3), during which time Jesus' faithful followers reign with him a thousand years (20:4–6).

Satan is then released from his temporary prison only to join the two beasts in eternal torment (20:7–10). The dead are judged by the One who sits on the great white throne. Anyone whose name is not found written in the book of life is also thrown into the lake of fire (20:11–15). At this point death itself is judged.

Having judged sin, Satan, and death, God ushers in the eternal state of glory. There is a general description of the new heaven and new earth in 21:1–8, followed by a more detailed presentation in 21:9–22:5. The Old Testament promise that God will live among his people finds its ultimate fulfillment here (21:3). There is no Temple in this city of God because God Almighty and the Lamb are its Temple (21:22). God's victory is complete, and the fellowship he desired with Adam and Eve is now recovered in a restored Garden of Eden, complete with a tree of life (22:1–2). The curse of sin is removed and redeemed humanity is once again able to walk with God and see his face (22:4).

(10) *Conclusion (22:6–21)*. Revelation closes with a final blessing on those who keep "the words of the prophecy in this book" (22:7) and a warning for those who practice sexual immorality, idolatry, and other sinful acts (22:15). The book is an authentic revelation from God and should be read faithfully to the churches (22:6, 16). Jesus assures his people that his return is imminent (22:7, 12, 20). John responds with a prayer statement that Christians of all times can make their own: "Come, Lord Jesus" (22:20). In the meantime, John writes, "the grace of the Lord Jesus be with God's people. Amen" (22:21).

Theological Message

Revelation transforms its hearers by immersing them in God's story, a story with seven main theological themes. These themes weave together the main characters and the central storyline in a way that culminates in challenging the readers to make a decision to either "keep the words of this prophecy" or "practice falsehood." The seven themes are as follows:

(1) *The God of the story*. Revelation asserts that God is sovereign, worthy of worship, and an ever-present help. The salutation (Rev. 1:4–8) anchors the letter in God's sovereign control of all history through a vivid, threefold description of God: the "Alpha and the Omega" (beginning and the end), "the one who is and who was and who is to come" (God of the

past, present and future), and "the Lord God, the Almighty" (ruler over the universe).

The throne room vision of Revelation 4–5 supplies perhaps the most magnificent portrait of God's sovereignty. The centrality of the throne signifies God's sovereign rule as the centerpiece of ultimate reality around which everything else revolves. All subsequent visions in the book emerge from these introductory visions of God's sovereignty. The faithful witness and suffering of believers, the rebellion and punishment of unbelievers, and the fulfillment of God's promise to redeem his people and live among them are all under God's control.

Because God alone is supreme over his creation, he alone is worthy of worship. The heavenly beings surrounding the throne worship God because he has created all things, "You are worthy, our Lord and God, to receive glory and honor and power, for you created all things, and by your will they were created and have their being" (Rev. 4:11; cf. 4:8; 14:7; 19:6). God is also worshiped for his role in redemption. The One who sits on the throne grips the scroll of his divine plan firmly in his right hand (5:1), and the only One worthy to open the scroll (i.e., to carry out God's plan) is the Lamb who was slaughtered. The cross emerges as God's way of bringing salvation (5:11–14; 7:9–12). In addition (and perhaps a surprise for those who have not faced persecution), God is worshiped in Revelation for his judgment of evil and vindication of his people (4:8; 15:3–4; 16:5–7; 19:1–2).

Along with being the Judge, God is revealed as an ever-present help for his people. God protects his people from his wrath by sealing them (Rev. 7:2–3; 14:1). He shelters his people (7:15), wipes away their tears (7:17; 21:4), and abolishes death, mourning, crying, and pain (21:4). He has not forgotten his children; rather, he is making all things new for them to enjoy in his Presence.

In the second time that God is actually quoted in Revelation, he announces the fulfillment of a longstanding, three-part promise to live among his people: "He said to me: 'It is done. I am the Alpha and the Omega, the Beginning and the End. To him who is thirsty I will give to drink without cost from the spring of the water of life. He who overcomes will inherit all this, and I will be his God and he will be my son'" (Rev. 21:6–7; cf. Ex. 29:45–46; Lev. 26:11–12; Ezek. 37:37; Zech. 2:10–11). God's desire for eternal intimacy with his people comes into full view in Revelation 22:1–5, where his servants see his face (22:4). God's children are given unhindered access to and fellowship with their Father.

(2) *The enemies of God.* While God is seated on the throne as the high king and receives worship from all who submit to his rule, he does have enemies who oppose him and his people. The dragon (also known as Satan, the devil, the serpent, the accuser), God's chief enemy, amasses and empowers worldly empires and systems in an attempt to thwart God's purposes. Revelation 12 offers the most complete picture of this cosmic conflict. The great dragon is defeated and thrown to earth, where he turns his anger against the woman and the rest of her offspring. As Revelation 12 closes the dragon is seen taking his stand on the shore of the sea.

The dragon's partners in evil take the form of two beasts. The first beast (traditionally known as the "Antichrist") rises out of that same sea (Rev. 13:1) and is empowered by Satan (13:2, 4; 16:13–14) to carry out his purposes of blaspheming God (13:1, 5–6) and destroying God's people (13:7). John's readers would have identified this sea beast as Rome, the dominant pagan empire at the time, but the reference most likely extends beyond the first century. Any politico-economic power that demands absolute allegiance (or "worship") in place of loyalty to God fits the description.

The second beast (called the "false prophet" in Rev. 19:20 and 20:10) rises out of the earth. Also deriving its power from Satan, this second beast represents religious power and propaganda organized in support of the evil politico-economic system. The false prophet's main task is to deceive people into worshiping the first beast through the use of great and miraculous signs (13:11–15). The dragon, the beast from the sea (Antichrist), and the beast from the earth (false prophet) constitute the satanic trinity.

People who choose to follow the evil trio are usually referred to as "inhabitants of the earth." Because they have been deceived (Rev. 13:14), they give themselves over to sin (17:2) and worship of the beast (13:8, 12). These earth dwellers gladly participate in persecuting Christians (6:10; 11:10), but their celebration is short-lived. They do not have their names written in the Lamb's book of life and will suffer God's judgment (8:13).

(3) *The Lamb of God.* John prefers the designation "Lamb" for Jesus since it communicates vividly his central role in the story of salvation. It is the Lamb of God who takes away the sin of the world. Revelation speaks of the Lamb as God, the Lamb as the triumphant sacrifice, and the Lamb as the returning Warrior-Judge.

John consistently emphasizes the Lamb's oneness with God. Jesus appears in the opening greeting with its reference to the Trinity (Rev. 1:4–5). As John presents his vision of "one like a son of man" (1:13), he uses terms that are often found in the Old Testament when referring to God himself (e.g., the description of God as the "Ancient of Days" in Dan. 7:9–10). Throughout Revelation expressions that refer to God are also used of Jesus, thereby affirming Jesus' deity (e.g., "Alpha and Omega," "Lord"). The primary indication of the Lamb's divine identity in Revelation is that he shares in the authority, glory, and worship reserved for God (5:6, 9–14; 7:10, 17; 12:10; 21:22–23; 22:1, 3).

The Lamb is also presented as the triumphant sacrifice in Revelation. He is worthy to open the scroll because he was slain and with his blood "purchased men for God from every tribe and language and people and nation" (Rev. 5:9). The divine paradox is that the Lamb's victory comes through suffering and sacrifice. He "freed us from our sins by his blood" (1:5). The Lamb is faithful in his witness unto death (1:5, 18) and this sacrificial death becomes the crucial event in God's ultimate victory over evil. The Lamb's death is, of course, followed by his resurrection (1:17–18). As the slaughtered, yet risen Lamb, he is able to empathize with his people, who now endure tribulation as part of their identification with him (1:9; 12:17; 20:4). And he has promised to return as the Warrior-Lamb to bring ultimate deliverance and restoration.

Jesus came to earth the first time as the sacrificial Lamb, but he promises to return a second time as the Warrior-Judge. His return is mentioned as early as the letter's salutation (Rev. 1:7). Jesus promises the church at Philadelphia that he is "coming soon" (3:11), and when the sixth angel pours out his bowl of judgment, Jesus announces, "Behold, I come like a thief!" (16:15).

Revelation 19:11–21 offers the most captivating account of the return of the Warrior-Judge. Jesus is identified here not as the Lamb, but as the one who "judges and makes war" (19:11). He is mounted on a white stallion. His eyes are a flame of fire. He is crowned with many crowns and wears a robe dipped in blood. Out of his mouth comes a sharp sword, and he will rule the nations with a rod of iron. He "treads the winepress of the fury of the wrath of God the Almighty" (19:15). He is called "Faithful and True," "the Word of God," and "King of kings and Lord of lords" (19:11, 13, 16; cf. 17:14).

The famous battle that follows is reported in a single statement: "But the beast was captured, and with him the false prophet" (Rev. 19:20). The Antichrist and the false prophet are then condemned to the lake of burning sulfur (19:20), and their followers become the banquet meal for the birds of prey (contrast the wedding supper of the Lamb in 19:9).

4. *The people of God.* John uses a variety of expressions and images to portray God's people: "church" (e.g., Rev. 1:4, 11; 2:1; 3:1; 22:16), "saints"

(e.g., 5:8; 13:10; 14:12; 17:6), the "144,000" (7:4; 14:1, 3), the "great multitude" (7:9; 19:1, 6), the "bride" of the Lamb (18:23; 21:2, 9; 22:17), and the "new Jerusalem" (21:2, 10), just to name a few. Above all, what sets these people apart is that they have been redeemed by the blood of the slaughtered Lamb (1:5; 5:9; 14:3–4). In spite of fierce opposition, they have continued to rely on the Lamb's sacrificial death on their behalf. The seven occurrences of the fourfold formula — every "tribe, language, people and nation" — indicate that the Lamb's redemptive sacrifice has created a genuinely multicultural people of God (5:9; 7:9; 10:11; 11:19; 13:7; 14:6; 17:15).

Along with being a truly multicultural redeemed people, God's people are also a persecuted people. The book clearly bears out what Jesus said to his disciples, "In this world you will have trouble [or tribulation]" (John 16:33). His followers face persecution because of their identification with their suffering Savior (Rev. 1:9; 2:9–10; 7:14). This is real spiritual warfare as God's people are mocked and mistreated (11:9–10), deprived economically (13:16–17), falsely accused (12:10), and sometimes even put to death (6:9–11; 16:6; 17:6; 18:24; 19:2) for following the Lamb and refusing to worship the evil powers (13:15; 20:4).

God's people are at war with Satan (Rev. 12:17; 13:7), and while their defeat may at times appear certain (11:7; 13:7), the God of life will himself give them life and victory. No wonder that the saints' prayers in Revelation are focused on asking God to vindicate his people and judge the ungodly (5:8; 6:9–11; 8:3–4). The reality of persecution demands endurance and faithfulness on the part of the saints (13:10).

After being thrown out of heaven, the dragon makes war on those who "obey God's commandments and hold to the testimony of Jesus" (Rev. 12:17). The importance of faithfulness is emphasized in two main ways. (a) God's people are characterized throughout the book as those who are obedient to the commands of God (1:2, 9; 6:9; 12:17; 14:12; 20:4; 22:9). They have not defiled themselves (14:4–5), but have put on righteous deeds consistent with their relationship to the Lamb (19:8; 22:11, 14). (b) They faithfully witness to the testimony of/for Jesus (1:2, 9; 6:9; 19:10; 20:4). Put simply, they "follow the Lamb wherever he goes" (14:4).

In spite of their faithfulness, God's people face temptation. Revelation has its share of pointed warnings, calling the saints to endure in faith (Rev. 13:10; 14:12). One of the most vivid warnings occurs in chapter 18, when the heavenly voice urges believers to separate from Babylon and her idolatry: "Come out of her, my people, so that you will not share in her sins" (18:4). God's people are reminded to stay alert for Christ's return

(16:5) and to conquer evil by holding fast to their confession, even to the point of death (12:11).

(5) *The judgment of God.* In the central section of Revelation God's judgment of evil is played out in three series of seven judgments: the seals (Rev. 6:1–8:1), the trumpets (8:2–11:19), and the bowls (16:1–21). While the judgments grow more intense and severe, all three series arrive at the final end, although not in strict chronological order (cf. 6:12–17; 11:15–19; 16:17–21). To a large extent many of these judgments are modeled on the plagues of Egypt in Exodus: hail, darkness, sores, locusts, and frogs and bodies of water turning to blood. In Revelation as in Egypt, God sends the plagues on his enemies to show his power and to vindicate his people. These powerful images, drawn from the most familiar of Old Testament stories, overwhelm the reader and force a decision. Unbelievers are warned to repent or face the ultimate exile, while believers are reminded that God will be victorious over evil.

The interlude of Revelation 14 contains the theme of God's judgment. The war between God and the beast presents a clear choice for humanity —either fear God and give him glory (14:7) or face God's terrible judgment reserved for Babylon and those who worship the beast (14:8–9). God's judgment will be inescapable and eternal (14:11). Two images dramatize the impending judgment: the grain harvest (14:14–16) and the winepress (14:17–20). The gruesome details of the beast followers being crushed in "the great winepress of God's wrath" drive home the point that God's judgment of evil will be absolute (14:19; cf. 19:15).

Revelation 17:1–19:6 reports in greater detail God's final judgment on "Babylon the great, the mother of prostitutes." In contrast to the new Jerusalem as the bride of Christ, Babylon constitutes the worldly system that blasphemes God and puts Christians to death. At the end of chapter 17 the reader is told that part of God's judgment on these enemies is that "the Lamb will overcome them" (17:14). When Babylon falls, God's people rejoice because his judgment demonstrates not only his justice, but also the validity of their faith.

The final battle is recorded in detail in Revelation 19:11–21. Throughout history, the forces of evil make war against God's people and appear to conquer them. But when they make war against the Lamb, they pick on the wrong opponent. Jesus captures the Antichrist and the false prophet and throws them alive into the lake of fire (19:20). Eventually Satan himself is doomed to the same fate (20:10). The satanic trinity suffers God's eternal wrath as a result of their rebellion as they are "tormented day and night forever and ever" (20:10).

In contrast to the resurrection of the righteous in Revelation 20:5–6, there is a second "resurrection" of the wicked to face the condemnation of God. With the devil and both beasts condemned, these people now stand before God with no place to hide and no evil power to delay their judgment. Any person whose name is not found in another book, "the book of life," is thrown into the lake of fire to experience the second death (20:14–15; see BOOK OF LIFE). Finally, Death and Hades are thrown into the lake of fire, paving the way for the restoration of creation.

(6) *The paradise of God.* The story of God's ultimate restoration of his people and his creation is recounted in detail in Revelation 21–22. What God begins to do in Genesis, he now completes in Revelation (see chart in GENESIS, BOOK OF). As Revelation 22 opens, the sea that produced the beast is no more, and there appears a "river of life" flowing from the throne of God and of the Lamb. This recalls the inaugural visions of Revelation 4–5 and the focus on God's throne, a symbol of his sovereign rule over all of reality. The centrality of the throne vision has proven true: God has kept his promise to conquer his enemies, vindicate his people, and restore his creation.

Instead of toiling with a cursed ground to get their food (Gen. 3:17–19), God's people may now eat freely of the tree of life that grows beside the river of life and bears fruit throughout the year. This scene has much in common with the book of Ezekiel, which also envisions a restored garden where water flows from the sanctuary and nurtures fruit-bearing trees. In Ezekiel 47:12 the "fruit will serve for food and their leaves for healing" (see EZEKIEL, BOOK OF). Revelation 22:2 adds the phrase "of the nations" to the word "healing" to show that redeemed peoples from the various nations will be permitted to reside in the heavenly city.

The heart of the Abrahamic Covenant in Genesis 12 that God would bless "all the peoples on earth" in him is being fulfilled. What God initiated with Abraham and expanded at Pentecost, he now consummates with the restored multicultural community living in the new heaven and new earth (see ABRAHAMIC COVENANT). The curse has been totally and completely abolished. All that remains is blessing.

The celestial city is identified primarily as the place where God lives with his people: "They will see his face, and his name will be on their foreheads" (Rev. 22:4). The communion that God desired with Adam and Eve is finally realized with those who have been redeemed by Jesus Christ, the last Adam. In the restored paradise, there will be no more Satan, no more sin, and no more pain or death. God's glory will completely banish all night and darkness. He will live among his people, and they will know him face to face. They will join the multitude of angels worshiping God forever and ever for all the good he has done.

(7) *The battle of God.* The future is bright for God's people, but what about the present? What about the pressure to participate in the imperial cult, to deny Christ to avoid economic disaster, or to convert to a "safe" religion? What does Revelation say about the living God's story here and now? Revelation clearly shows that God and his people are at war with the forces of evil. The Creator has enemies who advocate sin and attempt to thwart his plan and destroy his people. Through his life, death, and resurrection, Jesus Christ has dealt a death blow to sin and Satan. Those who follow Jesus are promised eternal life in a new heaven and new earth, yet the Lamb's followers continue to live in enemy territory and face choices that will test their true identity. The promises are genuine, but overcoming is prerequisite to inheriting the promises.

The word translated "overcome" or "conquer" (*nikaō*) is a battle term Jesus uses to challenge all seven churches at the beginning of the book. The promises he makes to those who overcome are all associated with ultimate restoration: eternal life, provision, justice, participation in Christ's victory, and the very presence of God. Then at the end of the book in the vision of the new heaven and new earth, the term reappears to describe those who will inherit God's eternal kingdom, "He who overcomes will inherit all this, and I will be his God and he will be my son" (Rev. 21:7).

While Jesus challenges people to overcome in the book's introduction and rewards those who have overcome in the conclusion, what it means is clearly summarized in Revelation 12:11: "They [Christians] overcame him [Satan] by the blood of the Lamb and by the word of their testimony; they did not love their lives so much as to shrink from death." While Christians may suffer earthly defeat at the hands of Satan through persecution and even death, they actually conquer him by holding fast to their testimony of Christ crucified and resurrected. Satan's seeming victory over them is at the same time their victory over Satan. They overcome in the same way that their Lord overcame—victory through suffering (cf. 3:21; 5:5–6).

But what exactly does overcoming entail for the people of God? The seven beatitudes (or "blessings") of Revelation offer insight into the specific nature of what it means to overcome. The blessing of God is given to those who hear and obey his Word, turn away from sin, and persevere in following the Lamb to the end.

1:3	**Blessed** is the one who reads aloud the words of the prophecy, and **blessed** are those who hear and who keep what is written in it; for the time is near.
14:13	**Blessed** are the dead who from now on die in the Lord. Yes, says the Spirit, they will rest from their labors, for their deeds follow them.
16:15	See, I am coming like a thief! **Blessed** is the one who stays awake and is clothed, not going about naked and exposed to shame.
19:9	**Blessed** are those who are invited to the marriage supper of the Lamb.
20:6	**Blessed** and holy are those who share in the first resurrection. Over these the second death has no power.
22:7	See, I am coming soon! **Blessed** is the one who keeps the words of the prophecy of this book.
22:14–15	**Blessed** are those who wash their robes, so that they will have the right to the tree of life and may enter the city by the gates. Outside are the dogs and sorcerers and fornicators and murderers and idolaters, and everyone who loves and practices falsehood.

In addition, Jesus defines overcoming at the end of the messages to the seven churches. Overcoming necessitates following Jesus by rejecting false teaching, abstaining from sexual immorality, resisting idolatry, and refusing to compromise. Positively, it demands both faith and the good works that demonstrate its authenticity, along with patient endurance that will almost certainly involve suffering and perhaps even death. Overcoming involves making ethical decisions in everyday life that please God. To overcome, therefore, means to follow the Lamb with one's whole life until the end, however that end may come.

Conclusion

Whenever false religion partners with ungodly political power to form a system that demands total allegiance, the historical situation faced by John's first readers finds a parallel. The responses will vary. For those who stand strong and face persecution, Revelation offers a prophetic perspective on what is real. The result is a hope that empowers perseverance. For those who are compromising with the evil system to avoid trouble, Revelation offers a sober warning of coming judgment. The intended result is repentance leading to life.

Revelation no doubt offered hope to its original readers. The book also contains significant portions that look to future fulfillment. As the final chapter in God's plan to defeat the powers of evil, he will reverse the curse of sin, restore his creation, and live among his people forever in perfect community. For those living between the first century and the last century, Revelation supplies an empowering vision for following Jesus. While many of the details of this fascinating book remain a mystery, the main idea is clear: God wants his people to live faithfully in a fallen world until Jesus returns. To fulfill God's purpose, people need a vision powerful enough to transform how they think and how they live. They need to hear afresh the message of Revelation.

Rewards

While the Scriptures stress that salvation is a gift from God, they also indicate that believers will be rewarded or recompensed according to their deeds. The idea of reward appears early in the biblical story when God assures Abraham: "Do not be afraid, Abram. I am your shield, your very great reward" (Gen. 15:1). At the conclusion of the biblical story Jesus promises to return with his reward: "Behold, I am coming soon! My reward is with me, and I will give to everyone according to what he has done. I am the Alpha and the Omega, the First and the Last, the Beginning and the End" (Rev. 22:12–13; cf. Isa. 40:10; 62:11). While the theme of rewards runs throughout the Bible, the Old Testament and New Testament concepts are not identical.

In the Old Testament God rewards those who turn away from evil and pursue righteousness through obedience to his commands (e.g., Ps. 1). Rewards are based on a fear of the Lord (Ps. 112; Prov. 11:18; 22:4) as demonstrated through conduct or behavior (Ps. 62:12; Jer. 17:10; 32:19). The Old Testament consistently carries the theme of God's rewarding the righteous with good things *in this life*, things such as children, blessings from the land, long life, success, riches, and honor (e.g., Deut. 28:1–14; 1 Sam. 26:23; 2 Sam. 22:21, 25; Ps. 18:20, 24; 19:11; Prov. 13:21). Even most narratives convey the idea that God rewards the righteous (e.g., Abraham and Sarah with a promised son, Joseph with authority and honor in Egypt, David with a mighty kingdom, and in the end, even Job with twice as much as he had possessed prior to suffering). The writer of the New Testament book of Hebrews, however, makes it clear that these Old Testament figures did not always receive in this life all that they were pursuing (Heb. 11:1–40). Generally speaking, the Old Testament emphasizes the immediate and earthly nature of God's rewards given to those who walk in his ways.

The New Testament theme of rewards shifts away from the immediate and earthly and instead spotlights the eternal and heavenly. Although there are places where Jesus speaks of rewards in this life (Mark 10:28–31; Luke 18:28–30), these are exceptions to the rule. Rewards are usually connected with the age to come. In the Sermon on the Mount the blessings Jesus pronounces on his followers are for the most part reserved for the heavenly kingdom (e.g., being comforted by God, seeing God, inheriting the kingdom of heaven and a heavenly reward; cf. Matt. 5:1–12; Luke 6:20–26). Jesus says that "men will have to give account on the day of judgment for every careless word they have spoken" (Matt. 12:36). When the Son of Man comes "in his Father's glory with his angels ... then he will reward each person" (Matt. 16:27). In his Olivet Discourse (Matthew 24–25) Jesus clearly emphasizes the heavenly timing of rewards (e.g., Matt. 25:34—"Then the King will say to those on his right, 'Come, you who are blessed by my Father; take your inheritance, the kingdom prepared for you since the creation of the world' ").

Likewise, the apostle Paul points to the final judgment as the time when rewards are given. In 2 Corinthians 5:10 he notes that "we must all appear before the judgment seat of Christ, that each one may receive what is due him for the things done while in the body, whether good or bad." Paul himself anticipates receiving his rewards on "that day"—the day of Christ's return (2 Tim. 4:8). In the book of Revelation the time of reward is clearly marked as the day when Christ returns. John reports in Revelation 11:18 that "the time has come for judging the dead, and for rewarding your servants the prophets and your saints and those who reverence your name, both small and great—and for destroying those who destroy the earth" (cf. also Rev. 22:12, cited above). What is done during our time on earth will be rewarded in eternity (see JUDGMENT; JUDGMENT SEAT OF CHRIST).

Although the various Greek terms are used on occasion to describe negative rewards (e.g., Matt. 5:26; 6:1–2, 5, 16; 12:36; 18:30, 34; Acts 1:18; Rom. 1:27; 12:19; Col. 3:25; 2 Thess. 1:6; Heb. 10:30; 1 Peter 4:5; Rev. 11:18), the majority of the time these carry a positive sense of rewards for the righteous. Rewards represent God's recognition of the righteous character possessed by an individual (Matt. 10:41–42; Mark 9:41).

Character qualities such as humility, goodness, faithfulness, and generosity are displayed through outward conduct and behavior. This outworking of one's inward relationship with and obedience to the Lord becomes the basis or standard of reward.

Consequently, the New Testament stresses that at the end of time each person will be rewarded for his or her deeds. Jesus said that at his coming he will "reward each person according to what he has done" (Matt. 16:27) and "give to everyone according to what he has done" (Rev. 22:12). Paul contends that on the Day of Judgment God will "give to each person according to what he has done" (Rom. 2:6; cf. Ps. 62:12; Prov. 24:12). Again, we know that "the Lord will reward everyone for whatever good he does" (Eph. 6:8). We will appear before the judgment seat of Christ, where "each one may receive what is due him for the things done while in the body, whether good or bad" (2 Cor. 5:10). The term "bad" (*phaulos*) in this context refers to a work that is worthlessness or "good-for-nothing," rather than one that is inherently evil. In the parallel context of 1 Corinthians 3, Paul conveys the idea that believers play different roles in building (or growing) God's kingdom. Some "plant" and others "water" but "each will be rewarded according to his own labor" (1 Cor. 3:8).

The many clear New Testament references to God's rewarding of his people on the basis of their deeds raises an important question: Can a person be redeemed or saved on the basis of good works? The consistent New Testament answer to that question is "No, salvation is by grace, not by works" (e.g., Rom. 3:27–28; Gal. 2:15–16; Eph. 2:8–9). Paul touches on this issue indirectly in 1 Corinthians 3:10b–15, when he writes about God's use of various people to build up the body of Christ:

> But each one should be careful how he builds. For no one can lay any foundation other than the one already laid, which is Jesus Christ. If any man builds on this foundation using gold, silver, costly stones, wood, hay or straw, his work will be shown for what it is, because the Day will bring it to light. It will be revealed with fire, and the fire will test the quality of each man's work. If what he has built survives, he will receive his reward. If it is burned up, he will suffer loss; he himself will be saved, but only as one escaping through the flames.

Here Paul indicates that good works will survive the judgment and bring reward, whereas bad or worthless works will be burned up and result in loss of reward (cf. 2 John 8). A person's eternal destiny is distinct from a person's reward or loss of reward. Paul seems to imply that a worthless work is one that is performed apart from the direction and power of the Spirit (e.g., with wrong motives), while good works are outward displays of an inward obedience empowered by the Spirit. Rewards are bestowed by God's grace on the basis of the believer's willingness to follow the lead of the Spirit and walk in good works (Eph. 2:10).

The New Testament puts side by side the theological truths of salvation by grace and judgment by works (e.g., Matt. 16:27; Rom. 2:6; 14:12; 1 Cor. 3:12–15; 2 Cor. 5:10; 11:15; 2 Tim. 4:14; 1 Peter 1:17; Rev. 2:23; 11:18; 14:13; 22:12). Justification by faith and reward according to works (not justification by works) are complementary concepts calling believers to work out (or "walk out") their faith (Gal. 5:6; Eph. 2:8–10; Phil. 2:12–13; 1 Thess. 1:3). Good works demonstrate that a person has already entered into a genuine relationship with the Lord on the basis of grace.

There is some New Testament evidence for levels or degrees of reward, but not enough to make this a central doctrine. Jesus speaks of those who demonstrate certain qualities receiving a "great reward" (Matt. 5:12; Luke 6:23, 35). In the parable of the pounds (Luke 19:11–17), the servants receive different rewards corresponding to their levels of faithfulness (cf. Matt. 25:14–30). If there are degrees of reward (and this remains a debated topic), this does not suggest that certain individuals are more valuable than others. Rather, it only suggests that some allowed the Spirit to work more deeply in their lives. Those who have delighted more deeply in the Lord while on earth would likely be the last ones to focus on the rewards themselves. Instead, their attention is directed to the reward Giver.

The ultimate reward for every believer is God himself. In the Old Testament God is already known to be the supreme reward (e.g., Gen. 15:1; Ps. 63:3; Isa. 62:10–12). Jesus encourages his disciples to pursue the Father's unseen approval as the chief motivation for practicing righteousness (Matt. 6:4, 6, 18). When the Lord appears on the final day he will award the "crown of righteousness" to "all who have longed for his appearing" (2 Tim. 4:8; cf. Heb. 11:6). These faithful followers will be longing for the Lord himself more than for any reward he might give. In fact, in the "sheep and goats" passage of Jesus' Olivet Discourse, when the righteous are rewarded, they seem to be unaware of what they have done to deserve it (Matt. 25:37–39). In the closing chapters of Revelation the ultimate reward is for God's people to dwell in God's very presence (Rev. 21:3–7; 22:3–5). Although rewards are important for God's people, the chief goal remains to please and glorify the Giver of the rewards.

Rewards function as God's instruments of comfort and hope so that we do not lose heart during difficult times. The writer of Hebrews puts it this way: "So do not throw away your confidence; it will be richly rewarded.

You need to persevere so that when you have done the will of God, you will receive what he has promised" (Heb. 10:35–36). Each of the messages to the seven churches in Revelation 2–3 concludes with a promise of heavenly reward for those who overcome. The hope of receiving and enjoying rewards (or perhaps the threat of their loss) should motivate believers to turn from sinful ways and live lives pleasing to the Lord. (See HEAVEN; SEVEN CHURCHES OF REVELATION).

Right Hand of God

The "right hand of God" is a common metaphor in the Old Testament for God's power and authority (Ex. 15:6, 12; Ps. 18:35; 20:6; 63:8; Isa. 41:10; 48:13). "Right hand of God" in New Testament prophecy is associated with Jesus' fulfillment of Psalm 110:1: "The LORD says to my Lord, 'Sit at my right hand until I make your enemies a footstool for your feet'" (see especially Matt. 22:41–23:7; Mark 12:35–40; Luke 20:41–47; Acts 2:34–36 [cf. 5:31; 7:55–56]; Rom. 8:34; 1 Cor. 15:25–26; Eph. 1:20; Col. 3:1; Heb. 1:3; 8:1; 10:12; 12:2; Rev. 5:5; 22:16).

Classical dispensationalists believe that Psalm 110:1 will only be fulfilled at Jesus' second coming, when he is enthroned as King in Jerusalem (see DISPENSATIONALISM, CLASSICAL). Only then will he be seated on David's throne, the right hand of God. Progressive dispensationalists and most other schools of interpretation, however, argue that Psalm 110:1 is applied by the New Testament to Jesus at his resurrection and/or ascension. Thus he sits enthroned at the right hand of God now (see DISPENSATIONALISM, PROGRESSIVE).

River of Life

The "river of the water of life" mentioned in Revelation 22:1 provides the water supply for the new Jerusalem. The image calls to mind the river in the original garden of God (Gen. 2:10) as well as prophetic references to water flowing from the temple in Ezekiel 47 (cf. also Joel 3:18; Zech. 14:8). This end-time river is crystal clear (symbolic of purity and holiness) and full of the "water of life" (either water that is life or water that gives life). Perhaps most significantly, the river flows "from the throne of God and of the Lamb," indicating the source of the water. Since the water is life or life-giving, the "river of life" primarily signifies the eternal life and fellowship that God gives fully and abundantly to his people (cf. the Holy Spirit as "living water" in John 7:37–39). (See NEW JERUSALEM; THRONE.)

Rome/Roman Empire

Rome was the leading city of the Italian Peninsula and the capital of the Roman Empire. The "city set on seven hills" was founded about 753 B.C. as a small settlement on the east bank of the Tiber River. It was ruled by kings until 509 B.C., when it became a republic governed by a senate. The republic ended and the Roman Empire proper began in 31 B.C. when Octavian (Augustus) defeated Marc Anthony at the Battle of Actium. Augustus brought peace to the Roman Empire after two civil wars.

The *pax Romana* or "Roman peace" describes the stable political conditions throughout the empire from the time of Augustus until the middle of the second century A.D. Augustus claimed to have discovered Rome as a city of bricks and left it as a city of marble, so extensive were his restoration efforts. The boundaries of the empire were the Atlantic Ocean, the English Channel, and the North Sea to the west, the Euphrates River to the east, the Rhine and Danube Rivers to the north, and the Sahara Desert of Africa to the south.

The early Roman Empire was led by two dynasties of emperors: Julio-Claudian (Augustus, Tiberius, Gaius Caligula, Claudius, and Nero) and the Flavian (Vespasian, Titus, Domitian), separated by a period of one year when three lesser-known emperors ruled briefly (Galba, Otho, Vitellius; see chart in EMPERORS). Several Roman emperors are mentioned directly or indirectly in the New Testament: Augustus (Luke 2:1), Tiberius (3:1), Claudius (Acts 11:28; 18:2), and Nero (Acts 25:10–12; 27:24; 2 Tim. 4:16–17). The emperor was an autocratic leader whose word was law.

Many emperors were offered divine honors, most after their death, but some while they were still living. For example, although Tiberius was eager to attribute deity to Augustus, he refused veneration for himself. But Caligula proclaimed strongly that he was a god (the incarnation of Jupiter) and demanded worship, but he was not deified by the Senate after his assassination. While Claudius refused divine honors during his lifetime, Nero had him deified after his death. Nero was depicted on coins as a god and allowed his statue to be set up in the Temple of Mars.

Although Vespasian declined worship, a temple was built in Rome after his death ascribing deity to him. Domitian honored his brother Titus, who preceded him, but insisted that his subjects address himself as "our lord and god." A temple to Domitian in Ephesus with a massive statue of the emperor became the center of the imperial cult in Asia Minor. Throughout the first century there was an increasing tendency to stress the emperor's deity. Since Roman religion was closely connected to politics and economics, people who refused to worship the emperor (e.g., Christians) suffered financially, socially, and sometimes physically (see IMPERIAL CULT).

In addition to the imperial cult, Romans embraced a plurality of religious expressions. They worshiped national gods and goddesses such as Apollo, Juno, Jupiter, Mars, and Minerva, along with foreign gods and goddesses such as Cybele, Isis, Mithras, and Asclepius. Rome, as well as the large cities of Asia Minor, was filled with temples to various gods along with statues of emperors. The one thing the Roman worldview could not tolerate was religious exclusivism as found in the monotheistic religions, such as Judaism and Christianity. For Rome, religion was a concern of the state, and new movements were allowed as long as their ultimate allegiance was to Rome and as long as they participated in the veneration of the Roman emperors.

With a first-century population of around one million people, the city of Rome was a collection of people from a variety of ethnic backgrounds and regions (e.g., Spain, Germany, Syria, Asia Minor, Africa). It is estimated that by the first century A.D. there were almost fifty thousand Jews in Rome. Whether or not Judaism was given the status as a "legal religion" (*religio licita*), Jews were allowed to meet for worship in their synagogues.

Most likely Christianity came to Rome as a result of Pentecost (Acts 2:10), and these Jewish Christians probably maintained some connection to the synagogue for a time. When Claudius expelled the Jews from Rome in A.D. 49, this action affected some Jewish Christians as well (e.g., Priscilla and Aquila in Acts 18:2). By the time of Paul's first visit to Rome (A.D. 60) and the great fire of A.D. 64 when Nero used Christians as the scapegoat, Christianity had publicly broken with Judaism. By the time Paul wrote Romans (ca. A.D. 57) the church in Rome (likely a group of house churches from the references to various households in Rom. 16:5, 10, 11, 14, 15) had become an important church (1:8).

Many interpreters believe that "Babylon" as used in Revelation refers at least in part to first-century Rome (Rev. 14:8; 16:19; 17:5; 18:2, 10, 21; cf. "the great city" in 11:8; 16:19; 17:18; 18:10, 16, 18, 19, 21; cf. also 1 Peter 5:13). Originally Babylon was the wicked Old Testament empire that destroyed Jerusalem and its Temple and exiled Israel. As a system of ungodly religious, social, political, and economic power, Rome paralleled Babylon as a wicked force that sought to enslave God's people.

As a symbol of Rome and perhaps subsequent world powers in opposition to God, Babylon is the "mother of prostitutes" (Rev. 17:5), who made the nations drink "the maddening wine of her adulteries" (14:8) and became "drunk with the blood of the saints" (17:6). She will be made to drink "the cup filled with the wine of the fury of his [God's] wrath" (16:19) as her materialism, idolatry, and immorality come to an end under God's judgment (ch. 18). (See BABYLON/BABYLONIANS; EMPERORS; IMPERIAL CULT.)

Rosh

Rosh is the common Hebrew word in the Old Testament for "head"; it occurs nearly six hundred times. It can refer to the literal head of a person, but it can also refer to the head priest (2 Kings 25:18, i.e., chief priest), the head of a family (Num. 7:2), or the chief or primary city or city-state in a district (Josh. 11:10).

These are common usages, and this appears to be the sense in which *rosh* is used in Ezekiel 38:2. The NIV translates the verse in this sense, reading, "Son of man, set your face against Gog, of the land of Magog, the chief [*rosh*] prince of Meshech and Tubal" (see GOG AND MAGOG; MESHECH AND TUBAL). Besides the NIV, those translations that understand *rosh* as "chief" and translate it similarly include the KJV, the NRSV, the NAB, the NLB, the HCSB, and the ESV.

A few translations, however, have understood *rosh* in Ezekiel 38:2 as a place. Thus the NASB translates this verse, "Son of man, set your face toward Gog of the land of Magog, the prince of *Rosh*, Meshech, and Tubal." Also understanding *rosh* in this manner was the nineteenth-century German scholar Wilhelm Gesenius, who suggested that *rosh* in this verse referred to modern-day Russia. This view was popularized in the early twentieth century by the *Scofield Reference Bible*, and it is still held by many popular writers today.

However, the evidence for this view is weak, and there is no substantial scholarly evidence for this view. Some writers have pointed out that the foe in Ezekiel 38 is said to come from the "far north" (Ezek. 38:6, 15) and thus conclude that the reference is to Russia, since Russia is indeed to the north of Israel. But, as archaeologist Barry Beitzel observes, the basic way for almost any enemy to attack ancient Israel, which lay at the bottom of the Fertile Crescent, was from the north, regardless of where the foe resided.[92] For example, Beitzel observes that the Bible labels the following ancient enemies of Israel as from the north, even though they were located to the east: Assyrians (Zeph. 2:13), Babylonians (Jer. 1:13–15; 6:22; Zech. 2:6–7), and Persians (Isa. 41:25; Jer. 50:3) (see FOE FROM THE NORTH).

Old Testament scholars today are virtually unanimous in their rejection of the view that connects Ezekiel 38:2 to modern Russia. Historian Edwin Yamauchi notes that even if one transliterates the Hebrew *rosh* as a proper name, it can have nothing to do with modern Russia: "This would be a gross anachronism, for the modern name is based upon the name *Rus*, which was brought into the region of Kiev, north of the Black Sea, by the Vikings only in the Middle Ages."[93] Other top evangelical scholars on Ezekiel agree. Daniel Block writes, "The popular identification of Rosh with Russia is impossibly anachronistic and based on a faulty etymology, the assonantal similarities between Russia and Rosh being purely accidental."[94] Iain Duguid concurs, noting that such identification contains several factual flaws and pointing out that Russia is "etymologically unrelated to the Hebrew term."[95]

Samuel

Samuel is one of the central characters in 1 Samuel 1 – 19. He is an important transitional figure, for he bridges the gap between the time of the judges (Judges) and the time of the kings (1 – 2 Samuel, 1 – 2 Kings).

Samuel is dedicated to God by his mother Hannah and is given to the high priest Eli to be raised as a priest (1 Sam. 1). However, as Samuel grows up, he functions not only as a priest but also as a judge and a prophet. In essence Samuel is the last judge and the first of the traditional prophets who appear in 1 – 2 Samuel and 1 – 2 Kings. The well-known story of the LORD revealing his word to Samuel while he is still a small child (1 Sam. 3:1 – 18) is an early proof of Samuel's call as a prophet.

Immediately after that event, the Scriptures state that the LORD is with Samuel as he grows up and that "all Israel from Dan to Beersheba recognized that Samuel was attested as a prophet of the LORD" (1 Sam. 3:19 – 20). Likewise, 19:18 – 24 portrays Samuel later in life as the leader of a band of prophets residing at Ramah.

Throughout 1 – 2 Samuel and 1 – 2 Kings one of the major roles of the true prophets of God is to declare the word of God to the king. That is, the prophets become God's spokesmen to the kings. When the kings are faithful to God and listen to the prophet, that prophet becomes a critical ally and advisor to the king, guiding him and assisting him. However, all too often the kings disobey, defying the true prophet of God and following other gods. When that happens, the prophet proclaims God's judgment on the king.

Samuel carries out both roles. As God directs, Samuel anoints the first king Saul and supports him (1 Sam. 9–11). But after Saul repeatedly disobeys Samuel and the LORD, Samuel rebukes Saul and anoints David (1 Sam. 13–16). Throughout the reign of Saul and into the time of David, Samuel frequently functions in the role of true prophet, presenting God's word to the king. Samuel's death is recorded in 1 Samuel 25:1.

Sardis

Jesus addresses the church at Sardis as a church with a "reputation of being alive," when in reality it is "dead" (Rev. 3:2). In spite of being quite religious, Sardis was a city immersed in paganism. There was a large and influential Jewish community in Sardis. After the time of Revelation, they built a new synagogue and connected it to the city gymnasium and bath houses—a visible indication of the historical friendship between Judaism and paganism in Sardis. The patron deities of Sardis were Cybele and Artemis, and one can still see the remains of the Artemis temple.

Since persecution is never mentioned in this message, most people in the church in Sardis were apparently compromising with the pagan culture. Only a few there had not "soiled their clothes," a metaphor for impurity and idolatry. The prophetic command to Sardis to "wake up" (NIV) can also be translated "watch," a warning that Jesus commonly uses in his teachings on last things (cf. Matt. 24:42–43; 25:13; Mark 13:34–37). If they refuse to "wake up" or "watch," Jesus will come unexpectedly "like a thief," another image that recalls his end-times teachings (cf. Matt. 24:43; Luke 12:39; see also 1 Thess. 5:2–4; 2 Peter 3:10). The one who remains faithful will be "dressed in white" (an image of purity), will never be erased from the book of life, and will be acknowledged by Jesus before the Father. (See SEVEN CHURCHES OF REVELATION.)

Satan

The Hebrew word śāṭān means "accuser, adversary." Since the doctrine of Satan is less developed in the Old Testament, there is some debate about whether to translate the term as a title ("the satan/accuser") or as a proper name ("Satan"). In both Job 1–2 and Zechariah 3:1–2 the word is used with the definite article—"the satan."

In Job "the accuser" presents himself before God as a member of the divine assembly and as the one responsible for accusing, investigating, or testing humans. When God boasts of Job's blameless character and devotion, the satan proposes two tests for Job. In Zechariah 3 the satan accuses the high priest Joshua before being strongly rebuked by the Lord. Then in 1 Chronicles 21:1, Satan (this time without the definite article) rises up against Israel and incites David to take a census. Although the identity of the accuser in Job is more ambiguous, the later Old Testament references are moving toward the New Testament understanding of Satan as the personal, evil, demonic being who stands as God's primary adversary (the books of Chronicles are the last books in the Hebrew Bible).

The New Testament clearly and repeatedly portrays Satan as the head of the demons and as God's chief opponent and the enemy of all humanity, especially of those who belong to Jesus Christ. The New Testament also refers to Satan by a host of other names: the devil (Matt. 4:1; 25:41), the serpent (2 Cor. 11:3; Rev. 12:9; 20:2), the dragon (Revelation 12), Beelzebub (Matt. 10:25; 12:24, 27), the ruler of this world (John 12:31; 14:30; 16:11), the evil one (Matt. 13:19; 1 John 2:13), the prince of demons (Matt. 9:34; 12:24), the accuser (Rev. 12:10), the enemy (Luke 10:19; 1 Peter 5:8), and the prince of the power of the air (Eph. 2:2).

Satan has a twofold mission: to oppose God and to destroy humanity. (1) Just as Satan tempted Adam and Eve to sin (Gen. 3), so he tempted Jesus to sin in hopes of destroying God's rescue mission (Matt. 4). Satan is the source of sin and the chief tempter. He was a murderer and liar from the beginning (John 8:44) and "has been sinning from the beginning" (1 John 3:8).

Nowhere is Satan's animosity toward God and his purposes more vividly described than in Revelation 12. In this colorful chapter a sign appears in heaven—a woman about to give birth to a male child (Jesus). Waiting to devour the child is a great red dragon. (Here the Old Testament sea monster or dragon is equated with Satan as well as the ancient serpent of Gen. 3.) To the dragon's surprise, after the child is born, he is snatched up and taken away to God (likely a reference to the resurrection and ascension of Jesus). The woman flees from the dragon to the desert, where she is nourished and protected by God for 1,260 days.

Beginning in Revelation 12:7 John retells the same story from the vantage point of a war in heaven, where Michael and his angels fight against the devil and his angels. The great dragon is defeated and is thrown out of heaven to the earth (perhaps an allusion to Isa. 14:3–21), where he turns his wrath against the woman and the rest of her children (lit., *sperma*, "seed"; cf. Gen. 3:15; see SEED OF THE WOMAN). As Revelation 12 closes, the dragon takes his stand on the shore of the sea, out of which the first beast of Revelation 13 emerges. The impression left by Revelation 12 is that Satan is indeed the archenemy of God and God's people.

(2) The other aspect of Satan's mission is to destroy humanity, as 1 Peter 5:8 makes clear: "Your enemy the devil prowls around like a roaring lion looking for someone to devour." Satan's evil activities include influencing a person's thinking (Matt. 16:23; Mark 8:33), tempting people to sin (Acts 5:3; 1 Cor. 7:5), deceiving them (2 Cor. 11:14; Rev. 12:9; 20:3, 8, 10), accusing them (Rev. 12:10), attacking them (Luke 22:31), temporarily hindering God's work (1 Thess. 2:18), and working through enemies of the gospel (John 8:44; 2 Thess. 2:9; Rev. 2:9, 13; 13:2). Satan is resourceful and active, using his demonic army to harm God's people.

Besides direct temptation, Satan uses lies, deceit, anger, fear, confusion, sickness, slander, trickery, and even religion to carry out his cause. As a result, Christians are engaged in an ongoing conflict that calls for discernment, wisdom, courage, and endurance.

While Satan is powerful and cunning, believers are not left defenseless against his attacks. Paul instructs believers to "put on the full armor of God so that you may take your stand against the devil's schemes" (Eph. 6:11). The "armor" includes truth, righteousness, the gospel of peace, faith, salvation, the Word of God, and prayer. Believers are to engage in the spiritual battle by forgiving (2 Cor. 2:10–11), dealing with anger (Eph. 4:27), relying on God's faithfulness (1 Cor. 10:13), resisting the devil (1 Peter 5:9; Jas. 4:7), exercising the authority provided by Jesus (2 Cor. 10:3–4), responding with God's Word (Matt. 4:1–11), and remaining faithful to the Lord Jesus and his gospel.

The New Testament clearly teaches the final destruction of Satan and his demonic forces. An "eternal fire" is prepared for the devil and his angels (Matt. 25:41). Jesus has already dealt the death blow through his incarnation, crucifixion, and resurrection (Luke 10:18; John 12:31; 16:11; Heb. 2:14; 1 John 3:8). Having been cast down from heaven to earth (Rev. 12:9), Satan will be forced to descend even further at the second coming of Christ. Jesus will first cast Satan from the earth "into the Abyss" (Rev. 20:3), and then from the Abyss into the lake of burning sulfur (20:10) to seal his eternal doom. (See DRAGON; REVELATION, BOOK OF)

Scroll

In Revelation 5 John sees the One sitting on the throne holding a "scroll with writing on both sides and sealed with seven seals" (Rev. 5:1). Only the Lamb who triumphed through sacrifice is worthy to take the scroll and open its seals (5:2–8:1).

Later in Revelation another mighty angel comes from heaven to earth holding a "little scroll," which lies open in his hand (Rev. 10:1–2). John is instructed to take the scroll and eat it (10:8–10). The chain of revelation related to the scroll (God–Jesus–an angel–John) is the same as in 1:1.[96] The background for the scroll image in Revelation appears to be Ezekiel's experience of eating a scroll with writing on both sides (Ezek. 2:8–3:7). For both John and Ezekiel the experience of eating the prophetic scroll is sweet to the taste but bitter to the stomach.

Scholars have debated the exact nature of the scroll and whether the "scroll" (biblion) of Revelation 5 and the "little scroll" (biblaridion) of Revelation 10 are the same. (1) There are several possibilities for the identity of the scroll:[97]

- the Lamb's book of life containing all the names of the redeemed
- the true meaning of the Old Testament
- the last will and testament specifying the inheritance of the saints
- a doubly-written contract deed containing God's Covenant promises
- a book detailing the events of the Great Tribulation
- a heavenly book containing God's plan of judgment and redemption

While good arguments can be made for most of the alternatives, the final option appears to offer the best explanation. The scroll signifies God's plan for judging evil and redeeming his people, a plan foreshadowed in the Old Testament, anchored in the death and resurrection of the Lamb, and consummated at his return. The double-sided writing and the seven seals signify the fullness of the divine plan. The scroll of Revelation 5 is not opened until all seven seals have been broken, showing that the scroll itself concentrates on what is described in the subsequent trumpet and bowl judgments as well as the events of Revelation 17 on.

(2) Is the "scroll" in chapter 5 the same as the "little scroll" in chapter 10? There are differences between the two books to be sure (e.g., the one who holds or receives the scroll, or the specific location of the scene), but the similarities are even more prominent.[98] Consequently, most scholars see a strong connection between the two scrolls, although they do not appear to be absolutely identical. The "little scroll" of chapter 10 gives a deeper and sharper focus to what precedes in Revelation 5–9. At the heart of this narrowed focus lies the suffering of the church in the plan of

God. The prophetic message is "sweet" because God is in charge and his sovereign plan to redeem his people and judge evil is rapidly unfolding. But the message is also "bitter" because God's people can expect to suffer persecution and even martyrdom.

Sea

The image of the sea plays a significant role in prophetic literature and especially in the book of Revelation, where the word itself is used twenty-six times. Often in Revelation the "sea" simply refers to a literal body of water that is a natural part of God's creation (e.g., Rev. 5:13; 7:1–3; 8:8–9; 14:7). On a few occasions, however, "sea" is used figuratively to symbolize something more than literal water (4:6; 13:1; 15:2; 21:1).

John's description of God's throne in Revelation 4 includes "something like" or "what appears to be" a sea of glass: "Before the throne there was what looked like a sea of glass, clear as crystal" (Rev. 4:6). John's reference to the heavenly sea probably draws on Ezekiel 1:22: "Spread out above the heads of the living creatures was what looked like an expanse, sparkling like ice, and awesome." Ezekiel 1 seems to reflect Genesis 1:6–7, where the heavenly sea is separated from the earthly sea. Because heaven in Revelation appears like a temple, other scholars see the bronze basin of water (i.e., "sea") of Solomon's temple as the background of Revelation 4:6 (1 Kings 7:23–26). Whatever the source, the "crystal clear" character of this sea symbolizes the radiance and purity of God's glory (cf. Rev. 21:11, 18, 21).

The beast of Revelation 13:1 arises "out of the sea," a picture reminiscent of Daniel 7:3, where four beasts arise from the sea. In the ancient world, the sea was commonly associated with chaos and evil and was the home of the great mythical sea monster Leviathan or Rahab (or the dragon). As God defeated the ancient monster (e.g., Job 26:12; Ps. 74:13–14; 89:9–10; Isa. 27:1; 51:9–10), so he will defeat the "beast from the sea" and cast him into the lake of fire (Rev. 19:20) (see BEASTS OF REVELATION; CHAOSKAMPF).

Before the seven bowls of God's wrath are poured out in Revelation 15–16, we read of those who were victorious over the beast standing beside "what looked like a sea of glass mixed with fire," singing the song of Moses and of the Lamb (15:2–3). This reference to the sea compares Christ's victory over the beast in the end times to God's victory over Pharaoh at the time of the exodus (cf. the plagues of 15:1, the song of Moses of 15:3, and "the tabernacle of the Testimony" in 15:5). In the Old Testament the evil sea monster lived in the Red Sea (Ps. 74:12–14) and "fire" typically indicates divine judgment in Revelation (e.g., Rev. 8:5–8, 11:5; 14:10, 18). Consequently, the sea is the place where the Lamb judges the powers of evil (cf. Jesus' defeat of the demonic sea in Mark 4:35–41; 6:45–56).

In the new heaven and the new earth, there is "no longer any sea" (Rev. 21:1). In the new creation there will no longer be any evil powers lurking below or any evil threat that can bring death or crying or pain (21:4). Noting the verbal parallels between 21:1 and 21:4, Greg Beale concludes:

> The evil nuance of the sea metaphorically represents the entire range of afflictions that formerly threatened God's people in the old world. Uppermost in John's mind would have been tribulations resulting from oppression by the ungodly world. There will be no trial over which to weep in the final order of things.[99]

The disappearance of the sea conveys God's victory over all evil that it represents. Replacing the sea in the new heaven and new earth is the fresh, life-giving water of the river of life that flows from the throne of God (Rev. 22:1). (See BEASTS OF REVELATION; CHAOSKAMPF; GARDEN; NEW HEAVEN AND NEW EARTH; RIVER OF LIFE.)

Seal of the Living God

In contrast to the "mark of the beast" stands the "seal of the living God" (Rev. 7:2, 3, 4, 5, 8; 9:4). Just as the beast puts his mark on the foreheads of his followers, so God marks his servants on their foreheads (7:3; 9:4; see MARK OF THE BEAST). That both marks are symbols of ownership is evident by how Revelation compares the seal to the "name" of God and the Lamb (see 2:3, 13, 17; 3:8, 12; 11:18; 14:1; 21:12, 14; 22:4) in contrast to the "name" of the beast (13:17; 14:11; 15:2).

As a result, the followers of the beast bear his name and his mark, just as the followers of God and the Lamb bear his name and his seal. (In 2 Tim. 2:19 both God's "seal" and "name" identify those who belong to God.) The seal is from "the living God" (i.e., God as the source of life), a reminder that the names of true believers have been written in the book of life (3:5; 13:8; 17:8; 20:12, 15; 21:27; also 2:7, 10–11; 20:4; 21:6; 22:1–2, 14, 17, 19).

The most important background for the image of the divine seal is Ezekiel 9. There God commands an angel to put a mark on all true believers to protect them from his coming wrath to be inflicted through the Babylonians

(9:4, 6). God instructs other angels to kill the unfaithful Israelites who have not been marked (9:5–10). Likewise, in Revelation only those who are sealed by God can withstand his coming wrath (Rev. 6:17). In Revelation 9, as the fifth angel sounds his trumpet, an army of locusts tortures "those people who did not have the seal of God on their foreheads" (9:4). As a result, the "seal" of God indicates both ownership and protection.

The seal of God is the safeguard of God's protective presence in the lives of all genuine believers. Those who are sealed have been "redeemed" and "purchased," showing a close connection between the divine sealing and their salvation (Rev. 14:3–4). The sealing enables them to endure trials and to respond in faith, rather than losing their faith. God's seal does not exempt believers from persecution, suffering, even death (as is seen throughout Revelation), but it does empower them to remain loyal to Christ rather than to compromise when pressured by the powers of evil, both human and demonic.

Although believers may suffer and even lose their physical lives (Rev. 6:9; 12:11; 20:4), the seal keeps them from losing their spiritual and eternal lives. Those who are not sealed are deceived into worshiping the beast (13:8; 19:20), and they will suffer the eternal wrath of God (14:9–11). In contrast, those who are sealed are protected from final judgment of God and are given eternal life.

Although Revelation never explicitly makes the connection, the "seal" is identified as the Holy Spirit in other parts of the New Testament. Paul teaches that the Spirit is God's "seal of ownership" put in our hearts "as a deposit, guaranteeing what is to come" (2 Cor. 1:22). In Ephesians, he writes: "And you also were included in Christ when you heard the word of truth, the gospel of your salvation. Having believed, you were marked in him with a seal, the promised Holy Spirit" (Eph. 1:13). And again, "Do not grieve the Holy Spirit of God, with whom you were sealed for the day of redemption" (4:30).

To the believer, God's seal communicates that we belong to God, that God will protect us spiritually from evil even though we may suffer persecution, and that God will fulfill his promise of living eternally with him. (See MARK OF THE BEAST; ONE HUNDRED FORTY-FOUR THOUSAND; WRATH OF GOD.)

Seal Judgments

The majestic throne-room scene of Revelation 4–5, where the Lamb is shown worthy to unseal the scroll, unfolds into the central section of the book: Revelation 6–16. This middle section highlights the role of judgment in God's master plan. The seal judgments are the first of three series of judgments—seals, trumpets, and bowls—that contain seven parts each (see the summary chart on p. 407).

In all three series of seven, the first four judgments focus on the earth, while the last three are more cosmic in nature. The seals and trumpets follow a 4 + 2 + 1 pattern, while the bowls follow a 4 + 3 pattern. There is an interlude between the sixth and seventh seals and the sixth and seventh trumpets, but no interlude between the sixth and seventh bowls as the pace becomes too intense.

Some see a chronological progression among the three series as the seventh seal turns into the seven trumpets and the seventh trumpet expands into the seven bowls. Others see more repetition and overlap between the three series because of the four-three grouping and the fact that each series culminates at the end of time with a storm-earthquake. Clearly, there is both a degree of overlap and a degree of intensification (e.g., the absence of an interlude in the bowl series or the change from one-fourth of humanity in the seals to one-third in the trumpets to everyone in the bowls).

Osborne identifies seven major themes in the three judgment series of seals, trumpets, and bowls.[100] (1) These judgments are poured out on unbelievers, while believers are protected (Rev. 3:10; 7:1–8; 9:4; 16:2). (2) These judgments are God's response to the prayers of the saints for justice and vengeance (5:8; 6:9–11; 8:3–5). (3) The sovereignty of God is emphasized throughout. (4) God does not command evil to do his will; he simply allows it to operate. (5) Unbelievers (often referred to as "inhabitants of the earth") respond by refusing to repent and by cursing God; this demonstrates their depravity (9:20–21; 16:9, 11). (6) Most debatable, these judgments are acts of mercy, providing a final opportunity to repent (9:20; 14:6–7; 16:9, 11). (7) There is a progressive dismantling of creation, preparing for the final consummation.

The first four seal judgments (popularly known as the "Four Horsemen of the Apocalypse"; see FOUR HORSEMEN OF THE APOCALYPSE) are grouped together as judgments operating throughout history as a result of the sinfulness of humanity. John adapts imagery from Zechariah 1:7–11 and 6:1–8, where four riders on different colored horses (or four chariots drawn by different-colored horses) serve as the Lord's patrol. In Revelation 6, however, the riders unleash judgments, and the color of the horses corresponds roughly to the nature of the judgment (e.g., red = bloodshed). The first four seal judgments include military conquest, violent bloodshed, famine, and death. These four also parallel the "beginnings of birth pains" mentioned by Jesus in his Olivet Discourse—wars, nations rising against nations, earthquakes, famines, and pestilence (Matt. 24:6–8; Mark 13:5–8; Luke 21:8–11).

The last three seal judgments encompass cosmic events much broader than the first four. When the fifth seal is opened, instead of seeing another divine judgment, John sees a human response to suffering: "I saw under the altar the souls of those who had been slain because of the word of God and the testimony they had maintained" (Rev. 6:9). Although there is only one altar in Revelation, the image here recalls the altar of burnt offerings in the Temple, under which the blood or "life" of sacrifices was poured (Ex. 29:10–14; Lev. 4:3–12). Like Christ himself (Rev. 5:6, 9), these martyrs have been "slain" or slaughtered. They have been persecuted to death because of their faithfulness to God's Word (i.e., their testimony about Jesus; cf. 1:2, 9; 12:17; 14:2; 20:4). Yet, their primary activity was witnessing, not dying; martyrdom was simply the result (see MARTYRDOM).

The martyrs cry in a loud voice to God for vindication: "How long, Sovereign Lord, holy and true, until you judge the inhabitants of the earth and avenge our blood?" (Rev. 6:10). Their plea "How long?" runs throughout Scripture as a common prayer of the righteous awaiting vindication (e.g., Ps. 13:1–2; 74:9–11; 89:46; Hab. 1:2; Zech. 1:12). They ask God to "judge the inhabitants of the earth and avenge our blood." The phrase "inhabitants of the earth" is a synonym for "unbeliever" in Revelation (Rev. 3:10; 8:13; 11:10; 13:8, 12, 14; 17:2, 8) and refers here to human beings opposed to God and God's people. Since the martyrs have suffered unjustly at the hands of God's enemies, they plead for justice. They appeal to "the Sovereign Lord, holy and true," but if God fails to punish the wicked, his character will be called into question. The focus is not on personal revenge but on whether God will prevail over evil.

God responds to their request in two ways. (1) He gives them "a white robe," a symbol of purity and innocence as a recognition that he has heard their prayer. (2) He tells them that they will have to "wait a little longer" before they receive their answer, "until the number of their fellow servants and brothers who were to be killed as they had been was completed" (Rev. 6:11). The phrase "a little longer" indicates an unknown, but not an unlimited amount of time (10:6; 12:12; 17:10; 20:3). God is assuring these martyrs that he has heard their prayer and that he will answer it according to his sovereign schedule. This divine plan includes additional persecution and martyrdom for a number of God's people. The promise

	Seals (6:1–17; 8:1)	Trumpets (8:6–9:21; 11:14–19)		Bowls (16:1–21)
1	White horse— military conquest	Hail and fire, mixed with blood, burn up ⅓ of earth		Sores on those with beast's mark
2	Red horse— violent bloodshed	Burning mountain causes ⅓ of sea to turn to blood and destroys ⅓ of creatures and ships		Sea turns to blood and everything in it dies
3	Black horse— famine	Blazing star (Wormwood) turns ⅓ of fresh water bitter, killing many people	Interlude: 12:1–14:20	Rivers and springs turned to blood
4	Pale horse— Death and Hades bring death to ¼ of earth	⅓ of sun, moon, and stars turned dark		Sun scorches people with fire and they curse God
5	Martyrs cry out to God for vindication and are told to wait	Fallen star opens Abyss, releasing locust-scorpions to harm those without seal of God for five months		Throne of beast cursed with darkness. Again, people in agony curse God
6	Shaking of entire cosmos, followed by the wicked attempting to hide from wrath of God and Lamb	Release of four angels bound at Euphrates, who then raise an army of serpent-lions to kill ⅓ of people on earth		River Euphrates dries up as demonic forces gather kings of earth for Armageddon
	Interlude: 7:1–17	Interlude: 10:1–11:14		No Interlude
7	Silence + seven trumpets

Storm-earthquake at 8:3–5 | Christ's kingdom arrives as elders thank God for his judgment, rewarding of saints, and vindication of his people.

Storm-earthquake at 11:19 | Interlude: 12:1–14:20 | Voice from temple says, "It is done," followed by storm-quake and destruction of Babylon by God. Islands and mountains disappear and huge hailstones fall on people who respond by cursing God.

Storm-earthquake at 16:18 |

recalls Peter's words to other first-century believers (2 Peter 3:8–15a; cf. Matt. 24:14; Mark 13:9–10):

> But do not forget this one thing, dear friends: With the Lord a day is like a thousand years, and a thousand years are like a day. The Lord is not slow in keeping his promise, as some understand slowness. He is patient with you, not wanting anyone to perish, but everyone to come to repentance.
>
> But the day of the Lord will come like a thief. The heavens will disappear with a roar; the elements will be destroyed by fire, and the earth and everything in it will be laid bare.
>
> Since everything will be destroyed in this way, what kind of people ought you to be? You ought to live holy and godly lives as you look forward to the day of God and speed its coming. That day will bring about the destruction of the heavens by fire, and the elements will melt in the heat. But in keeping with his promise we are looking forward to a new heaven and a new earth, the home of righteousness.
>
> So then, dear friends, since you are looking forward to this, make every effort to be found spotless, blameless and at peace with him. Bear in mind that our Lord's patience means salvation.

With the opening of the sixth seal, an answer to the martyr's prayer is forthcoming as the Day of the Lord arrives. This judgment includes the shaking of the entire cosmos. The great eschatological earthquake combined with the moving of mountains and islands leaves no hiding place for the wicked. The sun turns black and the moon blood red, the stars fall, and the sky is rolled back as a scroll—all common elements in Old Testament accounts of the end (Isa. 13:9–11; 24:1–6; 19–23; 34:4; Ezek. 32:6–8; 38:19–23; Joel 2:10, 30–31; 3:15–16; Zech. 14:5). In Jesus' teachings, the dissolution of the cosmos occurs at the return of Christ (Mark 13:24–27).

God's shaking of the cosmos terrifies unbelievers, who attempt to hide from his presence (Isa. 2:19; Hos. 10:8). Seven groups of people are specified in Revelation 6:15, signifying the all-inclusive nature of God's judgment: kings of the earth, princes, generals, rich, mighty, every slave, and every free person (cf. 13:16; 19:18). All, Caesar included, must stand before God. They are desperately afraid as they even plead for a violent death rather than face their Creator.

But not even death can exempt them from God's judgment (Rev. 20:11–14). The great day of the wrath of both God and the Lamb has come. The meek, sacrificial Lamb returns as the Conqueror-Judge Lamb, a frightening image.

This seal closes with an all-important question: "Who can stand?" meaning "Who can survive or endure the wrath of God?" The cosmic judgment scene of Joel 2:10–11 closes with a similar question related to the Day of the Lord, "Who can endure it?" The interlude of Revelation 7:1–17 supplies the answer: only the "servants of God" can survive because they will experience God's salvation rather than his wrath (7:3, 14–17).

With the breaking of the seventh and last seal, the scroll is ready to be opened. Following the climactic sixth seal and the interlude of Revelation 7, anticipation runs high. Yet when the seventh seal is opened, there is a surprising "silence in heaven." What is the significance of the silence? The silence could allow the prayers of the saints to be heard (8:3–5). It may be a dramatic pause that anticipates what God will do next in the trumpet judgments. Or it may represent the world's reaction before God at the last judgment (Zeph. 1:17; Zech. 2:13; Rev. 18:22–23). Since the offering of incense and sacrifices were made in silence, the silence in Revelation 8:1 may prepare for the sacrifice in 8:1–6.

Whatever the significance of the silence (the options above are not mutually exclusive), it marks a transition on a number of levels from the seal judgments to the trumpet judgments that follow. (See BOWL JUDGMENTS; EARTHQUAKES; TRUMPET JUDGMENTS; WRATH OF GOD.)

Second Advent

The term *advent* means "coming" or "arrival" and refers to Jesus' first coming to earth when he secured and offered salvation through his life, death, and resurrection. Just before Christmas many Christians celebrate "Advent" to remember and honor the first coming of Christ. The "second advent" anticipates Jesus' second coming or return to earth at the end of history to raise the dead, reward the faithful, condemn the wicked, and destroy God's enemies (see SECOND COMING).

Second Coming

The expression "second coming" refers to Jesus' personal return to earth at the end of history to raise the dead, reward the faithful, condemn the wicked, and destroy God's enemies. Three main Greek words are used in the New Testament to describe Jesus' second coming. Each points to the same event, although they highlight different aspects of his return.

- The word *parousia* means "presence, arrival" and was used in ancient times to describe the arrival of a ruler or king (e.g., Matt. 24:3, 27, 37, 39; 1 Cor. 15:23; 1 Thess. 3:13; 4:15; 5:23; 2 Thess. 2:1, 8, 19; Jas. 5:7–8; 2 Peter 3:4, 12; 1 John 2:28).
- The word *apocalypsis* refers to an "unveiling" or "revealing" of Jesus Christ at the end of the age (Rom. 2:5; 1 Cor. 1:7; 2 Thess. 1:7; 1 Peter 1:7, 13; 4:13; Rev. 1:1; see APOCALYPSE).
- The word *epiphaneia* speaks of an "appearing" or "manifestation" and refers to the visible, earthly appearance of Jesus (2 Thess. 2:8; 1 Tim. 6:14; 2 Tim. 1:10; 4:1, 8; Titus 2:13) (see EPIPHANY).

Jesus himself clearly predicted his second coming in his Olivet Discourse, in answer to the disciples' question about the signs of his return and the end of the age. The main theme of this teaching section is the return of the Son of Man and its implications for believers. After teaching on what will happen prior to his coming, Jesus concludes by saying, "At that time the sign of the Son of Man will appear in the sky, and all the nations of the earth will mourn. They will see the Son of Man coming on the clouds of the sky, with power and great glory" (Matt. 24:30; see THE OLIVET DISCOURSE). Jesus uses the verb "come" in this discourse to speak about his return (24:39, 42, 43, 44, 46; 25:19, 27, 31). His return is also predicted by angels (e.g., Acts 1:11) and apostles (Acts 3:20–21; 1 Cor. 11:26; Phil. 3:20; Heb. 9:28).

The New Testament describes certain events that will precede his coming. There will be wars, famines, earthquakes, and other cosmic disturbances (Matt. 24:6–8, 29). Believers will be persecuted and hated (24:9–13, 21–22). Many "believers" will turn away from the faith (24:10–13; 1 Tim. 4:1; 2 Tim. 3:1–5; 2 Peter 3:3–4). There will be false Christs and false prophets who will deceive many through signs and wonders (Matt. 24:11, 23–26). The "man of lawlessness" (sometimes referred to as the Antichrist) will be revealed (2 Thess. 2:1–12). In addition, the gospel will be preached to all nations (Matt. 24:14).

While Christ's coming is certain, the exact time of his coming is uncertain in the sense that it cannot be predicted. Jesus himself said that "no one knows about that day or hour, not even the angels in heaven, nor the Son, but only the Father" (Matt. 24:36). He warned his followers that it was not for them "to know the times or dates the Father has set by his own authority" (Acts 1:7). Jesus will return at God's appointed time (3:21). While scoffers may question the reality of his return, the delay reveals God's patience and desire that many will come to repentance and faith (2 Peter 3:4, 8–9).

When he comes again, Christ's return will be "visible to all, like lightning in the east is visible in the west" (Matt. 24:27). The last trumpet will announce his coming in awesome power and great glory with his holy angels (16:27; 24:30–31; 25:31; 1 Cor. 15:52; 1 Thess. 3:13; 4:16; 2 Thess. 1:7; 2:8; Jude 14). His coming will also be sudden and unexpected, "like a thief in the night" (Matt. 24:43–44; 1 Thess. 5:1–2; 2 Peter 3:10; Rev. 16:15). With respect to the idea of suddenness, Jesus draws a comparison to the days of Noah, when people were so consumed with routine activities that they neglected righteousness. As a result, they were spiritually unprepared when the "flood came and took them all away" (Matt. 24:37–39).

Jesus will come again for several eternally significant reasons. He will raise the dead (John 5:28–29; 1 Cor. 15:22–23, 52; 1 Thess. 4:16) and separate the wicked from the righteous (Matt. 24:40–41; 25:31–32). He will transform the bodies of believers into glorious, resurrection bodies (1 Cor. 15:51–53; Phil. 3:20–21), gather his followers to himself (1 Thess. 4:17; 2 Thess. 2:1), and reward them for their faithfulness (Matt. 16:27; 24:46–47; 1 Thess. 2:19; 2 Tim. 4:8; 1 Peter 5:4; Rev. 22:12; see REWARDS). The suffering of believers will be replaced with the Lord's praise (2 Thess. 1:7; 1 Peter 1:7; 4:13) and the full experience of salvation (Heb. 9:28).

By contrast, Jesus' second advent means wrath for the wicked (Matt. 24:51; Rom. 2:5; 2 Thess. 1:8–9; Jude 15; Rev. 20:11–15) and destruction for God's enemies (1 Cor. 15:25–26; 2 Thess. 2:8; Rev. 19:11–21; 20:7–10). His coming also means that the present age is replaced by the messianic age (Matt. 24:3; Acts 3:21; 1 Cor. 15:24; 2 Peter 3:10–13; Rev. 21). Is it any wonder that the unrighteous will react to his coming with mourning (Matt. 24:30), while the righteous will marvel (2 Thess. 1:10)?

Much of what the New Testament says about Jesus' coming is summarized in 2 Peter 3:4, 8–14:

> They will say, "Where is this 'coming' he promised?...
>
> But do not forget this one thing, dear friends: With the Lord a day is like a thousand years, and a thousand years are like a day. The Lord is not slow in keeping his promise, as some understand slowness. He is patient with you, not wanting anyone to perish, but everyone to come to repentance.
>
> But the day of the Lord will come like a thief. The heavens will disappear with a roar; the elements will be destroyed by fire, and the earth and everything in it will be laid bare.
>
> Since everything will be destroyed in this way, what kind of people ought you to be? You ought to live holy and godly lives as you look forward to the day of God and speed its coming. That day will bring about the destruction of the heavens by fire, and the elements will melt in the

heat. But in keeping with his promise we are looking forward to a new heaven and a new earth, the home of righteousness.

So then, dear friends, since you are looking forward to this, make every effort to be found spotless, blameless and at peace with him.

This summary passage touches on a key New Testament theme regarding Jesus' return: the need for believers to be spiritually alert and prepared. Jesus strongly urges his disciples to be watchful and ready (Matt. 24:42–44; 25:10). Since his coming is imminent but its timing uncertain, believers should eagerly expect his return at any time (1 Cor. 1:7; Phil. 3:20; Jas. 5:7–8). Remaining watchful and ready consists of being faithfully engaged in doing what Jesus instructs (Matt. 24:46; Matt. 25:14–30; 1 John 2:28), even if this means suffering (Matt. 24:13; 1 Peter 1:6–7). We are called to live holy and blameless lives in anticipation of meeting Jesus face-to-face (1 Thess. 3:13; 5:23; 1 Tim. 6:14; 1 Peter 1:13; 2 Peter 3:11–14; 1 John 2:28–29; 3:2–3). The promise of Jesus' return becomes a motivation for mission (2 Tim. 4:1–2; 2 Peter 3:12).

Christians wait for the "blessed hope—the glorious appearing of our great God and Savior, Jesus Christ" (Titus 2:13). The book of Revelation ends on this note of hope. Following a description of the new Jerusalem, Jesus says: "Behold, I am coming soon! Blessed is he who keeps the words of the prophecy in this book" (Rev. 22:7). And again, "Behold, I am coming soon! My reward is with me, and I will give to everyone according to what he has done" (22:12). Jesus' promise elicits a welcoming response: "The Spirit and the bride say, 'Come!' Let the one who hears this say, 'Come!'" (22:17). As the book closes, Jesus again promises, "Yes, I am coming soon," and the resounding response is "Amen. Come, Lord Jesus!" (22:20; cf. 1 Cor. 11:26; 16:22). (See JUDGMENT; JUDGMENT SEAT OF CHRIST; LAST JUDGMENT; RESURRECTION.)

Second Resurrection

Revelation 20:1–6 describes the millennial saints as being included in the first resurrection; consequently, they will not be hurt by the second death, which will befall the beast and his evil followers (20:7–15). Those who interpret 20:1–6 as referring to a literal one-thousand-year reign of Christ on earth view the first resurrection as raising Christians to life to participate in the kingdom of God while the lost remain in their graves (see MILLENNIUM). At the end of the millennium, the text implies that the lost will be raised to face judgment at the Great White Throne of God, along with Satan and the beast.

Those who do not interpret the millennium as a future event but rather as the present reign of Christ in his kingdom believe that the first resurrection refers to the current spiritual conversion of Christians while the second death refers to the lost who will appear (or be raised) at the second coming of Christ to be judged by God.

Seed of Abraham

The Hebrew word for "seed" (*zera^c*) plays an important role in the theology surrounding the Abrahamic Covenant (see ABRAHAMIC COVENANT). The word literally refers to the seeds of plants, but it is used often figuratively to refer to human descendants. English translations such as the NIV frequently translate the term as "descendants" or "offspring." The word "seed" is singular, but the term can be used to refer to either an individual or to a corporate group, or sometimes even to both.

As part of God's covenantal promise to Abraham, God makes several promises regarding Abraham's seed (or descendants). He will give the land of Canaan to them (Gen. 12:7; 13:14–17; 15:13–21; 17:8); they will be numerous, like the stars of the sky, the dust of the earth, or the sand on the seashore (13:16; 15:5; 22:17); all the nations of the earth will be blessed through Abraham's seed. Note that at the beginning of the promise to Abraham, God declares that "all peoples on earth will be blessed through you" (12:3). This promise is made more specific in 22:17, where God states, "and through your seed all nations on earth will be blessed." God repeats this promise to Isaac as well (26:3–5).

In the New Testament, Paul explains how the Old Testament promise concerning the seed of Abraham is fulfilled through Christ. First, Paul notes that Christ himself is the ultimate seed of Abraham that fulfills the promise (Gal. 3:16). He then explains the connection between the seed and the promise of blessings for the nations. With Christ being the ultimate seed of Abraham, Paul points out the relationship between all believers (Jewish and Gentile) and Abraham through Christ: "If you belong to Christ, then you are Abraham's seed, and heirs according to a promise" (3:29), reaffirming the earlier statement in 3:7, "those who believe are the children of Abraham."

Paul also explains that the spread of the gospel to the Gentiles fulfills the Abrahamic promise regarding the blessing for all the nations. He writes, "The Scriptures foresaw that God would justify the Gentiles by faith, and announced the gospel in advance to Abraham, 'All nations will be blessed through you.' So those who have faith are blessed along with Abraham, the man of faith" (Gal. 3:8–9). Paul also connects this Abrahamic promise of blessing on all the nations to the role of the Spirit in the life of all believers, including Gentiles: God "redeemed us in order that the blessing given to Abraham might come to the Gentiles, through Christ Jesus, so that by faith we might receive the promise of the Spirit" (Gal. 3:14).

Seed of the Woman

The Hebrew word for "seed" (*zera*ᶜ) literally refers to the seed of plants. However, in a figurative sense, it is used frequently to refer to one's offspring or descendants. Several English versions of the Bible translate this term as "offspring" or "descendants." The term can carry either a corporate meaning or an individual meaning.

In Genesis 3:15, as part of the curse God pronounced on the serpent, God states, "I will put enmity between you and the woman and between your seed [offspring] and hers; he will crush your head and you will strike his heel." Christians have traditionally understood the serpent in Genesis 3 to represent Satan. The interpretation of the "seed of the serpent" is not as clear, but it probably refers to all those throughout history who are "of Satan." That is, it refers to those who are evil and opposed to God.

Thus on one hand, in a corporate sense, Genesis 3:15 points to the continuous enmity and warfare that occurs throughout history between good and evil, or between those of Satan and those of God. On the other hand, in an individual sense, the verse can be taken to refer to Christ, who ultimately crushes the head of Satan, the great serpent. Because of this messianic understanding, many theologians throughout church history have labeled this verse as the *protoevangelion* ("the first good news"), that is, the first proclamation of the gospel.

As with so many other theological themes introduced in Genesis, the book of Revelation connects back to this theme to bring it to its climactic conclusion. Revelation 12 is tightly linked with Genesis 3, and in particular with 3:15. The dragon in Revelation 12 is identified as Satan, but is also called the "ancient serpent," a clear allusion to the serpent in the Garden of Eden. Moreover, both the individual and corporate aspects of the "seed of the woman" are present in Revelation 12. In 12:5 the woman bears a male child, who represents Jesus Christ. But in 12:17, the text refers to "the rest of her seed [offspring]," referring to the corporate understanding of "seed," that is, faithful believers of the church. The dragon/serpent attempts to kill the child (Christ), but the forces in heaven war against Satan to protect the child. As a result the dragon is thrown down from heaven to earth, where he wages war against the faithful (12:17; see WOMAN OF REVELATION 12). Eventually, in Revelation 20, Satan, called the "ancient serpent" once again, is finally destroyed as Christ triumphs over all.

Seer

There are two different Hebrew words that mean "to see." Both words can be formed into nouns, thus yielding "the seer" or "the seeing one." The word for "vision" also comes from one of these Hebrew words. Thus the term "seer" implies one who can see things, especially things of God or future things. The term was apparently an older designation for a prophet, occurring more frequently in the early history of Israel.

Note the explanation given in 1 Samuel 9:9, "the prophet of today used to be called a seer." Several times Samuel is called a "seer" (9:9; 1 Chron. 26:28; 29:29). In Amos 7:12 the priest Amaziah calls Amos a "seer," but Amos answers, "I was neither a prophet nor a prophet's son" (7:14). "Seer" is used primarily in 1–2 Chronicles, where in addition to Samuel it is used of the following people: Gad (1 Chron. 21:9), Heman (1 Chron. 25:5), Iddo (2 Chron. 9:29), Hanani (16:7), Asaph (29:30), and Jeduthun (35:15). In some instances the individual is identified as both a seer and a prophet. For example, in 2 Samuel 24:11 Gad is identified as "the prophet, David's seer."

Seraphim

The Hebrew word *seraphim* means "burning ones." Its only occurrence is in Isaiah 6:2–3, 6–7, where that prophet receives a vision of the Lord enthroned in heaven, accompanied by creatures with six wings (two of which covered their faces, two more of which covered their feet, and two more for flying). Their role seems to be that of focusing on God's holiness, hence their designation "burning ones." Thus one of the seraphs touches Isaiah's mouth with a hot coal to purify him. These heavenly beings are similar to the cherubim and four living creatures that attend the throne of God (see Ezek. 1:10; Rev. 4–5; see CHERUBIM; FOUR LIVING CREATURES).

Serpent

See DRAGON.

Servant of the LORD

See SERVANT SONGS.

Servant Songs

On several occasions in Isaiah the coming Messiah is referred to as "the servant of the LORD." Four passages in particular focus on this coming Servant. These four are called the Servant Songs: Isaiah 42:1 – 7; 49:1 – 6; 50:4 – 9; 52:13 – 53:12. In them God declares that he delights in his Servant and puts his Spirit on him. The Servant will establish justice and righteousness, will regather the people of Israel, will be a light and a covenant to the nations/Gentiles (see LIGHT TO THE NATIONS/GENTILES), and will provide life for God's people. Yet, ironically, the Servant will also come quietly and humbly. He will be mocked and rejected by his people. He will bear the sins of his people and suffer for their iniquities. Through him many will be made righteous. Ultimately, he will be exalted to his proper place.

Throughout history there has been much discussion as to the identity of the Servant. Much of the time Isaiah refers to the Servant as an individual, but in Isaiah 49:3 "servant" refers to the nation of Israel. Also note the puzzlement of the Ethiopian eunuch in Acts 8:32 – 34 regarding the identity of this individual in the fourth Servant Song (Isa. 52:13 – 53:12). He asks of Philip, "Who is the prophet talking about, himself or someone else?" Starting with that text, Philip explains to him all about Jesus the Messiah.

Thus the Servant of the LORD in Isaiah refers primarily to the coming Messiah, Jesus Christ. However, there is a sense in which Jesus also represents the ideal Israel; that is, unlike Old Testament Israel, Jesus is completely obedient and fulfills many of the things that the nation itself failed to complete. So the nation Israel can be called "the servant," but only Jesus as the ideal Servant of the LORD fulfills all that Isaiah prophesies in the Servant Songs.

Seven

See NUMBERS, NUMEROLOGY.

Seven Churches of Revelation

Revelation 2 – 3 contains the letters (or messages) to seven churches of Asia Minor: Ephesus, Smyrna, Pergamum, Thyatira, Sardis, Philadelphia, and Laodicea. This revelation comes ultimately from Jesus, the one described in Revelation 1 as gloriously standing and walking among these churches. A map of the seven cities shows that they form a loop, beginning with Ephesus and moving clockwise. The person who carried the letter of Revelation to each church probably traveled this circular route to deliver the larger letter (Revelation) with its more specific message to each of the seven churches.

Each letter is Jesus' prophetic word given through the Spirit who is inspiring John (e.g., "these are the words" is literally "these things say," a common introductory formula to the word of the Old Testament prophets. Craig Keener observes that the letters stand in the tradition of Old Testament prophetic letters (e.g., 2 Chron. 21:12–15; Jer. 29) and prophetic oracles (e.g., Isa. 13–23; Jer. 46–51; Ezek. 25–32; Amos 1–2).[101] Greg Beale notes further that the letters use a covenant pattern with blessings and curses like those of Exodus and Deuteronomy, except that this New Covenant pattern is specifically defined by Jesus, who is now described with attributes of Yahweh (the LORD).[102] All the messages to the seven churches follow a similar literary pattern:

"To the angel of [specific church], write ..."
A description of Jesus (usually drawing imagery from Rev. 1)
A commendation of the church's good works
Jesus' accusation against the church because of some sin
Exhortation followed by a warning and/or an encouragement
An admonition to listen to what the Spirit says
A promise to the overcomers

Overall the letters indicate that the churches of Asia Minor are in poor condition spiritually. Lukewarm Laodicea receives no praise at all, while every other church except Smyrna and Philadelphia is portrayed as having serious problems. The letters emphasize the church's responsibility to be salt and light in the surrounding culture. Some churches are proving faithful to that task and, as a result, are facing persecution. Other churches, however, are in danger of losing not only their influence, but also their very identity as churches because of their willingness to compromise with their culture. These churches receive a prophetic warning from the risen Christ in hopes that they will return to a path of faithfulness.

Each church is called to "overcome," a predominant theme in Revelation. Overcoming relates directly to the church's influence on its culture versus the culture's influence on the church. Often the areas of struggle

Command to write to an angel of a church	Description of Jesus	Commendation of good works	Accusation related to sin
2:1–7: To the angel of the church in Ephesus write:	These are the words of him who holds the seven stars in his right hand and walks among the seven golden lampstands:	I know your deeds, your hard work and your perseverance. I know that you cannot tolerate wicked men, that you have tested those who claim to be apostles but are not, and have found them false. You have persevered and have endured hardships for my name, and have not grown weary.... But you have this in your favor: You hate the practices of the Nicolaitans, which I also hate.	Yet I hold this against you: You have forsaken your first love.
2:8–11: To the angel of the church in Smyrna write:	These are the words of him who is the First and the Last, who died and came to life again.	I know your afflictions and your poverty—yet you are rich! I know the slander of those who say they are Jews and are not, but are a synagogue of Satan. Do not be afraid of what you are about to suffer. I tell you, the devil will put some of you in prison to test you, and you will suffer persecution for ten days. Be faithful, even to the point of death, and I will give you the crown of life.	
2:12–17: To the angel of the church in Pergamum write:	These are the words of him who has the sharp, double-edged sword.	I know where you live— where Satan has his throne. Yet you remain true to my name. You did not renounce your faith in me, even in the days of Antipas, my faithful witness, who was put to death in your city— where Satan lives.	Nevertheless, I have a few things against you: You have people there who hold to the teaching of Balaam, who taught Balak to entice the Israelites to sin by eating food sacrificed to idols and by committing sexual immorality. Likewise you also have those who hold to the teaching of the Nicolaitans.

Exhortation + warning and/or encouragement	Admonition to listen	Promise to Overcomers
Remember the height from which you have fallen! Repent and do the things you did at first. If you do not repent, I will come to you and remove your lampstand from its place.	He who has an ear, let him hear what the Spirit says to the churches.	To him who overcomes, I will give the right to eat from the tree of life, which is in the paradise of God.
	He who has an ear, let him hear what the Spirit says to the churches.	He who overcomes will not be hurt at all by the second death.
Repent therefore! Otherwise, I will soon come to you and will fight against them with the sword of my mouth.	He who has an ear, let him hear what the Spirit says to the churches	To him who overcomes, I will give some of the hidden manna. I will also give him a white stone with a new name written on it, known only to him who receives it.

Command to write to an angel of a church	Description of Jesus	Commendation of good works	Accusation related to sin
2:18–29: To the angel of the church in Thyatira write:	These are the words of the Son of God, whose eyes are like blazing fire and whose feet are like burnished bronze.	I know your deeds, your love and faith, your service and perseverance, and that you are now doing more than you did at first.	Nevertheless, I have this against you: You tolerate that woman Jezebel, who calls herself a prophetess. By her teaching she misleads my servants into sexual immorality and the eating of food sacrificed to idols. I have given her time to repent of her immorality, but she is unwilling. So I will cast her on a bed of suffering, and I will make those who commit adultery with her suffer intensely, unless they repent of her ways. I will strike her children dead. Then all the churches will know that I am he who searches hearts and minds, and I will repay each of you according to your deeds.
3:1–6: To the angel of the church in Sardis write:	These are the words of him who holds the seven spirits of God and the seven stars.	I know your deeds; you have a reputation of being alive …Yet you have a few people in Sardis who have not soiled their clothes. They will walk with me, dressed in white, for they are worthy.	… but you are dead.

Exhortation + warning and/or encouragement	Admonition to listen	Promise to Overcomers
Now I say to the rest of you in Thyatira, to you who do not hold to her teaching and have not learned Satan's so-called deep secrets (I will not impose any other burden on you): Only hold on to what you have until I come.	He who has an ear, let him hear what the Spirit says to the churches.	To him who overcomes and does my will to the end, I will give authority over the nations— "He will rule them with an iron scepter; he will dash them to pieces like pottery"—just as I have received authority from my Father. I will also give him the morning star.
Wake up! Strengthen what remains and is about to die, for I have not found your deeds complete in the sight of my God. Remember, therefore, what you have received and heard; obey it, and repent. But if you do not wake up, I will come like a thief, and you will not know at what time I will come to you.	He who has an ear, let him hear what the Spirit says to the churches.	He who overcomes will, like them, be dressed in white. I will never blot out his name from the book of life, but will acknowledge his name before my Father and his angels.

Command to write to an angel of a church	Description of Jesus	Commendation of good works	Accusation related to sin	
3:7–13: To the angel of the church in Philadelphia write:	These are the words of him who is holy and true, who holds the key of David. What he opens no one can shut, and what he shuts no one can open.	I know your deeds. See, I have placed before you an open door that no one can shut. I know that you have little strength, yet you have kept my word and have not denied my name. I will make those who are of the synagogue of Satan, who claim to be Jews though they are not, but are liars—I will make them come and fall down at your feet and acknowledge that I have loved you. Since you have kept my command to endure patiently, I will also keep you from the hour of trial that is going to come upon the whole world to test those who live on the earth. I am coming soon. Hold on to what you have, so that no one will take your crown.		
3:14–22: To the angel of the church in Laodicea write:	These are the words of the Amen, the faithful and true witness, the ruler of God's creation.		I know your deeds, that you are neither cold nor hot. I wish you were either one or the other! So, because you are lukewarm—neither hot nor cold—I am about to spit you out of my mouth. You say, 'I am rich; I have acquired wealth and do not need a thing.' But you do not realize that you are wretched, pitiful, poor, blind and naked.	

Exhortation + warning and/or encouragement	Admonition to listen	Promise to Overcomers
	He who has an ear, let him hear what the Spirit says to the churches.	Him who overcomes I will make a pillar in the temple of my God. Never again will he leave it. I will write on him the name of my God and the name of the city of my God, the new Jerusalem, which is coming down out of heaven from my God; and I will also write on him my new name.
I counsel you to buy from me gold refined in the fire, so you can become rich; and white clothes to wear, so you can cover your shameful nakedness; and salve to put on your eyes, so you can see. Those whom I love I rebuke and discipline. So be earnest, and repent. Here I am! I stand at the door and knock. If anyone hears my voice and opens the door, I will come in and eat with him, and he with me.	He who has an ear, let him hear what the Spirit says to the churches."	To him who overcomes, I will give the right to sit with me on my throne, just as I overcame and sat down with my Father on his throne.

relate to the overlap in that culture between political power, religious power, and economic power (see EMPERORS; IMPERIAL CULT). The risen Christ, who walks among his churches, offers them a clear but difficult prophetic choice: Listen to his voice and persevere in spite of persecution, or reject his voice, assimilate to the culture, and face his coming judgment in spite of temporary comfort.

Perhaps that explains why each letter closes with an age-old prophetic admonition to listen: "Hear what the Spirit says to the churches." Keener wisely observes, "When pagans charged that Rome fell because of its conversion to Christianity, Augustine responded that it fell rather because its sins were piled as high as heaven and because the commitment of most of its Christian population remained too shallow to restrain God's wrath."[103] (See EPHESUS; SMYRNA; PERGAMUM; THYATIRA; SARDIS; PHILADELPHIA; LAODICEA.)

There is a once commonly held view of the seven churches in Revelation that they represent various periods of church history. For a description of this view and brief analysis, see HISTORICIST VIEW OF REVELATION.

Seven Spirits of God

The expression "seven spirits" occurs four times in Revelation (Rev. 1:4; 3:1; 4:5; 5:6). While the phrase could refer to seven angels mentioned elsewhere in the book, most scholars see it as a reference to the Holy Spirit. The number seven symbolizes perfect wholeness or completeness in Revelation so that the "seven spirits" represent the sevenfold Spirit or the Spirit manifested in his perfect fullness.

In the opening greeting of the letter (Rev. 1:4–5, "grace and peace to you"), the "seven spirits" appear with the Father ("him who is, and who was, and who is to come") before his throne and with Jesus Christ ("the faithful witness, the firstborn from the dead, and the ruler of the kings of the earth"). John clearly sees the blessing as coming from the triune God. Stephen Smalley suggests that the unusual order (Father, Spirit, Son) is determined by the order of their appearance in the heavenly vision of Revelation 4–5.[104]

In Revelation 3:1 Christ "holds the seven spirits of God," showing that he is the Spirit of Christ and is distinct from the seven angels. In 4:5 the "seven lamps" that are blazing before the throne of God are identified as the seven spirits of God. In 5:6 the seven spirits appear as characteristics of the Lamb himself: "He had seven horns and seven eyes, which are the seven spirits of God sent out into all the earth."

The background of the "seven spirits" is likely in Zechariah 3–4. The "seven eyes" of Revelation 5:6 reflect the seven eyes of the Lord mentioned in Zechariah 3:9 and 4:10, where the eyes are said to "range throughout the earth." The "seven lamps" of Revelation 4:5 reflect the lampstand with seven lights referred to in Zechariah 4:2. When asked to identify the symbols, the angel answered, "This is the word of the LORD to Zerubbabel: 'Not by might nor by power, but by my Spirit,' says the LORD Almighty" (4:6), thus connecting the images to the Spirit of God.

Another possible, though less likely, background of the image of "seven spirits" in Revelation is found in Isaiah 11:2. In the Greek translation of the Old Testament (the Septuagint), this verse has added the quality of "godliness" to the list of six other virtues, so that the promised Davidic ruler will possess seven virtues of the Spirit.

The Holy Spirit is mentioned a number of times in Revelation simply as "the Spirit" (Rev. 1:10; 2:7, 11, 17, 29; 3:6, 13, 22; 4:2; 14:13; 17:3; 21:10; 22:17; cf. also 11:11; 19:10; 22:6). Why is the image of the "seven spirits" used on four occasions? The context suggests that "seven spirits" is used when the Spirit's union with the Father and Son becomes the focus — joining with the Father and Son in giving grace and peace (1:4), serving as the Spirit of Jesus in confronting the church (3:1), connected to the throne of God (4:5), and describing the Lamb who is worthy to take the scroll (5:6). The "seven spirits" image portrays a member of the Godhead in all his sovereignty, power, and fullness. (See SEVENTY SEVENS; NUMBERS, NUMEROLOGY; SPIRIT.)

Seventy Sevens

Daniel 9:24–27 is one of the most puzzling prophetic texts to decipher. Its history of interpretation text can be divided into three major views: premillennial, amillennial, and historical. The critical issue involves determining the meaning of the three time-related references: the first unit of seven "sevens" or forty-nine years, the second unit of sixty-two "sevens," or 434 years; and the last "seven" or seven years. The total period is seventy "sevens" or 490 years. The following chart encapsulates the three views:

The first two interpretations can be analyzed together because, although they differ with respect to whether there is a long gap between Daniel's sixty-ninth week and the seventieth week (so premillennialists) or a short one (so amillennialists), both approaches equate the cutting off of the "anointed one" with the death of Jesus Messiah in A.D. 33. However,

Unit 1: 49 years ("7 weeks")	Unit 2: 434 years ("62 weeks")	Unit 3: 7 years ("1 week")
1. Premillennial		
445 B.C. (Artaxerxes' decree to rebuild Jerusalem)	Completed in A.D. 33 with the death of Jesus Christ (allowing for leap years and a 360-day year)	Long gap after 69th week (church age), then 70th week = 7-year Tribulation with Antichrist in control
2. Amillennial		
445 B.C. (Artaxerxes' decree to rebuild Jerusalem)	Completed in A.D. 33 with the death of Jesus Christ	Short gap after 69th week (the death of Christ), then 70th week = A.D. 70 destruction of Jerusalem
3. Historical		
587/586 B.C. (beginning Babylonian Captivity) to 538 B.C. (Joshua the high priest)	605 B.C. (date of Jeremiah's prophecy) to 171 B.C. (murder of high priest, Onias III)	171 B.C. (Antiochus Epiphanes's persecution of the Jews') to 164 B.C. (the restoration of the temple)

most New Testament scholars date Christ's death to A.D. 30, thus throwing off the math of this approach by three years, not to mention the difficulty of factoring leap years and a 360-day calendar year into the equation.

The historical view, by contrast, nicely accounts for the sixty-two weeks (434 years) stretching from 605 B.C. (Jeremiah's prophecy) to the murder of Onias III in 171 B.C., as well as the last seven years from 171 B.C. to 164 B.C.. But the problem with the historical perspective is that, in subsuming the first seven weeks of years (forty-nine years) under the sixty-two weeks plus the seventieth week only adds up to sixty-three weeks of years or 441 years, not seventy weeks of years or 490 years.

Seventy Years of Exile

In describing the destruction of Jerusalem and Judah by the Babylonians, Jeremiah writes, "This whole country will become a desolate wasteland,

and these nations will serve the king of Babylon seventy years" (Jer. 25:11). Later, in Jeremiah's letter to the exiles in Babylon, he writes, "This is what the LORD says, 'When seventy years are completed for Babylon, I will come to you and fulfill my gracious promise to bring you back to this place'" (Jer. 29:10).

Several other biblical writers quote Jeremiah. Thus Daniel states, "I, Daniel, understood from the Scriptures, according to the word of the LORD given to Jeremiah the prophet, that the desolation of Jerusalem would last seventy years" (Dan. 9:2). Zechariah also is probably alluding to Jeremiah when he states, "How long will you withhold mercy from Jerusalem and from the towns of Judah, which you have been angry with these seventy years?" (Zech. 1:12). Likewise 2 Chronicles 36:20–23 relates the time of the exile to Jeremiah's seventy years:

> He [Nebuchadnezzar] carried into exile to Babylon the remnant, who escaped from the sword, and they became servants to him and his sons until the kingdom of Persia came to power. The land enjoyed its Sabbath rests; all the time of its desolation it rested, until the seventy years were completed in fulfillment of the word of the LORD spoken by Jeremiah.
>
> In the first year of Cyrus king of Persia, in order to fulfill the word of the LORD spoken by Jeremiah, the LORD moved the heart of Cyrus king of Persia to make a proclamation throughout his realm.

The term "seventy years" appears to be used both for the time that the Israelites would be in exile in Babylon and for the time that the Babylonians would be in power. In addition the end point of the seventy years in some texts is brought about by the decree of Cyrus (538 B.C.) that allowed the exiles to return home to Jerusalem. Thus it is difficult to determine precisely which events begin and end the seventy years. Several chronologies have been suggested:

- From the fall of Nineveh (i.e., the rise of Babylon) (612 B.C.) to the fall of Babylon (539 B.C.) equals 73 years.
- From the fall of Nineveh (i.e., the rise of Babylon) (612 B.C.) to the decree of Cyrus (538 B.C.) equals 74 years.
- From the victory of the Babylonians over the Assyrians at the battle of Carchemish (605 B.C.) to the fall of Babylon (539 B.C.) equals 66 years.
- From the victory of the Babylonians over the Assyrians at the battle of Carchemish (605 B.C.) to the decree of Cyrus (538 B.C.) equals 67 years.

- From the fall of Jerusalem and the beginning of the exile (587/586 B.C.) to the reconstruction of the Temple (520–515 B.C.) equals 70+/- years.

When Jeremiah writes to the exiles (Jer. 29:10) to tell them that they won't come back for seventy years, the main point is probably that seventy years is a lifetime; none of those who were adults when they went into exile will be alive when the return occurs. Thus most scholars lean toward the view that the term "seventy years" as used by Jeremiah and others, is a general or approximate time span, corresponding to "a lifetime" (cf. Ps. 90:10). Indeed, whether one looks at the length of the Babylonian Empire or at the end of the exile signaled by the decree of Cyrus, the length of time is about seventy years.

Shemaiah

Shemaiah means "The LORD has heard." It is a common name in the Old Testament (twenty-nine different people bear this name). One of these is Shemaiah the prophet, who prophesies during the reign of Rehoboam, son of Solomon. After Solomon dies, the country erupts into civil war. As Ahijah the prophet predicted (1 Kings 11:26–40; see AHIJAH THE SHILONITE), the ten northern tribes break away from Judah to form the new northern kingdom Israel. Rehoboam mobilizes his troops and prepares to attack them. Shemaiah, called "the man of God" (see MAN OF GOD), tells Rehoboam not to attack but to go home, and Rehoboam complies (12:22–24).

In 2 Chronicles 12, Shemaiah, now called "the prophet," appears, again to Rehoboam. Because Rehoboam disregards the law, God raises up Shishak king of Egypt to attack Jerusalem. Shemaiah tells Rehoboam and the leaders of Judah that God is delivering them over to Shishak because they have abandoned God (12:5). Rehoboam and the leaders acknowledge Shemaiah's words and humble themselves, at which point Shishak withdraws, content with taking gold from the Temple as tribute (12:6–11). In fact, in the Egyptian historical annals of Shishak, Jerusalem is not listed as one of the cities he conquered.

At the end of the texts describing Rehoboam's reign is an interesting verse: "As for the events of Rehoboam's reign, from the beginning to end, are they not written in the records of Shemaiah the prophet and Iddo the seer that deal with genealogies?" (2 Chron. 12:15). The records mentioned in this verse are not biblical books, but rather royal court records. But it is interesting to note that one of the roles of prophets on occasion was that of recording history.

Shepherds

In the ancient Near East, because shepherds were known for the care and protection of their sheep, the image of shepherd is often used to refer to the king or to other top leaders. The Old Testament frequently uses the image of shepherds in the same way. The prophets often employ the shepherd imagery in reference to both good leaders and bad leaders. Thus the prophets will speak of good (just, righteous, faithful) shepherds and bad (unjust, self-seeking, lazy, unfaithful) shepherds.

The prophets often criticize the leaders of Israel or Judah (the king, the priests, the nobility, the false prophets), and they often use the shepherd imagery to do this. In numerous texts, the prophets declare that the shepherds of Israel/Judah are bad, unfaithful shepherds and that severe judgment is therefore coming upon them (Jer. 10:21; 12:10; 23:1–2; Zech. 11:17). Note, for example, Jeremiah 23:1, where God declares, "Woe to the shepherds who are destroying and scattering the sheep of my pasture!" Likewise in Ezekiel 34:2 God orders the prophet, "Prophesy against the shepherds of Israel ... Woe to the shepherds of Israel who only take care of themselves! Should not shepherds take care of the flock?"

However, as the prophets look to the future messianic era, they declare that God will bring an end to this inept, corrupt, selfish leadership and will instead provide leadership that is just and righteous. The prophets likewise use shepherd imagery to describe this coming righteous and caring leader. Sometimes God declares that he will raise up a righteous leader who will shepherd his flock with strength and care (Mic. 5:4). In other texts God indicates that he himself will shepherd the flock (Isa. 40:10–11). The shepherd image is especially appropriate because it combines the attributes of powerful protection, self-sacrifice, and loving, tender care.

Ezekiel spends an entire chapter developing the shepherd imagery (Ezek. 34). In 34:1–10 God condemns the unfaithful and selfish shepherds (i.e., leaders) of Israel and pronounces judgment on them. Then in 34:11–31 God repeatedly states that "I myself" will shepherd the flock, protecting them, strengthening the weak, providing for them, and ruling with justice. Finally God declares, "I will place over them one shepherd, my servant David, and he will tend them" (34:23).

Jesus probably draws directly from Ezekiel 34 when he proclaims, "I am the good shepherd" (John 10:11, 14). In similar fashion to Ezekiel 34, Jesus presents an extensive discussion that contrasts thieves and robbers (the bad leaders) with himself, the good shepherd who cares for and protects the sheep. Indeed, Jesus as the "good shepherd" fulfills the Old

Testament prophetic promises and embodies the virtues that the prophets attribute to this coming Shepherd — powerful protection, self-sacrificing, and tender, loving care.

At the climax of history, Revelation 7:17 uses the shepherd imagery as well, declaring (ironically) that Jesus is both the Lamb and the Shepherd: "For the Lamb at the center of the throne will be their shepherd; he will lead them to springs of living water. And God will wipe away every tear from their eyes."

Sheshach

See ATBASH.

Signs of the Times

See MESSIANIC WOES.

Singing

Throughout the Bible singing unites the two important themes of joy and worship. Especially in the book of Psalms, God's people are frequently exhorted to sing joyfully in worship because of the wonderful things that God has done for them. The Old Testament prophets in general, and Isaiah in particular, use the theme of singing in a similar way. As they look to the wonderful future time of restoration and to the coming of the Messiah, they describe God's people as responding to his saving action with joyful, worshipful singing (Isa. 12:5 – 6; 35:10; 51:3, 10). Because the coming messianic age will be exciting and new, Isaiah calls on those future redeemed people to "sing to the LORD a new song" (42:10).

In Revelation 5 singing once again merges together the two responses of joy and worship, this time not just from redeemed people, but from all creation. John sees the Lamb (Jesus Christ; see LAMB) standing on the throne in heaven. The four living creatures and the twenty-four elders fall down before the throne and sing "a new song": "You are worthy ..." (5:8 – 10; see FOUR LIVING CREATURES; TWENTY-FOUR ELDERS). Then thousands upon thousands of angels circle the throne and likewise sing: "Worthy is the Lamb ..." (5:11 – 12). Finally every creature in heaven and on earth joins in to sing: "To him who sits on the throne and to the Lamb be praise and honor and glory and power, for ever and ever!" (5:13).

Six Hundred Sixty-Six

The mark of the beast of Revelation 13 is also the name of the beast, and the name has a numerical value— "his number is 666" (13:18). There has been much speculation about how to solve this apocalyptic riddle.

Some turn to the ancient Jewish practice of *gematria*, which calculated the numerical value of words by assigning numbers to letters of the alphabet (see GEMATRIA). For instance, the numerical value of the name "Jesus" in Greek (*IHSOYS*) is 888 (I = 10, H = 8, S = 200, O = 70, Y = 400, S = 200).

The most popular option for 666 using this approach is "Nero Caesar," whose name equals "666" if transliterated from Greek into Hebrew and only consonants are used: *N* (e) *r* (o) *n*—*K* (ai) *s* (a) *r* (N = 50, r = 200, n=6, K = 100, s = 60, r = 200). But why does the name have to be transliterated into Hebrew for an audience that is mainly Greek-speaking? The numerical value of *Nerōn Kaisar* in Greek is 1005, not 666. John does use Hebrew words elsewhere in key places (e.g., Rev. 9:11; 16:16), but does this provide a sufficient explanation for the shift to Hebrew?

Because of the long list of names that can add up to 666 and the arbitrary manner in which the method is often applied, this approach remains uncertain.[105] Others have suggested that the number refers to Domitian, arrived at by abbreviating his titles found on Roman coins— Autokrator Kaisar Dometianos Sebastos Germanikos. Abbreviated as A.KAI.DOMET.ZEB.GE., the total comes to 666. The problem is that no single coin has been discovered up to this time on which all five titles occur together. If John was calling for the use of *gematria* to solve the riddle, the best option is the word "beast" (*thērion*), which comes out to 666 when transliterated into Hebrew as "*TRYVN*."

Smyrna

Along with Ephesus and Pergamum, Smyrna was one of the leading cities of Asia Minor and an important center of the imperial cult. The city had a strong tradition of being faithful to Rome and in A.D. 23 was granted the privilege of building a temple to Emperor Tiberius. Among the seven churches mentioned in Revelation 2–3, only Philadelphia and Smyrna receive all praise and no blame.

The message to Smyrna begins with Jesus' reassurance that he knows their "afflictions," their "poverty," and the "slander" they are experiencing from those who claim to be Jews, but in reality constitute the "synagogue of Satan" (Rev. 2:8–9). Often the prophetic word to God's people who are suffering is a word of encouragement and comfort. Jews were exempt from worshiping the Roman emperor as god because they were tolerated as an ancient, ethnic, monotheistic religion. For a time Christianity enjoyed a degree of protection because it was closely associated with Judaism. "Slander" (2:9) probably refers to Jewish "informers" or "accusers" who made the Romans aware of the Christians in their midst (see IMPERIAL CULT). This led to Roman persecution of believers who refused to worship Caesar as Lord.

Jesus encourages the church to remain "faithful, even to the point of death" (Rev. 2:10) and assumes that some Christians will not only be imprisoned but also executed. The Jewish accusation of Christians continued into the second century when they betrayed Polycarp, a disciple of the apostle John and bishop of Smyrna, resulting in his martyrdom. Jesus, "the First and the Last, who died and came to life again," promises the martyrs of Smyrna "the crown of life" and protection from "the second death" (2:8, 10–11). The church at Smyrna is not promised exemption from persecution but resurrection from the dead after being faithful unto death. As with other messages to the seven churches, Jesus' promises to the overcomers are predominantly eschatological rather than immediate. (See MARTYRDOM; SEVEN CHURCHES OF REVELATION.)

Sodom and Gomorrah

Jude 7 and 2 Peter 2:6–10 both draw on the Old Testament's account of divine judgment on the infamous cities of Sodom and Gomorrah because of their sexual perversions (Gen. 18–19). They view this incident as a type of judgment to come in the end times (see TYPOLOGY). They therefore perceive in the false teachers of their day who promote sexual promiscuity and perversion the antitype or fulfillment of the Genesis story. In other words, the false teachers are a sign that the last days are here. Second Peter 2:6–10 adds a detail from Genesis 18–19 not recorded in Jude 7, namely, that God's deliverance of Lot from Sodom and Gomorrah is a type of the coming deliverance of the righteous in the end times.

Son of Man

In the four Gospels, Jesus' favorite title for himself is "Son of Man." His first-century Jewish audience would probably have understood this term in light of the Old Testament usage of the title as well as its usage in Jewish apocalyptic literature.

There are four common traits of such a personage that occur frequently in both biblical apocalyptic literature and pre-Christian Jewish apocalyptic literature (see APOCALYPTIC LITERATURE; PARABLES OF ENOCH): (1) a heavenly, superhuman figure (Dan. 7:13; 11; Matt. 25:31; Mark 14:62; John 1:51; Rev. 1:12–18; 14:14); (2) a ruler given eternal dominion and authority (Dan. 7:14; Matt. 16:27; 25:34; cf. John 12:23; Rev. 1:5; 3:21; 5:12–13; 17:14); (3) a judge who executes the final, righteous judgment of God (Matt. 13:41–43; 16:27; 19:28; 25:31–46; Rev. 1:18; 14:14 [as reaper]; cf. 2:22–23; 19:11); and (4) a warrior victorious over the forces of evil (Rev. 2:16; 3:21; 17:17; 19:11; cf. John 12:20–36; 14:30–31; 16:8–11).

Jesus' self-designation as "Son of Man" has as its background the heavenly apocalyptic Son of Man in ancient Judaism—that is, the Messiah. Jesus' usage of this title as recorded in the Gospels can be classified into three groups of sayings: (1) the earthly Son of Man (ten times, e.g., Matt. 9:6; 12:8; Mark 2:10; Luke 5:24; 6:5); (2) the suffering Son of Man (nine times, e.g., Matt. 17:12; Mark 8:31; 9:12; Luke 9:22); and (3) the apocalyptic Son of Man (some twenty-four times, e.g., Matt. 16:27; Mark 8:38; John 1:51; 12:20–36).

The Gospel of Mark makes the connection among these three groups of sayings that the other Gospels basically follow. Before Peter's confession that Jesus is the Christ, Jesus only referred to himself in the third person as the earthly Son of Man (the Messiah). But after Peter's confession Jesus predicts that he, the Son of Man, will suffer and die. After that he will be raised, something associated with the heavenly, apocalyptic Son of Man expected in Judaism, and he will someday return in heavenly glory and power to rule the world.

Sons of the Prophets

Many of the Old Testament prophets are portrayed as solitary individuals prophesying by themselves against a corrupt Israelite king. In the Elisha narratives of 2 Kings 2–9, however, there are several references to a group of prophets living and traveling together in the northern kingdom Israel who are called "the sons of the prophets" (2 Kings 2:3, 5, 7, 15; 4:1, 38; 5:22; 6:1; 9:1). The NIV and the NRSV translations render this phrase as "the company of the prophets," while the NLB translates it as "group of prophets." They appear to be a community or "guild" of prophets who look first to Elijah and then to Elisha as their leader.

This group of prophets seems to be of significant size. When they first appear, there are at least fifty of them (2 Kings 2:7), and they apparently also have wives and families (4:1). The text in 6:1 implies that they grow in number during the leadership of Elisha. Throughout the Elisha narratives the implication is that the "sons of the prophets" have withdrawn from the normal society and are living frugally; that is, they are a rather poor group economically (4:1, 38–41).

During the time of Samuel (150 years earlier), there were also groups of prophets traveling together (1 Sam. 10:5; 19:20), but they are not called "the sons of the prophets." Thus it is not certain if the two groups are connected. In 10:5 the prophets in this group played musical instruments and prophesied as they traveled. Likewise the prophets in 19:20 are described as prophesying aloud together. The "sons of the prophets" in 2 Kings 2–9 are never described in quite this fashion, so they are perhaps serving as prophets in a different manner than this earlier group.

When the prophet Amos declares that he is not "a son of a prophet" (Amos 7:14), he is likely referring to the same organized group or guild that appears in 2 Kings 2–9. Amos prophesies only about forty years after the death of Elisha, so he probably uses the expression "a son of a prophet" in a similar fashion to the usage of "the sons of the prophets" in 2 Kings 2–9. Amos is thus declaring that he is not part of the organized, professional guild of prophets that existed in the northern kingdom Israel at that time (see AMOS, BOOK OF).

Speaking in Tongues

At Pentecost, the Holy Spirit comes upon the believers gathered together in Jerusalem and they begin to "speak in other tongues" (Acts 2:1–13). Regardless of one's view on "speaking in tongues" for the church today, it is important to appreciate the role that speaking in tongues plays in biblical prophecy. In Acts 2:14–21, Peter identifies the phenomenon of tongue speaking as a fulfillment of Joel 2:28–32, a prophecy regarding the last days in which God will pour out his Spirit on all people (see JOEL, BOOK OF). Likewise, throughout Acts, the phenomenon of tongue speaking becomes proof that the Gentiles have been included in the salvation provided by Christ. Thus the statement in Joel 2:28 that God will pour out his Spirit "on all people" finds fulfillment in the inclusion of the Gentiles (see LIGHT TO THE NATIONS/GENTILES). This likewise fulfills Genesis 12:3, in which God promises blessings on the nations/Gentiles (see GENESIS, BOOK OF).

Also of interest is Acts 2:5–12, which lists the many different nations represented at Pentecost, underscoring the numerous languages involved in the tongue-speaking event. One of the significances of Pentecost is that it reversed the result of the Tower of Babel (Gen. 11; see BABYLON/BABYLONIANS). Just as sin resulted in the scattering of people and confusion of language (Gen. 10–11), so the coming of the Spirit in Acts 2 allowed all believers to proclaim the gospel and praise God together, unhindered by different languages.

This event foreshadows the ultimate reversal of Genesis 10–11, which occurs in Revelation. In Revelation 7:9–10, John describes a great multitude of people "from every nation, tribe, people and language, standing before the throne." They are praising God together in a loud voice, indicating an end to the divisions created in Genesis 10–11.

Spirit

In the Old Testament the Spirit of God is tightly interconnected with three main interrelated themes: the presence of God, the power of God, and the revelation of God. (1) The Spirit of God implies the presence of God, which brings with it divine power and enablement (see PRESENCE OF GOD).

(2) At various points in the Old Testament the Spirit of God implies the power to sustain, support, and protect God's people. It is also connected with the power or enablement to create. The implication is always that all this power comes from the presence of God.

(3) In the Old Testament the Spirit is also related to revelation from God. The presence of God leads to power/enablement, which in turn leads to revelation, oracles, wisdom, and prophecy. The Spirit of God often functions as the channel by which God transfers to his people not only power, but also knowledge. The Spirit was not given to all of God's people, as it is in the New Testament, but only on special occasions to specially selected individuals, usually a king or a prophet.

Thus as the Old Testament prophesies about the Messiah, the coming King, it describes him as One who will be especially empowered by the Spirit of God. As King David was empowered by the Spirit, so will the Messiah, only more so. Isaiah 11:2 states: "The Spirit of the LORD will rest on him—the Spirit of wisdom and of understanding, the Spirit of counsel and power, the Spirit of knowledge and of the fear of the LORD."

However, the prophets Joel and Ezekiel add a radically new dimension to the coming messianic era. In both Joel 2:28–29 and Ezekiel 36:27 God promises that in the coming time of restoration he will pour out his Spirit on all his people. Note that in Ezekiel one of the central themes is the loss of God's presence in the Temple because of Israel's great sin (Ezek. 8–10). In contrast to that loss, Ezekiel 36 promises a restoration of God's presence, this time involving placing the Spirit of the LORD within God's people.

In Jeremiah 31:33–34 God promises that under the coming New Covenant he will write his law in his people's minds and on their hearts and that they will all know him. But Jeremiah does not explain how this will happen; Joel 2 and Ezekiel 36 provide the answer, that God will put his Spirit in all of his people. This Spirit will empower people to know God, to be obedient to him, and to speak prophetically of him.

In the New Testament the Spirit plays an important role in the life of Jesus. The Spirit empowers him, leads him, and reveals God's will to him. The powerful activity by the Spirit in Jesus' life is cited as evidence that he is indeed the promised Messiah, empowered by the Spirit as the prophets predicted (Isa. 11:1–4; 61:1–2; Luke 4:16–21).

In his farewell discourse of John 13–17 Jesus explains in more detail the role that the Spirit will play in believers' lives. Jesus refers to the Spirit as the "Counselor" or advocate and describes his special role—the "personal presence of Jesus in the Christian while Jesus is with the Father." The Spirit will be both teacher and revealer, given to Jesus' followers to remind them of his teaching and to interpret it to them.[106]

In Acts 2 the Spirit fills the followers of Christ in fulfillment of Joel 2 and Ezekiel 36. Peter quotes directly from Joel 2:28–32 to explain this event at Pentecost. The outpouring of the Spirit on all believers and the empowering by the Spirit of the early Christians throughout Acts underscore that the messianic age has indeed come. Throughout Acts the Spirit both empowers believers and reveals God's guidance and direction to them. Furthermore, it is always closely interconnected to the conversion/salvation experience. The presence of the Spirit also functions as an authentication of true salvation, proving beyond a shadow of a doubt that salvation has come to the Gentiles as well as to the Jews who believe.

Paul points out in Galatians 3:14 that the gift of the Spirit is part of the fulfillment of the Abrahamic Covenant with its promised blessing to the nations. In Paul's letters the role of the Spirit (in regard to God's presence, God's power, and God's communication of his will) is fundamental to just about every aspect of Christian theology and Christian living.

In Revelation the Spirit often plays a role in revealing prophetic truth to people, similar to the role the Spirit played in the Old Testament. Also, several times Revelation mentions the "seven spirits," which is probably a symbolic reference to the Holy Spirit, pointing to the Spirit in its perfect fullness (see SEVEN SPIRITS OF GOD).

Temple

In the Old Testament the Temple was first and foremost the place where God's presence resided. Because of that, it also functioned as a meeting place between God and his people, a place where they could sacrifice to him and worship him (see PRESENCE OF GOD). In 587/586 B.C., however, because of the continued apostasy of Judah and Jerusalem, God's presence departed from the Temple, and the Babylonians destroyed it (see EZEKIEL, BOOK OF).

After the destruction of the Temple, prophecies about future hope and restoration often included the promise of a new, restored Temple. The hope for a new Temple appeared not only in Old Testament books like Ezekiel, but also in other Jewish literature written between the close of the Old Testament and the beginning of the New Testament era. This includes nonbiblical Jewish apocalyptic literature as well as the Dead Sea Scrolls. Three main types of Temple expectations occur in this literature.

(1) The most common type of Temple expectation had to do with a rebuilt, earthly temple in Jerusalem. This fervent hope arose after the fall of Jerusalem to the Babylonians in 587/586 B.C. along with the destruction of Solomon's temple. Zerubbabel's Temple in 519 B.C. tried in vain to recapture the splendor of the earlier Temple. Even the massive refurbishing of King Herod's Temple, beginning in 20 B.C. and ending in A.D. 64, failed to satisfy Israel's nostalgia for the past glory of the first Temple. In any event, Herod's Temple was destroyed by the Romans in A.D. 70.

(2) The disappointment at the destruction of Solomon's Temple prompted Ezekiel to predict a new, end-time Temple (Ezek. 40–48), one

more glorious and even larger than Solomon's temple. This hope was kept alive in Jewish apocalyptic circles (see APOCALYPTIC LITERATURE).

(3) Alongside these two expectations (physical and eschatological temples) developed the belief that God's people, not a building, would constitute the true Temple of God. This is reflected in the literature of the Dead Sea Scrolls (see DEAD SEA SCROLLS).

The New Testament indicates that, to some degree, all three types of Temple expectations are fulfilled in Jesus. (1) His resurrection body has replaced the physical Temple, the dwelling place of God (see Mark 14:58; John 2:19). (2) The true "temple of the living God" is that sacred "place" to which Christians are now joined by the Spirit as the new people of God's dwelling (1 Cor. 3:11–17; 2 Cor. 6:14–7:1; Eph. 2:19–22). (3) According to Revelation 21–22, when Christ comes again, the eschatological Temple of God will dwell with humankind. This was the prototype and goal of the earthly Tabernacle and Temple (cf. Ex. 25:40; 2 Cor. 5:1–10; Gal. 4:26; Heb. 9:23–24).

Some scholars, however, maintain that the Old Testament prophecies of Ezekiel and others concerning a future Temple will be fulfilled literally by a new rebuilt Temple located on the Temple Mount in Jerusalem (see NEW TEMPLE).

Temple Mount

The Temple Mount is the name given to the twenty-six-acre raised platform on which Herod's Temple rested (19 B.C. to A.D. 70), which was twice as large as that on which Zerubbabel's Temple was situated. Herod's Temple Mount was artificially built up by underground arches (the present "Solomon's Stables") and fill. It was held in place by massive forty-foot stone retaining walls (the Wailing Wall, as it is called today, is a part of Herod's Western retaining wall). The Temple Mount itself was surrounded by a high wall.

The principal gates leading onto the platform were reached by way of arches from the west side and steps from the southern side. The Eastern Gate may have been the Beautiful Gate of the New Testament era (Acts 3:2, 10), perhaps located where the Golden Gate is today. Around the inside of the walled platform ran porches. The finest one was the Royal Porch on the south side, showcasing 162 magnificent white marble columns in the Corinthian style. The eastern porch was called Solomon's Colonnade (John 10:23; Acts 3:11; 5:12). Near the northwest corner of the temple mount was the Roman fortress Antonia. It overlooked the

Temple grounds (see Paul's sermon from there in Acts 21:31–22:21) and was manned by Roman soldiers vigilant to stamp out any signs of Jewish rebellion, especially during feast days.

Today, the Dome of the Rock, a sacred Muslim shrine, is located where the Temple once stood, according to most biblical scholars (see DOME OF THE ROCK). Many dispensationalists believe the Jewish Temple will be rebuilt during the Great Tribulation (2 Thess. 2:4; Rev. 11), which will necessitate the removal of the Dome of the Rock (see DISPENSATIONALISM, CLASSICAL). Indeed, the Jewish Temple Institute in Jerusalem is preparing for such a day. Nondispensationalists, however, believe that Christ and his church have replaced the Temple as the dwelling place of God; thus, there is no reason for a future rebuilt Temple in the holy city (see Heb. 8–10; Rev. 21–22).[107]

Ten-Horned Beast

The "ten-horned beast" is a prophetic image that occurs in Daniel (Dan. 7:7–8, 20, 24) and Revelation (Rev. 12:3; 13:1; 17:3–16). There are two major approaches to identifying the ten-horned beast: (1) The beast is a symbol of a future European organization, such as the European Union; (2) the beast was a historical entity (such as Rome) opposed to the people of God. Neither view is without difficulty.

The European Union View

Many popular prophecy writers argue that the ten-horned beast prophecy will be fulfilled by the present-day European Union. They have assumed (1) that the beast refers to a revived Roman Empire, (2) that Europe is the new embodiment of that empire, (3) that the ten horns refer to nations, and (4) that these must be European nations. Many of these writers have pointed to the European Union (usually the European Common Market in earlier literature) as proof that this interpretation is correct (see EUROPEAN UNION). Is this valid?

In 1973, the European Union had nine members (Belgium, Germany, France, Italy, Luxembourg, the Netherlands, Denmark, Ireland, and the United Kingdom) and appeared to be close to fulfilling the ten-nation coalition portrayed in Daniel 7. In 1981, Greece joined the European Union, bringing the number to ten! Many popular doomsday writers of the 1970s and 1980s believed that the ten-member European Union was proof that the events of the end times were under way and that the revived Roman Empire would emerge from this union.

However, time passed. The end did not come. Instead, in 1986, two more countries (Spain and Portugal) joined the union. The EU now had twelve members. Then in 1995, three more countries joined (Austria, Finland, and Sweden), and the membership swelled to fifteen. In 2004 ten additional countries were added (Cyprus, the Czech Republic, Estonia, Hungary, Latvia, Lithuania, Malta, Poland, Slovakia, and Slovenia). At the present time the membership of the European Union stands at twenty-five members and is still growing. Bulgaria and Romania are expected to join in 2007. Croatia and Turkey are currently seeking membership. Thus, the argument that the European Union is a fulfillment of the prophecy of Daniel 7 and signals the rise of a ten-member revived Roman Empire has proven to be misleading. Clearly, the twenty-five-member European Union doesn't seem to fulfill a prophecy about a ten-horned beast.

Furthermore, the assumption that modern Europe is the equivalent of a revived Roman empire is faulty on two counts. (1) Numerous countries now in the EU or accepted as new members in the EU were not part of the Roman Empire in the first century (and most of them were never in the Roman Empire). These countries include most of Germany and most of the Netherlands, as well as Denmark, Ireland, Finland, Sweden, the Czech Republic, Estonia, Latvia, Lithuania, Poland, and the Slovak Republic.

(2) Extensive tracks of territory that were critical parts of the Roman Empire in the first century A.D. are not part of Europe and are not part of the EU. These countries (such as Egypt and Libya) were much more important to the economic health of Rome (they provided most of the food) than some of the fringe provinces such as Britain. Other countries that were part of the Roman Empire but are not connected to Europe or the European Union include Morocco, Algeria, Tunisia, Israel, Jordan, Lebanon, Syria, and Turkey (although Turkey has applied for membership in the EU). It is simply historically and geographically incorrect to assume that Europe is a modern-day Roman Empire.

Ancient History View

The other major interpretation of the ten-horned beast looks to ancient history for its identification. (1) According to one view, Daniel 7:7–8, 20, 24–25 predicts the coming victory of Alexander the Great, who conquered the then-known world. After his death, the Greek Empire was divided among Alexander's four generals: Antipater, Cassander, Seleucus I, and Ptolemy I. Ten provinces constituted the territories of these four generals: Macedonia, Pergamum, Bithynia, Pontus, Cappadocia, Armenia, Bactria, Parthia, Seleucia, and Ptolemies (Dan. 7:7–8, 20). Furthermore, the Seleucid king, Antiochus the Great, defeated three of these provinces

(Cappadocia, Armenia, Parthia, 7:24). Antiochus was replaced by his son Antiochus Epiphanes, who wreaked havoc with the Jewish people in 167 B.C., the little big horn (7:24–25).

(2) With regard to the ten-horned beast in Revelation, the usual historical reading of that book is that the seven hills equated to the beast's seven heads (Rev. 17:9) refer to the seven hills of ancient Rome (Capitol, Aventine, Caelian, Esquiline, Quirinal, Viminal, and Palatine). The ten horns, then, are the first ten Roman Caesars: Julius (101–44 B.C.); Augustus (27 B.C.–A.D. 14), Tiberius (A.D. 14–37), Gaius (sometimes called Caligula, A.D. 37–41), Claudius (A.D. 41–54), Nero (A.D. 54–68), brief civil war, Vespasian (A.D. 69–79), Titus (A.D. 79–81), Domitian (A.D. 81–96), and Nerva (A.D. 96–98). Some suggest that the ten horns could have been the ten provinces of the Roman Empire, or perhaps ten client kings. According to this view, therefore, the ten-horned beast in Revelation was the Roman imperial cult against which John preached.

The problem with the historical view as a whole is twofold. (1) Two different identifications of the beast are assigned, one for Daniel and another for Revelation: ten Greek provinces, especially Antiochus Epiphanes, in the former, and the Roman imperial cult in the latter. (2) Not all agree with the identification of the ten Caesars in Revelation. Some argue that the three emperors during Rome's civil war should be counted (Galba, Otho, Vitellius [A.D. 68–69]) while Nerva should not, because he came after Revelation was written. If this argument is correct, then there are twelve Caesars, not ten. Furthermore, Revelation 17:12 states that the ten kings had not yet received authority, which was not true of the ancient Caesars of the first century A.D.

Thessalonians, 1 and 2

The founding of the church at Thessalonica is recorded in Acts 17:1–9. During Paul's second missionary trip in A.D. 50–51 (15:36–18:22) he and Silas visited Thessalonica, the capital of the ancient province of Macedonia (modern Greece), a city of 200,000. There the two preached the gospel in the local synagogue, comprised of both Jews and God-fearers (uncircumcised Gentile believers in God, 17:4).

Paul's message was a prophetic one, namely, that the Old Testament predicted the suffering and resurrection of the Messiah and that Jesus Christ fulfilled these prophecies (Acts 17:2–3). Probably Isaiah 53 factored heavily in his sermon. While some in the audience were persuaded by the message, unfortunately other Jews from the synagogue rejected the message of Paul and Silas, accusing them of promoting a rival king to the Roman Caesar (Acts 17:4–8). An uproar ensued, and Paul and Silas were forced to leave Thessalonica in haste. However, even though Paul could only preach the gospel for three Sabbaths in that city, it was enough time for a church to be established.

The messages of 1 and 2 Thessalonians are eschatological through and through; thus practically every chapter makes reference to the second coming of Christ. In 1 Thessalonians 1–3, each chapter closes with a reference to the imminent return of Christ, the hope of which empowers the Thessalonian Christians to be faithful to the gospel despite severe persecution. Depending on one's view, such affliction might be equated with the Great Tribulation (the messianic woes). First Thessalonians 4:13–18 contains Paul's famous words about the rapture, the return of Christ, and the comfort these events brings to Christians mourning the loss of their believing loved ones. Chapter 5 describes the end times in terms reminiscent of the signs of the times predicted in the Olivet Discourse. But such wrath will not fall on Christians (5:9; cf. 1:10; 2:15 [by way of contrast with disobedient Jews, who will experience divine wrath]).

Pretribulationists appeal to this passage as support of their view that the rapture will take the church out of this world *before* the Great Tribulation begins (1 Thess. 4). Midtribulationists think the church will undergo the first half of the Tribulation but will be raptured away to heaven before the onslaught of the Great Tribulation. Posttribulationists argue that the church will undergo the entire Great Tribulation but that God will preserve his people through that time. Thus this view does not distinguish the rapture from the second coming.

In 2 Thessalonians, a new problem had arisen. Some had taught the Thessalonian Christians that Christ's second coming and the Day of the Lord had already occurred (2 Thess. 2:1–2). Paul corrects that misinformation by pointing out that the signs of the times, especially the apostasy of believers and the rise of the Antichrist, which were precursors to the second coming, had not yet happened (see also 2 Thess. 1 for Paul's description of the visible, glorious second coming of Jesus, which had not occurred yet for all to see). Therefore, Paul states that Christians should continue to be faithful at their jobs, in their homes, and in their service to the Lord while awaiting Christ's return (2 Thess. 3).

Two critical issues surface in modern discussions of 1 and 2 Thessalonians. (1) As mentioned above, the question of the nature and time of the rapture in 1 Thessalonians 4:13–17 is hotly debated by pretribulationists, posttribulationists, and to a lesser degree by midtribulationists. The pretribulationist distinguishes between 4:13–17 (secret rapture before the advent of the signs of the times) and 5:1–11/2 Thess. 1–2 (signs of the times immediately prior to the public second coming of Christ; see also the Olivet Discourse, especially Matt. 24). In other words, they maintain that the church will be raptured to heaven by a secret coming of Christ (1 Thess. 4), after which will begin the signs of the times and the Great Tribulation, culminating in the visible, glorious second coming of Christ (1 Thess. 5:1–11; 2 Thess. 1–2). This is what Paul intended when he said that the church will be saved from the wrath to come (1 Thess. 1:10; 5:9).

Posttribulationists, and to a certain extent midtribulationists, argue to the contrary, that 1 Thessalonians 4:13–17 is undeniably connected with 5:1–11, 2 Thessalonians 2–3, and Matthew 24. That is, the two are the same; the rapture is the second coming. The posttribulationists point to the parallels between Matthew 24 (the Olivet Discourse) and 1–2 Thessalonians as proof of this connection. They offer the following chart as evidence:[108]

Olivet Discourse	Event	Paul
Matt. 24:5	warning about deception	2 Thess. 2:2
Matt. 24:5, 11, 24	lawlessness, delusion of the nonelect, signs and wonders	2 Thess. 2:6–11
Matt. 24:12	apostasy	2 Thess. 2:3
Matt. 24:15	Antichrist in the Temple	2 Thess. 2:4
Matt. 24:21–22	tribulation preceding the end	2 Thess. 1:6–10
Matt. 24:30–31	Parousia of Christ, on clouds at the time of a trumpet blast, with angelic accompaniment	1 Thess. 4:14–16
Matt. 24:30–31	in power	2 Thess. 2:8
Matt. 24:31	gathering of believers	1 Thess. 4:16; 2 Thess. 2:1
Matt. 24:36, 42, 44, 50; 25:13	unexpected and uncertain	1 Thess. 5:1–4
Matt. 24:42–25:13	exhortation to watch	1 Thess. 5:6–8

(2) The other critical issue raised by modern interpreters of 1 and 2 Thessalonians is in regard to authorship. Some deny that Paul wrote 2 Thessalonians because, they argue, the eschatologies of the two letters are contradictory. First Thessalonians, so it is said, contains no timetable of events preceding the Parousia (or second coming) while 2 Thessalonians does, thus casting doubt on the genuineness of the latter letter. But both pretribulationists and posttribulationists (both of whom are conservatives theologically) disagree with this view, arguing in their own ways that the two letters are consistent in their teaching about future things.

Thus, pretribulationists posit a twofold coming of Christ: a secret rapture (1 Thess. 4:13–17) and the Parousia (5:1–11; 2 Thess. 2–3). Posttribulationists, for their part, argue that 2 Thessalonians 2–3 are not designed to provide a list of events leading up to the Day of the Lord; rather, these chapters serve as proof that Christ's second coming had not yet transpired. Nor does 1 Thessalonians 4–5 teach that the Day of the Lord will come without the attendant signs of the times but, rather, that it will come suddenly on *non-Christians* (see MIDTRIBULATION RAPTURE; POSTTRIBULATION RAPTURE; PRETRIBULATION RAPTURE; RAPTURE.)

Thousand-Year Reign

See CHILIASM; MILLENNIAL KINGDOM; MILLENNIALISM; MILLENNIUM.

Throne

The throne of God is the Bible's way of asserting God's sovereignty over earth and heaven. The Old Testament prophets were privileged to see God on his throne surrounded by the heavenly court (1 Kings 22:19–23; Isa. 6:1–3; Ezek. 1:4–28; Dan. 7:9–10). From such a vantage point, they could hear the deliberations of God in his council and announce the divine decision on earth.

Revelation mentions the heavenly throne forty times, mostly with reference to God (e.g., Rev. 4:2, 9; 5:13; 7:10, 15; 19:4; 20:11), but also in connection with Christ (e.g., 3:21; 5:13). Early on this book draws attention to the throne as a central image. Alongside the vision of Christ among the seven churches on earth (chs. 1–3) stands the vision of God's throne room in heaven (chs. 4–5). The centrality of the throne signifies God's sovereign rule as the centerpiece of ultimate reality around which everything else revolves.[109] All subsequent visions in the book emerge from these introductory visions of God's sovereignty. The faithful witness and suffering of believers, the rebellion and punishment of unbelievers, and the fulfillment of God's promise to redeem his people and live among them are all under God's control. Because only God is supreme over his creation, he alone is worthy of worship.

As the vision of Revelation 4 moves into Revelation 5, the throne image expands with reference to who is seated on the throne. Here the Lamb is also pictured "standing in the center of the throne" (5:6). He takes the scroll from the right hand of "him who sat on the throne." In the rest of Revelation 5 both God and the Lamb receive enthusiastic worship for their work of redemption. John's message is clear in all of this: Jesus is God and will accomplish his will on earth.

In Revelation 21, after evil has been destroyed, the new Jerusalem, "the central symbol of the whole book"[110] descends from heaven to earth. This Jerusalem shows that God will live among his people. In the holy city the throne remains prominent:

> Then the angel showed me the river of the water of life as clear as crystal, flowing from the *throne* of God and of the Lamb down the middle of the great street of the city … The *throne* of God and of the Lamb will be in the city and his servants will serve him. They will see his face, and his name will be on their foreheads. There will be no more night. They will not need the light of a lamp or the light of the sun, for the Lord God will give them light. And they will reign for ever and ever."(Rev. 22:1–5; italics added)

Now it is no longer just the twenty-four elders and the four living creatures who have access to God's presence. Rather, all God's people are invited into his glorious presence where they find ultimate fulfillment in serving and worshiping the One on the throne and the Lamb.

Thyatira

In his message to the church at Thyatira, Jesus is described as the Son of God with blazing eyes and feet of burnished bronze (Rev. 2:18). John, along with echoing the opening vision in 1:14–15, is likely drawing on the story of Daniel for these images (Dan. 3; 6). In addition, the description of Jesus stands in direct contrast to the Roman emperors, who claimed to be divine, along with the various gods and goddesses promoted by the local culture (e.g., Apollo, Helios).

The church at Thyatira is commended for its love, faith, witness, perseverance, and growth. They are rebuked, however, for tolerating the false teachings of "Jezebel," presumably a local prophetess nicknamed after the biblical figure who led Israel into spiritual adultery (see JEZEBEL). Thyatira was a hub of economic life with a large number of powerful trade guilds connected to local deities (Acts 16:14). Evidently this Jezebel was a woman (or a group of false teachers) within the church who claimed to be a "prophetess" and offered "deep secrets" (Rev. 2:20, 24). Her teachings likely included an encouragement to participate in local business life even if it caused Christians to compromise with paganism. True prophets call people to confess the truth about Jesus and lead them to follow him faithfully even in a pagan culture.

To the overcomer Jesus promises a share in his messianic rule, a rule that is much greater than that of Rome or any earthly power (Rev. 2:26–28). (See SEVEN CHURCHES OF REVELATION.)

Times of the Gentiles

The phrase "times of the Gentiles" comes from Luke 21:24 and is similar in theme to Romans 11:25. Jesus prophesies in the Olivet Discourse about the fall of Jerusalem to the Romans in A.D. 70 (see DESTRUCTION OF THE JERUSALEM TEMPLE [A.D. 70]). From then on until Christ's return, Jerusalem will be under the rule of Gentiles (see Acts 1:6–7).

This negative portrayal of the Gentiles is given a positive twist by Paul in Romans 11:25. There the apostle to the Gentiles says that this present era is devoted to reaching the Gentiles with the gospel. When "the full number of the Gentiles has come in"—that is, when the divinely predetermined number of Gentiles comes to Christ—God will turn his attention once again to bringing Israel to faith in their Messiah. In actuality, declares Paul in 11:11–27, the Gentiles' conversion to Christianity is intended to stir Israel to jealousy in order to reclaim their Messiah, whom they once rejected.

Timothy, 2

Some scholars question Pauline authorship of 2 Timothy, claiming that this letter downplays the importance of eschatology and therefore does not contain the imminent expectation of Christ's return that pervades Paul's other letters. But a careful reading of this letter refutes such an assertion, for the signs of the times, or the messianic woes, that are expected to precede the Parousia (Jesus' second coming) form a pervasive theme in 2 Timothy. Thus 2 Timothy corresponds well with the Olivet Discourse. Note these parallels:

Olivet Discourse and the signs of the times	2 Timothy and the signs of the times
1. Arrival of last days (Matt. 24:22, 29; Mark 13:19–20; Luke 21:6, 23)	1. Arrival of last days (2 Tim. 3:1; 4:3; cf. 1 Tim. 4:1)
2. Persecution of believers (Matt. 24:9; Mark 13:9–12; Luke 21:12–13)	2. Persecution of believers (2 Tim. 2:8–13; 3:10–12; 4:4–6)
3. False teachers of deception (Matt. 24:11, 23–24; Mark 13:5, 6, 21–22; Luke 21:8)	3. False teachers of deception (2 Tim. 2:17–18; 3:6; 4:3, 4; cf. 1 Tim. 4:1–5)
4. Apostasy (Matt. 24:12; Mark 13:22a; Luke 21:6)	4. Apostasy (2 Tim. 3:5–9; etc.)
5. Parousia and judgment (Matt. 24:30; Mark 13:26–27; Luke 21:27)	5. Parousia and judgment (2 Tim. 4:1, 8, 18)

Moreover, it is clear from the preceding statements that Paul in 2 Timothy believes he is living in the midst of the signs of the times and that Christ may come back at any moment. This leads one to the rightful conclusion, therefore, that Paul indeed is the author of 2 Timothy, for it matches his view of the last things elsewhere in his writings as well as that presented in the Gospels by Christ at the Olivet Discourse.

Tower of Babel

See BABYLON/BABYLONIANS.

Transfiguration

"Transfiguration" in the Bible refers to Jesus' inward, hidden glory becoming visible for his inner circle disciples (Peter, James, and John; see Matt. 16:28–17:8; Mark 9:1–8; Luke 9:27–36; 2 Peter 1:16–21). Immediately after Peter confesses that Jesus is the Christ, Jesus predicts that some of his disciples will not see death until they taste of the kingdom of God. Some six days later (Luke rounds it off to eight days, Luke 9:28) Jesus takes Peter, James, and John to a mountaintop (perhaps Mount Hermon because it was close to Caesarea Philippi, the place of Peter's confession).

There, suddenly, the inward hidden glory of Jesus shines through his body and he converses with Moses and Elijah (see ELIJAH; MOSES). Peter wants his companions to build booths (i.e., temporary shelters) to prolong the visit of the three heavenly personages: Moses, the representative of the law; Elijah, the representative of the prophets; and Jesus, the Messiah. But God the Father mildly rebukes Peter, announcing that Jesus is his beloved Son; he is preeminent and must be heard.

In 2 Peter 1:16–21 Peter cites himself as an eyewitness of the transfiguration; he heard a divine voice proclaiming Jesus to be the Son of God. This is the same voice speaking through him in his letter, confirming that the second coming of Christ will truly happen.

Several prophetic themes emerge from the transfiguration episode as recorded in the preceding texts. (1) Some of the disciples do indeed taste of the kingdom of God during their lifetime, for the transfiguration provides for them a foretaste of the glorious splendor that will accompany Christ at his second coming, the Parousia.

(2) Moses and Elijah conversing with Jesus on the mountain indicate perhaps that the Law (Moses) and the Prophets (Elijah) find their fulfillment in Jesus the Messiah.

(3) The transfiguration itself conveys a prophetic word, namely, that Jesus must first suffer and die after which he will enter heavenly glory. According to Luke 9:31 Moses and Elijah converse with Jesus about his "exodus" in Jerusalem—that is, his death and resurrection, the basis of a new exodus for the people of God. This is confirmed by Jesus' words to his disciples as they descend the Mount of Transfiguration that they should tell no one what they have seen until he rises from the dead (Matt. 17:9; Mark 9:9; cf. Luke 9:44).

(4) The presence of Elijah at the transfiguration also confirms the disciples' recent conclusion that Jesus is the Messiah because the Old Testament taught that Elijah was to be the forerunner of the Messiah (Mal. 4:5). Jesus agrees, pointing out to the three disciples that Elijah has indeed come in the person of John the Baptist and that he, like Jesus, must first suffer before entering into the glory of the messianic kingdom.

Transformation of Nature

In Genesis 3 Adam and Eve disobey God and are banished from the garden and from accessing the tree of life (see TREE OF LIFE). Theologians refer to this event as "the fall," and the consequences of the fall reverberate throughout Scripture. In fact, the overarching biblical story (i.e., the story of redemption) is in reality a story of how God restores the human race back to the close relationship they had with him in the garden in the beginning prior to the fall.

However, the sin of humankind and the resulting fall have serious consequences not only for the human race (death) but also for nature (decay, wildness). The implication of Genesis 3:17–19 is that the fall brings about a curse on nature itself, changing it from the ideal it was prior to the fall. Prior to the fall, humanity lived at peace with nature. Because of the fall, sin changes that situation so that strife and tension exist between people and nature. The natural world has changed from a peaceful, wonderful, idyllic place to live into a difficult and dangerous place that constantly threatens death. A reminder of that tension can be seen throughout the Old Testament by the presence and threat of wild animals (see WILD ANIMALS).

Part of the promise of ultimate restoration, therefore, involves restoring the natural world to a situation of peace and harmony between nature and humanity. Some scholars suggest that Isaiah's vision of wild animals living at peace with domestic animals and even with people is an allusion to the future time when nature will be restored (Isa. 11:6–9; 65:25).

The clearest expression of the decayed state of nature and the hope of nature's transformation is found in Romans 8:19–25. Douglas Moo summarizes this passage: "Creation, helplessly enslaved to the decay that rules this world after the Fall, exists in the hope that it will be set free to participate in the eschatological glory to be enjoyed by God's children."[111] Scholars are divided over when this transformation will take place. Many premillennialists place it at the beginning of the millennial kingdom; during this time God's people and nature will live in peace and harmony (see MILLENNIAL KINGDOM). Other scholars maintain that Paul is referring to something that happens as part of the eternal state, when the "new heaven and new earth" of Revelation 21–22 are established (see NEW HEAVEN AND NEW EARTH).

An interesting point made by some scholars is that ancient people developed culture, and especially cities—the main expression of culture in the ancient world—in an attempt to counter the wild, hostile forces of nature. Yet because of fallen humanity, cities themselves became fallen expressions of culture. The story of Sodom and Gomorrah (Gen. 18–19) is a good prototypical example. Thus, not only nature but also culture/cities needed to be transformed. The description of the new Jerusalem in

Revelation 21–22 combines both a transformed natural world (the garden) with a transformed culture (the city), which thus brings about a total restoration and perfect blend of both living situations.[112]

Tree of Life

In Genesis 2 God establishes the Garden of Eden. In its center he plants two trees: "the tree of life and the tree of the knowledge of good and evil" (Gen. 2:9). God tells Adam that he is free to eat of any tree in the garden except the tree of the knowledge of good and evil (2:16–17). This command seems to imply that it is alright for Adam and Eve to eat of the tree of life. Also implied in Genesis is that access to the tree of life provided immortality. Thus as long as Adam and Eve have access to this tree, they enjoy immortality.

However, after Adam and Eve disobey God and eat from the tree of the knowledge of good and evil, God banishes them from the garden, removing them from access to the tree of life, thus taking away their immortality and introducing the human race to death. God then places cherubim to guard the way back into the garden, stating explicitly that the cherubim are to keep them from accessing the tree of life (Gen. 3:24). The theological implication of this action is that the human race is now excluded from access to the tree of life and that all people, therefore, will experience death.

The tree of life emerges again in Revelation, where access to it once again represents eternal life or immortality. In Revelation 2:7, God tells the church at Ephesus that "to him who overcomes, I will give the right to eat from the tree of life, which is in the paradise of God." The tree of life reappears at the end of the book. John describes the new Jerusalem in Revelation 21, and the description of the garden in chapter 22 is an extension of that picture (see NEW JERUSALEM).

The scene in Revelation 22 has many connections to Ezekiel 47, but it also alludes back to Genesis 2. At the culmination of history God's redeemed people are once again back in the garden, enjoying the presence of God. Central to John's description of this ultimate paradisal garden is the river of life, which flows from the throne of God and of the Lamb (see RIVER OF LIFE). This river waters the tree of life, stressing the connection between the powerful presence of God and human immortality. Also, note that the tree of life stands on both sides of the river. Not only has this tree increased from one to many (probably an entire grove), but John stresses how plentiful and available the fruit will be. Even the leaves are valuable, providing healing for the nations (probably a reference to salvation). Access to this tree will provide eternal life for all God's people.

Tribulation

Tribulation refers to the distress, trouble, persecution, and suffering experienced by God's people as a part of living faithfully in a world opposed to God. Words for "tribulation" occur fifty-five times in the New Testament (the verb *thlibō* occurs ten times and the noun *thlipsis* forty-five times) in five main ways:

- the troubles or hardships of life in general
- the present persecutions and trials experienced by Christians as a part of following Christ
- the period of intense persecution at the end of the age (see GREAT TRIBULATION)
- the "afflictions of Christ"
- the judgment on the wicked

While "tribulation" can refer to troubles of life in general (Acts 7:10–11; 1 Cor. 7:28; 1 Tim. 5:10; Jas. 1:27), most of the time it refers to persecutions and trials experienced by Christians. Jesus warns that those who desire to follow him in discipleship should expect tribulation. In the parable of the sower, he mentions people whose commitment will be short-lived because of the trouble or persecution they encounter (Matt. 13:21; Mark 4:17). In his Upper Room Discourse on the night before his crucifixion, Jesus compares his disciples' grief at his leaving to the "anguish" or pain of childbirth (John 16:21). He then tells his disciples plainly, "In this world you will have trouble [*thlipsis*]. But take heart! I have overcome the world" (John 16:33).

The book of Acts also uses *thlypsis* to refer to the "persecution" associated with Stephen's martyrdom (Acts 11:19) and to Paul's near-death experience at Lystra as examples of the "hardships" that believers must endure to enter the kingdom (14:22). Likewise, the Spirit warns Paul that he will encounter tribulation in every city (20:23).

Paul speaks often of tribulations, hardships, and trouble. He does not hesitate to talk about the persecutions that are part of his apostolic ministry (2 Cor. 1:8; 4:8; 6:4; 7:5; Eph. 3:13; Phil. 1:17; 4:14; 1 Thess. 3:3, 4, 7). He mentions the trials of a particular congregation (2 Cor. 8:2, 13; 1 Thess. 1:6; 2 Thess. 1:4, 6, 7) or the troubles associated with relating to a congregation (2 Cor. 1:6; 2:4). Yet Paul is quick to add that a believer's tribulations are "light and momentary" when compared to God's weighty glory (2 Cor. 4:17; 7:4). Since tribulation cannot separate believers from the love of Christ (Rom. 8:35), Paul encourages patience (12:12) and even joy in the endurance process (5:3), knowing that God will give comfort (2 Cor. 1:4).

Other New Testament writers also speak of Christians experiencing tribulation or persecution. The writer of Hebrews alludes to the "persecution" experienced by his readers (Heb. 10:33) and the faithful examples who preceded them (11:37). In Revelation, John testifies that he too shares in the suffering or tribulation that his readers are facing (Rev. 1:9). Jesus assures the church at Smyrna that he knows their "afflictions" and warns them to prepare for "persecution" (imprisonment or even death) at the hands of the devil (2:9–10).

In addition to the many references to the present persecutions and trials experienced by Christians, "tribulation" can also refer to the intensification of trial and trouble in the last days. Jesus warns his own disciples that they will be handed over to be "persecuted and put to death" because of their loyalty to Jesus (Matt. 24:9). He then warns of a "great distress, unequaled from the beginning of the world until now—and never to be equaled again" (Matt. 24:21; Mark 13:19). After that period of distress, the end will come (Matt. 24:29; Mark 13:24). This "Great Tribulation" represents an intense time of suffering at the end of history.

The only place in the book of Revelation where "tribulation" is explicitly mentioned in the sense of eschatological suffering is 7:14. John sees a great multitude in heaven praising God when one of the elders asks him a question about their identity. John pleads ignorance and the elder then answers his own question: "These are they who have come out of the Great Tribulation; they have washed their robes and made them white in the blood of the Lamb." Revelation 7:14 explicitly draws on Daniel 12:1 to describe this end-time Tribulation. Craig Keener uses first-century reference points to explain this graphic picture of blessedness for those who have been through the Tribulation:

> These people refused to deify the enthroned emperor; now they are before God's throne (7:15). They resisted the temples of Caesar and other false gods; now they serve continually in God's temple (7:15). They suffered economic deprivation for refusing to serve the world system (13:17); now they are freed from suffering and sorrow, and all their needs are provided (7:16–17).[113]

Interestingly, the "afflictions of Christ" mentioned by Paul in Colossians 1:24 probably also represent end-time afflictions. This single reference to Christ's afflictions occurs in the context of Paul's own apostolic ministry: "Now I [Paul] rejoice in what was suffered for you, and I fill up in my flesh what is still lacking in regard to Christ's afflictions [lit., the afflictions of Christ], for the sake of his body, which is the church" (cf. 1 Peter 4:12–13). On the basis of the immediate context of this passage with its eschatological tone and the background of Old Testament and Jewish apocalyptic, Peter O'Brien concludes that "the afflictions of Christ" here are synonymous with the afflictions or tribulations of God's people in the last days.[114] The afflictions of Christ have already begun (triggered by the death and resurrection of Christ), and when they are filled up or completed, the present age will end and God's kingdom will come in all its fullness. All Christians participate in the "birth pains" out of which the messianic age is born (Matt. 24:8; Mark 13:8). Since God had set a limit on these afflictions (Mark 13:19–24), Paul saw his own sufferings as contributing to this appointed total and the arrival of the future kingdom (cf. God's answer to the martyrs in Rev. 6:9–11).

Tribulation, therefore, is already a present reality for God's people. From the first coming of Christ until his return, believers will experience tribulation, persecution, or trouble (John 16:33). In addition, there will be a time of intense Tribulation at the end of the age just before the arrival of the kingdom of God in all its glory (see GREAT TRIBULATION). The appropriate response to present troubles is hope, joy, and perseverance on our part, knowing that God will ultimately conquer evil. Believers should also remember that God is never the source of their suffering and distress.

In other words, although God's people will experience the wrath of evil powers, they will never face God's wrath (1 Thess. 5:9). Ironically, while God's people will experience tribulation for a time at the hands of God's enemies, they help to defeat those enemies by their endurance in faithfulness. By contrast, while God's enemies persecute his people, in the end they will face tribulation and suffering that comes directly from the hand of God (Rom. 2:9; Rev. 2:22). (See GREAT TRIBULATION; WRATH OF GOD.)

Trilateral Commission

The Trilateral Commission is an organization formed in 1973 by private citizens of Europe, Japan, and the United States to foster discussions by nongovernment people regarding the challenges and responsibilities of the strongest democratic industrialized areas of the world. Some popular end-time writers point to the Trilateral Commission as evidence of the development of the one-world government that they expect to come soon, but such claims lack convincing evidence.

Trumpet Judgments

Along with the seals and bowls, the trumpets (Rev. 8:6–9:21; 11:15–19) constitute the three sets of judgments occupying the central section of Revelation. Each of these series has seven parts that form two groups: judgments 1–4 and judgments 5–7 (see SEAL JUDGMENTS for a summary chart). More specifically, the seals and trumpets follow a 4 + 2 + 1 pattern and the bowls follow a 4 + 3 pattern. Like the seal judgments, there is an interlude between the sixth and seventh trumpets, and like the subsequent bowl judgments, the trumpets draw on the plagues of the Exodus. While the first six trumpets deal with various disasters and judgments, the seventh trumpet describes the final arrival of the kingdom of God.

1st trumpet (Rev. 8:7)	Hail and fire mixed with blood	7th plague (Ex. 9:22–25)	Hail and lightning
2nd trumpet (Rev. 8:8–9)	Burning mountain turns sea to blood	1st plague (Ex. 7:14–21)	Nile turned to blood
3rd trumpet (Rev. 8:10–11)	Blazing star makes fresh water bitter	1st plague	
4th trumpet (Rev. 8:12–13)	Sun, moon, and stars darkened	9th plague (Ex. 10:21–23)	Darkness covers Egypt
5th trumpet (Rev. 9:1–11)	Hoard of scorpion-locusts	8th plague (Ex. 10:1–20)	Massive swarm of locusts

The first four trumpets (and even the fifth) draw on the plagues of the Exodus as background for describing how God will pour out his judgment on the earth. The purpose is to convey God's sovereign power through his control over nature, his judgment of human wickedness and idolatry, and his offer of a final opportunity to repent. These judgments are more intense and severe than the seals (e.g., one-third of the earth is affected compared to one-fourth in the seal judgments). The figure of "a third" used in each of the first four trumpets reveals that God's judgments are partial and destructive, but not yet final. The fourth trumpet ends with a plague of darkness, a regular symbol of judgment and destruction (e.g., Isa. 13:10 – 11; Joel 2:1 – 2; Amos 5:18; Mark 13:24).

Following the fourth trumpet, Revelation 8:13 offers an introduction to the remaining three trumpets, describing them as "woes": "As I watched, I heard an eagle that was flying in midair call out in a loud voice: 'Woe! Woe! Woe to the inhabitants of the earth, because of the trumpet blasts about to be sounded by the other three angels!'" While the first four trumpets are directed at nature, the fifth and sixth trumpets are directed against the "inhabitants of the earth" (i.e., unbelievers).

The lengthy description of the fifth and sixth trumpets emphasizes the seriousness of God's judgment against idolatry. God permits demonic forces associated with these false gods to torture their followers. The hideous images are meant to terrify unbelievers and turn them back to the Lord. In the end, however, they refuse to repent in spite of the torment they have suffered. Those who have been sealed (Rev. 7:1 – 8; 9:4, 20 – 21) are protected from these demonic attacks, just as Israel was protected from the plagues on Egypt (Ex. 8:22 – 23; 9:26).

At the sounding of the fifth trumpet, a fallen star opens the Abyss to release a plague of locust-scorpions that will torture unbelievers for five months (a limited time). Although these invaders could be human, their gruesome appearance (faces like humans, teeth like lions, and tails like scorpions, cf. Rev. 9:7 – 10) favors a demonic identity. These attackers are led by a demonic leader — an angel from the Abyss named Abaddon (Heb. for "the place of death and destruction") or Apollyon (Gk. for "destroyer"). Because of their pain and suffering, the earth-dwellers will desperately try to die, but death will elude them. John draws on both the eighth plague against Egypt, the plague of locusts (Ex. 10:1 – 20), and the invading army of locusts in Joel 1 – 2 to describe this judgment. Yet these locusts cannot harm those bearing the seal of God.

The fifth trumpet also provides evidence of God's sovereign ability to use evil for his ultimate purposes. The divine passive "was given" signals God's control (Rev. 9:1, 3, 5). The demonic army tortures unbelievers — an example of using evil to punish evil. God puts limits on the attackers (9:4, 5, 6, 10) and forbids them from attacking those who belong to him (9:4). Overall, the terrifying depiction of the fifth trumpet judgment reassures believers and attempts to persuade unbelievers to repent.

When the sixth angel sounds his trumpet (Rev. 9:13), John hears a heavenly voice from the golden altar, reminding the readers that God continues to answer the prayers of his people (cf. 8:3 – 5). That voice calls for the release of four angels who are bound at the great River Euphrates.

Their "binding" likely points to their demonic nature (cf. 20:2, 7, where Satan is bound). Upon their release they become leaders of a demonic cavalry of (lit.) "two myriads of myriads" (i.e., "two hundred million"). This unfathomable number represents an army almost beyond calculation in its immensity. In addition to the number, the detailed description of these fierce demonic warriors in 9:17–19 (cf. a similar description of demonic scorpion-locusts in 9:7–10) intensifies the impact of the vision.

While the first four trumpet judgments destroyed a portion of nature and the fifth brought torment to unbelieving humanity, the sixth trumpet culminates in death for a third of the earth's population. Throughout the trumpet judgments, God has dramatically warned the rest of humanity: Repent, or else you too will face my wrath! As Craig Keener reminds us, "the death of one-third of the world is judgment, but it is also mercy."[115]

Much like the pharaoh of the exodus, who hardens his heart in response to God's plagues of judgment (Ex. 7:13, 22), the people who experience these judgments refuse to repent:

> The rest of mankind that were not killed by these plagues still did not repent of the work of their hands; they did not stop worshiping demons, and idols of gold, silver, bronze, stone and wood—idols that cannot see or hear or walk. Nor did they repent of their murders, their magic arts, their sexual immorality or their thefts. (Rev. 9:20–21)

This brief description of the sins of unrepentant humanity—demon worship, idolatry, murders, magic arts, sexual immorality, and thefts—connects idol worship with demonic activity (cf. also the list in Rev. 21:8 that describes those who will experience the second death and in 22:15 that explains who will be excluded from the new Jerusalem). Those in the churches of Asia Minor who compromise with the surrounding pagan culture need to hear that demonic forces stand behind such practices and that they will result in God's judgment.

The seventh trumpet follows the lengthy interlude of Revelation 10:1–11:13 and offers an unexpected vision. Instead of more demonic creatures torturing or killing unbelievers, the seventh seal opens to the sound of a heavenly choir praising God and celebrating the arrival of his kingdom. The twenty-four elders once again fall on their faces in worship:

> We give thanks to you, Lord God Almighty,
>> the One who is and who was,
> because you have taken your great power
>> and have begun to reign.

The nations were angry;
   and your wrath has come.
The time has come for judging the dead
   and for rewarding your servants the prophets
and your saints and those who reverence your name,
   both small and great—
and for destroying those who destroy the earth. (Rev. 11:17–18)

The elders reaffirm God's sovereignty and thank him for setting up his final kingdom. God has finally answered the martyrs' question in Revelation 6:10 and the saints' prayers in 8:3–5. The wrath of God has come—through judging the dead, rewarding his servants, and destroying those who destroy the earth. After condemning evil and rewarding the faithful, God's heavenly Temple is opened so that all can see his presence, symbolized by the Ark of the Covenant (cf. 21:3; 22:3–4). The series of seven trumpets closes with a storm earthquake (11:19), communicating God's sovereign majesty. (See BOWL JUDGMENTS; REVELATION, BOOK OF; SEAL JUDGMENTS.)

Tubal

See MESHECH AND TUBAL.

Turkey (Anatolia)

Modern Turkey encompasses the geographical region that historians refer to as Anatolia. Throughout the biblical era this region has a complex and varied history, with numerous people migrations and invasions. Anatolia was originally the home of the Hittites, but numerous other groups settled and/or fought there.

Regarding biblical prophecy this region comes into the discussion especially in Ezekiel 38. Here Ezekiel prophesies of a coalition of countries that will attack unsuspecting Israel. Several of the countries mentioned in this chapter are located in Anatolia. There is strong historical evidence that Meshech and Tubal (Ezek. 38:2–3) are both located in Anatolia. Some biblical scholars also argue that Gog should be translated as a place and not a personal name and that it is also located in Anatolia. Several popular eschatology writers state that Gomer (Ezek. 38:6) refers to Turkey, but historical evidence is strong that Gomer refers to an ancient people/region further north across the Black Sea.

Some popular writers maintain that Ezekiel 38 describes a Russian-led coalition of Muslim Arabs who will attack Israel in the near future.

Most Old Testament scholars, however, are doubtful of this view, even though it continues to be popular. There is no substantial evidence that Ezekiel 38 has anything to do with modern Russia (see GOG AND MAGOG; MESHECH AND TUBAL). Also, for most of the late twentieth century the modern country of Turkey has been a member of NATO and thus allied with the Western countries against the Soviet Union/Russia. At the time of this writing Turkey is still a member of NATO and still host to the US Air Force at Incirlik Airbase. Likewise, while the Turks are primarily Muslim, they are not Arabs.

Most understand Ezekiel 38 to be a symbolic description of the archetypal enemy who will rise up against God's people. In this chapter there are seven nations from the far north, south, east, and west, probably representing all of the worldwide enemies of God's people.[116]

Twenty-Four Elders

In the heavenly court scene of Revelation 4–5, surrounding the throne of God are twenty-four other thrones with "twenty-four elders" seated on them. These elders have been identified as (1) Old Testament saints, (2) patriarchs and apostles representing the Old and New Testament saints together, (3) the whole community of believers based on the twenty-four orders of the priesthood in 1 Chronicles 24:4–5, (4) angels who represent the saints, (5) angelic members of the heavenly court, or (6) some combination of the above. Their function in this book supports the conclusion that the elders are angels that in some way represent all of God's people.

The number twenty-four probably derives from the twelve tribes and the twelve apostles or from the twenty-four orders of priests. Both possible backgrounds indicate a representative role for the elders. Note that the elders only appear in Revelation in heavenly contexts: the opening throne scene (Rev. 4:4, 10; 5:5, 6, 8, 11, 14), in interludes that bring a heavenly perspective (7:11, 13; 11:16; 14:3), and at the beginning of the final heavenly vision (19:4).

The primary role or function of the twenty-four elders is to worship God (Rev. 4:10; 5:14; 7:11; 11:16; 19:4). Their worship often includes falling down before him in praise and adoration (4:10; 5:8, 14; 7:11; 11:16; 19:4). They verbalize praise (4:9, 11; 7:12; 11:16; 19:4), lay their crowns before God's throne (4:10), and sing songs of praise (5:9–14).

The elders also play a mediating role in serving the saints. One of the elders comforts John as he weeps in despair at the thought of no one being able to open the scroll: "Then one of the elders said to me, 'Do not weep!

See, the Lion of the tribe of Judah, the Root of David, has triumphed. He is able to open the scroll and its seven seals' " (Rev. 5:5). On another occasion, one of the elders explains to John the identity of the great multitude clothed in white robes (7:9): "These are they who have come out of the great tribulation; they have washed their robes and made them white in the blood of the Lamb" (7:14). The elders are also portrayed as holding the golden bowls that contain the prayers of the saints (5:8) and as forming an audience with God and the four living creatures to hear the song of the 144,000 (14:3; see FOUR LIVING CREATURES).

Two-Covenant Theory

Extreme dispensationalists and some others believe that the Bible contains two different covenants to salvation from God. Jews today are under the old covenant of the Mosaic Law, whereupon, if they keep it, God will accept them into his kingdom; Gentiles are under the New Covenant of faith in Christ apart from the law.

This bold theory rests on three basic arguments. (1) Romans 11 discusses the final salvation of Israel without mentioning the name of Christ. Those who hold the two-covenant theory maintain that this implies that the Jews' justification is not based on Christ. (2) Since Paul's letters are addressed to only Gentiles, his remarks about not being justified by the law are applicable only to the Gentiles and not to Jews. (3) When Paul criticizes Israel, he does so because they have refused, not to become Christians, but to recognize Christ as God's means of righteousness for the Gentiles.

Such a view, however, is easily refuted by Romans alone. Donaldson summarizes that letter with the above three arguments in mind:

> Certainly Romans 11, with its evident concern for the ongoing validity of election and the ultimate certainty of Israel's salvation, needs to be given full weight. But the chapter does not exist in a vacuum. Prior to this point, Paul has argued that Jews as well as Gentiles are under sin and guilty before God (1:18–3:18; 5:12–21); declared that the law does not exempt Jews from this universal plight (3:19–20; 5:20); stated that the righteousness of God, testified to by law and prophets, has been manifested in Christ (3:21–22); declared that all without distinction, can attain the righteousness not available through the law by being "of the faithfulness" of Jesus (3:22–26); argued that only those who walk according to the Spirit of Christ (8:9–11) can fulfill the just requirement of the law (8:1–4); and lamented over Israel, because they have not recognized that righteousness is to be found in Christ (9:30–10:4) and

have not believed the message of salvation in Christ (10:9, 14–21). By the time one arrives at chapter 11, then, Paul has established a christocentric semantic range for the key vocabulary of this seemingly nonchristological discourse, for example, "saved" (vv. 14, 26; cf. 10:9–13); "unbelief" (v. 20; cf. 10:17); "foreknew" (v. 2; see 8:29).[117]

In reality, Paul and the New Testament teach only one covenant, namely, that faith in Christ alone brings salvation to both Jew and Gentile. It is that message that Israel will receive in the last days, according to Paul in Romans 11:25–33.

Two Witnesses

In Revelation 11 John is told to "measure the temple of God and the altar," but to "exclude the outer court," which has been given to the Gentiles. God will empower two witnesses who will "prophesy for 1,260 days, clothed in sackcloth." The witnesses are then identified as "the two olive trees and the two lampstands that stand before the Lord of the earth" (11:4). They are empowered by God to do spiritual battle, to perform miracles, and to call down God's judgment (11:5–6). After they finish their testimony, the beast attacks and kills them. Their bodies lie unburied in the great city for three and a half days as the "inhabitants of the earth" celebrate their defeat and death (11:7–10). After the period of days the "breath of life from God" enters them and they are taken to heaven as their terror-stricken enemies look on.

The identity of the two witnesses is much debated. The Old Testament background lies in Zechariah 4:1–14, where the two olive trees (likely referring to the king and the priest) are empowered by the Spirit to lead God's people. The lamp/lampstand image in Zechariah 4 may refer to God's presence among his people through his empowering Spirit (4:2, 6). However, since Revelation regularly transforms Old Testament images, knowing the background does not fully answer the question about the identity of the two witnesses.

Some suggest that the two witnesses are actual people who will appear at the end of history during the Great Tribulation. If the beast in Revelation 11:7 and 13:1 is an individual rather than a symbol, then the two witnesses are also likely individuals. Also, their death and resurrection supports identifying them as literal individuals. A common suggestion is that the two persons will come "in the Spirit and power of" Moses and Elijah, because their actions seem similar to those of the two Old Testament figures (cf. Luke 1:17). Moses has the God-given power to turn water into blood and bring on plagues while Elijah has the power to prevent rain (11:6). In the midst of the Great Tribulation, these two witnesses are God's instruments for confronting a wicked world.

Others prefer to see the two witnesses as symbolic of the witnessing church. The lampstands (Rev. 11:4) have already been identified as churches (1:20). Joshua and Zerubbabel as the high priest and king symbolize the church as a kingdom of priests (1:6; 5:10). They witness for 1,260 days, a period of time signifying the entire Christian era. The whole world sees their death and resurrection, which suggests their presence throughout the world. Note that other "individuals" in Revelation are interpreted to symbolize groups (e.g., the women in Rev. 12 and 17). The witnessing of these two witnesses parallels the pattern throughout Revelation, where the world system has the power to kill God's witnesses, but the witnesses triumph through their faithful sacrifice and future resurrection (6:9; 12:11, 17; 19:10; 20:4). There are two witnesses because two is the number required for valid testimony (Deut. 17:6; 19:15); they represent the two figures of Zechariah 4, and they stand in contrast to the two evil leaders of Revelation 13.

The two figures, however they are identified, emphasize the role of prophetic witness in Revelation. They are empowered by God to carry out a difficult mission (Rev. 11:2–3). God uses them to do miraculous deeds and confront a wicked world (11:5–6). They are temporarily conquered and put to death by the powers of evil (11:7–10). In the end, however, they overcome by God's life-giving power and their own faithfulness, and they are ushered into the safety of God's presence (11:11–12). (See GREAT TRIBULATION; NEW TEMPLE.)

Typology

A *type* can be defined as "a biblical event, person or institution which serves as an example or pattern for other events, persons or institutions."[118] The Old Testament flows into the New Testament as part of a continuous salvation-history story. What is promised in the Old is fulfilled in the New. This can be accomplished through prophetic word or through prophetic action/event. The use of prophetic action/event to predict or foreshadow future actions/events involves typology. Typology is part of the promise-fulfillment scheme that connects the two Testaments together.

Typological interpretation of the Old Testament is different from allegorizing a text, for the former restricts itself to the meaning intended by the original author while the latter reads things into the Old Testament passage (usually in connection with messianic prophecy) not initially intended. It should be noted, of course, that the Old Testament authors may not have always fully comprehended the far-view fulfillment of their prophecies.

Thus, for example, Psalm 22 reveals King David's trials and tribulations, which are later viewed by New Testament authors as applicable to the crucifixion of Christ (see the quotation of Ps. 22:18 in Matt. 27:34–38, Mark 15:24–25, the soldiers' casting of lots for Jesus' clothes). David probably did not envision his situation as predictive of the sufferings of the coming Messiah, but the Holy Spirit did, who later helped the Gospel authors make the connection (see PSALMS, BOOK OF).

Thus typology is a special form of biblical prophecy, which Christ seemed to use extensively. Thus the "type" occurs in the Old Testament and its "antitype" in the New Testament. R. T. France summarizes Jesus' usage of Old Testament types in the following way:

> He uses *persons* in the Old Testament as types of himself (David, Solomon, Elijah, Elisha, Isaiah, Jonah) or of John the Baptist (Elijah); he refers to Old Testament *institutions* as types of himself and his work (the priesthood and the covenant); he sees in the *experiences* of Israel foreshadowings of his own; he finds the *hopes* of Israel fulfilled in himself and his disciples, and sees his disciples as assuming the *status* of Israel; in Israel's *deliverance* by God he sees a type of the gathering of men into his church, while the *disasters* of Israel are foreshadowings of the imminent punishment of those who reject him, whose *unbelief* is prefigured in that of the wicked in Israel and even, in two instances, in the arrogance of the Gentile nations.
>
> In all these aspects of the Old Testament people of God Jesus sees foreshadowing of himself and his work, with its results in the opposition and consequent rejection of the majority of the Jews, while the true Israel is now to be found in the new Christian community. Thus in his coming the history of Israel has reached its decisive points. The whole of the Old Testament is gathered up in him. He himself embodies in his own person the status and destiny of Israel, and in the community of those who belong to him that status and destiny are to be fulfilled, no longer in the nation as such.[119]

The rest of the New Testament continues Jesus' typological interpretation of the Old Testament, seeing in him the supreme antitype of Old Testament symbolism. Thus, for example, Paul sees Christ as the "second Adam" (Rom. 5:12–21), whose church is the new Israel (1 Cor. 10:1–13; cf. Gal. 6:16). Matthew perceives Jesus to be the new Moses (Matt. 1–10). Luke understands Jesus to be the new David (Luke 2–3). Hebrews believes

Christ has inaugurated the New Covenant (Heb. 8) and is the true priest-hood (7–8; 10), whose death is the fulfillment and replacement of the sacrificial system of the Old Testament (9–10). Revelation 21–22 confirms that Jesus is the new Temple.

Ultradispensationalism

Classical dispensationalism distinguishes between Israel and the church and points to Pentecost in Acts 2 as the beginning of the church and the point at which God's plan changed from one form of administration or dispensation to another. Ultradispensationalism (or extreme dispensationalism) claims that the church did not begin at Pentecost, but rather with Paul's ministry at some later point in Acts.

Ultradispensationalists strongly disagree among themselves about where to locate this official beginning point in Acts (e.g., Acts 9; 13; 28). In effect they have inserted another dispensation between Israel and the church. There are now two "churches": the completely Jewish "bride of Christ" (a transitional dispensation) and the body of Christ that began with Paul's ministry and includes Gentiles.

According to ultradispensationalists, relocating the birth of the church from Acts 2 to later in Acts has significant implications for contemporary Christian practices, including one's view of Scripture. Ultradispensationalists do not recognize the ministry of the twelve apostles as a continuation of Christ's ministry, they do not accept the Great Commission as relevant to the Gentile church, and they view Israel (rather than the church) as the bride of Christ. They reject water baptism and many also reject the Lord's Supper as applicable church ordinances. Finally, they accept only the Pauline letters (and some accept only the Pauline Prison Letters) as written to the Gentile church.

Ultradispensationalism began in England with E. W. Bullinger (1837–1913), who taught that during the time of the Gospels the message was only preached to Jews (and authenticated by water baptism). The Gospels and Acts are under the dispensation of the law, and the church actually began with Paul's ministry after Acts 28. Bullinger believed that the Gentile church was only related to Christ through Spirit baptism. A more moderate group of ultradispensationalists was composed of C. R. Stam, Charles F. Baker, and others associated with the Grace Bible College in Grand Rapids, Michigan, and the ministries of Grace Gospel Fellowship and Worldwide Grace Testimony. They favor the middle part of Acts as the beginning point of the church (Acts 9, 11, or 13).

The strengths of ultradispensationalism are difficult to identify and its weaknesses are too numerous to discuss in detail. The vast majority of evangelical interpreters fault their biblical exegesis on many levels. All that Jesus taught indicates that the ministry of the twelve apostles is a continuation of his ministry. The entire scope of Acts points to Acts 2 as the beginning of the church. The early church portrayed in Acts is comprised of both Jews and Gentiles. Both Peter (Acts 10) and Paul (Acts 16) endorsed water baptism for Gentile converts. The image of the bride in the New Testament certainly applies to the whole church. Paul himself teaches that all Scripture is inspired and useful for believers (2 Tim. 3:16). Classical and progressive dispensationalists alike reject ultradispensationalism as a viable theological system. (See DISPENSATIONALISM, CLASSICAL; DISPENSATIONALISM, PROGRESSIVE.)

United Nations

Many popular writers deduce from Revelation that in the end times the entire world will be controlled by one central world government. Since many of these writers also believe that the end is near, they frequently examine the world today to see if there are signs that point to a one world government. Some of these writers predict that the United Nations is such a sign and that it will evolve into the end-time world government that the Antichrist will control. Some have posited that the United Nations is planning to split the world up into ten administrative districts (the ten-horned beast) and to move the UN headquarters to a small town in Iraq (site of ancient Babylon, see BABYLON/BABYLONIANS). Other writers argue for identifying the ten-horned beast with different organizations such as the European Union (see EUROPEAN UNION) or the Club of Rome (see CLUB OF ROME CONFERENCE).

However, critics of such views point out that at the present time there is no evidence or documentation that the United Nations is planning to move its headquarters from New York to Iraq or that it is planning to split the world up into ten administrative districts.

United States

Because many American popular writers firmly believe that the end times are near and since the United States is such a prominent player in geopolitics today, many wonder if biblical prophecy refers to the United States in any way. The answer to that question is "no." There are no discernable references to the United States in biblical prophecy. A few popular writers, however, have nonetheless argued that the Bible does include the United States in the end-time scenario. Some have argued that "Babylon" in Revelation 18–19 refers to New York and thus to the United States. Others maintain that the term "merchants of Tarshish" in Ezekiel 38:13 actually refers to the United States (or to the US and Britain). Then again, other popular writers maintain that Isaiah 18:1–2 is referring to the United States.

None of these views and arguments has any merit. None of the places mentioned has any connection to the United States.

Valley of Dry Bones

In Ezekiel 37 God takes the prophet Ezekiel to a valley filled with dry human bones. The text does not say how the bones actually came to be there. Most scholars assume that a significant battle was probably fought in that valley and the slain soldiers were simply left unburied on the field where they fell. Over time, scavengers had picked the bones clean and the sun had dried and bleached them.

The obvious point about the dry bones is that these people are really, really dead. Thus, it is astonishing when God tells Ezekiel to prophesy to the bones in order that they might come to life. Note that there is a running wordplay in this story. The same Hebrew word can be used for "spirit," "wind," and "breath." God says that he will put his "breath" (or "spirit"?) in the bones to give them life. He tells Ezekiel to prophesy to the four "winds" to come fill the bones with "breath." Indeed, the "breath/wind/spirit" comes and fills the bones, and they come to life.

In Ezekiel 37:11 – 14 God explains to Ezekiel what this event means. Just as God is powerful enough to bring dead, dry bones back to life, so he is powerful enough to bring shattered and scattered Israel back to life. God is here promising restoration, resurrection, and the indwelling of the Spirit.

Virgin Birth

The virgin birth in biblical prophecy has to do with Matthew's application of Isaiah 7:14 to Jesus' conception and birth. Matthew 1:23 reads: "The virgin will be with child and will give birth to a son, and they will call him Immanuel."

There are two issues involved in Isaiah's prophecy. (1) Should the Hebrew ʿalmah be translated "virgin" (as Matt. 1:23 does, following the Septuagint [the Greek translation of the Old Testament, ca. 250 B.C.] of Isa. 7:14) or "young woman"? It does seem that "young woman" is the more accurate rendering of ʿalmah in Isaiah 7:14.

(2) When was Isaiah 7:14 fulfilled? Most likely this Old Testament text was partially fulfilled in Isaiah's day (with reference to King Ahaz's unnamed son or to Isaiah's son, Maher-Shalal-Hash-Baz [see 8:1]), but it found its ultimate fulfillment in Jesus, as Matthew 1:23 points out (see ISAIAH, BOOK OF).

Vision

"Vision" in biblical prophecy is often the means by which God reveals the future to his prophets (e.g., Dan. 2; 7; Rev. 4:1–2), whether on earth or by way of mystic journey to heaven. Most of the time the visions are interpreted to the seer by an angel.

Some scholars argue, however, that the apocalyptic visions are *vaticinia ex eventu* ("pronouncements after the event"); that is, they are historical descriptions recast as predictive prophecy. They argue, for example, that Daniel 9, even though it purports to predict hundreds of years in the future from Daniel's day (about 550 B.C.), actually comes from an unnamed author assuming the pseudonym of Daniel who lived during the time of conflict between Jews and Antiochus Epiphanes (167 B.C.; see ANTIOCHUS EPIPHANES). But evangelical scholars disagree that this notion of pseudonymity is applicable to biblical authors and reaffirm that God uses biblical visions to predict the future and to encourage his people, through his spokespersons, that they will overcome their trials and enter the kingdom of God (see ORACLE; SEER).

Wild Beasts

Wild animals are mentioned frequently in the prophetic texts of the Bible. The Hebrew language of the Old Testament uses two primary phrases to refer to wild (and dangerous) animals. The most common term literally translates "animals of the field." These animals are clearly distinguished from domesticated animals, for which Hebrew has a different word. The "animals of the field" are dangerous and are always a threat to kill people — lions, bears, leopards, hyenas, snakes, and so on. Another term for wild animals in the Old Testament literally translates "bad animals" or "animals that can cause harm." The NIV usually translates both of these Hebrew phrases as either "wild animals" or "wild beasts." Sometimes the NIV uses "beasts of the field" and "beasts of the earth."

When the Hebrew Old Testament was translated into Greek (the Septuagint), the translators used the same Greek term for all of these Hebrew references to wild animals. This word *thērion* simply means "beast," but it implies a wild and dangerous animal. The New Testament uses this word in Mark 1:13 (NIV "wild animals"), Acts 28:4–5 (NIV "snake"), and throughout Revelation (see BEASTS OF REVELATION).

Wild Animals in the Old Testament

God created the wild animals in Genesis 1:25 and saw this creation as "good." When God declared in 1:26, 28 that humankind should rule over the creation, however, the wild animals are not specifically mentioned. Yet in 2:19–20 God brings all of the wild animals to Adam to name, implying that he was given power to rule over them (naming implies power over something).

The serpent in Genesis 3:1 is described as being the most crafty of the wild animals. Thus it should be viewed as part of the "wild animal" category. When Adam and Eve yield to the serpent (Satan), besides blatantly disobeying God, they are giving up their right to rule and to control creation. As a result of the fall of humanity in Genesis 3, nature itself changes and the wild animals become hostile and dangerous to people (see TRANSFORMATION OF NATURE).

Throughout the Old Testament, controlling the wild animals in a given region was considered a critical part of subduing that area. In Exodus 23:29 and in Deuteronomy 7:22 God states that he will not drive out the Canaanites from the Promised Land too quickly because if he did, the wild animals would fill the land and be too numerous for the Israelites to control. Thus conquering and controlling the Promised Land involved not only dealing with the Canaanites but also dealing with the wild animals. Wild animals may be used here figuratively for other kings and nations, but it seems more likely that the text is referring to actual wild animals.

Thus, the presence and power of hostile wild animals came to be associated with the loss of control and rule of an area. The prophetic writers use wild animals figuratively to represent devastation and destruction of the land. The prophets often include wild animals along with one or more of their other central terms for desolation—the sword, plague, and famine. They proclaim that the presence of wild animals roaming the land and dominating the inhabitants is part of the coming judgment on disobedient Israel and Judah.

Yet the prophets often also declare that the wild animals are under God's control. God sends them as part of his decreed judgment on Israel (Jer. 15:3; Ezek. 14:15–16) as well as on other sinful nations. In fact, when God raises up the Babylonian king Nebuchadnezzar to inflict judgment on sinful and disobedient Judah, God states that even the wild animals will be subject to Nebuchadnezzar (Jer. 27:6; 28:14), implying that Nebuchadnezzar will use them for judgment.

As is frequently the case, when the prophets switch from images of judgment to images of messianic restoration, they often reverse the images of destruction into images of blessing. Thus when the Messiah comes, the prophets declare, the wild animals will be transformed into peaceful animals that no longer kill and devour (Isa. 11:6–9; 65:25). Some prophets say that wild animals will be removed altogether from the land (Ezek. 34:25, 28).

In Ezekiel 34 God declares that the bad shepherds of Israel (their leaders) have allowed the people to be scattered and devoured by wild animals (34:5). God then promises to become their shepherd himself and to give his people rest and safety (Jesus connects to this chapter when he describes himself as the good shepherd; see SHEPHERDS). God then promises to make a Covenant of Peace (see COVENANT OF PEACE) with his people, in which he will rid the land of wild animals, allowing his sheep (his people) to sleep in peace and safety.

Wild Animals (Beasts) in the New Testament

The New Testament makes several connections to the wild animals of Genesis and the prophetic books. Mark 1:13 is about the temptation of Jesus: "and he (Jesus) was in the desert forty days, being tempted by Satan. He was with the wild animals and angels attended him." Although not all scholars agree, some maintain that the grammar of this verse implies that Jesus was with the animals peacefully.[120] That is, although Satan was tempting him, the Lord had subdued, and was at peace with, the wild animals. At any rate, a strong connection between the temptation of Christ and the temptation of Adam is implied. Adam failed and thus lost control of the wild animals (especially the serpent, i.e., Satan). Jesus, however, does not fall to the temptation, but instead emerges victorious. Thus the animals fall under his rule and control, although the final crushing of Satan (the serpent) does not take place until the end of Revelation.

In Acts 28 the Greek word for beast (*thērion*) is used again, although this time the NIV translates it as "snake." Scholars are divided over the significance of this usage. In Acts 28:3, Paul, shipwrecked on the island of Malta, is bitten by a poisonous "viper." The word used here clearly refers to a snake. Yet when Paul shakes it off into the fire (28:5), the text uses the word *thērion*, although clearly referring back to the snake. Thus 28:5 literally says, "Paul shook the beast off into the fire." The passage indicates clearly that Paul had power over the bite of this snake. But the passage may also be pointing out the fact that ultimately the followers of Christ have power over the hostile wild animals (the beasts), especially as they are represented by the snake (i.e., Satan). It may also foreshadow the ultimate fiery destruction of "the beast" in Revelation.

The Greek word *thērion* occurs thirty-eight times in Revelation. The first usage is in Revelation 6:8. Here God is using the wild animals again as part of his judgment on the earth. In this passage the four horsemen are "given power over a fourth of the earth to kill by sword, famine and plague, and by the wild beasts of the earth." The role of the wild beasts as agents of judgment sent by God parallels the usage of the wild beasts by the Old Testament prophets (note the similar connection to sword, famine, and plague).

Throughout the rest of Revelation, *thērion* is translated as "beast" and regularly refers to either Satan or one who works for him (see BEASTS OF REVELATION). Ultimately, however, as part of Christ's final victory, Satan (called "the ancient serpent") and his beast are thrown into the lake of fire and destroyed. Furthermore, in Revelation 21:25 the new Jerusalem will never close its gates, not even at night (see GATES). Thus the ultimate picture of peace and safety from all enemies, including wild animals both literal and figurative, is established by the victorious Christ, and humankind lives at peace with God in their midst once again in the garden (22:1–5).

Woman of Revelation 12

The book of Revelation features four women: Jezebel (Rev. 2, see JEZEBEL), the great prostitute (chs. 17–18, see GREAT PROSTITUTE), the bride of the Lamb (chs. 19; 21–22, see BRIDE OF THE LAMB), and the woman of Revelation 12. The "great and wondrous sign" involving the woman of Revelation 12 is of major importance, but who is this woman?

Although some have identified her as Mary, the mother of Jesus, nowhere is the woman named Mary, and the description that follows (12:2–6, 13–17) goes well beyond what can be said of Mary. The woman is a positive figure who stands in contrast to Jezebel and the great prostitute. The woman is said to be "clothed with the sun, with the moon under her feet and a crown of twelve stars on her head" (12:1). In Genesis 37:9 we read of the sun, moon, and eleven stars representing Jacob (Israel), his wife, and the eleven tribes of Israel, who bow down to Joseph, the twelfth. Therefore, the woman of Revelation 12 has some connection to Israel.

The woman's primary role is to give birth to a "male child, who will rule all the nations." The child is subsequently "snatched up to God and to his throne" (Rev. 12:5)—a likely reference to the ascension/exaltation of Jesus Christ. The prophets speak of restored Israel as a woman (Isa. 54:1–6; 62:1–5; 66:7–13), an image John integrates with the bride of Christ in Revelation 21–22. In some sense, then, the woman should be seen as the mother community of Jesus, the Messiah.

After the birth of her son, the woman is attacked by the dragon, but she is protected by God for 1,260 days (Rev. 12:6, 14). The figure of 1,260 days (or "a time, times, and half a time") in 12:14 signifies an indefinite, but not unlimited, amount of time. In Jewish history the desert is connected with the Exodus event as the place where God guided and cared for his people following their deliverance from captivity.

The Exodus imagery continues in Revelation 12:15–16 as torrential waters from the dragon's mouth threaten to destroy the woman before they are swallowed by the earth (cf. Ex. 15:10, 12). Many scholars believe that the water from the dragon's mouth represents deceit, slander, and false teaching launched at God's people. God offers spiritual protection and refuge for his faithful community against the onslaughts of Satan and his followers.

The chapter ends with a note about the woman's other children: "Then the dragon was enraged at the woman and went off to make war against the rest of her offspring—those who obey God's commandments and hold to the testimony of Jesus" (Rev. 12:17; cf. Gen. 3:15). The context clearly defines these other "offspring" as true disciples of Jesus Christ (cf. Rev. 1:2, 9; 12:11; 14:12; 19:10; 20:4).

Taken as a whole, Revelation 12 identifies the woman as the community of God's people to whom the Messiah was given. There is a strong connection to the faithful remnant of Israel or true Israel, since the woman's children are identified as genuine followers of Jesus. (See BRIDE OF THE LAMB; DRAGON; SEED OF THE WOMAN.)

Women Prophets

Female prophets are known in non-Israelite cultures of the ancient Near East during the Old Testament era. In addition, several women in the Bible are called prophets. (1) Miriam, the sister of Moses, is called a prophetess and leads the Israelite women in a song of celebration and praise in Exodus 15:20–21. Micah 6:4 refers to Miriam as one of the leaders whom God raised up for Israel (see MIRIAM).

(2) Deborah, one of the judges, is called a prophetess in Judges 4:4 (see DEBORAH).

(3) In 2 Kings 22:11–20, after King Josiah recovers the book of Deuteronomy and hears of the warnings in the book, he sends his advisers to the prophetess Huldah to inquire of the LORD what will happen to them. Huldah, in the true prophetic tradition, tells Josiah that although God is definitely going to judge Judah and Jerusalem because of their sin, nonetheless, because of Josiah's repentant, humble attitude, Josiah himself will be delivered and will not see the judgment (see HULDAH).

(4) In Nehemiah 6:14 there is a brief reference to a prophetess named Noadiah, who causes trouble for Nehemiah.

(5) Another woman referred to as a prophetess is Isaiah's wife (Isa. 8:3). Some scholars suggest that this woman is called a prophetess simply because she is married to Isaiah the prophet. Others disagree, noting that there is nothing in the context or culture that indicates that she is not a prophet in her own right (cf. the prophetic role of Huldah).

The New Testament too notes several women who prophesy or are called prophets. (1) A prophetess named Anna recognizes the baby Jesus in the temple as the Messiah (Luke 2:36–38) (see ANNA). (2) Acts 21:7 states that Philip the evangelist had four unmarried daughters with the gift of prophecy (see DAUGHTERS OF PHILIP). (3) In a negative light, Revelation 2:20 commends the church at Thyatira because they cannot tolerate the woman Jezebel, who calls herself a prophetess (see JEZEBEL; THYATIRA).

Wrath of God

The "wrath of God" refers to God's holy and righteous response to sin and evil. On occasion Jesus speaks about God's coming wrath (Matt. 3:7; Luke 3:7; 21:23). Paul refers to God's wrath as a present reality (e.g., Rom. 1:18; 1 Thess. 2:16), a future reality (e.g., Rom. 2:5, 8; 1 Thess. 1:10; cf. also Heb. 3:11; 4:3), and a certainty for the disobedient, without an emphasis on the time of wrath (e.g., Rom. 9:22; 12:19; Eph. 2:3; 5:6; Col. 3:6). Paul also clearly teaches that Jesus rescues believers from God's present and future wrath (e.g., Rom. 5:9; 1 Thess. 1:10; 5:9; cf. also John 3:36). The biblical teaching on God's wrath comes into sharpest focus in Revelation, which draws on a variety of Old Testament prophetic images.

Revelation uses two primary words for wrath: *orgē* (Rev. 6:16, 17; 11:18; 14:10; 16:19; 19:15) and *thymos* (12:12; 14:8, 10, 19; 15:1, 7; 16:1, 19; 18:3; 19:15). In three instances both terms are used together, probably for added intensity (14:10; 16:19; 19:15). Ironically, *thymos* is also used to describe Satan's wrath aimed at the followers of Jesus (12:12, 17) and Babylon's "wine of the passionate desire [*thymos*] of her immorality" (14:8; 18:3). In a sense Revelation portrays a battle of two opposing wraths —God's wrath versus that of Satan and Babylon. The diabolical "wrath" consists of a willful opposition to God that results in the rejection and persecution of God's people. The emphasis in Revelation, however, falls on the victorious wrath of God.

Who will experience God's wrath? With the opening of the sixth seal, the end of the age has arrived and unrepentant people from every social order attempt to hide themselves from "the face of him who sits on the throne and from the wrath of the Lamb. For the great day of their wrath has come" (Rev. 6:16–17). After the sounding of the seventh trumpet, the twenty-four elders worship God by celebrating the coming of God's wrath, which includes "destroying those who destroy the earth" (11:17–18). Those who worship the beast and his image "will drink of the wine of God's fury [*thymos*], which has been poured full strength into the cup of his wrath [*orgē*]" (14:10; cf. Ps. 75:8; Isa. 51:17; Jer. 25:15–16).

The wicked of the world are also in view in Revelation 14:19, where they are trampled in "the great winepress of God's wrath" (cf. Isa. 63:3; Lam. 1:15; Joel 3:13) and in Revelation 15:1, 7; 16:1, when the seven golden bowls filled with God's wrath are poured out on the earth. At the end of Revelation 16 when the seventh bowl is poured out, the end arrives with lightning, thunder, and a great earthquake. The earthquake destroys Babylon, and 16:19 reports that "God remembered Babylon the Great and gave her the cup filled with the wine of the fury [*thymos*] of his wrath [*orgē*]." Jesus appears in Revelation 19 as the supreme holy Warrior to conquer the wicked nations. One of his actions is to tread "the winepress of the fury [*thymos*] of the wrath [*orgē*] of God Almighty" (19:15). Those who experience God's wrath are the wicked who have deliberately opposed God and his people.

God's people will never experience his wrath. In almost every case where God's wrath is mentioned, there are contrasting statements or predictions about the positive fate of believers. After describing how the wicked will attempt to hide from the wrath of God and of the Lamb, Revelation 6 ends with this question: "For the great day of their wrath has come, and who can stand?" Revelation 7 provides the answer—only those who have been sealed (7:3). The wrath of God on the nations is followed by a reward for the saints:

> The nations were angry;
>> and your wrath has come.
> The time has come for judging the dead,
>> and for rewarding your servants the prophets
> and your saints and those who reverence your name,
>> both small and great. (Rev. 11:18)

After hearing that those who worship the beast will face the wrath of God, the faithful and obedient are encouraged to endure patiently, and those who have died receive a blessing: " 'Blessed are the dead who die in the Lord from now on.' 'Yes,' says the Spirit, 'they will rest from their labor, for their deeds will follow them' " (Rev. 14:12–13). In climactic fashion, following the account of God's wrath coming on the great city

Babylon (16:17–21) and the wicked nations (19:11–21), we read of the new Jerusalem, the holy city of God (chs. 21–22).

Unlike arbitrary, unjustified human anger, God's wrath is the deliberate and intentional expression of his righteous and holy character. As the full and final judgment of all that is unholy and wicked, God's wrath enables the defeat of evil, the vindication of his people, the triumph of his perfect character, and eternal fellowship with his redeemed creation in the new heaven and the new earth (see DAY OF THE LORD; JUDGMENT).

Z

Zechariah, Book of

Zechariah is one of the postexilic prophets (see POSTEXILIC PROPHETS). His prophetic ministry takes place in Jerusalem among the postexilic community. That is, many of the descendants of the Jews carried off in exile to Babylon because of their disobedience to God have returned to Jerusalem and are trying to rebuild the city and the Temple. Both Zechariah and his contemporary Haggai are concerned especially with rebuilding the Temple.

Zechariah ties the dates of his prophecies to the reign of the Persian kings who still rule Israel, a reminder that the preexilic prophecies of restoring Israel to prominence under a Davidic king are not yet being fulfilled. The return of the exiles to Jerusalem is perhaps a partial fulfillment of the preexilic prophecies, but it falls short—extremely short—of the glorious vision that Isaiah, Jeremiah, and Ezekiel prophesied regarding the restoration. But there is a sense in which the return during Zechariah's day is a partial fulfillment, similar to a "near view" fulfillment, which still looks forward to the consummate "far view" fulfillment (see NEAR VIEW–FAR VIEW).

The book of Zechariah is comprised primarily of eight night visions (Zech. 1:7–6:15) and two oracles (Zech. 9–14). Portions of the book are in apocalyptic form (see APOCALYPTIC LITERATURE), while other portions are similar to standard Old Testament prophetic material and form. Zechariah brings a message of both rebuke and encouragement. He points out that the people are falling into the same sins as their forefathers. He exhorts them to participate in true worship through spiritual renewal and to be actively concerned with social justice.

The New Testament Gospels cite from Zechariah frequently to demonstrate that Jesus is the Messiah that the Old Testament prophesied. Matthew 21:4–5 and John 12:14–15 cite Zechariah 9:9–10 regarding the Messiah's humble entry into Jerusalem mounted on a donkey. Zechariah 13:7 ("strike the shepherd and the sheep will be scattered") is cited in Matthew 26:31. John 19:37 states that the spear-piercing of Jesus on the cross is the fulfillment of Zechariah 12:10. Likewise, Zechariah 11:12–13 (thirty pieces of silver being thrown to the potter) is connected along with a prophecy from Jeremiah to Judas's betrayal of Jesus (Matt. 27:9).

Like the other Old Testament prophets Zechariah speaks of a future time when salvation will come to Israel (Zech. 9:16) through the work of a servant-king who is first rejected by Israel (11:4–17). Like Isaiah, Zechariah refers to the Messiah as the "Branch" (3:8; 6:12). Intertwined with the salvation theme is the restoration of both Israel and Judah (10:9–12; 12:1–9; 14:1–5).

The culmination of the restoration, however, moves beyond the boundaries of Israel as God establishes a new world order where he himself rules from a new Jerusalem over all the earth (14:6–15).[121] Indeed, Zechariah 2:11 and 14:16–21 are part of the Old Testament prophetic background for the climactic fulfillment seen in Revelation 7:9–17 and in Revelation 20–22. Many of the fulfillments, images, and analogies in Revelation are drawn from Zechariah and merged with material from Genesis, Psalms, Isaiah, Ezekiel, and Daniel.

Zephaniah, Book of

The name Zephaniah means "the LORD treasures." Zephaniah, a contemporary of Jeremiah, lived and preached in the southern kingdom Judah during the reign of Josiah (640–609 B.C.). His prophecy is one of the Minor Prophets (see MINOR PROPHETS).

Much of Zephaniah deals with imminent judgment on Judah and on several neighboring nations, a judgment that found fulfillment in the invasions by the Babylonians (see BABYLON/BABYLONIANS). One of the central themes of Zephaniah is "the day of the LORD" (see DAY OF THE LORD). This phrase refers to that time when God will intervene dramatically into human history to bring about his decreed plan. It thus has two contrasting aspects: judgment on the unbelieving and disobedient ones, but blessing on the true believers.

After prophesying destruction on various nations and destruction on Jerusalem, Zephaniah turns to the LORD's great plan of restoration for both groups. Zephaniah 3:9–13 is a promise of salvation for both the people of Israel (3:11–13) and for all the peoples of the earth (3:9–10). Interestingly, the terms used in 3:9–10 appear to echo terms found in the Tower of Babel story in Genesis 11. The languages (lit., "lips") of the peoples were confused in Genesis 11, but Zephaniah prophesies a time when they will be purified; thus in the prophetic future the effects of the Tower of Babel will be reversed. The phrase "my scattered people" (Zeph. 3:10) may also connect to the scattering of people in Genesis 11.

Similar to Isaiah, Zephaniah paints a picture of a new world order in which there is unity of the nations based on a universal recognition of the LORD. This picture focuses on a region "beyond the rivers of Cush," from which the LORD's scattered people (those from Gen. 10–11 as well as people of Israel) will stream to the LORD to worship him. The rivers of Cush probably refer to the natural significant rivers in the region of Cush (the White Nile, the Blue Nile, and the Atbara). "From beyond the rivers of Cush" then refers to Cush itself and black Africa beyond to the south (see CUSH/ETHIOPIA). Thus for Zephaniah, Cush becomes a paradigm for the inclusion of foreign people into the future people of God. The mixing of Africans shoulder to shoulder with the remnant of Israel in worship of the LORD is at the core of the prophetic imagery regarding the fulfillment of God's great salvific plan for the ages.

Zion

Originally "Zion" referred to the ridge or mount in Jerusalem above the Kidron Valley. When David became king, as he moved to complete the abandoned conquest, he captured the city of Jerusalem from the Jebusites. In describing this action, 2 Samuel 5:7 states, "David captured the fortress of Zion, the City of David." Apparently Zion was the top of the ridge that lay to the immediate south of the future Temple Mount. In 1 Kings 8 Solomon brought up the Ark from "Zion, the City of David" to its new location in the Temple, which was just to the north. From then on, the Temple Mount is also called Zion.

However, throughout the Old Testament prophets, Zion is used both literally and metaphorically. It can refer to the ridge on which the Temple was built, but it is also frequently used in a metaphorical sense to refer to the Temple itself, the entire city of Jerusalem, or to the inhabitants of Jerusalem.

Phrases such as "the daughter of Zion" usually refer to the inhabitants of Jerusalem. In Psalms "Zion" often refers to the entire nation.

When the Old Testament prophets speak of the glorious future reign of God, they often describe God as reigning in Zion. Micah, for example, declares, "The LORD will rule over them in Zion" (Mic. 4:7). The prophets often use "Zion" as a synonym for Jerusalem or as the place within Jerusalem from where God rules (Isa. 24:23). Yet the prophets also use the term to refer to the inhabitants of Jerusalem (e.g., 40:9).

The New Testament writers use Zion in a similar way. Matthew 21:5 cites Zechariah 9:9, using the phrase "Daughter of Zion" to refer to the inhabitants of Jerusalem. Sometimes the New Testament uses Zion to refer to the "heavenly Jerusalem." The writer of Hebrews declares, "But you have come to Mount Zion, to the heavenly Jerusalem, the city of the living God" (Heb. 12:22). Likewise in John's vision of the end times, the Lamb (Jesus Christ) is described as standing on Mount Zion (Rev. 14:1).

Zionism

While "Zion" is a biblical term, "Zionism" is a nonbiblical, modern term that first appeared toward the end of the nineteenth century. Zionism refers to the Jewish political movement of the late nineteenth century and early twentieth century that organized, campaigned for, and implemented the creation of a Jewish state in Palestine.

The movement began slowly around 1860; at the end of the nineteenth century the World Zionist Organization was formed. The First International Zionist Congress met in 1897. Among many Orthodox Jews the religious eschatological-messianic hope for a large-scale return to the land of Israel, accompanied by the creation of a theocratic (i.e., religious) Jewish state, had always been—and for some continues to be—part of their faith. Such a state, they believed, would be brought into being by God himself, and the best way for Jews to facilitate this coming event would be to meticulously obey the Torah.

Zionism developed into a modern political and social movement that "increasingly secularized and politicized the religious." Many of the Jews moving to Palestine wanted a secular Jewish state, a social democracy, and they believed that the way to achieve it was "from below," that is, by human planning and organizing.[122] As the first half of the twentieth century progressed, the Zionist movement, although secular in its leadership, often appealed to the Bible and to Jewish religious traditions. Indeed, by

World War II the movement had melded the religious vision and the secular vision together, creating a tension that still exists in Israel today.

Throughout the first half of the twentieth century, the Zionist movement organized and pushed vigorously for Jewish immigration to Palestine. The Zionist movement and key Zionist leaders like David ben Gurion were a major force that brought about the creation of the modern Jewish state of Israel in 1948 (see ISRAEL, MODERN STATE OF).

NOTES

The following abbreviations pertain to these endnotes:

AB	Anchor Bible
BEC	Baker Exegetical Commentary
NICOT	New International Commentary on the Old Testament
NIGTC	New International Greek Testament Commentary
NIVAC	NIV Application Commentary
TDNT	*Theological Dictionary of the New Testament*
WBC	Work Biblical Commentary

1. J. Scott Duvall and J. Daniel Hays, *Grasping God's Word*, 2nd ed. (Grand Rapids: Zondervan, 2005), 188.
2. Craig S. Keener, *Revelation* (NIVAC; Grand Rapids: Zondervan, 2000), 73.
3. Richard Bauckham, *The Theology of the Book of Revelation* (Cambridge: Cambridge Univ. Press, 1993), 27–28.
4. Stephen Smalley, *The Revelation of John: A Commentary on the Greek Text of the Apocalypse* (Downers Grove: InterVarsity, 2005), 573.
5. See Robert B. Stimple, "Amillennialism," in *Three Views on the Millennium and Beyond*, ed. Darrell L. Bock (Grand Rapids: Zondervan, 1999), 118–29.
6. Brent D. Sandy, *Plowshares & Pruning Hooks: Rethinking the Language of Biblical Prophecy and Apocalyptic* (Downers Grove, IL: InterVarsity Press, 2002), 108–9.
7. Ibid., 169–89.
8. Bauckham, *Theology*, 5–12, 17–22.
9. Ibid., 17–18.
10. Gregory K. Beale, *The Book of Revelation: A Commentary on the Greek Text* (NIGTC; Grand Rapids: Eerdmans, 1999), 175.
11. See Duvall and Hays, *Grasping God's Word*, 288–94.
12. Beale, *Revelation*, 840.
13. David E. Aune, *Revelation 6–16* (WBC 52B; Dallas: Word, 1997), 417.
14. Albert Schweitzer, *The Mysticism of Paul the Apostle*, trans. W. Montgomery (New York: Macmillan, 1955), 147.
15. See C. Marvin Pate and Douglas W. Kennard, *Deliverance Now and Not Yet: The New Testament and the Great Tribulation* (New York: Lang, 2003).
16. Hans Küng, *Judaism: Between Yesterday and Tomorrow*, trans. John Bowden (New York: Crossroad, 1992), 288–89.

NOTES

17. Richard Bauckham, *Climax of Prophecy: Studies on the Book of Revelation* (Edinburgh: T. &.T. Clark, 1993), 424–25.
18. Michael Drosnin, *The Bible Code* (New York: Simon & Schuster, 1997), 15–19.
19. See Michael Weitzman, review of *The Bible Code*, in *The Jewish Chronicle*, 1997.
20. See B. McKay et al., "Solving the Bible Code Puzzle," *Statistical Science*, 1999.
21. Drosnin, *The Bible Code*, 35.
22. See the critique in Duvall and Hays, *Grasping God's Word*, 198–202.
23. David E. Aune, *Revelation 1:1–5:14* (WBC 52a; Dallas: Word, 1997), 224.
24. K. L. and M. A. Schmidt, "πωρόω, πώρωσις," *TDNT*, 5:1022–28.
25. Bruce W. Longenecker, "Different Answers to Different Issues: Israel, the Gentiles and Salvation History in Romans 9–11," *Journal for the Study of the New Testament* 36 (1999): 95–123.
26. Daniel Block, *The Book of Ezekiel, Chapters 25–48* (NICOT; Grand Rapids: Eerdmans, 1998), 303–7.
27. R. H. Lightfoot, *The Gospel Message of St. Mark* (Oxford: Clarendon, 1950), 48–49.
28. Dale C. Allison, *The End of the Ages Has Come: An Early Interpretation of the Passion and Resurrection of Christ* (Philadelphia: Fortress, 1985), 37.
29. Ibid., 38.
30. N. T. Wright, *Jesus and the Victory of God* (Minneapolis: Fortress, 1996).
31. J. Daniel Hays, *From Every People and Nation: A Biblical Theology of Race* (Downers Grove, IL: InterVarsity Press, 2003), 105–39, 172–79.
32. Joyce G. Baldwin, *Daniel* (TOTC; Downers Grove, IL; InterVarsity Press, 1978), 23–28.
33. C. Marvin Pate, ed., *Four Views on the Book of Revelation* (Grand Rapids: Zondervan, 1998), 210.
34. See Craig A. Blaising and Darrell L. Bock, *Progressive Dispensationalism* (Wheaton, IL: Victor, 1993).
35. See Robert L. Saucy, *The Case for Progressive Dispensationalism* (Grand Rapids: Zondervan, 1993).
36. Mark Strauss and Steven A. Austin, "Earthquakes and the End Times: A Geological and Biblical Response to an Urban Legend," *Christian Research Journal* 21 (1999): 30–39.
37. See Colin Hemer, *The Letters to the Seven Churches of Asia in Their Local Setting* (Biblical Resources Series; Grand Rapids: Eerdmans, 1989), 134.
38. Keener, *Revelation*, 29.
39. Ibid., 113.
40. Iain M. Duguid, "Exile," in *New Dictionary of Biblical Theology*, ed. T. Desmond Alexander et al. (Downers Grove, IL: InterVarsity Press, 2000), 475.
41. Leland Ryken, *How to Read the Bible as Literature* (Grand Rapids: Zondervan, 1984), 99–100.
42. Barry Beitzel, *The Moody Atlas of Bible Lands* (Chicago: Moody Press, 1985), 4.

43. John Walton, "The Four Kingdoms of Daniel," *Journal of the Evangelical Theological Society* 29 (1986): 30.

44. Ibid., 33–34.

45. Keener, *Revelation*, 204.

46. Bruce Metzger, "The Fourth Book of Ezra," in *The Old Testament Pseudepigrapha*, James H. Charlesworth, ed. (London: Darton, Longman, & Todd, 1985), 2:521.

47. John Davis, *Biblical Numerology: A Basic Study of the Use of Numbers in the Bible* (Grand Rapids: Baker, 1968), 36–40, 140–49.

48. C. Marvin Pate et al., *The Story of Israel: A Biblical Theology* (Downers Grove, IL: InterVarsity Press, 2004), 271–72.

49. Iain Duguid, *Ezekiel* (NIVAC; Grand Rapids: Zondervan, 1999), 452.

50. Smalley, *Revelation*, 441.

51. See Grant Osborne, *Revelation* (BEC; Grand Rapids: Baker, 2002), 722.

52. John Walvoord, *The Revelation of Jesus Christ* (Chicago: Moody Press, 1966), 52.

53. See Hemer, *The Letters to the Seven Churches*.

54. Quoted in C. K. Barrett, *The New Testament Background: Selected Documents* (New York: Harper & Row, 1961), 167.

55. Küng, *Judaism*, 296–97.

56. Raymond E. Brown, *The Gospel According to John I-XII* (AB 29; Garden City, NY: Doubleday, 1966), cxv.

57. Leon Morris, "Judgment, Day of," in *Evangelical Dictionary of Biblical Theology*, ed. Walter Elwell (Grand Rapids: Baker, 1996), 438.

58. Martin Luther, *Luther's Works*, ed. Lewis W. Spitz (St. Louis: Concordia, 1963–64), 334, 336–37.

59. Ernst Käsemann, "The Righteousness of God in Paul," in *New Testament Questions of Today*, trans. W. J. Montague (Philadelphia: Fortress, 1969), 168–82.

60. N. T. Wright, *What Saint Paul Really Said* (Grand Rapids: Eerdmans, 1997), 103.

61. Ibid., chs. 5–7.

62. Wright, *Jesus and the Victory of God*, 536ff.

63. Beale, *Revelation*, 206.

64. J. G. Millar, "Land," *New Dictionary of Biblical Theology*, ed. T. Desmond Alexander et al. (Downers Grove, IL: InterVarsity Press, 2000), 623.

65. Walter Brueggemann, *The Land: Place as Gift, Promise, and Challenge in Biblical Faith* (Overture to Biblical Theology; Minneapolis: Fortress, 2002), 157–72.

66. Hemer, *The Letters to the Seven Churches*, 202–7.

67. James Leo Garrett, *Systematic Theology: Biblical, Historical, and Evangelical*, 2 vols. (Grand Rapids: Eerdmans, 1990, 1995), 2:780.

68. John Walvoord, *The Millennial Kingdom* (Grand Rapids: Zondervan, 1971), 276–95.

69. Stephen Smalley, "Excursus: Vengeance in the Apocalypse," in *Revelation*, 160–64.

70. Bauckham, *Theology*, 93.
71. R. T. France, "Messiah in the NT," *New Bible Dictionary*, 760–61.
72. This summary chart is from Bauckham, *Theology*, 131–32.
73. See the comprehensive study by Greg Beale, *The Temple and the Church's Mission: A Biblical Theology of the Dwelling Place of God* (New Studies in Biblical Theology; Downers Grove, IL: InterVarsity Press, 2004).
74. See Beale, *Revelation*, 251, 260, for evidence that these three groups are closely related.
75. See Davis, *Biblical Numerology*.
76. See Leland Ryken, et al., *Dictionary of Biblical Imagery: An Encyclopedic Exploration of the Images, Symbols, Motifs, Metaphors, Figures of Speech, and Literary Patterns of the Bible* (Downers Grove, IL: InterVarsity Press, 1998), 774–75.
77. Ibid., 307–8.
78. See Hemer, *The Letters to the Seven Churches*, 86.
79. Keener, *Revelation*, 125.
80. William W. Klein, Craig L. Blomberg, and Robert L. Hubbard, *Introduction to Biblical Interpretation*, rev. ed. (Nashville: Nelson, 2004), 274.
81. Ibid., 279.
82. Duvall and Hays, *Grasping God's Word*, 349–60.
83. Kenneth Gentry, "Postmillennialism," in Bock, ed., *Three Views*, 13–14.
84. Ibid., 19.
85. Robert H. Gundry, *The Church and the Tribulation* (Grand Rapids: Zondervan, 1973), 172–88.
86. See H. B. Huffmon, "Prophecy (ANE)," *Anchor Bible Dictionary*, 5:477–82.
87. Willem A. VanGemeren, "Psalms," *Expositor's Bible Commentary* (Grand Rapids: Zondervan, 1991), 5:586–89.
88. Hans-Joachim Kraus, *Theology of the Psalms* (Minneapolis: Augsburg, 1986), 180–85.
89. Ibid., 185–88.
90. Ibid., 188–90.
91. J. M. Lunde, "Repentance," *New Dictionary of Biblical Theology*, ed. T. Desmond Alexander et al. (Downers Grove, IL: InterVarsity Press, 2000), 726–27.
92. Beitzel, *Moody Atlas*, 4.
93. Edwin Yamauchi, *Foes from the Northern Frontier* (Grand Rapids: Baker, 1982), 19–27.
94. Block, *The Book of Ezekiel: Chapters 25–48*, 434.
95. Duguid, *Ezekiel*, 453.
96. Bauckham, *Theology*, 81–82.
97. See Beale, *Revelation*, 339; Osborne, *Revelation*, 248–50.
98. See Beale, *Revelation*, 527.
99. Ibid., 1043.
100. Osborne, *Revelation*, 270–71.

101. Keener, *Revelation*, 105.
102. Beale, *Revelation*, 227.
103. Keener, *Revelation*, 110.
104. Smalley, *Revelation*, 34.
105. Beale, *Revelation*, 718–28.
106. M. Turner, "Holy Spirit," *New Dictionary of Biblical Theology*, ed. T. D. Alexander et al. (Downers Grove, IL: InterVarsity Press, 2000), 555–56.
107. See *New International Bible Dictionary*, ed. J. D. Douglas and Merrill C. Tenney (Grand Rapids: Zondervan, 1987), 995–96.
108. Douglas Moo, in *Rapture: Pre-, Mid- or Post-Tribulational?* by Douglas Moo et al. (Grand Rapids: Zondervan, 1984), 194.
109. See Bauckham, *Theology*, 31.
110. Ibid., 141–42.
111. Douglas Moo, *The Epistle to the Romans* (Grand Rapids: Eerdmans, 1996), 517.
112. Richard Bauckham and Trevor Hart, *Hope against Hope: Christian Eschatology at the Turn of the Millennium* (Grand Rapids: Eerdmans, 1999), 148–53.
113. Keener, *Revelation*, 245.
114. Peter T. O'Brien, *Colossians-Philemon* (WBC; Waco, TX: Word, 1982), 78–80.
115. Keener, *Revelation*, 272.
116. Duguid, *Ezekiel*, 448; Block, *The Book of Ezekiel: Chapters 25–48*, 436.
117. Terence L. Donaldson, *Paul and the Gentiles: Remapping the Apostle's Convictional World* (Minneapolis: Fortress, 1997), 233.
118. A quote from Douglas Moo, cited in Duvall and Hays, *Grasping God's Word*, 186.
119. R. T. France, *Jesus and the Old Testament* (Downers Grove, IL: InterVarsity Press, 1971), 75–76.
120. See, e.g., Robert Guelich, *Mark 1:1–8:26* (WBC; Dallas: Word, 1989), 38.
121. Andrew E. Hill and John H. Walton, *A Survey of the Old Testament* (Grand Rapids: Zondervan, 2000), 541.
122. Küng, *Judaism*, 283.

SCRIPTURE INDEX
(WITH APOCRYPHA)

Ezekiel

John

Acts

Romans